Asian/Oceanian Historical Dictionaries
Edited by Jon Woronoff

Asia

1. *Vietnam*, by William J. Duiker. 1989
2. *Bangladesh*, 2nd ed., by Craig Baxter and Syedur Rahman. 1996
3. *Pakistan*, by Shahid Javed Burki. 1991
4. *Jordan*, by Peter Gubser. 1991
5. *Afghanistan*, by Ludwig W. Adamec. 1991
6. *Laos*, by Martin Stuart-Fox and Mary Kooyman. 1992
7. *Singapore*, by K. Mulliner and Lian The-Mulliner. 1991
8. *Israel*, by Bernard Reich. 1992
9. *Indonesia*, by Robert Cribb. 1992
10. *Hong Kong and Macau*, by Elfed Vaughan Roberts, Sum Ngai Ling, and Peter Bradshaw. 1992
11. *Korea*, by Andrew C. Nahm. 1993
12. *Taiwan*, by John F. Copper. 1993
13. *Malaysia*, by Amarjit Kaur. 1993
14. *Saudi Arabia*, by J. E. Peterson. 1993
15. *Myanmar*, by Jan Becka. 1995
16. *Iran*, by John H. Lorentz. 1995
17. *Yemen*, by Robert D. Burrowes. 1995
18. *Thailand*, by May Kyi Win and Harold Smith. 1995
19. *Mongolia*, by Alan J. K. Sanders. 1996
20. *India*, by Surjit Mansingh. 1996
21. *Gulf Arab States*, by Malcolm C. Peck. 1996
22. *Syria*, by David Commins. 1996
23. *Palestine*, by Nafez Y. Nazzal and Laila A. Nazzal. 1997
24. *Philippines*, by Artemio R. Guillermo and May Kyi Win. 1997

Oceania

1. *Australia*, by James C. Docherty. 1992
2. *Polynesia*, by Robert D. Craig. 1993
3. *Guam and Micronesia*, by William Wuerch and Dirk Ballendorf. 1994
4. *Papua New Guinea*, by Ann Turner. 1994
5. *New Zealand*, by Keith Jackson and Alan McRobie. 1996

New Combined Series

25. *Brunei Darussalam*, by D. S. Ranjit Singh and Jatswan S. Sidhu. 1997
26. *Sri Lanka*, by S. W. R. de A. Samarasinghe and Vidyamali Samarasinghe. 1998
27. *Vietnam*, 2nd ed., by William J. Duiker. 1998
28. *People's Republic of China: 1949–1997*, by Lawrence R. Sullivan, with the assistance of Nancy Hearst. 1998
29. *Afghanistan*, 2nd ed., by Ludwig W. Adamec. 1997
30. *Lebanon*, by As'ad AbuKhalil. 1998
31. *Azerbaijan*, by Tadeusz Swietochowski and Brian C. Collins. 1999
32. *Australia*, 2nd ed., by James C. Docherty. 1999
33. *Pakistan*, 2nd ed., by Shahid Javed Burki. 1999
34. *Taiwan (Republic of China)*, 2nd ed., by John F. Copper. 2000

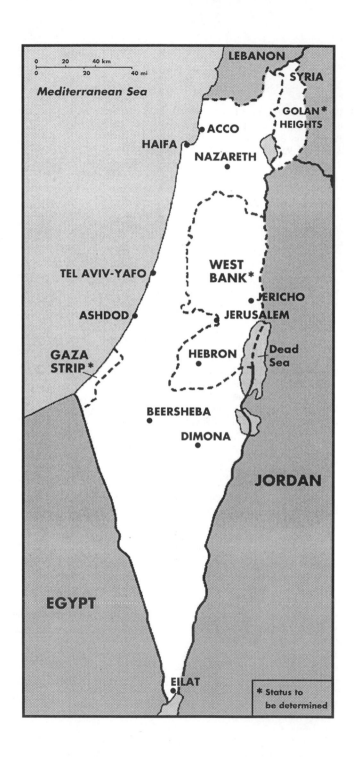

LEBANON

SYRIA

Mediterranean Sea

GOLAN *
HEIGHTS

ACCO

HAIFA

NAZARETH

WEST
BANK *

TEL AVIV-YAFO

JERICHO

JERUSALEM

ASHDOD

GAZA
STRIP *

HEBRON

Dead
Sea

BEERSHEBA

DIMONA

JORDAN

EGYPT

EILAT

* Status to
be determined

0   20   40 km
0   20   40 mi

Political Dictionary of Israel

Bernard Reich and
David H. Goldberg

The Scarecrow Press, Inc.
Lanham, Maryland, and London
2000

SCARECROW PRESS, INC.

Published in the United States of America
by Scarecrow Press, Inc.
4720 Boston Way, Lanham, Maryland 20706
http://www.scarecrowpress.com

4 Pleydell Gardens, Folkestone
Kent CT20 2DN, England

British Library Cataloguing in Publication Information Available

Library of Congress Cataloging-in-Publication Data

Reich, Bernard.
    Political dictionary of Israel / Bernard Reich and David H. Goldberg.
      p.   cm.
    Includes bibliographical references.
    ISBN 0-8108-3778-1 (cloth : alk. paper)
    1. Israel—Politics and government—Dictionaries. 2. Israel—History—
Dictionaries. I. Goldberg, David H. II. Title.

    DS126.5 .R385 2000
    956.94′003—dc21   00-021979

DEDICATIONS

BR: To the Blessed Memory of Rosalyn and Moe Reich

DHG: To the Blessed Memory of Shirley Sara Goldberg

CONTENTS

EDITOR'S FOREWORD

From the outset, political life in Israel was defined by a combination of challenges over and above the normal stresses and strains that affect all modern countries. Central to these was the ongoing need of overcoming the often tragic history of the Jewish people, culminating with the annihilation of much of European Jewry in the Nazi Holocaust. Additional challenges included inculcating a sense of a common identity among the more than two-and-one-half million immigrants absorbed from all corners of the world; and building a democratic political process and modern socioeconomic system even as it was compelled to construct a powerful military security infrastructure capable of defending the state against persistent existential security threats. In Israel's first half-century of independent statehood, the effort to reconcile these competing pressures created a vibrant, sometimes unruly, political system.

Today, political life in Israel remains very much still "a work in progress." Although the vast majority of Israelis view with favor the prospects of normalized relations with their immediate neighbors, they continue to debate actively the price Israel will be required to pay to achieve this elusive goal. And domestically, Israelis continue to debate such core issues as the role of religion in political affairs, the integrating into Israeli political culture of concepts such as pluralism and multiculturalism, and adapting a tightly centralized socialist-based economy into one capable of succeeding in the interconnected international market place of the twenty-first century.

The purpose of this *Political Dictionary of Israel* is to provide the reader with a detailed and comprehensive guide to the past, present, and future of political life in Israel, with an emphasis on the important events, issues, political parties, and players. The dictionary is complemented by a brief introduction, a chronology of important dates in Israel's political history, and an extensive bibliography organized on a thematic basis.

This volume was written by Bernard Reich and David H. Goldberg. Dr. Reich is Professor of Political Science and International Affairs at George Washington University in Washington, DC. He is also a consultant to government and business on Middle Eastern affairs. Among the many books he has authored, coauthored or edited, special mention should be made of the *Historical Dictionary of Israel*, the companion to the present volume. Dr. Goldberg is the Director of Research and Education for the Canada-Israel Committee in Toronto. He has authored or coedited four books on themes relating to Israeli political and security affairs. Between them they have produced an extremely useful resource guide to Israeli politics at a particularly significant juncture in the country's evolution.

Jon Woronoff
Series Editor

PREFACE

Few countries of its size have attracted more attention, and aroused more controversy, than Israel. It is a country beset by conflict in its region and faced with the need to integrate immigrants and to weld individuals of disparate backgrounds and ethnicity into a modern and advanced state. And, although small in size and population, it has played a significant role in international relations. The State of Israel has been a magnet for attention. It has preoccupied students and observers, scholars and journalists, since its independence in 1948. Israel and its politics, hotly and vigorously debated both at home and abroad, have been the subject of a substantial, and often highly partisan—both supportive and critical—literature.

This book is designed to provide, in a single source, a comprehensive and up-to-date reference volume with detailed information about every aspect of the political life of contemporary Israel and to serve as a comprehensive guide to the complexities and nuances of contemporary Israeli politics. Although its scope is more political and contemporary, this volume builds on the earlier *Historical Dictionary of Israel* (published by Scarecrow Press in 1992) and other writings by the two authors. It seeks to fill a gap in the literature by providing comprehensive information about the various diplomatic and political personalities, institutions, organizations, events, concepts, and documents that together define the political life of the Jewish state. This dictionary is designed to include the references needed by the student, scholar, and journalist, as well as the general reader, to understand Israeli politics and policy. Hundreds of entries of varying lengths are alphabetically arranged and cross-referenced, by the use of an asterisk (*). In addition to a general bibliography of items designed to facilitate further reading and research on the broader subjects and themes of Israeli politics, there are also bibliographies appended to particular entries where there is substantial specific literature that refers to the subject at hand. There is a chronology of major events, tables of leading personalities, and other basic information. We trust this work will be a useful addition to the literature and will provide both students and scholars with information and descriptions, as well as bibliographical references, for further study and serve as a basic research tool containing factual information.

To ensure both scholarly comprehensiveness (especially given the extensive subject matter appropriate for discussion) and conciseness (to create a "user-friendly" volume), the authors made difficult but necessary choices concerning terms, names, topics and issues to be included or excluded. These choices were based on their knowledge and understanding of Israeli politics and on the judgements of others who, through their questions, writings, comments and observations, suggested the need to further explain various elements of politics and policy in contemporary Israel.

Israeli politics have always been intense and frenetic encompassing, directly or indirectly, virtually all aspects of life in the state. We have sought to capture these developments by a continuous revision of all entries through the date of submission of the manuscript to the publication process in February 2000.

ACKNOWLEDGMENTS

Two former students at The George Washington University were particularly helpful in the preparation of this work. Stuart Hershfeld and Adam Segal reviewed earlier versions of the manuscript and offered suggestions for revisions of entries and for the composition of the book. Other colleagues, who prefer anonymity, offered criticism and suggestions that helped to shape the final work.

The manuscript was prepared for publication in copy-ready format by NBR Computer Consulting of Alexandria, Virginia.

ABBREVIATIONS AND ACRONYMS

ADP   Arab Democratic Party

AIPAC   American Israel Public Affairs Committee

AMAN   Agaf Modiin (Intelligence Branch)

BCE   Before the Common Era (BC)

c.   *circa* (about)

CRM   Citizens' Rights and Peace Movement (Hatnua Lezhuiot Haezrah)

DA   Democracy and Aliyah

DASH   (See DMC)

DFPE   Democratic Front for Peace and Equality

DMC (DASH)   Democratic Movement for Change (Hatnua Hademocratit Leshinui)

DMI   Director of Military Intelligence

DOP   Declaration of Principles (Israel and the PLO, 1993)

GAHAL   Gush Herut Liberalim (Herut Liberal bloc)

HABAD   Hokhmah, Binah, Daat (wisdom, comprehension, knowledge)

HADASH   Hazit Demokratit Leshalom Uleshivyon (Democratic Front for Peace and Equality)

IAI   Israel Aircraft Industries

IBA   Israel Broadcasting Authority

IDF (ZAHAL)   Israel Defense Forces (Zvah Hagana Leyisrael)

JNF   Jewish National Fund

LEHI (LHY)   Fighters for the Freedom of Israel or Stern Group (Lohamei Herut Yisrael)

MAFDAL (NRP)   Miflaga Datit Leumit (National Religious Party)

MAHAL   Mitnadvei Hutz Laeretz (foreign volunteers)

MAPAI   Workers Party of the Land of Israel (Mifleget Poalei Eretz Yisrael)

MAPAM   United Workers Party (Mifleget Poalim Hameuchedet)

MK   Member of the Knesset

MOU   Memorandum of Understanding

NAHAL   Fighting Pioneering Youth (Noar Halutzi Lohaim)

NRP   National Religious Party

NUG   National Unity Government

NZO   New Zionist Organization

PA   Palestinian Authority

PFLP   Popular Front for the Liberation of Palestine

PIJ   Palestine Islamic Jihad

PLO   Palestine Liberation Organization

PLP   Progressive List for Peace

PNC   Palestine National Council

RAFI   Reshimat Poalei Israel (Israel Labor List)

RAKAH   New Communist List (Reshima Konumistit Hadasha)

RATZ   Hatnua Lezhuiot Haezrah UleShalom (Citizens' Rights and Peace Movement)

SHABAK   Sherut Bitahon Klali, Shin Bet (General Security Services)

SHAI   Sherut Yediot (information service)

SHAS   Sephardi Torah Guardians

SLA   South Lebanese Army

TAAS   Taasiya Tzvait (military industry)

TAMI   Movement for a Traditional Israel (Tenuah Lemassoret Israel)

TIPH   Temporary International Presence in Hebron

UAL	United Arab List
UAR	United Arab Republic
UIA	United Israel Appeal
UJA	United Jewish Appeal
UNDOF	United Nations Disengagement Observer Force
UNEF	United Nations Emergency Force
UNIFIL	United Nations Interim Force in Lebanon
UNGA	United Nations General Assembly
UNSC	United Nations Security Council
UNSCOP	United Nations Special Committee on Palestine
UNTSO	United Nations Truce Supervision Organization
UPA	United Palestine Appeal
UTJ	United Torah Judaism
WIZO	Women's International Zionist Organization
WOJAC	World Organization of Jews from Arab Countries
WZO	World Zionist Organization
ZAHAL	(See IDF)

CHRONOLOGY

c.17th Century BCE   The period of the Jewish Patriarchs: Abraham, Isaac, Jacob.

c.1250-1210 BCE   The Exodus of the Jews from Egypt; wandering in the desert of Sinai and the conquest of Canaan under Joshua.

c.1020-1004 BCE   King Saul. Establishment of the Israelite kingdom.

c.1004-965 BCE   King David. Consolidation and expansion of the kingdom.

c.961-928 BCE   King Solomon. The Temple is built in Jerusalem.

c.928 BCE   Division of the state and the establishment of Kingdoms of Judah and Israel.

c.722 BCE   Assyrian conquest of Samaria, Kingdom of Israel; large number of Jews exiled.

c.586 BCE   Jerusalem is conquered and the Temple is destroyed. Mass deportation of Jews to the Babylonian captivity.

c.520-515 BCE	The Temple is rebuilt.
c.167-160 BCE	Hasmonean rebellion under Judah Maccabee.
164 BCE	Jerusalem is liberated and the Temple is rededicated.
37-4 BCE	Reign of Herod.
c.19 BCE	The Temple is rebuilt.
AD/CE 66	Jewish revolt against Rome.
70	Siege of Jerusalem; Destruction of the Temple by Romans. Direct Roman rule is imposed until 395. Beginning of the Jewish Diaspora.
73	Fall of Massada.
132-135	Bar Kochba War.
135	Jews are expelled from "Palestine," a name given to Judea by Rome.
395-638	Byzantine rule.
638	Arab Muslim armies conquer Jerusalem.
c.636-1072	Arab rule.
1072-1099	Seljuq rule.
1099	Jerusalem captured by the Crusaders.
1099-1291	Crusader rule with interruptions.
1187	Jerusalem is captured by Saladin.
1291-1516	Mameluke rule.

c.1517-1917	Ottoman Turkish rule.
1878	Petah Tikva is founded.
1882-1903	First Aliya.
1882	Hibbat Zion Movement started. Rishon Le-Zion is founded.
1894	Dreyfus trial in France.
1896	Publication of *Der Judenstaat* by Theodor Herzl.
1897	First Zionist Congress is held in Basle, Switzerland. The World Zionist Organization is established.
1901	Jewish National Fund is established.
1904	Herzl dies.
1904-1914	Second Aliya.
1909	Kibbutz Degania is founded. Tel Aviv is established.
1917	British army captures Jerusalem.
November 2	The Balfour Declaration is issued.
1919-1923	Third Aliya.
1920	The British Mandate over Palestine is granted at San Remo although it is not formalized until 1922. Herbert Samuel is appointed High Commissioner for Palestine. The Histadrut and Hagana are founded.
1921	Moshav Nahalal is founded.

1922   Churchill White Paper.

July   Palestine Mandate ratified by League of Nations.

1924-1928   Fourth Aliya.

1925   Hebrew University is inaugurated on Mt. Scopus, Jerusalem.

1929   Arab riots take place in Jerusalem and massacres occur in Hebron and Safed.

1929-1939   Fifth Aliya.

1935   The Revisionist movement, headed by Vladimir Zeev Jabotinsky, secedes from the World Zionist Organization and establishes the new Zionist Organization.

1937   Peel Commission Report; first proposal to partition Palestine.

1939   British White Paper further limits Jewish immigration to Palestine and Zionist land purchases.

1942 May   Biltmore Program promulgated by Zionists at conference in New York.

1945 November   Anglo-American Committee of Inquiry established.

1946 July 22   British headquarters in King David Hotel, Jerusalem, bombed.

1947   Great Britain turns the Palestine issue over to the United Nations. The United Nations Special Committee on Palestine (UNSCOP) examines the problem and recommends solutions.

November 29   The United Nations General Assembly adopts a
                   resolution (UNGA Res 181 (II)) providing for an
                   independent Jewish state in Palestine to be united
                   economically with an independent Arab state. An
                   international regime is to be established in
                   Jerusalem. U.S. and USSR support the partition
                   plan.

December   Jewish-Arab communal warfare in Palestine
                   intensifies after adoption of partition plan.

1948 May 14   Proclamation of the independence of the State of
                   Israel. U.S. extends de facto recognition. Ben-
                   Gurion becomes first Prime Minister of Israel.

May 15   The British Mandate for Palestine is terminated;
                   Arab armies of Egypt, Iraq, Jordan, Lebanon, and
                   Syria invade and the first Arab-Israeli War
                   (Israel's War of Independence) officially begins.
                   The United States and the Soviet Union recognize
                   Israel.

June 11   The first truce in the Arab-Israeli hostilities
                   begins.

July 8   The truce ends.

July 18   The second truce begins.

October 15   The truce ends.

December 11   UNGA adopts Resolution 194.

1949 January 25   Election for the First Knesset.

February 14   First Knesset opens in Jerusalem.

February 16   Chaim Weizmann is elected the first President of
                   Israel.

February 24	The Armistice Agreement with Egypt is achieved.
March 8	The first session of the Knesset begins in Tel Aviv.
March 10	The first regular Government is established under David Ben-Gurion as Prime Minister.
March 23	Armistice Agreement with Lebanon.
April 3	Armistice Agreement with Jordan.
May 11	Israel becomes a member of the United Nations.
July 20	Armistice Agreement with Syria.
September 12	Compulsory Education Law passed.
November 2	The Weizmann Institute of Science is inaugurated.
December	Abdullah annexes that part of Palestine occupied by the Arab Legion (West Bank) and East Jerusalem. (Annexation ratified by Jordanian parliament in April 1950.)
December 13	A resolution to transfer the Knesset and the Government to Jerusalem is adopted.
December 26	The Knesset session resumes in Jerusalem.
1950 January	Egyptians occupy the islands of Tiran and Sanafir at the southern entrance to the Gulf of Aqaba, thus blocking passage to the Israeli port of Eilat.
January 4	The Knesset ratifies a Government statement opposing the internationalization of Jerusalem.
May 25	Tripartite Declaration (Britain, France, U.S.) regulates arms to the Middle East.

June 13	The Knesset adopts a resolution on the manner in which a Constitution for the state is to be devised.
July	Beginning of large-scale immigration to Israel from Iraq.
July 5	The Law of Return, confirming the right of every Jew to settle in Israel, is passed by Knesset.
September 24	The airlift of Jews from Yemen to Israel is concluded.
1951 March	Israel launches a three-year plan to drain the Huleh swamps for irrigation and for generation of hydroelectric power.
July	The airlift of Jews from Iraq to Israel is completed.
July 20	King Abdullah of Jordan is assassinated, ostensibly because of negotiations with Israel. Talal becomes king.
July 30	Election for the Second Knesset.
August 14	The 23rd Zionist Congress opens in Jerusalem.
August 20	The Second Knesset opens.
September 1	The United Nations Security Council condemns Egyptian anti-Israel blockade in Suez Canal.
1952 July 23	Free Officers coup ousts King Farouk of Egypt.
August 11	Talal is replaced by his son Hussein as King of Jordan.
November 9	President Chaim Weizmann dies.
December 8	Yitzhak Ben Zvi is elected the second President of Israel.

1953   Ben-Gurion resigns as Prime Minister. Moshe
                    Sharett becomes Prime Minister.

June 18   Republic of Egypt is declared.

September 2   Israel initiates the second phase of the Jordan
                    Development Plan.

October 14   Israel Defense Forces (IDF) troops carry out a
                    reprisal raid against the Jordanian village of Kibya.

1954   Moshe Dayan becomes Chief of Staff of IDF.
                    Nasser becomes Prime Minister and President of
                    Egypt. Lavon Affair occurs.

June 2   Hebrew University dedicates its new campus in
                    Jerusalem.

July 19   The Yarkon-Negev pipeline, to irrigate 25,000
                    acres in the Negev, is opened.

September 28   Egypt seizes the *Bat Galim*, an Israel-flag
                    merchant vessel, at Suez when it attempts to transit
                    the Suez Canal, and its crew is imprisoned.

October 12   Thirteen Jews are indicted in Egypt on charges of
                    espionage.

1955 February 28   Israel raids Gaza Strip in retaliation for guerilla
                    activity against Israel.

July 26   Election for the Third Knesset.

August 15   The Third Knesset opens. David Ben-Gurion
                    becomes Prime Minister.

September 27   Premier Gamal Abdul Nasser of Egypt signs an
                    agreement with Czechoslovakia to obtain vast
                    quantities of arms.

October 3	Czechoslovakia announces confirmation of an arms deal with Egypt. Later it is revealed to be a Soviet-Egyptian transaction.
November	Ben-Gurion again becomes Prime Minister of Israel.
1956 April 24	The 24th Zionist Congress opens in Jerusalem.
July 26	Egyptian President Gamal Abdul Nasser announces the nationalization of the Suez Canal Company.
October 29	Israel moves against Egyptian fedayeen bases and prepares for attack in the Sinai Peninsula to eliminate commando bases. Israel invades Sinai. Sinai/Suez War (second Arab-Israeli war) begins.
November 5	France and the United Kingdom invade the Suez Canal Zone.
November 6	Israel announces acceptance of a cease-fire in the Sinai Peninsula.
November 7	Egypt, France, and Britain accept the cease-fire.
December 22	Anglo-French troops complete their withdrawal from the Suez Canal Zone.
1957	Israel evacuates Sinai and the Gaza Strip. The United Nations Emergency Force (UNEF) is established.
January 22	Israel evacuates all of Sinai except Gaza and Sharm el-Sheikh.
March 1	Israel agrees to evacuate Gaza and Sharm el-Sheikh.
March 8	UNEF forces take over from Israel the garrisoning

	of Sharm el-Sheikh and the administration of the Gaza Strip.
March 25	The first large vessel arrives at the Israeli port of Eilat.
March 29	Convoy traffic resumes through the Suez Canal.
October 31	The Arid Zone Research Institute opens in Beersheba.
1958 January 16	The Beersheba-Eilat highway, Israel's "dry-land Suez Canal," opens.
February	United Arab Republic (UAR) of Egypt and Syria is established.
July 14	Revolution in Iraq.
December 4	The cornerstone of the new Knesset building is laid.
1959 November 3	Election for the Fourth Knesset.
November 18	Israeli Finance Minister Levi Eshkol announces that diversion of water from the Jordan River for irrigation purposes had become a priority project for Israel.
November 30	The Fourth Knesset opens.
1960 February 1	Israeli and Syrian forces clash in the demilitarized zone.
March	Prime Minister Ben-Gurion visits the United States and Great Britain.
April 26	Israel's National Water Council approves a plan for laying a giant conduit to carry water from the Sea of Galilee to southern Israel.

May 23	Adolf Eichmann is kidnaped from Argentina for trial in Israel.
1961 April 11	The Eichmann Trial opens in Jerusalem.
July 5	Israel launches its first meteorological space rocket.
July 30	The cornerstone of the deep-sea port of Ashdod is laid. The millionth immigrant since the establishment of the state arrives.
August 15	Election for the Fifth Knesset.
September 4	The Fifth Knesset opens.
September 29	Syria withdraws from the UAR.
1962 May 31	Adolf Eichmann is executed.
June 30	Ten years of activities of the United States Operations Mission in Israel are completed, both Governments agreeing that in view of Israel's progress, no special body is needed to administer U.S. technical aid.
September 27	The Foreign Ministry announces that the United States has agreed to supply Israel with Hawk ground-to-air missiles for defense. First direct sale of significant American weapons to Israel.
October 30	Yitzhak Ben Zvi is reelected for a third term as President of Israel.
November 21	The new town of Arad in the eastern Negev is officially inaugurated.
1963 March 20	The Knesset calls upon the Bonn Government to terminate the activities of German scientists in Egypt.

April 18   Work begins on construction of Carmiel, a new town in Galilee.

April 23   President Yitzhak Ben Zvi dies.

May 21   Shneur Zalman Shazar is elected by the Knesset as Israel's third President.

June 16   David Ben-Gurion resigns from his post as Prime Minister and Minister of Defense.

June 26   A new Government, with Levi Eshkol as Prime Minister, takes office.

July 11   *Shalom*, Israel's largest passenger liner, is launched in France.

October 21   Prime Minister Levi Eshkol announces far-reaching relaxations of military Government restrictions on Israel's Arab Citizens.

1964 January   The Palestine Liberation Organization (PLO) is created in Cairo. Ahmed Shukairi becomes first chairman.

January 1   Yitzhak Rabin becomes Chief of Staff of the Israel Defense Forces.

January 5   Pope Paul VI begins a pilgrimage to Christian holy sites in Israel.

June   National Water Carrier begins operation.

1965 January 1   Fatah is established and launches its first attack against Israel

November 2   Election for the Sixth Knesset.

November 22   The Sixth Knesset opens.

1966 January — Golda Meir resigns as Foreign Minister and is succeeded by Abba Eban.

August 30 — Knesset building is formally opened.

November 12 — An Israeli patrol car detonates a land mine near the Jordan frontier, killing three soldiers and injuring six. Israel complains to the United Nations Security Council.

November 13 — Israeli forces launch an attack on the Jordanian village of es-Samu in response to killing of Israelis.

1967 April 7 — During an air clash six Syrian MIG 21s are shot down by Israeli planes.

May 15 — The United Arab Republic puts its forces on a state of alert and begins extensive redeployment of military units.

May 18 — The United Arab Republic asks the United Nations to remove UNEF from the Egypt-Israel armistice line and the United Nations complies. Israel announces that it is taking "appropriate measures" in response to the UAR build-up in Sinai.

May 22-May 23 — UAR President Gamal Abdul Nasser announces an Egyptian blockade of the Gulf of Aqaba, cutting off Israel's access to the Red Sea through the port of Eilat.

May 24 — Jordan announces it has given permission for Iraqi and Saudi Arabian forces to enter Jordan and that general mobilization in Jordan has been completed.

June 1 — Prime Minister Levi Eshkol forms a broadly based "National Unity Government" in which former Chief of Staff Moshe Dayan becomes Minister of

Defense.

June 5   Hostilities commence between Israel and the Arab
                 states in the Six Day War (third Arab-Israeli war).

June 6   The UAR closes the Suez Canal to all shipping.
                 The UAR breaks relations with the United States
                 over allegations of U.S. support for Israel in the
                 war.

June 7   The Jordanian and Israeli Governments accept the
                 United Nations call for a cease-fire. At the
                 conclusion of hostilities, the Israelis had
                 established themselves at the Jordan River and had
                 control of the West Bank.

June 8   A cease-fire goes into effect between the UAR and
                 Israel. Israeli forces had occupied the Gaza Strip
                 and the Sinai Peninsula.

June 10   The USSR breaks diplomatic relations with Israel.
                 Other Soviet-bloc European countries, except
                 Romania, follow suit.

June 11   A cease-fire goes into effect between Israel and
                 Syria. The Israelis had penetrated beyond the
                 former demarcation line, establishing themselves
                 on the Golan Heights.

June 12   In a policy speech to parliament, Israeli Prime
                 Minister Levi Eshkol declares that Israel could not
                 return to the prewar situation and demands that the
                 Arabs make peace with Israel.

June 28   The Israeli Minister of the Interior announces new
                 municipal boundaries for Jerusalem, in accordance
                 with enabling legislation passed the previous day
                 by the Knesset; former Jordanian-held East
                 Jerusalem is included within the new municipal
                 jurisdiction.

1967 September 1	Arab Summit Meeting at Khartoum, Sudan declares no recognition, no negotiation, and no peace with Israel.
October 21	The Israeli destroyer *Eilat* is sunk by UAR patrol boats off the Sinai coast. In reprisal, on October 24, Israel shells Suez and its oil refineries.
November 22	The United Nations Security Council adopts Resolution 242.
December	Mission of Gunnar Jarring to implement UNSC Res 242 begins.
1968 January 27	The Israeli submarine *Dakar* disappears in the Mediterranean Sea.
December 26	Arab fedayeen, who had just arrived from Beirut, attack an EL AL plane at Athens airport.
December 28	Israeli helicopter-borne commandos attack aircraft at Beirut airport in retaliation for Palestinian aircraft hijacking and other aircraft attacks.
1969	The War of Attrition (the fourth Arab-Israeli war) begins along the Suez Canal.
February	Arafat becomes head of the PLO (Chairman of PLO Executive Committee).
February 26	Levi Eshkol dies.
March 7	Golda Meir becomes Prime Minister.
October 28	Election for the Seventh Knesset.
1970	Bar-Lev line is completed.
August 7	The War of Attrition is ended by a cease-fire.

September	Jordan civil war between armed forces and the PLO. PLO is ousted from Jordan by Hussein's army.
September 28	Nasser dies. Anwar Sadat becomes president of Egypt.
1972 May 30	Japanese gunmen, acting for the Popular Front for the Liberation of Palestine (PFLP), shoot up Lod Airport.
September 5	Munich Olympics massacre of Israeli athletes by Black September terrorists.
1973 April 10	Ephraim (Katchalski) Katzir is elected fourth President of Israel.
October	UNSC Resolution 338 is adopted.
October 6	The Yom Kippur or Ramadan War (fifth Arab-Israeli war) begins.
November	The Agranat Commission established.
November 11	Israel-Egypt cease-fire is signed at Kilometer 101.
December 21	Geneva Peace Conference is convened.
December 31	Election for the Eighth Knesset.
1974 January 17	Egypt-Israel Disengagement Agreement is signed at Kilometer 101.
April 10	Golda Meir resigns.
April 22	Yitzhak Rabin becomes Prime Minister.
May 15	Palestinian infiltrators hold school children hostage in Maalot; 21 children are killed.

May 31	Israel and Syria sign a Disengagement Agreement in Geneva.
October 28	Arab League summit meeting at Rabat, Morocco, declares the PLO as "sole legitimate representative of the Palestinian people."
November 13	Yasser Arafat addresses the UN General Assembly. PLO is later granted observer status.
1975	Egypt and Israel sign a Disengagement (Sinai II) Agreement.
June 5	Suez Canal reopens.
September 4	Egypt and Israel sign Sinai II disengagement agreement.
November 10	United Nations General Assembly resolution declares Zionism to be a form of racism.
1976 July 4	Israeli commandos free hostages at Entebbe Airport, Uganda.
1977 April	Rabin resigns as Prime Minister. Shimon Peres is selected as Labor Party leader.
April	May 17: Election for the Ninth Knesset. Likud, under the leadership of Menachem Begin, emerges as the largest party.
June 21	Begin forms the Government coalition with himself as Prime Minister, the first non-Labor Government in Israel.
November	President Anwar Sadat of Egypt announces to the Egyptian National Assembly his willingness to visit Israel to discuss peace; the Israeli Knesset overwhelmingly approves an invitation to Sadat. Sadat arrives in Jerusalem and addresses the Israeli

Knesset. Negotiations begin.

December 25-26   Begin meets Sadat in Ismailia, Egypt.

1978 March   Following an attack on an Israeli bus, Israel launches (on March 14) Operation Litani against Palestinian bases in Lebanon.

April 19   Yitzhak Navon is elected fifth President of Israel.

May   The United States Congress approves a weapons package for Israel, Egypt, and Saudi Arabia.

June 13   Israel completes the withdrawal of its armed forces from Lebanon and United Nations Interim Force in Lebanon (UNIFIL) takes up positions there.

July 18-19   The Leeds Castle Conference takes place.

September 5-17   Sadat, Begin, and Carter meet at the Summit at Camp David, Maryland. The Camp David Accords are signed on the 17th at the White House in Washington, DC.

October 12   Egypt and Israel begin peace negotiations at Blair House in Washington to implement the Camp David Accords.

December 10   Nobel Peace Prize is awarded jointly to Sadat and Begin.

1979 March 26   The Egypt-Israel Peace Treaty is signed in Washington.

April 30   First Israeli freighter passes through the Suez Canal.

May 25   Israel begins withdrawal from the Sinai Peninsula; Egypt and Israel begin discussion of autonomy issues.

October	Moshe Dayan resigns as Foreign Minister.
1980 February	Egypt and Israel exchange Ambassadors.
March	Yitzhak Shamir appointed Foreign Minister of Israel.
June 13	European Community issues Venice Declaration.
July 30	The Knesset adopts a Basic Law reaffirming united Jerusalem as Israel's capital.
1981 June 7	Israel destroys the Iraqi Osirak nuclear reactor near Baghdad.
June 30	Election for the 10th Knesset. Likud secures the largest number of seats. A Begin coalition Government secures a vote of confidence from the Knesset in August.
October 6	President Sadat of Egypt is assassinated.
November 30	The United States and Israel sign a Memorandum of Understanding on Strategic Cooperation.
December 14	Israel extends its "law and jurisdiction" to the Golan Heights.
1982 April 25	Israel completes its withdrawal from the Sinai Peninsula and returns it to Egypt.
June 6	War in Lebanon (Operation Peace for Galilee) begins. Israel invades Lebanon in an attempt to destroy PLO bases.
July-August	Israeli siege of Beirut.
September	Bashir Gemayel, president-elect of Lebanon, is assassinated. Massacres take place at the Sabra and Shatila refugee camps. The Kahan

	Commission is established to inquire into the massacres.
September 1	United States President Ronald Reagan outlines his "fresh start" initiative for peace in the Middle East.
September 20	Amin Gemayel becomes President of Lebanon.
1983 September 20	February: The Kahan Commission of Inquiry reports its findings. Ariel Sharon resigns as Defense Minister and is replaced by Moshe Arens.
March 22	Chaim Herzog is elected sixth President.
May 17	Israel and Lebanon sign an agreement concluded with the assistance of United States Secretary of State George Shultz.
September 16	Menachem Begin resigns as Prime Minister.
October	Yitzhak Shamir forms a new Government and takes office as Prime Minister.
1984 March 5	Lebanon abrogates the May 17, 1983, agreement with Israel.
July 23	Election for the 11th Knesset.
September	A Government of National Unity is formed with Shimon Peres as Prime Minister and Yitzhak Shamir as alternate Prime Minister and Foreign Minister. The mass immigration of Ethiopian Jews (Falashas) to Israel in Operation Moses takes place.
1985 January	Israel announces its intent to withdraw unilaterally from Lebanon.
July	The Israel Defense Forces (IDF) completes its

withdrawal from Lebanon. A security zone is established in southern Lebanon astride the Israeli-Lebanese frontier.

September 11-12   Prime Minister Shimon Peres and President Hosni Mubarak hold a summit meeting in Egypt.

October   *Achille Lauro* incident.

1986 July   Prime Minister Shimon Peres visits King Hassan II in Morocco.

October 20   The National Unity Government Rotation shifts Shamir to the position of Prime Minister and Peres to the post of Foreign Minister.

1987 December 8   An Israeli truck hits a Palestinian car in Gaza killing 4 people. Anti-Israeli violence erupts throughout Gaza.

December 9   An Arab uprising (intifada) begins in the West Bank and the Gaza Strip challenging Israel's authority in the territories.

1988 February   Hamas is created in Gaza.

September   Israel launches a space satellite.

September 29   Taba is awarded to Egypt by an international arbitration panel.

November 1   Election for the 12th Knesset.

November 15   The Palestine National Council (PNC), meeting in Algiers, declares an independent Palestinian state and issues ambiguous statements concerning acceptance of UNSC Resolutions 242 and 338.

December 13   Arafat, at press conference, recognizes Israel's right to exist, accepts UNSC Res. 242 and 338, renounces terrorism. U.S. announces that it will begin a dialogue with the PLO in Tunis.

December 22   Prime Minister Yitzhak Shamir presents his coalition Government to the Knesset. It is approved by a vote of 84 to 19 with three abstentions.

1989 March 15   Egypt takes control of Taba.

April 6   Shamir announces election plan for the occupied territories

May 14   The Cabinet formally approves "Shamir Plan" peace initiative.

July 28   An Israeli commando team seizes Sheik Abdul Karim Obeid, a leading figure of Hezbollah, in Lebanon.

November   Prime Minister Shamir visits the United States and meets with President George Bush to discuss the peace process.

1990 January   Soviet Jews begin to arrive in Israel in large numbers.

March 13   Prime Minister Yitzhak Shamir dismisses Deputy Prime Minister Shimon Peres from the Government and the other Labor Party cabinet ministers resign.

March 15   The Knesset passes a motion of no-confidence in the Government led by Yitzhak Shamir by a vote of 60 to 55.

April 26   Labor Party leader Shimon Peres returns the mandate to form a Government to President Chaim Herzog after failing in his efforts.

April 27   Acting Prime Minister Yitzhak Shamir accepts the
                            mandate to form a new Government.

June 11   The   Knesset   approves Yitzhak Shamir's
                            Government composed of Likud and right-wing
                            and religious parties.

June 20   President George Bush suspends the U.S. dialogue
                            with the PLO.

August   Iraq invades Kuwait.

September 30   Consular relations are reestablished between Israel
                            and the Soviet Union.

November 5   Rabbi Meir Kahane, leader of the Kach Party, is
                            assassinated in New York.

November 16   Agudat Israel joins the coalition Government of
                            Prime Minister Shamir.

November 25   The cabinet approves Gen. Ehud Barak to replace
                            Lt. Gen. Dan Shomron as Chief of Staff of the IDF
                            when Shomron's tenure ends in April 1991.

1991 January 16   Allied forces launch a massive air campaign
                            against Iraq (Operation Desert Storm). In the
                            ensuing conflict Iraq launches Scud missiles
                            against Israel and Saudi Arabia.

February 3   Rehavam Zeevi of Moledet joins the cabinet as
                            Minister without Portfolio.

October 18   Israel and the Soviet Union restore diplomatic
                            relations.

October 30   Peace conference organized by the United States
                            and the Soviet Union meets in Madrid, Spain.

December 10   Beginning of Washington rounds of bilateral

Arab-Israeli negotiations.

| December 16 | United Nations General Assembly repeals the "Zionism is Racism" resolution. |

1992 January 24   Israel and China establish diplomatic relations.

January 29   India announces it will establish formal diplomatic relations with Israel.

March 17   30 killed and over 200 wounded in bombing of Israel Embassy in Buenos Aires, Argentina.

March 18   The Knesset approves electoral reform that includes direct election of the Prime Minister.

May   First round of meetings of multilateral working groups established at Moscow conference; disputes arise over Palestinian representation.

June   Israel and South Korea renew diplomatic relations.

June 23   Election for the 13th Knesset. Israel Labor Party wins under leadership of Yitzhak Rabin.

July 13   Rabin's coalition with Meretz and Shas assumes power, with Rabin serving as Prime Minister and Defense Minister and Shimon Peres as Foreign Minister and Deputy Prime Minister.

August   Israel and the Vatican establish joint commission to examine normalization of relations.

August 24   Sixth round of bilateral peace talks convene in Washington, the first since Rabin's election.

September-   Second round of multilateral peace talks, first
November   since Israeli election; some progress reported despite continued disputes over Palestinian representation.

September 18   Israel and India sign industrial cooperation
                    agreement.

October 8   Israel withdraws its previous objection to the
                    participation of Palestinians from outside the West
                    Bank, Gaza Strip, and Jerusalem in multilateral
                    peace talks but it continues to bar PLO and
                    Palestinian National Council members..

December 1   Knesset takes initial step to repeal law prohibiting
                    contacts with the PLO.

December 4   Israeli academic Yair Hirschfeld and the PLO's
                    Ahmed Suleiman Karia (Abu Alaa) begin
                    backchannel discussions.

December 17   Israel orders temporary expulsion to Lebanon of
                    some 415 Muslim extremists in response to
                    terrorist attacks on Israeli soldiers.

1993 January 19   Knesset repeals legislation prohibiting PLO
                    contacts.

January-   Deputy Foreign Minister Yossi Beilin discloses
February   existence of Oslo talks to Peres, who in turn
                    informs Rabin. Oslo negotiators begin drafting
                    declaration of principles for interim Israel-PLO
                    agreement.

March 11   In meeting with Rabin U.S. President Clinton
                    pledges to "minimize risks" of peace for Israel.
                    Rabin reportedly accedes to U.S. request to permit
                    leading Arab Jerusalemite and PLO activist Faisal
                    Husseini to join Palestinian delegation to bilateral
                    talks in Washington.

March 23   Benjamin Netanyahu is elected leader of the Likud
                    Party, replacing Yitzhak Shamir.

March 24   Ezer Weizman elected seventh President of Israel.

May

Rabin agrees to upgrade Oslo talks to official level, sending Foreign Ministry Director-General Uriel Savir to negotiate on Israel's behalf. Rabin authorizes Foreign Ministry legal expert Yoel Zinger to draft new Declaration of Principles.

May 17

Peres begins first official visit in 40 years by an Israeli leader to India, signing 6 bilateral agreements on collaboration in science and technology, tourism and culture.

July 25

Israel launches bombardment of Hezbollah bases in southern Lebanon ("Operation Accountability"); US brokers cease-fire and agreement between Israel and Lebanon (acting on Hezbollah's behalf) to avoid firing on the other's civilian populations.

August 20

Israeli and PLO officials initial Declaration of Principles (DOP) in Oslo.

August 30

Israel cabinet approves DOP with no amendments allowed; 2 Ministers (Arye Deri of Shas and Labor's Shimon Shetreet) abstain from cabinet vote.

September 9

Rabin and Arafat exchange letters of mutual recognition on behalf of Israel and the PLO.

September 13

Israel-PLO DOP is signed by Peres and the PLO's Mahmoud Abbas (Abu Mazen) on the White House lawn in Washington. Prime Minister Rabin and PLO leader Arafat shake hands.

September 14

Israel and Jordan sign Common Agenda for future negotiations. Rabin meets with King Hassan II in Morocco.

September 23

Knesset approves DOP by vote of 61-50 with 8 abstentions.

October	Rabin visits Indonesia, the world's largest Muslim country, and meets with President Suharto in Jakarta.
October 4	A Palestinian drives a car rigged with explosives into an Israeli bus in the West Bank, wounding 29.
October 6	Rabin and Arafat meet with Egypt's Hosni Mubarak in Cairo to coordinate implementation of "Gaza-Jericho First" agreement.
November 2	Long-time Jerusalem Mayor Teddy Kollek is defeated by Likud's Ehud Olmert in municipal election.
November 13	Hikmet Cetin becomes first Turkish Foreign Minister to visit Israel.
December	Third round of Israel-Palestinian talks on implementing Oslo Accords occur in Cairo, Oslo, and Paris.
December 6	Palestinian gunman opens fire on a van outside the West Bank settlement of Kiryat Arba, killing a father and son.
December 10	Three Palestinians returning from work in Israel are shot dead in Tarqumiyah in the occupied West Bank. Settlers are suspected.
December 14	By vote of 155 to 3 (Iran, Syria and Lebanon) and 1 abstention (Libya), the UN General Assembly adopts resolution expressing "full support" for Israel-Palestinian peace process.
December 29	Peres and Mahmoud Abbas conclude draft agreement on security arrangements for Gaza and Jericho border crossings.
December 30	Israel and the Vatican sign Basic Agreement to

establish diplomatic ties.

1994 January	Israel, Jordan, and Egypt agree on joint program to control maritime pollution in Gulf of Aqaba.
late January	President Ezer Weizman becomes first Israeli Head of State to visit Turkey.
February 9	Peres and Arafat sign partial agreement on implementing Gaza-Jericho agreement.
February 9	Clinton reaffirms Washington's "ironclad" commitment to Israel's security.
February 25	Jewish settler Baruch Goldstein kills 29 Palestinian worshipers and wounds more than 100 others in Hebron's Tomb of the Patriarchs/Ibrahim Mosque in Hebron. Commission of Inquiry set up under Supreme Court President Meir Shamgar.
March 28	Six Palestinian members of Al Fatah, the PLO faction led by Yasser Arafat, are shot dead by undercover Israeli troops in Jabaliya in the occupied Gaza Strip.
March 31	Israel and PLO agree on Temporary International Presence in Hebron (TIPH).
April 6	9 are killed and 45 wounded in bus-bombing in Afula.
April 10	Peres meets in Ankara with Turkish Foreign Minister Hikmet Cetin, Prime Minister Tansu Ciller and President Suleiman Demirel.
April 13	6 are killed and 28 wounded in bus-bombing in Hadera.
April 27	Israel and China sign memorandum of understanding on energy.

April 29	Israel-PLO economic cooperation agreement signed in Paris.
April-May	Fifth round of multilateral peace talks.
May	Israel Air Force pilots conduct first joint exercise with Turkish counterparts.
May 4	Israel and the PLO sign the Cairo agreement for establishing self-rule in Gaza Strip and Jericho.
May 13	IDF withdraws from Jericho, transferring authority to PLO.
May 18	IDF completes withdrawal from Gaza Strip (except for security positions near handful of small settlements in the north); joint Israel-Palestinian security patrols in Gaza begin on May 21.
June 3	Israel and Turkey sign bilateral trade agreement.
June 12	Arrow 2 interceptor missile system successfully tested.
June 16	Israel and Vatican establish full diplomatic relations.
July 1	Arafat visits Gaza Strip for the first time in 27 years.
July 18	95 are killed and hundreds wounded in bombing of Jewish community offices in Buenos Aires, Argentina.
July 19	21 people, 12 of them Jews, are killed in bombing of Panamanian airplane; responsibility is claimed by Lebanon-based militant Shi'ite group.
July 25	Washington Declaration on Israel-Jordan peace is signed; Rabin and King Hussein address joint

session of U.S. Congress.

July 26   17 are wounded in separate bombings of Israeli Embassy and Zionist Federation offices in London, England.

August 3   Knesset, by vote of 77-9 with 4 abstentions, approves resolution reaffirming Jerusalem's status as the "eternal capital of Israel, and Israel alone."

August 8   Prime Minister Rabin visits King Hussein in Jordan in the first official visit to Jordan by an Israeli leader.

August 29   "Early empowerment" agreement on transfer of civilian authority in parts of West Bank and Gaza Strip is signed.

September 1   Israel and Morocco sign agreement to open liaison offices in Tel Aviv and Rabat.

October 1   Gulf Cooperation Council (GCC) announces suspension of secondary and tertiary applications of boycott of Israel.

October 6   Israel and Turkey reach draft agreement on joint efforts to combat terrorism, drug-trafficking, and organized crime.

October 9   IDF soldier Nahshon Waxman is kidnapped by Hamas cell demanding release of comrades in Israeli prisons.

October 9   A Palestinian blows himself up on a bus in Tel Aviv, killing 22 and wounding 48.

October 14   Kidnaped Israeli soldier Nahshon Waxman is killed during failed Israeli rescue attempt on a Hamas hideout. An Israeli officer and three Hamas kidnappers also die.

October 17   Israel and Jordan initial a peace treaty in Amman, Jordan.

October 19   Hamas bomber Saleh Abdel-Rahim Souwi kills himself and 23 people in suicide attack on an Israeli bus on Tel Aviv's main Dizengoff street.

October 26   Israel and Jordan sign Peace Treaty; King Hussein subsequently makes first official visit to Israel where he and Rabin formally exchange copies of the treaty.

October 30-   First Middle East/North Africa Economic Summit
November 2   convenes in Casablanca, Morocco.

November 2   Hani Abed, an Islamic Jihad activist, is killed when his car blows up in Gaza. Islamic Jihad blames Israel, which does not deny responsibility.

November 3   Tansu Ciller makes first visit by Turkish Prime Minister to Israel.

November 11   After riding his bicycle into an Israeli army post outside Netzarim in the Gaza Strip, a Palestinian from Islamic Jihad ignites the explosives, killing 3 Israelis and wounding 11 people.

November 18   Fourteen Palestinians are killed in clashes that erupt when Palestinian policemen open fire on Hamas demonstration in the Gaza Strip.

November 27   Israel and Jordan establish diplomatic relations.

December   IDF Chief of Staff Ehud Barak and his Syrian counterpart, Hikmat Shihabi, meet in Washington to discuss security arrangements for the Golan Heights and related matters.

December 10   Yitzhak Rabin, Shimon Peres, and Yasser Arafat receive the Nobel Peace Prize in Oslo, Norway.

December 11	Israel and Jordan open their respective embassies in Amman and Tel Aviv.
December 12-15	Rabin visits Japan and South Korea.
December 21	Israel and India sign wide-ranging trade agreement.
December 25	A Palestinian policeman belonging to Hamas blows himself up near a soldiers' bus stop in Jerusalem, wounding 14 people.
December 26	Rabin becomes first Israeli Prime Minister to visit Persian Gulf Sultanate of Oman.
December 26	Knesset, by vote of 56 to 6 (with 32 abstentions), passes "Gaza/Jericho Agreement Implementation Law (Limiting of Activities)," barring any PLO or Palestinian Authority political activity in eastern Jerusalem and the rest of Israel and areas of the West Bank and Gaza still under Israeli control.
1995 January 22	19 are killed and 62 wounded in bombing near Beit Lid; Palestine Islamic Jihad (PIJ) claims responsibility.
February 2	Leaders of Egypt, Israel, Jordan and the PLO hold summit meeting in Cairo, affirming cooperation against terrorism.
February 7-8	Officials from the U.S., Israel, Egypt, Jordan, and the PLO meeting in Taba, Egypt, sign joint declaration calling for end to boycott of Israel.
February 12	Experts from the U.S., Israel, Egypt, Jordan, and the PLO meet in Washington to coordinate fight against terrorism.
March 14	Israel and Syria agree to resume direct peace talks involving Israel's Ambassador to Washington,

Itamar Rabinovich, and his Syrian counterpart, Walid al-Moualem.

April	Ofek (Horizon) 3 satellite is launched by Israel.
April 9	An Islamic Jihad member attacks an Israeli convoy near the Kfar Darom settlement in Gaza. 7 Israeli soldiers and an American tourist are killed and 34 wounded.
May 24	U.S. officials announce progress toward Israeli-Syrian working agreement for security arrangements on the Golan Heights.
July 24	An unidentified suicide bomber activates a bomb aboard a bus in Ramat Gan, near Tel Aviv, killing six Israelis, wounding 28.
July 30	Successful test flight of Arrow 2 interceptor missile.
August 11	Israeli and Palestinian delegations meeting in Taba, Egypt, reach partial agreement on IDF redeployment in West Bank.
August 21	5 are killed and more than 100 wounded in Palestine suicide bus-bombing in Jerusalem.
September 19	Tomiichi Murayama makes first visit by a Japanese Prime Minister to Israel.
September 28	Israeli-Palestinian Interim Agreement on the West Bank and Gaza Strip ("Oslo II") is signed in Washington.
September 30	Peres and Omani Foreign Minister Yousuf Bin Alawi agree to establish interest offices in Muscat and Tel Aviv and to work toward economic and technical cooperation.

October 6   A paramilitary Egyptian police officer kills seven
                     Israeli tourists at the Egyptian Red Sea resort of
                     Ras Burka.

October 24   U.S. Congress passes "Jerusalem Embassy Re-
                     location Act," requiring transfer of embassy to
                     Jerusalem by May 1999.

October 25   Israeli troops begin withdrawing from six cities in
                     West Bank.

October 26   Fathi Shukaki, Secretary-General of the militant
                     Palestine Islamic Jihad, is assassinated in Malta.

October 29-31   Second Middle East/North Africa Economic
                     Summit convenes in Amman, Jordan.

November 1   Yossi Beilin and Mahmoud Abbas sign "document
                     of understanding" on terms of permanent status
                     arrangements between Israel and the Palestinian
                     Authority.

November 4   Yitzhak Rabin is assassinated by Yigal Amir in
                     Tel Aviv; Peres becomes Interim Prime Minister;
                     inquiry headed by retired Supreme Court President
                     Meir Shamgar finds serious lapse in security
                     around Rabin but no evidence of conspiracy.

November 20   Treaty of Association with European Union (EU)
                     is signed, institutionalizing political relations at
                     ministerial level, expanding the scope of EU-Israel
                     free trade zone, and granting Israel membership in
                     EU's research and development program. Treaty is
                     ratified by European Parliament in February 1996.

November 22   The Knesset votes its confidence in the new
                     Government of Shimon Peres by a vote of 62-8
                     with 32 abstentions.

December 4   Amir Peretz is chosen as chairman of Histadrut.

December 11	Peres and Clinton meet in Washington, the first time since Rabin's assassination.
December 11-27	IDF completes withdrawal from six major West Bank cities (Bethlehem, Jenin, Nablus, Qalqilya, Ramallah, and Tulkarem).
December 27	Israelis and Syrians meet at Wye Plantation in Maryland.
1996 January 5	The "engineer," Yahya Ayyash, mastermind of Hamas suicide bombings, is killed in Gaza, allegedly by Israeli agents.
January 20	Arabs in Gaza Strip and West Bank elect first Palestinian Legislative Council; candidates affiliated with Fatah and pro-Arafat independents win 67 of 88 seats (75%), with Yasser Arafat taking 88.1% in election for President.
January 27	Israel and Oman sign agreement to open liaison offices in Muskat and Tel Aviv.
February	Israel and Turkey sign agreement on joint military training.
February 12	Arafat is sworn in as President of Palestinian Authority.
February 20	David Levy announces the establishment of his new political party, Gesher (Bridge).
February 25	25 people, including 2 American tourists, are killed and 50 wounded in suicide bombing in Jerusalem.
February 25	1 soldier is killed and 30 wounded in bombing in Ashkelon.
February 26	1 is killed and 22 wounded in Jerusalem terrorist

	incident.
March	Israel and Turkey sign military and intelligence cooperation agreements.
March 3	19 are killed and 10 wounded in suicide-bombing on a bus in Jerusalem.
March 4	14 are killed and 200 wounded in suicide-bombing in Tel Aviv.
March 7	First meeting of Palestinian Legislative Council in Gaza.
March 13	"Summit of the Peacemakers" at Sharm el-Sheikh, Egypt.
April 14-16	13 are wounded by Katyusha rockets fired into northern Galilee from Hezbollah bases in Lebanon. In retaliation Israel launches air and missile barrage ("Operation Grapes of Wrath"), to push Hezbollah out of firing range of the Galilee and south Lebanon security zone.
April 18	IDF bombardment of suspected Hezbollah missile emplacements results in the death of 11 Lebanese civilians in the village of Nabatiya al-Fawqa, and 102 at UN refugee base at Kfar Qana; Israel is widely condemned for these deaths.
April 22	21st Palestinian National Council meeting in Gaza resolves that the PLO Charter is "hereby amended by canceling the articles that are contrary to the letters exchanged between the PLO and the Government of Israel 9-10 September 1993," and instructs its legal committee to present redrafted Charter within 6 months. Prime Minister Peres declares that the PLO has fulfilled its obligation to change the Charter; others disagree with that assessment.

May 5-6   First session of Israel-PLO permanent status talks
                 convenes at Taba, Egypt.

May 21   Israel opens its interests office in Muskat, Oman.

May 29   In the first direct election of the Prime Minister,
                 Benjamin Netanyahu defeats Shimon Peres by less
                 than 1% (50.4% to 49.5%), though among Jewish
                 voters there is an 11% differential (55.5% to
                 44.5%). Concurrent election to 14th Knesset is
                 held.

June 2   Major General Danny Yatom becomes head of the
                 Mossad.

June 17   New 6-party governing coalition (holding 66 of
                 120 seats) is presented to the Knesset.

June 22-23   Arab leaders threaten to reconsider relations with
                 Israel if the new Government forsakes the land-
                 for-peace formula; they also reiterate their demand
                 for Israel's withdrawal from "all the Arab territory
                 it captured in the 1967 war, including East
                 Jerusalem and the Golan Heights, as well as from
                 South Lebanon [Israel] must also dismantle
                 settlements and let the Palestinians set up an
                 independent Palestinian state in the West Bank and
                 Gaza Strip, with East Jerusalem as its capital."

July 10   In address to joint session of the U.S. Congress
                 Netanyahu talks about "three pillars of peace":
                 security, reciprocity, and democracy and human
                 rights, and pledges to reduce Israel's dependence
                 on U.S. financial assistance.

August 8   Oman opens its trade representative office in Tel
                 Aviv.

August 28   Israel and Turkey sign bilateral technical
                 agreement; among other things the agreement is

designed to alleviate Israel's concern about the status of bilateral ties under new Turkish Government headed by Prime Minister Necmetin Erbakan's fundamentalist Welfare Party.

September 4   Netanyahu and Arafat meet for the first time.

September 9   First meeting of Israeli-Palestinian Steering Committee since Israeli elections.

September 24-30   Israel cabinet approves opening of new exit to existing ancient tunnel running beneath Western Wall; Palestinian rioting ensues resulting in 59 Arab and 15 Israeli deaths.

October 1-2   Netanyahu and Arafat join King Hussein and Clinton at mini summit in Washington; Israeli and Palestinian leaders reaffirm commitment to abide by obligations undertaken in the Oslo Accords.

October 6   "Non-stop" talks toward implementing outstanding aspects of interim agreements begin between delegations headed by former IDF Chief of Staff Dan Shomron and chief Palestinian negotiator Saeb Erekat.

November   Netanyahu declares that the Palestinian entity to emerge from permanent status talks will be "on the model of a state like Puerto Rico or Andorra."

November 5   Israeli and Palestinian tourism bureaus announce plan to jointly market tourism to the region.

November 12-14   Third Middle East/North Africa Economic Summit convenes in Cairo, Egypt.

November 26   Palestinian Authority (PA) announces it will boycott meetings of multilateral working groups (except those dealing with refugee issue), to protest Israel's "lack of seriousness in implementing interim agreements."

December 6	Israel and Turkey sign $650 million agreement for Israel Aircraft Industries (IAI) to modernize Turkish air force.
December 22	Agreement to open Regional Desalination Center in Oman is signed, with Israel as full partner.
December 29	Ezer Weizman becomes first Israeli President to visit India, signing 4 bilateral trade and agricultural agreements and opening model high-tech farm to be administered by Mashav, the International Cooperation Department of Israel's Foreign Ministry.
1997 January 1	6 Palestinians are wounded when a deranged IDF soldier opens fire in Hebron. Israel cabinet gives formal approval to trade treaties with Canada, the Czech Republic, Slovakia, and Turkey.
January 15	Israel and Palestinian Authority conclude Protocol Concerning the Redeployment in Hebron; appended to the protocol are 2 additional documents: a "Note for the Record" listing outstanding obligations to be fulfilled by each side; and U.S. "Letter of Assurance" to Israel regarding terms of reference for further IDF redeployments.
January 16	By vote of 87 to 17 (with 1 abstention) the Knesset endorses the Hebron agreement.
January 22	Tourism bureaus of Israel, the Palestinian Authority, and Jordan launch joint marketing campaign.
January 25	Group of Likud and Labor MKs sign "National Agreement Toward Permanent Status Discussions with the Palestinians"; goal of bipartisan

discussions, headed by Michael Eitan (Likud) and Yossi Beilin (Labor) was to facilitate beginnings of "national consensus" among Israelis about contentious issues to be addressed in final status talks with the Palestinians.

February 4   73 Israeli soldiers die when two IDF helicopters collide near the Lebanon border.

February 13   Netanyahu and Clinton meet in Washington, the first time since the Hebron agreement.

February 17   Israeli-Palestinian talks on implementing interim agreements resume in Jerusalem.

February 26   Israel cabinet approves plan to build 6,500 housing units at the Har Homa district of eastern Jerusalem; Palestinian leaders warn that the start of construction could provoke renewed violence.

March 7   The U.S. vetoes proposed UN Security Council resolution criticizing Har Homa project.

March 7   Israel cabinet announces plan to redeploy from additional 9% of the West Bank; PA rejects proposal as insufficient.

March 9   Jordan's King Hussein sends letter to Netanyahu expressing "distress" over stalemate in negotiations with the Palestinians and questioning whether it is Netanyahu's "intent to destroy" the peace process.

March 11   Fourth successful test of Arrow 2 interceptor missile.

March 13   7 Israeli schoolgirls are killed when a deranged Jordanian soldier opens fire at Naharayim; King Hussein makes unprecedented condolence calls on families of the victims.

March 15   Arafat convenes meeting in Gaza to rally
                    international support against Har Homa project;
                    Israel criticizes the meeting as unnecessary and
                    calls on the PA to utilize dispute resolution
                    mechanism set up in Oslo Accords.

March 18   Israeli bulldozers begin construction work at Har
                    Homa.

March 21   The U.S. vetoes a second proposed UN Security
                    Council condemnation of Har Homa project.

March 21   3 Israelis are killed and several wounded in
                    suicide-bombing in Tel Aviv. Israel cabinet adopts
                    6 conditions for continuing peace talks: stronger
                    and improved security cooperation; prevention of
                    inciteful propaganda against Israel; an effective
                    war on terrorist organizations and their
                    infrastructure; the arrest, trial, and punishment of
                    terrorists; handling of requests for the extradition
                    of suspected terrorists to Israel; and the collection
                    of illegal arms and ammunition.

March 28   Jewish worshipers are temporarily evacuated from
                    the plaza in front of the Western Wall when
                    Palestinian demonstrators throw stones from the
                    Temple Mount above.

March 31   Arab foreign ministers recommend that Arab
                    countries cease normalizing relations with Israel
                    and restore the economic boycott, and that they
                    suspend participation in multilateral peace talks to
                    protest absence of progress in bilateral talks.

April 14   A Palestinian woman from the West Bank town of
                    Qalqilya opens fire at the Allenby Bridge crossing
                    point, wounding 2 Israeli security personnel and a
                    Palestinian bystander.

April 14   The Mufti of Istanbul, Turkey, Selhattin Kaya, declares that there is no Muslim religious objection to Israel's existence.

April 24   The UN General Assembly, meeting in a rare "emergency special session," adopts a resolution criticizing the Har Homa building project; Israel and the United States oppose the resolution as one-sided, unnecessary, and detrimental to the peace process.

May 16   Arafat implicitly endorses move by Palestinian Legislative Council to impose death penalty against Arabs suspected of selling property in eastern Jerusalem to Jews.

May 29   Israel and Jordan sign agreement to share international airports at Eilat and Aqaba; the "Shalom Airport" goes into service in November 1997.

July   Finance Minister Yaacov Ne'eman is appointed to head committee comprised of representatives of various streams of Judaism (Ultra-Orthodox, Orthodox, Conservative, and Reform) set up to achieve compromise on "Who is a Jew" controversy.

July 15   By vote of 131 to 3 (Israel, the U.S., and Micronesia), the UN General Assembly condemns continued work at Har Homa and makes veiled threats to apply partial economic sanctions and take steps to isolate Israel at the UN.

July 20   Two suicide bombers strike in Mahane Yehuda market in Jerusalem.

July 22   10 British and Canadian tourists are wounded in 2 separate terrorist attacks by the same person in Jaffa.

July 27

Israel cabinet freezes plans by U.S. millionaire Irving Moskowitz to build yeshiva and Jewish housing in Ras al-Amud, a largely Arab district of eastern Jerusalem.

August 6

In meetings with Jordan's Crown Prince Hassan and Prime Minister Abdul Salem Majali, Netanyahu affirms Israel's readiness to ease sanctions against Palestinians once PA fights terrorism.

August 25

Netanyahu meets with Chinese Deputy Prime Minister and Foreign Minister Qian Qichen during stopover in Beijing, eliciting pledge that China will not assist Iran's nuclear weapons program. The two leaders agree to establish committees on bilateral cooperation in the fields of agriculture, education, health, and culture. Minister Qichen accepts Netanyahu's invitation to visit Israel.

August 27

Israel and South Korea agree to establish $6 million joint technological research and development fund.

September

Madeleine Albright makes first visit to Middle East since becoming U.S. Secretary of State.

September 4

4 are killed and 200 wounded when 3 suicide bombs explode in Jerusalem's Ben Yehuda pedestrian mall.

September 22

Two staffers at the Israeli Embassy in Amman, Jordan, are wounded in terrorist attack.

September 25

Khalel Meshal, head of the Hamas political office in Jordan, is wounded in an assassination attempt in Amman; 2 Mossad agents, carrying forged Canadian passports, are arrested by Jordanian police. Jordanians react by temporarily suspending security cooperation. Israel acquiesces to King

Hussein's demand to release the founder and spiritual leader of Hamas, Sheik Ahmed Yassin, and other Hamas activists.

September 30   Turkey rejects appointment of new Israeli Ambassador to Ankara, Professor Ehud Toledano, for remarks made years earlier about World War I massacre of ethnic Armenians.

October 1   Israel frees Hamas spiritual leader Sheikh Ahmed Yassin.

October 8   Netanyahu and Arafat hold first one-on-one meeting in 8 months.

November 10   Israel and the Vatican sign agreement granting special legal status to institutions of the Catholic Church in Israel.

November 12   Israel's Agriculture Minister Rafael Eitan and his Chinese counterpart sign bilateral agreement providing for increased exchange of agriculture produce, technology, and investment.

November 16-18   Fourth Middle East/North Africa Economic Conference convenes in Doha, Qatar.

November 18   Netanyahu and King Hussein meet in London to resume bilateral security cooperation after the "Meshal Affair" and to coordinate response to Iraq-UN dispute over arms inspections.

November 25   Israeli and Jordanian navies hold joint search-and-rescue training exercises in the Gulf of Eilat.

November-
December   Israel agrees to have a portion of its U.S. foreign aid transferred to Jordan.

December 4   In an open letter to his Prime Minister, Jordan's King Hussein criticizes Netanyahu for his "unending attempt to destroy the Oslo Pact."

December 7	Organization of the Islamic Conference (OIC) adopts draft resolution criticizing Turkey-Israeli relations and calling for end to normalization steps with Israel to protest stalemate in talks with Palestinians.
December 22	Chinese Deputy Prime Minister and Foreign Minister Qian Qichen visits Israel to activate bilateral working committees and to establish political framework for visit by Chinese Prime Minister Li Peng.
1998 January 4	Defense Minister Yitzhak Mordechai declares Israel's readiness to negotiate IDF withdrawal from southern Lebanon on the basis of UN Security Council Resolution 425 (1978).
January 4	David Levy resigns as Foreign Minister and withdraws his Gesher faction from the governing coalition to protest stalemate in peace process and proposed budget cuts.
January 7	Israel, Turkey, and the U.S. hold joint naval search and rescue training exercises; "Reliant Mermaid" exercises are observed by the commander of the Jordanian navy.
January 16	In meeting at the Vatican with Government minister Moshe Katsav, Pope John Paul II expresses interest in visiting Israel; the Holy See also declares it has no intention of recognizing Palestinian sovereignty in east Jerusalem any more than it has recognized Israeli claims there.
January 20	Netanyahu meets with Clinton in Washington.
January 20	Zevulun Hammer, leader of the National Religious Party and Education Minister and Deputy Prime

Minister, dies.

January 27-28   In meetings in Washington Finance Minister Yaacov Ne'eman reaffirms goal of reducing dependence on U.S. financial aid.

February 18   Foreign Ministry Director-General, Eitan Bentsur, sends letter to his Palestinian counterpart detailing proposals for joint "People-to-People" projects.

February 23   Chief Israeli and Palestinian negotiators, Danny Naveh and Saeb Erekat, meet to coordinate continued efforts to implement interim agreements.

February 24   Mossad head Danny Yatom resigns.

March 4   Knesset reelects Ezer Weizman to second term as President of Israel; Weizman receives 63 votes to 49 for the Likud's Shaul Amor, with 8 abstentions.

March 8-10   Government ministers Ariel Sharon and Natan Sharansky make separate visits to Jordan, and Crown Prince Hassan makes first visit by Jordanian leader to Israel since the "Meshal Affair."

March 10   3 Palestinian workers are killed in incident with IDF soldiers at Tarkumiya checkpoint in the West Bank; sporadic rioting occurs in Hebron and elsewhere in reaction.

March 18   81 U.S. Senators sign letter to President Clinton expressing concern about reported White House pressure on Israel to make unsafe concessions in negotiations with the Palestinian Authority.

July 17   Israel (along with the United States and 5 other countries) votes against the Rome Convention, establishing an International Criminal Court; Israel objects to the implied inclusion of Jewish settlement activity in the West Bank and Gaza Strip in the draft treaty's definition of "war crimes."

October 9	Ariel Sharon is named Foreign Minister and Israel's chief negotiator of final-status agreements with the Palestinian Authority.
October 23	Netanyahu and Arafat conclude the Wye River Memorandum.
October 27	A resident of Kiryat Arba is killed by assailants who reportedly flee into Palestinian sector of Hebron.
October 29	2 are killed and 3 others wounded in attempted Hamas suicide-bombing of a Jewish school bus near the Gush Khatif junction in Gaza Strip.
October 31	The United States and Israel sign Memorandum of Agreement on strategic security cooperation (against the threat of nonconventional weapons of mass destruction and long-range ballistic missiles).
November 6	2 suicide-bombers are killed and 4 are wounded in attack in Jerusalem's Mahane Yehuda market; Palestine Islamic Jihad claims responsibility.
November 17	The Knesset ratifies the Wye River Memorandum by vote of 75-19, with 9 abstentions and 14 absent.
November 18	Foreign Minister Sharon and Palestinian Authority minister Abu-Mazen (Mahmoud Abbas) formally launch final-status negotiations.
November 20	Israel redeploys from areas between Jenin and Nablus in northern sector of the West Bank, implementing first phase of Wye River Memorandum.

November 29	First operational Arrow anti-missile missile system is transferred from Israel aircraft Industries to Defense Ministry's *Homa* ("Wall") project.
December 9	For the first time, the UN General Assembly includes anti-Semitism in its definition of racism.
December 14	At special meeting in Gaza, and in the presence of U.S. President Clinton, the Palestine National Council ratifies changes to the Covenant stipulated in Arafat's January 22, 1998, letter to Clinton. Israel calls the changes "satisfactory."
December 18	Finance Minister Yaacov Ne'eman resigns.
December 21	Faced with likely defections of key coalition partners in Knesset no-confidence vote over his Government's handling of the peace process, Netanyahu supports legislation to prepare for general elections. All-party agreement subsequently is reached setting May 17, 1999, as date for direct election of Prime Minister and election of the 15th Knesset.
December 22	Dan Meridor quits Likud, announcing intention to run for Prime Minister as head of a new centrist political party. This proposed party ultimately is subsumed within the new Center Party headed by Yitzhak Mordechai.
December 28	Ze'ev Binyamin Begin quits Likud, announcing intention to enter race for Prime Minister as head of New Herut (Herut Hahadasha) Party. This party subsequently is incorporated into new right-wing National Union coalition, with Begin as its candidate for Prime Minister.
1999 January 23	Prime Minister Netanyahu dismisses Defense Minister Yitzhak Mordechai.

March 25   Azmi (Ahmed) Bishara becomes first Israeli Arab to declare his candidacy for Prime Minister.

May 15-16   On the eve of general elections, Azmi Bishara, Yitzhak Mordechai, and Ze'ev Binyamin Begin, withdraw from prime ministerial race, creating two-way contest between Benjamin Netanyahu and Ehud Barak.

May 17   Israel Labor Party/One Israel leader Ehud Barak defeats the Likud's Benjamin Netanyahu in the direct election for Prime Minister, receiving 56.08% of the popular vote (1,791,020) compared to 43.92 (1,402,474) for Netanyahu. In elections for the 15th Knesset, One Israel wins 26 seats, Likud 19, and Shas 17.

May 28   Wreckage of submarine *Dakar* located in Mediterranean.

June 18   Employing a special presidential waiver, Bill Clinton delays for an additional six months implementing Congressional legislation requiring the transfer of the U.S. embassy from Tel Aviv to Jerusalem, citing national security and the interests of the Arab-Israeli peace process.

June 19-21   Hezbollah fires missiles into northern Galilee, ostensibly in retaliation for injuries suffered by Lebanese civilians when their village, just north of Israel's south Lebanon security zone, was hit by an IDF anti-tank missile.

June-July   Ehud Barak and Syria's President Hafez al-Assad exchange rare public compliments.

July 6   The Knesset approves Ehud Barak's Government and policy guidelines and he is sworn in as Prime Minister. Barak presents his seven party, 75-member governing coalition and its program before the Knesset for ratification; in his inaugural speech as Prime Minister, Barak urges Israel's Arab neighbors to resume pursuit of peace initiated by his mentor, Yitzhak Rabin. Labor MK Avraham Burg is elected speaker of the 15th Knesset.

July 14-15   Turkish President Suleyman Demirel makes an official visit to Israel.

July 25   Barak sends soldiers to remove mobile homes brought by settlers to expand a hilltop encampment in the West Bank that he called illegal. His office noted that "the Government will vigorously oppose any unilateral and illegal steps" by the settlers.

July 26   At the invitation of Knesset Speaker Avraham Burg, Ahmad Qurie (Abu Ala), Speaker of the Palestinian Legislative Council, conducts an official visit to the Knesset.

August 5   MK Nawaf Massalha is appointed to the post of Deputy Foreign Minister, the first Israeli Arab to hold that post.

August 10   An Arab drives his car into a group of Israelis at Nachshon Junction wounding at least 11 before being shot dead. An army spokesman called the driver an "Arab terrorist."

August 30   Morocco renews political contacts with Israel, frozen during Netanyahu years.

August 31   Two young Israelis are found murdered in the Megiddo Forest near the West Bank city of Jenin. An Israeli Arab is arrested for the crime, for which Hamas takes responsibility.

September 2   Ariel Sharon is elected leader of the Likud Party, defeating challengers Ehud Olmert and Meir Shitreet.

September 2 — In a plea bargain, Samuel Sheinbein admits committing premeditated murder in Maryland, and is sentenced to 24 years in an Israeli prison.

September 4 — Barak and Arafat sign agreement at Sharm el-Sheikh, to implement outstanding elements of the October 1998 Wye River Memorandum. A target date for completing final-status peace negotiations is set for September 2000, with a "framework agreement" scheduled for February 2000.

September 5 — In separate incidents in Tiberias and Haifa, 3 suicide-bombers are killed when their cars explode prematurely. The dead were discovered to be Israeli Arabs, members of the radical wing of the Islamic Movement in Israel.

September 8 — Cabinet approves Sharm el-Sheikh peace accord by a vote of 19 for, 1 against (Housing Minster Yitzhak Levy), with one abstention (Interior Minister Natan Sharansky) and with 4 ministers (all from Shas) absent.

September 9 — Knesset ratifies Sharm el-Sheikh agreement by 54-23 vote, with 2 abstentions, and with a number of coalition members, including Interior Minister Natan Sharansky, absent.

September 9 — 199 Palestinian prisoners are released.

September 13 — Foreign Minister David Levy and Palestinian negotiator Abu Mazen formally launch the final status peace talks between Israel and the Palestinians.

October 25 — Ehud Barak becomes the first Israeli Prime Minister since David Ben-Gurion to visit Turkey.

October 28	Mauritania establishes diplomatic ties with Israel, becoming the third Arab country (after Egypt and Jordan) to do so.
November 1	In a test flight, the Arrow anti-missile missile successfully finds and destroys a simulated Scud missile in mid-flight.
November 7	Pipe bomb explosions wound 27 in Netanya.
November 8	Israel and the PLO begin permanent status talks in earnest in Ramallah.
November 10	Barak Cabinet approves additional 5 percent redeployment in the West Bank, but Arafat refuses to sign the maps, claiming that the areas affected by the proposed redeployment are "not significant enough" for the Palestinians.
November 14	Jacob Frenkel resigns as Governor of the Bank of Israel, effective in early 2000.
December	Israel, Turkey, and U.S. participate in "Reliant Mermaid 1999" search-and-rescue navel exercises in the eastern Mediterranean.
December	Evidence is uncovered of President Ezer Weizman's having received substantial financial gifts; Weizman resists growing pressure to resign.
December 8	President Clinton announces agreement of Israel and Syria to resume formal talks.
December 15-16	Barak and Syrian Foreign Minister Farouk al-Sharaa meet with Clinton in Washington.
December 21	Barak and Foreign Minister David Levy meet with Arafat in Ramallah in an attempt to reconcile differences over a further 5 percent redeployment.

December 29   Israel releases 26 Palestinian security prisoners as Ramadan goodwill gesture.

2000 January   Dr. David Klein is appointed Governor of the Bank of Israel.

January 3-10   Barak and Sharaa and their respective delegations meet with U.S. mediators in Shepherdstown, West Virginia. Clinton presents a 7-page document designed to "bridge" differences between Israeli and Syrian positions on key issues, and to serve as a blueprint for a comprehensive peace treaty.

January 6   Israel concludes a scheduled redeployment from 5 percent of the West Bank.

January 16   Dr. David Klein is formally appointed Governor of the Bank of Israel.

January 20   Israel's Attorney General orders a criminal investigation of President Ezer Weizman over alleged financial improprieties. Weizman subsequently addresses the nation: "I do not intend to resign."

January 27   A criminal investigation is ordered into the fund-raising activities of Barak's One Israel coalition in the 1999 election campaign; simultaneous investigations are launched into the fund-raising activities of four other political parties. Barak and Justice Minister Beilin subsequently announce formation of public committee, headed by retired Supreme Court Justice Dov Levin, to examine campaign financing laws in Israel.

January 28   Appeal of former Shas leader Arye Deri's 1999 conviction for bribery and fraud begins.

February 1   Multilateral track of Middle East Peace Process negotiations is revived at conference in Moscow, after three-year hiatus; Syria and Lebanon continue to boycott the multilateral process.

February 2 Barak Cabinet approves maps for third IDF redeployment from 6 percent of the West Bank; Arafat hesitates to approve maps, reportedly over Palestinian demand that areas affected by redeployment should include Arab villages on the periphery of Jerusalem.

February 3 Barak and Foreign Minister David Levy meet with Arafat at Erez crossing in attempt to resolve differences over third redeployment; Palestinians declare "major crisis" in the negotiations blocking completion of the Framework Agreement on a permanent settlement by February 13 target date.

TABLES

TABLE 1

PRESIDENT

Chaim Weizmann	1949-1952
Yitzhak Ben Zvi	1952-1963
Shneor Zalman Shazar	1963-1973
Ephraim Katzir	1973-1978
Yitzhak Navon	1978-1983
Chaim Herzog	1983-1993
Ezer Weizman	1993-

TABLE 2

PRIME MINISTER

David Ben-Gurion	1948-1954
Moshe Sharett	1954-1955
David Ben-Gurion	1955-1963
Levi Eshkol	1963-1969
Golda Meir	1969-1974
Yitzhak Rabin	1974-1977
Menahem Begin	1977-1983
Yitzhak Shamir	1983-1984
Shimon Peres	1984-1986
Yitzhak Shamir	1986-1992
Yitzhak Rabin	1992-1995
Shimon Peres	1995-1996
Benjamin Netanyahu	1996-1999
Ehud Barak	1999-

TABLE 3

MINISTER OF FOREIGN AFFAIRS

Moshe Sharett	1948-1956
Golda Meir	1956-1966
Abba Eban	1966-1974
Yigal Allon	1974-1977
Moshe Dayan	1977-1979
Menahem Begin	1979-1980
Yitzhak Shamir	1980-1986
Shimon Peres	1986-1988
Moshe Arens	1988-1990
David Levy	1990-1992
Shimon Peres	1992-1995
Ehud Barak	1995-1996
David Levy	1996-1998
Benjamin Netanyahu	1998-1998
Ariel Sharon	1998-1999
David Levy	1999-

TABLE 4

MINISTER OF DEFENSE

David Ben-Gurion	1948-1954
Pinhas Lavon	1954-1955
David Ben-Gurion	1955-1963
Levi Eshkol	1963-1967
Moshe Dayan	1967-1974
Shimon Peres	1974-1977
Ezer Weizman	1977-1980
Menahem Begin	1980-1981
Ariel Sharon	1981-1983
Moshe Arens	1983-1984
Yitzhak Rabin	1984-1990
Moshe Arens	1990-1992
Yitzhak Rabin	1992-1995
Shimon Peres	1995-1996
Yitzhak Mordechai	1996-1998
Moshe Arens	1999-1999
Ehud Barak	1999-

TABLE 5

MINISTER OF FINANCE

Eliezer Kaplan	1948-1952
Levi Eshkol	1952-1963
Pinhas Sapir	1963-1968
Ze'ev Sharef	1968-1969
Pinhas Sapir	1969-1974
Yehoshua Rabinowitz	1974-1977
Simha Ehrlich	1977-1980
Yigael Hurvitz	1980-1981
Yoram Aridor	1981-1983
Yigal Cohen-Orgad	1983-1984
Yitzhak Moda'i	1984-1986
Moshe Nissim	1986-1988
Shimon Peres	1988-1990
Yitzhak Moda'i	1990-1992
Avraham Shochat	1992-1996
Dan Meridor	1996-1997
Yaacov Ne'eman	1997-1998
Meir Shitreet	1999-1999
Avraham Shochat	1999-

TABLE 6

ISRAEL DEFENSE FORCES: CHIEF OF STAFF

Yaacov Dori	1948-1949
Yigael Yadin	1949-1952
Mordechai Maklef	1952-1953
Moshe Dayan	1953-1958
Chaim Laskov	1958-1961
Zvi Tsur	1961-1964
Yitzhak Rabin	1964-1968
Chaim Bar-Lev	1968-1972
David Elazar	1972-1974
Mordechai Gur	1974-1978
Raphael Eitan	1978-1983
Moshe Levy	1983-1987
Dan Shomron	1987-1991
Ehud Barak	1991-1994
Amnon Lipkin-Shahak	1995-1998
Shaul Mofaz	1998-

TABLE 7

ATTORNEY GENERAL

Ya'acov Shimshon Shapira	1948-1950
Haim Cohen	1950-1960
Gideon Hausner	1960-1963
Moshe Ben Ze'ev	1963-1968
Me'ir Shamgar	1968-1975
Aharon Barak	1975-1978
Yitzhak Zamir	1978-1986
Yosef Harish	1986-1992
Michael Ben Ya'ir	1992-1996
Ronnie Bar-On	1997 (3 days)
Elyakim Rubinstein	1997-

TABLE 8

KNESSET: BEGINNING OF TERM

First Knesset	1949
Second Knesset	1951
Third Knesset	1955
Fourth Knesset	1959
Fifth Knesset	1961
Sixth Knesset	1965
Seventh Knesset	1969
Eighth Knesset	1973
Ninth Knesset	1977
Tenth Knesset	1981
Eleventh Knesset	1984
Twelfth Knesset	1988
Thirteenth Knesset	1992
Fourteenth Knesset	1996
Fifteenth Knesset	1999

TABLE 9A

IMMIGRATION TO PALESTINE AND ISRAEL
1882-1999
(PART 1 OF 2)

1882-1903	20,000-30,000
1904-1914	35,000-40,000
1919-1923	35,183
1924-1931	81,613
1932-1938	197,235
1939-1945	81,808
1945-1948, May 15	56,467
1948 (May 15-Dec 31)	101,819
1949	239,576
1950	170,215
1951	175,129
1952	24,369
1953	11,326
1954	18,370
1955	37,478
1956	56,234
1957	71,224
1958	27,082
1959	23,895
1960	24,510
1961	47,638
1962	61,328
1963	64,364
1964	54,716
1965	30,736
1966	15,730
1967	14,327
1968	20,544
1969	37,804

(continued)

TABLE 9B

IMMIGRATION TO PALESTINE AND ISRAEL
1882-1999
(PART 2 OF 2)

1970	36,750
1971	41,930
1972	55,888
1973	54,886
1974	31,981
1975	20,028
1976	19,754
1977	21,429
1978	26,394
1979	37,222
1980	20,428
1981	12,599
1982	13,723
1983	16,906
1984	19,981
1985	10,642
1986	9,505
1987	12,965
1988	13,034
1989	24,050
1990	199,500
1991	176,000
1992	77,100
1993	77,080
1994	82,000
1995	76,400
1996	70,605
1997	66,500
1998	56,700
1999 (as of September)	17,100

TABLE 10A

POPULATION AT END OF YEAR
(THOUSANDS)
(PART 1 OF 2)

	JEWS	MUSLIMS	CHRISTIANS	DRUZE & OTHERS	TOTAL
1948	758.7	--------------- 156.0 ---------------			
1949	1013.9	111.5	34.0	14.5	1173.9
1950	1203.0	116.1	36.0	15.0	1370.1
1951	1404.4	118.9	39.0	15.5	1577.8
1952	1450.2	122.8	40.4	16.1	1629.5
1953	1483.6	127.6	41.4	16.8	1669.4
1954	1526.0	131.8	42.0	18.0	1717.8
1955	1590.5	136.3	43.3	19.0	1789.1
1956	1667.5	141.4	43.7	19.8	1872.4
1957	1762.8	146.8	45.8	20.5	1976.0
1958	1810.2	152.8	47.3	21.4	2031.7
1959	1858.8	159.2	48.3	22.3	2088.7
1960	1911.3	166.3	49.6	23.3	2150.4
1961	1981.7	179.4	51.3	26.3	2234.2
1962	2068.9	183.0	52.6	27.3	2331.8
1963	2155.6	192.2	53.9	28.5	2430.1
1964	2239.2	202.3	55.5	28.6	2525.6
1965	2299.1	212.4	57.1	29.8	2598.4
1966	2344.9	223.0	58.5	31.0	2657.4
1967	2383.6	289.6	71.0	32.1	2776.3
1968	2434.8	300.8	72.2	33.3	2841.1
1969	2506.8	314.5	73.5	34.6	2929.5
1970	2582.0	328.6	75.5	35.9	3022.1
1971	2662.0	344.0	77.3	37.3	3120.7
1972	2752.7	360.7	73.8	37.8	3225.0

(continued)

TABLE 10B

POPULATION AT END OF YEAR
(THOUSANDS)
(PART 2 OF 2)

	JEWS	MUSLIMS	CHRISTIANS	DRUZE & OTHERS	TOTAL
1973	2845.0	377.2	76.7	39.3	3338.2
1974	2906.9	395.2	78.7	40.8	3421.6
1975	2959.4	411.4	80.2	42.2	3493.2
1976	3020.4	429.1	82.0	43.9	3575.4
1977	3077.3	446.5	83.8	45.6	3653.2
1978	3141.2	463.6	85.5	47.3	3737.6
1979	3218.4	481.2	87.6	49.0	3836.2
1980	3282.7	498.3	89.9	50.7	3921.7
1981	3320.3	513.7	91.5	52.3	3977.9
1982	3373.2	530.8	94.0	65.6	4063.6
1983	3412.5	542.2	95.9	68.0	4118.6
1984	3471.7	559.7	98.2	70.0	4199.7
1985	3517.2	577.6	99.4	72.0	4266.2
1986	3561.4	595.0	100.9	74.0	4331.3
1987	3612.9	614.5	103.0	76.1	4406.5
1988	3659.0	634.6	105.0	78.1	4476.8
1989	3717.1	655.2	107.0	80.3	4559.6
1990	3946.7	679.8	115.7	81.9	4821.7
1991	3947.0	680.0	116.0	79.0	4822.0
1992	4177.0	715.0	135.0	86.0	5113.0
1993	4335.2	751.2	149.2	90.6	5327.6
1994	4441.1	782.4	158.7	93.0	5471.5
1995	4549.5	814.7	162.9	95.5	5619.0
1996	4637.4	840.8	184.3	97.9	5759.4
1997	4731.8	879.1	188.8	100.0	5900.0
1998	4783.0	901.3	129.6	102.6	6037.0
1999	4900.0	936.0	131.0	253.0	6220.0

INTRODUCTION

Israel is an independent Jewish state, small in size and population, located at the southwestern tip of Asia on the eastern shore of the Mediterranean Sea. It achieved independence in 1948. Since Biblical times, Jews of the Diaspora have hoped that they would return to Zion, the "promised land," where the ancient Jewish state had been located, as described in the Bible. Over the centuries, Zionism focused on spiritual, religious, cultural, social, and historical links between Jews and the holy land. Political Zionism, with the establishment of a Jewish state as its goal, and Jewish immigration to Palestine both developed in nineteenth-century Europe, partly as responses to anti-Semitism. The defeat of the Ottoman Empire during World War I and its dismemberment during the subsequent peace conferences led to British administration of Palestine (under a League of Nations Mandate) and set the stage for the eventual independence of Israel.

Israel has achieved rapid development and impressive accomplishments in the social and scientific arenas. It has been the region's most politically and socially innovative state and has achieved prosperity for its people. Israel has built a democratic system unlike that of any other in the Middle East and has melded immigrants from more than seventy countries into a uniquely Israeli population. In a country almost devoid of natural resources, its people have achieved a high standard of living.

Israel's development has occurred despite the fact that it has been in a state of war since independence and continually must be ready to defend its existence. Despite peace treaties with Egypt and Jordan, an aborted agreement with Lebanon, and a series of interim agreements with the Palestine Liberation Organization (PLO) and periodic U.S.-sponsored talks with Syria, Israel's pursuit of permanent peace with its neighbors is far from complete. The continuing Arab-Israeli conflict and the potential for conflict with elements of the broader Muslim world remain central tests of Israel's foreign and defense policies.

GOVERNMENT AND POLITICS

Israel is a parliamentary democracy but has no formal written constitution. A series of Basic Laws have been enacted since independence that guide Israel's actions and which are intended, in time, to form portions of a consolidated constitutional document. Pressure has been building recently for the promulgation of a written constitution with a bill of rights.

The President is the head of state and is elected by the Knesset (parliament). The President's powers and functions are primarily ceremonial and his or her actual political power is very limited. The Prime Minister is head of government and, as the chief executive officer, wields considerable power. He or she is now chosen through direct popular election. The Prime Minister forms the Government (or Cabinet) whose members head the ministries. The Prime Minister determines the agenda of Cabinet meetings and has the final word in policy decisions, although such decisions are often arrived at through bargaining and compromise among the coalition of parties that, since independence, have constituted Israel's governments. Decisions by the Government determine the direction and policy of the state.

Legislative power resides in the Knesset, a unicameral body of one hundred twenty members that is the supreme authority in the state. The Knesset's main functions are similar to those of other modern parliaments and include votes of confidence or no confidence in the government, legislation, participation in the formulation of national policy, approval of budgets and taxation, election of the President, and general monitoring of the activities of the executive branch. All members of the Knesset are elected at-large in a national and general election in which seats are apportioned by a complex system of proportional representation.

The judiciary consists of secular and religious court systems. The Supreme Court is the highest court in the land and hears appeals from lower courts in civil and criminal cases and acts to protect the rights of Israeli citizens. While it does not have the power of judicial review, the Supreme Court has in recent years adopted a more activist role, both in invalidating administrative actions it regards as contrary to the law and in commenting on broader social issues. Each major religious community has its own religious courts that have jurisdiction over matters of personal status such as marriage and divorce, alimony, probate, and inheritance.

Israel has a large number of political parties that represent a wide spectrum of views, positions, and interests. There are also religious and special-issue parties that focus on a particular subject or theme. There are also political parties that represent the interests of Israeli Arabs and other minority and ethnic communities.

SOCIETY

At independence, Israel had some 806,000 citizens (650,000 Jews and 156,000 non-Jews). Israel's population by January 2000 stood at 6.2 million, some 80 percent of which were Jews. Israel's non-Jewish population has quadrupled since 1948, mostly as a result of high rates of natural growth. The Jewish population has increased more than fivefold since independence with more than 2.6 million Jewish immigrants, many of whom came from Arab and Islamic countries of the Middle East and North Africa. Beginning in the late 1980s, some 750,000 immigrants from the former Soviet Union added substantially to Israel's population while smaller but more dramatic immigrations came from Ethiopia. Under the Law of Return, any Jew, with some specific exceptions, may immigrate to Israel and receive citizenship. Immigrants are provided with housing and language and vocational training to speed their integration into the mainstream of Israeli society.

Israel's Jews are of a single religious faith and share a spiritual heritage and elements of historical experience. However, ethnically and culturally, they are heterogenous. The Jewish population is composed of immigrants from numerous countries and reflects a variety of ethnic and linguistic groups, degrees of religious observance, and cultural, historical, and political backgrounds. No single ethnic group constitutes even 20 percent of the total Jewish population, although one of the largest is of Moroccan origin.

The two main groups in Israel's Jewish population are the Ashkenazim (that is to say, Jews of central and east European origin) and the Sephardim or Orientals (Jews who came to Israel from the countries of the Middle East and the Mediterranean area). Although the overwhelming majority of the Jewish population was of Ashkenazi origin at independence, Israeli society is now almost evenly split between the Ashkenazim and Jews of Sephardic origin, who are also referred to as "Edot Hamizrach" (eastern or Oriental communities). Increasingly, ethnic divisions are becoming less relevant as the instances of cross-cultural marriages grow and as native-born Israelis identify themselves not as Ashkenazi or Sephardic but as "Sabra".

Geographically, Israel is an Oriental country, but its culture, society, and political system remain primarily Western in nature and orientation. The early Zionists laid the foundations for an essentially European culture in Palestine and subsequent immigration accelerated the trend. The Western immigrants created and developed the structure of land settlement, institutions, trade unions, political parties, and educational systems in preparation for a Western-oriented Jewish national state. Future immigrants from non-Western countries had to adapt to a society that had formed these institutions.

After the Holocaust and the creation of Israel, whole Jewish communities were transported to Israel from the countries of the Middle East and North Africa. This massive Oriental immigration created a situation in which a large portion of the population had societal and cultural traditions different from those of their Western coreligionists who constituted the majority and dominant element in Israel. The religious traditions of Judaism provide a common core of values and ideals, but there are major differences in outlook, frames of reference, levels of aspiration, and other social and cultural components. Although steps have been taken to alleviate the situation, Israel continues to suffer from ethnic-cultural cleavages and a socioeconomic gap and consequent inequalities within the

Jewish community.

Israel's non-Jewish citizenry, constituting about 20 percent of the total population, consists primarily of the Arabs who remained in what became Israel after the 1948-1949 Arab-Israeli War and their descendants. The Arab population is composed primarily of Muslims (about 80%) and is predominantly Sunni, although some 11 percent are Christian (mostly Greek Catholic and Greek Orthodox) and some 9 percent Druze.

Although their legal status is the same as Israel's Jewish population, Israel's Arab citizens are confronted by problems qualitatively different. Between 1948 and the mid-1960s, activities of the Arab community were regarded primarily as concerns of Israel's security system, and most of the areas inhabited by the Arabs were placed under military control. The restrictions were gradually modified, and in 1966 military government was abolished. Although Israeli Arabs vote, sit in the Knesset, serve in government offices, have their own schools and courts, and prosper materially, they face difficulties in adjusting to Israel's modern, Jewish and Western-oriented society. The Arabs tend to live in separate sections of major cities. They speak Arabic, attend a separate school system, and generally do not serve in the army. The Arab and Jewish communities in Israel have few points of contact, and those that exist are not intimate; they are separate societies that generally continue to hold stereotypical images of each other which often are reinforced by the tensions and problems generated by the larger Arab-Israeli conflict. There is mutual suspicion and antagonism, and there is still a Jewish fear of the Arabs—a result of wars and terrorism.

Israel is a Jewish state; nevertheless, it guarantees all of its citizens—in law and in practice—freedom of religion and conscience and considerable autonomy under the *millet* system derived from the Ottoman Empire. At the same time, there have been tensions and often open clashes between the religious and secular segments of the Jewish community and between the Orthodox and non-Orthodox denominations. At issue are the authority and power of the Orthodox and ultra-Orthodox religious authorities and their desire to mould Israeli society in their preferred image. Debate has focused on the appropriate relationship between religion and the state, between the religious and secular authorities, and between the Orthodox-dominated religious establishment and non-Orthodox movements (i.e., Conservative and Reform/Progressive Jewry). At the core of this debate is the contentious question of "Who is a Jew?" The issue has had philosophical, theological, political, and ideological overtones with specific practical dimensions in connection with immigration, marriage, divorce, inheritance, and conversion as well as in registration of identity cards and in the official collection of data and information. The question relates to the application of legislation such as the Law of Return, the Nationality Law, and others passed by the Knesset. Despite ongoing efforts, no permanent solution to the enduring "Who is a Jew" controversy has occurred.

GEOGRAPHY

Israel is a small country whose land borders (except with Egypt, Jordan, and the sea) are not permanent and recognized and whose size has not been determined precisely due to the absence of permanent and comprehensive peace. Within its current frontiers (established by armistice agreements signed in 1949 at the end of the first Arab-Israeli War), Israel is less than 8,000 square miles (some 20,700 square kilometers) and is bounded on the north by Lebanon, on the northeast by Syria, on the east by the West Bank, Jordan, and the Dead Sea, and on the west by the Mediterranean Sea. The country is 264 miles long and, at its widest, is some 70 miles.

Israel may be divided into four main natural land regions: the coastal plain, the highlands of Judea and Samaria, the Rift Valley, and the Negev Desert. The coastal plain lies along the Mediterranean and is composed of a generally narrow and sandy shoreline bordered by fertile farmland varying up to 25 miles in width from the northern border to the Israel-Egypt border in the southwest. Most Israelis live in the coastal plain and most of the industry and agriculture are located there. A series of mountain ranges run north-south from the Galilee to the Negev. The mountains of Galilee stretch southward to the Jezreel Valley, south of which are the mountains and hills of Samaria, Judea, and the Negev. Upper Galilee is the highest part of the country. Lower Galilee's hills are more broken. The highlands of Galilee are where most of Israel's Arabs live in a triangular-shaped area that includes the city of Nazareth. Mount Meron, Israel's highest mountain, is here. The Judean hills include Jerusalem. There is also the Carmel mountain range near Haifa.

The Rift Valley is part of the Great Syrian-African rift—the deepest valley on earth. In Israel, it includes the Jordan Valley, which is located between the mountains of Judea and Samaria in the west and the mountains of Jordan to the east; the Hula Valley between the mountains of Galilee and the Golan Heights; the Jezreel Valley between the mountains of Galilee and Samaria; and the Arava, a long and arid valley running from the Dead Sea to the Red Sea. Portions of the Arava were ceded to Jordan in the 1994 Peace Treaty and then leased back to Israeli farmers. The Dead Sea, a saltwater body, is part of the Rift Valley area and is the lowest land area on earth, about 1,286 feet below sea level. The Negev is an arid area of flatlands and limestone mountains that stretches southward from the Judean Desert, which lies between Jerusalem and the Dead Sea.

The Jordan River, the longest of Israel's rivers, flows north-south through the Sea of Galilee (also known as Lake Kinneret and Lake Tiberias) and empties into the Dead Sea. Most of Israel's other rivers are small and generally seasonal in nature, except for the Kishon (which is about 8 miles long and flows east to west and empties into the Mediterranean north of Haifa) and the Yarkon (which is about 16 miles long and flows east to west and empties in to the Mediterranean at Tel Aviv).

Israel's climate generally is Mediterranean in nature—marked by hot and dry summers and cool but relatively mild winters. There is sunshine from May through mid-October and no rain falls during this season. Periods of hot and dry weather brought by easterly winds occur at the beginning and end of the summer, usually in May and September. The hot, dry, sandy, easterly wind of Biblical fame is commonly known as *khamsin*, from the Arabic for "fifty." The rainy season begins about mid-October, but it is only in December that rainy days become frequent. Winter weather alternates between short but heavy rainy spells and sunshine. March and April are cool, with occasional rains of short duration. Nevertheless, there is a variation of climate by region, partly as a consequence of differences in altitude. North of Beersheba, Israel has a Mediterranean climate, but the Negev is generally arid and cultivation there is impossible without irrigation. The Jordan Valley is hotter and drier than the coastal plain. Tiberias and the Jordan Valley enjoy warm temperatures and little rainfall. In the hilly regions (including Jerusalem and the Upper Galilee), temperatures drop toward the freezing point, and brief snowfalls are not unusual.

ECONOMY

Israel's economy has made impressive progress and the economic well-being of its people has improved significantly since independence when Israel was a poor country with weak agricultural and industrial sectors and a dependence on imported consumer goods, raw materials, and food. Economic growth was stimulated by a massive influx of immigrants and large governmental and private capital flows from abroad. Although virtually bereft of natural resources and faced with substantial burdens of immigrant absorption and of defense, Israel achieved relatively prosperous economic levels by the late 1980s with a standard of living comparable to that in many Western European countries. Life expectancy is among the highest in the world; Israel has maintained a substantial level of social services for its population; and its gross national product (GNP) has made dramatic progress. Nevertheless, Israel's economy remains dependent on foreign assistance and is burdened with an extraordinarily heavy debt-repayment responsibility.

Israel's economy grew rapidly after independence. Between 1950 and 1972, the country maintained a real economic output rate of nearly 10 percent per year and its output per worker nearly tripled. This was accompanied by significant increases in the standard of living. Inflation became a problem as the economy reached double-digit inflation in the early 1970s and triple-digit inflation (more than 400%) by the 1984 election. It was subsequently brought down to some 15 percent by 1987 through the efforts of the 1984-1988 National Unity Government. Balance of payments problems also marked the economy in the 1980s.

Israel lacks substantial natural resources—it has limited amounts of various chemicals, such as potash and phosphates, and water supplies—but this has been offset by the unusually valuable asset Israel has in its human resources. Massive immigration created problems in Israel's early years, but it also endowed Israel with a motivated and skilled labor force. Israel has developed its own highly regarded educational and scientific establishment. Illiteracy is virtually nonexistent, and Israel's population is one of the most highly educated in the world. It is in the forefront of scientific accomplishment in fields such as irrigation and water usage, energy technology, and medical-scientific research.

Israel's only significant domestic energy source is solar power; it has no coal or hydroelectric power potential and possesses very little oil and natural gas. Energy requirements are met largely by crude oil and coal imports, and nuclear power is under study.

Israel has lacked the capital necessary for its economy to function efficiently and since 1948 it has relied on foreign capital inflows to finance the economy and for current expenditures. External sources have included loans, grants, contributions, outside investments, United States government aid, the sale of Israel Bonds, German reparations and restitution payments, and donations from Diaspora Jewish communities. These sources have permitted Israel to pursue a policy of rapid economic and demographic expansion.

The country's economy today is a mixture of state and private enterprise. The service sector remains large because of government and quasi-government activity, including the machinery to integrate large immigrant populations and the trade and transport functions connected with a high level of foreign imports. However, in the 1990s successive governments set as a priority the privatization of state-owned institutions and the opening-up of the economy to increased competition and foreign investment.

Agriculture (most often associated with the kibbutz) traditionally has occupied a position of prominence in Israel and in Zionist ideology greater than its economic contribution has warranted. Its central place in Zionist ideology, dominant role in the settlement of the country, important function in absorbing new immigrants, and security aspects have assured agriculture its priority in Israel's economic policies. The government has been involved in developing, subsidizing, and controlling agricultural activity, including fishing and forestry, since independence. The agricultural sector uses modern scientific methods and has significantly expanded the area under cultivation through irrigation drawn basically from the Jordan River. Agricultural research is extensive, and farmers are quick to adopt improved techniques and respond to changes in market conditions. Israel has become self-sufficient in food production and is an exporter of various foods, including citrus and other fruits, vegetables, and poultry products. In spite of its rapid growth, agriculture's prominent position has gradually eroded to the point where it contributes only about 5 percent of the GNP and it is a diminishing source of employment primarily because of improved techniques and mechanization. Farm organization is predominantly cooperative, with the moshav being the most popular, while private farming is primarily the domain of non-Jewish sectors, mostly Arabs and some Druze.

Industry became an important, diverse, and fast-growing sector of the economy that contributed about one-third of the GNP by the late 1970s and also became a major source of employment and of commodity exports. The manufacturing-sector output is similar in range, sophistication, and quality of products to that of smaller industrialized countries. Textile manufacturers produce a range of goods including knitwear and high-fashion clothing and there are also plastics, electronics, high-technology scientific and optical equipment, and food processing. The cutting and polishing of diamonds remains a major export industry. Israel's defense industries are dominated by government-owned plants, of which Israel Aircraft Industries is the largest. The mineral and chemical industry depends heavily on the Dead Sea, which is the country's leading mineral source and includes magnesium chloride, potassium chloride (potash), table salt, chlorine, and calcium and magnesium bromide. The Israel-Jordan Peace Treaty and interim agreements with the PLO both included provisions for the joint exploitation of minerals extracted from the Dead Sea region as well as tourism and manufacturing in the region.

Government policy supported industrial development with an export orientation to ease the country's chronic balance-of-payments problem. Emphasis was given to science-based industries with a large value added by domestic manufacturing, particularly since the 1960s. This was the kind of export (e.g., chemicals, metal products, machinery, and electronic equipment) that, along with polished gem diamonds, grew most rapidly in the 1970s. Diamonds are the only product in which Israel has more than a peripheral share in any foreign market, although Israeli-manufactured arms and weapons systems have become very popular internationally and have become an important dimension of the country's export policy.

The foreign markets for Israeli products, and even the pattern of industrial growth, were shaped by the Arab boycott that precluded the possibility of Israel developing close trade links to the economies of its immediate neighbors. Instead the country had to seek more distant markets. The peace agreements with Egypt and Jordan, and the accords with the PLO, led to a partial suspension of the Arab boycott in the early 1990s, which resulted in only modest improvements in the level and quality of commercial interaction between Israel and its neighbors. It is also a fact that there is limited compatibility between Israel's advanced industrial economy and those of its Arab and Muslim neighbors.

Israel's exports reached about $23.5 billion in 1999 and included such products as manufactured goods including high-tech electronics and computer software, diamonds, citrus and other fruits and other agricultural products, chemicals, plastics, rubber products, mining and quarrying, textiles, processed foods, wood products, paper, and jewelry. Tourism is also an important earner of foreign exchange. Israeli imports, valued at more than $30 billion in 1999, included raw materials; machinery; equipment and vehicles for investment; consumer goods; rough diamonds; fuels; and ships, aircraft, and other military equipment. Israel's major trading partners include the United States and the European Union. The establishment of free trade agreements with the U.S. and the EU were important for Israel's export market. Israel also has signed free trade zone agreements with Canada, Turkey, and several countries in eastern Europe, and it has made important economic inroads in the former Soviet Union and Asia. Israel's economy is fully interconnected with the global economy, to the extent that economic trends elsewhere in the world, such as in Russia and Asia, have a direct bearing on the well-being of the Israeli economy.

HISTORY

The new state of Israel came into being on May 14, 1948, with the termination of the British Mandate, but its creation was preceded by more than fifty years of efforts by Zionist leaders to establish an independent Jewish state in Palestine.

The modern history of Israel may be dated from the Jewish immigration to Palestine in the second-half of the nineteenth century from Europe, especially Russia and Poland. The practical and modern effort to establish a state began with the founding of the Zionist movement and the creation of the World Zionist Organization by Theodor Herzl at the end of the nineteenth century. Waves of state-sponsored anti-Semitism ("pogroms") in eastern Europe and incidents such as the "Dreyfus Affair" in western

Europe were important contributing factors in the development of modern political Zionism. Zionist aspirations were given impetus with the issuance of the Balfour Declaration (1917) in which the British Government expressed support for the establishment of a Jewish national home in Palestine. Jewish immigration to Palestine grew throughout this period, but with the advent of the Nazi regime in Germany and the Holocaust, the numbers escalated rapidly in the 1930s. With the end of World War II there was pressure for the remnants of European Jewry to be permitted to immigrate to Palestine despite British restrictions. The Arab reaction to the effort to create a Jewish state was negative and frequently violent.

On November 29, 1947, the United Nations General Assembly adopted the Partition Plan (Resolution 181) which called for the division of Palestine into a Jewish state and an Arab state (linked by an economic union) and for an international administration for Jerusalem. The Plan was accepted with reluctance by the Zionists but denounced by the Arab world which prepared for war to ensure that all of Palestine would be an Arab state. Between November 1947 and May 1948 the Arab community in Palestine, with the active encouragement of the neighboring Arab countries, waged a campaign of terror against the Jewish settlement ("yishuv") in an effort to prevent implementation of the partition plan. This Arab terror provoked small militant elements of the Zionist community to launch violent reprisals against the Arabs as well as against symbols of a British Mandatory Authority that was accused of siding with the Arabs. With the British withdrawal from Palestine in May 1948, the new Jewish state proclaimed its independence. David Ben-Gurion became the Prime Minister of the State of Israel and Chaim Weizmann was elected President. The new government was soon recognized by the United States and the Soviet Union, as well as by many other states. The Arab League declared war on Israel, and the neighboring Arab states announced that their armies would enter the former Palestine Mandate, ostensibly to "restore order." A long and bitter war ensued between Israel and armies from Egypt, Jordan, Syria, Lebanon, and Iraq with assistance from other Arab League members.

In the spring of 1949, armistice agreements were signed between Israel and each of the bordering states (Egypt, Syria, Jordan, and Lebanon) which established a frontier (armistice line) between Israel and each of the neighboring states and portions of these areas were demilitarized. Peace negotiations to resolve the Arab-Israeli conflict were to follow, but did not. As a consequence of the war, Israel encompassed more territory than had been allocated to it by the Partition Plan. At the same time, portions of the territory allocated to the Palestinian Arab state came under Egyptian (the Gaza Strip) and Jordanian (the West Bank) control. Jerusalem was divided between Israel and Jordan. Under the terms of the armistice with Jordan, Israelis and other Jews were to be accorded access to Jewish holy places in Jerusalem's Old City and in the West Bank. However, this did not occur; rather, the Jordanians permitted holy places to be desecrated and destroyed.

Israel has fought six major wars (in 1948-1949, 1956-1957, 1967, 1969-1970, 1973, and 1982) with the Arab states to secure its position, but formal peace has eluded Israel with all but Egypt and Jordan. In addition, Israel has signed a series of interim agreements with the PLO and has held sporadic substantive talks with Syria under U.S. sponsorship. But a comprehensive peace agreement with all of its neighbors appears still far away.

Soon after its independence, Israel moved to function as a regular state. Elections for a parliament (Knesset) were held January 25, 1949, and regular parliamentary and presidential elections have been held, as required by law, since then. But, Israel's progress in its domestic life was not matched by comparable developments with the Arab states; frequent border incidents and clashes characterized the early 1950s.

Tensions continued to increase and the situation was exacerbated by external (primarily Soviet) arms supplies and Palestinian terrorist incursions into Israel and Israeli retaliatory raids on *fedayeen* bases in Egyptian-controlled Gaza. In the summer of 1956, Egyptian President Gamal Abdul Nasser nationalized the Suez Canal and tensions grew. In late October, Israel invaded the Sinai Peninsula to destroy hostile Egyptian military positions and to reopen the blockaded Strait of Tiran. In a brief war, Israel captured the Gaza Strip and the Sinai Peninsula. Following a British and French ultimatum (coordinated in advance in top-level secret tripartite—British, French, and Israeli—meetings), their forces were interposed between Israel and Egypt along the Suez Canal. Eventually Israel was forced by U.S. pressure to withdraw from Egyptian territory and from the Gaza Strip. The United Nations Emergency Force (UNEF) was stationed on the frontier between the two states and helped ensure quiet along the border for the next decade. The sea lanes through the Strait of Tiran to Israel's port of Eilat were opened to Israeli shipping. But the hope that peace talks might follow was not realized. Although the other Arab states did not join in the 1956-1957 hostilities, they made no effort to reach a peace agreement with Israel and their territories often became bases for attacks across the border into Israel. Israel maintained its military posture and capability to deal with the Arab threat.

In 1966 and 1967, Israel again focused on the problems associated with the Arab-Israeli conflict. Border incidents became more serious and escalation toward conflict began in late 1966 and early 1967 as clashes between Israel and Syria contributed to regional tensions. In May 1967, President Nasser of Egypt demanded the partial removal of UN forces from Sinai and Gaza, mobilized the Egyptian military, and moved troops and equipment into demilitarized areas. Nasser also announced the closing of the Strait of Tiran to Israeli shipping. Other factors also contributed to the growing tensions. Finally, on June 5, 1967, Israel launched a preemptive military strike against Egypt. Other Arab states joined in the hostilities that spread to include Jordan, Syria, and Iraq, among other Arab participants.

The Six Day War of June 1967 substantially altered the nature and parameters of the Arab-Israeli dispute. The realities of Arab hostility, the nature of the Arab threat, and the difficulties of achieving a settlement became more obvious. The issues of the conflict changed with the extent of the Israeli victory: Israel occupied the Sinai Peninsula, the Gaza Strip, the West Bank, East Jerusalem, and the Golan Heights. Israel adopted the position that it would not withdraw from those territories until there were negotiations with the Arab states leading to peace agreements that recognized Israel's right to exist and accepted Israel's permanent position and borders. The Arab response to these terms of reference were the "three nos" adopted at the Khartoum, Sudan, meeting of the Arab League in September 1967: no peace with Israel, no recognition of Israel, no negotiations with Israel. Throughout the period between the Six Day War (1967) and the Yom Kippur War (1973), the focal point was the effort to achieve a settlement of the Arab-Israeli conflict and to secure a just and lasting peace based on United Nations Security Council Resolution 242 of November 22, 1967, which recommended an exchange of land for peace between Israel and the Arab states. Although some of the efforts were promising, peace was not achieved and there was little movement in that direction. The 1969-1970 War of Attrition (launched by Egypt against Israel along the Suez Canal in April 1969) marked the fourth round of hostilities between Israel and the Arabs; it was also unique in the sense of involving direct military engagements between Israelis and Soviet pilots flying Egyptian aircraft. It was also in this period that a restructured PLO emerged under the leadership of Yasser Arafat and posed new challenges to Israel's security, in the form of terrorist attacks inside Israel and on Israeli and Jewish targets internationally.

On October 3, 1973, Egyptian and Syrian military forces launched surprise attacks on Israeli positions along the Suez Canal and in the Golan Heights. Despite initial Arab advances on both fronts, Israel pushed Syria back beyond the 1967 cease-fire line and crossed the Suez Canal to take a portion of its west bank. The war increased Israel's dependence on the United States, as no other country would provide Israel with the vast quantities of modern and sophisticated arms required for war or for the political and moral support necessary to negotiate peace.

The 1973 War was followed by renewed and intensified efforts to achieve Arab-Israeli peace. An extended process of "shuttle diplomacy" launched by United States Secretary of State Henry Kissinger resulted in two disengagement of forces agreements in the Sinai (January 1974 and September 1975) and one disengagement agreement involving Israeli and Syrian forces on the Golan Heights (May 1974). However, efforts at building comprehensive peace out of these partial agreements did not succeed. A major step in this regard occurred in 1977 with the announcement by Egyptian President Anwar Sadat that he was prepared to negotiate peace directly with the Israelis. His November 1977 visit to Israel ultimately led to the Camp David Accords in September 1978 and the Egypt-Israel Peace Treaty signed on March 26, 1979 (both witnessed by U.S. President Jimmy Carter). "Normal relations" between Egypt and Israel began officially on January 26, 1980, when Israel completed its withdrawal from two-thirds of the Sinai Peninsula, as called for in the peace treaty, and land, air, and sea borders between the two states were opened. In late February, embassies were opened in Cairo and Tel Aviv, and on February 26, Ambassadors Eliahu Ben-Elisar of Israel and Saad Mortada of Egypt presented their credentials.

Despite the peace treaty with Egypt and its implementation, Israel's other borders remained tense and problems often emerged. The frontier with

Lebanon had been relatively quiet between the 1948-1949 war and the early 1970s, when the PLO was forced out of Jordan and ultimately took up positions in Lebanon. Cross-border PLO terrorist raids into northern Israel and Israeli retaliations (such as 1978's "Operation Litani" to push PLO forces out of firing range of northern Israel) escalated tensions. The PLO's presence in Lebanon exacerbated an already complicated balance among that country's indigenous political and military forces, an arrangement that broke down completely in 1975 with the start of civil war in Lebanon. In order to protect its interests, Syria became increasingly involved militarily in Lebanon. The continued presence in eastern Lebanon of surface-to-air missiles (SAM) that had been moved there by Syria in the spring of 1981 remained an Israeli concern, as were PLO attacks against Israeli and Jewish targets worldwide despite a U.S.-arranged cease-fire in the summer of 1981. On June 6, 1982, Israel launched a major military action against the PLO in Lebanon ("Operation Peace for Galilee"). The military objective was to ensure security for northern Israel, to destroy the PLO infrastructure that had established a state-within-a-state ("Fatahland") in Lebanon, to eliminate a center of international terrorism, and to eliminate a base of operations from which Israel could be threatened; the success of the military operation also involved the early neutralization of the Syrian SAM emplacements in eastern Lebanon. But the political objectives of the operation were not so precise. In many respects, the results were ambiguous. Under U.S. and international protection, the PLO was permitted to withdraw most of its forces from Lebanon in August 1982. Israel's northern border was temporarily more secure, but the Israeli troops that remained in Lebanon became targets of Iranian-backed Hezbollah terrorists and others, and numerous casualties resulted. A May 1983 agreement between Israel and Lebanon that would have facilitated a withdrawal of Israeli forces was abrogated a year later by Lebanon under pressure from Syria. In 1985, the bulk of Israeli forces were withdrawn unilaterally from Lebanon but a narrow "security zone" north of the border was manned by Israeli soldiers and members of the Israeli-backed South Lebanese Army (SLA). The costs of the War in Lebanon were high, as have been the costs of Hezbollah's continuing war of attrition against Israeli and Israeli-backed targets in the security zone.

With the departure of the PLO forces from Lebanon, attention focused on divisions among Israelis over the status of the West Bank and Gaza Strip. Although the internal debate over these territories had been a core issue since they were occupied by Israel in the 1967 Six Day War, their status took on new immediacy in the wake of the Palestinian rioting in the West Bank and Gaza that began in early December 1987. However, while it prompted extensive public debate, the *intifada* did not facilitate agreement among Israelis about a clear policy option for addressing the complex set of disputes with the Palestinians, a problem exacerbated by the continuation of a widespread Arab consensus on avoiding relations with Israel.

The August 1990 Iraqi invasion of Kuwait and the participation of Arab confrontation states in the multilateral coalition that fought the Persian Gulf War (January-February 1991) caused the first discernible cracking (since the Egypt-Israel Peace Treaty) in the Arab consensus concerning Israel. This helped create the atmosphere for the Madrid Middle East Peace Conference (October 1991) that set in motion bilateral and multilateral processes of negotiations cosponsored first by the United States and the U.S.S.R. (later Russia). These negotiations, while unprecedented in their scope, did not generate any immediate substantive progress. Such progress was produced through secret back-channel communications—and then formal negotiations—involving Israelis and PLO representatives in the spring and summer of 1993 that were held under the good offices of the foreign minister of Norway. The exchange of letters of recognition between Prime Minister Yitzhak Rabin and PLO Chairman Yasser Arafat (September 9, 1993) and the signing of the Israel-PLO Declaration of Principles (September 13, 1993) set in motion a series of interim agreements affecting parts of the West Bank and Gaza Strip. However, these interim agreements—first with the PLO and then with the Palestinian Authority (elected in January 1997)—did not ameliorate the protracted debate among Israelis over the final political status of the West Bank and Gaza Strip or the Arab and Jewish populations there. To the contrary, the internal debate was exacerbated by widespread terrorism against Israelis in the spring of 1996 by Muslim extremist groups, such as Hamas and Islamic Jihad, and by secular Palestinian groups opposed to the Oslo Accords—terrorism that the Palestinian Authority under the leadership of Yasser Arafat seemingly was unable or unwilling to combat.

Despite their inherent instability and uncertainty, the Israel-PLO interim agreements established an atmosphere in which substantive progress involving Israel and other Arab parties could be achieved. Principal among these was the Common Agenda for future negotiations signed with Jordan on September 14, 1993, which laid the groundwork for the Washington Declaration (July 25, 1994) and the Israel-Jordan Peace Treaty (October 26, 1994). There were also diplomatic and/or commercial openings with a number of Arab countries, including Morocco, Tunisia, Oman, and Qatar; the secondary and tertiary aspects of the Arab economic boycott of Israel were officially suspended by the Gulf Cooperation Council (GCC); and periodic high-level talks, under U.S. sponsorship, were held with Syria about security arrangements on the Golan Heights and related issues. While some of these developments were important in and of themselves, all were part of a long-term process that has yet to provide Israel with permanent peace and normalized relations with all of its neighbors. Militating against this goal were a number of factors, including the continued threat of terrorism emanating from the West Bank and Gaza Strip; a protracted war of attrition waged by Iranian-backed Hezbollah and other Muslim extremist groups against Israeli forces in southern Lebanon; the continued domination of Lebanon by Syria, as well as Syrian support for groups opposed to the Arab-Israeli peace process; threats by a number of Arab countries to link normalizing of relations with Israel to the depth of Israeli political and territorial concessions in interim and final-status agreements with the Palestinian Authority; and the long-term strategic threat to Israel posed by active efforts by several Arab and Islamic regimes to acquire and deploy weapons of mass destruction and the long-range ballistic missile capability to deliver those weapons on targets throughout Israel.

ISRAEL IN THE INTERNATIONAL COMMUNITY

Since independence, Israel has sought positive relations with the members of the international community. It has joined and participated in the work of international organizations (despite longstanding efforts by the Arabs and their supporters to isolate and ostracize Israel at the United Nations and in other international fora) and it has sought to establish and maintain friendly relations with as many states as possible. Within the framework of this broad effort, there has been a particular focus on relations with the United States and the Soviet Union (and subsequently, with Russia).

Israel had a variable relationship with the Soviet Union and the members of the Eastern bloc since before independence. Although the Soviet Union supported the United Nations Partition Plan of 1947 and Israel's independence in 1948, relations deteriorated rapidly and the Soviet Union shifted to a pro-Arab position, including providing economic assistance and arms to front-line Arab states such as Egypt and Syria by the mid-1950s. Since 1967, when the Soviet Union and the Eastern bloc states, except Romania, broke diplomatic relations with Israel, the questions of a Soviet role in the Arab-Israeli conflict and the peace process and the status of Jews in the Soviet Union were central themes in Israel-Soviet relations. Under Mikhail Gorbachev a thaw developed and relations between Israel and the Soviet camp improved in a number of spheres. Formal diplomatic relations between Israel and the Soviet Union were restored in October 1991 in conjunction with the start of the Madrid Middle East Peace Conference under joint U.S. and Soviet sponsorship. Moscow permitted the migration of Soviet Jews to Israel, a process that ultimately swelled to some 750,000 Jewish immigrants in the 1990s.

The special but central and complex relationship between Israel and the United States has been more significant. The relationship revolves around a broadly conceived ideological factor. Moreover, it is based on substantial positive perception and sentiment evident in public opinion and official statements and manifest in political-diplomatic support and military and economic assistance. However, the U.S.-Israeli relationship has not been enshrined in a legally binding commitment joining the two states in a formal alliance. Undergirding the relationship is a general agreement on broad policy goals. The two states maintain a remarkable degree of parallelism and congruence on such objectives as the need to prevent major war in the Middle East, to achieve a negotiated resolution of the Arab-Israeli conflict that does not endanger Israeli security, and to strengthen Israel's economic and social well-being. Nevertheless, there have been instances of noncongruence of policy between Washington and Jerusalem on specific issues which have derived from various differences of perspective; for example, disputes with the Begin and Shamir governments over West Bank settlement activity, and differences between the Netanyahu government and the Clinton Administration over the depth and pace of Israeli redeployment in the West Bank. These differences aside, the United States is an indispensable ally that provides Israel with economic, technical, military, political, diplomatic, and moral support. It was seen as the ultimate protector against the Soviet Union in the Cold War and, since the demise of the Soviet Union, against militant Islamist terrorism and rogue regimes, and it is the primary (if not sole) guarantor of Israel's qualitative military advantage over its regional adversaries.

Israel has seen Europe and the developing world (especially Africa and Latin America) as important components of its overall policy. It has sought to maintain positive relations with Europe based on the commonality of the Judeo-Christian heritage and the memories of the Holocaust. The European Union is also an important trading partner for Israel given the long-standing refusal of its immediate neighbors to engage in normal commercial relations. Israel's approach to the developing world has focused on its ability to provide technical assistance in the development process. Despite substantial effort in those sectors, the growing centrality of the United States as the primary facilitator of assistance to Israel, as well as of mediation in Arab-Israeli peacemaking, has caused Israelis to focus increasingly on solidifying relations with the United States.

ISRAEL FACES THE FUTURE

At the heart of Israel's agenda for the future is the continuing Arab-Israeli conflict, with its dimensions of potential conflict and of peace, but placed within the context of numerous territorial and political disputes still to be resolved. Israel's need and desire for peace is not a subject for debate among Israelis, although the means to that end are. Nevertheless, the quest for peace remains a central theme of national life and Israelis are preoccupied with survival and security.

Israel has fought six major wars and countless skirmishes with the Arabs, has built an impressive and highly sophisticated but costly military capability, and holds a strategic edge over its neighbors. Despite, or perhaps because of, its battlefield successes and the specter of future combat, Israelis continuously recalculate the increasingly sophisticated military balance between themselves and the Arab and Islamic worlds and concerns about weapons acquisitions, force structure, and capability, as well as willingness of Arab and Islamic nations to engage in battle with Israel, are never far from the center of attention. Factors in these assessments include the post-Gulf War build up of conventional weapons by several of Israel's immediate neighbors as well as the transfer of nonconventional (nuclear, biological, and chemical) weapons and weapons technology and long-range missiles by extra-regional actors (such as Russia, China, and North Korea) to militant Arab countries (such as Iraq, Libya, and Syria) and to Iran. The possibility of war with potentially high levels of casualties and other unbearable costs remains a matter of deep public concern.

For most Israelis, the prospects for a future in which they will live in peace with their immediate and more distant neighbors in the Middle East seems to lie at a point beyond the immediate future. This perception was not significantly affected by the process of negotiations ensuing from the Madrid Peace Conference or by the completion of interim agreements with the PLO or the signing of the peace treaty with Jordan, despite the fact that each of these events may be viewed as part of a long-term process that will lead to a comprehensive resolution of the Arab-Israeli conflict. Israelis also hope that an eventual end of the conflict with the Arabs will allow them to address a multitude of domestic challenges—relating, *inter alia*, to the role of religion in the state, social and economic disparities among Jewish Israelis, and the political status of Israel's non-Jewish citizenry—most of which were subsumed during the first fifty years of statehood to the more immediate challenge of protecting the state against existential external threat.

DICTIONARY

A

ABBAS, MAHMOUD (ABU MAZEN). Elected to the first Palestinian Legislative Council* in 1996, he was a principal negotiator of the 1993 Oslo Accords* with Israel and signed the Israel-PLO* Declaration of Principles* on behalf of the Palestinians. Born in Safed, Palestine*, in 1935, he studied at universities in Syria* and the USSR*. He became a member of the Fatah* Central Committee and was elected to the PLO Executive Committee in 1980. A close adviser to the PLO leader, Yasser Arafat*, he was involved in various rounds of negotiations with Israeli officials toward implementing the Oslo Accords. In 1995 he conducted a series of secret talks with Labor* MK and Deputy Foreign Minister Joseph (Yossi) Beilin* on the framework for a permanent Israeli-Palestinian settlement. In 1997 he was named by Arafat as his designated successor. He wrote a book published in Arabic under the title *The Path to Peace* in which he claimed that senior Israel Labor Party officials held secret talks with the PLO before the 1992 Israeli elections, when contacts with the organization were still illegal. According to Abbas, the purpose of these talks was to stall the Israeli-Palestinian talks in Washington (initiated following the Madrid Peace Conference*), thereby forcing a diplomatic crisis between the Yitzhak Shamir*-led Likud* Government and the United States* on the eve of the Israeli elections, a circumstance that would in turn help influence the outcome of the elections in Labor's favor. While acknowledging that they had had secret contacts with Palestinian officials, senior Labor Party officials denied Abbas's allegation about trying to torpedo the Washington talks. His book was subsequently translated into English and published under the title *Through Secret Channels* (London: Garnet Publishing, 1995).

ABU GHOSH. An Arab village west of Jerusalem* on the road to Tel Aviv* whose inhabitants were known for their friendly relations with their Jewish neighbors. During Israel's War of Independence* they did not participate in the fighting.

ABUHATZEIRA, AHARON. Born in Morocco in 1938, he immigrated to Israel in 1949 and studied history and Hebrew* literature at Bar Ilan University*. A teacher by profession, he served as Mayor of Ramle from 1971 to 1977. He was first elected to the Knesset* on the National Religious Party* list in December 1973, and was reelected to the Ninth Knesset on the same ticket in 1977. From June 1977 to August 1981 he served as Minister of Religious Affairs. Following a split with the National Religious Party (based primarily on the party's alleged bias against Sephardim*), Abuhatzeira was elected to the Tenth Knesset in 1981 as the head of the Tami Party* list and on August 5, 1981, he was sworn in as Minister of Labor and Social Welfare and Minister of Immigrant Absorption. In 1984 he was again elected to the Knesset as the leader of the Tami Party. In 1988 he was elected to the Knesset on the Likud* list.

For further information see: Daniel J. Elazar, *The Other Jews: The Sephardim Today* (New York: Basic, 1989); Calvin Goldscheider, *Israel's Changing Society: Population, Ethnicity, and Development* (Boulder, CO: Westview, 1996).

ABU MAZEN *see* MAHMOUD ABBAS

ACRE (AKKO). A coastal city in western Galilee* located along the Mediterranean Sea at the north end of Haifa* Bay. The city has a long history but became well known during the British Mandate* period because the British authorities used the medieval fortress as the country's central prison for political prisoners as well as criminals.

ADMINISTERED AREAS *see* OCCUPIED TERRITORIES

THE AFFAIR *see* LAVON AFFAIR

AGAF MODIIN (AMAN) *see* DIRECTOR OF MILITARY INTELLIGENCE (DMI)

AGRANAT, SHIMON. Born in Louisville, Kentucky, in 1906 he migrated to Palestine* in 1930 where he settled in Haifa*. He was appointed a justice of the Supreme Court* in 1950 and served on the five-member panel that adjudicated the trial of Nazi war criminal Adolf Eichmann* in 1962. He became Chief Justice of the Supreme Court in 1965. He served as head of the Agranat Commission of Inquiry*, established by the Government in 1973.

For further information see: Pnina Lahav, *Judgement in Jerusalem: Simon Agranat and the Zionist Century* (Berkeley: University of California Press, 1997).

AGRANAT COMMISSION OF INQUIRY. In November 1973 the Government of Israel appointed a five-man Commission of Inquiry to investigate the events leading up to the Yom Kippur War*, including information concerning the enemy's moves and intentions, the assessments and decisions of military and civilian bodies regarding this information, and the Israel Defense Forces'* deployments, preparedness for battle, and actions in the first phase of the fighting. The Commission was composed of Supreme Court* Chief Justice Shimon Agranat*; Justice Moshe Landau* of the Supreme Court; State Comptroller Yitzhak Nebenzahl; and two former chiefs of staff of the Israel Defense Forces, Yigael Yadin* and Chaim Laskov*. The Commission issued an interim report in April 1974 which focused primarily on events prior to the outbreak of hostilities and the conduct of the war during its early stages. Among its findings were that Prime Minister Golda Meir* and Defense Minister Moshe Dayan* were not responsible for Israel's lack of preparation for the Yom Kippur War and that faulty intelligence analysis was the primary failure. Lieut. General David Elazar* subsequently resigned as Chief of Staff of the IDF and Major General Yitzhak Hofi was named as his temporary replacement. The Commission's report also called for a new director of military intelligence to replace Major General Zeira and the reassignment of three other intelligence officers.

For further information see: S. Z. Abramov, "The Agranat Report and Its Aftermath," *Midstream* 20 (June-July 1974): 16-28; Chaim Herzog, *The War of Atonement: October 1973* (Boston: Little, Brown, 1975); Howard M. Sachar, *A History of Israel: From the Rise of Zionism to Our Time* (New York: Knopf, 1979).

AGREEMENT OF MAY 17, 1983, BETWEEN ISRAEL AND LEBANON *see* ISRAEL-LEBANON AGREEMENT OF MAY 17, 1983

AGRICULTURE. Agriculture and settlement on the land had been stressed by the immigrants to Palestine* and Israel since the beginning of modern political Zionism* and the establishment of the Zionist movement. In the early years of Israel's development agriculture was an important factor in assuring self-sufficiency in food and later it became an important source of foreign exchange earnings. Although declining in terms of revenues earned and people employed (due to increased mechanization and other efficiencies) agriculture remains an important sector of the Israeli economy. *See also* KIBBUTZ; MOSHAV.

AGUDA *see* AGUDAT ISRAEL

AGUDAT ISRAEL (ASSOCIATION OF ISRAEL). Agudat Israel (the Aguda) is a movement which views the Torah* as the only legitimate code of laws binding upon the Jews. It is a religiously oriented political party representing the interests of a section of ultra-Orthodox Jewry living both in and outside the Jewish state. The Aguda was established and its policies and programs delineated in Kattowitz (Katowice), Poland, in 1912 during a conference of the major East European and German-Austro-Hungarian Orthodox rabbis. It was formed, to a significant extent, in reaction to the growth of political Zionism* with its secular majority. The original concept was to unite Orthodox groups in Eastern and Western Europe into a united front in opposition to Zionism and its efforts to alter Jewish life. But there were different perspectives on a number of issues. The Aguda was to be a Torah movement directed by a Council of Torah Sages*, which was to be the supreme authority in all matters.

Originally, Agudat Israel was ambivalent concerning resettlement of Palestine*. Jewish law and tradition supported settling in Palestine and the Holocaust* made it a practical necessity, but there was a problem because many of the new settlers did not observe Jewish law. Agudat Israel was held aloof from Zionism and dissociated itself from the World Zionist Organization* and the Jewish Agency* because of its conviction that by cooperating closely with such irreligious elements, it would fail in the supreme aim of imposing the absolute rule of Jewish religion upon Jewish life. It opposed the concept of a Jewish National Home and of a Jewish State not founded on Jewish law and tradition. Agudat Israel opposed the Zionist view that Jews had to leave the Diaspora*, settle in Palestine, and build a new society there in order to live a proper Jewish life. The Orthodox groups held that the concept of "the ingathering of the exiles"* and the return to Zion could not be separated from the Messianic redemption, for which the time had not yet come.

In Palestine, Agudat Israel acquired land, founded the settlement of Mahane Yisrael, and established schools. It carried on an active anti-Zionist political campaign in British circles and in the world press in the 1920s. In Great Britain*, it denied the Jewish Agency's right to act as the representative of the Jewish people and demanded recognition, but was turned down. In Palestine, Agudat Israel was opposed to the organization of the Jewish community along the lines of Zionist ideology and opted out of the officially recognized Jewish community (Knesset Yisrael). It also did not recognize the authority of the Chief Rabbinate* established by the British and set up its own rabbinical court. However, in the late 1920s, with the arrival of significant numbers of new Agudat Israel members from Europe who wanted to participate in the economic and social development of the Yishuv* and who could not accept the idea of complete isolation from the World Zionist Organization and the Zionist movement, the Agudat Israel leadership in Palestine was reorganized. The end result was that some of the older and more conservative elements broke away from the movement and later formed the Neturei Karta*.

The genocide of European Jewry helped to convince Agudat Israel of the value of Zionism and the Aguda granted de facto recognition to the Yishuv. At the same time it retained its reservations concerning the establishment of an independent Jewish state. Prior to Israel's independence, an arrangement was concluded with David Ben-Gurion*, then chairman of the Jewish Agency, in which Agudat Israel agreed to support the state on condition that the status quo* in religious matters be maintained. Agudat Israel then joined the Provisional Council of State and participated in Israel's first Government. Although it boycotted the institutions of the Jewish community in Palestine, it eventually became a political party in 1948. Since independence it has contested the various Knesset* elections and has been represented in it. It now accepts the state, but without ascribing any religious significance to it. It has been represented in parliament since 1948 and has supported most of the coalition governments but since 1952 it has refused to accept a cabinet portfolio.

The movement's voting strength lies in Jerusalem* and Bnai Brak and consists mostly of Ashkenazim*. All crucial policy decisions are made not by the party's Knesset members or its membership, but by the 12-member Council of Torah Sages. Besides the Council, the party's central institutions are: the Great Assembly, composed of representatives of the local branches; the Central World Council; and the World Executive Committee. It has a youth movement (Tzeirei Agudat Yisrael), a women's movement (Neshei Agudat Yisrael), and its own school and yeshiva network in which religious instruction is a major part of the curriculum. The government supplies most of the funds for the school system. Agudat Israel is primarily concerned with enhancing the role of religion in the state and is opposed to all forms of secularism. Historically, its support for coalition governments was secured only after the construction of lengthy coalition agreements containing numerous concessions to the group's religious perspectives, e.g., strict Sabbath laws and revision of legislation to accommodate Orthodox Jewish principles.

During the 1988 Knesset election campaign, the political fortunes of Agudat Israel were strengthened by the intervention of the Lubavitcher* Rebbe, Rabbi Menachem Mendel Schneerson*, and by the Vishnitzer Rebbe and the Gerer Rebbe. Some observers attributed the winning of three Knesset seats to this support.

Long-standing personal and political rivalries between factions of Agudat Israel headed by Rabbi Schneerson and Rabbi Eliezer Shach* led to the formation of a breakaway faction of ultra-Orthodox Ashkenazi Jews known as Degel HaTorah* which ran a separate list in the 1988 Knesset election. In 1992 and 1996 Agudat Israel and Degel HaTorah agreed to submit joint slates of candidates under the banner of the United Torah Judaism* party, winning four seats in each election. Consistent with their non-Zionist political orientation, the leaders of United Torah Judaism agreed to join the Likud*-led coalition headed by Benjamin Netanyahu* but refused to sit as members of the cabinet, although party leader Rabbi Meir Porush did serve as deputy minister in the powerful Ministry of Housing and Construction. In the elections to the 15th Knesset held on May 17, 1999, United Torah Judaism won five seats. Despite their success at the ballot box, the rivalry between the leaders of Agudat Israel and Degel HaTorah continues. Moreover, the strong influence of Ashkenazi Jews in Agudat Israel contributed to the formation of a breakaway faction of ultra-Orthodox Sephardic* Jews known as Shas (Sephardi Torah Guardians*) prior to the 1984 Knesset election. One of the most significant changes in Israeli politics in the 1980s and early 1990s was the growing "nationalism" of Agudat Israel, manifested most prominently in its active support for West Bank* settlers and its opposition to territorial concessions in peacemaking.

For further information see: Eliezer Don-Yehiya, "Origins and Development of the *Aguda* and *Mafdal* Parties," *Jerusalem Quarterly*, No. 20 (Summer 1981): 49-64; Gershon R. Kieval, *Party Politics in Israel and the Occupied Territories* (Westport, CT: Greenwood, 1983); Emil Marmorstein, *Heaven at Bay* (London: Oxford University Press, 1969); Stewart Reiser, "The Religious Parties and Israel's Foreign Policy," in *Israeli National Security Policy: Political Actors and Perspectives*, edited by Bernard Reich and Gershon R. Kieval (New York: Greenwood, 1988): 105-122; Gary S. Schiff, *Tradition and Politics: The Religious Parties of Israel* (Detroit: Wayne State University Press, 1997).

AGUDAT YISRAEL *see* AGUDAT ISRAEL

AHAD HAAM ("ONE OF THE PEOPLE"). The pseudonym used by Asher Zvi Ginzberg, founder and proponent of the "cultural Zionism*" movement. Born in Skvira, near Kiev, in Russia in 1856, he began to learn Hebrew* as a youngster and developed a substantial background in Jewish literature and lore. He later settled in Odessa and engaged in commerce but came to the conclusion that the plight of Russian Jewry could only be alleviated by settlement in Palestine*. He joined the Central Committee of the Hoveve Zion* movement, but criticized its ideas and methods. In 1895 he turned to writing as a profession and soon began editing *Hashiloah,* a Hebrew monthly. Ahad Haam became an opponent of the World Zionist Organization* established in 1897 and he rejected the Jewish state as an immediate object of national policy. He sought instead a truly "Jewish" state that could be achieved only after a substantial period of national education and after the establishment of a cultural center for Jewish life in Palestine. This focus on cultural issues was in strong contrast to the political and practical Zionism of the mainstream of the Zionist movement. In 1908 he moved to London where he engaged primarily in business activities. In 1922 he settled in Tel Aviv* and died there in 1927.

For further information see: Shlomo Avineri, *The Making of Modern Zionism: The Intellectual Origins of the Jewish State* (New York: Basic, 1981); Arthur Hertzberg, editor, *The Zionist Idea: A Historical Analysis and Reader* (New York: Atheneum, 1977); Hans Kohn, editor, *Nationalism and the Jewish Ethic: Basic Writings of Ahad Haam* (New York: Schocken, 1962); Steven Zipperstein, *Elusive Prophet: Ahad Haam and the Origins of Zionism* (Berkeley: University of California Press, 1993).

AHDUT (UNITY). A political party, led by Victor Tayar created to contest the 1988 Knesset* election. It did not secure the minimum number of votes to gain a seat in parliament.

AHDUT HAAVODA (UNITY OF LABOR). A Zionist socialist association of Jewish workers in Palestine*. It was established in 1919 by a majority of the members of the Poalei Zion (Workers of Zion) Party*, along with some members of Hapoel Hatzair*. Its ambition was to unite all Jewish workers in Eretz Israel* and all federations and parties in the Jewish labor movement and the Zionist* movement abroad. Ahdut Haavoda joined the World Alliance of Poalei Zion. It was active in aliya*, immigrant absorption, and public works.

AHDUT HAAVODA-POALEI ZION (WORKERS OF ZION). A political party established in 1946 following an earlier split in Mapai* by the merger of Poalei Zion* (Workers of Zion) and smaller socialist Zionist groups. In 1948 it united with Mifleget Poalim-Hashomer Hatzair* to form Mapam* and, as such, contested the 1949 and 1951 Knesset* elections. In the early 1950s it split with Mapam and reestablished itself as an independent party and, as such, won 10 seats in the 1955 elections, seven in 1959, and eight in 1961. It formed the Alignment* with Mapai and contested the 1965 and subsequent Knesset elections in that political unit.

AL-AKSA MOSQUE. Considered by Muslims to be the third holiest site in Islam (after Mecca and Medina, both in Saudi Arabia), it was initially constructed in the year 638 on Jerusalem's* Temple Mount overlooking the Western Wall* and on land believed by Jews to be the site of the First and Second Temples. It suffered from neglect and disrepair under Ottoman rule. Under the British Mandate* responsibility for the care of the mosque was granted to Abdullah, the Emir of Transjordan, who appointed a *waqf* (Islamic holy trust) to administer it and other Muslim holy places in Jerusalem. Though designated in the 1947 UN Partition Plan* to be under international administration, the mosque along with the rest of Jerusalem's Old City was occupied by Jordan* between 1948 and 1967. The areas fell to Israeli control in the 1967 Six Day War*. Owing to Muslim sensitivities, Defense Minister Moshe Dayan* ordered the removal of the Israeli flag from the minaret above Al-Aksa Mosque and forbade Israeli soldiers from setting foot on any part of the mosque or the surrounding Temple Mount. Pledging to Muslim and Christian authorities that their religious rights in Jerusalem would be respected under Israeli administration, Dayan took steps to ensure that control over the administration of Al-Aksa Mosque remained in the hands of the Jordanian-dominated *waqf*.

Despite Israeli efforts to abide by these commitments, the mosque and the Temple Mount are a source of protracted tension between Arabs and Israelis and the setting for several violent incidents. In January 1984 Israeli security forces discovered a cache of weapons and explosives hidden near the mosque; these were to be used in an attack by ultra-Orthodox Jewish militants (members of the "Temple Mount Faithful") determined to start construction of a Third Temple there. In October 1990 violent clashes involving stone-throwing Palestinian youths, Jewish religious zealots, and Israeli forces resulted in the deaths of 19 Arabs and the wounding of more than 140 others; some Israeli soldiers and civilians as well as tourists praying at the Western Wall directly below the Temple Mount were also wounded in the incident. The Al-Aksa Mosque is also a source of inter-Arab rivalry. In the Israel-Jordan Peace Treaty* of 1994 it was stipulated that in any permanent peace agreement consideration would be given to Jordan's special interest in the mosque and in other Muslim holy places in Jerusalem. This provision was perceived by the PLO* as a direct challenge to its political interests in Jerusalem. In reaction, the PLO established its own *waqf* over Jerusalem to compete with the Jordanian-sponsored one, and pro-Jordanian journalists and newspapers in the West Bank* and Gaza Strip* were harassed by Palestinian officials. Also involved in the inter-Arab rivalry over Al-Aksa is the government of Saudi Arabia, which seeks to justify its claim over the mosque by virtue of Saudi administration over Mecca and Medina. *See also* JERUSALEM.

For further information see: M. A. Aamiry, *Jerusalem: Arab Origins and Heritage* (London: Longman, 1978); Ziad Abu-Amr, "The Significance of Jerusalem: A Muslim Perspective," *Palestine-Israel Journal of Politics, Economics and Culture* 2:2 (1995); Martin Gilbert, *Jerusalem: Illustrated History Atlas* (Jerusalem: Steimatsky, 1997); Abraham Rabinovich, *Jerusalem on Earth: People, Passions, and Politics in the Holy City* (New York: Free Press, 1988); Andrew Sinclair, *Jerusalem: The Endless Crusade: The Struggle for the Holy City from Its Foundation to the Modern Era* (New York: Crown, 1995); A. L. Tibawi, *Jerusalem: Its Place in Islam and Arab History* (Beirut: The Institute for Palestine Studies, 1969); Zvi Weblowsky, *The Meaning of Jerusalem to Jews, Christians, and Muslims* (Jerusalem: Intratypeset, 1977).

AL GALGALIM (ON WHEELS). A political party advocating improved working conditions for taxi cab drivers, headed by Herzl Haham, that sought election to the 13th Knesset* (1992) and failed to secure a seat.

ALIGNMENT (MAARACH). A political bloc formed in 1965 between Mapai* and Ahdut Haavoda*. In 1968 it joined with Rafi* to form the Israel Labor Party*. An Alignment subsequently was formed with Mapam* to contest the election of the Seventh Knesset*, although both Mapam and the Israel Labor Party retained their own organizations and memberships. The Alignment led Israel's government coalitions between 1965 and 1977 when it lost the election and became the opposition in parliament. In September 1984 it joined in the National Unity Government* with Likud*. As a consequence, Mapam and Yossi Sarid* of the Labor Party withdrew from the Alignment while Ezer Weizman's* Yahad* joined the Alignment.

For further information see: Asher Arian, *The Second Republic: Politics in Israel* (Chatham, NJ: Chatham House, 1998): chapter 5; Gershon R. Kieval, *Party Politics in Israel and the Occupied Territories* (Westport, CT: Greenwood, 1983); Bernard Reich and Gershon R. Kieval, *Israel:*

Land of Tradition and Conflict, Second Edition (Boulder, CO: Westview, 1993): chapter 4.

ALIYA. (Derived from the Hebrew* word for "Ascent" or "Going Up"). The immigration of Jews from the Diaspora* to the Holy Land (Palestine*, and later, Israel). Jewish immigration to and settlement in the Land of Israel is a central concept in Zionist* ideology, and the "ingathering of the exiles"* was the primary objective of the Zionist movement. However, even before the founding of the Zionist movement, there was immigration to Eretz Israel*, the Holy Land. Throughout Jewish history prior to the modern political Zionist movement, small numbers of Jews had always migrated to the Holy Land in keeping with the Jewish religion's concept that to live and die in the Holy Land was an important precept. Over the centuries Jews migrated to Eretz Israel and lived in the four holy cities: Jerusalem*, Safed*, Tiberias*, and Hebron*. With the practical and political Zionism of the nineteenth century, beginning in the 1880s, the numbers of Jewish immigrants to Palestine grew dramatically but they also varied in number depending on practical conditions both in their countries of origin and in Palestine (and later Israel).

Immigration to Palestine traditionally has been divided into five major phases or aliyot (waves of immigration) between the 1880s and World War II. During the First Aliya (1882-1903) some 20,000 to 30,000 individuals immigrated to Palestine, primarily in groups organized by the Hoveve Zion* and Bilu* movements in Russia and Romania. Some arrived on their own, mostly from Galicia. The Second Aliya* (1904-1914) involved some 35,000 to 40,000 young pioneers, mostly from Russia. In the Third Aliya (1919 1923) some 35,000 young pioneers immigrated to Palestine from Russia, Poland, and Romania. The Fourth Aliya (1924-1931) involved mainly middle-class immigrants from Poland, numbering some 88,000. The Fifth Aliya (1932-1938) consisted of some 215,000 immigrants, mainly from Central Europe. During World War II (1939-1945), immigration to Palestine continued both legally and illegally and totaled some 82,000. After World War II (1945) until the independence of Israel in May 1948, there were severe British Mandatory* restrictions on Jewish immigration to Palestine, but still some 57,000 Jews arrived. After Israeli independence the flow of immigrants to Palestine grew dramatically as Israel allowed free immigration and whole communities opted to move to the Holy Land. Beginning in 1989,

large-scale immigration brought to Israel some 750,000 Jews from the
former Soviet Union* and Ethiopia*.

For further information see: Ehud Avriel, *Open the Gates! A Personal
Story of "Illegal" Immigration to Israel* (New York: Atheneum, 1975);
Shlomo Barer, *The Magic Carpet* (London: Secker and Warburg, 1952);
Yehuda Bauer, *Flight and Rescue: Brichah* (New York: Random House,
1970); Zeev Ben-Sira, *Immigration, Stress, and Readjustment* (Westport,
CT: Praeger, 1997); Ephraim Dekel, *B'riha: Flight to the Homeland*
(New York: Herzl, 1973); Shlomo Deshen and Moshe Shokeid, *The
Predicament of Homecoming: Cultural and Social Life of North African
Immigrants in Israel* (Ithaca, NY: Cornell University Press, 1974);
Samuel N. Eisenstadt, *The Absorption of Immigrants* (Glencoe, IL: Free
Press, 1955); Robert Owen Freedman, "Soviet Foreign Policy toward the
United States and Israel in the Gorbachev Era: Jewish Emigration and
Middle East Politics," in *The Decline of the Soviet Union and the
Transformation of the Middle East*, edited by David H. Goldberg and Paul
Marantz (Boulder, CO: Westview, 1994): 53-95; Moshe Gat, *The Jewish
Exodus from Iraq, 1948-1951* (London: Frank Cass, 1997); Zvi Gitelman,
*Becoming Israelis: Political Resocialization of Soviet and American
Immigrants* (New York: Praeger, 1982); Calvin Goldscheider, *Israel's
Changing Society: Population, Ethnicity, and Development* (Boulder, CO:
Westview, 1996); Calvin Goldscheider, "Creating a New Society:
Immigration, Nation-Building, and Ethnicity in Israel," *Harvard
International Review* 20 (Spring 1998): 64-69; David H. Goldberg,
"Soviet Jewish Immigration: The Challenges for Israel," *Middle East
Focus* 12:1 (Summer 1990): 2-5; Ruth Gruber, *Rescue: The Exodus of the
Ethiopian Jews* (New York: Atheneum, 1988); David Horovitz and Vince
Beiser, "The End of Aliya?" *The Jerusalem Report* (July 24, 1997): 12-
15; Harold R. Isaacs, *American Jews in Israel* (New York: J. Day, 1966);
Clive Jones, "Arab Responses to Soviet Jewish Aliya, 1989-1992," *Israel
Affairs* 1:2 (Winter 1994): 267-287; Yossi Klein Halevi, "Suddenly, It's
Raining Jews," *The Jerusalem Report* (June 13, 1991): 12-19; Jon
Kimche and David Kimche, *The Secret Roads* (New York: Farrar, Straus,
and Cudahy, 1955); Elazar Leshem and Judith T. Shouval, editors,
Immigration to Israel: Sociological Perspectives (New Brunswick, NJ:
Transaction, 1998); "Refugee Settlement and Resettlement in Israel,"
Refuge: Canada's Periodical on Refugees (Special Issue) 14:6
(November 1994); Stewart Reiser, *Soviet Jewish Immigration to Israel:
Political and Economic Implications* (Los Angeles: The Susan and David

Wilstein Institute of Jewish Policy Studies, Spring 1992); Howard M. Sachar, *Aliyah: The Peoples of Israel* (Cleveland: World, 1961); Avraham Shama and Mark Iris, *Immigration without Integration: Third World Jews in Israel* (Cambridge, MA: Schenkman, 1977); Naomi Sheppard, "Ex-Soviet Jews in Israel: Asset, Burden, or Challenge?" *Israel Affairs* 1:2 (Winter 1994): 245-266; Moshe Shokeid, *The Dual Heritage: Immigrants from the Atlas Mountains in an Israeli Village* (Manchester, UK: Manchester University Press, 1971); Judith T. Shuval, *Immigrants on the Threshold* (New York: Atheneum, 1963); Hayim Tawil and Steven Miodownik (with Pierre Goloubinoff), *Operation Esther: Opening the Door for the Last Jews of Yemen* (New York: Balkis Press, 1998); Alex Weingrod, *Reluctant Pioneers: Village Development in Israel* (Ithaca, NY: Cornell University Press, 1966); Alex Weingrod, "Styles of Ethnic Adaptation: Interpreting Iraqi and Moroccan Settlement in Israel," in *Israel: The First Decade of Independence*, edited by S. Ilan Troen and Noah Lucas (Albany: State University of New York Press, 1995): 523-542; Dov Weintraub, et al., *Immigration and Social Change: Agricultural Settlement of New Immigrants in Israel* (Jerusalem: Israel University Press, 1971); Shmuel Yilma, *From Falasha to Freedom: An Ethiopian Jew's Journey to Jerusalem* (Jerusalem: Gefen, 1996).

ALIYA BET. A term for the illegal immigration of Jews into Palestine* under the British Mandate* in defiance of official British restrictions.

For further information see: Ehud Avriel, *Open the Gates! A Personal Story of "Illegal" Immigration to Israel* (New York: Atheneum, 1975); Yehuda Bauer, *Flight and Rescue: Brichah* (New York: Random House, 1970); Jon Kimche and David Kimche, *The Secret Roads* (New York: Farrar, Straus, and Cudahy, 1955).

ALLENBY BRIDGE. Also known as the King Hussein Bridge, it was named for Sir Edmund Allenby, the British General who commanded the Egyptian Expeditionary Force during World War I. It spans the Jordan River* just north of the Dead Sea*. It was central to the open bridges policy* instituted after the 1967 Six Day War* whereby Israelis and Jordanians maintained a high level of commercial contact even in the absence of formal peace. According to the Cairo Agreement* of May 1994 access to the bridge is now controlled by Jordan* on the east bank and by the Palestinian Authority* on the West Bank* with Israeli officials maintaining a presence on the Palestinian side for purposes of security.

The bridge remains a principal point of contact between Israelis, Palestinians, and Jordanians.

ALLON, YIGAL (FORMERLY PAICOVITCH). Born at Kfar Tabor (Mesha) in lower Galilee* on October 10, 1918, he was educated at local schools, graduating in 1937 from the Kadourie Agricultural School. He later studied at Hebrew University* and St. Antony's College, Oxford. In 1937, he helped to found and became a member of Kibbutz Ginnosar. During the Arab riots of 1936-1939 in Palestine*, he served in the underground defense forces commanded by Yitzhak Sadeh*. In 1941 he helped found Palmah*, a commando unit which assisted in Allied surveillance and sabotage operations in Syria* and Lebanon*. In 1942 he headed an underground intelligence and sabotage network in Syria and Lebanon. The following year he became the deputy commander of Palmah and, in 1945, became its commander, a post he retained until 1948 when the Palmah was integrated into the newly formed Israel Defense Forces (IDF)*. In this capacity he directed sabotage against civil and military installations of the British Mandatory* government, and supported Aliyah Bet*, the illegal immigration of Jews into Palestine. He was commander of the southern front in the latter phases of Israel's War of Independence* and drove the Arab armies out of the Negev*. After Prime Minister David Ben-Gurion* dissolved the Palmah, Allon entered politics. In 1954 he was elected to the Knesset* and served as Minister of Labor from 1961 to 1967. In June 1967 he participated in the inner war cabinet which helped to plan the strategy of the Six Day War*. He was also the author of the "Allon Plan"*. In July 1968 he became Deputy Prime Minister and Minister for Immigrant Absorption. From 1969 to 1974 he served as Deputy Prime Minister and Minister of Education and Culture, and from 1974 to 1977 was Deputy Prime Minister and Minister of Foreign Affairs. He died in 1980.

For further information see: Yigal Allon, "The Arab-Israeli Conflict: Some Suggested Solutions," *International Affairs* 40 (April 1964): 205-218; Yigal Allon, *Curtain of Sand* (Tel Aviv: Hakibbutz Hameuchad, 1962, Hebrew); Yigal Allon, "Israel: The Case for Defensible Borders," *Foreign Affairs* 55 (October 1976): 38-53; Yigal Allon, "The Making of Israel's Army: The Development of Military Conceptions of Liberation and Defense," in *The Theory and Practice of Wars*, edited by Michael Howard (New York: Praeger, 1965); Yigal Allon, *Shield of David: The Story of Israel's Armed Forces* (London: Weidenfeld and Nicolson,

1970); Yigal Allon, *The Making of Israel's Army* (London: Valentine, Mitchell, 1970).

ALLON PLAN. A proposal developed by Yigal Allon* to establish peace and secure borders for Israel after the Six Day War*. Essentially the plan called for the return of the densely populated areas in the West Bank* and Gaza Strip* to Arab control as well as a return of most of the Sinai Peninsula* to Egypt*. Israel would retain control of the Jordan River* valley and mountain ridges where it could establish settlements and early warning systems (of radar and other devices) to provide warnings against attacks from the east. There would be adjustments to the 1949 armistice lines and Israel would retain Jerusalem* and the Etzion Bloc* of settlements south of Jerusalem. Other specifics were included in the detailed plan. The plan was never adopted as the official policy of Israel, but the Labor* party-led governments of Israel until 1977 pursued its settlement policy using the Allon plan as its guideline.

In 1996 a new political party, The Third Way*, ran on a policy platform regarding the future status of the West Bank that borrowed heavily from the Allon Plan. In late 1996 and 1997, the Likud*-led Government of Benjamin Netanyahu* articulated a vision of a permanent settlement with the Palestinians derived from the original Allon Plan and with adjustments to reflect then-current realities in the territories, a vision that Netanyahu called the "Allon Plan Plus."

For further information see: Yigal Allon, "Israel: The Case for Defensible Borders," *Foreign Affairs* 55 (October 1976): 38-53; Elisha Efrat, "Jewish Settlements on the West Bank: Past, Present and Future," *Israel Affairs* 1:1 (Autumn 1994): 135-148; Herb Keinon, *Israeli Settlements: A Guide* (New York: Anti-Defamation League, 1995); David Newman, "Boundaries in Flux: The 'Green Line' Boundary between Israel and the West Bank—Past, Present and Future," in *Boundary and Territory Briefing* 1:7 (Durham, UK: University of Durham Press, 1995).

ALONI, SHULAMIT. Born in 1929 in Tel Aviv*, she is a writer, lawyer, and prominent figure in Israel's women's liberation movement. A committed secularist and civil libertarian, she has fought the rigid control exercised by the Orthodox rabbinate over such issues as marriage, divorce, and other areas of personal status. She was elected to parliament on the Labor Party* list in 1965 but was dropped from the list for the

1969 and 1973 elections. She ran independently and led the Citizens' Rights Movement* in the 1973 elections where it secured three seats. It subsequently joined the coalition Government led by Prime Minister Yitzhak Rabin* in 1974 with Aloni serving as Minister without Portfolio, but it withdrew from the coalition in October of that year to protest the entry into the coalition of the National Religious Party (NRP)*. Her resignation from the coalition was based on the fact that her party was pledged to a program of separation of state and religion and that the inclusion of the NRP in the Government would lead to a strengthening of religious control over matters of personal status. Aloni headed the Meretz* coalition of left-wing Zionist parties that won 12 seats in the 1992 Knesset* election. Between 1992 and 1996 she held ministerial portfolios in the Labor-led coalition and in that capacity introduced a number of measures that upset the ultra-Orthodox member of the coalition, Shas*. Aloni retired from party politics prior to the 1996 election.

ALTALENA. In June 1948 a ship arrived on the coast of Israel from France* with immigrants and arms and ammunition for delivery to the Irgun*. The Government under Prime Minister David Ben-Gurion* ordered that the ship and its cargo be placed at its disposal, but the Irgun refused. In the subsequent battle between the army and the Irgun, the Government prevailed, and the ship was sunk. Soon afterward the Irgun was disbanded and its members were incorporated into the Israel Defense Forces*. The incident made it clear that the Government would not tolerate challenges to its authority or the existence of armed forces competing with the IDF. The incident contributed to the personal animosity between Menachem Begin* and Ben-Gurion that characterized Israeli politics in subsequent years.

For further information see: Michael Bar-Zohar, *Ben-Gurion: A Biography* (New York: Delacorte, 1979); Menachem Begin, *The Revolt: The Story of the Irgun* (New York: Nash, 1951): chapters XI-XII; Joseph Heller, "The Zionist Right and National Liberation: From Jabotinsky to Avraham Stern," *Israel Affairs* 1:3 (Spring 1995): 85-109; Samuel Katz, *Days of Fire: The Secret History of the Irgun Tzva'i Le'umi* (New York: Doubleday, 1968); Shlomo Nakdimon, *Altalena* (Jerusalem: Edanim, 1978 [in Hebrew]); Joseph Schechtman and Yehuda Benari, *A History of the Revisionist Movement* (Tel Aviv: Hadar, 1970); Yaacov Shavit, *Revisionism in Zionism* (Tel Aviv: Yariv, 1978); Ehud Sprinzak, *Brother*

Against Brother: Violence in Israeli Politics from the Altalena *Tragedy to the Rabin Assassination* (New York: Free Press, 1999).

ALTER, SIMCHA BUNIM. Rabbi Simcha B. Alter was born in 1897 in Gora Kalwaria, Poland, and emigrated to Palestine* in 1934. He was named the head of the Ger (or Gur) Hasidic dynasty in 1977. He was an influential figure behind the scenes in Israeli politics as leader of one of the largest Orthodox Jewish dynasties and as head of the Council of Torah Sages*, the spiritual adviser to Agudat Israel*. He campaigned for strict religious legislation in Israel. He died in 1992. His role as head of the Ger Hasidic community was taken by his half-brother, Rabbi Pinchas Menachem Alter, who in turn died in March 1996.

AM ECHAD *see* **ONE PEOPLE**

AMIR, YIGAL. The assassin of Prime Minister Yitzhak Rabin*. Raised in Herzliya in a religiously observant Sephardic* family, he was educated in Orthodox schools affiliated with the Ashkenazi*-dominated Agudat Israel* movement. Following high school he studied in the Karem Dyaneh yeshiva (part of the national religious Hesder yeshiva system combining Orthodox religious studies with military service). Part of his military service was spent in the elite Golani infantry brigade. After the military he studied law and computer science at Bar Ilan University* and won a place in the university's prestigious Institute for Advanced Jewish Studies. He murdered Rabin at the conclusion of a peace rally in Tel Aviv* on the evening of Saturday, November 4, 1995. He explained that he was motivated by an intense displeasure over the territorial concessions made by the Rabin Government in the context of the Oslo peace accords*. On March 27, 1996, he was convicted and sentenced to life in prison for the murder. On March 28, 1996, a commission of inquiry headed by the former President of the Supreme Court* of Israel, Justice Meir Shamgar*, concluded that Amir had acted alone in assassinating Rabin.

For further information see: Michael Karpin and Ina Friedman, *Murder in the Name of God: The Plot to Kill Yitzhak Rabin* (Jerusalem: Metropolitan Books, 1998); Uri Milstein, *The Rabin File: An Unauthorized Expose* (Jerusalem: Gefen, 1999); Avraham Rotem, *Ha-emet, Haver* (The Invisible Syndrome: How the Mythical Shin Bet Failed to Prevent the Assassination of Israel's Prime Minister) (Jerusalem: Bar-Keren Publishers, 1999).

AMIT, MEIR (FORMERLY SLUTZKY). Born in 1921 in Tiberias*, he joined the Hagana* in 1936 and was a member of Kibbutz Alonim between 1939 and 1952. He served in Israel's War of Independence*, was appointed commander of the Golani Brigade in 1950, and the head of Southern Command in 1955. He later served as commander of the Northern Command and studied business administration in the United States*. He was head of the Mossad* from 1963 to 1968 and was Managing Director of Koor Industries* until 1977. He was one of the founding members of the Democratic Movement for Change* in 1976 and served in the Knesset*. He served as Minister of Transport in the 1977 Government led by Menachem Begin*, but in 1978 left the Government and joined Shinui*. In 1980 he joined the Labor Party*. He has worked as a manager of corporations since the late 1970s.

AMITAL, RABBI YEHUDA. Born in 1925 in Transylvania. As a boy he studied in *heder* and yeshiva and had virtually no formal secular education. In 1943 the Nazis deported him to a labor camp. His family perished in Auschwitz. He immigrated to Palestine* in December 1944, and joined the Hagana*, participating in the battles of Latrun* and the western Galilee* during the War of Independence*. He resumed his yeshiva studies in Jerusalem* where he was ordained as a rabbi. Founder and dean (Rosh Yeshiva) of the Orthodox Har Etzion Yeshiva located in the West Bank* settlement of Alon Shvut. Founder of the national-religious Hesder yeshiva system which combines Orthodox religious studies with military service. Founder and chairman of the Meimad* (Movement for the Religious Center) Party that broke away from the National Religious Party* in 1988 to protest the NRP's shift to the political right on many domestic and foreign policy issues. Under his leadership Meimad ran lists in the 1988 and 1992 elections but in each instance the party failed to win a sufficient share of the vote to take seats in the Knesset*. He agreed to serve as Minister without Portfolio in the Government formed by Shimon Peres* after the November 1995 assassination of Yitzhak Rabin*. He seeks to promote dialogue and to lessen polarization within Israeli society on both domestic and security policy issues. On matters of peace and security he supports the principle of territorial compromise based on the notion that "the good of the people and State of Israel takes precedence over political control over the entire Land of Israel." While wishing to see increased adherence to Halacha* among Israeli Jews, he opposes what he terms the "religious coercion" exerted by the ultra-Orthodox political parties in seeking to force through legislation affecting the status quo agreement* over religious affairs. He advocates maximum tolerance among Israelis and between Israelis and Diaspora Jewish communities with regard to the contentious "Who is a Jew"* debate. *See also* STATUS QUO AGREEMENT.

AMOR, SHAUL. Born in 1941 in Morocco, he immigrated to Israel in 1956. Formerly head of the Migdal Ha'emek Local Council. Likud* MK since 1988, he was his party's candidate for President* of Israel in 1998 but was defeated by the incumbent, Ezer Weizman*. In January 1999 Amor was named Minister without Portfolio in the Government of Benjamin Netanyahu*. In May 1999 he was appointed Ambassador to Belgium and Luxembourg, though this appointment was challenged on the grounds that it was made on the eve of national elections to compensate Amor for having been bumped from a secure slot on the Likud list of candidates contesting the May 17, 1999, elections to the 15th Knesset*.

ANGLO-AMERICAN COMMITTEE OF INQUIRY. A committee of British and American representatives appointed by their respective governments in November 1945 to study the question of Jewish immigration to Palestine⁺ and the future of the British Mandate⁺. After numerous meetings and hearings in the region and elsewhere it issued a report on April 20, 1946. The recommendations included among others the immediate issuing of 100,000 immigration certificates for Palestine to Jewish victims of Nazi and Fascist persecution. Although United States* President Harry Truman accepted much of the report, especially the recommendation concerning Jewish immigration, the British Government did not accept the report. The Palestine problem was turned over to the United Nations.

For further information see: Joseph Heller, "The Anglo-American Committee of Inquiry in Palestine (1945-1946): The Zionist Reaction Reconsidered," in *Essential Papers on Zionism*, edited by Jehuda Reinharz and Anita Shapira (New York: New York University Press, 1996): 689-723; Amikam Nachmani, *Great Power Discord in Palestine: The Anglo-American Committee of Inquiry into the Problems of European Jewry and Palestine, 1945-1946* (London: Frank Cass, 1987); Allen H. Podet, *The Success and Failure of the Anglo-American Committee of Inquiry, 1945-1946: Last Chance in Palestine* (Lewiston, NY: Edwin Mellen, 1986); Evan Wilson, *Decision on Palestine: How the*

US Came to Recognize Israel (Stanford, CA: Hoover Institution Press, 1979).

ANTI-SEMITISM. The hatred of the Jewish people, either by individuals, groups, or states. One of the major factors motivating modern Zionism*. The founder of political Zionism, Theodor Herzl*, was an assimilated Austrian Jew who was drawn to the notion of independent Jewish statehood by the discriminatory treatment of a Jewish French army officer, Alfred Dreyfus*. Herzl and other political Zionists—especially those from eastern Europe who had experienced pogroms and other forms of state-sponsored anti-Semitism—came to the conclusion that the only solution to the centuries' old Jewish Question* confronting European society was for the Jews to have a state of their own.

AQABA, GULF OF *see* GULF OF AQABA

ARAB BOYCOTT OF ISRAEL. An Arab economic boycott was imposed on the Yishuv* soon after the founding of the League of Arab States* in 1945 and maintained by the Arab states against Israel since the establishment of the state. The boycott had primary, secondary, and tertiary applications and was part of the Arab effort designed to weaken and ultimately to destroy Israel. Until 1950 the boycott barred Arab businesses from dealing with Israel. After April 1950 foreign shippers carrying goods or immigrants to Israel were warned that they were subject to blacklisting in Arab states and would be denied access to Arab port facilities. Later, firms represented in Israel were added to the boycott list. Implementation of the boycott regulations by the Arab states against the targets varied substantially from country to country and from time to time. In the 1970s the United States* Congress adopted legislation outlawing compliance by American businesses with the boycott. Egypt*, since 1979, openly deals with Israel and some trade takes place unofficially and informally between Israel and other Arab partners. The secondary and tertiary applications of the boycott were formally suspended by the Gulf Cooperation Council (GCC) in the early 1990s, but the primary political boycott remained formally in effect.

For further information see: Dan S. Chill, *The Arab Boycott of Israel: Economic Aggression* (New York: Praeger, 1976); W. H. Nelson and T. Prittie, *The Economic War against the Jews* (New York: Random House, 1977); *The Arab Economic Boycott of Israel* (New York: Anti-

Defamation League memorandum, April 1997); Nancy Turck, "The Arab Boycott of Israel," *Foreign Affairs* 55:3 (April 1977): 472-493; Howard Stanislawski, "Ethnic Interest Group Activity in the Canadian Foreign Policy Making Process: A Case Study of the Arab Boycott," in *The Middle East at the Crossroads: Regional Forces and External Powers*, edited by Janice Gross Stein and David B. Dewitt (Oakville, Ontario: Mosaic, 1983): 200-220.

ARAB COOPERATION AND BROTHERHOOD. An Arab political party that won seats in the Knesset* in the elections of 1959, 1961, and 1965.

ARAB DEMOCRATIC LIST. An Arab political party that contested and won seats in the Knesset* elections of 1949, 1951, and 1955.

ARAB DEMOCRATIC PARTY. A political party formed in 1988 by former Labor Alignment* member of the Knesset*, Abd El-Wahab Darawshe*, that contested the 1988 Knesset election. Its platform called for appropriate and active representation for Arabs in Israel in all state institutions. In foreign policy it called for the recognition of the right of the Palestinian Arab people to self-determination. It advocated convening an international peace conference with the participation on an equal basis of all the parties involved, including the Palestine Liberation Organiza-tion* as the sole legitimate representative of the Palestinian people. The party called for the withdrawal of Israel from all the territories occupied in the Six Day War* and the establishment of a Palestinian state in Judea*, Samaria*, Gaza*, and East Jerusalem*. It won one seat in the 1988 election, two in 1992, and four in 1996 when it ran on a joint slate with the United Arab List*. The joint United Arab List-Arab Democratic Party, headed by Taleb a-Sanaa, won five seats in the May 17, 1999, elections to the 15th Knesset.

ARAB FARMERS AND DEVELOPMENT PARTY. An Arab political party that contested the Knesset* elections of 1951, 1955, and 1959 and won a single seat in each instance.

ARAB-ISRAELI CONFLICT. The Arab-Israeli conflict has been and continues to be the central concern and focus of Israel and affects all aspects of national life. In the period prior to Israel's independence the Arabs of Palestine* actively opposed Zionist efforts to create the Jewish state through attacks on Jewish settlers and settlements, through riots and demonstrations, and by opposition to Jewish immigration and land purchase. Arab opposition to the United Nations Partition Plan* of November 1947, which led to Israel's independence, was followed by a de facto war in Palestine until the termination of the British Mandate*. With the formal end of Great Britain's* role and the establishment of an independent Israel in May 1948, the first of six major Arab-Israeli wars began.

Israel and the Arabs have fought in Israel's War of Independence (1948-1949)*; the Sinai War (1956)*; the Six Day War (1967)*; the War of Attrition (1969-1970)*; the Yom Kippur War (1973)*; and the War in Lebanon (1982)*. In addition, there have been countless border and terrorist incidents and strikes against Israeli and Jewish targets abroad. Beginning in December 1987 Israel was confronted with widespread Palestinian disturbances (intifada*) in the West Bank* and Gaza Strip*. There was also a war of attrition between Hezbollah and other Muslim extremist groups and Israeli and Israel-backed forces in southern Lebanon*, as well as ongoing terrorism by militant Palestinian factions such as Hamas and Palestine Islamic Jihad against Israeli targets in the occupied territories* and in major Israeli cities. Substantial efforts to end the conflict and achieve peace, often involving outside, especially United States*, efforts, have yielded armistice agreements (1949)*; cease-fires at the end of the several conflicts; disengagement of forces agreements* in 1974 and 1975; the Camp David Accords of 1978*; the Egypt-Israel Peace Treaty of 1979*; the Declaration of Principles* and Oslo Agreements* with the PLO* beginning in 1993; and the Israel-Jordan* Peace Treaty* of 1994. While Israel is formally at peace with Egypt* and Jordan* and has a de facto working arrangement with some other Arab states and with the PLO, permanent resolution of the conflict has eluded Israel. *See* individual entries for the various elements and components of the conflict and the peace efforts.

For further information see: David Ben-Gurion, *My Talks with Arab Leaders*, edited by Misha Louvish (Jerusalem: Keter, 1972); Neil Caplan, "Negotiations and the Arab-Israeli Conflict," *The Jerusalem Quarterly* 6 (Winter 1978): 3-19; Neil Caplan, *Futile Diplomacy, Volume 1: Early Arab-Zionist Negotiation Attempts, 1913-1931* (London: Frank Cass, 1983); Neil Caplan, *Futile Diplomacy, Volume 2: Arab-Zionist Negotiations and the End of the Mandate* (London: Frank Cass, 1986); Michael J. Cohen, *The Origins and Evolution of the Arab-Zionist Conflict*

(Berkeley: University of California Press, 1998); Aharon Cohen, *Israel and the Arab World* (Boston: Beacon, 1976); Laura Zittrain Eisenberg and Neil Caplan, *Negotiating Arab-Israeli Peace: Patterns, Problems, Possibilities* (Bloomington: Indiana University Press, 1997); Robert O. Freedman, editor, *The Middle East and the Peace Process: The Impact of the Oslo Accords* (Gainesville: University Press of Florida, 1998); Shlomo Gazit, "Israel and the Palestinians: Fifty Years of Wars and Turning Points," *The Annals of the American Academy of Political and Social Science* 555 (January 1998): 82-96; Martin Gilbert, *The Arab-Israeli Conflict: Its History in Maps* (London: Weidenfeld and Nicolson, 1985); Yehoshafat Harkabi, *Arab Attitudes to Israel* (Jerusalem: Keter, 1972); Yehoshfat Harkabi, *The Palestinian Covenant and Its Meaning* (London: Valentine, Mitchell, 1979); Yehoshafat Harkabi, *Israel's Fateful Hour* (New York: Harper and Row, 1988); Chaim Herzog, *The Arab-Israeli Wars* (New York: Random House, 1982); Mark A. Heller, *A Palestinian State: The Implications for Israel* (Cambridge, MA: Harvard University Press, 1983); Mark A. Heller and Sari Nusseibeh, *No Trumpets, No Drums: A Two-State Solution of the Israeli-Palestinian Conflict* (New York: Hill and Wang, 1991); David Kimche, *After Nasser, Arafat and Saddam Hussein: The Last Option: The Quest for Peace in the Middle East* (London: Weidenfeld and Nicolson, 1991); Walter Laqueur and Barry Rubin, editors, *The Israel-Arab Reader: A Documentary History of the Middle East Conflict*, Fifth Edition (New York: Penguin, 1995); David Makovksy, *Making Peace with the PLO: The Rabin Government's Road to the Oslo Accord* (Boulder, CO: Westview, 1996); Ilan Peleg, editor, *The Middle East Peace Process: Interdisciplinary Perspectives* (Albany: State University of New York Press, 1998); William B. Quandt, *American Diplomacy and the Arab-Israeli Conflict since 1967* (Berkeley: The Brookings Institution/University of California Press, 1993); Itamar Rabinovich, *The Road Not Taken: Early Arab-Israeli Negotiations* (New York: Oxford University Press, 1991); Itamar Rabinovich, *The Brink of Peace: The Israeli-Syrian Negotiations and the Israeli-Arab Peace Process* (Princeton, NJ: Princeton University Press, 1998); Gideon Rafael, *Destination Peace: Three Decades of Israeli Foreign Policy* (New York: Stein and Day, 1981); Bernard Reich and Gershon R. Kieval, editors, *Israeli National Security Policy: Political Actors and Perspectives* (New York: Greenwood, 1988); Barry Rubin, "The Arab-Israeli Conflict Is Over," *Middle East Quarterly* III:3 (September 1996): 3-12; Nadav Safran, *From War to War: The Arab-Israeli Confrontation, 1948-1967* (New York: Pegasus, 1969); Uriel

Savir, *The Process: 1,100 Days That Changed the Middle East* (New York: Random House, 1998); Ze'ev Schiff, *Israel: Preconditions for Palestinian Statehood* (Washington, DC: Washington Institute for Near East Policy, Research Memorandum No. 39, May 1999); Samuel Segev, *Crossing the Jordan: Israel's Hard Road to Peace* (New York: St. Martin's, 1998); Avraham Sela, *The Decline of the Arab-Israeli Conflict: Middle East Politics and the Quest for Regional Order* (Albany: State University of New York Press, 1998); Mark Tessler, *A History of the Israeli-Palestinian Conflict* (Bloomington: Indiana University Press, 1994); Mohammed Z. Yakah, "From War to Peace: The Middle East Peace Process," *Israel Affairs* 3:3&4 (Spring/Summer 1997): 133-169; *The Palestinian-Israeli Peace Agreement: A Documentary Record*, Second Edition (Washington, DC: The Institute for Palestine Studies, 1994).

ARAB-ISRAELI WARS, ISRAEL'S WAR OF INDEPENDENCE (1948-1949) *see* WAR OF INDEPENDENCE

ARAB-ISRAELI WARS, SINAI WAR (1956) *see* SINAI WAR

ARAB-ISRAELI WARS, SIX DAY WAR (1967) *see* SIX DAY WAR

ARAB-ISRAELI WARS, WAR IN LEBANON (1982) *see* WAR IN LEBANON

ARAB-ISRAELI WARS, WAR OF ATTRITION (1969-1970) *see* WAR OF ATTRITION

ARAB-ISRAELI WARS, YOM KIPPUR WAR (1973) *see* YOM KIPPUR WAR

ARAB LEAGUE (LEAGUE OF ARAB STATES). Founded on March 22, 1945, in Alexandria, Egypt*, to coordinate increased Arab economic, cultural, and political unity. Its highest decision-making body is the Arab League Council, comprised of the heads of member states and based on equal representation. Six commissions were subsequently established to further the goal of strengthened relations, and a number of cooperative accords were signed over the years in the areas of mutual defense and trade. The Arab League has played a central role in the conflict with Israel. In 1946 it instituted a boycott on trade with the Zionist community in Palestine* (this embargo was applied to the State of Israel after independence in May 1948). On December 17, 1947, the Arab League formally rejected the UN Partition Plan*, called for an independent Arab state in all of Palestine, and resolved (on February 9, 1948) to prevent the birth of Israel. In January 1964, at a summit meeting in Cairo, the League endorsed the creation of the Palestine Liberation Organization*. At the Khartoum Conference* of September 1967 it issued its infamous "three noes"—no peace with Israel, no recognition of Israel, no negotiations with Israel. At its Rabat Conference (October 1974) the League recognized the PLO as "the sole legitimate representative" of the Palestinians. It opposed the Camp David Accords* of September 1978, expelling Egypt and "temporarily" moving its headquarters to Tunis from Cairo. The Arab League became increasingly fragmented over inter-Arab disputes (such as the Lebanon civil war, the rise of Muslim fundamentalism, and Iraq's August 1990 invasion of Kuwait) as well as over developments on the peace front with Israel, including the peace treaties with Egypt (1979) and Jordan* (1994) and the Israel-PLO Declaration of Principles* (1993). Also impinging on the internal unity and effectiveness of the Arab League was the growing tendency of member states to place their individual national interests over pan-Arab considerations, especially but not exclusively in regard to relations with Israel.

For further information see: Michael N. Barnett, editor, *Dialogues in Arab Politics: Negotiations in Regional Order* (New York: Columbia University Press, 1998); Boutros Boutros-Ghali, "The Arab League," *International Conciliation*, No. 498 (May 1954): 387-448; Hussein A. Hassouna, *The League of Arab States and Regional Disputes: A Study of Middle East Conflicts* (Dobbs Ferry, NY: Oceana Publications, 1975); Michael Hudson, editor, *Middle East Dilemma: The Politics and Economics of Arab Integration* (New York: Columbia University Press, 1999); Robert W. MacDonald, *The League of Arab States: A Study in the Dynamics of Regional Organization* (Princeton, NJ: Princeton University Press, 1965).

ARAB MOVEMENT FOR RENEWAL. A one-man Knesset* faction established when Ahmed Tibi* broke away from Azmi Bishara's National Democratic Alliance-Balad* Party in December 1999.

ARAB POLITICAL PARTIES. Arab political parties have been a part of the Israeli political scene since independence, and the Arabs of Israel* have been represented on a regular basis in the Knesset*. In the elections for the Knesset between 1949 and 1969, the majority of Israeli Arabs supported the dominant Jewish party or the Arab political party lists affiliated with it. In 1973 and 1977 this support declined; the mixed Arab and left-wing Jewish Communist Party* secured nearly 50% of the Arab votes in 1977. To a great extent, this reflected growing Arab nationalism and support for the Palestinians, causes espoused by the Communists. Overall Arab participation in the political process also declined during the same period. In 1981 the Alignment* tripled its vote among the Arabs of Israel compared to 1977; this was seen as a vote for the best of the bad alternatives. Much of the turn to Labor was seen as anti-Begin* and anti-Likud* and grew out of disappointment with Menachem Begin's ignoring the Arab problem in Israel. There was an unexpectedly low turnout of Arabs voters and a sharp decline in support for Rakah*. In the 1988 election Rakah won four seats. In 1992 the Arab and mixed Arab-Jewish parties won five Knesset seats; while 47% of Arab votes went to the Arab parties, 30% went to center-left Zionist parties (Labor 20.3%, Meretz 9.7%). In 1996 the vast majority of Arabs casting valid ballots voted for Shimon Peres* for Prime Minister; in the Knesset vote, the United Arab List-Arab Democratic Party* won four seats while the Israel Communist Party-Hadash* took five mandates. In the elections of May 17, 1999, Arab political parties won a total of 10 seats in the 15th Knesset, with the United Arab List-Arab Democratic Party* taking five, the Democratic Front for Peace and Equality-Hadash* three; and the National Democratic Alliance-Balad* two.

For further information see: Majid Al-Haj, "The Political Behavior of the Arabs in Israel in the 1992 Elections: Integration versus Segregation," in *The Elections in Israel 1992*, edited by Asher Arian and Michael Shamir (Albany: State University of New York Press, 1995): 141-160; Asher Arian, *The Second Republic: Politics in Israel* (Chatham, NJ: Chatham House, 1998): chapter 5; Hillel Frisch, "The Arab Vote in the 1992 Elections: The Triviality of Normality; The Significance of Electoral Power," in *Israel at the Polls 1992*, edited by Daniel J. Elazar and Shmuel Sandler (Lanham, MD: Rowman and Littlefield, 1995): 103-126; Hillel Frisch, "The Arab Vote: The Radicalization of Politicization?" *Israel Affairs* (Special Issue: "Israel at the Polls 1996") 4:1 (Autumn 1997): 103-120; Calvin Goldscheider, *Israel's Changing Society: Population, Ethnicity, and Development* (Boulder, CO: Westview, 1996); Gershon R. Kieval, *Party Politics in Israel and the Occupied Territories* (Westport, CT: Greenwood, 1983); Bernard Reich and Gershon R. Kieval, *Israel:*

Land of Tradition and Conflict, Second Edition (Boulder, CO: Westview, 1993).

ARAB PROGRESS AND WORK. An Arab political party that contested the 1951, 1955, 1959, 1961, and 1965 Knesset* elections and won seats in parliament.

ARABS IN ISRAEL. Israel's non-Jewish citizenry is composed mainly of the Arabs who remained in what became Israel after the 1949 Armistice Agreements* and their descendants. By 1999 that group had grown to some 1.2 million, primarily as a result of a high birthrate. The Muslim population, which constitutes about three-fourths of the non-Jewish population, is predominantly Sunni. The Christians constitute about 14% of the non-Jewish population. Greek Catholics and Greek Orthodox constitute more than 70% of that number, but there are also Roman Catholics, Maronites, Armenians, Protestants, and Anglicans.

The non-Jewish communities have special positions, similar to those enjoyed under the Ottoman millet system. After Israel's War of Independence* and the 1949 Armistice Agreements*, the activities of the Arab community were regarded primarily as concerns of Israel's security system, and most of the areas inhabited by the Arabs were placed under military control. Military government was established in those districts, and special defense and security zones were created. Israel's Arabs were granted citizenship with full legal equality, but were forbidden to travel into or out of security areas without permission of the military. Military courts were established in which trials could be held in closed session. With the consent of the Minister of Defense, the military commanders could limit individual movements, impose restrictions on employment and business, issue deportation orders, search and seize, and detain a person if that were deemed necessary for security purposes. Those who argued in support of the military administration saw it as a means of controlling the Arab population and of preventing infiltration from neighboring hostile Arab states, sabotage, and espionage. It was argued that the very existence of the military administration was an important deterrent measure. However, as it became clear that Israel's Arabs were not disloyal and as Israel's security situation improved, pressure for relaxation and then for total abolition of military restrictions on Israel's Arabs grew in the Knesset* and in public debate. The restrictions were gradually modified, and on December 1, 1966, military government was abolished.

Functions that had been exercised by the military government were transferred to relevant civilian authorities.

The non Jewish community has undergone other substantial changes since 1948. Education has become virtually universal. Local authority has grown, and through the various local authorities the Arabs have become involved in local decision making and provision of services. The traditional life of the Arab has been altered by new agricultural methods and increased employment in other sectors of the economy—especially industry, construction, and services. Social and economic improvements have included more urbanization, modernization of villages, better infrastructure, improved health care, and expansion of educational opportunities. *See also* DRUZE.

For further information see: Majid Al-Haj, *Education, Empowerment, and Control: The Case of the Arabs in Israel* (Albany: State University of New York Press, 1995); Majid Al-Haj and Henry Rosenfeld, *Arab Local Government in Israel* (Boulder, CO: Westview, 1990); Ismael Abu-Saad, "The Education of Israel's Negev Bedouin: Background and Prospects," *Israel Studies* 2:2 (Fall 1997): 21-40; Abner Cohen, *Arab Border Villages in Israel: A Study of Continuity and Change in Social Organization* (Manchester, UK: Manchester University Press, 1972); Calvin Goldscheider, *Israel's Changing Society: Population, Ethnicity, and Development* (Boulder, CO: Westview, 1996): chapters 2 and 4; Amiram Gonen and Rassem Khamaisi, *The Arabs in Israel in the Wake of Peace* (Jerusalem: The Florsheimer Institute for Policy Studies, November 1993); David Grossman, *Sleeping on a Wire: Conversations with Palestinians in Israel* (Translated by Haim Watzman) (New York: Farrar, Straus, and Giroux, 1993); Aziz Haidar, *On The Margins: The Arab Population in the Israeli Economy* (New York: St. Martin's, 1995); Sabri Jiryis, *The Arabs in Israel* (New York and London: Monthly Review Press, 1976); David Kretzmer, *The Legal Status of the Arabs in Israel* (Boulder, CO: Westview, 1990); Jacob M. Landau, *The Arabs in Israel: A Political Study* (London: Oxford University Press, 1969); Victor Lavy, *Variations in Resources and Outcomes in the Arab Educational System in Israel* (Jerusalem: The Florsheimer Institute for Policy Studies, May 1995); Ian Lustick: *Arabs in the Jewish State: Israel's Control of a National Minority* (Austin: University of Texas Press, 1980); Emanuel Marx, *Bedouin of the Negev* (New York: Praeger, 1968); David Newman, "Bedouin Inequality," *Jerusalem Post,* July 8, 1998; Ilan Pappe, "An

Uneasy Coexistence: Arabs and Jews in the First Decade of Statehood,"
in *Israel: The First Decade of Independence*, edited by S. Ilan Troen and
Noah Lucas (Albany: State University of New York Press, 1995): 617-
658; Arye Rattner and Gideon Fishman, *Justice For All? Jews and Arabs
in the Israeli Criminal Justice System* (Westport, CT: Praeger, 1998); Elie
Rekhess, editor, *Arab Politics in Israel at a Crossroads* (Tel Aviv: Moshe
Dayan Center for Middle Eastern and African Studies, 1996); Nadim
Rouhana, "The Test of Equal Citizenship: Israel between Jewish
Ethnocracy and Bi-National Democracy," *Harvard International Review*
20 (Spring 1998): 74-78; Nadim Rouhana and As'ad Hhanem, "The
Democratization of a Traditional Minority in an Ethnic Democracy: The
Palestinians in Israel," in *Democracy, Peace, and the Israeli-Palestinian
Conflict*, edited by E. Kaufman, S. Abed, and R. Rothstein (Boulder, CO:
Lynne Rienner, 1993): 163-184; Walter Schwartz, *The Arabs in Israel*
(London: Faber and Faber, 1959); Sammy Smooha, *Arabs and Jews in
Israel Volume I: Conflicting and Shared Attitudes in a Divided Society*
(Boulder, CO: Westview, 1989), *Volume II: Change and Continuity in
Mutual Intolerance* (Boulder, CO: Westview, 1992); Sammy Smooha,
"Arab-Jewish Relations in Israel in the Peace Era," *Israel Affairs* 1:2
(Winter 1994): 227-244; Sammy Smooha, "Ethnic Democracy: Israel as
an Archtype," *Israel Studies* 2:2 (Fall 1997): 198-241; Sammy Smooha,
*Social Research on Arabs in Israel, 1948-1977: Trends and an Annotated
Bibliography* (Ramat Gan, Israel: Turtledove, 1978); Sammy Smooha,
The Orientation and Politicization of the Arab Minority in Israel (Haifa,
Israel: University of Haifa, 1981); Elia T. Zureik, *The Palestinians in
Israel: A Study of Internal Colonization* (London: Routledge, 1979).

ARAD, RON. Missing Israeli airman believed to be held by Iran* or by
Iranian-backed Lebanese militant groups. On October 16, 1986, an Israeli
Air Force Phantom aircraft was downed by mechanical problems over
Sidon in southern Lebanon*. The pilot and the navigator bailed out and
landed safely. The pilot was rescued by an Israeli helicopter patrol.
However the navigator, Captain Ron Arad, was taken prisoner by a local
cell of the Amal Shi'ite organization. Direct responsibility for Arad's
welfare was passed to Mustafa Dirani, the head of Amal's security
service. At the beginning of 1988 Dirani split from Amal over ideological
differences, forming a pro-Iranian group called "the Faithful Resistance"
and taking Arad with him. Dirani's group was subsequently incorporated
into the pro-Iranian Hezbollah movement, and there is speculation that
Arad was transferred to Iranian forces in Lebanon or perhaps moved to

Iran itself. Neither Iran nor Hezbollah have formally acknowledged that they are holding Arad. But in July 1998 a senior Hezbollah official publicly pledged to search for information about him. Arad's name is frequently mentioned in negotiations over prisoner exchanges involving Israel and Hezbollah and other Lebanese-based guerrilla factions, and indeed, over the years Israeli forces have captured top Hezbollah and Amal officials in part in the hope of acquiring reliable information about Arad's status and/or exchanging the officials for him. Ron Arad remains a very sensitive issue for many Israelis.

ARAFAT, YASSER (ABU AMMAR). Born in August 1929, either in Jerusalem*, Gaza*, or Cairo. While acquiring a degree in civil engineering in Egypt* he became involved in Palestinian politics as President of the General Union of Palestinian Students and as a member of a fedayeen* guerrilla group. He also received training in sabotage at an Egyptian army college. From 1958 to 1962 he worked in Kuwait but then moved to Beirut and then Damascus where he helped found the Fatah* guerrilla movement. In 1968 he moved his base of operations to Jordan*, near the village of Karameh. In February 1969 Fatah secured control of a majority of seats on the Palestinian National Council* and Arafat became chairman of the Palestine Liberation Organization (PLO)* Executive Committee. In September 1970 he helped organize a civil war in Jordan, the goal being to oust the regime of King Hussein* and replace it with a PLO-dominated government. When this failed, the PLO moved to Lebanon*, where it set up a state-within-a-state in Beirut and much of southern Lebanon and waged an international campaign of terror against Israel and against Israeli and Jewish targets worldwide. These attacks provoked major Israeli retaliatory operations against PLO bases in Lebanon (e.g., Operation Litani* in 1978, and Operation Peace for Galilee* in 1982). The PLO's presence in Lebanon also disrupted the country's delicate balance of political forces and directly contributed to the outbreak of civil war in 1975.

After being forced out of Lebanon at the end of Operation Peace for Galilee, Arafat moved his base of operations to Tunis, from where he continued to coordinate the PLO's military campaign against Israel. Arafat ran a parallel political and diplomatic offensive designed to solidify the PLO's status as the "sole legitimate representative of the Palestinian people" in their struggle against Israel. In February 1985 he signed an accord with Jordan's King Hussein* that established a framework for a joint PLO-Jordanian approach for negotiations with Israel. At a November 1988 meeting of the Palestine National Council in Algiers, Arafat unilaterally declared independent Palestinian statehood and issued ambiguous statements implying the PLO's acceptance of UN Security Council resolutions 242* of 1967 and 338* of 1973 as the basis for negotiations with Israel; in subsequent days and weeks Arafat, under U.S.* prodding, provided greater clarification on these matters as well as on the PLO's renunciation of terror. His international credibility was adversely effected by his decision to publicly embrace Saddam Hussein following Iraq's* August 1990 invasion of Kuwait, and by the participation of non-PLO West Bank* Palestinians at the Madrid Peace Conference* and in early rounds of bilateral negotiations with Israel in Washington. However, the consummate political survivor, he weathered these political storms and soon reasserted personal control over the Palestinian movement and over Palestinian diplomacy. He approved the secret discussions with Israel in the spring and summer of 1993 that culminated with the Oslo Accords*, and he achieved his long-standing goal of being recognized as an international statesman by representing the Palestinian nation at the signing of the Israel-PLO Declaration of Principles* on September 13, 1993, and by being awarded the 1994 Nobel Peace Prize* (along with Israel's Yitzhak Rabin* and Shimon Peres*). In January 1996 he was elected President of the Executive Committee of the Palestinian Legislative Council*.

Since the signing of the Declaration of Principles and the election of the Palestinian Legislative Council, Arafat had to balance a number of competing political pressures. Central to these was the tension inherent in his commitment to help fight terror emanating from areas of the West Bank and Gaza Strip* being transferred to Palestinian control on the one hand, and on the other his desire to coopt militant secular and religious elements of the Palestinian movement opposed to the Oslo process*. The delicacy of this balancing act came to a head with the string of suicide bombings inside Israel committed by Hamas and Palestine Islamic Jihad activists in February and March of 1996. In addition, Arafat was subjected to growing internal criticism for his dictatorial leadership methods; the opulent lifestyles of senior members of his cabinet amid the continuing economic squalor in the Palestinian autonomous areas in the West Bank and Gaza Strip; the inefficiency, duplication of efforts, and corruption rampant in the Palestinian governmental institutions; and the human rights abuses and other excesses committed by elements of the multilayered Palestinian security forces.

Despite his advancing age and rumors of serious illness, Arafat showed no sign of either slowing the pace of his activities or ending his practice of micro-managing all aspects of the Palestinian struggle.

For further information see: Helena Cobban, "Yasser Arafat," in *Political Leaders of the Contemporary Middle East and North Africa*, edited by Bernard Reich (Westport, CT: Greenwood Press, 1990): 44-51; Samih K. Farsoun (with Christina E. Zacharia), *Palestine and the Palestinians* (Boulder, CO: Westview, 1997); Andrew Gowers and Tony Walker, *Behind the Myth: Yasser Arafat and the Palestinian Revolution* (New York: Olive Branch Press, 1992); Alan Hart, *Arafat: A Political Biography* (Bloomington: Indiana University Press, 1989); Nancy Hasanian, "Yasser Arafat," in *An Historical Encyclopedia of the Arab-Israeli Conflict*, edited by Bernard Reich (Westport, CT: Greenwood Press, 1996): 41-43; Thomas Kiernan, *Arafat, the Man and the Myth* (New York: Norton, 1976); Barry Rubin, *Revolution Until Victory? The Politics and History of the PLO* (Cambridge, MA: Harvard University Press, 1994); Janet Wallach and John Wallach, *Arafat in the Eyes of the Beholder* (New York: Carol Publishing Group/Lyle Stuart, 1990).

ARAVA. A part of the Negev*, it is a narrow and arid plain about 100 miles long and some 10 miles wide stretching north-south from the Dead Sea* to Eilat*. The frontier between Israel and Jordan* runs through the Arava from north to south. Portions of the Arava were ceded to Jordan in the 1994 Israel-Jordan Peace Treaty* and then leased back to Jewish farmers.

ARBELI-ALMOZLINO, SHOSHANA. Born in Iraq*, she has been a Labor Alignment* member of the Knesset* since 1965 and served as Deputy Speaker of the Knesset from 1977 to 1981.

ARENS, MOSHE. Moshe Arens was born in 1925 in Kovno, Lithuania. In 1939 his family immigrated to the United States* and he served in the United States Army during World War II. He secured a BS degree from the Massachusetts Institute of Technology but went to Israel at the outbreak of the War of Independence*, and served in the Irgun* led by Menachem Begin*. After the war he settled in Mevo Betar but returned to the United States in 1951 and secured an MA degree from the California Institute of Technology in aeronautical engineering in 1953. He then worked for a number of years on jet engine development in the United States. In 1957 he took a position as an Associate Professor of Aeronautical Engineering at the Technion*. He joined Israel Aircraft Industries* in 1962, where he was Vice President for Engineering, while continuing his relationship with the Technion. He won the Israel Defense Prize in 1971. He was active in Herut Party* politics from the outset. He was elected to the Knesset* in 1974 and after the Likud* victory of 1977, he became chairman of the Knesset Foreign Affairs and Defense Committee. He voted against the Camp David Accords*, but subsequently supported the Egypt-Israel Peace Treaty* as an established fact. He was appointed Ambassador to Washington in February 1982 and there introduced Benjamin Netanyahu* as an embassy staff member and into Likud politics. Arens became Defense Minister in 1983 after Ariel Sharon* resigned the post. Arens was a well-regarded technocrat and gained substantial kudos for his activities as Ambassador to Washington. His record as Defense Minister gained him similar positive reactions. He served as Minister without Portfolio in the National Unity Government* established in 1984 until he resigned when the Government decided to halt production of the Lavi* fighter aircraft. Arens served again as Minister without Portfolio from April to December 1988 when he became Foreign Minister in the Likud-led National Unity Government. In June 1990 he became Minister of Defense in a Likud-led Government, a position he held throughout the Persian Gulf War*. He retired from party politics after the 1992 Knesset election. He became actively involved in a bipartisan group of elder statesmen dedicated to lobbying for the repeal of the Basic Law: The Government providing for the direct election of the Prime Minister. On January 11, 1999, Arens left retirement to challenge Benjamin Netanyahu for the leadership of the Likud Party, but was soundly defeated by him in the party primary held on January 26, 1999. Arens was subsequently appointed interim Defense Minister, replacing the fired Yitzhak Mordechai*, and he was elected to the 15th Knesset on the Likud list, on May 17, 1999.

For further information see: Moshe Arens, *Broken Covenant: American Foreign Policy and the Crisis between the U.S. and Israel* (New York: Simon and Schuster, 1995); Merrill Simon, *Moshe Arens: Statesman and Scientist* (Middle Island, NY: Dean Books, 1988).

ARGENTINA. From the outset, Israel's relations with Argentina were characterized by mistrust. Argentina abstained from voting on the United Nations Palestine Partition Plan* of November 1947, and accorded official recognition to Israel only in 1949. Early efforts to enhance bilateral relations were complicated by the capture in Buenos Aires of Nazi war criminal Adolf Eichmann* by Israeli agents in 1960, and by long standing allegations that after World War II Argentina became a haven for other Nazi war criminals. A subtle positive change in the relationship began to occur in the second half of the 1970s and the early 1980s, typified by Argentina's November 1975 vote against United Nations General Assembly Resolution 3379*(describing Zionism to be a form of racism), and by substantial Israeli sales of military hardware to Argentina. However, most analysts attributed this shift in Middle East policy less to a pro-Israel orientation among Argentina's leaders than to their desire to improve relations with the United States*. Moreover, there was in this period increased sympathy on the part of Argentina for Arab states in international forums, perhaps in an effort to win Arab and Muslim backing for Argentina's 1982 war against Great Britain* over the Falkland Islands. Nevertheless, in 1991 Carlos Saúl Menem became the first Argentine head of state to make an official visit to Israel. Moreover, President Menem sought in this period to mediate Syrian*-Israeli negotiations over the Golan Heights* and offered his assistance in uncovering information about the status of Israeli soldiers missing in action in neighboring Arab countries. In the early 1990s bilateral relations with Argentina were severely compromised by two terrorist attacks in Buenos Aires: the March 17, 1992, bombing of the Israeli embassy, which left 29 dead and some 230 others wounded; and the July 18, 1994, attack on the building housing the offices of the Argentine Jewish Mutual Agency (AMIA) that killed 86 and wounded 200. These attacks—and the apparent laxness on the part of Argentine officials to identify and arrest the culprits—caused considerable anxiety on the part of the country's 300,000 Jews. In May 1998 Argentine investigators announced that there was "very damning evidence" linking the Government of Iran* and Iranian-backed Muslim terrorists to the 1992 and 1994 bombings. Nevertheless, it was only on December 4, 1998, that Argentine officials arrested one Iranian citizen residing in Argentina on suspicion of complicity in the two attacks. In April 1995 Israeli and Argentine officials signed a memorandum of understanding concerning bilateral trade in the high-tech sector.

For further information see: Joel Barromi, "Israeli Policies towards Argentina and Argentinian Jewry during the Military Junta, 1977-83," *Israel Affairs* 5:1 (Autumn 1998): 27-44; Michael Curtis and Susan Aurelia Gitelson, editors, *Israel in the Third World* (New Brunswick, NJ: Transaction Books, 1976); Edy Kaufman, Yoram Shapira, and Joel Barromi, *Israel-Latin American Relations* (New Brunswick, NJ: Transaction, 1979).

ARIDOR, YORAM. Born in Tel Aviv* in 1933, Yoram Aridor holds a BA degree in Economics and Political Science and an MJur from the Hebrew University of Jerusalem*. He was first elected to the Knesset* on behalf of the Herut Party* faction of Gahal* in October 1969, and reelected to subsequent Knessets as a member of the Likud* bloc. He served on the Knesset Constitution and Law Committee and as Chairman of the Knesset Interior and Environment Committee. He also served as the Chairman of the Herut faction in the Histadrut* from 1972 to 1977, was a member of the Herut Central Committee since 1961, and served as Chairman of the Herut Secretariat since October 1979. From July 1977 to January 1981 he served as Deputy Minister in the Prime Minister's Office. For varying lengths of time during this period he was also responsible for the activities of the Ministries of Justice; Labor and Social Welfare; Transport, Communications, and Industry; and Commerce and Tourism. In January 1981 he was appointed Minister of Communications. He later became Minister of Finance in the Government of Menachem Begin* and also served as the original Finance Minister of the new Government of Yitzhak Shamir* (1983). He resigned in October 1983 after substantial furor developed in response to his proposal that Israel link its economy directly to the United States* dollar. After Aridor resigned on October 13, 1983, Prime Minister Shamir sought to calm public concerns and distanced himself from Aridor and his proposals. Aridor subsequently served as Israel's Ambassador to the United Nations.

ARMED FORCES *see* HAGANA; ISRAEL DEFENSE FORCES

ARMISTICE AGREEMENTS (1949). Agreements concluded between Israel and the neighboring Arab states after the War of Independence*. In the spring of 1949 Israel and each of the neighboring states signed an armistice agreement terminating the hostilities of Israel's War of Independence. Iraq*, although a participant in the conflict, refused to do so. The agreements were to end the hostilities and pave the way for negotiations for peace. The latter did not occur. The armistice negotiations were held under the auspices of the United Nations Acting Mediator for Palestine, Ralph Bunche. Egypt* signed the armistice agreement with Israel on February 24, 1949; Lebanon* on March 23, 1949; Jordan* on April 3, 1949; and Syria* on July 20, 1949.

For further information see: David Brook, *Preface to Peace: The United Nations and the Arab-Israel Armistice System* (Washington, DC: Public Affairs Press, 1964); Shabtai Rosenne, *Israel's Armistice Agreements with the Arab States: A Juridical Interpretation* (Tel Aviv: Blumstein's Bookstores, 1951).

ARROW MISSILE. A sophisticated anti-missile missile system designed to intercept ground-to-ground ballistic missiles. Developed jointly by Israel and the United States*, research on the Arrow was initiated in the mid-1980s as part of the U.S. Strategic Defense Initiative ("Star Wars") and was continued in the context of the Pentagon's Tactical High Energy Laser (THEL) program. Interest in the Arrow grew significantly after Iraqi Scud missile* attacks during the 1991 Persian Gulf War* drew attention to gaps in Israel's missile defense capabilities. Its radar system, developed by a subsidiary of Israel Aircraft Industries*, is designed to track missiles and guide the anti-missile missile at a speed of nearly three km (two miles) per second to within four meters (13 ft) of an incoming target. The Arrow is designed to intercept missiles between 10 km and 40 km above the ground. In August 1997 a test of the Arrow had to be aborted, and the missile destroyed in mid-flight, after a malfunction caused it to deviate off course. In August 1998 the Defense Minister, Yitzhak Mordechai*, approved the accelerated development of the Arrow against the background of Iran's* testing of a new ballistic missile system. The new plan was to enable the Israel Air Force to deploy an operational Arrow anti-missile missile battery during the year 2000. In April 1998 Defense Secretary William Cohen announced the U.S. decision in principle to fund development of a third battery of Arrow missiles for Israel; a formal agreement to that effect was signed by Israeli and American officials in June 1998. The Arrow's three components—the missile, the radar system (for tracking incoming missiles), and the fire control system—were successfully tested together for the first time, against a simulated target, on September 14, 1998. The first operational Arrow missile was transferred from Israel Aircraft Industries (IAI) to the headquarters of the Defense Ministry's "Homa" ("Wall") Project on

November 29, 1998. In a test, on November 1, 1999, an Arrow missile successfully found and destroyed a simulated Scud* missile in mid-flight.

For further information see: Shai Feldman, *The Future of US-Israel Strategic Cooperation* (Washington, DC: The Washington Institute for Near East Policy, 1996).

ASEFAT HANIVCHARIM *see* ASSEMBLY OF THE ELECTED

ASHKENAZI JEWS (PL. ASHKENAZIM). Jews of Eastern and Central European extraction. Ashkenazi Jews were the main components of the first waves of Zionist immigration to Palestine*, where they encountered a small Jewish community that was primarily Sephardi* in nature. The Ashkenazi Jews had fled from the Jewish ghettos of Europe (including Russia) and sought to build a new society, primarily secular and socialist in nature.

In both the Yishuv* and independent Israel, the dominant members of the political elite were of Ashkenazi origin. Although geographically and demographically Israel is an Oriental country; culturally, socially, and politically it is Western in nature and orientation. The early Zionists laid the foundations for an essentially European culture in Palestine, with the attendant concepts, ideals, and ideologies and subsequent immigration accelerated the trend. The Western immigrants created and developed the Yishuv structure of land settlement, institutions, trade unions, and political parties, as well as an educational system—with its attendant assumptions and promises—all in preparation for a Western-oriented Jewish national state. This Ashkenazi influence and leadership remains paramount even as Sephardic* Jews continue to expand their roles and power.

ASSEMBLY OF THE ELECTED (ASEFAT HANIVCHARIM). During the British Mandate* period, the Jewish community in Palestine*, known as the Yishuv*, established and developed institutions for self-government and procedures for implementing political decisions, thereby laying the foundations for the future state of Israel. All significant Jewish groups belonged to the organized Jewish community (with the exception of the ultra-Orthodox Agudat Israel*, then anti-Zionist, which refused to participate) and by secret ballot chose the Assembly of the Elected as its representative body. It was first elected in 1920. It met at least once a year, and between sessions its powers were exercised by the National Council (Vaad Leumi)*, which it elected. The Assembly was formally abolished in February 1949, and its functions and authority were transferred to the Knesset*.

ASSOCIATION OF ISRAEL *see* AGUDAT ISRAEL

ATID (FUTURE). A new political party registered in January 1998. Setting freedom from religious coercion at the top of its agenda, it sought to present itself as a centrist alternative to the existing political parties. Among its other founding principles were the following: the affirmation of Israel as a democracy in which all citizens have equal rights; the supremacy of the rule of law and freedom of conscience; the attachment between Israel and Diaspora* Jewry; and the need to improve the status of Israelis residing in poor urban neighborhoods and in disadvantaged development towns. In the area of foreign and security policy, the party urged the continued pursuit of peace with the Palestinians and with other Arab negotiating partners while assuring security for Israelis. It was generally understood that the party was founded as a springboard for an anticipated run for Prime Minister on the part of the former Likud* MK and cabinet minister and outgoing Mayor of Tel Aviv*, Ron Milo*. Atid was eventually subsumed into the new Center* Party founded by Milo, along with former Likud Knesset* members and cabinet ministers Dan Meridor* and Yitzhak Mordechai* and former IDF* chief of staff Amnon Lipkin-Shahak*, that won six seats in the 15th Knesset.

ATOMIC RESEARCH AND DEVELOPMENT. During his tenure as Prime Minister, David Ben-Gurion* suggested that Israel's scientists begin to develop atomic energy as a source of power for a country essentially devoid of natural resources and as a component of broader scientific research. This included training scientists and engineers. In 1956 it was decided to establish a research reactor at Nahal Sorek, which went critical on June 16, 1960. It became a major facility for research and teaching. It was decided to build a second experimental reactor near Dimona* in the Negev* which became operational in 1964. Israeli scientists established an international reputation for their work in the peaceful uses of atomic energy, but there has been more focus on whether or not Israel has developed a nuclear weapon for potential use by its defense forces. It is generally believed that Israel possesses the scientific and technological know-how, the necessary components and nuclear material, as well as the capability to develop and to deliver a nuclear weapon, but Israel has never confirmed (nor specifically denied) its existence. Preferring a policy of "constructive ambiguity," successive Israeli governments have declared that Israel will not be the first to introduce nuclear weapons into the Middle East. On December 24, 1965, the Minister for Labor, Yigal Allon*, was quoted as saying that "Israel will not be the first to introduce nuclear weapons into the Middle East, but it will not be the second either." On May 18, 1966, Prime Minister Levi Eshkol* told the Knesset*: "Israel has no atomic arms and will not be the first to introduce them onto our region." In 1974 President Ephraim Katzir* stated that Israel "has the potential" to build nuclear weapons and could do so "within a reasonable period of time." On September 7, 1975, Prime Minister Yitzhak Rabin*, speaking on the ABC television program *Issues and Answers*, said that Israel was "a non-nuclear country" and "it will not be the first to introduce nuclear weapons into the area". On September 29, 1980, Yitzhak Shamir*, Israel's Foreign Minister, stated in the United Nations General Assembly that "Israel will not be the first to introduce nuclear weapons into the Arab-Israel dispute." It should be noted, however, that in the past Israeli officials have on occasion categorically denied the possession or intention to employ nuclear weapons. Thus, Prime Minister Golda Meir* stated in May 1969: "Israel has no nuclear bomb, Israel has no intention of using nuclear bombs."

Thus, in its declared policy, Israel has not categorically renounced nuclear weapons. But neither has it chosen to make a demonstration of its nuclear explosive capability, nor has it developed a demonstrable nuclear armament force. Furthermore, at the thirty-fifth session of the United Nations General Assembly, Israel for the first time joined the consensus vote on General Assembly Resolution 35/147, entitled "Establishment of a nuclear-weapon-free zone in the region of the Middle East." More recently, Israeli officials have tacitly linked the reduction or elimination of their country's conventional and nonconventional weaponry to the reduction or elimination of similar weaponry possessed by Israel's Arab and Muslim neighbors; optimally, this reciprocal reduction would be achieved in the framework of a comprehensive regional peace settlement and be based on transparent means of verifiability.

When India and Pakistan conducted nuclear tests in 1998 the reaction in Prime Minister Benjamin Netanyahu's* office was to reiterate the standard Israeli response to any inquiry about its nuclear program—"We

will not be the first to introduce nuclear weapons into the Middle East"
and to direct attention to Iran*, which is believed to be working on a
nuclear weapon.

There was the sense that the "nuclear ambiguity" introduced by the
construction of the Dimona nuclear reactor in the Negev in the 1950s and
1960s has served Israel well over the last three decades in "creating fear
without creating anger," as the policy has been defined, and is in no need
of change.

Israel's possession of nuclear weapons has been widely suspected for
decades. But by refusing to acknowledge them, Israel has spared the
United States* the need to impose sanctions under the Nuclear Non-
Proliferation Treaty. Shimon Peres, who as a young official was
instrumental in building Dimona, said in a recent interview: "We managed
to create sufficient suspicion for there to be deterrent without having
gotten to a status of clarity which would behoove sanctions against us."

In December 1995 Mr. Peres, then Prime Minister, came closest of any
Israeli official to acknowledging that Israel had the bomb and suggested
that it could get rid of it once it was at peace with all its neighbors. *See
also* MORDECHAI VANUNU.

For further information see: Shlomo Aronson (with Oded Brosh), *The
Politics and Strategy of Nuclear Weapons in the Middle East: Opacity,
Theory, and Reality, 1960-1991: An Israeli Perspective* (Albany: State
University of New York Press, 1992); Louis René Beres, "Israel's Bomb
in the Basement: A Second Look," *Israel Affairs* 2:1 (Autumn 1995):
112-136; Louis René Beres, editor, *Security or Armageddon: Israel's
Nuclear Strategy* (Lexington, MA: Lexington Books, 1986); Avner
Cohen, *The Opaque Bomb: The Political History of the Israeli Nuclear
Bomb* (Cambridge, MA: Harvard University Press, 1996); Avner Cohen,
Israel and the Bomb (New York: Columbia University Press, 1998); Alan
Dowty, "Nuclear Proliferation: The Israeli Case," *International Studies
Quarterly* 22 (March 1978): 79-121; Yair Evron, "Israel and the Atom:
The Uses and Misuses of Ambiguity, 1957-1967," *Orbis* 17 (Winter
1974): 1326-1343; Yair Evron, *Israel's Nuclear Dilemma* (Ithaca, NY:
Cornell University Press, 1994); Shai Feldman, *Israeli Nuclear
Deterrence: A Strategy for the 1980s* (New York: Columbia University
Press, 1982); Shai Feldman, *Nuclear Weapons and Arms Control in the*

Middle East (Cambridge, MA: MIT, 1997); Lawrence Freedman, "Israel's Nuclear Policy," *Survival* 17 (May/June 1975): 114-120; Seymour M. Hersh, *The Samson Option: Israel's Nuclear Arsenal and American Foreign Policy* (New York: Vintage Books, 1993); Efraim Inbar, "The Israeli Basement—With Bombs or Without?" *Crossroads* No. 8 (Winter-Spring 1982): 81-106; Fuad Jabber, *Israel and Nuclear Weapons: Present Options and Future Strategies* (London: Chatto and Windus, 1971); Ariel Levite and Emily B. Landau, "Arab Perspectives of Israel's Nuclear Position, 1960-1967," *Israel Studies* 1:1 (Spring 1996): 34-60; Efraim Inbar and Shmuel Sandler, "Israel's Deterrence Strategy Revisited," *Security Studies* 3 (Winter 1993/1994): 330-358; Peter Pry, *Israel's Nuclear Arsenal* (Boulder, CO: Westview Press, 1984); George H. Quester, "Israel," in Jed C. Snyder and Samuel F. Wells, Jr., *Limiting Nuclear Proliferations* (Cambridge, MA: Ballinger, 1985): 43-58; George H. Quester, "Israel and the NPT," *Survival* 11 (October 1969): 317-323; Zaki Shalom, "Kennedy, Ben-Gurion and the Dimona Project, 1960-1963," *Israel Studies* 1:1 (Spring 1996): 3-33; Avner Yaniv, "Non-Conventional Weapons and the Future of Arab-Israeli Deterrence," *Israel Affairs* 2:1 (Autumn 1995): 137-152.

ATTORNEY-GENERAL. The Attorney-General is the chief legal officer of the state and the formal legal advisor to the Government*. He is appointed by the Government based on the nomination of the Minister of Justice and performs the functions of legal advisor to the Government, legal draftsman of all bills proposed by the Government to the Knesset*, and the representative of the state before all courts. He is administratively, but not professionally, subordinated to the Minister of Justice who is a politician representing his party in the Government. The office of Attorney-General was created in order to ensure that the Government receives independent nonpolitical advice and representation.

For further information see: Asher Arian, *The Second Republic: Politics in Israel* (Chatham, NJ: Chatham House, 1998): chapter 9; Itzhak Zamir and Allen Zysblat, editors, *Public Law in Israel* (Oxford: Clarendon, 1996).

B

BADER-OFER PROCESS. The popular name given to a 1973 amendment to the Basic Law: Knesset Elections*, providing a complicated formula for distributing "surplus votes" that frequently occur as a result of Israel's proportional representation electoral system. Based on the "d'Hondt" system widely used in Western Europe, the Bader-Ofer process (named for the Likud* and Labor-Alignment* politicians who jointly sponsored the amendment) is the method used for allocating the share of the popular vote that went to parties that failed to achieve the minimum percentage required to win seats in the Knesset (the threshold was raised from 1% to 1.5% with the 1992 election). A form of this system was applied in the 1949 Knesset election and in all elections since 1973. Between 1961 and 1969 the party with the largest "remainder" of votes won the vacant seat or seats. Approval of the Bader-Ofer amendment of 1973 was forced through the Knesset by the Labor-Alignment and Likud over the objections of most smaller parties, who charged that the formula favored the large parties and as such worked against the principle of equal representation. *See also* KNESSET ELECTIONS.

For further information see: Asher Arian, *The Second Republic: Politics in Israel* (Chatham, NJ: Chatham House, 1998); Avraham Brichta, "Proposed Electoral Reform in Israel," *Jewish Journal of Sociology* 33:2 (1991); Gregory S. Mahler, *Israel: Government and Politics in a Maturing State* (San Diego: Harcourt Brace Jovanovich, 1990); Bernard Reich and Gershon R. Kieval, *Israel: Land of Tradition and Conflict*, Second Edition (Boulder, CO: Westview, 1993).

BAHAI. A religion founded in Persia in 1862 by Mirza Hussein Ali "Baha'ullah (Glory of God)" who was exiled from Persia in 1853 and subsequently imprisoned by the Ottoman government in Akko (Acre)*. After his death in Acre in 1892 the leadership of the movement passed to his son, Abdul-Baha. It grew out of Babism, one of the sectarian deviations of Shiite Islam. Bahai's main holy places are in Haifa* (Tomb of the Bab) and in Bahji, near Acre (site of the Tomb of Baha'ullah). The principles of Bahaism stress the "unity of all religions, world peace, and universal education." It claims to be an all-embracing world religion. On June 8, 1999, the world's first academic chair in Bahai studies was dedicated at the Hebrew University of Jerusalem*.

For further information see: William M. Miller, *The Baha'i Faith: Its History and Teachings* (South Pasadena, CA: W. Carey Library, 1974).

BALAD *see* NATIONAL DEMOCRATIC ALLIANCE-BALAD

BALFOUR DECLARATION. The Balfour Declaration was issued by the British Government on November 2, 1917. Substantial effort by the Zionist organization, with a special role played by Chaim Weizmann*, preceded the Government's decision, made after lengthy discussion and some divisiveness. The Declaration took the form of a letter from Arthur James Balfour, the Foreign Secretary, to Lord Rothschild, a prominent British Zionist leader. It stated: "His Majesty's Government view with favour the establishment in Palestine of a national home for the Jewish people, and will use their best endeavours to facilitate the achievement of this object, it being clearly understood that nothing shall be done which may prejudice the civil and religious rights of existing non-Jewish communities in Palestine, or the rights and political status enjoyed by Jews in any other country."

The Declaration was vague and sought to assuage the fears of prominent Jews in Great Britain* as well as those of the non-Jewish inhabitants of Palestine*. Nevertheless, it engendered much controversy, then and since. Among the problems was the Balfour Declaration's apparent conflict with arrangements made during World War I by the British with the French and the Arabs concerning the future of the Middle East after the termination of hostilities. Foremost among those was the Hussein-McMahon Correspondence, which the Arabs saw as a promise that an independent Arab kingdom would include all of Palestine, although the British later argued that they had excluded the territory west of the Jordan River* from that pledge. The Balfour Declaration provided a basis for Zionist claims to Palestine.

For further information see: George Antonius, *The Arab Awakening: The Story of the Arab National Movement* (New York: Capricorn, 1965); Norman Bentwich, "The History of the Balfour Declaration 1917-1948," *Contemporary Review* 211 (August 1967): 74-81; Michael J. Cohen, *The Origins and Evolution of the Arab-Zionist Conflict* (Berkeley: University of California Press, 1987); D. Z. Gillon, "The Antecedents of the Balfour Declaration," *Journal of Middle Eastern Studies* 5 (May 1969): 131-150; Sahar Huneidi, "Was Balfour Policy Reversible? The Colonial Office and

Palestine 1921-1923," *Journal of Palestine Studies* 27 (Winter 1998) 23-41; J.M.N. Jeffries, "Analysis of the Balfour Declaration," in *From Haven to Conquest: Readings in Zionism and the Palestine Problem until 1948*, edited by Walid Khalidi (Washington, DC: The Institute for Palestine Studies, 1987): 173-188; Rashid Khalidi, *Palestinian Identity: The Construction of Modern National Consciousness* (New York: Columbia University Press, 1997); "Lord Balfour's Personal Position on the Balfour Declaration," *The Middle East Journal* 22 (Summer 1968): 340-345; Jehuda Reinharz, "The Balfour Declaration in Historical Perspective," in *Essential Papers on Zionism*, edited by Jehuda Reinharz and Anita Shapira (New York: New York University Press, 1996): 587-616; Leonard Stein, *The Balfour Declaration* (New York: Simon and Schuster, 1961); Mayir Vérété, "The Balfour Declaration and Its Makers," *Middle Eastern Studies* 6 (January 1970): 48-76.

BANK OF ISRAEL. The central bank of the State of Israel established in accordance with the Bank of Israel Law in 1954. Its primary functions are in the area of monetary policy, where it administers, regulates, and directs the currency system and also supervises and directs the funds made available as loans to the public. It also regulates and supervises the work of commercial and other banks, including their foreign activities, in order to ensure sound practices and to protect the public interest.

For further information see: Yair Aharoni, "The Changing Political Economy of Israel," *The Annals of the American Academy of Political and Social Science* 555 (January 1998): 147-162.

BAR ILAN UNIVERSITY. An independent, coeducational university founded in 1955 and located in Ramat Gan*, a suburb of Tel Aviv*. The university, named for Rabbi Meir Bar Ilan, was established under the auspices of the Religious Zionists of America. The university's purpose is to train students in both Jewish and secular studies.

BAR KOCHBA WAR. In 63 BCE the Roman leader Pompey conquered Judea* and Jerusalem*, inaugurating a period of relative calm that ended with a revolt in AD 66. The revolt was put down, and Titus, commander of the Roman forces, conquered Jerusalem and destroyed the Temple in AD 70. After the revolt of Simon Bar Kochba (132-135), Jerusalem was destroyed, large numbers of Jews were killed or enslaved, and Jewish sovereignty over the area was terminated. Many Jews were dispersed throughout the world (a scattering known as the Diaspora*), and the idea of an ultimate return to the Promised Land went with them. Bar Kochba is credited with organizing a nearly total popular revolt against the Roman Emperor Hadrian which lasted for some three years. The rebuilding of Jerusalem as a Roman colony and the prohibition of circumcision were contributory factors, but it had been developing for a considerable period. The Roman counterattack, with an army of 35,000, began in 133. In 134-135, the Romans invaded Betar, Bar Kochba's last stronghold, and gradually reduced the remaining hill and cave strongholds. Bar Kochba was killed when Betar fell; records speak of the destruction of 50 fortresses and 985 villages, and of 580,000 Jewish casualties besides those who died of hunger and disease. As a result of the revolt, Judea fell into desolation, its population was annihilated, and Jerusalem was barred to Jews. This war became a focal point of substantial popular discussion when the respected military and strategic analyst Yehoshafat Harkabi wrote a book suggesting that this was a disaster that had modern day parallels in the dealings of Israel and the Arabs.

For further information see: Yehoshafat Harkabi, *The Bar Kochba Syndrome* (New York: Russell Books, 1983).

BAR LEV, HAIM. Born on November 16, 1924, in Vienna, Austria, he emigrated to Palestine* in 1939 from Zagreb, Yugoslavia. He graduated from the Mikveh Yisrael agricultural school. While still in school he joined the Hagana*. He later joined and served in the Palmah* (from 1942 to 1948), and during the War of Independence* he commanded a battalion of the Negev* Brigade which repulsed the Egyptian attack. In the 1956 Sinai War*, he was a colonel in command of the Armored Corps and his unit was among the first to reach the Suez Canal. From 1957 to 1961, Bar Lev was Commander of the Armored Corps. He spent time studying for his MBA at Columbia University in New York. He became commanding officer of the Northern Command in 1962. From 1964 until May 1966, when he went to Paris for advanced military courses, he served as Chief of the General Staff Branch Operations of the Israel Defense Forces*. He returned to Israel in May 1967 and was appointed Deputy Chief of Staff. Between January 1, 1968, and 1972, he served as Israel's eighth Chief of Staff. He became Chief of Staff during a period in which the Israel Defense Forces had to convert from an attack-oriented army into a defensive one without forfeiting any of its offensive qualities and capabilities. In response to continuing attacks and the escalation by

President Gamal Abdul Nasser of Egypt* in the War of Attrition*, he created what came to be known as the Bar Lev Line*—the fortification system along the Suez Canal. During the 1973 Yom Kippur War*, he served as Commander of the Egyptian Front. Since his election in 1973, Bar Lev served as a member of Knesset* for the Alignment-Labor Party*. He served as Minister of Commerce, Industry and Development between 1972-1977. In 1978 he was elected Secretary-General of the Labor Party. From 1984-1988 he served as Minister of Police in the National Unity Government and he was reappointed to that post in the Government established in December 1988. In 1992 he retired from party politics and was appointed Ambassador to Russia. He died in May 1994.

For further information see: Michael Bar-Zohar, editor, *Lionhearts: Heroes of Israel* (New York: Warner, 1998).

BAR LEV LINE. A defensive system on the east bank of the Suez Canal constructed by the Israel Defense Forces* during the tenure of Haim Bar Lev* as Chief of Staff. The Bar Lev line was essentially a series of fortifications and strong points constructed along the Suez Canal to withstand artillery shelling and other weapons and tended to reduce Israeli manpower requirements and potential casualties along the Suez Canal. It was overrun by the Egyptian army in the early hours of the Yom Kippur War*. *See also* WAR OF ATTRITION.

BARAK, AHARON. Aharon Barak was born in 1936 in Lithuania, immigrated to Palestine* in 1947. He studied law, economics, and international relations at the Hebrew University of Jerusalem*, receiving an MA in law in 1958 and a doctorate in law in 1963, he was appointed professor of law at Hebrew University in 1968, named dean of the university's law faculty in 1974 and awarded the Israel Prize* in legal sciences in 1975. In that same year he succeeded Meir Shamgar* as Attorney General*, a position he held until 1978. Part of Israel's legal team at the Camp David* talks in 1978, he was instrumental in crafting key provisions of the peace accords with Egypt*. He was appointed a justice of the Supreme Court of Israel* in 1978, and Deputy President of the court in 1993. He became President of the Court on August 13, 1995, again succeeding Meir Shamgar. Barak was instrumental in promoting the Supreme Court's increased activism and the "constitutional revolution" experienced in Israel in the 1990s. Several of his controversial judgments, especially with regard to religious affairs and the balance between

Halacha* and secular law, made him the object of much derision, including threats to his personal security emanating primarily from the Haredi (ultra-Orthodox) sector of Israeli society.

BARAK, EHUD. Born in 1942 as Ehud Brog in Kibbutz Mishmar Hasharon, his parents emigrated in the 1930s from Lithuania and Poland. He enlisted in the Israel Defense Forces (IDF)* in 1959 and was schooled in various military educational courses and held a number of significant military assignments. His education included undergraduate studies in physics and mathematics at Hebrew University* and a master's degree from Stanford University in California in systems analysis. He served as Director of Military Intelligence* (1985-1986) and later as Deputy Chief of Staff of the Israel Defense Forces (May 1987). He became Chief of Staff in April 1991. He retired from the IDF in 1994 and immediately entered Labor Party* politics. Yitzhak Rabin* appointed him Minister of the Interior and he became Foreign Minister in the Peres*-led Government established following Rabin's assassination. In June 1997 he replaced Shimon Peres as Labor Party chairman. As the leader of the expanded One Israel* Party, Barak was elected Prime Minister on May 17, 1999, defeating Benjamin Netanyahu*. On July 6, 1999, he presented his governing coalition before the Knesset* for ratification, with himself serving as both Prime Minister and Defense Minister and Acting Minister of Agriculture. After taking office, Barak set out an ambitious program, especially in the diplomatic arena. With Yasser Arafat*, he set February 13, 2000, as the target date for preparing a Framework Agreement for an Israeli-Palestinian permanent peace settlement (the completion of which was targeted for September 13, 2000). Barak reaffirmed his campaign pledge to withdraw the IDF from Lebanon within one year of taking office. He participated in formal talks (in Washington, DC, and in Shepherdstown, West Virginia) with Syria's Foreign Minister Farouk al-Sharaa, while reiterating his commitment to hold a national referendum on a final agreement affecting the Golan Heights*. Domestically, he was faced with a series of challenges on social and religious matters, and in late January 2000, Barak was caught up in a scandal relating to illegal fund-raising in a support of his 1999 election campaign.

For further information see: Ehud Barak, "A Vision of the Future: Realizing the Promise of the Promised Land," *Harvard International Review* 20 (Spring 1998): 60-63.

BARAM, UZI. Born in 1937 in Jerusalem* and educated in political science and sociology at Hebrew University*. Member of the Knesset* on the Labor Alignment* party list. Served as Secretary General of the Labor Party from 1984 until he resigned in January 1989, ostensibly because of his concern that Labor would lose its "identity" by joining in a National Unity Government led by Yitzhak Shamir* and that this would be a political disaster for the Labor Party in future elections. In May 1996 Baram was reelected on the Labor list, and, on May 17, 1999, he was reelected to the 15th Knesset on the One Israel* list.

BAR-ON, MORDECHAI. He served in various capacities in the Israel Defense Forces*, including the post of Chief Education Officer. He was among the founders of the Peace Now* movement. He served his first term as a member in the 11th Knesset* elected on the Ratz (Citizens' Rights Movement)* list. Retired from party politics, he remains a prominent peace activist.

For further information see: Mordechai Bar-On, *The Gates of Gaza: Israel's Road to Suez and Back, 1955-1957* (London: Macmillan, 1996); Mordechai Bar-On, *In Pursuit of Peace: A History of the Israeli Peace Movement* (Washington, DC: U.S. Institute of Peace, 1996).

BAR-ON, RONNIE. In January 1997, Prime Minister Benjamin Netanyahu* announced that Ronnie Bar-On was to be Israel's next Attorney General*. Bar-On was a Jerusalem*-based criminal lawyer and an active member of the Likud*. A scandal followed and Bar-On resigned. It was soon reported that the Bar-On appointment was in fact extortion on the part of Arye Deri*. Reportedly Deri had conditioned the voting of Shas* for the Hebron* Agreement on Bar-On's appointment and threatened to bring down the Government if Bar-On was not chosen. Netanyahu denied the report but suggested that the police open an investigation. The police recommended four indictments. However, State Attorney Edna Arbel and Attorney General Elyakim Rubinstein* decided there was insufficient evidence that would stand up in court against Netanyahu and Justice Minister Hanegbi*. On June 15, 1997, the Israeli Supreme Court* upheld the decision of the Attorney General not to prosecute Netanyahu or his Justice Minister in this matter.

BASIC LAW. As early as 1947, the Executive of the Vaad Leumi* appointed a committee headed by Zerah Warhaftig to study the question of a constitution for the new state. In December 1947 the Jewish Agency* Executive entrusted Dr. Leo Kohn, professor of international relations at the Hebrew University of Jerusalem*, with the task of preparing a draft constitution. On July 8, 1949, the Provisional Council of State appointed a Constitutional Committee. The First Knesset* devoted much time to a profound discussion of the issue of a constitution for the State of Israel. The major debate was between those who favored a written document and those who believed that the time was not appropriate for imposing rigid constitutional limitations. The latter group argued that a written constitution could not be framed because of constantly changing social conditions, primarily the result of mass immigration and a lack of experience with independent governmental institutions. There was also concern about the relationship between state and religion and the method of incorporating the precepts and ideals of Judaism into the proposed document. The discussion of these issues continued for over a year, and on June 13, 1950, the Knesset adopted a compromise that postponed the real issue indefinitely. It was decided in principle that a written constitution would be adopted ultimately, but that for the time being there would be no formal and comprehensive document. Instead, a number of fundamental, or basic, laws would be passed dealing with specific subjects, which might in time form chapters in a consolidated constitution. A number of Basic Laws dealing with various subjects have been adopted: The Knesset (1958); The Lands of Israel (1960); The President (1964); The Government (1968); The State Economy (1975); The Army (1976); Jerusalem, The Capital of Israel (1980); The Judiciary (1984); The State Comptroller (1988); Human Dignity and Liberty (1992); Freedom of Occupation (1992). The Basic Laws thereby provide a definitive perspective of the formal requirements of the system in specific areas of activity, a "written" framework, in a sense, for governmental activity.

BASIC LAW: THE KNESSET. Passed on February 12, 1958, by the Third Knesset*. It does not define the powers of the Knesset, but states that it is the house of representatives of the state, that its seat is in Jerusalem and that upon election it should include 120 members. The law deals with the electoral system, the right to vote and be elected, the Knesset's term of office, the principles relating to the Knesset elections, the service of Knesset members, the parliamentary immunity of the Knesset members and the Knesset buildings and well as the work of the Knesset and its committees. Amendment No 9 of the law, passed on July 31, 1985, states that a list may not participate in the elections if there is in its goals or actions a denial of the existence of the State of Israel as the state of the Jewish people, a denial of the democratic nature of the state, or incitement to racism.

Among other provisions, the law provides: "The Knesset is the parliament of the State. ... The Knesset shall, upon its election, consist of one hundred and twenty members. ... The Knesset shall be elected by general, national, direct, equal, secret and proportional elections, in accordance with the Knesset Elections Law; this section shall not be varied save by a majority of the members of the Knesset. ... The term of office of the Knesset shall be four years from the day on which it is elected. ... If the seat of a member of the Knesset falls vacant, it shall be filled by the candidate who, in the list of candidates which included the name of the late member, figured immediately after the last of the elected candidates. ... A candidates' list shall not participate in elections to the Knesset if its objects or actions, expressly or by implication, include one of the following: (1) negation of the existence of the State of Israel as the state of the Jewish people; (2) negation of the democratic character of the State; (3) incitement to racism."

BASIC LAW: ISRAEL LANDS. Passed on July 25, 1960, by the Fourth Knesset*. The basis of the law is the special relationship between the People of Israel and the Land of Israel and its redemption. The law ensures that the state lands, which constitute about 90% of the lands in the state, should remain national property. The law prohibits the transfer of ownership over lands owned by the state, the Development Authority, or the Jewish National Fund*, either by sale or by any other means, with the exception of types of land or transactions, that have been specified in the law.

BASIC LAW: THE PRESIDENT OF THE STATE. Passed on June 16, 1964, by the Fifth Knesset*. The law was basically a reenactment of previous instructions which were scattered in other laws. It deals with the status of the President* of the state, his election by the Knesset, his qualifications and powers, and the procedures of his work.

Among other provisions the law provides: "A President shall stand at the head of the State. ... The place of residence of the President of the State shall be Jerusalem. ... The President of the State shall be elected by the

Knesset for five years. ... The election of the President of the State shall be by secret ballot at a meeting of the Knesset assigned only for that purpose. ... The candidate who has received the votes of a majority of the Members of the Knesset is elected. .... (a) The President of the State (1) shall sign every Law, other than a Law relating to its powers; (2) shall take action to achieve the formation of a Government and shall receive the resignation of the Government in accordance with Law; (3) shall receive from the Government a report on its meetings; (4) shall accredit the diplomatic representatives of the State, shall receive the credentials of diplomatic representatives sent to Israel by foreign states, shall empower the consular representatives of the State and shall confirm the appointments of consular representatives sent to Israel by foreign states; (5) shall sign such conventions with foreign states as have been ratified by the Knesset; (6) shall carry out every function assigned to him by Law in connection with the appointment and removal from office of judges and other office-holders. (b) The President of the State shall have power to pardon offenders and to lighten penalties by the reduction or commutation thereof. (c) The President of the State shall carry out every other function and have every other power assigned to him by Law."

BASIC LAW: THE STATE ECONOMY. Passed on July 21, 1975, by the Eighth Knesset*. The law lays down the framework for the budget laws and the basic rule, according to which no taxes, compulsory loans, other compulsory payments and fees may be imposed, or their rates changed, except by law or in accordance with it. Regulations imposing compulsory payments are subject to the approval of the Knesset or one of its committees. In addition, the law deals with the authority to reach agreements involving state assets, the acquisition of rights and the undertaking of obligations in the name of the state, the state budget and its formulation, the printing of bank-notes and the minting of coins. The law also states that: "the state economy is subject to the control of the State Comptroller".

BASIC LAW: THE ARMY. Passed on March 31, 1976, by the Eighth Knesset*. Until the Basic Law was passed, the constitutional and legal basis for the operation of the Israel Defense Forces (IDF)* was to be found in the IDF Ordinance of 1948. The Basic Law follows that ordinance, adding instructions regarding the subordination of the military forces to the Government, the status of the Chief of Staff, and other instructions on issues dealt with by the Agranat Commission*, which investigated the circumstances of the outbreak of the Yom Kippur War*. The law states that the IDF is the army of the state, and deals with the compulsory military service and enlistment, as well as the instructions of the army and its orders. It states that "outside the Israel Defense Forces no armed force is to be set up or maintained, except in accordance with the law."

Among other provisions the law provides: "The Defence Army of Israel is the army of the State. ... (a) The Army is subject to the authority of the Government. (b) The Minister in charge of the Army on behalf of the Government is the Minister of Defence. ... (a) The supreme command level in the Army is the Chief of the General Staff. (b) The Chief of the General Staff is subject to the authority of the Government and subordinate to the Minister of Defence. (c) The Chief of the General Staff shall be appointed by the Government upon the recommendation of the Minister of Defence. ... The duty of serving in the Army and recruitment for the Army shall be as prescribed by or by virtue of Law. ... The power to issue instructions and orders binding in the Army shall be prescribed by or by virtue of Law. ... No armed force other than the Defence Army of Israel shall be established or maintained except under Law."

BASIC LAW: JERUSALEM, CAPITAL OF ISRAEL. Passed on July 30, 1980, by the Ninth Knesset*. The intention of the law is to establish the status of Jerusalem* as the capital of Israel, to secure its integrity and unity and concentrate all the instructions, which were scattered in various laws, regarding the location of national institutions. The law deals with the holy places, secures the rights of the members of all religions, and declares that Jerusalem will be granted special preferences with regard to its development.

Among other provisions the law provides: "Jerusalem, complete and united, is the capital of Israel. Seat of the President, the Knesset, the Government and the Supreme Court. ... Jerusalem is the seat of the President of the State, the Knesset, the Government and the Supreme Court. ... The Holy Places shall be protected from desecration and any other violation and from anything likely to violate the freedom of access of the members of the different religions to the places sacred to them or their feelings towards those places. ... (a) The Government shall provide for the development and prosperity of Jerusalem and the well-being of its inhabitants by allocating special funds, including a special annual grant to the Municipality of Jerusalem (Capital City Grant) with the approval of the Finance Committee of the Knesset. (b) Jerusalem shall be given special priority in the activities of the authorities of the State so as to further its development in economic and other matters. (c) The Government shall set up a special body or special bodies for the implementation of this section."

BASIC LAW: THE JUDICIARY. Passed on February 28, 1984, by the 10th Knesset*. The law deals with the judicial authority, the institutions of the judiciary, the principle of independence on matters of judgment, the openness of judicial proceedings, the appointment of judges, their qualifications and tenure of office, the powers of the Supreme Court*, the right of appeal, further hearing, retrial and the principle of settled law. The law does not deal with the authority of the courts to examine the legality of laws. This will be dealt with in the Basic Law: Legislation, when it is enacted. The law includes an instruction regarding its permanence and protection from changes by means of emergency regulations.

Among other provisions the law provides: "(a) Judicial power is vested in the following courts: (1) the Supreme Court; (2) a District Court; (3) a Magistrate's Court; (4) another court designated by Law as a court. In this Law, "judge" means a judge of a court as aforesaid. (b) Judicial power is vested also in the following: (1) a religious court (beit din); (2) any other court (beit din); (3) another authority all as prescribed by Law. (c) No court or court (beit din) shall be established for a particular case. ... A person vested with judicial power shall not, in judicial matters, be subject to any authority but that of the Law. ... Only an Israeli national shall be appointed judge. ... (a) The seat of the Supreme Court is Jerusalem. (b) The Supreme Court shall hear appeals against judgments and other decisions of the District Courts. (c) The Supreme Court shall sit also as a High Court of Justice. When so sitting, it shall hear matters in which it deems it necessary to grant relief for the sake of justice and which are not within the jurisdiction of another court (beit mishpat or beit din). (d) Without prejudice to the generality of the provisions of subsection (c), the Supreme Court sitting as a High Court of Justice shall be competent - (1) to make orders for the release of persons unlawfully detained or imprisoned. (2) to order State and local authorities and the officials and bodies thereof, and other persons carrying out public functions under law, to do or refrain from doing any act in the lawful exercise of their functions or, if they were improperly elected or appointed, to refrain from acting; (3) to order courts (batei mishpat and batei din) and bodies and persons having judicial or quasi-judicial powers under law, other than courts dealt with by this Law and other than religious courts (batei din), to hear, refrain from hearing, or continue hearing a particular matter or to void a proceeding improperly taken or a decision improperly given; (4) to order religious courts (batei din) to hear a particular matter within their jurisdiction or to refrain from hearing or continue hearing a particular matter not within their jurisdiction, provided that the application under this paragraph is the applicant that did not raise the question of jurisdiction at the earliest opportunity; and if he had no measurable opportunity to raise the question of jurisdiction until a decision had been given by a religious court (beit din), the court may quash a proceeding taken or a decision given by the religious court (beit din) without authority. (e) Other powers of the Supreme Court shall be prescribed by Law."

BASIC LAW: THE STATE COMPTROLLER. Passed on February 15, 1988, by the 12th Knesset*. Most of the law is a reenactment of previous instructions, which were scattered in other laws. The law deals with the powers, tasks, and duties of the State Comptroller in his/her supervision of government bodies and as ombudsman, the manner in which s/he is elected (by the Knesset) and the budget of the comptroller's office. The law states that the State Comptroller is responsible solely to the Knesset.

Among other provisions the law provides: "The State Audit shall be implemented by the State Comptroller. ... (a) The Comptroller will audit the economy, the property, the finances, the obligations and the administration of the State, of Government Ministries, of all enterprises, institutions, or corporations of the State, of Local Authorities, and of bodies or other institutions which were defined as law subject to audit by the State Comptroller. (b) The State Comptroller shall inspect the legality, integrity, managerial norms, efficiency and economy of the audited bodies, as well as any other matter which he deems necessary. ... The State Comptroller will investigate complaints from the public about bodies and persons, as provided by law: in this capacity the State Comptroller shall bear the title "Commissioner for Complaints from the Public". ... In carrying out his functions, the State Comptroller shall be accountable only to the Knesset and not to the Cabinet. ... (a) The State

Comptroller shall be chosen by the Knesset in a secret ballot; the exact arrangements shall be set by law."

BASIC LAW: HUMAN DIGNITY AND LIBERTY. Passed on March 17, 1992, by the 12th Knesset*. Sections of it were subsequently integrated into the 1994 version of the Basic Law: Freedom of Occupation. In view of the fact that the Knesset was unsuccessful in its endeavors to enact the Basic Law: Human Rights in its entirety, due to the opposition of the religious parties to some of its provisions, it was decided to enact those sections of the law on which there were no basic differences of opinion. Until the dissolution of the 13th Knesset two Basic Laws were passed, which will eventually constitute part of the complete law: the Basic Law: Human Dignity and Liberty, and the Basic Law: Freedom of Occupation. The Basic Law: Human Dignity and Liberty declares that the basic human rights in Israel are based on recognition of the value of man, the sanctity of his life, and the fact that he is free. The goal of the law is "to defend Human Dignity and Liberty, in order to establish in a Basic Law the values of the State of Israel as a Jewish and democratic state." The law defines human freedom in Israel as being the right to leave the country and enter it, to privacy and intimacy, refraining from searches relating to one's private property, body, and possessions, and avoidance of violations of the privacy of one's speech, writings, and notes. Violation of the dignity or freedom of man is permitted only in accordance with the law. The law includes an instruction regarding its permanence and protection from changes by means of emergency regulations.

Among its provisions are: "The purpose of this Basic Law is to protect human dignity and liberty, in order to establish in a Basic Law the values of the State of Israel as a Jewish and democratic state. ... There shall be no violation of the life, body or dignity of any person as such. ... There shall be no violation of the property of a person. ... All persons are entitled to protection of their life, body and dignity. ... There shall be no deprivation or restriction of the liberty of a person by imprisonment, arrest, extradition or otherwise. ... All governmental authorities are bound to respect the rights under this Basic Law."

Basic Law: Human Dignity and Liberty—Amendment In the Basic Law: Human Dignity and Liberty (5752 - 1992)

Section 1 shall be preceded by the following section: "Basic principles 1. Fundamental human rights in Israel are founded upon recognition of the value of the human being, the sanctity of human life, and the principle that all persons are free; these rights shall be upheld in the spirit of the principles set forth in the Declaration of the Establishment of the State of Israel."

BASIC LAW: THE GOVERNMENT. Its new version, which replaced the law of 1968, was passed on March 17, 1992, by the 12th Knesset*. The law lays down the rules and conditions for the direct election of the Prime Minister simultaneously with the Knesset elections, as of the elections to the 14th Knesset. In addition, the law deals with the principles regarding the service of the elected Prime Minister and his or her Government, the formation of the Government and the qualifications for becoming minister, the procedures leading up to the formation of a Government, its actual formulation, the way it functions, the distribution of functions amongst its members, its work procedures, its powers and the powers of the Ministers and Deputy Ministers, the tenure of office of the Ministers and their salary, the continuity of the Government, the conditions for the resignation or removal of the Prime Minister, which lead to new general elections or new elections for the Prime Minister. Only a majority of the Knesset members can amend the law.

Among other provisions the law provides: "The Government is the executive authority of the State. ... The seat of the Government is Jerusalem. ... (a) The Government is comprised of the Prime Minister and Ministers. (b) The Prime Minister serves by virtue of his being elected in the national general elections, to be conducted on a direct, equal, and secret basis in compliance with The Election Law (The Knesset and The Prime Minister). (c) The Ministers will be appointed by the Prime Minister; their appointment requires the approval of the Knesset. (d) Should the Knesset reject the Prime Minister's proposal regarding the composition of the Government, it will be regarded as an expression of no confidence in the Prime Minister, and the provisions of section 19(b) will apply. ... Persons entitled to vote in the elections to the Knesset shall be entitled to vote in the elections for the Prime Minister. ... The period of service of the Prime Minister and the Ministers shall be equal to the period of service of the Knesset to which they were elected; in special elections for the period of service of the Knesset serving at that time, unless specified differently in this Basic Law. ... (a) The elected Prime

Minister will be the candidate receiving more than half of the valid votes, provided that he is also a Knesset Member. (b) If no one of the candidates receives the number of votes prescribed in section (a), repeat elections will be held on the first Tuesday after the passage of two weeks from the publication of the results of the first elections. (c) In the return elections the candidates standing for election will be the two candidates who received the largest number of valid votes in the first elections, and who are Knesset Members; in the return elections, the candidate receiving the largest number of valid votes will be the chosen candidate. (e) Should there be a sole candidate, whether in the first elections or in the return elections, the elections will be conducted by way of a vote either for him or against him, and he will be elected if the number of valid votes for him exceeds the number of valid votes against him. (f) If no candidate is elected according to the provisions of this section, special elections will be held. ... (a) Within 45 days of the publication of the election results the Prime Minister elect will appear before the Knesset, present the Ministers of the Government, announce the division of tasks and the guiding principles of the Government's policies, and the Prime Minister and the Ministers will begin their service, provided that the provisions of section 33(a) and (b) have been complied with. As soon as possible after that the Prime Minister and the Ministers will make their declarations of allegiance before the Knesset in the version specified in subsection (c). ... (a) The Knesset may by means of a majority of its members adopt an expression of no confidence in the Prime Minister. (b) An expression of no confidence in the Prime Minister will be deemed to be a Knesset decision to disperse prior to the completion of its period of service. ... (a) The Prime Minister may, after notifying the Government of his decision to do so, resign by way of submitting his written resignation to the President of the State; the resignation will go into force 48 hours after the letter of resignation is submitted to the President, unless the Prime Minister retracts prior to such time. (b) A Prime Minister who has resigned will give notice thereof to the Speaker of the Knesset, and the Speaker of the Knesset will then give notice to the Knesset. (c) Should the Prime Minister resign, special elections will be conducted. ... Should the Prime Minister cease to function as a member of the Knesset, he will be deemed to have resigned. ... Should the Prime Minister die or be permanently incapacitated, special elections will be held. ... (a) Should the Prime Minister die, be permanently incapacitated, or be removed from office, the Government will empower one of the Ministers who is also a Knesset member, to serve as acting Prime Minister until the new Prime

Minister takes office. ... (a) Should the Prime Minister be absent from the country, meetings of the Government will be convened and conducted by the Minister delegated by the Prime Minister. ... (a) A Prime Minister who has resigned or in whom the Knesset expressed no confidence, will continue in office until the newly elected Prime Minister assumes office. ... (a) The Government shall not exceed eighteen members in number and not be less than eight. (b) At least one half of the Ministers shall be Knesset members. (c) A Minister shall be appointed over an office, but a Minister may be a Minister without portfolio. (d) The Prime Minister may also function as a Minister appointed over an office. (e) Subject to the provisions of subsections (a) and (b), the Prime Minister may add extra Ministers to the Government after its establishment; the commencement of service of a Minister so added to the Government shall be with the submission of notice from the Prime Minister to the Knesset regarding his appointment; immediately afterwards, the new Minister will submit his declaration of allegiance in accordance with the version prescribed in section 14 (c). ... (a) The Prime Minister may: (1) Determine the roles of the Ministers; (2) Change the division of roles amongst the Ministers; (3) Transfer authorities and duties not specified in the Law from one Minister to another; (4) Transfer areas of actions from one office to another; (5) Establish the Government offices, unite or divide them, abolish them or establish new offices, and having done so give notice thereof to the Knesset; (6) Establish permanent or temporary Ministerial committees for particular matters; after the appointment of a committee the Government may conduct its operations through it; (b) Authority granted by law to a particular Minister may be transferred by the Prime Minister either totally or partially to another Minister; a decision according to this section must be approved by the Government; (c) The Prime Minister will conduct the functioning of the Government and will set work procedures and voting procedures in the Government and its committees; (d) Government decisions will be adopted by a majority vote; should the vote be drawn, the Prime Minister will have an additional vote. ... The Government will, according to the proposal of the Prime Minister, appoint a Government Secretary and specify his duties. ... (a) The state may only begin a war pursuant to a Government decision. (b) Nothing in the provisions of this section will prevent the adoption of military actions necessary for the defence of the state and public security. (c) Notification of a Government decision to begin a war under the provision of subsection (a) will be submitted to the Knesset Foreign Affairs and Security Committee as soon as possible; the Prime Minister also will give notice to the Knesset plenum as soon as possible; notification regarding military actions as stated in subsection (b) will be given to the Knesset Foreign Affairs and Security Committee as soon as possible."

BASIC LAW: FREEDOM OF OCCUPATION. In its new version, which replaced the law of 1992 and was passed on March 9, 1994, by the 13th Knesset*. The law lays down the right of "every citizen or inhabitant to engage in any occupation, profession or trade" unless "a law which corresponds with the values of the State of Israel, and which was designed for a worthy end" determines otherwise. The law includes an instruction regarding its permanence and protection from changes by means of emergency regulations. Only a majority of the Knesset members can amend the law.

Among other provisions the law provides: "Fundamental human rights in Israel are founded upon recognition of the value of the human being, the sanctity of human life, and the principle that all persons are free; these rights shall be upheld in the spirit of the principles set forth in the Declaration of the Establishment of the State of Israel. ... The purpose of this Basic Law is to protect freedom of occupation, in order to establish in a Basic Law the values of the State of Israel as a Jewish and democratic state. ... Every Israel national or resident has the right to engage in any occupation, profession or trade."

For further information see: Joseph Badi, editor, *Fundamental Laws of the State of Israel* (New York: Twayne, 1961); Henry E. Baker, *The Legal System of Israel*, Revised Edition (Jerusalem, London, New York: Israel Universities Press, 1968); Aharon Barak, "The Constitutional Revolution: Human Rights Protected," *Law and Government in Israel* 1:1 (August 1992, Hebrew); Martin Edelman, *Courts, Politics, and Culture in Israel* (Charlottesville: University Press of Virginia, 1994); Reuven Y. Hazan, "Legislative-Executive Relations in an Era of Accelerated Reform: Reshaping Government in Israel," *Legislative Studies Quarterly* 22:3 (August 1997); Ran Hirschl, "The Constitutional Revolution and the Emergence of a New Economic Order in Israel," *Israel Studies* 2:1 (Spring 1997): 136-155; Peter Y. Medding, *The Founding of Israeli Democracy, 1948-1967* (New York: Oxford University Press, 1990); Philippa Strum, "The Road Not Taken: Constitutional Non-Decision-Making in 1948-1950 and Its Impact on Civil Liberties in the Israeli Political Culture," in *Israel: The First Decade of Independence*, edited by

S. Ilan Troen and Noah Lucas (Albany: State University of New York Press, 1995): 83-104; Gad Yaacobi, *The Government of Israel* (New York: Praeger, 1982); Itzhak Zamir and Allen Zysblat, editors, *Public Law in Israel* (Oxford: Clarendon, 1996).

BASLE PROGRAM. On August 23, 1897, in Basle (or Basel), Switzerland, Theodor Herzl* convened the first World Zionist Congress* representing Jewish communities and organizations throughout the world. The Congress established the World Zionist Organization* (WZO) and founded an effective, modern, political, Jewish national movement with the goal, enunciated in the Basle Program, the original official program of the WZO, that "Zionism seeks to establish a home for the Jewish people in Palestine secured under public law." Zionism* rejected other solutions to the Jewish Question* and was the response to centuries of discrimination, persecution, and oppression. It sought redemption through self-determination. Herzl argued in *Der Judenstaat*: "Let the sovereignty be granted us over a portion of the globe large enough to satisfy the rightful requirements of a nation; the rest we shall manage for ourselves." For the attainment of the aims of the Basle Program, the Congress envisaged the promotion of the settlement of Palestine* by Jewish agriculturalists, artisans, and trades people; the organization and unification of the whole of Jewry by means of appropriate local and general institutions in accordance with the laws of each country; the strengthening of Jewish national sentiment and national consciousness; and preparatory steps toward securing the consent of governments, which is necessary to attain the aim of Zionism. *See also* JERUSALEM PROGRAM.

For further information see: Shlomo Avineri, *The Making of Modern Zionism: The Intellectual Origins of the Jewish State* (New York: Basic, 1981): chapter 9; Shmuel Ettinger and Israel Bartal, "The First Aliya: Ideological Roots and Practical Accomplishments," in *Essential Papers on Zionism*, edited by Jehuda Reinharz and Anita Shapira (New York: New York University Press, 1996): 63-93.

BEGIN, BENNY *see* BEGIN, ZE'EV BINYAMIN

BEGIN, BINYAMIN *see* BEGIN, ZE'EV BINYAMIN

BEGIN, MENACHEM. Menachem Begin was born the son of Zeev-Dov and Hassia Begin in Brest-Litovsk, White Russia (later Poland), on August 16, 1913. He was educated in Brest-Litovsk at the Mizrachi Hebrew School and later studied and graduated in law at the University of Warsaw. After a short association with Hashomer Hatzair*, he became a devoted follower of Vladimir Zeev Jabotinsky*, the founder of the Revisionist Zionist* movement. At the age of 16 he joined Betar*, the youth movement affiliated with the Revisionists*, and in 1932 he became the head of the Organization Department of Betar in Poland. Later, after a period of service as head of Betar in Czechoslovakia, he returned to Poland in 1937 and in 1939 became head of the movement there. Upon the outbreak of World War II, he was arrested by the Russian authorities and confined in concentration camps in Siberia and elsewhere until his release in 1941. He then joined the Polish army and was dispatched to the Middle East. After demobilization in 1943, he remained in Palestine* and assumed command of the Irgun Tzvai Leumi*. For his activities against the British authorities as head of that organization, he was placed on their "most wanted" list, but managed to evade capture by living underground in Tel Aviv*.

With the independence of Israel in 1948 and the dissolution of the Irgun, Begin founded the Herut (Freedom) Party* and represented it in the Knesset* since its first meetings in 1949. He became Herut's leader, retaining that position until he resigned from office as Prime Minister and retired from public and political life in 1983. Herut was known for its right-wing, strongly nationalistic views, and Begin led the party's protest campaign against the reparations agreement with West Germany in 1952. He was instrumental in establishing the Gahal* faction (a merger of Herut and the Liberal Party*) in the Knesset in 1965. He developed a reputation as a gifted orator, writer, and political leader. He remained in opposition in parliament until the eve of the Six Day War* of June 1967, when he joined the Government of National Unity as Minister without Portfolio. He and his Gahal colleagues resigned from the Government in August 1970 over opposition to its acceptance of the peace initiative of United States* Secretary of State William Rogers, which implied the evacuation by Israel of territories occupied in the course of the Six Day War. Later, Gahal joined in forming the Likud* bloc in opposition to the governing Labor Alignment*, and Begin became its leader.

In June 1977 Begin became Israel's first non-socialist Prime Minister when the Likud bloc secured the mandate to form the Government after the May Knesset election. He also became the first Israeli Prime Minister to meet officially and publicly with an Arab head of state when he welcomed Egyptian* President Anwar Sadat* to Jerusalem* in November 1977. He led Israel's delegations to the ensuing peace negotiations and signed, with Sadat and United States President Jimmy Carter*, the Camp David Accords* in September 1978. In March 1979 he and Sadat signed the Egypt-Israel Peace Treaty*, with Carter witnessing the event, on the White House lawn. Begin and Sadat shared the 1978 Nobel Peace Prize* for their efforts. For Begin and Israel, it was a momentous but difficult accomplishment. It brought peace with Israel's most populous adversary and significantly reduced the military danger to the existence of Israel by neutralizing the largest Arab army with whom Israel had fought five wars. But, it was also traumatic given the extensive tangible concessions required of Israel, especially the uprooting of Jewish settlements in Sinai*.

The Knesset election of June 30, 1981, returned a Likud-led coalition Government to power in Israel, contrary to early predictions which projected a significant Labor Alignment victory. Menachem Begin again became Prime Minister and his reestablished Government coalition contained many of the same personalities as the outgoing group and reflected similar perspectives of Israel's situation and appropriate government policies. He also served as Minister of Foreign Affairs in 1979-1980 and as Minister of Defense from May 1980 to August 1981.

The 1982 War in Lebanon* occasioned debate and demonstration within Israel, resulted in substantial casualties, and led, at least initially, to Israel's increased international isolation and major diplomatic clashes with the United States. Many of the outcomes were muted over time, but the war left a legacy that continued to be debated long after Begin retired from public life. It was also a factor in Begin's decision to step down from the Prime Minister's office, but it was a decision he chose and was not forced to make. He resigned on September 16, 1983.

Within Israel, Begin's tenure was marked by prosperity for the average citizen, although there were indicators (such as rising debt and inflation levels) that this might prove costly in the long term. The standard of living rose, as did the level of expectations. The religious parties enhanced their political power and secured important concessions to their demands from a coalition which recognized their increased role in maintaining the political balance and from a Prime Minister who was, on the whole, sympathetic to their positions.

The relationship with the United States underwent significant change during Begin's tenure. The ties were often tempestuous as the two states disagreed on various aspects of the regional situation and the issues associated with resolution of the Arab-Israeli conflict*. Nevertheless, United States economic and military assistance and political and diplomatic support rose to all-time high levels.

Begin's political skills were considerable and apparent. Despite his European origins and courtly manner, he was able, through his powerful oratorical skills, charismatic personality, and political and economic policies, to secure and maintain a substantial margin of popularity over other major political figures, particularly the opposition leaders. At the time of his resignation he was the most popular and highly regarded of Israeli politicians, as the public opinion polls regularly indicated.

Menachem Begin's decision to resign as Prime Minister of Israel brought to an end a major era in Israeli politics. It was a surprise and a shock to Israelis, notwithstanding Begin's earlier statements that he would retire from politics at age 70. Although no formal reason for his resignation was forthcoming, Begin apparently believed that he could no longer perform his tasks as he felt he should and he seemed to be severely affected by the death of his wife the previous year and by the continuing casualties suffered by Israeli forces in Lebanon. He died in March 1992.

For further information see: Menachem Begin, *White Nights: The Story of a Prisoner in Russia* (New York: Harper and Row, 1979); Menachem Begin, *The Revolt: Story of the Irgun* (New York: Nash, 1981); Dan Caspi, Abraham Diskin, and Emanuel Gutmann, *The Roots of Begin's Success: The 1981 Israeli Elections* (London: Croom Helm, 1984); Thurston Clarke, *By Blood and Fire: The Attack on the King David Hotel* (New York: Putnam, 1981); Robert O. Freedman, editor, *Israel in the Begin Era* (New York: Praeger, 1982); Frank Gervasi, *The Life and Times of Menachem Begin: Rebel to Statesman* (New York: Putnam, 1979); Eitan Haber, *Menachem Begin: The Legend and the Man* (New York: Delacorte, 1978); Samuel Katz, *Days of Fire: The Secret History of the*

Irgun Tzva'i Le'umi (New York: Doubleday, 1968); Ilan Peleg, "Jabotinsky's Legacy and Begin's Foreign Policy," *Reconstructionist* 39 (October 1983): 9-14; Ilan Peleg, *Begin's Foreign Policy, 1977-1983: Israel's Move to the Right* (Westport, CT: Greenwood, 1987); Amos Perlmutter, *The Life and Times of Menachem Begin* (New York: Doubleday, 1987); Eric Silver, *Begin: The Haunted Prophet* (New York: Random House, 1984); Ned Temko, *To Win or Die: A Personal Portrait of Menachem Begin* (New York: Morrow, 1987).

BEGIN, ZE'EV BINYAMIN. Born in Jerusalem* in 1943, he is the son of former Prime Minister Menachem Begin*. He earned his BSc and MSc from the Hebrew University of Jerusalem* and his PhD in geology from the University of Colorado and in 1965 began working for the Israel Geological Survey prior to entering politics. A member of the Knesset* representing Likud* since 1988, he was a member of the Knesset Foreign Affairs and Defense Committee and its Subcommittee on National Defense Policy, and he was a member of the Knesset Committee on Constitution, Law and Justice. He was appointed Minister of Science in 1996 but resigned in January 1997 to protest the agreement to withdraw Israeli soldiers from much of the West Bank* city of Hebron*. On December 28, 1998, Begin formally quit the Likud and announced the formation of the New Herut* (Herut Hahadasha) Party, with himself at its leader and candidate for Prime Minister. This party subsequently joined with Moledet* and Tekuma* to form the right-wing National Union* Party, with Begin as its leader and prime ministerial candidate. On the eve of the May 17, 1999, elections, Begin withdrew from the race for Prime Minister. He retired from political life when his National Union Party won only four seats in the 15th Knesset, calling himself "a cantor without a congregation."

For further information see: Ze'ev B. Begin, "The Likud Vision for Israel at Peace," *Foreign Affairs* 70 (Fall 1991): 21-35; Ze'ev Binyamin Begin, "The Oslo Process: A View from the Opposition," *Peacewatch: Special Policy Forum Report* (Washington, DC: The Washington Institute for Near East Policy, February 16, 1996).

BEILIN, JOSEPH (YOSSI). Born in 1948 in Petah Tikva, Joseph Beilin has been a Labor* MK since 1988. He earned a PhD in political science at Tel Aviv University, and while working as a reporter for *Davar** he met and impressed Shimon Peres*, who hired him to be Labor Party spokesman.

He served in various governmental capacities, including the following: Cabinet Secretary (1984-1986); Director-General for political affairs in the Ministry of Foreign Affairs (1986-1988); Deputy Minister of Foreign Affairs (1988-1990); Minister of Economics and Planning (July-November 1995); Minister without Portfolio in the Prime Minister's Office (November 1995-June 1996). As Deputy Foreign Minister he was indirectly involved in the secret talks with Palestinian officials in the spring and summer of 1993 which culminated with the Israeli-PLO Declaration of Principles*. In 1995 he conducted a series of secret talks with Palestinian official Mahmoud Abbas (Abu Mazen)* on the framework for a permanent Israeli-Palestinian settlement. He sought the leadership of the Labor Party in 1997 but was defeated by former IDF* Chief of Staff Ehud Barak*. On May 17, 1999, Beilin was reelected to the 15th Knesset on the One Israel* list. He was appointed Justice Minister in the governing coalition headed by Ehud Barak*. He is the author of several books, including *Touching Peace: From the Oslo Accords to a Final Agreement*, translated by Philip Simpson (London: Weidenfeld and Nicolson, 1999).

BEIRUT AIRPORT RAID (1968). On December 28, 1968, Israeli helicopter gunships raided the international airport in Beirut, Lebanon*, destroying 13 or 14 commercial aircraft belonging to Lebanon's Middle East Airways. The raid was in retaliation for an attack the previous day on an El Al aircraft in Athens, Greece, by members of George Habash's Popular Front for the Liberation of Palestine (PFLP). It was part of an Israeli strategy to pressure the Lebanese central government to apply sovereign authority over the border region and to prevent the Palestine Liberation Organization (PLO)* and other militant factions from using the region as a base for terrorist strikes against Israel and against Israeli and Jewish targets internationally. However, the Lebanese government was too weak and the Israel Defense Forces (IDF)* ultimately had to take matters into its own hands, launching a series of small (and a few larger) initiatives to push the Palestinian groups out of firing range. *See also* LEBANON.

BEN YEHUDA, ELIEZER (FORMERLY PERLMAN). The pioneer of the restoration of Hebrew* as a living, spoken language. He is generally considered "the father of the Hebrew language." He was born in Lushky, Lithuania, in 1857 and died in Jerusalem* in 1922. Ben Yehuda became interested in the restoration of the Jews to their ancient homeland and in the revival of the Jewish language. In 1881 he settled in Palestine* with his wife and began editing and publishing dailies, weeklies, and periodicals in Hebrew. In 1889, together with several others, he established the Vaad Halashon Haivrit, the Hebrew Language Council, whose main task was the coining of new Hebrew words. Ben Yehuda developed a comprehensive dictionary of the Hebrew language containing words ranging from those found in the Bible to those in modern Hebrew literature.

For further information see: Robert St. John, *Tongue of the Prophets: The Life Story of Eliezer Ben Yehuda* (New York: Doubleday, 1952).

BEN ZVI, YITZHAK (FORMERLY SHIMSHELEVITZ). Born in Poltava, Ukraine, Russia, on December 6, 1884, he was educated at a *heder* and then at a Russian gymnasium. He early joined Zionist groups and in 1904 made his first visit to Palestine* and helped to found the Poalei Zion Party*. He entered Kiev University in 1905, but then strikes closed down the university for that year. During the pogroms of November 1905 he participated in Jewish self-defense groups in Poltava. In 1906 he was among the participants at the first meeting of Poalei Zion—Zionist Social Democrats of Russia. In June 1906, while his family was imprisoned by Russian police for illegal possession of weapons, he escaped to Vilna, where he attempted to coordinate Poalei Zion activities in different countries. He settled in Palestine in 1907 and that same year was the Poalei Zion delegate to the Eighth Zionist Congress at the Hague. He helped found the Hebrew* socialist periodical *Ahdut* (Unity) in 1910. After his deportation from Palestine, he traveled to New York and, in 1915, founded the Hehalutz movement in America.

During World War I, Ben Zvi and David Ben-Gurion* organized a volunteer movement for Jewish battalions in the United States*. Ben Zvi then served as a soldier in the Jewish Legion* of the British Royal Fusiliers. After returning to Palestine in 1918, he was appointed to the Palestine Advisory Council in 1920, but resigned the following year after riots in Jaffa. He was one of the founders of the Histadrut* in 1920. He joined the Vaad Leumi* and remained a member until Israel was established as a state. He was a member of the Knesset* from 1948 to 1952 and also served on the Jerusalem* Municipal Council. A signer of Israel's Declaration of Independence*, Ben Zvi was elected to the First Knesset in 1949 and to the Second Knesset in 1951. After Chaim Weizmann's* death, he was elected President in 1952 and reelected in

1957. In 1962 he was elected for a third term, but died in office in April 1963. As President, he encouraged intellectual gatherings at his residence to discuss literary, academic, and artistic concerns.

For further information see: Yitzhak Ben Zvi, *The Exiled and the Redeemed* (Philadelphia: Jewish Publication Society of America, 1961).

BEN-AMI. SHLOMO. Born in Morocco in 1943, he immigrated to Israel in 1955. From the mid-1970s until 1987 he served as professor of history at Tel Aviv University, specializing in the modern history of Spain and European fascism. He was appointed ambassador to Spain in 1987; in this capacity he was involved in planning the Madrid Middle East Peace Conference* of October 1991. He returned briefly to Tel Aviv University in 1992, but then left again to run for the 14th Knesset* on the Israel Labor* Party list. Contested to replace Shimon Peres* as Labor Party leader in June 1997. He lost to Ehud Barak* but garnered an impressive 15% of the vote among party members. A leading member of Labor's dovish wing, he was instrumental in encouraging Barak to modify traditional party policy in order to attract support from sectors that did not normally vote for Labor (e.g., Sephardim*, Russian immigrants, and residents of development towns in the Negev*). Ranked third in internal party primaries for the 15th Knesset (1999), behind only Barak and Peres. He ultimately placed fourth on the expanded One Israel* list that won 26 seats in the Knesset elections held on May 17, 1999. On July 6, 1999, Ben-Ami was named Internal Security Minister in the Barak-led governing coalition.

BEN-ELIEZER, BINYAMIN ("FUAD"). Born in Iraq* in 1936, he immigrated to Israel in 1949. A career officer in the Israel Defense Forces*, he served as a commander in the 1967 Six Day War* and the 1973 Yom Kippur War*. A member of the IDF Military Mission to Singapore from 1970-1973. In 1977 he was appointed first Commanding Officer in Southern Lebanon*, serving as the IDF liaison with the local Christian community. From 1978-1981, he served as IDF Commander in Judea* and Samaria*, and in 1983-1984 he was Government Coordinator of Activities in the Administered Areas. He was first elected to the Knesset* in 1984 on Ezer Weizman's Yahad* list, which subsequently joined with the Labor Alignment*. Reelected in 1988 and 1992, he served as Minister of Construction and Housing from 1992-1996. Reelected to the 15th Knesset on May 17, 1999, on the One Israel* list, he was appointed Minister of Construction and Housing by Ehud Barak* on July 6, 1999. On July 11, 1999, he was named Deputy Prime Minister.

BEN-ELISAR, ELIAHU (FORMERLY GOTTLIEB). Born in Radom, Poland, on February 2, 1932, Ben-Elisar immigrated to Palestine* in 1942. His original family name was Gottlieb but when he changed it to Hebrew*, he did so by combining the first half of his father's two names (Eliezer Yisrael) to create Ben-Elisar. He was educated at the University of Paris in political science and international law and during his time in Paris he was enlisted by the Mossad* where he worked until 1965. In 1965 he left the Mossad to pursue his doctorate at the University of Geneva where he wrote on the Jewish factor in the foreign policy of the Third Reich. It was published as a book in 1969. He returned to Israel and worked as a correspondent for several European newspapers. He also became involved in Herut Party* political activities and in 1971 began to serve as head of the Information Department of the Herut Movement. He served as Director General of Prime Minister Menachem Begin's* office and as Israel's first Ambassador to Egypt*. A member of the Knesset* on the Likud list*, he served as Chairman of the Foreign Affairs and Security Committee of the 10th Knesset. In 1996-1997 he served as Ambassador to Washington. In April 1998 he was named Ambassador to Paris.

BEN-GURION, DAVID (FORMERLY GRUEN). Born in Plonsk, Poland, on October 16, 1886, under the influence of his father and grandfather, he became a committed Zionist in childhood. He arrived in Jaffa* in September 1906. He was elected to the central committee of the Poalei Zion (Workers of Zion)* and began organizing workers into unions. In 1910 he joined the editorial staff of a new Poalei Zion paper, *Ahdut* (Unity) in Jerusalem* and began publishing articles under the name Ben-Gurion. He joined a group of young socialist Zionists who went to study at Turkish universities and moved in 1912 to the University of Constantinople, where he earned a law degree with highest honors. In 1914 he returned to Palestine* and resumed his work as a union organizer, but in 1915 was exiled by Ottoman authorities. In May 1918 he enlisted in a Jewish Battalion of the British Royal Fusiliers and sailed to Egypt* to join the expeditionary force. From 1921 to 1935, Ben-Gurion was the Secretary General of the Histadrut* and was instrumental in the founding of the United Labor Party, which eventually became Mapai*.

In the 1920s and 1930s, Chaim Weizmann*, the head of the World Zionist Organization* and chief diplomat of the Zionist movement, ran overall Zionist affairs while Ben-Gurion headed Zionist activities in Palestine where his major rival was Vladimir Jabotinsky*. Convinced that Revisionist Zionists* under Jabotinsky were endangering the drive toward eventual statehood, Ben-Gurion sought to undermine and discredit Revisionism. When Menachem Begin* became the leader of Revisionism in the 1940s and increased militant actions against the British, Ben-Gurion intensified his efforts to discredit Revisionism and its leader. In 1935 he defeated the forces of Chaim Weizmann and was elected Chairman of the Jewish Agency* Executive, a post in which he served from 1935 to 1948. Recognized as the founder of Israel, he served as Prime Minister from 1948 to 1963, except for two years from December 1953 to 1955 when he voluntarily retired to Sde Boker* in the Negev* to seek respite from the rigors of his long political career and to dramatize the significance of pioneering and reclaiming the desert. In 1955, when Pinhas Lavon* was forced to resign as Minister of Defense, Ben-Gurion left Sde Boker to become Minister of Defense in the Government headed by Moshe Sharett*. After the election of 1955, Ben-Gurion undertook to form a new Government. However, the eruption of the Lavon Affair* in 1960 brought disarray to Mapai* and Ben-Gurion's political strength eroded. He resigned as Prime Minister in June 1963. In 1965 he founded a new political party, Rafi*, and remained in the Knesset* until he resigned in 1970. He died on December 1, 1973.

For further information see: Avraham Avi-Hai, *Ben-Gurion: State-Builder: Principles and Pragmatism, 1948-1963* (New York: Wiley, 1974); Michael Bar-Zohar, *Ben Gurion: The Armed Prophet* (Englewood Cliffs, NJ: Prentice-Hall, 1966); Michael Bar-Zohar, *Ben-Gurion: A Biography* (New York: Delacorte, 1979); Michael Bar-Zohar, *Lionhearts: Heroes of Israel* (New York: Warner, 1998); David Ben-Gurion, *Rebirth and Destiny of Israel* (New York: Philosophical Library, 1954); David Ben-Gurion (with Moshe Pearlman), *Ben-Gurion Looks Back* (New York: Simon and Schuster, 1965); David Ben-Gurion, *Israel: A Personal History* (New York: Funk and Wagnalls, 1971); David Ben-Gurion, *My Talks with Arab Leaders* (Jerusalem: Keter, 1972); Eliezer Don-Yehiya, "Political Religion in a New State: Ben-Gurion's *Mamlachtiyut*," in *Israel: The First Decade of Independence*, edited by S. Ilan Troen and Noah Lucas (Albany: State University of New York Press, 1995): 171-192; Maurice Edelman, *David: The Story of Ben-Gurion* (New York:

Putnam, 1965); Dan Kurzman, *Ben-Gurion: Prophet of Fire* (New York: Simon and Schuster, 1983); Barnett Litvinoff, *Ben-Gurion of Israel* (New York: Praeger, 1954); Robert St. John, *Ben-Gurion: The Biography of an Extraordinary Man* (New York: Doubleday, 1959); Shabtai Teveth, *Ben-Gurion and the Palestinian Arabs: From Peace to War* (New York: Oxford University Press, 1985); Shabtai Teveth, *Ben-Gurion: The Burning Ground 1886-1948* (Boston: Houghton-Mifflin, 1987); Shabtai Teveth, *Ben-Gurion's Spy: The Story of the Political Scandal That Shaped Modern Israel* (New York: Columbia University Press, 1996); Shabtai Teveth, *Ben-Gurion and the Holocaust* (New York: Harcourt Brace, 1996); Ze'ev Tzahor, "Ben-Gurion's Mythopoetics," *Israel Affairs* 1:3 (Spring 1995): 61-84; Nathan Yanai, "The Citizen as Pioneer: Ben-Gurion's Concept of Citizenship," *Israel Studies* 1:1 (Spring 1996): 127-143.

BEN-GURION UNIVERSITY. Located in Beersheva*, the capital of the Negev*, it was founded in 1969 with a mandate to spearhead social, agricultural, and industrial growth in Israel's arid southern region.

BENE ISRAEL OF INDIA *see* BNAI ISRAEL OF INDIA

BENIZRI, SHLOMO. Born in Haifa* in 1937; received Orthodox religious education in Sephardic* institutions. He was first elected to the 13th Knesset* in 1992 on the Sephardic Torah Guardians/Shas* list and later appointed Deputy Minister of Health by Benjamin Netanyahu* (July 1996-June 1999). Reelected to the 15th Knesset on the Shas list, on July 6, 1999, he was appointed Minister of Health in the Government headed by Ehud Barak*.

BERMAN, YITZHAK. Born in Russia in 1913 Berman immigrated to Palestine* in 1921. After completing his schooling in Jerusalem*, he studied law in London. He served in the British army from 1942 to 1945. He joined the Irgun* and served in the Israel Defense Forces*. He then entered the world of business, in which he was active until 1954, when he opened a private law practice. In 1968 he became active in the Liberal Party*. He was first elected to the Ninth Knesset* on behalf of the Liberal Party faction of the Likud* bloc in May 1977, and he served as Chairman of the House Committee until his election to the position of Speaker of the Knesset on March 12, 1980. After being reelected to the 10th Knesset, he was sworn in as Minister of Energy and Infrastructure on August 5, 1981, and served until 1982 when he resigned.

BERNADOTTE PLAN. The Bernadotte Plan, submitted by Count Folke Bernadotte of Sweden to the United Nations* in 1948, called on Israel to relinquish control over the southern Negev*, in return for retention of western and central Galilee*. The Plan also called for the repatriation of all Arab refugees who had fled from Palestine* during the War of Independence*, the merger of the Arab part of Palestine with Jordan*, and that Haifa* be made an international port. The proposal raised opposition from both Jews and Arabs, and was rejected by the Political Committee of the United Nations General Assembly in early December 1948. Bernadotte was assassinated in Jerusalem* on September 17, 1948. The assassins were never apprehended, but they were believed to be associated with the militant Stern Group (also known as Lohamei Herut Israel or LEHI*).

For further information see: Menachem Begin, *The Revolt: Story of the Irgun* (New York: Nash, 1981); Joseph Heller, "The Zionist Right and National Liberation: From Jabotinsky to Avraham Stern," *Israel Affairs* 1:3 (Spring 1995): 85-109; Samuel Katz, *Days of Fire: The Secret History of the Irgun Tzva'i Le'umi* (New York: Doubleday, 1968); Katy Marton, *A Death in Jerusalem* (New York: Pantheon, 1993); Howard M. Sachar, *A History of Israel: From the Rise of Zionism to Our Time* (New York: Knopf, 1979); Joseph Schechtman and Yehuda Benari, *A History of the Revisionist Movement* (Tel Aviv: Harad, 1970); Yaacov Shavit, *Revisionism in Zionism* (Tel Aviv: Yariv, 1978).

BETAR. Hebrew acronym for Brit Yosef Trumpeldor (Joseph Trumpeldor* Pact). A Revisionist* Zionist youth movement founded in 1923 in Riga, Latvia, named after Joseph Trumpeldor, and affiliated with the Revisionist Movement. The movement's ideological mentor was Vladimir Zeev Jabotinsky*. Betar's ideological tenets were: Jewish statehood; territorial integrity of the homeland; ingathering of the exiles*; the centrality of the Zionist idea; cultivation of the Hebrew* language; social justice; military preparedness for defense; national service; and *hadar*—a code of honor and strict personal behavior. Following Israel's War of Independence*, Betar founded agricultural and rural settlements. It also supports a sports society by the same name.

BETHLEHEM. A town in the West Bank*, it lies about five miles (eight kilometers) south of Jerusalem* and is the birthplace of Jesus Christ. Bethlehem is chiefly a religious shrine with many churches and other religious institutions. Bethlehem was a walled city during the time of King David*, who was born there. Christian crusaders captured it in the first Crusade, but later lost it to Turkish Muslims. The Ottoman Turks gained control of the area in the 1500s. In 1917, during World War I, British forces led by General Allenby took the town. It was part of the West Bank area annexed by Jordan* in 1949. Israel took control of the city during the Six Day War* of 1967. Control of the city was transferred to the Palestinians in late 1995 within the context of the Oslo II* Interim Agreement.

BIALIK, HAIM NAHMAN. One of the most influential Hebrew* poets and writers of modern times. He was born in Radi, Russia, in 1873 and died in Vienna in 1934. In many of his poems he stressed the vital role of the Beit Hamidrash (House of Study) and extolled the tradition of learning in Jewish life, but his main preoccupation was with the rebirth of the Jewish people and their return to Zion*. In 1924 he settled in Palestine* and played an important and active role in numerous cultural institutions and was also a President of the Vaad Halashon Haivrit, the Hebrew Language Council.

For further information see: David Aberbach, *Bialik* (London: Peter Halban, 1988); Arthur Hertzberg, editor, *The Zionist Idea: A Historical Analysis and Reader* (New York: Atheneum, 1979): 278-288; Eliezer Schweid, "The Rejection of the Diaspora in Zionist Thought: Two Approaches," in *Essential Papers on Zionism*, edited by Jehuda Reinharz and Anita Shapira (New York: New York University Press, 1996): 133-160.

BILTMORE PROGRAM. After World War I, when the British Mandate* replaced Ottoman rule in Palestine*, the focus of Zionist political and diplomatic endeavor was Great Britain*. However, during and after World War II, political necessity and reality resulted in a shift in focus to the United States*. The Biltmore Program was adopted by the Extraordinary Zionist Conference in New York on May 11, 1942, in response to Britain's policy toward the Jewish national home, particularly the restrictions on land sales and immigration to Jews imposed in the White Paper* of 1939. The Program became the basis for Zionist effort until Israel's independence and was a harbinger of change. It rejected efforts to restrict Jewish immigration and settlement in Palestine and called for the fulfillment of the Balfour Declaration* and the mandate, urging that "Palestine be established as a Jewish Commonwealth." The Biltmore Program reflected the urgency of the situation in which the Jewish leadership found itself as a consequence of the Holocaust* and the need to provide for the displaced Jews of Europe.

BILU MOVEMENT. A Zionist society and movement of Palestinian pioneers from the nonreligious, Jewish-Russian intellectual leadership, founded in Kharkov in 1882, who spearheaded the First Aliya*. It derived its name from the Hebrew* acronym of the biblical verse: "Bet Yaakov Lkhu Vnelha" ("House of Jacob, come ye and let us go," Isaiah 2:5), which served as its slogan. Its aim was the national renaissance of the Jewish people, the development of its productiveness, and its return to agriculture. The society was founded after the pogroms of 1882, and the first group of Bilu settlers in Palestine* arrived in July 1882. Although their concrete achievements of establishing settlements were limited, the moral and historical effect of the movement was substantial because the ideals it represented continued to inspire successive generations.

For further information see: Shmuel Ettinger and Israel Bartal, "The First Aliya: Ideological Roots and Practical Accomplishments," in *Essential Papers on Zionism,* edited by Jehuda Reinharz and Anita Shapira (New York: New York University Press, 1996): 63-93; Hayyim Hisin, *A Palestine Diary: Memoirs of a Bilu Pioneer* (New York: Herzl, 1976); Walter Laqueur, *A History of Zionism* (London: Weidenfeld and Nicolson, 1972): chapter 6; Howard M. Sachar, *A History of Israel: From the Rise of Zionism to Our Time* (New York: Knopf, 1979): chapter 2; Nahum Sokolow, *Hibbath Zion (The Love of Zion)* (Jerusalem: Rubin Mass, 1941); Nahum Sokolow, *History of Zionism, 1600-1918* (New York: Ktav, 1969).

BISHARA, AZMI (AHMED). Born in 1956 in Nazareth to Christian Arab parents, he was educated in East Germany. He became professor of philosophy at Bir-Zeit University in the West Bank* and founder and head of the National Democratic Alliance-Balad* Party. He was first elected to the Knesset* in 1996 on the list of the Democratic Front for Peace and Equality-Hadash* Party. He subsequently broke from Hadash, and Balad stood independently in the 14th Knesset. In 1999 he became the first Arab citizen to run to become Israel's Prime Minister, campaigning for the extending of full civil and political rights to the Arab community and demanding that Israel be transformed into "a state of all its citizens" and not simply "a Jewish state." Bishara also criticized Israeli policy toward the Golan Heights* during highly publicized meetings in Damascus with the President of Syria*, Hafez al-Asad, and by expressing sympathy for Hezbollah and other groups waging a war of attrition against IDF* personnel in southern Lebanon*. He withdrew from the prime ministerial race on the eve of the May 17, 1999, elections, throwing his support to the candidacy of One Israel* leader Ehud Barak*. The National Democratic Alliance-Balad won two seats in the 15th Knesset. *See also* ARAB POLITICAL PARTIES.

BITON, CHARLEY. Born in Casablanca, Morocco, in 1947 Biton emigrated to Israel in 1949. One of the founders of the Black Panthers* movement, he was elected to the 11th and 12th Knessets* on the Democratic Front for Peace and Equality* list. He led a campaign to have amnesty granted to prisoners (mainly poor Sephardim*) incarcerated in Israeli prisons in 1998 to mark the country's fiftieth anniversary.

BLACK HEBREWS. The name applied to a community of African-Americans that arrived in Israel in the late 1960s and early 1970s claiming to be the "rightful inheritors of Jerusalem* and the Holy Land", and have remained in the country illegally ever since. Founded in the Black ghettos of Chicago in the early 1960s, its members claimed to be the "true descendants" of Abraham and the biblical Israelites; they rejected the legitimacy of the State of Israel and predicted that "by 1977, the lands and the institutions now being controlled by the illegal government occupying that land [Israel] will be in the hands of Black people from America, with the authority of the Original African Hebrew Israelite Nation of Jerusalem." The first group of 39 Black Hebrews arrived in Israel, via Liberia, on December 21, 1969. They asked to be granted immediate immigrant status under the Law of Return*. Befuddled Israeli immigration officials deferred responding to this request until the religious status of the group's members could be clarified; in the meantime they were granted tourist visas, were settled in the Negev* development town of Dimona*, and given assistance in obtaining housing, employment, Hebrew language instruction, and other support usually provided to new immigrants. Shortly thereafter, other Black Hebrews arrived in two groups and joined their colleagues in Dimona. In due course, Israeli rabbinical authorities determined that the Black Hebrews were not Jewish and the Interior Ministry began expulsion proceedings against those who had either entered the country illegally or whose tourist visas had expired. On appeal, an Israeli court ruled that since the Black Hebrews were not Jewish they could not benefit from the Law of Return, and that the Interior Ministry was acting legally in ordering the deportation of those living in the country illegally. Despite this ruling, successive Israeli Governments avoided deporting the group's members, seemingly fearful of eliciting charges of racism and of provoking tensions between American Jewish and Black communities. In the meantime, the Black Hebrew community in Israel grew to some 3,000 members, most of whom lived in squalid conditions in Dimona, Arad, and Mitzpeh Ramon. See also LAW OF RETURN.

For further information see: Israel J. Gerber, *The Heritage Seekers: Black Jews in Search of Identity* (Middle Village, NY: J. David, 1977).

BLACK PANTHERS. Although there had been riots in the Oriental* neighborhood of Wadi Salib* in 1959, no significant political movement developed in the Oriental community until the 1970s. Then a militant protest group formed by some young Orientals of North African background, who chose to call themselves Black Panthers, took to the streets to oppose what they regarded as discrimination against the Oriental Jewish community. They helped to generate awareness and a plethora of public investigation and study commissions. Demands for more educational and social services were part of the effort to achieve improvement in the Oriental community's socioeconomic status. These efforts achieved some amelioration of the situation, but they did not effect substantial change.

For further information see: Daniel J. Elazar, *The Other Jews: The Sephardim Today* (New York: Basic, 1989); Calvin Goldscheider, *Israel's Changing Society: Population, Ethnicity, and Development* (Boulder, CO: Westview, 1996): chapter 2; David J. Schnall, *Radical Dissent in Contemporary Israeli Politics: Cracks in the Wall* (New York: Praeger, 1979); Yael Yishai, *Land of Paradoxes: Interest Politics in Israel* (Albany: State University of New York Press, 1991).

BNAI ISRAEL OF INDIA. A Jewish community indigenous to western India* near Bombay whose origins are a mystery. In 1947 there were some 24,000 members of the community living in India, but most subsequently immigrated to Israel. In 1961 a controversy erupted in Israel as to whether the Bnai Israel were Jews according to Jewish law. The controversy ended in 1964 when Prime Minister Levi Eshkol* declared adherents of the Bnai Israel as Jews in every respect.

For further information see: Joan G. Roland, *The Jewish Communities of India: Identity in a Colonial Era*, Second Edition (New Brunswick, NJ: Transaction, 1998).

BRIT SHALOM. A Jewish organization based in Mandatory Palestine* and devoted to the promotion of a working arrangement between Zionism* and Arab nationalism. The main goal was to promote a binational state in Palestine rather than a Jewish state. It was a small and loosely shaped organization composed primarily of Jewish intellectuals and other well-known Jewish figures and reached its peak in the 1920s and 1930s. In many respects it was more of a debating society and study group than an active political organization. Martin Buber* and Judah Magnes* were among its prominent members.

For further information see: Norman Bentwich, *For Zion's Sake: A Biography of Judah L. Magnes* (Philadelphia: Jewish Publication Society of America, 1954); Martin Buber, *A Land of Two Peoples: Martin Buber on Jews and Arabs* (New York: Oxford University Press, 1983); Susan Lee Hattis, *The Bi-National Idea in Palestine during Mandatory Times* (Haifa: Shikmona, 1970); Rael Jean Isaac, *Israel Divided: Ideological Politics in the Jewish State* (Baltimore: Johns Hopkins, 1976); Hagit Lavsky, "German Zionists and the Emergence of Brit Shalom," in *Essential Papers on Zionism*, edited by Jehuda Reinharz and Anita Shapira (New York: New York University Press, 1996): 648-670; Judah L. Magnes, *Like All Nations?* (Jerusalem: Weiss Press, 1930).

BRITISH MANDATE FOR PALESTINE (BRITISH MANDATE, MANDATE). At the end of World War I the great powers dismantled the Ottoman Empire. Great Britain* was granted control over Palestine* under the League of Nations Mandate system and retained control of the territory from 1922 to 1948. It was during the Mandatory period that most of the political, economic, and social institutions of Israel were formed, its political parties launched, and the careers of its political elite begun. In the spring of 1947, the British turned the problem of the future of the

Mandate over to the United Nations which established a Special Committee on Palestine (UNSCOP)* to review the situation and to offer suggestions for disposition of the territory. UNSCOP's majority report, which called for the partition of Palestine, was adopted by the United Nations General Assembly on November 29, 1947. The British terminated the Mandate and its presence in Palestine on May 15, 1948.

For further information see: George Antonius, *The Arab Awakening: The Story of the Arab National Movement* (New York: Capricorn, 1965); Neil Caplan, *Futile Diplomacy, Volume 1: Early Arab-Zionist Negotiations Attempts, 1913-1931* (London: Frank Cass, 1983); Neil Caplan, *Futile Diplomacy, Volume 2: Arab-Zionist Negotiations and the End of the Mandate* (London: Frank Cass, 1986); *Great Britain and Palestine: 1915-1945*, Third Edition (London: Royal Institute of International Affairs, 1946); Dan Horowitz and Moshe Lissak, *Origins of the Israeli Polity: Palestine under the Mandate* (Chicago: University of Chicago Press, 1978); Walid Khalidi, editor, *From Haven to Conquest: Readings in Zionism and the Palestine Problem until 1948* (Washington, DC: The Institute for Palestine Studies, 1987); Baruch Kimmerling and Joel S. Migdal, *Palestinians: The Making of a People* (New York: Free Press, 1993); William Roger Louis and Robert W. Stookey, editors, *The End of the Palestine Mandate* (Austin: University of Texas Press, 1986); Yehoshua Porath, *The Emergence of the Palestinian-Arab National Movement, 1918-1929* (London: Frank Cass, 1974); Howard M. Sachar, *A History of Israel: From the Rise of Zionism to Our Time* (New York: Knopf, 1979); A. J. Sherman, *Mandate Days: British Lives in Palestine 1918-1948* (London: Douglas and McIntyre, 1998); Alan R. Taylor, *Prelude to Israel: An Analysis of Zionist Diplomacy 1897-1947*, Revised Edition (Beirut: The Institute for Palestine Studies, 1970); Mark Tessler, *A History of the Israeli-Palestinian Conflict* (Bloomington: Indiana University Press, 1994); David Vital, *Zionism: The Formative Years* (New York: Oxford University Press, 1982); Bernard Wasserstein, "Patterns of Communal Conflict in Palestine," in *Essential Papers on Zionism*, edited by Jehuda Reinharz and Anita Shapira (New York: New York University Press, 1996): 671-688.

BROTHER DANIEL CASE. A 1962 ruling by the Supreme Court of Israel* affecting the "Who is a Jew"* issue. Daniel Rufeisen was born in 1922 and reared in Poland as a Jew named Osvald Rufeizin (Oswald Rufeisen). He was hidden by Roman Catholics during World War II and converted to Catholicism and became a Carmelite monk. He moved to Israel, settling in Haifa, and claimed citizenship and special benefits restricted to Jewish immigrants under the Law of Return* based on the fact that he was born to a Jewish mother. The Interior Minister, Moshe Shapira of the National Religious Party*, rejected this appeal, arguing that although by a strict definition of Halacha* Brother Daniel was indeed born Jewish, the fact that he had willingly converted to another religion meant that he had forfeited his claims as a Jew. If he wanted to immigrate to Israel under the terms of the Law of Return, he would have to consent to be "reconverted" to Judaism. In 1962 the Supreme Court ruled against Brother Daniel's appeal, although the Court emphasized that it was basing its judgment on secular grounds rather than an Orthodox interpretation of Halacha. Brother Daniel was later accorded Israeli citizenship by the Interior Ministry. He died in August 1998.

For further information see: Gary S. Schiff, *Tradition and Politics: The Religious Parties of Israel* (Detroit: Wayne State University Press, 1977).

BUBER, MARTIN. A Jewish religious philosopher born in Vienna in 1878 and died in Jerusalem* in 1965. Buber was the author of many books on Jewish philosophy, general philosophy, Hasidism*, theology, Zionist theory, and the Bible. His fame, which was greater in the non-Jewish world than in Israel itself, was based primarily on his philosophy of a dialogue between God and man, as expressed in his books *Between Man and Man* (1947) and *I and Thou* (1958). He joined Judah Magnes* and the Ihud* movement and advocated Arab-Jewish rapprochement as well as an Arab-Jewish binational state in Palestine*.

For further information see: Martin Buber, *Israel and Palestine: The History of an Idea* (London: East and West Library, 1952); Martin Buber, *Israel and the World: Essays in a Time of Crisis*, Second Edition (New York: Schocken, 1963); Martin Buber, *A Land of Two Peoples: Martin Buber on Jews and Arabs* (New York: Oxford University Press, 1983); Arthur Hertzberg, editor, *The Zionist Idea: A Historical Analysis and Reader* (New York: Atheneum, 1979): 450-465; Aubrey Hodes, *Martin Buber: An Intimate Portrait* (New York: Viking, 1973).

BURG, AVRAHAM. Born in Jerusalem* in 1955, he was the son of veteran National Religious Party* politician Yosef Burg*. A graduate of the Orthodox Hesder yeshiva system, he began his political career in 1985 as advisor to Prime Minister Shimon Peres* on Israel-Diaspora* affairs. First elected to the Knesset*, on the Labor* Party list, in 1988 and reelected in 1992, he served as Chairman of the Knesset Education Committee but did not stand for election in 1996. In June 1995 he was elected Chairman of the Executive of the Jewish Agency for Israel* and the World Zionist Organization*, replacing Simha Dinitz*. In December 1997 he was reelected to a second two-year term. A proponent of religious tolerance among Israeli Jews, continuing peace negotiations with the Palestinians, and the streamlining of the Jewish Agency and the WZO to reflect current political and financial circumstances affecting the Israel-Diaspora relationship, he reentered party politics in the spring of 1999, winning a seat in the Knesset on the Labor/One Israel* list. He was elected Speaker of the 15th Knesset on July 6, 1999, defeating the only other candidate, Hadash* Party leader Mohammed Barakei, by 100 votes to 10.

For further information see: Avraham Burg, *Brit Am—A Covenant of the People: Proposed Policy Guidelines for the National Institutions of the Jewish People* (Jerusalem: The Jewish Agency for Israel, 1995).

BURG, YOSEF. Born in Dresden, Germany*, in 1909, from 1928 to 1931 he completed his rabbinical studies at the seminary in Berlin and studied in the Faculty of Humanities at Berlin University. In 1933 he received a PhD from the University of Leipzig. In 1938 he emigrated to Palestine* and, from 1939 to 1951, he served as a member of the World Zionist Council*. Between 1946 and 1949 he carried out a number of rescue missions in Europe. Initially elected on behalf of the National Religious Party* to the First Knesset* in January 1949, Dr. Burg was reelected to subsequent Knessets. He served as Deputy Speaker in the First Knesset; as Minister of Health from 1951 to 1952; Minister of Posts from 1952 to 1958; Minister of Social Welfare from 1959 to 1970; and as Minister of the Interior from 1970 to 1984. On August 5, 1981, in addition to his post as Minister of the Interior and as Chairman of the Ministerial Committee on Negotiations for Autonomy for the Arab Residents of Judea*, Samaria*, and the Gaza District*, Dr. Burg assumed the post of Minister of Religious Affairs. In the Government of National Unity*, he served as Minister of Religion from 1984 until his resignation from the post in 1986. He later served as World Chairman of the Mizrachi* movement. He died in Jerusalem on October 14, 1999.

C

CABINET. The cabinet or Government is the central policy-making body of the Israeli governmental system. In the past, the President* was empowered to designate a member of Knesset*, almost always the leader of the party holding the most seats, to form a Government. Pursuant to the revised Basic Law: The Government (1992)*, the cabinet is now appointed by the Prime Minister* who is chosen through direct popular election. The Prime Minister must be a citizen of Israel of at least 30 years of age and a member of the Knesset. Ministers are usually, but not necessarily, members of the Knesset. The number of ministers, including the Prime Minister, may not exceed 18 nor be less than eight. In 1999 the number was increased to 24. The Prime Minister-elect has 45 days within which to form a Government and present that Government and its guiding principles before the Knesset for a vote of confidence. If within that period a Government cannot be formed, a brief extension may be granted, after which time new elections for both the Prime Minister and Knesset must be held.

The Government is constituted upon obtaining a vote of confidence from the Knesset, which must approve the composition of the Government, the distribution of functions among the ministers, and the basic guidelines of its policy. The cabinet is collectively responsible to the Knesset, reports to it, and remains in office as long as it enjoys the confidence of that body. Until March 1990 there had never been a successful motion of no-confidence by the Knesset causing the ouster of a Government. Under the new Basic Law: The Government, there are several ways to terminate a cabinet's tenure. The first is a vote of no-confidence motion in the Prime Minister, which requires a majority of 61 members of the Knesset to pass. If such a motion passes, the Knesset must dissolve and new elections must be held for both the Prime Minister and Knesset within 60 days. There is also the possibility of ousting the Prime Minister without terminating the Knesset. This requires a special motion supported by 80 Knesset members. The third possibility is for the Prime Minister himself or herself to inform the President that the Government cannot continue to function properly; the President is then empowered to call for both prime ministerial and Knesset elections. There is also the outside possibility of members of Knesset filing a bill calling for the dissolution of the Knesset.

It was through this mechanism that the Government of Benjamin Netanyahu* fell in late December 1998 and new elections for both Prime Minister and the Knesset were set for May 17, 1999.

The cabinet decides Israel's policies in all spheres, subject to Knesset approval, and it generally initiates the largest portion of legislation. Increasingly much of the cabinet's work has been conducted by a small and select group of ministers meeting informally in "kitchen cabinets*", for example, as occurred when Golda Meir* was the Prime Minister, or in ministerial committees on issues such as security and defense.

Ministries are divided among the parties forming the coalition in accordance with the agreement reached by the parties and generally reflect their size and influence. The most important positions in the cabinet aside from the Prime Minister tend to be Defense Minister, Foreign Minister, and Finance Minister.

To date, no party has received enough Knesset seats to be able to form a Government by itself (that is to say, at least 61 seats of the 120-seat Knesset). Thus, all Israeli Governments have been based on coalitions between two or more parties, with those remaining outside the Government making up the opposition. The coalition is based on agreement among the parties that make up the Government, defining common policy goals and the principles which are to guide its activities. The coalition agreement is not a legally binding document. Though one of the goals behind the change to the direct election of the Prime Minister was to make the coalition-formation process more stable and less vulnerable to coalition pressures, this has yet to be proven to be the case in practice. In the summer of 1996 Prime Minister-elect Benjamin Netanyahu formed a coalition composed of six parties representing six diverse political interests and demands on the system and on the Prime Minister. One Israel* leader Ehud Barak* presented his coalition Government—comprised of seven parties—and its program to the Knesset for confirmation on July 6, 1999.

For further information see: Asher Arian, *The Second Republic: Politics in Israel* (Chatham, NJ: Chatham House, 1998): chapter 9; *Basic Law: The Government* (Jerusalem: Government Printing Office); Avraham Brichta, "The New Premier-Parliamentary System in Israel," *The Annals of the American Academy of Political and Social Science* 555 (January

1998): 180-192; Reuven Y. Hazan, "Presidential Parliamentarianism: Direct Popular Election of the Prime Minister, Israel's New Electoral and Political System," *Electoral Studies* 15 (1996): 21-37; Gad Yaacobi, *The Government of Israel* (New York: Praeger, 1982).

CAMP DAVID ACCORDS. Egyptian President Anwar Sadat's* historic visit to Jerusalem* in November 1977 was followed by negotiations in which the United States*—and President Jimmy Carter* personally—played an active and often crucial role. In September 1978, President Carter, President Sadat of Egypt*, Prime Minister Menachem Begin* of Israel, and their senior aides held an extraordinary series of meetings for 13 days at Camp David, Maryland, during which they discussed the Arab-Israeli conflict*. On September 17, 1978, at the White House they announced the conclusion of two accords that provided the basis for continuing negotiations for peace: a "Framework for Peace in the Middle East" and a "Framework for the Conclusion of a Peace Treaty between Egypt and Israel." The Middle East framework set forth general principles and some specifics to govern a comprehensive peace settlement, focusing on the future of the West Bank* and the Gaza Strip*. It called for a transitional period of no more than five years during which Israel's military government would be withdrawn (although Israeli forces could remain in specified areas to ensure Israel's security) and a self-governing authority would be elected by the inhabitants of these areas. It also provided that "Egypt, Israel, Jordan and the representatives of the Palestinian people" should participate in negotiations to resolve the final status of the West Bank and Gaza, Israel's relations with Jordan based on United Nations Security Council Resolution 242*, and Israel's right to live within secure and recognized borders. The Egypt-Israel framework called for Israel's withdrawal from the Sinai Peninsula* and the establishment of normal, peaceful relations between the two states. In addition to the two frameworks, there was a series of accompanying letters clarifying the parties' positions on certain issues. The Egyptian cabinet approved the accords on September 19 and on September 28 the Israeli Knesset* voted 84-19 (with 17 abstentions) to endorse them. The Camp David Accords led to further negotiations and the Egypt-Israel Peace Treaty*.

For further information see: Yaacov Bar-Siman-Tov, *Israel and the Peace Process 1977-1982: The Search of Legitimacy for Peace* (Albany: State University of New York Press, 1994); Zbigniew Brzezinski, *Power and Principles: Memoirs of the National Security Adviser 1977-1981*

(New York: Farrar, Strauss, and Giroux, 1983); Jimmy Carter, *Keeping Faith: Memoirs of a President* (New York: Bantam, 1982); Jimmy Carter, *The Blood of Abraham* (Boston: Houghton-Mifflin, 1985); Moshe Dayan, *Breakthrough: A Personal Account of the Egypt-Israel Peace Negotiations* (New York: Knopf, 1981); Marius Deeb, "Anwar Sadat," in *Political Leaders of the Contemporary Middle East and North Africa*, edited by Bernard Reich (Westport, CT: Greenwood Press, 1980): 453-460; Eitan Haber, Zeev Schiff, and Ehud Yaari, *The Year of the Dove* (New York: Bantam, 1979); William B. Quandt, editor, *Camp David: Peacemaking and Politics* (Washington, DC: The Brookings Institution, 1986); Ezer Weizman, *The Battle for Peace* (New York: Bantam, 1981); Laura Zittrain Eisenberg and Neil Caplan, *Negotiating Arab-Israeli Peace: Patterns, Problems, and Possibilities* (Bloomington: Indiana University Press, 1998).

CARTER, JIMMY. President of the United States* from 1977 to 1981 who played an active role in negotiations between Israel and Egypt* that led to the Camp David Accords* and the Egypt-Israel Peace Treaty*.

For further information see: Jimmy Carter, *Keeping Faith: Memoirs of a President* (New York: Bantam, 1982); Jimmy Carter, *The Blood of Abraham* (Boston: Houghton-Mifflin, 1985).

CASINO PARTY. Another single issue party, the Casino Party believed that the casino in Jericho which has drawn Israelis to gamble outside of Israel should result in the legalization of gambling in Israel. Led by Ezra Tissona, a man who made his career in gambling, this party failed to win a seat in the 15th Knesset. Also in favor of reduced taxes and fighting crime and drugs.

CENTER LIBERAL PARTY *see* LIBERAL CENTER PARTY

CENTER PARTY. A centrist political party formed in late 1998 to contest the May 17, 1999, election to the 15th Knesset*. Its founders were former Likud* members of Knesset* and cabinet ministers Dan Meridor*, Ronnie Milo*, and Yitzhak Mordechai*, and former Israel Defense Forces* Chief of Staff Amnon Lipkin-Shahak*. In seeking to create a third political constituency, the party's founders were responding to strong popular support for a political party that would occupy the ideological middle ground between the Likud and Labor* parties and their respective alliance partners. On foreign and security policy, the Center Party platform advocated "examining Palestinian interests, including their aspiration for a state, in the framework of [final status] negotiations, while maintaining [Israel's] vital interests." With regard to relations with Syria* and Lebanon*, it envisioned "a new strategic situation in the north with territorial compromise on the Golan." Its domestic policy platform promised increased national unity based on a more equitable distribution of resources to all segments of Israeli society; efforts to improve the country's educational system; the promulgation of a formal, written constitution; and an end to "religious coercion" practiced by the ultra-Orthodox political parties. The Center Party selected as its leader the former Defense Minister, Yitzhak Mordechai, who also was its candidate for Prime Minister until the eve of the May 17, 1999, elections, when he withdrew and threw his support to One Israel* candidate Ehud Barak*. The party won six seats in the 15th Knesset and joined the governing coalition announced by Barak on July 6, 1999, with Mordechai as Transportation Minister and Amnon Lipkin-Shahak as Minister of Tourism.

CENTER-SHINUI MOVEMENT. A political bloc made up of three parties: Shinui*, the Independent Liberals*, and the Liberal Center*. Shinui was formed in 1974 by Tel Aviv University law professor Amnon Rubinstein*. In 1976 it joined with other groups to form the Democratic Movement for Change (DMC)*, a centrist party headed by Yigael Yadin* that won 15 seats in the 1977 Knesset* election. With the demise of the DMC, Shinui set out on its own, winning two seats in 1981 and three in 1984. It was a junior partner in the 1984-1988 National Unity Government*. It joined with the Independent Liberal and Liberal Center parties to form the Center-Shinui Movement and won two seats in the 1988 election. In 1988 it campaigned on a platform that claimed it was the only political body combining an aspiration for peace based on compromise, a socio-economic concept encouraging a free and enterprising economy, the protection of individual rights, and opposition to religious coercion. It also claimed that it would not join a coalition government formed by the Likud* and the religious parties*. It also differed from the Labor Alignment* in its approach to the economy and focused on a free economy encouraging growth and creativity rather than the failed bureaucratic approaches of the Labor Alignment. In the political realm the movement favored a peace agreement with the Arabs, arguing that this would free Israel from the cycle of war and bloodshed and prevent it from becoming a binational state which would rule over another people. Such a peace agreement would be based on the principle of land for peace. Israel's security would be guaranteed by secure border adjustments, security arrangements, and the demilitarization of evacuated areas.

In 1992 the Center-Shinui Movement joined with two other Zionist left-wing parties (Citizens' Rights Movement* and Mapam*) to form the Meretz/Democratic Israel* coalition that won 12 seats in the 13th Knesset and participated in the Labor-led coalition Governments headed by Yitzhak Rabin and Shimon Peres.

For further information see: David H. Goldberg, *Democracy in Action 1999: A Guide to the Participants and Issues in Israeli Politics* (Toronto: Canada-Israel Committee, May 1999); Gershon R. Kieval, *Party Politics in Israel and the Occupied Territories* (Westport, CT: Greenwood, 1983); Amnon Rubinstein, *A Certain Political Experience* (Jerusalem: Idanim, 1982, Hebrew); Yael Yishai, "Interest Groups and Political Parties in the 1992 Elections: Rivals, Partners or Clients?" in *Israel at the Polls 1992*, edited by Daniel J. Elazar and Shmuel Sandler (Lanham, MD: Rowman and Littlefield, 1995): 229-250.

CHEN (WOMEN'S ARMY CORPS). Women have served in the Israel Defense Forces (IDF)* since its inception. During the War of Independence* women soldiers participated occasionally in combat, but since 1949 no women have been allowed to do so. Women generally serve in the army for two years. However, women over 24, married women, and women with religious objections are exempt from military service. The Women's Corps is responsible for the placement, conditions of service, and well-being of women in the service. Women serve as clerks, drivers, radar operators, nurses, medical doctors, social workers, teachers, instructors at the various service branch schools, and in various intelligence duties, in the legal service of the IDF, and in administrative capacities. In the mid to late 1990s steps were taken to gradually integrate women soldiers into some front-line units of the IDF.

For further information see: Stuart A. Cohen, "Towards a New Portrait of the (New) Israeli Soldier," *Israel Affairs* 3:3&4 (Spring/Summer 1997): 77-114; Calvin Goldscheider, *Israel's Changing Society: Population, Ethnicity, and Development* (Boulder, CO: Westview, 1996):

chapter 8; Yael Yishai, *Between the Flag and the Banner: Women in Israeli Politics* (Albany: State University of New York Press, 1997).

CHINA. Israel was among the first countries in the world to recognize the People's Republic of China in January 1950, but official relations were established only in 1992. Since then substantial links have been created between the two countries as many agreements were signed in the areas of trade, aviation, culture, scientific, and military cooperation. A binational research and development foundation was established; bilateral agricultural, dual-taxation, and investment encouragement agreements also were signed. Numerous reciprocal visits have taken place.

For further information see: Jonathan Goldstein, editor, *China ad Israel: A Fifty Year Retrospective* (Westport, CT: Praeger, 1999).

CIECHANOVER COMMISSION. A commission established by the Netanyahu* Government to investigate the Mossad's* botched attempted assassination of Hamas official Khaled Mashaal* on September 25, 1997, in Amman, Jordan*. Officially designated as a "clarification" committee that was to report to the Cabinet alone, it was chaired by Joseph Ciechanover, former legal adviser to the Defense Ministry and director-general of the Foreign Ministry, and chairman of the Board of Directors of El Al*. Its other members were to have been Rafi Peled, former National Police Chief, and director-general of the Israel Electric Corporation; and Nahum Admoni, former Mossad chief, and director-general of the Mekorot Water Company. However, Admoni soon resigned amidst suggestions of a conflict-of-interest and he was replaced on the committee by Don Tolkovsky, former commander of the Israel Air Force and a retired businessman. The committee's final report was submitted to the Government in mid-February 1998. It was highly critical of all aspects of the failed Mashaal operation, calling it "amateurish" and "negligent." While it absolved Prime Minister Benjamin Netanyahu* of responsibility for the actual operation, it did rebuke him for approving an attempted assassination on Jordanian soil. The report laid much of the blame for the botched operation at the feet of Mossad chief Danny Yatom* and his director of operations. (The latter, whose name was withheld for security reasons, had already resigned on November 14, 1997.) Among its findings were that the Mossad did not inform its representative in Amman of the planned attempt. Many of the details of the plan were left vague. There were not enough agents or enough escape vehicles. The Mossad did not expect Mashaal to have bodyguards, and the agents surrendered immediately when caught. The committee was divided on whether Yatom should be fired for his role in the debacle, leaving it up to the Prime Minister and cabinet to determine his fate; Yatom resigned as Mossad chief on February 24, 1998. Finally, the Ciechanover Commission recommended the appointment of a special intelligence adviser in the Prime Minister's Office to advise the Prime Minister on all clandestine operations and to liaise between the PMO, the Mossad, and other branches of the intelligence and security community.

CITIZENS' RIGHTS AND PEACE MOVEMENT (CRM—HATNUA LEZHUIOT HAEZRAH ULESHALOM—RATZ). The Citizens' Rights Movement is a social-liberal political party established by Shulamit Aloni*, a former Labor Party* member and civil rights activist, in August 1973, although it began to develop following the Yom Kippur War* when there was substantial discontent with the Labor Party. It called for electoral reform; the introduction of a Basic Law* protecting human rights; recognition of a Palestinian entity and the Palestinian right to self-determination; the separation of religion and state; and equal rights for women. In the elections to the 8th Knesset*, which took place on December 31, 1973, the CRM won three seats and joined the Government coalition for a brief period in 1974. It gained only one seat in the elections to both the 9th Knesset (1977) and the 10th Knesset (1981), but following the 1981 elections Aloni joined the Alignment* so that it would have the same number of seats (48) as the Likud* bloc and thus it would be blocked in its efforts to form the new Government. The tactic failed and in 1984 the CRM struck out on its own, taking with it a number of young Labor Party activists (such as Yossi Sarid*) who had become disenchanted with the party's infighting and its perceived gradual shift away from its founding ideological convictions. The CRM won three Knesset seats in 1984 and five in 1988. In 1992 it joined with Mapam* and Center-Shinui* to form the Meretz/Democratic Israel* faction that won 12 Knesset mandates and participated in the 1992-1996 Labor-led coalition Government.

The party changed character in the 1980s, becoming a party whose membership is drawn from a variety of older groups. The party is now composed of the historical CRM, including liberals and secularists; the academics of the "group of 100" (including former Peace Now* and Labor Party doves); and former Shelli* members. Its constituency is primarily the "middle class" Ashkenazi* population, and its platform emphasizes civil rights for all Israelis. Its original focus was on human and civil rights and it opposes discrimination based on religion, sex, or ethnic identification. It advocates a peace settlement with the Arabs and the Palestinians. Beginning with the 1988 Knesset election it supported a platform which recognized the right of the Palestinian people to self-determination and called on the Palestine Liberation Organization* to recognize Israel's right to a sovereign and secure existence, so that the PLO would be able to participate in peace negotiations as the representative of the Palestinian people. It believes that the Palestinian people should ultimately decide what form their self-determination should take. On domestic issues, it stood for the separation of religion and state.

In 1996 the long-time leader of the CRM and Meretz, Shulamit Aloni, retired from party politics and was succeeded by Yossi Sarid. In the election to the 14th Knesset (1996) the CRM and Meretz won nine seats, down from 12 in 1992. The CRM and Meretz made two significant changes to their foreign policy platform for the May 17, 1999, election to the 15th Knesset: they called for the unilateral withdrawal of Israeli forces from the south Lebanon* security zone*; and, while promoting the national consensus in favor of the continued unified status of Jerusalem* under Israeli sovereignty, they called for greater respect for Palestinian representatives and institutions in the city. In 1999 the party also campaigned aggressively against the special privileges accorded by the incumbent Netanyahu*-led Government to the ultra-Orthodox political parties and their constituents. The party won 10 seats in the 15th Knesset and joined the governing coalition headed by Ehud Barak*, with Yossi Sarid as Education Minister and Ran Cohen as Industry and Trade Minister.

For further information see: Asher Arian, *The Second Republic: Politics in Israel* (Chatham, NJ: Chatham House, 1998); David H. Goldberg, *Democracy in Action 1999: A Guide to the Participants and Issues in Israeli Politics* (Toronto: Canada-Israel Committee, May 1999); Gershon R. Kieval, *Party Politics in Israel and the Occupied Territories* (Westport, CT: Greenwood, 1983).

CIVIL RIGHTS MOVEMENT *see* CITIZENS' RIGHTS AND PEACE MOVEMENT

COHEN, GEULA. Geula Cohen was born in Tel Aviv* in 1925 to parents of Yemenite and Moroccan background. In her youth she was a member of Betar* and the Irgun* and in 1943 she joined LEHI*. Later she was arrested and sentenced to prison by the British authorities in Palestine*. She graduated from Hebrew University* and worked as a journalist. After the Six Day War* she became involved in the question of Soviet Jewry and in 1970 joined Herut*. She was elected to the Eighth Knesset*. She left Herut in June 1979 in opposition to the Camp David Accords* and the Arab-Israeli peace process. She was elected to the 10th and subsequent Knessets on the Tehiya* ticket, a party she helped to found and to lead. The failure of Tehiya to pass the threshold for winning seats in the 13th Knesset (1992) led Cohen to retire from party politics. Nevertheless, she remained a strong supporter of nationalist positions and has been active in promoting Jewish settlement in Judea* and Samaria*. A resident of the West Bank* settlement of Kiryat Arba*, Cohen is a vigorous opponent of the Oslo* peace process. She is the mother of Tzahi Hanegbi*, Likud* MK and Government minister from 1996 to 1999.

For further information see: Aaron D. Rosenbaum, "Tehiya as a Permanent National Phenomenon," in *Israeli National Security Policy: Political Actors and Perspectives*, edited by Bernard Reich and Gershon R. Kieval (New York: Greenwood, 1988): 147-167.

COHEN, RAN. Born in Iraq in 1937, Ran Cohen immigrated to Israel in 1950. Chairman of the Beit Or Aviova organization for the rehabilitation of drug users, he was first elected to the Knesset* in 1984 on the Citizens' Rights Movement (Ratz)* list. He was a member of the CRM Executive Committee and chairman of the party's faction in the Histadrut*and served as Deputy Minister of Construction and Housing from June 1992-January 1993. On May 17, 1999, he was reelected to the 15th Knesset on the Meretz/Democratic Israel* list, and was appointed Minister of Industry and Trade in the Government headed by Ehud Barak*.

COHEN-ORGAD, YIGAL. Born in Tel Aviv*, Yigal Cohen-Orgad is an economist who was trained at Hebrew University* and served as a member of the Knesset* from the Likud*. He served as Finance Minister from the fall of 1983 until the Government of National Unity* acceded to power in the fall of 1984. As Finance Minister, he introduced austerity measures and sought to strengthen the balance of payments through export-led growth and a cut in imports. In order to promote this growth, public and private consumption had to be restricted, and he sought to promote those sectors focusing on production and export. He initiated a variety of budgetary cuts, including the slashing of subsidies, in order to reduce government expenditures. He also initiated new revenue-raising measures, including education fees, taxes on early pensions, higher income tax in the higher brackets, and a cut in fringe benefits for civil servants and public-sector workers. A hardliner on foreign policy, he opposed the Camp David Accords* and the Egypt-Israel Peace Treaty* and promoted continued Jewish settlement in the West Bank* and Gaza Strip*.

COMMISSIONS OF INQUIRY. The Basic Law: Knesset* provides for the creation of Commissions of Inquiry to investigate matters determined by the Knesset. "The Knesset may appoint commissions of inquiry—either by empowering one of the permanent committees in that behalf or by electing a commission from among its members—to investigate matters designated by the Knesset; the powers and functions of a commission of inquiry shall be prescribed by the Knesset; every commission of inquiry shall include also representatives of party groups which do not participate in the Government, in accordance with the relative strength of the party groups in the Knesset." Among the more prominent have been the Agranat*, Ciechanover*, Kahan* and Shamgar* Commissions.

COMMUNIST PARTY. The Communist movement began in Palestine* in 1919 during the British Mandate* and has existed continuously since that time, although it has been plagued by internal divisions and splits. Although isolated from the mainstream of political life and prevented from joining the Government, Communist parties have been legal in Israel since independence and have been represented in the Knesset* continuously. On average, the Communists secure four or five seats in the Knesset.

The Israel Communist Party (Miflaga Kommunistit Yisraelit; Maki) was founded in 1948 and split in 1965. The splinter group, the New Communist List* (Reshima Komunistit Hadasha; Rakah) was pro-Moscow, strongly anti-Zionist, and primarily drew its membership from Israel's Arab population. In 1977 a merger of the Communist Party and the Black Panthers* resulted in the creation of the Democratic Front for Peace and Equality* or Hadash Party*. Drawing on support from disadvantaged classes of Jewish and Arab Israelis, Hadash won four seats in each of the 1981, 1984 and 1988 Knesset* elections. It took three seats in 1992 and five in 1996. Its domestic policy platform focuses on measures to improve the lot of all disadvantaged Israelis and the extension of full rights and opportunities to Israeli Arabs. In foreign and security policy it was among the first political parties to advocate open contacts with the PLO* and complete Israeli withdrawal from the West Bank* and Gaza Strip* and the establishment there of an independent Palestinian state. Since the first Knesset the Communist Party was led by Meir Wilner*, a signer of the Declaration of Independence*. In 1990 the leadership of the party was taken over by Towfik Ziad, the former mayor of the Arab city of Nazareth, who in turn was succeeded by Hashem Mahameed, the former mayor of the Arab village of Umm el Fahm. In November 1997 Mahameed resigned as chairman of Hadash's ruling council, citing his frustration over internal divisions within the party. As the Democratic Front for Peace and Equality-Hadash, the party contested the May 17, 1999, elections under the leadership of Mohammed Barakei, winning three seats in the 15th Knesset.

For further information see: Moshe M. Czudnowski and Jacob M. Landau, *The Israeli Communist Party and the Elections for the Fifth Knesset, 1961* (Stanford University: The Hoover Institution on War, Revolution, and Peace, 1965); Kevin Devlin, *Communism in Israel* (New York: Research Institute on Communist Affairs, Columbia University, 1969); Maurice Friedberg, "The Split in Israel's Communist Party," *Midstream* 12 (February 1966): 19-28; Alain Greilsammer, "Communism in Israel: 13 Years After the Split," *Survey*, 104:3 (Summer 1977-78): 172-92; Walter Z. Laqueur, *Communism and Nationalism in the Middle East*, Second Edition (New York: Frederick A. Praeger, 1957): 73-119; Peretz Merhav, *The Israeli Left: History, Problems, and Documents* (San Diego: A. S. Barnes, 1980); Dunia H. Nahas, *The Israeli Communist Party* (London: Croom Helm, 1976); Sandra Miller Rubenstein, *The Communist Movement in Palestine and Israel, 1919-1984* (Boulder, CO: Westview, 1985).

CONSTITUENT ASSEMBLY. The name applied to the first Knesset* that was elected in January 1949. In March 1948 a temporary National Council of State assumed administrative responsibility over areas of Palestine under Jewish control. It was this body, under the leadership of David Ben-Gurion* and serving as a Provisional Government, that proclaimed Israel's independence on May 14, 1948. It directed the war against the Arab states, levied taxes, and established governmental institutions and social service agencies. It functioned from May 14, 1948 until early 1949. On November 18, 1948, the Provisional Government passed the Constituent Assembly Elections Ordinance, calling for the election of a Constituent Assembly. Two months later the transition ordinance was adopted and the Provisional Government transferred its authority to the Constituent Assembly that was elected on January 25, 1949, and convened for the first time on February 14. Three weeks later it declared itself the First Knesset. On February 16, the Constituent Assembly enacted the Transition Law. For all intents and purposes this law was a mini-constitution, containing chapters on the Knesset, the President, the Government, and other institutions. But the Assembly never formally debated a written constitution. It did table a draft constitution authored by Leo Kohn, a political advisor to Prime Minister David Ben-Gurion, but it did not take up the issue again until it met as the First Knesset.

CONSTITUTION *see* BASIC LAW

CORFU, HAIM. Haim Corfu was born in Jerusalem* in 1921 and studied law at the Hebrew University*. He served on the Jerusalem City Council. In the Seventh and Eighth Knessets* he was a member of the Finance Committee, and in the Ninth Knesset he was a member of both the Defense and Foreign Affairs Committees and the House Committee, as well as being the Coalition Chairman. He is a member of the Herut* Executive. On August 5, 1981, he was sworn in as Minister of Transport and served in that position in the Government of National Unity*.

COUNCIL OF STATE (MOETZET HAMEDINA HAZMANIT). Israel's Declaration of Independence* provided for the transformation of the 37-member People's Council into the Provisional State Council, which was to serve as the country's provisional legislature for the first nine months of independence. The executive arm of the People's Council, the People's Administration, consisting of 13 members, became the Provisional Government by the same instrument. In keeping with its provisional functions, the Council sought to confine its legislative activity to a minimum. Its first enactment was for the continuance in force of virtually the whole body of mandatory law as well as of the regulations and orders that had been issued by the Jewish Agency* for Palestine. Nevertheless, in meeting emergent demands of the new state, the Council, during its short life of 40 weekly sittings, passed 98 ordinances, including important organic laws, fiscal measures, and amendments to mandatory ordinances. The Council met for the last time on February 10, 1949, and ceased to exist with the convocation of the Constituent Assembly* on February 14, 1949.

COUNCIL OF TORAH SAGES (MOETZET GEDOLEI HATORAH). The supreme authority in all matters relating to Agudat Israel*. The Council, instituted in the 1920s, is a group of revered scholars and rabbis, heads of mainly Ashkenazi Yeshivas (religious schools), and members of Hasidic* dynasties who represent the various factions of the Aguda movement. Council members are chosen for their scholarly merit and prestige in the realm of Orthodox Jewry. The Council of Torah Sages continues to be the supreme decision-making body for Aguda adherents, and its decisions are sovereign in all questions affecting the membership, including religious and political matters, such as joining or remaining in a Government coalition. This authority derives from the personal standing and reputation of its members, who have achieved recognition as qualified interpreters of Halacha* and are viewed with high esteem by members of Aguda. The Council traditionally has not permitted its representatives in the Knesset* to accept ministerial appointments, but they have held important committee chairmanships. *See also* SIMCHA BUNIM ALTER.

For further information see: Charles S. Liebman and Asher Cohen, "Synagogue and State: Religion and Politics in Modern Israel," *Harvard International Review* 20 (Spring 1998): 70-73; Gary Schiff, *Tradition and Politics: The Religious Parties of Israel* (Detroit: Wayne State University Press, 1977).

CRM *see* CITIZENS' RIGHTS AND PEACE MOVEMENT

CUNNINGHAM, ALAN GORDON. Born in Dublin in 1887, he was a soldier who served as the last British High Commissioner for Palestine*. He had a distinguished military career and achieved the rank of General in 1945 and in that year was appointed High Commissioner for Palestine. He left Palestine on May 14, 1948, when the State of Israel declared its independence.

For further information see: Zeev Sharef, *Three Days: An Account of the Last Days of the British Mandate and the Birth of Israel* (New York:

Doubleday, 1962); A. J. Sherman, *Mandate Days: British Lives in Palestine 1918-1948* (London: Douglas and McIntyre, 1997).

CZECHOSLOVAKIAN-EGYPTIAN ARMS DEAL. On September 27, 1955, Egyptian President Gamal Abdel Nasser announced an agreement to have Egypt* purchase some $320 million worth of Soviet-built weapons from Czechoslovakia. Payment on an interest-free basis would be spaced out over 12 years in shipments of Egyptian cotton. In addition to the weapons, Czech and Soviet instructors would be sent to Egypt. In a parallel treaty, Syria* purchased from Soviet-bloc countries tanks, MiG jet fighters, artillery pieces, and armored vehicles. The implications of the arms sale were great. Among other things, it emboldened Nasser to continue his hostile behavior toward Israel (including sponsoring and giving safe haven to Palestinian fedayeen* groups operating against Israel from bases in the Egyptian-held Gaza Strip*, and taking steps to re-militarize parts of the Sinai Peninsula* in violation of the 1949 armistice agreement with Israel). These actions in turn caused a heightened sense among Israel's leadership about the long-term security threat posed by Egypt and the need to preempt this threat, thereby accelerating the slide toward war in the fall of 1956. *See also* SINAI WAR.

For further information see: Mordechai Bar-On, *The Gates of Gaza: Israel's Road to Suez and Back, 1955-1957* (London: Macmillan, 1994); Neil Caplan, *Futile Diplomacy, Volume Four: Operation Alpha and the Failure of Anglo-American Coercive Diplomacy in the Arab-Israeli Conflict, 1954-1956* (London: Frank Cass, 1997); Motti Golani, *Israel in Search of a War: The Sinai Campaign 1955-1956* (Brighton, UK: Sussex Academic Press, 1998).

D

DA (DEMOCRACY AND ALIYA, YES). (Russian initials for Demokratia v'Aliyah—democracy and immigration and the Russian word for "yes"). A political party formed in February 1992 by Yuli Kosharovski to represent the interests of Jewish immigrants from the former Soviet Union*. It focused its platform on deregulation of the economy, passage of a civil rights law, separation of religion and politics, and more assistance for Soviet immigrants. It participated in the 1992 election but failed to win seats in the Knesset*.

For further information see: Bernard Reich, Meyrav Wurmser, and Noah Dropkin, "Playing Politics in Moscow and Jerusalem: Soviet Jewish Immigrants and the 1992 Knesset Elections," in *Israel and the Polls 1992*, edited by Daniel J. Elazar and Shmuel Sandler (Lanham, MD: Rowman and Littlefield, 1995): 127-154.

DAKAR. Israeli submarine that sank on its maiden voyage on January 27, 1968. The *Dakar* was built in 1945 and was bought from Great Britain* in June 1965. Along with other craft, it underwent extensive renovations in Portsmouth harbor. On January 8, 1968, the sub left Portsmouth for Haifa, its new home port. It never reached Israel. On January 24, as it was believed to be passing south of Crete, it lost radio contact. There were 69 Israelis on board when it sank. A series of naval searches turned up no trace of the vessel. Thirteen months later, one of its emergency buoys washed ashore in Egypt, but since then there had been nothing. Searches off the Egyptian coast, made possible in the 1980s after relations between Israel and Egypt improved, were unsuccessful. So was a reported expedition near Rhodes, a Greek island that lies close to Turkey's Mediterranean coast. Because the submarine was lost only months after Israel fought a war against Egypt, some theorized that it might have been attacked by Egyptians or their Soviet allies. There was no evidence to support that theory, however, and Israeli experts contend there could have been a collision, fire, mechanical failure, or other accident. Despite the time that had passed, Israel kept the investigation active. Families of the victims banded together in a loose support group, and assembled each year at a memorial that stands in a Jerusalem military cemetery. The wreckage was finally found on May 28, 1999, in the Mediterranean Sea between Crete and Cyprus.

DARAWSHE (DAROUSHA), ABD EL-WAHAB. Born in 1943 in Kfar Iksal, Darawshe is an Israeli Arab* member of the Knesset* who resigned from the Labor Alignment* in March 1988 and was recognized as a one-man parliamentary faction. His Arab Democratic Party* contested the 1988 Knesset election, and he won a seat in parliament. Darawsha's ADP won two seats in the 13th Knesset (1992) and four in the 14th (1996) when it ran on a joint electoral slate with the United Arab List*. The United Arab

List-Arab Democratic Party won five seats in the May 17, 1999, elections to the 15th Knesset. *See also* ARAB POLITICAL PARTIES.

DAVAR (THE WORD). A daily Hebrew*-language newspaper published in Tel Aviv*. It was founded in 1925 by the Histadrut* and was the third Hebrew daily newspaper to appear in Palestine* under the British Mandate*. As a result of the dominance of the labor movement in the leadership of the World Zionist Organization* and the Jewish Agency* under the Mandate and in the Government of Israel after independence, *Davar* became, for all practical purposes, the unofficial organ of the leadership and Government of Israel. It ceased publication in the mid-1990s.

DAYAN, MOSHE. Moshe Dayan was born in Kibbutz Degania* on May 20, 1915, but grew up in Nahalal*. Dayan was one of the first to join the Palmah* when it was established, on May 18, 1941, and served under Orde Wingate in his "night squads" (mobile bands of fighters created to deter night-time Arab terror attacks on isolated Jewish settlements). From 1939 to 1941 Dayan was detained by the British in Acre*, but was released in order to take part in an allied venture against the Vichy French in Syria* in 1941. On June 7, 1941, Dayan headed a squad of Hagana* members who joined the British in an operation which was intended to destroy bridges in Syria. During an assault on a police station he lost his left eye. In July 1948 he was made the commanding officer of Jerusalem*, while it was under siege. In that capacity he took part in informal negotiations with King Abdullah of Jordan* and later served as a member of the Israeli delegation to the armistice negotiations in Rhodes. Between 1950 and 1953 Dayan served as Commander of the Southern and Northern commands of the Israel Defense Forces* and later head of the General Branch of Operations in the General Staff. In December 1953 he was appointed Chief of Staff. He was nominated after a stormy cabinet defense committee meeting, and with David Ben-Gurion's* support.

Dayan led the IDF during the Sinai War of 1956* and was discharged from the IDF in January 1958. In November 1959 he was elected as a member of the Knesset* on the Mapai* list and became Minister of Agriculture in Prime Minister David Ben-Gurion's Government. In 1963 Ben-Gurion left his party over the Lavon Affair* and established Rafi*. After much hesitation Dayan joined Ben-Gurion and Shimon Peres* (who served during this period as Deputy Defense Minister). Nevertheless, he continued to serve as Minister of Agriculture under Prime Minister Levi Eshkol*. Dayan brought to Israeli agriculture methods of long-range planning and national allocation of resources such as water. He resigned from the cabinet on November 4, 1964, when Eshkol tried to prevent him from participating in the formulation of defense policy. In 1965 he was elected to the Sixth Knesset on the Rafi ticket. Dayan went briefly to Vietnam to observe and write about the war.

Just prior to the Six Day War*, by popular demand, Prime Minister Levi Eshkol was forced, against his expressed will, to appoint Dayan to the post of Minister of Defense. Although Dayan did not have time to change the IDF's operational plans, his position as Minister of Defense inspired the country with confidence and helped Eshkol to decide on a preemptive strike. After the war Dayan supported the research and development functions of the Ministry of Defense as a means of replenishing the equipment and ammunition of the IDF, in light of the French arms embargo. He also initiated the open bridges* policy providing an infrastructure for coexistence between Israel and the Arabs. When Eshkol died suddenly in February 1969 and was succeeded by Golda Meir*, Dayan remained as Minister of Defense. He was among those blamed by the public for the delay in the mobilization of Israel's reserve forces at the time of the Yom Kippur War*. Nevertheless, Dayan continued to serve under Meir's leadership after the elections of December 31, 1973.

When Golda Meir resigned in April 1974, however, new Prime Minister Yitzhak Rabin* did not include Dayan in the cabinet. Between 1974 and 1977, Dayan served as a member of the Knesset and was active in archaeological excavations. When Menachem Begin* became Prime Minister after the May 1977 elections Dayan joined the Government as Foreign Minister and in that capacity played a crucial role in the negotiations that led to the Camp David Accords* and the Egypt-Israel Peace Treaty*. Dayan resigned in 1979 over differences of viewpoint and policy between himself and the Prime Minister in regard to autonomy negotiations. On April 4, 1981, Dayan established a new political party, Telem*, which had as one of its primary goals to support Dayan's proposals concerning the occupied territories*. The party secured two mandates in the 1981 Knesset elections. Dayan died on October 16, 1981.

For further information see: Michael Bar-Zohar, *Lionhearts: Heroes of Israel* (New York: Warner, 1998); Moshe Dayan, *Diary of the Sinai*

Campaign (New York: Harper and Row, 1966); Moshe Dayan, "Israel's Border and Security Problems," *Foreign Affairs* 33 (January 1955): 250-267; Moshe Dayan, *Story of My Life* (New York: Morrow, 1976); Moshe Dayan, *Breakthrough: A Personal Account of the Egypt-Israel Peace Negotiations* (New York: Knopf, 1981); Moshe Dayan (with A. Schweitzer), *Israel: The Changing National Agenda* (London: Dover, 1986); Yael Dayan, *My Father, His Daughter* (London: Weidenfeld and Nicolson, 1985); Gabriella Heichal, "Moshe Dayan," in *Political Leaders of the Contemporary Middle East and North Africa*, edited by Bernard Reich (Westport, CT: Greenwood, 1990): 142-150; Pinchas Jorman, editor, *Moshe Dayan: A Portrait* (New York: Dodd Mead, 1969); Naphtali Lau-Lavie, *Moshe Dayan: A Biography* (London: Valentine Mitchell, 1969); Curtis Bill Pepper, "Moshe Dayan: Reflections on a Life of War and Peace," *New York Times Magazine*, May 4, 1980: 36-39, 108, 110-114, 116, 132; Shabtai Teveth, *Moshe Dayan: The Soldier, The Man, The Legend* (Boston: Houghton-Mifflin, 1973); Natan Yanai, *Moshe Dayan on the Peace Process and the Future of Israel* (Tel Aviv: The Defense Military Publishing House, 1988, Hebrew).

DAYAN, YAEL. Born in Palestine* in 1939. Daughter of Moshe Dayan.* Labor* MK. Writer and journalist by profession. Outspoken peace activist, civil libertarian, and feminist.

DEAD SEA. The lowest point on earth. Located about 30 miles east of Jerusalem* and shared by Jordan* and Israel, it is 49 miles long and 11 miles wide, has a 1,309 foot maximum depth, and is 1,299 feet below sea level. Its salty water has a high content of minerals and other chemical elements including: magnesium chloride (52%); sodium chloride (cooking salt, 30%); calcium chloride (12%); potassium chloride (4.36%); and magnesium bromide (1.46%). One of Israel's major industries is the extraction of these minerals from the Dead Sea. The Dead Sea has also become a major tourist attraction for both Israeli and international visitors who seek to benefit from the medicinal value of its mineral waters. The peace treaty with Jordan and interim agreements with the PLO* included provisions for the joint exploitation of Dead Sea minerals and tourism ventures.

DECLARATION OF INDEPENDENCE. The United Nations partition plan* of November 1947 provided for the establishment of a Jewish state in Palestine*. The date of the termination of the British Mandate* was set for May 15, 1948, and with that date nearing, the Zionist General Council decided that the Jewish people would establish an independent regime in their homeland. This decision, put forth in a resolution, paved the way for the Declaration of Independence. A five-man committee was established to prepare the Declaration, and a four-man committee, including David Ben-Gurion*, worked out the final draft. The Declaration of Independence was read on May 14, 1948, and went into effect the following day. The Declaration provides for a Jewish state in the Land of Israel and it recalls the religious and spiritual connection of the Jewish people to the Land of Israel, but it does not mention boundaries. Nevertheless it notes that "it will guarantee freedom of religion and conscience, of language, education, and culture." The document does not address the meaning of a Jewish state or the roles that would be played by religious forces and movements (especially by their political parties) in such an entity.

DECLARATION OF THE ESTABLISHMENT OF THE STATE OF ISRAEL

ERETZ ISRAEL [the Land of Israel] was the birthplace of the Jewish people. Here their spiritual, religious and political identity was shaped. Here they first attained to statehood, created cultural values of national and universal significance and gave to the world the eternal Book of Books.

After being forcibly exiled from their land, the people kept faith with it throughout their Dispersion and never ceased to pray and hope for their return to it and for the restoration in it of their political freedom.

Impelled by this historic and traditional attachment, Jews strove in every successive generation to re-establish themselves in their ancient homeland. In recent decades they returned in their masses. Pioneers, *ma'pilim* [immigrants coming to Eretz Israel in defiance of restrictive legislation] and defenders, they made deserts bloom, revived the Hebrew language, built villages and towns, and created a thriving community, controlling its own economy and culture, loving peace but knowing how to defend itself, bringing the blessings of progress to all the country's inhabitants, and aspiring towards independent nationhood.

In the year 5657 (1897), at the summons of the spiritual father of the Jewish State, Theodor Herzl, the First Zionist Congress convened and proclaimed the right of the Jewish people to national rebirth in its own country.

This right was recognized in the Balfour Declaration of the 2nd November, 1917, and re-affirmed in the Mandate of the League of Nations which, in particular, gave international sanction to the historic connection between the Jewish people and Eretz-Israel and to the right of the Jewish people to rebuild its National Home.

The catastrophe which recently befell the Jewish people—the massacre of millions of Jews in Europe—was another clear demonstration of the urgency of solving the problem of its homelessness by re-establishing in Eretz-Israel the Jewish State, which would open the gates of the homeland wide to every Jew and confer upon the Jewish people the status of a fully-privileged member of the comity of nations.

Survivors of the Nazi holocaust in Europe, as well as Jews from other parts of the world, continued to migrate to Eretz-Israel, undaunted by difficulties, restrictions and dangers, and never ceased to assert their right to a life of dignity, freedom and honest toil in their national homeland.

In the Second World War, the Jewish community of this country contributed its full share to the struggle of the freedom- and peace-loving nations against the forces of Nazi wickedness and, by the blood of its soldiers and its war effort, gained the right to be reckoned among the peoples who founded the United Nations.

On the 29th November, 1947, the United Nations General Assembly passed a resolution calling for the establishment of a Jewish State in Eretz-Israel; the General Assembly required the inhabitants of Eretz-Israel to take such steps as were necessary on their part for the implementation of that resolution. This recognition by the United Nations of the right of the Jewish people to establish their State is irrevocable.

This right is the natural right of the Jewish people to be masters of their own fate, like all other nations, in their own sovereign State.

ACCORDINGLY WE, MEMBERS OF THE PEOPLE'S COUNCIL, REPRESENTATIVES OF THE JEWISH COMMUNITY OF ERETZ-ISRAEL AND OF THE ZIONIST MOVEMENT, ARE HERE ASSEMBLED ON THE DAY OF THE TERMINATION OF THE BRITISH MANDATE OVER ERETZ-ISRAEL AND, BY VIRTUE OF OUR NATURAL AND HISTORIC RIGHT AND ON THE STRENGTH OF THE RESOLUTION OF THE UNITED NATIONS GENERAL ASSEMBLY, HEREBY DECLARE THE ESTABLISHMENT OF A JEWISH STATE IN ERETZ-ISRAEL, TO BE KNOWN AS THE STATE OF ISRAEL.

WE DECLARE that, with effect from the moment of the termination of the Mandate, being tonight, the eve of Sabbath, the 6th Iyar, 5708

(15th May, 1948), until the establishment of the elected, regular authorities of the State in accordance with the Constitution which shall be adopted by the Elected Constituent Assembly not later than the 1st October, 1948, the People's Council shall act as a Provisional Council of State, and its executive organ, the People's Administration, shall be the Provisional Government of the Jewish State, to be called "Israel."

THE STATE OF ISRAEL will be open for Jewish immigration and for the Ingathering of the Exiles; it will foster the development of the country for the benefit of all inhabitants; it will be based on freedom, justice and peace as envisaged by the prophets of Israel; it will ensure complete equality of social and political rights to all its inhabitants irrespective of religion, race or sex; it will guarantee freedom of religion, conscience, language, education and culture; it will safeguard the Holy Places of all religions; and it will be faithful to the principles of the Charter of the United Nations.

THE STATE OF ISRAEL is prepared to cooperate with the agencies and representatives of the United Nations in implementing the resolution of the General Assembly of the 29th November, 1947, and will take steps to bring about the economic union of the whole of Eretz-Israel.

WE APPEAL to the United Nations to assist the Jewish people in the building-up of its State and to receive the State of Israel into the comity of nations.

WE APPEAL—in the very midst of the onslaught launched against us now for months—to the Arab inhabitants of the State of Israel to preserve peace and participate in the upbuilding of the State on the basis of full and equal citizenship and due representation in all its provisional and permanent institutions.

WE EXTEND our hand to all neighbouring states and their peoples in an offer of peace and good neighbourliness, and appeal to them to establish bonds of cooperation and mutual help with the sovereign Jewish people settled in its own land. The State of Israel is prepared to do its share in common effort for the advancement of the entire Middle East.

WE APPEAL to the Jewish people throughout the Diaspora to rally round the Jews of Eretz-Israel in the tasks of immigration and upbuilding and to stand by them in the great struggle for the realization of the age-old dream—the redemption of Israel.

PLACING OUR TRUST IN THE ALMIGHTY, WE AFFIX OUR SIGNATURES TO THIS PROCLAMATION AT THIS SESSION OF THE PROVISIONAL COUNCIL OF STATE, ON THE SOIL OF THE

HOMELAND, IN THE CITY OF TEL-AVIV, ON THIS SABBATH EVE, THE 5TH DAY OF IYAR, 5708 (14 MAY, 1948).

DECLARATION OF PRINCIPLES (SEPTEMBER 13, 1993). A document signed at the White House in Washington, DC, by Israel and the Palestine Liberation Organization*, concluding months of secret negotiations in Olso, Norway, and elsewhere in Europe. The document was signed by Foreign Minister Shimon Peres* and PLO Executive Committee member Mahmoud Abbas (Abu Mazen)*. The signing was witnessed by U.S. President Bill Clinton, Israeli Prime Minister Yitzhak Rabin*, PLO Chairman Yasser Arafat*, U.S. Secretary of State Warren Christopher, and Russian Foreign Minister Andrei Kozyrov. Key provisions of the Declaration of Principles included the following: Israel and the PLO exchanged recognition; the PLO accepted UN Security Council resolutions 242* and 338* as the basis for negotiations and renounced the use of terrorism and violence to resolve outstanding disputes with Israel; the parties agreed to the formation of a Palestinian Interim Self-Government Authority* that would administer areas of the West Bank* and Gaza Strip* during a five-year transitional period leading to a permanent settlement; and there was an agreement to defer until the final status phase of negotiations* (to begin no later than the third year of the interim period) decisions about Jerusalem*, refugees, settlements, security arrangements, borders, relations and cooperation with other neighbors, and other issues of common interest. The Declaration of Principles went into effect on October 13, 1993, and subsequent negotiations led to further interim agreements affecting the Gaza Strip and the West Bank town of Jericho*; the transfer of authority over civil affairs in major Arab population centers in the West Bank; the election of a Palestinian legislative council* and executive committee in January 1996; and the IDF's redeployment from much of the West Bank town of Hebron* in January 1997. *See also* CAIRO AGREEMENT; EARLY EMPOWERMENT AGREEMENT; OSLO ACCORDS; OSLO TWO ACCORDS; WYE RIVER MEMORANDUM.

DEGANIA. The first kibbutz*. In 1909 a group of Russian immigrants built a cooperative worker's settlement located at the exit of the Jordan River* from Lake Kinneret* on a site which commanded the approach to Galilee* and Haifa*, on land purchased by the Jewish National Fund*. Degania was established as a completely integrated communal settlement where its members lived and worked together. Part of the original land was given to another group of settlers who founded Degania Bet in 1919. Subsequently the original settlement became known as Degania Aleph. Degania served as a prototype for all subsequent communal settlements.

For further information see: Henry Near, *The Kibbutz Movement: A History*, 2 volumes (London: The Littman Library of Jewish Civilization, 1992, 1997).

DEGEL HATORAH. A mainly Ashkenazi* ultra-Orthodox religious political party which broke away from Agudat Israel* and secured two seats in the 1988 Knesset* election. The party was founded by Rabbi Eliezer Shach*, the head of the Ponevesher Yeshiva and a former member of the presidium of the Council of Torah Sages* who decided that Agudat Israel* was not loyal to its original ideals and objectives. Among Agudat Israel's faults was its connection to the Chabad Hasidim* and its leader, Rabbi Menachem Mendel Schneerson*, the Lubavitcher Rebbe, which Rabbi Shach considered heretical. The party supported the Likud*-led Government established in June 1990. In 1992 Degel Hatorah agreed to participate with Agudat Israel on a joint electoral list known as United Torah Judaism*, which won four seats in the 13th Knesset. United Torah Judaism took four seats in 1996 and agreed to join the coalition Government headed by Benjamin Netanyahu*, though consistent with its non-Zionist orientation it declined to accept full cabinet portfolios (its leader, Rabbi Meir Porush, served as Deputy Minister of Housing and Construction). Degel Hatorah, again running on a joint platform with Agudat Israel under the United Torah Judaism banner, won a total of five seats in the 15th Knesset in elections held on May 17, 1999. It agreed to join the governing coalition headed by Ehud Barak*, though it would not accept a cabinet portfolio.

DEMJANJUK, JOHN (IVAN THE TERRIBLE). Demjanjuk had entered the United States* after World War II and became an auto worker in Cleveland. He was extradited to Israel in 1985 and lost his U.S. citizenship after the U.S. Justice Department built a case that he was "Ivan the Terrible", the gas chamber operator at the Nazi death camp of Treblinka in World War II. In 1981 his U.S. citizenship was revoked and in 1986 he was extradited to Israel. In 1988 he was found guilty and sentenced to death. He appealed the verdict. On July 29, 1993, the Israeli Supreme Court* nullified the death sentence and overturned his conviction of war crimes on grounds that new evidence from the former

Soviet Union* had created reasonable doubt that he was Ivan the Terrible. He was thus free to leave Israel.

DEMOCRATIC FRONT FOR PEACE AND EQUALITY (HADASH). In 1977 Rakah* and some members of the Israeli Black Panthers* joined to form the Hadash* (acronym for Hazit Demokratit Leshalom Uleshivyon) political party. Hadash, the Democratic Front for Peace and Equality, contested Knesset* elections beginning in 1977. Its program has called for: Israeli withdrawal from all the territories occupied in the Six Day War*; the establishment of an independent Palestinian state; recognition of the Palestine Liberation Organization* as the representative of the Palestinians; and a number of measures to improve the situation of the disadvantaged classes in Israel. The party won three seats in the 15th Knesset and five seats in the 14th Knesset. *See also* COMMUNIST PARTY.

DEMOCRATIC MOVEMENT. One of the remaining units of the Democratic Movement for Change* after it disintegrated in 1978. The Movement remained in the Government coalition, but the party ceased to exist in 1981.

DEMOCRATIC MOVEMENT FOR CHANGE (HATNUA HADEMOCRATIT LESHINUI) (DMC). The DMC was a political party formed in 1976 in order to contest the 1977 Knesset* election. In May 1976 Professor Yigael Yadin* appeared on Israeli television and announced that he would form a new political party to contest the next election with a program that concentrated on domestic political reform. He suggested that the party would play a key role in any future Government coalition. He had decided to enter politics and create the party because, he said, the country urgently needed certain reforms to enable it to combat social and economic ills. Yadin believed that electoral reform must be the nation's first priority because the electoral system, which was based on proportional representation, had created a leadership crisis. He called for reductions in the number of Government ministries and drastic cuts in the Government budget.

The nucleus of the party was soon formed around academic and governmental personalities. The Shinui (Change)* Movement headed by Amnon Rubinstein* joined and the party took the name of Democratic Movement for Change. The DMC contested the 1977 election and won a surprising 15 seats. The unexpected Likud* victory provided the base for the DMC's efforts to influence the nature and direction of Israeli politics. The main goal of the DMC was still to become a partner in the coalition with a significant political role. During the 1977 election campaign it stressed a number of crucial points: it wanted a significant reduction in the number of government ministries; an economic program designed to reduce inflation; programs for disadvantaged areas; electoral reform; and support for DMC views on foreign policy. The DMC soon entered into negotiations to enter the Likud-led Government coalition, but there were problems resulting from divergent foreign policy views and positions. Ultimately the DMC would join the coalition. Unlike other political parties, however, its membership cut across the spectrum of political ideologies and party affiliations. After joining the coalition Government, the party split into several smaller groups and disintegrated by the time of the 1981 Knesset elections.

For further information see: Asher Arian, *The Second Republic: Politics in Israel* (Chatham, NJ: Chatham House, 1998); Miri Bitton, "Third Reformist Parties," PhD Dissertation (City University of New York Press, 1995); Gershon R. Kieval, *Party Politics in Israel and the Occupied Territories* (Westport, CT: Greenwood, 1983); Gregory S. Mahler, *Israel: Government and Politics in a Maturing State* (San Diego: Harcourt Brace Jovanovich, 1990): chapters 5 and 6; Nachman Oricli and Amnon Barzilai, *The Rise and Fall of the DMC* (Tel Aviv: Reshafim, 1982, Hebrew); Bernard Reich and Gershon R. Kieval, *Israel: Land of Tradition and Conflict*, Second Edition (Boulder, CO: Westview, 1993); Amnon Rubinstein, *A Certain Political Experience* (Jerusalem: Idanim, 1982, Hebrew).

DER JUDENSTAAT. Theodor Herzl* was the driving force for the creation of the political ideology and worldwide movement of modern political Zionism*. Herzl wrote *Der Judenstaat (The Jewish State),* published in Vienna on February 14, 1896, in which he assessed the situation and problems of the Jews and proposed a practical plan for resolution of the Jewish question. It contains an examination of the status of the Jewish people and a detailed plan for creating a state in which Jews would reconstitute their national life in a territory of their own. Herzl set forth his concept of a Jewish homeland, believing this was the only solution to the Jewish problem. Herzl's pamphlet was the catalyst for a campaign to influence European leaders on behalf of the Zionist cause. As a result of this initiative, the first World Zionist Congress* was convened in Basle* in 1897, at which the World Zionist Organization* was established. Subsequently, Herzl traveled widely to publicize and gain support for his ideas.

For further information see: Shlomo Avineri, *The Making of Modern Zionism: The Intellectual Origins of the Jewish State* (New York: Basic, 1981): chapter 9; Ben Halpern, *The Idea of the Jewish State*, Second Edition (Cambridge, MA: Harvard, 1970); Joseph Heller, *The Zionist Idea* (New York: Schocken, 1949); Arthur Hertzberg, editor, *The Zionist Idea: A Historical Analysis and Reader* (New York: Atheneum, 1979); Jacques Kornberg, *Thedor Herzl: From Assimilation to Zionism* (Bloomington: Indiana University Press, 1993); Robert Wistrich, "Theodor Herzl: Zionist Icon, Myth-Maker, and Social Utopian," *Israel Affairs* 1:3 (Spring 1995): 7-37.

DERECH ERETZ (MANNERS). A political party, led by Tal Urbach, created to contest the 1969 Knesset* election. It failed to secure the votes necessary to gain a seat in parliament.

DERI, RABBI ARYE. Born in Morocco in 1959, Deri was brought to Israel by his family in 1968. He was educated at Porat Yosef Talmudic College and Yeshivat Hebron in Jerusalem*. He became Secretary General of the Shas* Party in 1985, and has remained in that position since. He became Minister of the Interior in the Government established in December 1988 although he was not a member of the Knesset*, and retained that position in the Government established in June 1990. Under Deri's leadership Shas won six seats in the 13th Knesset (1992) and agreed to join the governing coalition headed by Yitzhak Rabin*, with Deri serving as Interior Minister. However, Shas soon left the coalition over differences with Meretz* about religious policy and because of criminal charges against Deri. These charges precluded Deri's participation in the coalition Government formed by Benjamin Netanyahu* in 1996. On March 17, 1999, at the conclusion of one of the longest trials in Israeli judicial history, Deri was found guilty of charges of bribery, corruption, and abuse of the public trust. The court found that he had developed and sustained an illegal relationship with his old yeshiva friends once in government. The court found that from 1985 to 1989 Deri accepted $155,000 in bribes in exchange for steering substantial public funds to the yeshiva. The directors paid him off partly with the public funds thus diverted. The court determined that the bribes included cash payments as well as trips to New York and London and helped in buying a luxury apartment in Jerusalem. He was also accused of obstruction of justice during the nine-year case. The verdict outraged ultra-Orthodox Sephardic* Jews who see him as a champion of their underclass community. They proclaimed Deri to be a victim of bias against religious Jews and Sephardic Jews of Middle Eastern and North African origin. On April 15, 1999, he was sentenced to four years in prison along with a substantial fine. The conviction was appealed. Deri's conviction became a key issue in the 1999 election campaign, with opposition politicians emphasizing Deri's close personal relationship with Prime Minister Netanyahu as a symbol of the government's overall inefficiency and corruption; with secularist politicians (such as Shinui's* Yossi (Tommy) Lapid*) linking Deri's crimes to the alleged overall corruption of the ultra-Orthodox political parties; and with many of Deri's supporters rallying around him and Shas in the belief that his conviction was a politically motivated act designed to discriminate against both Sephardi* and ultra-Orthodox segments of Israeli society. During the 1999 election campaign, One Israel* leader Ehud Barak* declared his determination not to invite Shas into his coalition Government so long as Arye Deri remained the party's political leader. This declaration posed a serious dilemma for Rabbi Ovadia Yosef* and other leaders of Shas: They could retain Deri as their political leader but remain outside of government (and hence, without direct access to power and influence), or they could distance themselves from Deri in order to join the Barak-led coalition. After much soul-searching, Deri announced his formal resignation from the Knesset and from all of Shas's political activities, on June 16, 1999. This decision was approved by Rabbi Yosef and the other members of Shas's Council of Torah Sages, thereby opening the way for Shas to enter the Government on July 6, 1999. Meanwhile, Deri awaited the results of the appeal of his conviction. Deri began to make an impact on the Israeli political system while still in his twenties.

DEVELOPMENT TOWNS. Towns built in Israel since independence, primarily in regions remote from the old population centers. They were begun in the 1950s and had several goals. These included the dispersal of population and industry for both economic and security reasons and the development of administrative and economic centers for the more rural areas of the country. The idea was to create new urban centers, as opposed to additional farming villages which had been the pattern in the pre-state period. This would also provide facilities for the absorption and integration of the large numbers of new immigrants to the country. Among the development towns are Kiryat Shmona, Maalot, Karmiel, Migdal Haemek, Bet Shemesh, Ashdod*, Netivot, Arad*, Dimona*, and Mitzpe Ramon.

For further information see: Calvin Goldscheider, *Israel's Changing Society: Population, Ethnicity, and Development* (Boulder, CO: Westview, 1996); Calvin Goldscheider, "Creating a New Society: Immigration, Nation-Building, and Ethnicity in Israel," *Harvard International Review* 20:2 (Spring 1998): 64-69; Arie Shachar, "Reshaping the Map of Israel: A New National Planning Doctrine," *The Annals of the American Academy of Political and Social Science* 555 (January 1998): 209-218.

DIASPORA. A Greek word meaning "scattering," that has been used since the Babylonian exile of 586 BCE to refer to the dispersion of the Jews and the Jewish communities outside of Israel. It is interchangeable with the Hebrew* term *Golah*. The "ingathering of the exiles," the return of Jews in the Diaspora to the spiritual homeland in biblical Eretz Israel*, is a driving force in Jewish liturgy and in modern political Zionism. The relationship between Israel and Diaspora Jewish communities has gone through various emotional phases, ranging from ambivalence and mutual mistrust to limited and guarded cooperation to dependence. Although complex, the present relationship may be best described as "interdependent," in which Israelis receive the benefits of financial, political, and moral support of their coreligionists in Jewish communities outside of Israel, at the same time that Diaspora Jewry draws spiritual strength, pride, and a sense of unity from the tremendous accomplishments of the Jewish State.

For further information see: Arthur Hertzberg, "Israel and the Diaspora: A Relationship Reexamined," *Israel Affairs* 2:3&4 (Spring/Summer 1996): 169-183; Charles S. Liebman, "Restoring Israeli-Diaspora Relations," *Israel Studies* 1:1 (Spring 1996): 315-322; Gabriel Sheffer, "Israel-Diaspora Relations in Comparative Perspective," in *Israel in Comparative Perspective: Challenging the Conventional Wisdom*, edited by Michael N. Barnett (Albany: State of New York Press, 1996): 53-83; David Vital, "Israel and the Jewish Diaspora: Five Comments on the Political Relationship," *Israel Affairs* 1:2 (Winter 1994): 171-187.

DIMONA. A development town in the central Negev*. Founded in 1955, its name is derived from the book of Joshua in the Bible. It has become a center for textile and other manufacturing activities. Israel, with French technical assistance, established a uranium/heavy water nuclear reactor in Dimona in 1964.

DINITZ, SIMHA. Born in Tel Aviv* in June 1929, Simha Dinitz was educated in the United States* (University of Cincinnati and Georgetown University) where he received bachelors and masters degrees. He served as political adviser to Prime Minister Golda Meir*, Director General of Prime Minister Meir's office (1969-1973) and Ambassador to the United States (1973-1978). Later he served as Vice President of Hebrew University* and then as a Labor Alignment* member of the Knesset*. He then became Chairman of the World Zionist Organization* and Jewish Agency*, a position which he was subsequently compelled to relinquish in the context of charges of financial impropriety. His conviction on these charges was reversed on appeal to the Supreme Court*.

For further information see: David Horovitz, "Chairman of the Bored: He's Been Cleared of Fraud Now, but Former Jewish Agency Head Simha Dinitz Knows There's No Resurrecting His High-flying Career," *The Jerusalem Report* (December 25, 1997): 24-25; Golda Meir, *My Life* (London: Weidenfeld and Nicolson, 1975): chapter 14; Tom Sawicki, "Dinitz and $: The Jewish Agency at a Crossroads," *Moment* (December 1993): 45-49, 92-95.

DIRECTOR OF MILITARY INTELLIGENCE (DMI). The Director of Military Intelligence heads the Intelligence Branch (AMAN, acronym for Agaf Modiin) of the Israel Defense Forces* General Staff. Its function is to provide intelligence for the planning of Israel's defense policy and for war and to provide intelligence to the IDF and other government bodies, especially the cabinet. The first head of AMAN was Isar Beeri (1948-1949). He was followed by Chaim Herzog* (1949-1950 and 1959-1962). Benjamin Gibli served from 1950 to 1955. Yehoshafat Harkabi held the post from 1955 to 1959. Subsequent Directors included: Meir Amit, 1962 to 1964; Aharon Yariv, 1964 to 1972; Eliahu Zeira, 1972 to 1974; Shlomo Gazit, 1974 to 1978; Yehoshua Saguy, 1978 to 1983; Ehud Barak*, 1983 to 1985; Amnon Lipkin-Shahak*, 1986-1991; Uri Saguy, 1991-1995; Moshe Ya'alon, 1995-May 1998; and Amos Malcha, May 1998- .

DISENGAGEMENT OF FORCES *see* ISRAEL-EGYPT DISENGAGEMENT OF FORCES AGREEMENT (1974); ISRAEL-SYRIA DISENGAGEMENT OF FORCES AGREEMENT (1974)

DMC *see* DEMOCRATIC MOVEMENT FOR CHANGE

DOP *see* ISRAEL-PLO DECLARATION OF PRINCIPLES

DORI, YAACOV. Born in Odessa, Russia, in 1899 he was brought to Palestine* as a child and joined the Jewish Legion*. He later studied engineering in Belgium. After returning to Palestine he joined the Technical Department of the Zionist Executive and became active in the Hagana*. He became Chief of Staff of the Hagana in 1938 and in 1948-1949 he was Chief of Staff of the Israel Defense Forces*. In this capacity he commanded the Israeli army in the War of Independence*. From 1951 to 1965 he served as president of the Technion*.

DOR SHALOM (AN ENTIRE NATION DEMANDS PEACE). An extraparliamentary interest group advocating continuation of the peace process with the Palestinians on the basis of the Oslo Accords*. It also advocated reconciliation among Israeli Jews on religious issues and equality among all Israelis in education and social and economic affairs. One of its founders and public spokesmen was Yuval Rabin, son of the assassinated Prime Minister, Yitzhak Rabin*.

DREYFUS, ALFRED. A French Jew and artillery captain attached to the general staff of the French army. In 1894, he was accused of selling military secrets to Germany and placed on trial for espionage and treason. He was tried by a military court and sentenced to life in prison. His sentence was contested by a minority group consisting mainly of intellectuals, called "Dreyfusards," who claimed the evidence against Dreyfus was based on forged documents. Among other developments, it led Emile Zola to write his famous article *"J'accuse"* in 1898. Public opinion became so aroused that the military was forced to reopen the case. Dreyfus was again found guilty, but the sentence was reduced to ten years in prison. Dissatisfaction with the verdict persisted, and in 1906 Dreyfus was exonerated. The sharp controversy which the case triggered caused a wave of anti-Semitic demonstrations and riots throughout France. The Dreyfus trial was considered an important indicator of growing anti-Jewish sentiment in Europe and helped to awaken a Jewish nationalistic feeling. Theodor Herzl* covered the first Dreyfus trial as a newspaper correspondent and later said that this convinced him that assimilation was not the solution to the problem of anti-Semitism*.

DRUCKMAN, HAIM. Born in Poland in 1933 and immigrated to Palestine* in 1944, he was one of the founders of the Bnai Akiva youth movement. He split from the National Religious Party* and helped to establish the Morasha (Heritage) Party*. He was elected to the Eleventh Knesset* on the Morasha list. A founder of the militant Gush Emunim*, he is a forceful opponent of territorial compromise in the occupied territories*, suggesting that it is consistent with Halacha* (Jewish law) for soldiers to disobey orders to evacuate Jewish settlements. In 1997 and 1998 Rabbi Druckman headed a committee of representatives of various streams of Judaism mandated to achieve compromise on the status of adopted children converted to Judaism outside of Israel. Druckman was inserted into the number two slot on the NRP's list of candidates for the May 17, 1999 elections to the 15th Knesset and was reelected.

DRUZE (DRUSE). The Druze are a self-governing religious community that broke from Islam in the 11th century, whose members live primarily in Syria* and Lebanon*. They number some 90,000 (about 9% of Israel's non-Jewish population). Their religious practices are highly secretive and complex and the community is very tightly knit. The Druze are considered a separate community by the state of Israel, and they are the only Arabs conscripted into the Israel Defense Forces*. Druze soldiers have fought in all the Arab-Israeli wars for Israel.

For further information see: Gabriel Ben-Dor, *The Druzes in Israel: A Political Study* (Jerusalem: Magnes, 1979); Gabriel Ben-Dor, "An Overview of Israeli-Druze Relations," in *The Constitutional and Political Status of Minorities in Israel: The Druze Community*, edited by Shari Hillman (Washington, DC: The Israel Colloquium, May 1994); Nissim Dana, *The Druze: A Religious Community in Transition* (Jerusalem: Turtledove, 1980); Philip K. Hitti, *The Origins of the Druze People and Religion, with Extracts from their Sacred Writings* (New York: AMS Press, 1969); Sami N. Makerem, *The Druze Faith* (New York: Caravan, 1974); Laila Parsons, "The Palestinian Druze in the 1947-1949 Arab-Israeli War," *Israel Studies* 2:1 (Spring 1997): 72-93.

DULZIN, ARYE LEON. Born in Minsk, Russia*, on March 31, 1913, he emigrated to Mexico in 1928 where he became active in Zionist matters. He served as Secretary General of the Zionist Federation of Mexico and as its President (from 1938 to 1942). He settled in Israel in 1956 and became a member of the Executive of the Jewish Agency*. He served on a number of other boards and in various executive positions and was involved in the activities of the Liberal Party*. In 1969 he became Minister without Portfolio. He served as Treasurer of the Jewish Agency from 1968 to 1978 and was elected Chairman of the World Zionist Organization* and Jewish Agency in 1978. He retired in 1987. In 1986 he broke with the Liberal Party* and helped to form the Liberal Center Party*. He died in Tel Aviv in September 1989.

E

EARTHQUAKE. The Yom Kippur War* resulted in an Israeli military victory, but unleashed tensions in the economic, political, and psychological arenas in Israel. Protest groups focusing on various aspects of the resulting situation were formed. Israelis were concerned with war losses, the failure of military intelligence, initial battlefield reverses, questions about war-associated political decisions, and deteriorating economic and social conditions at home accompanied by diplomatic reverses abroad. This malaise affected the body politic during much of the tenure of Yitzhak Rabin* as Prime Minister (1974 to 1977), but seemed to reach a crucial level in conjunction with the 1977 Knesset* election when many of the forces set in motion by the Yom Kippur War and its aftermath seemed to coalesce, causing a major fissure in the political landscape in Israel. The body politic gave the largest number of votes to the Likud*, led by Menachem Begin*, and Labor* lost a substantial number of seats compared to the 1973 election. The results ended Labor's dominance of Israeli political life that had begun in the Yishuv* period. Menachem Begin subsequently formed a Likud-led coalition Government. This sudden shift in political direction, together with the aftershocks it caused, have been likened to an "earthquake," the descriptive term often attached to this period in Israeli political development.

EAST FOR PEACE (HAMIZRACH LESHALOM). An Oriental-based peace group organized by a group of intellectuals after the War in Lebanon* in part to counter the hardline image of Oriental Jews*. This group believes that peace is essential for Israel and that Oriental Jews should play a role in the effort to achieve it.

EAST JERUSALEM *see* JERUSALEM

EBAN, ABBA (FORMERLY AUBREY). Born in Cape Town, South Africa, in 1915 to Lithuanian-Jewish parents, he grew up in England. While a student of Oriental languages and classics at Cambridge University, he founded the University Labour Society, was president of the Students' Union, and was active in debating and Zionist* circles. During World War II, he served as a major to the British minister of state in Cairo and then as an intelligence officer in Jerusalem*. In 1946 he became the political information officer in London for the Jewish Agency*, and in the following year, the liaison officer for the Jewish Agency with the United Nations Special Committee on Palestine*. In May 1948, he became Israel's permanent delegate to the United Nations. From 1950 to 1959, he served as both Israel's Ambassador to the United States* and to the United Nations. In 1959, he was elected to the Knesset* on the Mapai* list. He served as Minister of Education and Culture from 1960 to 1963, and was Deputy Prime Minister in 1964 to 1965. He also served as President of the Weizmann Institute of Science* at Rehovot from 1959 to 1966. In 1966, he became Minister of Foreign Affairs, a position which he held until 1974. He served as chairman of the Knesset Committee for Security and Foreign Affairs from 1984 to 1988. In 1988 the Labor Party* dropped him from its list of candidates for the Knesset election. Retired from party politics, he continued to be a keen observer of and prolific commentator about foreign and security policy and Israel's place in the international system.

For further information see: Abba Eban, *Voice of Israel* (New York: Horizon, 1957); Abba Eban, *The Tide of Nationalism* (New York: Horizon, 1959); Abba Eban, *My People: The Story of the Jews* (New York: Random House, 1969); Abba Eban, *An Autobiography* (New York: Random House, 1977); Abba Eban, *The New Diplomacy: International Affairs in the Modern Age* (New York: Random House, 1983); Abba Eban, *Personal Witness: Israel through My Eyes* (New York: Putnam's, 1982); Abba Eban, *Diplomacy for the Next Century* (New Haven, CT:

Yale University Press, 1998); Robert St. John, *Eban* (New York: Doubleday, 1972).

EDELSTEIN, YULI (YOEL). Born in 1958 in Chernovitz, USSR*, he studied foreign languages at the Moscow Institute for Teacher Training. In 1977 he asked for an exit visa from the Soviet Union but was refused. Eventually he was sent to prison as a Prisoner of Zion*. He was set free on the eve of Israeli Independence Day in 1987 and he immigrated to Israel. In 1990 he graduated from the Jerusalem Fellows Program, and from 1990-1993 he was a department head at the Melitz Center for Zionist Education. In 1993-1994, he served as an adviser to then opposition leader Benjamin Netanyahu*. A founding member of the Israel B'Aliya* Party in 1996, he was first elected to the 14th Knesset* on the party's list. He served as Minister of Immigrant Absorption under Netanyahu from 1996 to June 1999. He was reelected to the 15th Knesset on May 17, 1999.

EDOT HAMIZRACH *see* ORIENTAL JEWS

EDRI, RAPHAEL. Born in Morocco in 1937, he served as Director General of Shikun Ovdim housing company. He served as a Labor Party* member of the Knesset* beginning in 1981. He became Minister without Portfolio in the Government established in December 1988.

EDUCATION. Education has been a priority for Israel since independence although there was already a substantial growth of Jewish education under the British Mandate*. During its initial years the educational system was characterized by tremendous expansion, which resulted from large-scale immigration (primarily from the Middle East and North Africa with large numbers of children) and the Compulsory Education Law of 1949. The educational system required facilities and teachers to deal with these needs and initially there were shortages of both. The system faced additional challenges created by the substantial immigration from numerous countries with different linguistic and educational backgrounds. The challenge to revive Hebrew* as a living language and the centerpiece of the system was compounded by the need to blend the cultures of the numerous immigrants from the various countries of the world.

Education is a basic element of Jewish tradition and is given a high priority in Israeli society. In 1949 the Knesset* passed the Compulsory

Education Law which made regular school attendance obligatory for all children from age five to 14 and tuition fees were abolished in government schools for these nine years. Since 1978 school attendance has been mandatory to age 16 and free to age 18.

Because of the special characteristics of Israel's major communities—Jewish, Arab*, and Druze*—which differ in language, history, and culture, two basic school systems are maintained: the Jewish system (which is itself separated into a "secular" and a religious system), with instruction in Hebrew; and the Arab/Druze system, with instruction in Arabic. Both systems are financed by and accountable to the Ministry of Education and Culture, but enjoy a large measure of internal independence. The Arab/Druze education system, with separate schools for Arab and Druze pupils, provides the standard academic and vocational curricula, adapted to emphasize Arab or Druze culture and history. Religious instruction in Islam or Christianity is provided by Arab schools if the community elders so determine. Due to the Compulsory Education Law and changes in traditional Arab/Druze attitudes toward formal education, there has been a substantial increase in general school attendance, particularly at the high school level, as well as in the number of female pupils. Higher education was begun during the British Mandate with the establishment of the Hebrew University* in Jerusalem* in 1925; the Technion*, known also as the Israel Institute of Technology in Haifa* in 1924; and the Weizmann Institute of Science* in Rehovot in 1934. Since independence additional institutions have been created including Bar-Ilan University* (1955), Tel Aviv University (1956), Haifa University (1963), and Ben-Gurion University* (1969).

Israel has one of the highest rates of post-secondary education in the world, as well as significant achievements in academic-based scientific and industrial research and development.

For further information see: Walter Ackerman, "Making Jews: An Enduring Challenge in Israeli Education," *Israel Studies* 2:2 (Fall 1997): 1-20; Daniel J. Elazar, "Education in a Society at a Crossroads: An Historical Perspective of Israeli Education," *Israel Studies* 2:2 (Fall 1997): 40-65; Yaacov Iram and Mirjam Schmida, *The Educational System of Israel* (Westport, CT: Greenwood Press, 1998).

EFRAT (ALSO KNOWN AS EFRATA). A middle-class settlement community located in the hills of Judea* between Jerusalem* and Hebron*. Founded in 1980, it is the "urban center" of the Etzion Bloc* of settlements. It is essentially a "bedroom community," with many of its 6,000 residents commuting daily to workplaces in Jerusalem and elsewhere inside the Green Line*. Efrat is also considered one of the most "American" of all settlements; one of its founders—and its spiritual leader—is Shlomo Riskin, a U.S.-born rabbi who brought many of his congregants with him to Israel.

EGYPT. Israel's neighbor to the west and the southwest with which it fought in the War of Independence*, the Sinai War*, the Six Day War*, the War of Attrition*, and the Yom Kippur War*.

During the War of Independence Egyptian forces succeeded in retaining a portion of the territory that was to have been a part of the Arab state in Palestine* and known since as the Gaza Strip*. Egypt retained the territory under military control until 1967, except for a brief period in 1956-1957 when Israel held the territory during and immediately after the Sinai War. Following the Egyptian revolution and the accession of Gamal Abdul Nasser to power in the 1950s the stage was set for a second round of warfare. Cross-border raids from Gaza into Israel and a substantial increase in the armaments of the Egyptian army (via the Czech-Egypt* arms deal of 1955), as well as the increased activism of the Nasser regime, helped to provide the context for the Sinai War. The conclusion of that conflict was followed by a decade of relative calm along the Egypt-Israel frontier which was broken by the Six Day War, in which Israel took the Gaza Strip and the Sinai Peninsula*. The War of Attrition* initiated by Nasser in the spring of 1969 was terminated by a cease-fire in the summer of 1970. The Egyptian- and Syrian-initiated Yom Kippur War of October 1973 was followed by movement in the direction of a settlement. United States* Secretary of State Henry Kissinger helped to arrange an Israeli-Egyptian disengagement agreement*, which was signed in January 1974 and the Sinai II* agreement of September 1975. Following the 1977 initiative of President Anwar Sadat*, Israel and Egypt began negotiations for peace, which led to the Camp David Accords* in September 1978 and the Egypt-Israel Peace Treaty* of March 1979. Peace and the normalization of relations followed—ambassadors were exchanged, trade and tourism developed, and continued contacts were sustained between the two states. Nevertheless, the relationship between the two countries could best be characterized by the concept of a "cold peace" in which formal ties exist and some intercourse occurs but links could not be characterized as friendly or warm in nature. There are continuing differences between Cairo and Jerusalem over the peace talks with the Palestinians as well as over Egyptian concerns about Israel's place in a "new Middle East," one premised on economic strength and industrial productivity.

For further information see: Yaacov Bar-Siman-Tov, *Israel and the Peace Process 1977-1982: The Search of Legitimacy for Peace* (Albany: State University of New York Press, 1994); Moshe Dayan, *Breakthrough: A Personal Account of the Egypt-Israel Peace Negotiations* (New York: Knopf, 1981); Shawn Pine, "Myopic Vision: Whither Israeli-Egyptian Relations?" *Israel Affairs* 3:3&4 (Spring/Summer 1997): 321-334; Howard Sachar, *Egypt and Israel* (New York: Marek, 1981); Kenneth W. Stein, "Continuity and Change in Egyptian-Israeli Relations, 1973-1997," *Israel Affairs* 3:3&4 (Spring/Summer 1997): 296-320.

EGYPT-ISRAEL DISENGAGEMENT OF FORCES AGREEMENT (1974) *see* ISRAEL-EGYPT DISENGAGEMENT FORCES AGREEMENT

EGYPT-ISRAEL PEACE TREATY (1979). A peace treaty signed in Washington, in March 1979, between the Arab Republic of Egypt and the State of Israel, under the auspices of the United States* which ended the state of war between the two countries. *See also* MENACHEM BEGIN; CAMP DAVID ACCORDS; JIMMY CARTER; ANWAR SADAT.

For further information see: Yaacov Bar-Siman-Tov, *Israel and the Peace Process 1977-1982: The Search of Legitimacy for Peace* (Albany: State University of New York Press, 1994); Zbigniew Brzezinski, *Power and Principles: Memoirs of the National Security Adviser 1977-1981* (New York: Farrar, Strauss, and Giroux, 1983); Jimmy Carter, *Keeping Faith: Memoirs of a President* (New York: Bantam, 1982); Moshe Dayan, *Breakthrough: A Personal Account of the Egypt-Israel Peace Negotiations* (New York: Knopf, 1981); Eitan Haber, Zeev Schiff and Ehud Yaari, *The Year of the Dove* (New York: Bantam, 1979); Ezer Weizman, *The Battle for Peace* (New York: Bantam, 1981).

EHRLICH, SIMHA. Born in Lublin, Poland, in 1915, Simha Ehrlich received a traditional Jewish education and at an early age became an active member of the General Zionist Youth Movement, emigrating to Palestine* at the age of 19. During his first years in the country he worked as an agricultural laborer and studied commerce and economics. He began his public and political career in the Union of General Zionists and rose through its ranks. He was elected to the Tel Aviv* Municipal Council in 1955 and continued to serve on it until his election to the 7th Knesset* in 1969. In 1962 he became Deputy Mayor of Tel Aviv. He also became President of the National Secretariat of the Liberal Party* and later, Chairman of its National Secretariat and member of the Gahal* Executive Committee. During the 7th and 8th Knessets, Ehrlich served on the Knesset Finance Committee and was Chairman of its Subcommittee for the Defense Budget. In the 9th Knesset, he served as Minister of Finance from June 1977 until November 1979 when he was appointed Deputy Prime Minister. While serving as Finance Minister he declared a new economic plan designed to eliminate the government from the economy and apply free market principles. The plan sought to modify the existing socialist system, check inflation, cut the foreign trade deficit, increase the growth rate, and promote foreign investment. On August 5, 1981, following his reelection to the 10th Knesset, he was sworn in as Deputy Prime Minister and Minister of Agriculture. He died in 1983.

EICHMANN, ADOLF. Born in Solingen, Germany, on March 19, 1906, Adolf Eichmann was a German SS officer who presided over the implementation of Adolf Hitler's "final solution," the extermination of European Jews. Captured by the Americans at the end of the war, Eichmann escaped to Argentina* where he was recaptured by Israeli agents in 1960. Eichmann was tried in public on charges of crimes against the Jewish people and war crimes against humanity. The trial began in Jerusalem* on April 11, 1961, and on December 11, 1961, the court found him guilty and sentenced him to death. After appeals he was executed on May 31, 1962. The trial focused world attention on the tragedy of European Jewry and the systematic efforts of Nazi Germany to exterminate the Jewish communities of Europe in the Holocaust*.

For further information see: Hannah Arendt, *Eichmann in Jerusalem: A Report on the Banality of Evil* (New York: Viking, 1964); Isser Harel, *The House on Garibaldi Street: The First Full Account of the Capture of Adolph Eichmann* (New York: Viking, 1975); Gideon Hausner, *Justice in Jerusalem* (New York: Harper and Row, 1966); Pnina Lahav, *Judgement in Jerusalem: Simon Agranat and the Zionist Century*

(Berkeley, CA: University of California Press, 1997); Dewey W. Linze, *The Trial of Adolf Eichmann* (Los Angeles: Holloway House, 1961); Henry A. Zeiger, editor, *The Case against Adolf Eichmann* (New York: New American Library, 1960).

EILAT (ELAT, ELATH). Israel's southernmost city, it is a deepwater port on the Gulf of Aqaba* connecting Israel with the Red Sea and the Indian Ocean. It is named for the ancient city of Eilat which is mentioned in the Bible as a city through which the Israelites passed during their desert wanderings. It later served as a port city for numerous empires and conquerors of the area. Prior to the opening of the Suez Canal to Israeli shipping, Eilat was Israel's major gateway for goods from the Far East, the Indian Ocean, Asia, and East Africa. Eilat's natural beauty and seaside location make it a year-round resort. Modern Eilat was founded in 1948. Its importance increased after 1950 when Egypt* banned Israeli ships from the Suez Canal. Without the canal, the Gulf of Aqaba became Israel's only outlet to the Red Sea. But Egypt also blocked the entrance to the Gulf at the Strait of Tiran*. The Gulf was opened as a result of the Sinai War of 1956*. Eilat then grew rapidly in both size and importance. Egypt's blockade of the Gulf in 1967 was a major cause of the Six Day War*. Eilat also serves as an important center for oil distribution; a pipeline carries oil from the city to Israel's Mediterranean coast and from there it is either exported or sent to a refinery in Haifa*.

EITAN, RAPHAEL (FORMERLY KAMINSKY; NICKNAMED "RAFUL"). Born in 1929 in Tel Adashim, he pursued a military career. He was educated at Tel Aviv* and Haifa universities. He joined the Palmah* at the age of 17. He served as chief of staff of the Israel Defense Forces* from 1978 to 1983. He first joined the Knesset* in 1984 on the Tehiya*-Tsomet* list. In 1988 Eitan and Tsomet ran as a separate electoral list, winning two Knesset seats. In June 1990 Tsomet joined the Shamir*-led coalition, with Eitan serving as Minister of Agriculture. Initially expressing an interest in running for the direct election of the Prime Minister in 1996, Eitan ultimately agreed to withdraw his candidacy and to have Tsomet enter into a joint electoral list along with Likud* and Gesher*. Eitan served as Minister of Agriculture and Rural Development, Minister of the Environment, and Deputy Prime Minister in the Government formed after the May 1996 election. He and Tsomet failed to pass the threshold for winning seats in the elections to the 15th Knesset held on May 17, 1999.

EL AL (UPWARD). Israel's national airline. One of the first decisions of the new State of Israel after independence was to establish a national airline to ensure that the country surrounded by hostile neighbors, would have an air link to the outside world. Among its first activities was flying whole communities of immigrants to Israel. It has grown to become a significant international air carrier.

On September 30, 1948, Chaim Weizmann*, flying from Geneva to be sworn in as Israel's first President, arrived aboard an Israeli Air Force DC-4 repainted and re-registered one day earlier as a commercial aircraft bearing the name El Al. On November 15, 1948, El Al was legally incorporated as Israel's national airline. On July 22, 1968, Palestinian skyjackers forced an El Al jetliner to land in Algeria. On December 26, 1968, terrorists attacked an El Al jet at the airport in Athens, prompting the airline to use special guards as its regular security force. On February 18, 1969, terrorists attacked an El Al airliner at Zurich airport. On September 6, 1970, El Al security repelled an attempted skyjacking by a Palestinian terrorist group. On June 6, 1994, a Cabinet committee recommended the sale of 51% of El Al to private investors; the offering was postponed in late 1995 after the assassination of Prime Minister Yitzhak Rabin*.

ELAZAR, DAVID (NICKNAMED "DADO"). Born in Zagreb, Yugoslavia, in 1925, he was brought to Palestine* as part of the Youth Aliya* in 1940. In 1946 he joined the Palmah*. In the War of Independence* he participated in the fighting for Jerusalem* and later in the Sinai Peninsula*. After a period as a training officer and as an operations officer in the Central Command he took a leave of absence in 1953 to study economics and Middle Eastern studies at Hebrew University*. In the Sinai War of 1956* he fought in the Gaza Strip*. In 1961 he was promoted to the rank of Major General. In November 1964 he was appointed Commander of the Northern Command which, during the 1967 war, captured the Golan Heights*. He was appointed head of the Staff Branch in 1969 and he served as the chief of staff of the Israel Defense Forces* from January 1972 until April 1974. He resigned in April 1974 after the release of the findings of the Agranat Commission of Inquiry* which blamed him for the initial setbacks at the beginning of the Yom Kippur War*, for excessive confidence in the ability of the army to contain the Egyptian and Syrian attacks without calling up the reserves, and for incorrect assessments and a lack of preparedness of the IDF at the outbreak of the war. The commission recommended the termination of his role as Chief of Staff. He later joined the ZIM shipping company as Managing Director and died in April 1976.

ELIAV, ARIE (NICKNAMED "LOVA"). Born in Moscow in 1921 he immigrated to Palestine* with his parents in 1924. Eliav was educated at Herzliya High School* in Tel Aviv*. He served in the Hagana* from 1936 to 1940 and from 1940 to 1945 with the British army. He served in the IDF* during the War of Independence*. From 1958 to 1960 Arie Eliav served as the First Secretary in the Israeli Embassy in Moscow. He served as the Secretary General of the Labor Party* from 1969 until 1971. Following the Six Day War*, Eliav became increasingly critical of the Labor Party, particularly its policies toward the Arab population. He eventually split from Labor, and formed a leftist group called the Independent Socialists. In 1977 this party joined other leftist groups and formed the Shelli (Peace for Israel) Party*. The party advocated the establishment of an Arab Palestinian state alongside Israel, Israel's withdrawal to pre-1967 borders, and negotiations with the Palestine Liberation Organization*. After serving in the Knesset* for 13 years, Eliav resigned in 1977. He rejoined the Israel Labor Party in 1986 and was elected to the Knesset in 1988 on the Maarach* list. He received the Israel Prize* in 1988.

EMIGRATION. Despite the fact that since 1948 Israel successfully absorbed some 2.7 million immigrants, there was also the phenomenon of emigration from the country. Essentially, persons leaving the country for long-term absences and de facto emigration belonged to one of three distinct groups: former immigrants returning to their country of origin; former immigrants emigrating to a third country; emigrants who were born and raised in Israel. Historically, the number of emigrants was always only a small proportion of the overall population and was outweighed by the number of immigrants to the country. Nevertheless, relatively large expatriate communities (totalling some 500,000 by 1997) arose in the United States* (350,000), Canada (40,000), France* (40,000), Great Britain* (30,000), South Africa (20,000), Germany* (8,000), and Australia (5,000). Inasmuch as it was inconsistent with the core principles of Zionism*, emigration from Israel was always treated derisively (indeed, the term used to describe the act of leaving the country, *yerida*, translates literally as "going down" or "descending", as in "going down from Zion"). Nevertheless, over the years efforts were made to entice Israelis residing outside the country to return home. Some of these efforts bore fruit, especially in the early 1990s as the economy grew and the prospects for peace improved. *See also* DIASPORA.

For further information see: Calvin Goldscheider, *Israel's Changing Society: Population, Ethnicity, and Development* (Boulder, CO: Westview, 1996).

ENGLAND *see* GREAT BRITAIN

ENTEBBE AIRPORT RAID *see* ENTEBBE OPERATION

ENTEBBE OPERATION. On July 4, 1976, an Israeli commando operation, codenamed "Thunderbolt," freed 103 hostages taken from a hijacked jetliner and held at Entebbe airport, Uganda. The jetliner, Air France flight 139 originating in Tel Aviv*, was hijacked on June 27, 1976, by Arab and German terrorists on a flight between Athens and Paris. The plane was flown to Uganda, then under the control of Idi Amin. Israel refused to give in to the hijackers' demands for the release of numerous terrorists held in Israel. They also sought the release of six terrorists in West Germany, five in Kenya, and others in France* and Switzerland. After a week of negotiations, Israeli commandos, under the command of Brigadier General Dan Shomron*, staged a dramatic and successful raid that later was renamed "Operation Jonathan" in memory of Jonathan (Yoni) Netanyahu, an Israeli officer who was killed during the rescue.

For further information see: Yehoshua Ben-Porat, Eitan Haber, and Zeev Schiff, *Entebbe Rescue* (New York: Dell, 1976); Max Hastings, *Yoni: Hero of Entebbe* (New York: Dial, 1979); Jonathan Netanyahu, *Self-Portrait of a Hero: From the Letters of Jonathan Netanyahu* (New York: Warner, 1997); Yehuda Ofer, *Operation Thunder: The Entebbe Raid* (London: Penguin, 1976); William Stevenson, *90 Minutes at Entebbe* (New York: Bantam, 1976); Tony Williamson, *Counter-Strike Entebbe* (London: Collins, 1976).

ERETZ ISRAEL (OR ERETZ YISRAEL). Eretz Israel or Eretz Yisrael is a Hebrew term meaning "Land of Israel," used to refer to Palestine*. The term is found in the Bible, Talmud*, and later literature, and refers to the land of ancient Israel: all of Palestine, including Judea* and Samaria*.

ESHKOL, LEVI (FORMERLY SHKOLNIK). Levi Eshkol was born in Oratovo in the Kiev district of the Ukraine, on October 25, 1895. In January 1914 he set out as part of a contingent representing the Zionist youth organization Hapoel Hatzair (The Young Worker)* to the port of Trieste where he sailed for Jaffa*. At first he served as a common farm laborer and watchman, but soon became involved in the building of a pumping station and was elected to the Workers' Agricultural Council of Petah Tikva*. He entered military service in the Jewish Legion* and upon demobilization in 1920 he helped to create Kibbutz Degania Bet*. When the Histadrut* was created in 1920 Eshkol joined the Executive Board and when Mapai* was founded in 1929 he was elected to its Central Council. David Ben-Gurion* became a powerful figure in the party and with him Eshkol was drawn into the party leadership. Eshkol increasingly was seen as a political appendage to Ben-Gurion because of the parallels in their careers and their friendship.

After Israel's independence Eshkol was appointed Director-General of the Ministry of Defense. He was appointed head of the Land Settlement Department of the Jewish Agency* in 1949. In 1951 he became Minister of Agriculture and Development and the following year Minister of Finance. Eshkol replaced Ben-Gurion as Prime Minister in June 1963 and served in that position until his death on February 6, 1969. He and Ben-Gurion split over the Lavon Affair*, which led to the defection of Ben-Gurion from Mapai and the creation of Rafi*. Eshkol was known for his contributions to Israel's economic development in a crucial period and for his skills as a compromiser. He led Israel through the Six Day War* and the crisis that preceded it. He was considered one of the more dovish of Israel's leaders, and did not wish to formally annex areas inhabited by large numbers of Arabs. Nevertheless, on June 27, 1967, he issued an administrative order to apply Israeli law and administration to east Jerusalem*.

For further information see: Michael Brecher, *The Foreign Policy System of Israel: Setting, Images, Process* (New Haven, CT: Yale, 1972); Michael Brecher (with Benjamin Geist), *Decisions in Crisis: Israel, 1967 and 1973* (Berkeley: University of California Press, 1980); Henry M. Christman, editor, *The State Papers of Levi Eshkol* (New York: Funk and Wagnalls, 1969); Terence Prittie, *Eshkol: The Man and the Nation* (New York: Putnam, 1969); Sanford R. Silverberg, "Levi Eshkol," in *Political*

Leaders of the Contemporary Middle East and North Africa, edited by
Bernard Reich (Westport, CT: Greenwood, 1990): 166-174.

ETHIOPIA, ETHIOPIAN JEWS. Sometimes called Falashas, meaning
strangers. Folklore in Ethiopia and in some traditional Jewish circles
explains the existence of the community as deriving from the 10th century
BCE union of Israel's King Solomon and the Queen of Sheba. Others say
Jews have been in Ethiopia since the destruction of the first temple in 586
BCE, and that they could be descendants of the lost tribe of Dan. In
Ethiopia the Jews lived primarily in small villages in the mountainous
regions where they were subsistence farmers, with a close-knit social
structure and family life. The largest concentration of Ethiopian
immigrants came to Israel in two major waves: Operation Moses* in the
early and mid 1980s (8,000 immigrants) and Operation Solomon* in 1991
(14,500 immigrants). Other immigrants arrived before Operation Moses
(3,500) and between Operation Moses and Operation Solomon (13,500)
as well as after the end of Operation Solomon (6,000). Approximately
10,000 children have been born to Ethiopian Jewish parents in Israel.
Today there are a total of some 56,000 Ethiopian Jews in Israel.

In Israel, the immigration of Ethiopian Jews raised some major
challenges, in particular how this group could become an integral part of
Israeli society. Those who came in the course of Operation Moses were
a smaller group who arrived over a number of years at a time when total
immigration was low. The number who came during Operation Solomon
was much larger, the bulk of them coming over a single weekend. They
came at the peak of the massive immigration to Israel from the former
Soviet Union. Most of those who came in Operation Moses came together
as families; in Operation Solomon, in many cases family members were
left behind in Ethiopia and many children arrived without their parents.
Israel sought to achieve their integration into Israeli society.

Israel's relationship with Ethiopia began in the pre-state period when,
acting on behalf of the British Government, the Zionist community in
Palestine provided military and technical assistance to the forces of
Emperor Haile Selassie in their efforts to evict the Italian army which
invaded in 1935. The quality of bilateral relations expanded in 1960 when
Israel assisted Ethiopia in combatting the Arab-backed rebellion in the
breakaway province of Eritrea. In return for this assistance, Ethiopia
granted Israel de jure recognition in 1961. Over the subsequent decade

Israel sent hundreds of military and economic advisors to Ethiopia and Israeli academics played a role in helping to establish the Haile Selassie I University in Addis Ababa. Ethiopia severed diplomatic relations with Israel in October 1973, under pressure from the Arab and Muslim oil-producing countries. In 1977 Israel agreed to airlift military and medical supplies to Ethiopia in exchange for Israel's being permitted to take about 200 Ethiopian Jews on the returning transport planes. Between 1980 and 1984 some 7,000 Ethiopian Jews fled the civil war in their country and made their way to Israel; many arrived only after spending many months in squalid refugee camps in neighboring Sudan. During a period of about two months beginning in November 1984 over 6,500 Ethiopian Jews were airlifted to Israel as part of Operation Moses. An additional 700 were transported to Israel in March 1985, in Operation Sheba*. In total, some 14,300 Ethiopian Jews reached Israel between 1972 and August 1985. In May 1991, Operation Solomon brought an additional 14,400 Ethiopian Jews to Israel, all in a 24-hour period. Though there were some serious problems in the early stages of their absorption, the vast majority of Ethiopian Jews rapidly became fully integrated into Israeli society. A total of 3,105 immigrants went to Israel from Ethiopia in 1998. These immigrants came from the Falash Moreh* compound in Addas Ababa. In a June 1997 cabinet decision concerning the Ethiopian Jews, the Interior Ministry decided to extend the mission of the special consul in Addis Ababa to examine the right to immigrate by the communities in Kwara (Qwara) and Gondar in accordance with the Law of Return*. The ministry also sought to expedite the immigration procedures. But conditions in Ethiopia led to fraudulent attempts to immigrate and lack of adequate records slowed the process. In May and June 1999 steps were undertaken to bring to Israel the remnants of the Jewish community residing in the Kwara (Qwara) province of Ethiopia.

The airlift of Ethiopian Jews to Israel resolved one issue but created problems in Israel itself. Beyond broad issues of discrimination the central question revolved around the issue of whether the Ethiopian Jews were in fact fully to be considered Jews under Israeli law and practice. The spiritual leaders of the Ethiopian community, known as *kessim* (singular, *kess*) were excluded from acting as rabbis in Israel despite their traditional role among the Ethiopians as rabbis. The *kessim* were prohibited from performing weddings.

In part the issue derives from the fact that the Ethiopian Jews were isolated from Jewish oral law and rabbinical interpretations and relied instead on the Torah as the basis of their beliefs. The Ethiopian Jews refer to themselves as *Beta Israel* (House of Israel). The chief rabbinate of Israel insisted that the *kessim* catch up on the oral law to be accepted as practicing rabbis in Israel.

In Ethiopia, the *kessim* presided over marriages, divorces, circumcisions, and funerals, and they sought the same rights in Israel. Israel's Chief Rabbinate refused until they studied relevant Jewish law and were appropriately certified. The Ethiopian Jewish tradition goes no further than the Bible, or Torah. The Talmud and the commentaries that form the basis of modern Jewish traditions never were incorporated into their system.

For further information see: Hanan S. Aynor, "Ethiopia, Relations with Zionism and Israel," in *New Encyclopedia of Zionism and Israel*, edited by Geoffrey Wigoder (Teaneck, NJ: Herzl Books, 1994): 396-397; Ruth Gruber, *Rescue: The Exodus of Ethiopian Jews* (New York: Atheneum, 1988); Steven Kaplan, "Ethiopian Jews in Israel," in *New Encyclopedia of Zionism and Israel*, edited by Geoffrey Wigoder (Teaneck, NJ: Herzl Press, 1994): 397-399; Kassim Shehim, "Israel-Ethiopia Relations: Change and Continuity," *Northeast Africa Studies*, 10:1 (1988): 25-37; Shmuel Yilma, *From Falasha to Freedom: An Ethiopian Jew's Journey to Jerusalem* (Jerusalem: Gefen, 1996).

ETZEL *see* IRGUN

ETZION BLOC (GUSH ETZION). A group of Jewish settlements in the hills of Judea* between Jerusalem* and Hebron* taken by Jordan* during the War of Independence*. The bloc included Kfar Etzion (the oldest of the settlements, founded in 1943), Massuot Yitzhak, Ein Tzurim, and Rvadim. After numerous attacks by the Jordanian Arab Legion and other Arabs, the Etzion Bloc fell on May 14, 1948. The area was recaptured by Israel during the Six Day War of 1967*. Subsequently settlements were reestablished in the area; many are considered hot-beds of Gush Emunim* and other opponents of territorial compromise in negotiations with the Palestinians. Virtually all Israeli peace formulas envision the permanent retention of the Etzion Bloc.

For further information see: Elisha Efrat, "Jewish Settlements in the West Bank: Past, Present and Future," *Israel Affairs* 1:1 (Autumn 1994): 135-148; David Newman, "Boundaries in Flux: The 'Green Line' Boundary between Israel and the West Bank—Past, Present and Future," *Boundary and Territory Briefing* 1:7 (Durham, UK: International Boundaries Research Unit, University of Durham Press, 1995); Ehud Sprinzak, *The Ascendance of Israel's Radical Right* (New York: Oxford University Press, 1991).

EXODUS **1947**. A ship bringing illegal immigrants to Palestine under the auspices of the Hagana* in 1947. The ship, originally named the *President Warfield*, was purchased by the Hagana to transport immigrants to Palestine*. It departed from France* in July 1947 with a shipload of immigrants, but the British escorted the ship to Haifa* and boarded it. The refugees were refused permission to enter Palestine and were forced to return in British ships to Europe, mostly to Germany*. *See also* ALIYA BET; BRITISH MANDATE FOR PALESTINE.

F

FALASH MURA. Descendants of Ethiopian Jews who either converted to Christianity or assimilated out of Judaism, but who still claim to be Jewish and generally are perceived as such by non-Jews in Ethiopia*. The Ministerial Committee on Absorption and Diaspora decided in July 1997 to enable the immigration of about 4,000 Falash Mura, living in transit camps in Addis Ababa, to immigrate to Israel over the coming year. The first group of Falash Mura immigrants from Ethiopia arrived in Israel on March 15, 1998.

FALASHAS (JEWS OF ETHIOPIA) *see* ETHIOPIA; ETHIOPIAN JEWS; OPERATION MOSES; OPERATION SOLOMON

FATAH (CONQUEST). The oldest and largest faction of the Palestine Liberation Organization*, its name is an acronym, reversed, for Harakat al-Tahrir al-Falistin (Movement for the Liberation of Palestine). It was founded in 1957 by a group of Palestinian students in Cairo and Kuwait that included Yasser Arafat*, Salah Khalaf (Abu Iyad), Farouk

Kaddoumi, Khalil al-Wazir (Abu Jihad), and Khalid al-Hassan (Abu Said). Its first armed action against Israel took place on January 1, 1965. However, it did not come into prominence until after the June 1967 Six Day War*. The movement's status was enhanced by the battle near the Jordanian village of Karameh* on March 21, 1968, in which Fatah fighters supported by Jordanian army forces held off a 15,000-man unit of the Israel Defense Forces*, inflicting substantial losses. Under Arafat's leadership Fatah joined the PLO in 1968 and won control over its executive committee a year later. It retains control over the PLO and its members are prominently placed in the Palestinian Legislative Council* and in the institutions of the Palestinian Self-Government Authority* established in the West Bank* and Gaza Strip* in the context of the Oslo Accords*.

For further information see: Helena Cobban, *The Palestinian Liberation Organization: People, Power and Politics* (New York: Cambridge University Press, 1984); Yasha Manuel Harari, "Fatah," in *An Historical Encyclopedia of the Arab-Israeli Conflict*, edited by Bernard Reich (Westport, CT: Greenwood, 1996): 159; Cheryl Rubenberg, *The Palestine Liberation Organization: Its Institutional Infrastructure* (Belmont, MD: Institute of Arab Studies, 1983); Barry Rubin, *Revolution Until Victory? The Politics and History of the PLO* (Cambridge, MA: Harvard, 1994); Ehud Ya'ari, *Strike Terror: The Story of Fatah* (New York: Sabra Books, 1970).

FATAHLAND. The name applied to the Arqub area of Lebanon* controlled by the Palestine Liberation Organization* from the late 1960s until Israel's 1982 Operation Peace for Galilee* when much of the PLO military was forced to leave the country. Indeed, the name is derived from Fatah*, the largest PLO faction, headed by Yasser Arafat*. The PLO occupied the area, located in the foothills of Mount Hermon and bordered by the Hasbani River to the west and Syria* to the east, when its leadership was evicted from Jordan* following the September 1970 civil war. Fatahland was the staging ground for terrorist attacks on northern Israel throughout the 1970s, attacks that provoked massive retaliations by the Israel Defense Forces (IDF)* such as Operation Litani* in 1978 and Operation Peace for Galilee in 1982. There was also a vast network of PLO-controlled schools, nurseries, hospitals, and industries that transformed Fatahland into a virtual "state-within-a-state" in southern Lebanon.

FEDAYEEN (THOSE WHO SACRIFICE THEMSELVES/MEN OF SACRIFICE). The term applied to Palestinian guerrilla units that were formed in the Palestinian refugee camps following the 1948-1949 Arab-Israeli War* and which, with Egyptian training and logistical support, launched terrorist raids from bases in the Gaza Strip* into Israel beginning in the summer of 1955.

For further information see: Yehoshafat Harkabi, *Fedayeen Action and Arab Strategy*, Adelphi Papers, No. 53 (London: Institute for Strategic Studies, 1968); Donald A. Pearson and John Fontaine, "Fedayeen," in *An Historical Encyclopedia of the Arab-Israeli Conflict*, edited by Bernard Reich (Westport, CT: Greenwood, 1996): 162-163; Ze'ev Schiff and Raphael Rothstein, *Fedayeen: Guerrillas against Israel* (New York: David McKay, 1972).

FIGHTERS FOR THE FREEDOM OF ISRAEL (LOHAMEI HERUT YISRAEL-LEHI) *see* STERN (GANG) GROUP

FIGHTERS LIST. A political party based largely on members and sympathizers of LEHI (the Stern Gang)*. It contested and won a seat in the First Knesset*, but did not contest the Second Knesset election and ceased to be a political force.

FINAL STATUS TALKS *see* OSLO ACCORDS

FIRST ALIYA *see* ALIYA

FLATTO-SHARON, SHMUEL. Born in Lodz, Poland, in 1930 and immigrating as a child to France*, he became a successful businessman. He ran for election in the 1977 Knesset* election and again in 1981. When he first ran for parliament he neither spoke nor understood Hebrew* as he was a new immigrant. France had requested his extradition to stand trial on charges of illegal financial transactions, embezzlement, and fraud. Nevertheless, he won more than enough votes to secure a seat in the parliament and as a member of the Knesset he gained immunity from extradition. He was later convicted in Israel of bribing voters in the 1977 election.

FRANCE. The relationship between France and Israel has evolved through a series of stages over the years as had France's relationship with the

Zionist movement in the earlier decades of the twentieth century. Although France voted for the Palestine Partition Plan* in November 1947 and recognized Israel in early 1949, relations between the two states remained cool. In 1950 France joined with the United States* and Great Britain* in a Tripartite Declaration that sought to stabilize the situation in the Middle East by limiting arms supply to the region. In subsequent years the relationship between the two states improved and by 1954-1955 France and Israel had signed a number of agreements relating to arms supply and nuclear energy. A political-military marriage of convenience between Israel and France developed as the revolt against France in Algeria gained support from President Gamal Abdul Nasser in Egypt* and Nasser clashed with France over the nationalization of the Suez Canal. France and Britain reached agreement with Israel, which led to the Sinai War* in October 1956. France became Israel's primary supplier of military equipment (including tanks and aircraft) until the Six Day War* and close links were established in other sectors as well. France also assisted Israel in the construction of a nuclear reactor at Dimona* in the Negev*.

However, after Charles de Gaulle came to power in France in 1958 and suggested a need to resolve the Algerian issue, relations between Israel and France began to cool—a trend that accelerated after the accord in 1962 that led to Algerian independence. The Six Day War of 1967 became a more significant watershed as France announced in early June an embargo on arms shipments to the Middle East, a decision that severely and negatively affected Israel since France was Israel's primary arms supplier. De Gaulle's antipathy to Israel and its policies grew after the 1967 war and the trend accelerated even further when Georges Pompidou became President. After Israel's raid on Beirut airport in December 1968 (following a terrorist attack on an El Al* aircraft in Athens, Greece), France imposed a total embargo on arms deliveries to Israel. In December 1969 Israel smuggled five gunboats (that had been built for Israel and paid for) out of Cherbourg harbor. This led to an intensification of the embargo and a deterioration in relations that was further compounded by growing French dependence on Arab oil and a desire to sell military equipment to the Arab states. Among the factors in the relationship were French efforts to secure the Venice Declaration of the European Community (that proposed a European consensus approach to resolution of the Arab-Israeli conflict) in 1980, which was condemned by Israel.

Relations improved when François Mitterrand became President and paid a state visit to Israel in early 1982. Relations in other sectors also improved in subsequent years despite some interruption in the trend as a result of the War in Lebanon* of 1982. Bilateral relations were again strained during the intifada* and as France, along with much of the rest of the European Union, adopted a perspective on the Arab-Israeli peace process that most Israelis interpreted as pro-Palestinian in orientation. At the same time, France continued to use its historical and commercial contacts with Syria* and Lebanon* in an effort to facilitate progress toward peace on those two fronts.

For further information see: Raymond Aron, *DeGaulle, Israel and the Jews* (New York: Praeger, 1969); Uri Bialer, *Between East and West: Israel's Foreign Policy Orientation, 1948-1956* (Cambridge: Cambridge University Press, 1990); Michael Brecher, *The Foreign Policy System of Israel: Setting, Images, Process* (New Haven, CT: Yale University Press, 1972); Sylvia K. Crosbie, *A Tacit Alliance: France and Israel from Suez to the Six Day War* (Princeton, NJ: Princeton University Press, 1974); Paul Marie de La Gorce, "Europe and the Arab-Israel Conflict: A Survey," *Journal of Palestine Studies* 24:3 (Spring 1997): 5-16; Edward A. Kolodziej, *French International Policy under de Gaulle and Pompidou: The Politics of Grandeur* (Ithaca, NY and London: Cornell University Press, 1974); Zach Levey, *Israel and the Western Powers, 1952-1960* (Chapel Hill, NC: University of North Carolina Press, 1997); Shimon Peres, *David's Sling* (Jerusalem: Weidenfeld and Nicholson, 1970); Ghassan Salame, "Torn between the Atlantic and Mediterranean: Europe and the Middle East in the Post-Cold War Era," *Middle East Journal* 48:2 (Spring 1994): 226-249; Howard M. Sachar, *Israel and Europe: An Appraisal in History* (New York: Knopf, 1999); S. Ilan Troen, "The Protocols of Sèvres: British/French/Israeli Collusion against Egypt, 1956," *Israel Studies* 1:2 (Fall 1996): 122-139; Pia Christina Wood, "France and the Israeli-Palestinian Conflict: The Mitterand Policies, 1981-1992," *Middle East Journal* 47:1 (Winter 1993): 21-40; Avner Yaniv, "The French Connection: A Review of French Policy towards Israel," *The Jerusalem Journal of International Relations* 1 (Spring 1976): 115-131.

FREE CENTER PARTY (HAMERKAZ HAHOFSHI). Founded by Shmuel Tamir* in 1967, when he and two other Knesset* members split from the Herut* party because of ideological differences. In 1973 the Free Center rejoined Herut. Subsequently, the larger portion of the Free Center, excluding Tamir, joined the La'am* faction (organized in 1977) within Likud. Tamir joined Yigael Yadin's* Democratic Movement*.

FREE TRADE AREA. The United States* Congress, in October 1984, authorized the President to negotiate a free trade area agreement with Israel. The idea was broached during a meeting between President Ronald Reagan and Prime Minister Yitzhak Shamir* in November 1983 and subsequently the President sought the requisite congressional approval to negotiate such an agreement. Under the arrangement, Israel became the first country in the world to enjoy a bilateral free trade arrangement with the United States. It allows Israel access to its largest single trading partner on substantially improved terms, thereby aiding its export capability. Israel eventually will gain virtually complete and permanent duty-free access to the world's largest market.

For further information see: Mitchell Bard, *US-Israel Relations: Looking to the Year 2000* (Washington, DC: AIPAC, 1991); Mitchell Bard, *Partners for Change: How US-Israel Cooperation Can Benefit America* (Chevy Chase, MD: American-Israeli Cooperation Enterprise, 1993); Wolf Blitzer, *Between Washington and Jerusalem: A Reporter's Notebook* (New York: Oxford University Press, 1985); Bernard Reich, *The United States and Israel: Influence in the Special Relationship* (New York: Praeger, 1984); Bernard Reich, "Reassessing the United States-Israeli Special Relationship," *Israel Affairs* 1:1 (Autumn 1994): 64-83; Bernard Reich, *Securing the Covenant: United States-Israel Relations after the Cold War* (New York: Greenwood, 1995).

FRENKEL, JACOB (YA'AKOV). He was appointed Governor of the Bank of Israel in August 1991. He holds a BA in economics and political science from the Hebrew University of Jerusalem* and an MA and PhD in economics from the University of Chicago. He also is a professor at Tel Aviv University, and in 1995 was appointed Chairman of the Board of Governors of the Inter-American Development Bank. Frenkel announced in November 1999 his decision to resign from his post as of January 2000. He was replaced by Dr. David Klein.

FUNDAMENTAL LAWS *see* BASIC LAWS

G

GABRIEL MISSILE. A missile, developed by Israel, which was the first operational sea-to-sea missile in the Western world. The Gabriel has since become a centerpiece of Israel's arms export industry, with lucrative sales throughout the world.

For further information see: Benjamin Beit-Hallami, *The Israeli Connection: Who Israel Arms and Why* (New York: Pantheon, 1987); Eitan Berglas, *Defense and the Economy: The Israeli Experience* (Jerusalem: The Maurice Falk Institute for Economic Research, January 1983); Aharon S. Klieman, *Israeli Arms Sales: Perspectives and Prospects* Jaffee Center for Strategy Studies Paper, No 24 (Tel Aviv University, February 1984); Aharon S. Klieman, *Israel's Global Reach: Arms Sales as Diplomacy* (McLean, VA: Pergamon-Brassey, 1985); Aharon S. Klieman and Reuven Pedatzur, *Rearming Israel: Defense Procurement through the 1990s* (Boulder, CO: Westview, 1991); Stewart Reiser, *The Israeli Arms Industry: Foreign Policy, Arms Transfers, and Military Doctrine of a Small State* (New York: Holmes and Meier, 1989).

GADNA (ISRAELI YOUTH CORPS). Gadna began operating some 10 years before the establishment of the state. Over the years it has had a variety of names and tasks, but its primary purpose has remained to (a) educate the youth on good citizenship, loyalty, and preparation for national service, (b) make youth aware of national security problems, and (c) develop the physical fitness of youth. During the riots in Palestine* in the period 1936-1939 the leaders of the Yishuv* reached the conclusion that all able-bodied individuals were essential and the mobilization of young boys was begun. A number of groups were established. In the summer of 1948 the chief of staff of the Israel Defense Forces* signed the order for the establishment of Gadna. The intent was not to send these youngsters into combat, but occasionally this was done during the War of Independence*. The basic purpose is to train and prepare Israeli youth between the ages of 14 and 18 for national duty.

For further information see: Stuart A. Cohen, "The IDF: From a 'People's Army' to a 'Professional Military'—Causes and Implications," *Armed Forces and Society* 21 (Winter 1995): 237-254; Stuart A. Cohen, "Towards a New Portrait of a (New) Israeli Soldier," *Israel Affairs* 3

(Spring/Summer 1997): 33-114; Moshe Lissak, "The Civilian Component of Israel's Civil-Military Relations in the First Decade," in *Israel: The First Decade of Independence*, edited by S. Ilan Troen and Noah Lucas (Albany: State University of New York Press, 1995); 575-592.

GAHAL. In 1965 Herut* was joined by the former General Zionists* in the Liberal Party* to form the parliamentary bloc Gahal (acronym for Gush Herut Liberalim—bloc of Herut and the Liberals), under the leadership of Menachem Begin*. The Gahal Agreement was signed on April 25, 1965. Among other elements, the agreement fixed the ratio of Herut and Liberal members of parliament and the locations of candidates from the two parties on the Gahal election list. Each of the parties got 11 of the first 22 slots on the list, one going to each party, with Herut getting the first, the Liberals the second, and so on. From that point to the fortieth position, Herut got 11 seats and the Liberals got seven. From that point on the agreement again provides for one each. This complex arrangement was disrupted by the joint electoral list involving Likud*, Tsomet*, and Gesher* for the 1996 election. Gahal joined the National Unity Government formed on the eve of the Six Day War* and was represented in the cabinet by Menachem Begin* and Joseph Saphir. Likud* (Unity) was formed in 1973 as a parliamentary bloc by the combination of Gahal and La'am* (Toward the People), and Menachem Begin retained his dominant role.

GALEI ZAHAL. Israel Defense Forces* Radio.

GALILEE. The northernmost section of Israel. Divided into an Upper Galilee (mostly mountainous) and a Lower Galilee (more hilly in nature). Encompassing some of the most fertile land in Israel (the Jordan and Jezreel valleys), it was one of the first areas to be settled by Jewish farmers. Today it encompasses the largest concentration of Israeli Arabs, including the city of Nazareth, although it is increasingly populated by Israeli Jews.

GALILI, ISRAEL (FORMERLY BERCZENKO). Born in Brailov, Ukraine, Russia in 1910, Israel Galili was taken to Palestine* at the age of four. There he became active in various Zionist and labor activities at a young age and remained active throughout his life. He helped found Kibbutz Naan where he remained a member. He joined the Hagana* and rose through the ranks to become Deputy Commander in Chief. In the

Provisional Government of Israel established in 1948, he served as Deputy Minister of Defense. He was a member of Ahdut Haavoda* and served in the Knesset* from its inception. In 1966 he became a member of the cabinet without portfolio. He played an especially important role in foreign policy and security decisions when Golda Meir* was Prime Minister and was a significant member of her "kitchen cabinet"*. He died in 1986.

GALILI DOCUMENT. A compromise brokered by Israel Labor* Party stalwart Israel Galili* in the summer of 1973 for the purpose of maintaining party unity. It committed Labor to supporting the establishment of settlements in the West Bank* and Gaza Strip* and the building of the town of Yamit* in the Sinai Desert*, and the integration of the economy of the occupied territories* with that of Israel. This compromise satisfied Labor Party hawks such as Moshe Dayan* (who had been threatening to bolt the party over its apparent softness on the issue of settlements), but it was opposed by moderates such as Abba Eban* who viewed it as a legitimization of the policy of "creeping annexation" advocated by the opposition Gahal* Party in the Knesset* headed by Menachem Begin*. The Galili Document was dropped by Labor following the Yom Kippur War* of October 1973 and replaced by a new 14-point platform, supported by Eban and the party's moderate wing, that made no explicit or implicit reference to the retention by Israel of any of the occupied territories, except Jerusalem*. The platform also referred, for the first time, to Labor's recognition of the need for Palestinian self-expression in a Jordanian-Palestinian state.

For further information see: Efraim Inbar, *War and Peace in Israeli Politics: Labor Party Positions on National Security* (Boulder, CO: Lynne Rienner, 1991); Gershon R. Kieval, *Party Politics in Israel and the Occupied Territories* (Westport, CT: Greenwood, 1983); Gershon R. Kieval, "The Foreign Policy of the Labor Party," in *Israeli National Security Policy: Political Actors and Perspectives*, edited by Bernard Reich and Gershon R. Kieval (New York: Greenwood, 1988): 19-54.

GALUT *see* DIASPORA

GAZA DISTRICT *see* GAZA STRIP

GAZA STRIP. The southernmost section of the coastal plain of Mandatory Palestine*. It is some 25 miles long and between 4 and 8 miles in width. Its major city is Gaza and there is substantial citrus agriculture. Although it lies between Israel and Egypt*, it belongs to neither and its disposition remains a matter of dispute between Israel and the PLO*. The territory, heavily populated by Palestinians, was to have been part of a Palestinian Arab state under the terms of the 1947 United Nations Partition Plan* for Palestine. However, it was taken by the Egyptian army during the 1948-1949 war with Israel and placed under Egyptian military administration. Held briefly by Israel in 1956-1957, the Gaza Strip was then returned to Egyptian control, where it remained until 1967 when Israel again occupied the area during the Six Day War*. Egypt did not claim sovereignty over the Gaza Strip as a part of the Egypt-Israel Peace Treaty*. Violence and protests directed at Israel and the Israeli administration in the area increased considerably since late 1987, and both Jews and Arabs were killed during the course of the intifada*. Pursuant to the Israel-PLO Gaza-Jericho First* implementing agreement (Cairo, May 1994), control over much of the Gaza Strip was transferred to the Palestinian self-rule authority, with the exception of a handful of small settlements in northern Gaza, which continued to be defended by the IDF. Its ultimate status is yet to be decided.

GENERAL FEDERATION OF JEWISH LABOR *see* HISTADRUT

GENERAL FEDERATION OF LABOR *see* HISTADRUT

GENERAL ZIONIST PARTY (HATZIONIM HAKLALIYIM). In June 1946, the General Zionists A and B, previously separate parties, joined to form the General Zionist Party. The General Zionists, Group A, in the main represented middle-class interests as well as members of the liberal professions. Group B was more outspokenly right wing. The social outlook of the party was largely determined by the fact that it relied for support mainly upon the industrialists, merchants, citrus growers, and landlords, and the various professional associations formed by them. When the General Zionist Party was created, its constituent elements survived within it as organized groupings and real cohesion was never achieved. After Israeli independence the rift between the two groups became greater. The crisis culminated in August 1948 with a split of the party when the former General Zionists A broke away to take part in the formation of the new Progressive Party*. The party represented a large section of the secular non-socialist element among the Jewish population of Israel and sought to portray itself as a center party in the early 1950s. It was represented in the Knesset* from 1949 to 1961.

GERMANY. The relationship between Israel and the Federal Republic of Germany (formerly West Germany) has been described by observers as "special." The complex relationship grows out of developments related to the Holocaust* and the crimes committed by the Germans against the Jews and the subsequent efforts on the part of Germany to normalize its relationship with Israel and to integrate itself into the international system.

Germany's approach to Israel had its origins in the views and policies of Germany's first postwar Chancellor, Konrad Adenauer, who believed that there should be reconciliation between Germany and the Jewish people. Adenauer admitted the crimes committed by Germany against the Jewish people and argued that the rehabilitation of the Jews through moral and material reparations by Germany was essential. After negotiations which began in the early 1950s, a restitution agreement (known as the Luxembourg Agreement) was signed by representatives of Israel and West Germany, and a second agreement was signed by Germany with the Conference on Jewish Material Claims against Germany in September 1952, despite strong Arab opposition. The agreement was of great importance to Israel as it provided substantial economic support at a crucial time for the young state. Germany subsequently became a supplier of military equipment to the Jewish state. Nevertheless and despite the significance of this agreement for Israel, there was strong opposition in Israel to any arrangement with Germany and diplomatic relations between the two states were not a realistic option. For Germany the agreement was crucial in helping to reestablish its international position and to help prepare the way for its reintegration into the Western European alliance structure.

Despite various high level meetings and continued economic assistance and military sales, a number of issues precluded substantial movement toward a diplomatic relationship between Israel and Germany for some time. These included the trial of Adolf Eichmann*, which rekindled old memories, and the activities of German scientists in assisting in the development of Arab military capabilities. Diplomatic relations were not established until 1965. Although many Israelis remained concerned about dealing with the successor state to Nazi Germany, contacts between Israel and Germany flourished in all sectors and at all levels. Germany has become a major trading partner and its aid to Israel has been indispensable to the economic growth of the state. Although Germany has become increasingly critical of some of Israel's policies concerning the Palestinians and the Arab-Israeli conflict*, the Holocaust factor continues to play a special role in Germany's approach to Israel.

For further information see: Nicholas Balabkins, *West German Reparations to Israel* (New Brunswick, NJ: Rutgers, 1971); Michael Brecher, *The Foreign Policy System of Israel: Setting, Images, Process* (New Haven, CT: Yale, 1972); Michael Brecher, *Decision in Israel's Foreign Policy* (New Haven, CT: Yale, 1975); Inge Deutschkeon, *Bonn and Jerusalem: The Strange Coalition* (Philadelphia: Chilton, 1970); Lily Gardner Feldman, *The Special Relationship between West Germany and Israel* (Winchester, MA: Allen and Unwin, 1984); Kurt R. Grossman, *Germany's Moral Debt: The German-Israel Agreement* (Washington, DC: Public Affairs Press, 1954); George Lavy, *Germany and Israel: Moral Debt and National Interest* (London: Frank Cass, 1996); Zach Levey, *Israel and the Western Powers, 1952-1960* (Chapel Hill: University of North Carolina Press, 1997); Aryeh Rubinstein, "German Reparations in Retrospect," *Midstream* 8 (Winter 1962): 29-42; James Feron, "A German Ambassador to Israel," *New York Times Magazine* (October 31, 1965): 102, 114, 117, 119, 120, 122; Howard M. Sachar, *Israel and Europe: An Appraisal in History* (New York: Knopf, 1999); Nana Sagai, *German Reparations: A History of the Negotiations* (Jerusalem: Magnes, 1980); Zaki Shalom, "Document: David Ben-Gurion and Chancellor Adenauer at the Waldorf Astoria on March 14, 1960," *Israel Studies* 2:1 (Spring 1997): 50-71; Shabtai Teveth, *Ben-Gurion and the Holocaust* (New York: Harcourt Brace, 1996); Angelika Timm, "The Burdened Relationship between the GDR and Israel," *Israel Studies* 2:1 (Spring 1997): 22-49; Angelika Timm, "Assimilation of History: The GDR and the State of Israel," *Jerusalem Journal of International Relations* 14 (March 1992): 33-47; Rolf Vogel, editor, *The German Path to Israel, A Documentation* (London: Oswald Wolff, 1969); Rolf Vogel, "Voices in the German-Israeli Dialogue: Adenauer, Strauss and Others," *Wiener Library Bulletin* 23:1 (Winter 1968/1968): 6-12.

GESHER (BRIDGE). A breakaway party from Likud* headed by David Levy*. Levy announced the formation of the party on February 20, 1996, when he quit Likud, claiming that the party leadership was biased against

Moroccans and other Sephardic* Jews. The party was to serve as a "bridge" in the social and political fields. Levy announced that the party would be a partner to any Government which accepts Gesher's principles. It was generally understood that the departure from Likud of the Levy faction was related to his personal rivalry with Benjamin Netanyahu* (who defeated Levy in a bitter 1993 race to succeed Yitzhak Shamir* as Likud Party leader). In addition to preparing to run a separate Gesher list for the 1996 Knesset elections, David Levy announced his candidacy for Prime Minister, thereby threatening to split the center-right vote. However, in mid-March 1996 Levy agreed to withdraw his candidacy and to have Gesher join the Likud and Tsomet* parties in a unified "national camp" list to contest the 1996 Knesset election. Gesher participated in the coalition Government established by Netanyahu in June 1996, with David Levy serving as both Foreign Minister and Deputy Prime Minister. However, the party left the coalition when Levy quit in January 1998 in a dispute with Netanyahu over proposed cuts to social spending and over the management of the Palestinian peace negotiations. In the spring of 1999, Gesher agreed to join with Labor* and Meimad* to form the One Israel* movement that won 26 seats in the elections to the 15th Knesset that occurred on May 17, 1999, and which dominated the governing coalition formed by Ehud Barak* on July 6, 1999, with David Levy once again serving as Foreign Minister and Deputy Prime Minister.

GIMLAIM (PENSIONERS) PARTY. A political party, led by Abba Gefen, that contested the 1988 Knesset* election but failed to gain sufficient votes for a mandate in parliament.

GINZBERG, ASHER ZVI *see* AHAD HAAM

GOLAN HEIGHTS. A zone east of the Huleh Valley* and the Sea of Galilee* that abuts Mount Hermon*. It is a sparse territory some 41 miles long and 15 miles wide. The border between Israel and Syria* has been in dispute since the establishment of the Jewish state in 1948. In 1949 the armistice agreement* designated small areas on the western side of the border as demilitarized zones. Many of the clashes between Syria and Israel between 1949 and 1967 developed from Israel's efforts to assert control over these parcels of land.

In the Six Day War*, Israel occupied the Syrian territory known as the Golan Heights and began to establish settlements there. It was placed under military administration. During the Yom Kippur War*, Syria briefly recaptured a portion of the Golan Heights, but Israel quickly took additional Syrian territory. The Israel-Syria Disengagement of Forces Agreement* of 1974 resulted in Syria's regaining some territory lost in 1967. No major incidents and only a few minor ones have occurred since 1974. Since the late 1970s the focus of Israeli-Syrian tension has been in Lebanon* because of the use by the Palestine Liberation Organization* and later Hezbollah of Syrian-controlled Lebanese territory for strikes against Israel.

On December 14, 1981, the Government of Israel presented a bill to the Knesset* which applied the law, jurisdiction, and administration of the state to the Golan Heights. The bill passed all three readings required in the Knesset and was adopted by a vote of 63 in favor and 21 against. Explaining this action, Prime Minister Menachem Begin* declared that, "in this matter of the Golan Heights there is a universal, or nearly universal, national consensus in Israel." Begin also stated that the law did not alter Israel's readiness to negotiate all outstanding issues with Syria, including the issue of final borders. The Government cited several reasons for proposing the bill to the Knesset. After 14 years of administration, the Syrians had rejected all efforts to bring them into a peace process. The Syrians had refused to accept the Camp David peace process, had installed missiles in Lebanon which were a direct threat to Israel, and in their occupation of Lebanon directly aided the PLO in its border attacks against Israel.

The action by the Knesset changed the status of the Golan Heights from military to civil jurisdiction. The Druze* farmers who live there had the option of receiving Israeli citizenship. The population of the Golan numbers about 17,000 Jews in 27 farms and villages, 12,000 Druze in four villages, and one village of 600 Alawite Muslims.

Following the Knesset vote on the Golan bill, the United States* condemned the act, stating that the swift nature of the Israeli action surprised the United States, was harmful to the peace process, and violated the Camp David Accords* and the letter and spirit of United Nations Security Council Resolutions 242* and 338* calling for the negotiated settlement of disputes based on the land-for-peace* formula. The State Department spokesman noted: "We continue to believe that the final status of the Golan Heights can only be determined through negotiations between Syria and Israel based upon Resolutions 242 and 338." On December 17, 1981, the United Nations Security Council adopted unanimously a resolution holding "that the Israeli decision to impose its laws, jurisdiction and administration in the occupied Syrian Golan Heights is null and void and without international legal effect; [and] Demands that Israel, the occupying power, should rescind forthwith its decision." The United States announced that it was suspending the U.S.-Israel Memorandum of Understanding on Strategic Cooperation*. Additionally, the U.S. administration canceled several bilateral economic agreements that would have provided Israel with opportunities to sell Israeli-made arms to nations friendly to the United States, using U.S. credit dollars. The administration also canceled several planned purchases of Israeli-made arms.

Following the Madrid Peace Conference*, Israeli and Syrian officials met periodically to discuss the status of the Golan Heights and related matters. Prime Minister Yitzhak Rabin* declared that the depth of Israel's withdrawal on or from the Golan Heights would be determined by the depth of peace and normalized relations offered in exchange by Syria. Rabin pledged to hold a national referendum on the issue. U.S.-sponsored talks in Washington and at the Wye Plantation* in Maryland, involving the chiefs of staff of the Israeli and Syrian militaries and Israel's ambassador to the United States and his Syrian counterpart, were reportedly proceeding well on the eve of Rabin's assassination. The talks stalemated after Rabin's death and broke down in the context of Syria's refusal to explicitly condemn the string of suicide bombings that rocked Israel in February and March of 1996. While Syrian officials played an important part in containing the damage caused by violent exchanges between Israel and Hezbollah in southern Lebanon in April 1996's Operation Grapes of Wrath*, Israeli officials continued to contend that Syria chose to permit a level of instability in southern Lebanon in the hopes of compelling Israel to cede sovereignty over all of the Golan Heights to Syria. On January 26, 1999, the Knesset passed a Golan Heights Law which required a majority Knesset vote in order to give up any part of Israeli sovereign territory. The law also required the drafting of a Basic Law on Popular Referendums after the May 1999 elections which would force any decision to relinquish Israeli land to be put to a referendum of Israeli voters in addition to the Knesset vote. After Ehud Barak* became Prime Minister in 1999 the status of the Golan Heights reemerged as a prominent public policy issue. Barak (who as IDF* Chief of Staff had participated in talks in the United States* with his Syrian counterpart) offered to resume negotiations over the Golan from the point where they had left off in the spring of 1996. Barak also reaffirmed Rabin's pledge to hold a national referendum over the future of the Golan. After months of behind-the-scenes diplomacy, Israel and Syria resumed discussions in Washington, DC, on December 15, 1999. The negotiations were headed by Prime Minister Ehud Barak and Syria's Foreign Minister, Farouk a-Sharaa.

For further information see: Jerry Asher, *Duel for the Golan* (New York: Morrow, 1987); M. Zuhair Diab, "Syrian Security Requirements in a Peace Settlement with Israel," *Israel Affairs* 1:4 (Summer 1995): 71-88; Efraim Inbar, "Israeli Negotiations with Syria," *Israel Affairs* 1:4 (Summer 1995): 89-100; David Eshel, "The Golan Heights: A Vital Strategic Asset for Israel," *Israel Affairs* 3:3&4 (Spring/Summer 1997): 225-238; Bruce A. Hurwitz, "The Legal Status of the Golan Heights," *Middle East Focus* 10:4 (Summer 1988): 6-11; Moshe Ma'oz, *Syria and Israel: From War to Peace-Making* (London: Oxford University Press, 1996); Muhammed Muslih, "The Golan: Israel, Syria, and the Strategic Calculation," *Middle East Journal* 47 (Autumn 1993); "Golan Residents Mark 30 Years of Settlement," *Ha'aretz,* July 18, 1997; Daniel Pipes, *Syria Beyond the Peace Process* (Washington, DC: Washington Institute for Near East Policy, 1996); Daniel Pipes, "The Word of Hafez al-Assad," *Commentary* (October 1999): 37-40; Itamar Rabinovich, *The Brink of Peace: The Israeli-Syrian Negotiations and the Israel-Arab Peace Process* (Princeton, NJ: Princeton University Press, 1998); Aryeh Shalev, *The Israel-Syria Armistice Regime 1949-1955* (Boulder, CO: Westview, 1993); Aryeh Shalev, *Israel and Syria: Peace and Security on the Golan Heights* (Boulder, CO: Westview, 1994); Eliav Shochetman, "Israel's Right to the Golan Heights," *Midstream* (August-September 1993); United Nations Security Council Resolution No. 497 (1981) of 17 December 1981: "Deciding That the Israeli Decision to Impose Its Laws, Jurisdiction and Administration in the Occupied Syrian Golan Heights Is Null and Void and without International Legal Effect"; Eyal Zisser, *Syria and Israel: From War to Peace* (Tel Aviv: The Moshe Dayan Center for Middle Eastern and African Studies, Monograph, December 1994).

GOLDSTEIN, BARUCH. The perpetrator of an attack at the Tomb of the Patriarchs (known by Muslims as the Ibrahim Mosque) in Hebron* on February 25, 1994, that left 29 Arab worshippers dead and more than 100 others wounded. Dr. Goldstein, an American-born resident of the nearby settlement of Kiryat Arba* and a follower of Rabbi Meir Kahane* and the Kach* movement, was killed by some of the survivors of the massacre. The attack resulted in a brief disruption in autonomy negotiations with the PLO*, and the imposition of a Temporary International Presence in Hebron (TIPH)*. A commission of inquiry headed by the President of the Supreme Court of Israel*, Justice Meir Shamgar*, concluded on June 26, 1994, that Goldstein had acted alone in committing this "base and murderous" massacre. *See also* HEBRON MASSACRE; SHAMGAR COMMISSION.

GONEN, SHMUEL (FORMERLY GORODISH). He came to Palestine* with his parents from Lithuania when he was three years old and attended a yeshiva. He joined the Hagana* in 1944 and rose through the ranks to become a general officer. He gained fame in the June 1967 Six Day War* when his tank brigade broke through Egyptian defenses in northern Sinai. After the Yom Kippur War* he was among those criticized by the Agranat Commission* and was suspended. The suspension was later reversed on condition that he not be appointed as a corps commander. He retired from the army in 1976 and went into private business. He died in September 1991.

"GOODBYE, FRIEND." A memorial bumper sticker distributed after the assassination of Prime Minister Yitzhak Rabin* and reflecting the sentiment spoken by U.S. President Bill Clinton in tribute to Rabin. In February 1996 new bumper stickers, as a response to this and to a terrorist attack, read "Goodbye, friends." This referred to the 25 people killed by two Palestinian suicide bombers in February 1996.

GORDON, AHARON DAVID. A Hebrew* writer and spiritual mentor of labor Zionists who believed in settlement of the land. Gordon was born in Troyanov, Russia, in 1856. He was given a position in the financial management of Baron Guenzburg's estate and remained in this position for 23 years. In 1903, because he had to find other employment, he decided to move to Palestine*, which he did the following year. Five years later he brought his family. He became involved in manual agricultural work but also, beginning in 1909, started writing articles concerning his outlook on labor, Zionism*, and Jewish destiny, which became known as "the religion of labor." He died in Degania* in 1922.

For further information see: Shlomo Avineri, *The Making of Modern Zionism: The Intellectual Origins of the Jewish State* (New York: Basic, 1981); Shmuel Ettinger and Israel Bartal, "The First Aliyah: Ideological Roots and Practical Accomplishments," in *Essential Papers on Zionism* (New York: New York University Press, 1996): 63-93; Ben Halpern, *The Idea of the Jewish State*, Second Edition (Cambridge, MA: Harvard, 1970); Arthur Hertzberg, editor, *The Zionist Idea: A Historical Analysis and Reader* (New York: Atheneum, 1979): 368-386.

GOREN, RABBI SHLOMO. Born in Poland in 1917 and immigrated to Palestine* in 1925, Shlomo Goren was educated at Hebrew University* and served as Chief Rabbi of Tel Aviv-Jaffa*. He also served as Chief Chaplain of the Israel Defense Forces* and as Ashkenazi Chief Rabbi* of Israel. In June 1967 he celebrated with IDF soldiers the reacquisition of Jerusalem at the Western Wall*. In the 1970s and 1980s he became increasingly associated with extreme factions of the West Bank* settler movement. In 1993 he created controversy when he ruled that it was permissible under Halacha for IDF soldiers to disobey orders to evacuate Jewish settlements. Goren died in October 1994.

GOVERNMENT *see* CABINET

GOVERNMENT OF NATIONAL UNITY. A coalition Government comprised of Labor* and Likud* following the 1984 Knesset* election, which produced no clear victor between the two leading parties. The coalition lasted until the 1988 Knesset election. Under the terms of the agreement, Labor's Shimon Peres* served as Prime Minister from 1984 to 1986 while Likud's Yitzhak Shamir* served as Foreign Minister and Deputy Prime Minister; the two rotated positions half way through the Government's tenure, in 1986. The Government of National Unity took important steps toward alleviating inflation and withdrew the IDF* from Labanon*. A variant of the National Unity Government was formed following the 1988 election, but it lasted only until the spring of 1990. *See also* ROTATION; WALL-TO-WALL COALITION.

GREAT BRITAIN. Israel's relationship with England (the United Kingdom, Great Britain) antedates Israel's independence. It can be traced to the period of World War I when, among other arrangements concerning Palestine*, the British Government issued the Balfour Declaration* which endorsed the concept of a national home for the Jewish people in

Palestine. The Declaration was seen as support for the Zionist claim to a Jewish state in Palestine. The British were granted the Mandate over Palestine after the end of the war and retained their control until the establishment of Israel's independence in May 1948. Britain did not support the establishment of the Jewish state and supplied arms to the Arab states during the War of Independence* in addition to supporting the Arab position in the United Nations. Britain recognized Israel in 1949.

In May 1950 Britain joined with France* and the United States* in a Tripartite Declaration to limit arms sales to the region in an effort to ensure regional stability. The ensuing years were marked by a coolness in relations while Britain retained close links with many of Israel's Arab neighbors. Nevertheless, in the fall of 1956 Britain joined with France and Israel in a tripartite plan to deal with the policies and activities of President Gamal Abdul Nasser of Egypt*. Nasser sought to accelerate the British withdrawal from Egypt and the Suez Canal zone and to undermine British influence elsewhere in the Arab world. In July 1956 he nationalized the Suez Canal which the British regarded as having economic value and strategic significance. Israel invaded Egypt at the end of October 1956 in the Sinai War* and Britain and France soon joined in after giving both Egypt and Israel an ultimatum. The convergence of interests and the marriage of convenience between Britain and Israel that resulted soon came apart under the pressure of the international community, especially the United States.

In the 1960s there was a small growth and improvement in relations between Israel and Britain which included the sale of some military equipment to Israel. At the same time, Britain was in the process of reordering its relationship with the Arab states of the Middle East, especially its former colonial territories. Sympathy for Israel was widespread in England at the outbreak of the Six Day War*. It was Britain's United Nations representative (Lord Caradon) who was instrumental in the drafting of United Nations Security Council Resolution 242*, but Britain did not play a major role in trying to achieve peace in the years immediately following the 1967 war.

The succeeding years saw a variation in the relationship with links alternately improving and declining, based on changes in personality in decision-making positions in both Britain and Israel. Britain's role in the European community and its advocacy of the Venice Declaration of 1980, which sought a resolution of the Arab-Israeli conflict on terms deemed problematic by Israel, remained an irritant in the relationship. Nevertheless other factors, such as a common opposition to Middle East-originated terrorism, proved to be positive factors in British relations with Israel. *See also* BALFOUR DECLARATION; BRITISH MANDATE FOR PALESTINE; SINAI WAR.

For further information see: Uri Bialer, *Between East and West: Israel's Foreign Policy Orientation, 1948-1956* (Cambridge: Cambridge University Press, 1990); Michael Brecher, *The Foreign Policy System of Israel: Setting, Images, Process* (New Haven, CT: Yale, 1972): chapter 2; Paul- Marie de La Gorce, "Europe and the Arab-Israel Conflict: A Survey," *Journal of Palestine Studies* 26 (Spring 1997): 5-16; Zach Levey, *Israel and the Western Powers, 1952-1960* (Chapel Hill, NC: University of North Carolina Press, 1997); Selwyn Lloyd, *Suez 1956: A Personal Account* (New York: Mayflower, 1978); Ghassan Salame, "Torn between the Atlantic and Mediterranean: Europe and the Middle East in the Post-Cold War Era," *Middle East Journal* 48 (Spring 1994): 226-249; Howard M. Sachar, *Israel and Europe: An Appraisal in History* (New York: Knopf, 1999); Zeev Sharef, *Three Days: An Account of the Last Days of the British Mandate and the Birth of Israel* (New York: Doubleday, 1962); A. J. Sherman, *Mandate Days: British Lives in Palestine 1918-1948* (London: Douglas and McIntyre, 1998); Christopher Sykes, *Crossroads to Israel, 1917-1948* (Bloomington: Indiana University Press, 1973); Alan R. Taylor, *Prelude to Israel: An Analysis of Zionist Diplomacy 1897-1947*, Revised Edition (Beirut: The Institute for Palestine Studies, 1970); S. Ilan Troen, "The Protocol of Sèvres: British/French/Israeli Collusion against Egypt, 1956," *Israel Studies* 1:1 (Fall 1996): 122-139; Harold Wilson, *The Chariot of Israel: Britain, America and the Story of Israel* (London: Weidenfeld and Nicolson, 1981).

GREATER ISRAEL. The concept of Israel's retaining permanently all of Eretz Israel*, including the territories occupied in the 1967 Six Day War* as well as parts of historic Palestine* "promised" to the Zionists in the Balfour Declaration* and the League of Nations Mandate for Palestine*. Inherited from the Zionist Revisionism* of Vladimir Ze'ev Jabotinsky*, it was the bedrock of Likud* ideology for many years. However, it also found expression among some veteran Mapai* activists as well as among Tehiya* and other right-wing and Orthodox political parties opposed to the territorial concessions made in the Camp David Accords* with Egypt and the concessions in the West Bank* and Gaza Strip* made by both Likud- and Labor-led governments in negotiations with the PLO* ensuing from the Oslo Accords*.

For further information see: Yehoshafat Harkabi, *Israel's Fateful Hour* (New York: Harper and Row, 1988); Rael Jean Isaac, *Israel Divided: Ideological Politics in the Jewish State* (Baltimore: Johns Hopkins, 1976).

GREEN LEAF PARTY. Boaz Wachtel, a former drug counselor, created this single-issue party as a means of attempting to legalize marijuana in Israel. The party did not win any mandates in the 15th Knesset.

GREEN LINE. The frontier lines between Israel and the neighboring Arab states (Egypt*, Jordan*, Lebanon*, Syria*) established by the Armistice Agreements of 1949 and lasting until the June 1967 Six Day War*.

For further information see: David Newman, "Boundaries in Flux: The 'Green Line' Boundary between Israel and the West Bank—Past, Present and Future," *Boundary and Territory Briefing* 1:7 (Durham, UK: International Boundaries Research Unit, University of Durham Press, 1995).

GULF OF AQABA. Israel also refers to it as the Gulf of Eilat, derived from the port city of Eilat* at its head. The Gulf of Aqaba is about 100 miles long with a coastline shared by Israel, Egypt*, Jordan*, and Saudi Arabia. At its northern end are the Israeli port of Eilat and the Jordanian port of Aqaba. At the southern end, where the Gulf meets the Red Sea, there are two islands: Tiran and Sanafir. The navigable channel is between Tiran and the coast of the Sinai Peninsula* and is three nautical miles wide. The point on the Sinai coast directly facing Tiran is Ras Nasrani, near Sharm el-Sheikh*. In the 1950s, Egypt set up gun emplacements there to prevent Israeli and Israeli-bound shipping through the Strait of Tiran*. Israel destroyed the guns on November 3, 1956.

Israel's use of the Strait of Tiran and the Gulf of Aqaba has been a factor in the relations between Egypt and Israel and in the Sinai* and Six Day Wars*. Since the Israeli occupation of the Sinai Peninsula in 1956 and later withdrawal in 1957, Israeli ships have used the Strait and the Gulf, except for a brief interruption in 1967. Nasser's announced blockade of the Strait in 1967 was considered by Israel as a war provocation and by the United States* as a major act leading to the conflict. To avoid a repetition of the blockade, the United Nations adopted Security Council Resolution 242* of November 1967, the basic document in the quest for an Arab-Israeli peace settlement. Resolution 242 called inter alia for freedom of navigation in international waterways, including the Strait of Tiran and Gulf of Aqaba.

The narrowness of the Gulf of Aqaba and the disparate claims by the coastal states have the potential to cause problems of maritime boundary delimitations. Both Egypt and Saudi Arabia have claimed 12-mile territorial seas and additional six-mile contiguous zones. Israel has claimed six-mile territorial seas, and Jordan has claimed three miles without any contiguous zones.

Since the Gulf of Aqaba is very deep and because no natural resources have been discovered in it, no disputes over exploitation rights have arisen, but disputes over navigation, mostly concerning shipping to and from Eilat, have occurred. After the Israeli occupation of the western shore of the Strait of Tiran in 1967, ships of all states again enjoyed the right of passage through the Strait and the Gulf. To ensure freedom of navigation the 1979 Egypt-Israel Peace Treaty* provided that, after Israel withdrew from the shores and entrances of the Gulf of Aqaba in 1982, the area would be controlled by a multinational force established by the concerned parties and stationed in the area of Sharm el-Sheikh.

For further information see: L. M. Bloomfield, *Israel and the Gulf of Aqaba in International Law* (Toronto: Carswell, 1957); Malcolm W. Cagle, "The Gulf of Aqaba—Trigger for Conflict," *US Naval Institute Proceedings* 85 (January 1959): 75-81; Paul A. Porter, *The Gulf of Aqaba: An International Waterway—Its Significance to International Trade* (Washington, DC: Public Affairs Press, 1957); Charles B. Selak, Jr., "A Consideration of the Legal Status of the Gulf of Aqaba," *The American Journal of International Law* 52 (1958): 660-698.

GULF OF EILAT *see* GULF OF AQABA

GUR, MORDECHAI (NICKNAMED "MOTTA"). Mordechai Gur was born in Jerusalem* on May 6, 1930. At the age of seventeen, he joined the youth battalion of the Hagana* during the Mandate* period and later served in the Palmah*. After the War of Independence* he attended Hebrew University* and studied politics and Oriental studies while still in the military. He became a paratrooper and helped to develop the Israeli style of commando raids on fedayeen* bases across the frontier lines before the Sinai War*. He commanded the elite Golani Brigade from 1961 to 1963. During the Six Day War* he commanded the paratroop brigade that captured East Jerusalem* and the walled city, reporting "The Temple Mount is in our hands." In August 1967 he became Commander of the Gaza Strip* and Northern Sinai. He was a graduate of the prestigious Ecole de Guerre in Paris. He served as military attaché in Washington from August 1972 until December 1973. He served as Chief of Staff of the Israel Defense Forces* from 1974 to 1978, taking over after David Elazar* resigned from that post in the wage of the Agranat Commission* report. As IDF Chief of Staff, Gur oversaw the planning of Operation Entebbe*, the July 4, 1976, rescue of hostages from the Entebbe* airport in Uganda. After leaving the IDF in 1978, he became Director General of a division of Koor industries*. In 1981 he ran for the Knesset* on the Labor Party* list and won a seat. He served as Minister of Health in the Government of National Unity* established in 1984 and became Minister without Portfolio in the Government established in December 1988. Gur served as Deputy Minister of Defense under Yitzhak Rabin* and as Rabin's chief liaison to Jewish settlers from 1992 until his death on July 16, 1995, from a self inflicted gunshot wound. He suffered from cancer. Gur was also well known in Israel for his children's books about a paratrooper unit and their fighting mascot, a dog named Azit.

For further information see: Yehoshua Ben-Porat, Eitan Haber, and Zeev Schiff, *Entebbe Rescue* (New York: Dell, 1976); Robert Moskin, *Among Lions: The Battle for Jerusalem, June 5-7, 1967* (New York: Arbor House, 1982).

GUSH EMUNIM (BLOC OF THE FAITHFUL). A movement which promotes the establishment of Jewish settlements in Judea*, Samaria*, and Gaza* as a means of promoting retention of these areas, especially the West Bank*. It is an aggressive (sometimes even illegal) settlement movement that combines religious fundamentalism and secular Zionism* to create a new political force. Its leaders assert a biblically based Jewish claim to Judea and Samaria. Gush Emunim became active after the Six Day War* in establishing Jewish settlements in the occupied territories*. But it was not until after the Yom Kippur War* that it organized politically in order to oppose further territorial concessions and to promote the extension of Israeli sovereignty over the occupied territories. The founding meeting of Gush Emunim took place in 1974 at Kfar Etzion, a West Bank kibbutz that had been seized by the Arabs in Israel's War of Independence* and which was recovered by Israel in the Six Day War. Among those playing leading roles in the movement's founding were: Rabbi Moshe Levinger*, the leader of the Kiryat Arba* settlers; Hanan Porat, one of the revivers of Jewish settlement in Gush Etzion*; Rabbi Haim Druckman*, educator, who was one of the leaders of the Bnai A'kiva religious youth movement and subsequently became a member of the Knesset*; Rabbi Eliezer Waldman; and Rabbi Yohanan Fried.

Gush Emunim began as a faction within the National Religious Party*, but because of distrust of the NRP's position concerning the future of Judea and Samaria, the Gush left the party and declared its independence. The Gush Emunim people—mostly yeshiva graduates, rabbis, and teachers—launched an information campaign to explain their position. Gush Emunim has since refused to identify with any political party and has gained a unique political status. During the tenure of the Government of Yitzhak Rabin* from 1974 to 1977, Gush Emunim protested the disengagement agreements with Egypt* and Syria*, staged demonstrations in Judea and Samaria to emphasize the Jewish attachment to those parts of the Land of Israel, and engaged in settlement operations in the occupied territories. Gush Emunim's primary commitment is to settlement beyond the 1949 Armistice Agreement* demarcation lines, which had served as the de facto borders between Israel and the Jordanian-annexed West Bank and between Israel and the Egyptian-administered Gaza Strip and Sinai from 1949 to 1967. Gush Emunim has continued to push for settlements in all parts of Eretz Israel*.

Gush Emunim's spiritual authorities and political leaders were educated in Yeshivat Merkaz Harav, whose founder was Avraham Yitzhak Hacohen Kook*, the first Ashkenazi* Chief Rabbi of Eretz Yisrael. Kook believed that the era of redemption for the Jewish people had already begun with the rise of modern Zionism* and the growing Zionist enterprise in Palestine*. Israel's victory in the Six Day War transformed the status of Kook's theology. It seemed clear to his students that they were living in the messianic age and believed that redemption might be at hand. Kook's views were expounded by his son, Rabbi Zvi Yehuda Kook*, who succeeded him as the head of Yeshivat Merkaz Harav. Gush

Emunim has become a highly complex social and institutional system comprised of a settlement organization, regional and municipal councils, and independent economic corporations. In addition, its spiritual leadership is composed of distinguished rabbis and scholars. Though a powerful force in Israeli politics, Gush Emunim never organized itself into a political party that would vie for seats in the Knesset. Increasingly, its interests in this regard were represented by the National Religious Party (NRP), which, by the 1980s, had entered into a close political association with the settler community in the West Bank generally and with the Gush Emunim in particular.

For further information see: Rael Jean Isaac, *Israel Divided: Ideological Politics in the Jewish State* (Baltimore: Johns Hopkins, 1976); Herb Keinon, *Israeli Settlements: A Guide* (New York: Anti-Defamation League, 1995); Rabbi Zvi Yehuda Kook, "Honest We Shall Be in the Land and in the Torah," in *A Land of Settlement*, edited by Yaacov Shavit (Jerusalem: Har Zion, 1977, Hebrew); David Newman, editor, *Gush Emunim: Political Inspiration and Settlement Objectives* (New York: St. Martin's Press, 1984); David Newman, editor, *The Impact of Gush Emunim: Politics and Settlements in the West Bank* (New York: St. Martin's, 1985); David Newman, "Gush Emunim between Fundamentalism and Pragmatism," *The Jerusalem Quarterly* 39 (1986): 33-43; David Newman, *Jewish Settlement in the West Bank: The Role of Gush Emunim* (Durham, UK: University of Durham Press, 1982); Zvi Raanan, *Gush Emunim* (Tel Aviv: Sifriyat Poalim, 1980, Hebrew); Amnon Rubinstein, *The Zionist Dream Revisited: From Herzl to Gush Emunim and Back* (New York: Schocken, 1984); Danny Rubinstein, *On The Lord's Side: Gush Emunim* (Tel Aviv: Hakibbutz Hameuchad, 1982, Hebrew); Ehud Sprinzak, "Extreme Politics in Israel," *The Jerusalem Quarterly* 5 (Fall 1977): 33-47; Ehud Sprinzak, *Gush Emunim: The Politics of Zionist Fundamentalism in Israel* (New York: American Jewish Committee, 1986); Ehud Sprinzak, "Gush Emunim: The Tip of the Iceberg," *The Jerusalem Quarterly* 21 (Fall 1981): 28-47; Ehud Sprinzak, "Extremist Inputs into Israel's Foreign Policy: The Case of Gush Emunim," in *Israeli National Security Policy: Political Actors and Perspectives*, edited by Bernard Reich and Gershon R. Kieval (New York: Greenwood, 1988): 123-146; Ehud Sprinzak, *The Ascendance of Israel's Radical Right* (New York: Oxford University Press, 1991); Ehud Sprinzak, "Extremism and Violence in Israel: The Crisis of Messianic Politics," *The Annals of the American Academy of Political and Social*

Science 555 (January 1998): 114-126; David Weisburd (with Vered Vinitzky), "Vigilantism as Rational, Social Control: The Case of Gush Emunim Settlers," in *Religion and Politics, Political Anthropology*, volume 3, edited by Myron Aronoff (New Brunswick, NJ: Transaction, 1983).

GUSH ETZION *see* ETZION BLOC

H

HA'ARETZ **(THE LAND)**. A daily Hebrew language newspaper not affiliated with any political party. It was founded as *Hadashot Ha'aretz,* and first appeared in Jerusalem* on June 18, 1919. It was later transferred to Tel Aviv*. It was the first Hebrew* language daily to be published in Palestine* after World War I. In 1997 it launched an English-language edition in coordination with the *International Herald Tribune.*

HABAD. Acronym for *Hokhmah, Binah, Daat* (wisdom, comprehension, knowledge). A central stream of Hasidut (whose adherents are called Hasidim*), its founder was Rabbi Shneur Zalman of Lyady. It began in Belorussia, in a town called Lubavitch (therefore these Hasidim are called Lubavitchers, and their rabbi is the Rabbi of Lubavitch—the Lubavitcher Rebbe). Its political interests in Israel are represented primarily through Agudat Israel*.

HABERFELD, HAIM. Former Labor* Party member of Knesset*, he served as chairman of the Histadrut* labor federation from 1992-1994, when his Labor Party list was defeated by the independent faction headed by former Labor MK Haim Ramon*, thereby ending Labor's 74-year control over the Histadrut.

HABIBI, EMILE. Israeli Arab author and former Israel Communist Party* member of Knesset* and recipient of the Israel Prize* for literature. Born in Haifa* on August 29, 1922. From 1941 to 1943 he was cultural affairs reporter and editor of the Arabic section of Broadcasting House in Jerusalem* and ran the network's cultural department. He joined the Communist Party in 1943. When the party split into Jewish and Arab factions in 1945, he helped establish the Arab Communists' League for National Liberation. After Israel's independence, Habibi was one of the founders of the Israel Communist Party, which reunited the Jewish and Arab factions, and represented the party in the Knesset from 1952 to 1972. After leaving the Knesset he concentrated on writing and on editing the Communist Party newspaper *Al-Ittihad*, which he edited until 1989, when he broke with the Communist Party in the wake of the political changes in the Soviet Union. He depicted the predicament of Arabs in Israel caught between Arab identity and Israeli citizenship and was one of the most popular and well-known authors in the Middle East. He received Israel's highest cultural award, the Israel Prize*, in 1992 despite protests by both Jews and Arabs, and the PLO's* Jerusalem Medal in 1990. He asserted his Arab identity but also advocated Jewish-Arab coexistence and mutual recognition between Israelis and Palestinians. He died in Nazareth on May 2, 1996. His most famous novel, *The Opsimist*, depicts the combination of optimism and pessimism that characterizes the lives of Israeli Arabs; it has been translated into many languages and staged in both Arabic and Hebrew.

HADASH *see* DEMOCRATIC FRONT FOR PEACE AND EQUALITY

HADASSAH. The organization of Zionist women in America, founded in 1912 at the instigation of Henrietta Szold. (The name Haddassah is the Hebrew name for Esther, a Jewish Queen who dedicated herself to the saving of her people. It is also the equivalent of myrtle, a plant indigenous to Israel). Its activities in Palestine* and Israel were limited at first to health and medical care, and then extended to include social and educational projects. At the Second Zionist Congress, Theodor Herzl* asked Mrs. Richard Gottheil to direct her energies to enlisting the interest of her American colleagues in the principles of Zionism*. Mrs. Gottheil joined a group of the Daughters of Zion which met in New York and introduced the name "Hadassah Circle." In 1907 Henrietta Szold joined this group and, in 1909, she and her mother visited Palestine. On her return Szold described the distressing social and health situation in Palestine and the group developed a program of action. On February 24, 1912, the national organization of "Daughters of Zion" was established and the New York chapter retained the name "Hadassah." At the suggestion of Professor Israel Friedlander, the Daughters of Zion adopted the motto "The healing of the daughter of my people." Hadassah began its involvement in health and medical services in Palestine and Israel in 1913 and has continued in those areas since.

For further information see: Michael Brown, "Henrietta Szold's Progressive American Vision of the Yishuv," in *Envisioning Israel: The Changing Ideas and Images of North American Jews*, edited by Allon Gal (Jerusalem: Magnes, 1996): 60-80; Naomi W. Cohen, *American Jews and the Zionist Idea* (New York: Ktav, 1975); Joan Dash, *Summoned: The Life and Times of Henrietta Szold* (New York: Harper and Row, 1979); Irving Fineman, *Woman of Valor* (New York: Simon and Schuster, 1961); Samuel Halperin, *The Political World of American Zionism* (Detroit: Wayne State University Press, 1961); Carol Bosworth Kutscher, "The Early Years of Hadassah," PhD Dissertation (Brandeis University, 1976); Marvin Lowenthal, *Henrietta Szold: Life and Letters* (New York: Viking, 1942); Melvin I. Urofsky, *American Zionism from Herzl to the Holocaust* (Garden City, NY: Anchor, 1975); Melvin I. Urofsky, *We Are One! American Jewry and Israel* (Garden City, NY: Anchor, 1978).

HADASSAH HOSPITAL. The largest medical facility in Israel, it is affiliated with the Hebrew University of Jerusalem*. Founded by the Women's Zionist Organization of America (WIZO)*, Hadassah's first hospital was opened in 1939 on Mount Scopus* in Jerusalem*. Throughout World War II it was used by the Allied authorities and, by the war's end, it had become the medical focal point not only for Palestine but for the entire region. On April 13, 1948, a convoy travelling to Mount Scopus from Jerusalem was ambushed by Arab guerrillas, leaving some 75 hospital personnel dead. Shortly afterward, civilians were evacuated and the hospital was left under guard of the Hagana* and later the IDF*. When Mount Scopus was demilitarized (as part of the 1949 Israel-Jordan Armistice Agreement*), its main access road was placed under the supervision of the United Nations. An Israeli police unit was stationed in the abandoned hospital and the adjoining Hebrew University facilities. Upon the reunification of Jerusalem in the June 1967 Six Day War* steps were immediately taken to reopen the Hadassah Hospital. Functions of the hospital are now split between Mount Scopus and the 300-acre facility at Ein Kerem.

HAGANA (DEFENSE). The security force of the Yishuv* was established in Palestine* in 1920 as a clandestine defense organization for the purpose of protecting Jewish life and property against Arab attacks. In

1941 it created a commando or "striking" force, the Palmah* (a full-time military force of volunteers, something of a professional and elite unit) which later provided a large proportion of the senior officers in the early years of the Israel Defense Forces*. Officially Hagana ceased to exist on May 31, 1948, when the Israel Defense Forces were constituted.

For further information see: Yigal Allon, *Shield of David: The Story of Israel's Armed Forces* (London: Weidenfeld and Nicolson, 1970); Yigal Allon, *The Making of Israel's Army* (London: Valentine, Mitchell, 1970); Yehuda Bauer, *From Diplomacy to Resistance* (Philadelphia: American Jewish Publication Society, 1970); Efraim Dekel, *SHAI: The Exploits of Hagana Intelligence* (New York: Yoseloff, 1959); Ben Zion Dinour, editor, *History of the Haganah*, 2 volumes (Tel Aviv: Ma'arakhot, 1956, 1964, Hebrew); Zerubavel Gilad, editor, *Hidden Shield: The Secret Military Efforts of the Yishuv during the War, 1939-1945* (Jerusalem: Jewish Agency, 1951); Dan Horowitz and Moshe Lissak, *Origins of the Israeli Polity: Palestine under the Mandate* (Chicago: University of Chicago Press, 1978); Moshe Pearlman, *The Army of Israel* (New York: Philosophical Library, 1950); Amos Perlmutter, *Military and Politics in Israel, 1948-1967: Nation-Building and Role Expansion* (London: Frank Cass, 1969); Ze'ev Schiff, *A History of the Israeli Army (1870-1974)* (New York: Simon and Schuster, 1974).

HAGANA BET see IRGUN

HAICHUD HALEUMI see NATIONAL UNION

HAIFA. A major deepwater port city on the Bay of Haifa on the eastern end of the Mediterranean Sea, it lies on and around Mount Carmel. It is the administrative center of the north of Israel and is an important manufacturing and cultural center. The city is composed of three sections: (1) the lower section, which spreads around the bottom of Mount Carmel, includes port facilities, warehouses, and apartment buildings; (2) the main business district covers most of the mountain slopes; and (3) the upper part of Haifa consists mostly of large houses, apartments buildings, and gardens and parks on top of the mountain.

Many religious landmarks are located in Haifa, including the Bahai* Temple, the Monastery of Our Lady of Mount Carmel, and Elijah's Cave. Haifa has two universities. The city's industries include oil refining and the manufacture of cement, chemicals, electronic equipment, glass, steel, and textiles. Haifa is also a shipping and railroad center. People lived in what is now the Haifa area about 3,000 years ago. Haifa was a small town until the mid-1850s, when it was first used as a port. By the mid-1990s Haifa had a population of about 250,000, roughly evenly split between Jews and Arabs.

HAKIBBUTZ HAARTZI. Hakibbutz Haartzi came into being as a settlement federation in 1927. Its ideological foundations are Zionism* and socialism. It advocates the combination of settlement with the class struggle, and for many years demanded of its members total identification with the kibbutz* federation's political philosophy, a concept which was termed "collective ideology." However, in the course of time the intensity of this collective ideology diminished, and today some members of Hakibbutz Haartzi publicly identify with other political parties (noticeably on the left). It was from this kibbutz movement that Hashomer Hatzair* developed, and this party founded with Sia Bet in 1949 the United Workers Party—Mapam*.

HAKIBBUTZ HADATI. The Federation of Religious Zionist Kibbutzim in Israel, affiliated since its inception in 1934 with the religious Zionist Mizrachi* movement and the National Religious Party*. The first religious kibbutz*, Tirat Tzevi, was established in 1930 by German-Jewish immigrants affiliated with religious Zionist youth movements such as Hashomer Hadati and B'nai Akiva. The movement's founders were motivated by a desire to integrate the labor-socialist principles central to early Zionist initiatives in Palestine* with Orthodox religious observance. It arose in part as an Orthodox response to the secularist tendencies exhibited by many of the early kibbutzim. Many of its earliest settlements, such as the Etzion bloc* south of Jerusalem*, were destroyed in the first Arab-Israeli War of 1948-1949*. After the 1967 War* it moved to immediately reestablish several of them. Elements of the religious kibbutz movement are affiliated with Gush Emunim*.

HAKIBBUTZ HAMEUHAD (UNITED KIBBUTZ). Hakibbutz Hameuhad was founded in 1927 by the association of Kibbutz En Harod and other kibbutz* settlements. Its program was finally crystallized in 1936: establishing large collective settlements that could grow even larger and which could engage in all spheres of industry. Each kibbutz was an autonomous unit. This kibbutz federation regards itself as fulfilling the historic mission of the Ahdut Haavoda* Party (founded in 1919) within the Mapai* Party and its heir—the Israel Labor Party*. Because of differences of opinion on ideological and political party matters, Hakibbutz Hameuhad split into two factions in 1951 and Ihud Hakvutzot Vehakibbutzim* was formed. Both are reunited in the United Kibbutz Movement*. Between 1944 and 1968 Hakibbutz Hameuhad provided the political base for the Sia Bet faction that split from Mapai in 1944 to form the Ahdut Haavoda Party. It united with Mapai and Rafi* to found the Israel Labor Party in 1968.

HAKOAH HASHAKET (THE QUIET FORCE). A political party created to contest the 1988 Knesset* election. Led by Yaacov Gross, it failed to secure a seat in parliament.

HALACHA. Jewish religious law. Debates over the interpretation of Halacha, and over the role of religious law in the affairs of the modern state, have bedevilled Israelis since before statehood.

HALEVY, EPHRAIM. Ephraim Halevy was born in England in 1943 and immigrated to Israel with his parents in 1948. He graduated in law from Hebrew University*. He joined the Mossad* in 1961. He served in the Mossad's operational unit, but spent most of his years in the "Tevel" (Hebrew for universe) division which operates as the liaison division charged with the Mossad's ties and contacts with its counterparts abroad, including those with which Israel has no official ties. In 1990 Halevy was appointed Deputy Mossad Chief and served for five years until he retired and was then appointed by Yitzhak Rabin* as his special intermediary with King Hussein* of Jordan*. He then became known as the secret channel between the Israeli Prime Minister and the royal court in Amman, prior to the signing of the Israel-Jordan Peace Treaty*. He was named head of the Mossad by Benjamin Netanyahu* in March 1998. He is said to maintain close and friendly relations with the royal court in Amman and was asked to help to mend fences with the monarchy following the aborted Maashal (Mashal*) affair in Amman.

HALUTZ (PIONEER). A term used in the Zionist* movement and in Israel to designate an individual who devoted himself or herself to the ideals of upbuilding Jewish Palestine* with physical labor, especially in agriculture.

HAMERCAZ *see* CENTER PARTY

HAMIZRACH LESHALOM *see* EAST FOR PEACE

HAMMER, ZEVULUN. Born in Haifa* in 1936, he received a BA in education and Jewish studies from Bar Ilan University* in 1964 and graduated from the National Defense College. A founder of the B'nai Akiva youth movement, Gush Emunim*, and the Hesder yeshiva system, Hammer was a strong proponent of religious Zionism*. First elected on behalf of the National Religious Party* to the Seventh Knesset* in October 1969, and reelected to subsequent Knessets, Hammer served as Deputy Minister of Education and Culture and was a member of the Defense and Foreign Affairs and Education and Culture Committees of the Knesset. Hammer served as Minister of Welfare from 1975 to 1976, and became Minister of Education and Culture from June 1977 to 1984 and Minister of Religious Affairs from October 1986 to December 1988. He again became Minister of Religious Affairs in the Government established in December 1988. In June 1990 he assumed the portfolio of Minister of Education and Culture. He served as Minister of Education, Culture, and Sport and Deputy Prime Minister from 1996 until his death in January 1998. Respected as one of the wiliest and most pragmatic of Israeli politicians, his death had implications for all segments of the political system suggesting a new dynamic in both intra- and inter-party negotiations.

HANEGBI, TZACHI. Born in Jerusalem* in 1957, he was educated at the Hebrew University of Jerusalem*. He managed the Likud* election campaign in 1984, and served as adviser to the Foreign Minister (1984-1986) and as director of the Prime Minister's Office (1986-1988). A member of Knesset*, for Likud*, since 1988. He served as Minister of Health from June to November 1996, and was named Minister of Justice in November 1996, a position that he held until July 1999. On May 17, 1999, he was reelected on the Likud list to the 15th Knesset. He is the son of Geula Cohen*, former MK and founder and head of the Tehiya* Party.

HAOLAM HAZEH. A political party founded in 1965, which focused on peace as the supreme aim and called for negotiations for a peace settlement between Israel and the Palestinian Arab state that should arise in the Land of Israel. It also called for free state welfare services for all.

It won one seat in the Knesset* elected in 1965 and two seats in the Knesset elected in 1969.

For further information see: David J. Schnall, *Radical Dissent in Contemporary Israeli Politics: Cracks in the Wall* (New York: Praeger, 1979).

HAPOEL HAMIZRAHI (WORKERS OF THE SPIRITUAL CENTER) *see* MIZRAHI

HAPOEL HATZAIR (THE YOUNG WORKER). A Zionist socialist political party established in 1905 by East European pioneers in Palestine*. In general it sought to distinguish itself from the other socialist groups, especially Poalei Zion*. It established Degania*—the first kibbutz*. In 1930 it joined with Ahdut Haavoda* to found Mapai*. Strongly committed to the idea that labor was a prerequisite for the realization of Zionist aspirations in Palestine, it also advocated the exclusive employment of Jewish labor (*Avoda Ivrit*). It was a founding institution of the Histadrut* labor federation, in 1920.

For further information see: Gershon R. Kieval, *Party Politics in Israel and the Occupied Territories* (Westport, CT: Greenwood, 1983); Peter Y. Medding, *MAPAI in Israel: Political Organization and Government in a New Society* (Cambridge, MA: Harvard, 1972); Peretz Merhav, *The Israeli Left: History, Problems, and Documents* (San Diego: A. S. Barnes, 1980).

HAREDI ("GOD FEARING", PL. HAREDIM). The term usually used to describe the ultra-Orthodox Jewish religious community in Israel, whose political interests are represented, in most cases, by parties such as Agudat Israel*, Degel Hatorah*, and Shas*. While this community is generally non-Zionist in political orientation—believing that the full national renewal of the Jewish people must await the arrival of the Messiah—most Haredim have come to terms with Zionism* and have, to one degree or another, become integrated into modern Israeli society. Only a small, extreme element of the Haredi community, represented by such groups as the Neturai Karta*, actually pursue a policy of noncontact with Israeli society and can be described as anti-Zionist. Demographically, the Haredim (along with the "modern Orthodox") are among the fastest growing segments of the Jewish-Israeli population.

For further information see: Charles S. Liebman, *Religion, Democracy and Israeli Society* (Amsterdam: Harwood Academic Publishers, 1997); Gary S. Schiff, *Tradition and Politics: Religious Parties of Israel* (Detroit: Wayne State University Press, 1977).

HAREL, ISSER (FORMERLY HALPERIN). One of the founders of the Israeli intelligence service. He was born in Russia in 1912 and immigrated to Palestine* in 1931. He was one of the original founders of Kibbutz Shfaim. During the War of Independence*, he headed the Hagana's Information Service (SHAI) and was a member of the National Command. In 1952, he was appointed head of the Mossad Lemodiin Vetafkidim Meyuhadim*, the central intelligence and security service of Israel. During his service in this post, he commanded the special operation to capture the Nazi war criminal Adolf Eichmann*. In 1963, he resigned his post over a disagreement with Prime Minister David Ben-Gurion* on the question of German scientists in Egypt*. In 1965, he was appointed an intelligence consultant to Prime Minister Levi Eshkol*, but he resigned this post after a short tenure.

For further information see: Michael Bar-Zohar, *Spies in the Promised Land: Isar Harel and the Israeli Secret Service* (Boston: Houghton-Mifflin, 1972); Efraim Dekel, *SHAI: The Exploits of Israel's Haganah Intelligence* (New York: Yoseloff, 1959); Dennis Eisenberg, *The Mossad: Israel's Secret Intelligence Service—Inside Stories* (London: Paddington, 1978); Tuviah Friedman, *The Hunter*, edited and translated by David C. Gross (New York: Macfadden, 1961); Isser Harel, *The House on Garibaldi Street: The First Full Account of the Capture of Adolf Eichmann, Told by the Former Head of Israel's Secret Service* (New York: Viking, 1975); Moshe Pearlman, *The Capture and Trial of Adolf Eichmann* (New York: Simon and Schuster, 1963); Dan Raviv and Yossi Melman, *Every Spy a Prince: The Complete History of Israel's Intelligence Community* (Boston: Houghton-Mifflin, 1990); Stewart Stevens, *The Spymasters of Israel* (New York: Macmillan, 1980).

HAR HOMA. Known to the Arabs as Jebel Abu-Ghneim. The area is primarily an uninhabited hilltop situation about 2 kilometers north of Bethlehem* on the southern outskirts of Jerusalem*. A rocky promontory, it is a blank spot in an increasingly dense urban landscape. At 2,500 feet above sea level and 3,900 feet above Dead Sea level, the site offers commanding vistas of Jerusalem's Old City and of the Judean desert.

Good new roads make it a 10-minute drive trip to Jerusalem's main shopping districts. It is located between Kibbutz Ramat Rahel and the Arab neighborhood of Beit Shaur, just beyond the "green line"*. Israeli proposals to build there predate the Oslo Accords* though plans had been deferred by the Rabin* and Peres* Governments for fear of upsetting the diplomatic process. The issue was revisited by the Netanyahu* Government. The project required the appropriation of land from both Jewish and Arab landowners. The High court of Justice* upheld the government's right to appropriate this land in order to meet the housing needs of the public at large. After the initial groundbreaking for the project in March 1997, the Palestinian authority angrily broke off peace talks, beginning an impasse that lasted until the negotiations at the Wye Plantation* in October 1998. The United Nations adopted resolutions of condemnation and, under Arab pressure, the General Assembly called upon the Government of Switzerland to convene an unprecedented meeting of the High Contracting Parties to the Fourth Geneva Convention to discuss ways of forcing Israel to apply the Convention in the occupied territories and in Jerusalem. Palestinians see Har Homa as part of an Israeli plan to encircle Arab sections of Jerusalem and to erect physical barriers between the city and areas of the West Bank* transferred to Palestinian control. Along with other neighborhoods of Jerusalem such as Ramot, Talpiot, and Gilo, Har Homa contributes to a ring of Jewish neighborhoods in Jerusalem.

HARMAN, AVRAHAM. Born in London, the son of a rabbi, he earned a law degree from Wadham College, Oxford. He moved to Jerusalem* in 1938 and held various positions with the Jewish Agency*. When Israel became independent, he was named Deputy Director of the Government Information Office. He held various diplomatic posts in Canada, at the United Nations, and in New York. He served as director of the Jewish Agency's information department before being sent to Washington to replace Abba Eban* where he served as ambassador from 1959 to 1968. Later he served, from 1968 to 1983, as president of Hebrew University* and as its chancellor until his death in 1992.

HAR-SHEFI, MARGALIT. In June 1998 Margalit Har-Shefi, a 23-year-old female friend of Yigal Amir* was found guilty by an Israel court of failing to prevent the 1995 assassination of Prime Minister Yitzhak Rabin*. She was a religious settler from Beit El who was a classmate of Amir at Bar Ilan University.

HASHOMER HATZAIR. Literally "the young guard." The oldest of the Jewish youth movements in Israel and abroad. The movement strives to instill in its members national values, Zionist* awareness, and socialist ideals, as well as to prepare them for kibbutz* life. Hakibbutz Haartzi* is its affiliate.

For further information see: Elkana Margalit, "Social and Intellectual Origins of the Hashomer Hatzair Youth Movement, 1913-1920," in *Essential Papers on Zionism,* edited by Jehuda Reinharz and Anita Shapira (New York: New York University Press, 1996): 454-472.

HASIDIM (THE PIOUS). A religious movement founded by Israel Baal Shem Tov around 1735. He was not a rabbi but journeyed widely as an itinerant preacher and proclaimed a philosophy of faith, love, and joy. His preaching was widely acclaimed and condemned. The Jewish leading authority of the day, the Vilna Gaon, excommunicated him. His philosophy spread throughout Eastern Europe where most Jews were concentrated at that time and had a revolutionary effect on Jewish life. It also generated strong opponents (the Mitnagdim). Hasidim are still a vital aspect of contemporary Judaism and numerous Hasidic dynasties of prominent rabbis continue to have large groups of followers in Israel and abroad.

HATIKVA (THE HOPE). Anthem of the Zionist* movement and the national anthem of the State of Israel which expresses the hope and yearning of the Jew for the return to Zion*. It was written by Naftali Herz Imber and first published in Jerusalem* in 1886.

HATNUA HAKIBBUTZIT HAMEUHEDET *see* UNITED KIBBUTZ MOVEMENT

HATZOFEH (THE OBSERVER). Hebrew* language daily newspaper published in Tel Aviv* representing an Orthodox religious perspective. Founded in 1937 by Rabbi Meir Bar-Ilan, it is affiliated with the Mizrachi* movement and the National Religious Party*. It serves as the NRP's organ. It has extensive coverage of religious parties and related orthodox groups.

HAUSNER, GIDEON M. An Israeli jurist who was born in Lvov, Poland, on September 26, 1915. He was brought to Palestine* in 1927. He graduated from the Hebrew University of Jerusalem* in 1940 and from the Jerusalem Law School in 1941. He was in private law practice from 1946 to 1960. From 1960 to 1963 he served as Attorney General* of the State of Israel. In that position he was the chief prosecutor at the Adolf Eichmann* trial. He was elected to the Knesset* on the Independent Liberal Party* ticket in 1965 and served until 1977. He died in November 1990. He wrote about his experiences during the Eichmann trial in *Justice in Jerusalem* (New York: Harper and Row, 1966; Schocken, 1968).

HAWK MISSILE. An anti-aircraft missile that was the first significant weapon system sold by the United States* to Israel, in 1962.

HAYERUKIM *see* ISRAEL GREEN PARTY

HAZIT DEMOKRATIT LESHALOM ULESHIYYON (HADASH) *see* DEMOCRATIC FRONT FOR PEACE AND EQUALITY

HEALTH. Palestine*, at the beginning of the twentieth century, was a backward area with substantial diseases, including malaria and numerous other ailments, as well as high infant mortality rates and other indicators of poor medical circumstances. Israel's situation is quite different. When the state was established in 1948, the Government created a Ministry of Health to serve as an administrative organ to supervise the functioning of the existing health organizations and to deal with the needs of the new state. Numerous health care-related organizations have been created. These include voluntary organizations such as the Kupat Holim*, the Hadassah* Medical Organization, the Magen David Adom*, and various other groups.

The basis of Israel's health care system was developed during the British Mandate* by the British authorities as well as by Jewish organizations in Palestine and in the Diaspora*. The tradition of health care provision antedates the founding of the state and in some instances even the Zionist movement. Jewish clinics established in Jerusalem* in the nineteenth century provided services to all citizens of the city and some have evolved into modern hospitals such as Bikur Holim and Shaare Zedek. In 1913 Hadassah sent two trained nurses to work in Jerusalem*—from this small beginning there eventually evolved the massive Hadassah-Hebrew University Medical Center with its attendant hospitals, clinics, and schools of medicine. Kupat Holim, Israel's first health insurance arrangement and the largest today, was established by the Histadrut* soon after the latter's founding in 1920 to provide health care for its members. More than 80% of Israel's population is insured through Kupat Holim today. Kupat Holim operates a vast network of facilities with thousands of staff throughout Israel. Thus, by the time Israel became independent there was a substantial health-services infrastructure. However, the post-independence wave of new immigrants, which included Holocaust* survivors from Europe as well as substantial immigration from developing countries, brought health problems that challenged the existing system both to meet their needs and to provide services that were new and different from those previously provided. From that starting point, Israel has created a modern health care system that rivals many of those in the most developed states, and Israel's achievements in the health field are among the most impressive in the world. Health insurance is voluntary, but virtually all of the population is insured under one or another health scheme. In the early 1990s the national health care system experienced radical restructuring and privatization.

For further information see: David P. Chinitz, "Reforming the Israeli Health Care Market," *Social Science and Medicine* 39 (1994): 1447-1457; Yael Yishai, "Physicians and the State in the USA and Israel," *Social Science and Medicine* 34 (1992): 129-139; Yair Zalmanovitch, "Public-Policy Management at the Margins of Government and Administration in Israel, Health Policy Making—The Israeli Case, 1970-1984," PhD Dissertation (The Hebrew University of Jerusalem, 1991, Hebrew); Yair Zalmanovitch, "Some Antecedents to Health Care Reform: Israel and the United States," Paper presented at conference on Israel in Comparative Perspective: The Dynamics of Change (University of California Press, Berkeley, September 1996); Yair Zalmanovitch, "Transitions in Israel's Policymaking Network," *The Annals of the American Academy of Political and Social Science* 555 (January 1998): 193-208.

HEBREW LANGUAGE. The official language of the State of Israel, Hebrew is a Semitic language in which most of the Bible, the Mishna and parts of the Talmud*, and much of rabbinic and secular Jewish literature are written. It is written from right to left. Until the Babylonian Exile (in 586 BCE) Hebrew was the sole language of the Jews. After the exile Aramaic came into widespread use although some Hebrew was still utilized. Both the Babylonian and Jerusalem* Talmuds are written in Aramaic rather than Hebrew. In countries of the Diaspora* the Jewish communities adopted local languages and substantially limited their use of Hebrew as a language of communication although it remained a language of Jewish literature and prayer. As the language of the Bible and prayer it was considered the sacred tongue. When the first pioneers came to Palestine* in the 1880s it seemed natural to use Hebrew as the vernacular language. The revival of the Hebrew language was closely associated with Eliezer Ben Yehuda* who arrived in Palestine in 1881 and sought to promote the use of Hebrew as a spoken language. There was opposition from skeptics who felt that the language was not rich enough to deal with contemporary matters and from the ultra-religious who objected to the use of the sacred tongue for practical everyday concerns. There was a vocabulary gap as a consequence of centuries of limited use. Ben Yehuda founded the Vaad Halashon Haivrit (Hebrew Language Council) in 1890 for the purpose of coining and creating new Hebrew words for modern usage. After the independence of Israel this body became the Akademiya Lalashon Haivrit (the Hebrew Language Academy). Hebrew made great strides among the pioneers who arrived in Palestine prior to 1948 and was well entrenched by the time of Israel's independence and the immigration to Israel of hundreds of thousands of new immigrants in the late 1940s and early 1950s who would have to learn Hebrew to become integrated into the society of the new state.

For further information see: Robert St. John, *Tongue of the Prophet: The Life Story of Eliezer Ben Yehuda* (New York: Doubleday, 1952).

HEBREW UNIVERSITY OF JERUSALEM. A prominent institution of higher learning located in Jerusalem*. Hebrew University was formally opened on April 1, 1925, on Mount Scopus* and remained there until the War of Independence* when in 1948 it became an enclave in Jordanian-held territory. The main focus of university life then was transferred to a new campus at Givat Ram. After Israel recaptured the surrounding areas and restored the Mount Scopus campus to the university during the Six Day War*, the university embarked on an ambitious scheme to dramatically increase its activities on the Mount Scopus campus. Judah Magnus* was instrumental in the creation of Hebrew University, serving as its first President.

HEBRON (HEVRON). Sometimes referred to as Kiryat Arba*. A town southwest of Jerusalem* in the hills of Judea*. It is one of the oldest cities in the world and played an important part in the ancient history of the Jewish people. It was the residence of the Jewish patriarchs and served as

King David's capital before he conquered Jerusalem. According to Jewish tradition, Abraham, Isaac, and Jacob and their wives (Sarah, Rebecca, and Leah) are buried in Hebron's Cave of the Patriarchs (Machpela). The traditional site of the cave, over which a mosque was erected, is one of the most sacred of Jewish shrines. The Arabs call it Al Halil. The meaning of the name Al Halil is "the friend" or "lover," the nickname given to Abraham, considered a holy man in Islam. His full nickname, Al Halil Al Rahman, means "the lover the God." In Isaiah's prophesy, God calls Abraham "my friend" (Isaiah, 41:8), and in the Book of Second Chronicles, he is called "Abraham, God's friend" (2 Chronicles, 20:7). In the Koran, it is written: "saintly Abraham, whom Allah himself chose to be his friend [in Arabic: Ibrahim Hallilian]" (Koran, 4, Women, 125). The Jewish legend finds in the name Hebron a combination of the two words Haver-Naeh, meaning a nice company or friend, which alludes to Abraham, since it was said, "a nice friend—that is Abraham" (Genesis, 4:13).

Small communities of devout Jews resided in Hebron, even during the centuries of Jewish exile from the Holy Land. In the late nineteenth century Hebron had a population of about 1,500 Jews; by 1910 their number had fallen to 700. In the 1929 Arab riots, 67 Jews were killed in Hebron, 60 others were wounded, and synagogues were destroyed. The surviving Jews left. Thirty-five families returned in 1931 but were evacuated by the British Mandatory Authority at the time of the resumed Arab riots of 1936-1939. Between 1948 and 1967 Israelis had no access to the city or the Cave of the Patriarchs. The city was captured by Israeli forces in the Six Day War.*

After the Six Day War* Israelis flocked to Hebron's religious sites, and it became a central focus of activity for Gush Emunim*. Rabbi Moshe Levinger* and his 450 or so followers, situated in a series of buildings in Hebron, along with the residents of the nearby settlement of Kiryat Arba, are among the strongest opponents of the Oslo Accords*. Hebron's Cave of the Patriarchs (Ibrahim Mosque) was the site of the massacre of 29 Arab worshipers by Dr. Baruch Goldstein* in February 1994. In January 1997 Israel and the PLO* concluded an agreement to transfer control of 80% of Hebron to Palestinian authority, with the Israel Defense Forces (IDF)* remaining in the other 20% to protect the city's Jewish population.

For further information see: "Hebron: Historical Background and Statistics" (Jerusalem: Israel Ministry of Foreign Affairs, October 28, 1976); "The Trouble with Hebron," *The Jerusalem Report* (July 25, 1996): 18-22.

HEBRON MASSACRE. On February 29, 1994, Dr. Baruch Goldstein*, a resident of Kiryat Arba*, opened fire with an assault rifle on Arab worshipers in Hebron's* the Tomb of the Patriarchs (known to Muslims as the Ibrahim Mosque), killing 29 and wounding more than 100 others. Goldstein was killed by survivors of the attack. It was one of the bloodiest single days in the occupied territories* since the Six Day War*. The attack was immediately condemned by the Government of Prime Minister Yitzhak Rabin* and by all parties in the Knesset*. A commission of inquiry headed by the President of the Supreme Court of Israel*, Justice Meir Shamgar*, concluded on June 26, 1994, that Goldstein had acted alone in committing this "base and murderous" massacre. The attack, which was condemned by the United Nations Security Council, caused a brief disruption in autonomy negotiations with the PLO*, and led to the imposition of a Temporary International Presence in Hebron (TIPH)* comprised of unarmed European observers. *See also* SHAMGAR COMMISSION.

For further information see: *Report of the State Investigative Committee in the Matter of the 1994 Massacre in Hebron's Cave of the Patriarchs* (Jerusalem: Government of Israel, June 26, 1994).

HERUT HAHADASHA *See* NEW HERUT

HERUT PARTY (TENUAT HAHERUT—FREEDOM MOVEMENT). A political party founded by the Irgun* in 1948 after the independence of Israel and the dissolution of the Irgun. Herut is descended from the Revisionist (New Zionist) movement* of Vladimir Ze'ev Jabotinsky*. The Revisionists advocated militant ultra-nationalistic action as the means to achieve Jewish statehood. Reacting to Great Britain's* decision to sever Transjordan from the original Palestine Mandate* in 1922, Revisionism called for the creation of a Jewish state in "Greater Israel" (all Palestine* and Jordan*); rapid mass immigration of Jews into Palestine; formation of a free-enterprise economy; rapid industrialization—as opposed to agricultural settlements—to increase employment opportunities; a ban on strikes; and a strong army. In order to effect these policies, and because they were outnumbered by leftist and moderate elements in the World Zionist Organization*, the Revisionists formed the New Zionist Organization in 1935. Their rejection of the socialist and liberal Zionist leadership and its conciliatory policy toward the mandatory power led Revisionists to form two paramilitary groups: Irgun Tzvai Leumi (Etzel)*, founded in 1937, and the even more radical LEHI (Stern Gang)*, founded in 1939-1940. The Irgun was commanded by Menachem Begin* after 1943. Betar*, the Revisionist youth movement, was founded by Jabotinsky in 1920 and continues as the Herut youth wing. Begin founded Herut in June 1948 to advocate the Revisionist program within the new political context of the State of Israel. Herut's political orientation has changed little over the years. It advocates the "inalienable" right of Jews to settle anywhere in Israel, in its historic entirety, including Judea* and Samaria* (the West Bank*). Herut advocates the unification of Eretz Israel* within its historic boundaries and favors a national economy based on private initiative and free competition. Other policies include a minimum of economic controls, a restructured free enterprise system to attract capital investment, and prohibiting the right to strike.

In 1965 Herut combined with the Liberal Party* to form Gahal*. In 1973 Gahal and several small parties combined to form Likud*. Within Herut and Likud*, Menachem Begin was the primary force from Israel's independence until his retirement in 1983. He was regarded by many as a heroic figure because of his role as a leader of the underground in the Israeli struggle for independence. Upon Begin's retirement, Yitzhak Shamir* became Prime Minister and party leader, although he was challenged within Herut, especially by David Levy* and Ariel Sharon*. Shamir retired from party politics after the 1992 election and was replaced as Herut and Likud leader by Benjamin Netanyahu*. Netanyahu resigned as party leader on May 17, 1999, following his defeat in the direct election for Prime Minister. He was succeeded on September 2, 1999, by Ariel Sharon.

For further information see: Dan Caspi, Abraham Diskin, and Emanuel Gutmann, editors, *The Roots of Begin's Success: The 1981 Israeli Elections* (London: Croom Helm, 1984); Ilan Peleg, "The Foreign Policy of Herut and the Likud," in *Israeli National Security Policy: Political Actors and Perspectives*, edited by Bernard Reich and Gershon R. Kieval

(New York: Greenwood, 1988): 55-78; Amos Perlmutter, *The Life and Times of Menachem Begin* (New York: Doubleday, 1987).

HERZL, THEODOR. The founder of modern political Zionism*, he was the driving force in the creation of the political ideology and the worldwide movement that led to the establishment of Israel. He was born in Pest, Hungary, on May 2, 1860. He was an assimilated Jew who later moved from Hungary to Vienna. He studied law but became involved in literature and wrote short stories and plays. He worked as the Paris correspondent of the Viennese daily newspaper *Neue Freie Presse* from 1891 to 1895. Growing anti-Semitism* in France contributed to Herzl's interest in the Jewish problem. As a journalist, he observed the trial of Alfred Dreyfus* and was affected by the false accusations leveled against the French Jewish army officer and by the episodes of anti-Semitism that accompanied the trial and the disgrace of Dreyfus. Herzl wrote *Der Judenstaat* (The Jewish State),* published in Vienna in 1896, in which he assessed the situation and problems of the Jews and proposed a practical plan—the establishment of a Jewish state for resolution of the Jewish Question*. Herzl argued: "Let the sovereignty be granted us over a portion of the globe large enough to satisfy the rightful requirements of a nation; the rest we shall manage for ourselves." Subsequently, Herzl traveled widely to publicize and gain support for his ideas. He found backing among the masses of East European Jewry and opposition among the leadership and wealthier segments of the Western Jewish communities.

On August 23, 1897, in Basle, Switzerland, Herzl convened the first World Zionist Congress* representing Jewish communities and organizations throughout the world. The congress established the World Zionist Organization (WZO)* and founded an effective, modern, political, Jewish national movement with the goal, enunciated in the Basle Program*, the original official program of the WZO: "Zionism seeks to establish a home for the Jewish people in Palestine secured under public law." Zionism rejected other solutions to the Jewish Question and was the response to centuries of discrimination, persecution, and oppression. It sought redemption through self-determination. Herzl died in Austria on July 3, 1904, and he was buried in Vienna. In August 1949 his remains were reinterred on Mount Herzl* in Jerusalem*.

For further information see: Shlomo Avineri, *The Making of Modern Zionism: The Intellectual Origins of the Jewish State* (New York: Basic, 1981); Alex Bein, *Theodor Herzl: A Biography* (Philadelphia: The Jewish Publication Society of America, 1948); Israel Cohen, *Theodor Herzl: Founder of Political Zionism* (New York: Herzl, 1959); Amos Elon, *Herzl* (New York: Holt, Rinehart and Winston, 1975); Ben Halpern, *The Idea of the Jewish State*, Second Edition (Cambridge, MA: Harvard, 1970); Joseph Heller, *The Zionist Idea* (New York: Schocken, 1949); Theodor Herzl, *Zionist Writings, Essays and Addresses*, 2 volumes (New York: Herzl Press, 1975); Arthur Hertzberg, editor, *The Zionist Idea: A Historical Analysis and Reader* (New York: Atheneum, 1979); Jacques Kornberg, *Theodor Herzl: From Assimilation to Zionism* (Bloomington: Indiana University Press, 1993); Walter Laqueur, *A History of Zionism* (London: Weidenfeld and Nicolson, 1972); Marvin Lowenthal, editor, *The Diaries of Theodor Herzl* (New York: Dial, 1956); David Vital, *The Origins of Zionism* (Oxford: Oxford University Press, 1975); Robert Wistrich, "Theodor Herzl: Zionist Icon, Myth-Maker, and Social Utopian," *Israel Affairs* 1:3 (Spring 1995): 7-37.

HERZLIYA HIGH SCHOOL (GYMNASIA HERZLIYA). First Hebrew* High School in Palestine*. It was founded in Jaffa* in 1905 for the purpose of providing a Jewish and secular education using Hebrew as the language of instruction. It was originally called the Gymnasia Ivrit of Jaffa and later renamed for Theodor Herzl*. It helped to educate generations of Jewish youth.

HERZOG, CHAIM. Born in Belfast, Ireland, on September 17, 1918, the son of Rabbi Isaac Halevi Herzog*, who later became the first Chief Rabbi of the State of Israel. He received an education in Ireland, at the University of London, at Cambridge, and at Hebron Yeshiva in Jerusalem*. He immigrated to Palestine* in 1935. During World War II, he served in the British army and became head of intelligence in the northern zone of Germany. During Israel's War of Independence* in 1948, he served as an officer in the battle for Latrun*. He was Director of Military Intelligence* from 1948 to 1950 and from 1959 to 1962. He served as military attaché in Washington from 1950-1954 and then became the commanding chief of the Jerusalem district from 1954-1957. He was chief of staff of the southern command from 1957-1959. After retiring from the army in 1962, he directed an industrial investment company. Beginning in 1967 with the Six Day War*, he was the leading military commentator for Israel Broadcasting Services. He was the first military commander of the West Bank* after the Six Day War. He served as Israel's representative at the United Nations from 1975 to 1978, and was elected to the 10th Knesset* in 1981. In 1983, he was elected President* of Israel and was reelected in 1988. He died in April 1997.

For further information see: Chaim Herzog, *Israel's Finest Hour* (Tel Aviv: Ma'ariv, 1967, Hebrew); Chaim Herzog, *The War of Atonement: October 1973* (Boston: Little, Brown, 1975); Chaim Herzog, *Who Stands Accused? Israel Answers Its Critics* (New York: Random House, 1978); Chaim Herzog, *The Arab-Israeli Wars* (New York: Random House, 1982); Chaim Herzog, *Living History: The Memoirs of a Great Israeli Freedom-Fighter, Soldier, Diplomat and Statesman* (London: Weidenfeld and Nicolson, 1997).

HERZOG, ISAAC HALEVI. Chief Rabbi of Palestine and Israel (1936-1959). He was born in Lomza, Russian Poland, in 1888 and died in Jerusalem* in 1959. He was educated in England* where he was ordained and attained a doctorate from the University of London. He served as a rabbi in Belfast and became Chief Rabbi of the Irish Free State in 1925. He was chosen Chief Rabbi of Palestine* in 1936. His son, Chaim Herzog*, became a significant figure in the Israel Defense Forces* and became President* of Israel, while his younger son, Ya'acov (Jacob David) Herzog, became an important figure in Israel's foreign policy and political establishment. *See also* CHIEF RABBINATE.

HESS, MOSES. Early Zionist thinker. Born in Bonn, Germany*, in 1812, he was one of the first to try to integrate two powerful ideological and political forces—socialism and Jewish nationalism. His book, *Rome and Jerusalem: The Last National Problem*, published in 1862, was a reaction to both nineteenth century European nationalism and blatant anti-Semitism*. It helped lay the intellectual foundations for Theodor Herzl* and other early proponents of modern political Zionism*. Hess died in Paris in 1875.

For further information see: Shlomo Avineri, *The Making of Modern Zionism: The Intellectual Origins of the Jewish State* (New York: Basic Books, 1981); Arthur Hertzberg, editor, *The Zionist Idea: A Historical Analysis and Reader* (New York: Atheneum, 1979); Jacob Katz, "The Forerunners of Zionism," in *Essential Papers on Zionism*, edited by

Jehuda Reinharz and Anita Shapira (New York: New York University Press, 1996): 33-45.

HEVRAT OVDIM. The cooperative association of all members of the Histadrut* organized in 1923. It serves as the ultimate authority—legislative, supervisory, and managerial—for all of the Histadrut's economic enterprises, as well as their official legal framework. These enterprises are independent, with Hevrat Ovdim supervising management, authorizing plans, and overseeing operations.

HIBBAT ZION MOVEMENT *see* HOVEVE ZION

HIGH COURT OF JUSTICE *see* SUPREME COURT

HILLEL, SHLOMO. Shlomo Hillel was born on April 23, 1923, the youngest of 11 children of a merchant in Baghdad, Iraq*. In 1933 he went to Palestine* and studied at the Herzliya High School* in Tel Aviv*. He was one of the founders of Kibbutz Maagen Michael. In 1946 he returned to Iraq to help organize the emigration of Iraqi Jews, and was active in the "illegal immigration" from Arab countries to pre-independence Israel. Following Israel's independence he was involved in the arrangements for the emigration in the early 1950s of virtually all of Iraq's Jewish community. He became a Mapai* member of the Knesset*, but resigned in 1959. He joined the Israeli diplomatic corps and served as Israel's Ambassador to a number of French-speaking African countries and in 1963 became head of the African division of the Foreign Ministry. He became Minister of Police in December 1969 and served as Minister of Interior and Police from 1973 to 1977. In 1984 he was elected Speaker of the Eleventh Knesset. He was reelected to parliament in 1988. Shlomo Hillel's experiences in helping to bring the Jews of Iraq to Israel were described in his book, *Operation Babylon* (New York: Doubleday, 1987).

HISTADRUT (GENERAL FEDERATION OF LABOR). The General Federation of Labor in Israel was founded in Haifa* in December 1920 as a federation of Jewish labor (Hahistadrut Haklalit Shel Ha'ovdim Ha'ivrim Be'eretz Yisrael). In 1966 the word Ha'ivrim (Hebrew) was dropped from the federation's name thus admitting Arabs to full membership. The purpose was to unite and organize all workers, to raise their standard of living, and to defend their economic interests, as well as to represent their interests in other areas. It is the country's biggest employer, controlling some 60% of the country's industry. It controls the Hapoel sports organization, the Naamat women's organization, and the biggest health insurance fund—Kupat Holim*. The Histadrut provides a wide range of services to its members. It cooperates with the government in numerous areas related to foreign and domestic policy and carries out many functions which are normally government activities in other modern states. Many of its leaders have served in major government posts (including that of Prime Minister) before and after working in Histadrut. Its decision-making bodies are organized along partisan political lines, and the organization as a whole has long been closely aligned with the leaders and policies of the Israel Labor Party*.

The Histadrut's constitution states: "The General Federation unites all workers in the land, as long as they live by their own toil without exploitation of another's labor, for the arrangement of all settlement and economic matters as well as cultural affairs of workers in the land, for the upbuilding of a Jewish workers' commonwealth in Eretz Israel." The founding convention also established a workers bank (now known as Bank Hapoalim), Israel's largest. The Histadrut evolved into a major institution in the Yishuv and in the State of Israel.

The Histadrut has a number of organs. The General Convention is the supreme authority of the Histadrut and is its legislature. Its decisions bind all members and all units of the organization. It is elected once every four years in general, direct, secret, and proportional elections. The convention chooses the Council (Moetzet Hahistadrut) whose composition is based on and reflects the political makeup of the Convention. The Histadrut Council is the supreme institution of the Histadrut between conventions. The Histadrut Executive is the governing executive body. It is chosen by the Council in keeping with the party makeup of the Histadrut Convention. It chooses the Central Committee and the Secretary General. The Histadrut Central Committee is its cabinet. It is chosen by the Executive and formally serves as its secretariat, conducting the day-to-day operations of the Labor Federation. It is composed only of members of the ruling coalition. The Histadrut Secretary General is chair of the Executive and of the Council and is extremely powerful.

However, the overall power and influence of the Histadrut declined due in large measure to efforts in the 1990s to breakup and privatize giant consortiums, efforts that pitted the Histadrut against Labor and Likud* governments alike. Though somewhat weakened by this trend as well as by significant changes and political divisions within the organization itself, the Histadrut remains very much a force to be reckoned with in Israeli economic, social, and political affairs. In the spring of 1999, Histadrut chairman (and former Labor* MK), Amir Peretz*, established a separate workers' political party, One Nation (Am Echad*), that won two seats in the elections to the 15th Knesset* that occurred on May 17, 1999.

Secretaries General of the Histadrut have included: David Ben-Gurion* (1921-1935), David Remez (1935-1945), Yosef Sprinzak (1945-1949), Pinhas Lavon* (1945-1950, 1955-1961), Mordechai Namir (1951-1955), Aharon Becker (1961-1969), Yitzhak Ben-Aharon (1969-1973), Yeruham Meshel (1973-1984), Israel Kessar*, Haim Haberfeld*, Haim Ramon*, and Amir Peretz*.

For further information see: Yitzhak Greenberg, "The Contribution of the Labor Economy to Immigrant Absorption and Population Dispersal during Israel's First Decade," in *Israel: The First Decade of Independence*, edited by S. Ilan Troen and Noah Lucas (Albany: State University of New York Press, 1995): 279-296; Nahum T. Gross, "The Economic Regime during Israel's First Decade," in *Israel: The First Decade of Independence*, edited by S. Ilan Troen and Noah Lucas (Albany: State University of New York Press, 1995): 231-242; Samuel Kurland, *Cooperative Politics: The Story of the Histadrut* (New York: Sharon Books for the National Committee for Labor of Palestine, 1947); David Levi-Faur, "State and Nationalism in Israel's Political Economy," *Israel Affairs* 3:1 (Autumn 1996): 143-160; Noah Malkosh, *Cooperative in Israel* (Tel Aviv: Histadrut, 1958); Noah Malkosh, *Histadrut in Israel: Its Aims and Achievements* (Tel Aviv: Histadrut, 1961); Ze'ev Tzahor, "The Histadrut: From Marginal Organization to 'State-in-the-Making,'" in *Essential Papers on Zionism*, edited by Jehuda Reinharz and Anita Shapira (New York: New York University Press, 1996): 473-508.

HOLOCAUST (THE SHOAH). Its origins were in Germany in January 1933 when the Nazis took power. It ended with the surrender of Nazi Germany at the end of World War II in May 1945. The period of Nazi control of Germany saw increasingly negative actions against Jews in the territories under Nazi Germany's control—an ever-increasing area as Adolf Hitler's military successes conquered more and more countries and their populations. Under Nazi Germany millions of European Jews lived in agony and fear and millions were tortured and killed. Israel remembers the Holocaust each year on the 27th day of Nisan of the Jewish calendar—known as Yom Hashoah. The Holocaust continues to have a major effect on Israel's collective psychology and on virtually every aspect of Israeli politics and foreign and security policy.

For further information see: Dan Bar-On, "The Holocaust Remembered: Israeli Society between the Culture of Death and the Culture of Life," *Israel Studies* 2:2 (Fall 1997): 88-117; Yehuda Bauer, *A History of the Holocaust* (New York: Franklin Watts, 1982); Judith Tydor Baumel, "'In Everlasting Memory': Individual and Communal Holocaust Commemoration," *Israel Affairs* 1:3 (Spring 1995): 146-170; Judith Tydor Baumel, "'Rachel Laments Her Children'—Representation of Women in Israeli Holocaust Memorials," *Israel Studies* 1:1 (Spring 1996): 100-126; Lucy S. Dawidowicz, *The War against the Jews, 1933-1945* (London: Weidenfeld and Nicolson, 1975); Evyatar Friesel, "The Holocaust and the Birth of Israel," *Wiener Library Bulletin* 32 (1979): 51-60; Dina Porat, "Attitudes of the Young State of Israel toward the Holocaust and Its Survivors: A Debate over Identity and Values," in *New Perspectives on Israeli History: The Early Years of the State*, edited by Laurence J. Silberstein (New York: New York University Press, 1991): 157-174; Joseph P. Schultz and Carla L. Klausner, *From Destruction to Rebirth: The Holocaust and the State of Israel* (Washington, DC: University Press of America, 1978); Shabtai Teveth, *Ben-Gurion and the Holocaust* (New York: Harcourt Brace, 1996); Yechiam Weitz, "Mapai and the 'Kasztner Trial,'" in *Israel: The First Decade of Independence*, edited by S. Ilan Troen and Noah Lucas (Albany: State University of New York Press, 1995): 195-210; Yechiam Weitz, "The Holocaust on Trial: The Impact of the Kasztner and Eichmann Trials on Israeli Society," *Israel Studies* 1:2 (Fall 1996): 1-26; Hannah Torok Yablonka, "The Silent Partner: Holocaust Survivors in the IDF," in *Israel: The First Decade of Independence*, edited by S. Ilan Troen and Noah Lucas (Albany: State University of New York Press, 1995): 557-574.

HOROWITZ, DAVID. Born on February 15, 1899, at Drogobych near Lvov in the Ukraine and educated at Lvov and Vienna, David Horowitz emigrated to Palestine* in 1920. He became a member of the Executive Committee of the Histadrut* in 1923, but also worked with a number of enterprises, served on government committees, and became director of the

Economic Department of the Jewish Agency*. After Israel's independence Horowitz became Director General of the Ministry of Finance. In 1954 he became Governor of the Bank of Israel*, a position in which he was responsible for the stability of Israel's currency at home and abroad and for the management of the public debt, among other functions.

For further information see: David Horowitz, *State in the Making* (New York: Alfred Knopf, 1953).

HOVEVE ZION (LOVERS OF ZION). A movement that was established in 1882, as a direct reaction to the widespread pogroms in Russia (especially Odessa) in 1881, for the purpose of encouraging Jewish settlement in Palestine* and achieving a Jewish national revival there. The founders concluded that the way to save the Jewish people was to return to Zion* and rebuild the land. They generally favored practical Zionism*—settlement in Israel. The members of the Hibbat Zion movement joined farm villages or established new ones (such as Rishon Le-Zion*, Zichron Yaakov, and Rosh Pina) in conformity with their view that immigration and settlement in Palestine would alleviate the problems of the Jewish communities in Europe.

For further information see: Shlomo Avineri, *The Making of Modern Zionism: The Intellectual Origins of the Jewish State* (New York: Basic, 1981); Shmuel Ettinger and Israel Bartal, "The First Aliyah: Ideological Roots and Practical Accomplishments," in *Essential Papers on Zionism*, edited by Jehuda Reinharz and Anita Shapira (New York: New York University Press, 1996): 63-93; Jacob Katz, "The Forerunners of Zionism," in *Essentials Papers on Zionism*, edited by Jehuda Reinharz and Anita Shapira (New York: New York University Press, 1996): 33-45; Nahum Sokolow, *Hibbat Zion* (The Love of Zion) (Jerusalem: Rubin Mass, 1941); Nahum Sokolow, *History of Zionism, 1600-1918* (New York: Ktav, 1969); David Vital, *The Origins of Zionism* (London: Oxford University Press, 1975).

HULEH VALLEY. A region in the upper and eastern portion of the Galilee*, bounding the Golan Heights*. Swamps were formed around Lake Huleh and were the cause of malarial conditions leading to high mortality rates and low living standards. Although earlier plans existed, Israel launched a major effort to drain the swamps beginning in 1951. By

1958 the project was concluded and successful; fertile land in the valley was reclaimed, water was made available for irrigation, and the threat of malaria was eliminated.

HUMAN DIGNITY AND FREEDOM *see* BASIC LAW: HUMAN DIGNITY AND FREEDOM

HURVITZ, YIGAEL. Born in Nahalat Yehuda in 1918, Yigael Hurvitz originally worked in agriculture, but became an industrialist. He was first elected to the Seventh Knesset* in October 1969 on the State List* and was reelected subsequently. He later served as chairman of the La'am* faction of the Likud*. He became Minister of Industry, Commerce and Tourism in 1977, but resigned in September 1978. He replaced Simha Ehrlich* as Minister of Finance in November 1979. He advocated hard-line economic policies, promoted austerity, and sought sharp cuts in subsidies, a reduction in civil service employment, some wage freezes, and other measures to reduce government expenditure. Under his stewardship, the Israeli pound was replaced by the shekel (the term drawn from the Bible), worth 10 Israeli pounds. Hurvitz later resigned his position and left Likud, and was elected to the Knesset in 1981 on Moshe Dayan's* Telem Party* list. In 1984 he entered the Knesset as the leader of the Ometz (Courage)* list. He served as Minister without Portfolio in the Government of National Unity* established in 1984. Hurvitz was elected to the Knesset on the Likud list in 1988. He retired from the Knesset in 1992, and died on January 10, 1995.

HUSSEIN, KING OF JORDAN (KING HUSSEIN, HUSSEIN IBN TALAL). Born in Amman, Jordan* on November 14, 1935, he died in Amman on February 7, 1999. He witnessed the assassination of his grandfather, King Abdullah I, at Jerusalem's* al-Alka mosque* on July 21, 1951. His father, Talal, ruled for only a brief period due to mental illness before Hussein was proclaimed King on Jordan on August 11, 1952. He continued to rule until his death. On the eve of the Six Day War* Hussein rejected an Israeli offer to maintain the status quo in Jerusalem and the West Bank* if Jordan agreed not to join the Arab military alliance confronting Israel; during the war Jordan lost control over these territories, although Israel permitted a degree of Jordanian influence to remain. In many years of secret contacts with Israelis, Hussein always reflected a pragmatism that contributed to the popularity of the idea of the "Jordan Option"* especially among elements of the Israel Labor Party*. Although he formally renounced Jordanian claims to the West Bank on July 31, 1988, Hussein remained actively engaged in diplomatic consultations about its final disposition and that of Jerusalem's Old City. On September 14, 1993 Israel and Jordan initialed a Common Agenda for future negotiations; the issuing of the Washington Declaration* on July 25, 1994, marked the completion of this Agenda. Hussein described the signing of the Israel-Jordan Peace Treaty* on October 26, 1994, and the warm personal relationship that he cultivated with Prime Minister Yitzhak Rabin*, as highlights of his political life. Hussein offered a moving tribute to Rabin at the latter's November 1995 funeral. He took the remarkable step of making personal condolence calls on the families of Israeli schoolgirls killed by a deranged Jordanian soldier in March 1997. Hussein interrupted his treatment for cancer to participate in the crucial final stages of Israeli-Palestinian negotiations that culminated with the Wye River Memorandum* of October 23, 1998.

For further information see: Peter Gubser, "Hussein Ibn Talal," in *Political Leaders of the Contemporary Middle East and North Africa*, edited by Bernard Reich (Westport, CT: Greenwood Press, 1990): 233-240; James Lunt, *Hussein of Jordan: Searching for a Just and Lasting Peace* (New York: William Morrow, 1989); Peter Snow, *Hussein: A Biography* (Washington, DC: Robert B. Luce, 1972); Gerald Sparrow, *Hussein of Jordan* (London: George C. Harrap, 1960).

I

IAI *see* ISRAEL AIRCRAFT INDUSTRIES

IDF *see* ISRAEL DEFENSE FORCES

IHUD. (Unity). A Jewish group in Palestine* during the British Mandate* that advocated an Arab-Jewish binational state in Palestine. Judah Magnes* believed that a determined effort should be made to avert a direct clash between Arabs and Jews. Along with others, such as Martin Buber*, he helped to form, in 1942, a group called Ihud. It advocated a binational solution to the problem of Palestine and argued for that view before the United Nations Special Committee on Palestine*. After the establishment of Israel, Ihud (and Magnes) argued for the establishment of a confederation in the Middle East that would include Israel and Arab states.

For further information see: Norman Bentwich, *For Zion's Sake: A Biography of Judah L. Magnes* (Philadelphia: Jewish Publication Society of America, 1954); Martin Buber, *A Land of Two Peoples: Martin Buber on Jews and Arabs* (New York: Oxford University Press, 1983); Susan Lee Hattis, *The Bi-National Idea in Palestine during Mandatory Times* (Haifa: Shikmona, 1970); Hagit Lavsky, "German Zionist and Emergence of Brit Shalom," in *Essential Papers on Zionism*, edited by Jehuda Reinharz and Anita Shapira (New York: New York University Press, 1996): 648-670; Judah L. Magnes, *Like All Nations?* (Jerusalem: Weiss Press, 1930).

IHUD HAKVUTZOT VEHAKIBBUTZIM. Founded in 1951 by the merger of Hever Hakvutzot with a group of kibbutzim* that broke away from Hakibbutz Hameuhad*. It provides economic, organizational, and social services to the kibbutzim of Oved Hatzioni and Poalei Agudat Israel*. Its members generally identify with the basic principles of the Israel Labor Party*.

IMMIGRATION *see* ALIYA

INDEPENDENCE, DECLARATION OF *see* DECLARATION OF INDEPENDENCE

INDEPENDENT LIBERAL PARTY (HALIBERALIM HAATZMAIM). A political party formed in 1965 by members of the Progressive* faction in the Liberal Party*. The Liberal Party split when the majority decided to join with Herut* to form Gahal*. Those who were concerned with the apparent rightward shift formed the new party. It contested the Knesset* elections beginning in 1965, and joined in the governments led by Labor* until 1977, when they lost their last Knesset seat. They later joined the Labor Alignment.

INDIA. India recognized Israel on September 18, 1950, but decided to establish full diplomatic relations only in January 1992. Israel had opened a consulate in Bombay in the early 1950s but its functions and jurisdiction were extremely limited and restricted. In the 1990s Israel and India developed mutually beneficial ties in the areas of trade and strategic cooperation. Ezer Weizman* became the first Israeli President* to visit India in 1996.

For further information see: P. R. Kumaraswamy, "Could Israel's Arrow End Up in India?," *Jane's Intelligence Review* (June 1999): 21-22; P. R. Kumaraswamy, *India and Israel: Evolving Strategic Partnership* (Ramat Gan: Begin-Sadat Center for Strategic Studies, Bar Ilan University, September 1998); P. R. Kumaraswamy, "India's Recognition of Israel, September 1950," *Middle Eastern Studies* (London) 31:1 (January 1955): 124-138; P. R. Kumaraswamy, "Prospects for Israeli-Indian Security Relations," *Survey of Arab Affairs* 37 (Jerusalem Center for Public Affairs, September 1, 1994).

INGATHERING OF THE EXILES (KIBBUTZ GALUYOT). The concept that the exiled Jewish communities in the Diaspora* would be gathered in Israel was derived from the Bible. The ingathering of the exiles became an important element in Zionism* during the pre-state period and was enshrined in the Law of Return* passed by the Knesset* after independence. *See also* ALIYA.

For further information see: Eliezer Schweid, "The Rejection of the Diaspora in Zionist Thought: Two Approaches," in *Essential Papers on Zionism*, edited by Jehuda Reinharz and Anita Shapira (New York: New York University Press, 1996): 133-160.

INTELLIGENCE. Given the existential military threats constantly confronting them, Israelis always have placed a high priority on military intelligence and, from the start of Jewish settlement in Palestine*, the Zionists relied on organized intelligence gathering and assessment. The intelligence service of the Hagana* (SHAI), initially concentrated on detecting threats to Yishuv* communities posed by local bands of Arabs, but also developed expertise about military and political affairs in the Arab world. During World War II, its personnel undertook intelligence and espionage activities in pro-Axis Arab countries in support of the British war effort. At the end of the war SHAI became actively engaged in Aliya Bet*, the illegal immigration of Jews to Palestine. By the spring of 1947 SHAI was preparing for the end of the British Mandate* by gathering detailed information about the political attitudes of local Arab villages and the military capabilities of the neighboring Arab countries that were massing troops on the borders of Palesitne. Today, intelligence functions are performed by a variety of agencies, including the IDF* (under the Director of Military Intelligence*), the General Security Services (Shin Bet*), the Political Research Department of the Foreign Ministry, and the Institute for Intelligence and Special Duties (Mossad*). Despite bureaucratic divisions of labor, intelligence gathering and assessment remains a vital element of Israel's national security doctrine.

For further information see: Zwy Aldouby and Jerrold Ballinger, *The Shattered Silence: The Eli Cohen Affair* (New York: Coward, McCann and Geoghegan, 1971); Michael Bar-Zohar, *Spies in the Promised Land: Isar Harel and the Israeli Secret Service* (Boston: Houghton Mifflin, 1972); Eli Ben-Hanon, *Our Man in Damascus* (Tel Aviv: A.D.M. Publishing House, 1967); Stanley Blumberg and Gwinn Owens, *The Survival Factor: Israeli Intelligence from World War I to the Present* (New York: G. P. Putnam's Sons, 1981); Richard Deacon, *The Israeli Secret Service* (New York: Tapliner, 1978); Ephraim Dekel (Krasner), *Shai: Historical Exploits of Haganah Intelligence* (New York: Yoseloff, 1959); Dennis Eisenberg, Uri Dan, and Eli Landau, *The Mossad Insider Stories: Israel's Secret Intelligence Service* (New York: Paddington, 1978); Isser Harel, *The House on Garibaldi Street: The First Full Account of the Capture of Adolf Eichmann, Told by the Former Head of Israel's Secret Service* (New York: Viking, 1975); Wolfgang Lotz, *The Champagne Spy: Israel's Master Spy Tells His Story* (New York: St. Martin's Press, 1972); Marcelle Ninio, Victor Levy, Robert Dassa, and Philip Natanson, *Operation Susannah* (New York: Harper and Row, 1978); Steve Posner, *Israel Undercover: The Secret Warfare and Hidden Diplomacy in the Middle East* (Syracuse: Syracuse University Press, 1987); Dan Raviv and Yossi Melman, *Every Spy a Prince: The Complete History of Israel's Intelligence Community* (Boston: Houghton Mifflin, 1990); Stewart Steven, *The Spymasters of Israel* (New York: Macmillan, 1980); Gordon Thomas, *Gideon's Spies: The Secret History of the Mossad* (New York: St. Martin's Press, 1999).

INTIFADA. Arab uprising in the West Bank* and Gaza Strip*, which began in December 1987 in strong and violent opposition to continued Israeli occupation of those territories. The Palestinian uprising became a test of wills and policy between Palestinians in the territories occupied by Israel in the Six Day War* and Israel. Israel sought to end the uprising and restore law and order in the West Bank and Gaza Strip. The Palestinians saw the uprising as a means to end Israeli occupation and to promote an independent Palestinian state. Palestinians sought to accelerate the political process and, in particular, to gain a representative role for the Palestine Liberation Organization* in negotiations with Israel and the United States*.

Confrontation and violence marked the evolution of the intifada with a growing toll of casualties on both sides. For the Palestinians the intifada seemed to provide a catharsis, but also a high cost in casualties, imprisonment, loss of education and employment, and growing divisions within the Palestinian population. For Israel the intifada posed a major challenge on a number of counts, including damage to its international image, divisions within the body politic on how to respond, the monetary costs of increased military reserve duty, and the costs of other disruptions of the economy.

The intifada began with a series of incidents (the stabbing to death of an Israeli by a Palestinian in Gaza City, a traffic accident in which four Palestinians were killed, and subsequent riots in the Jabaliya refugee camp) in early December 1987. Over the ensuing period the violence seemed to grow and to gain increasing international attention to the status of the Palestinians in the West Bank and Gaza Strip. Eventually Defense Minister Yitzhak Rabin* argued that this was not classical terrorism, but civilian violence carried out by a considerable portion of the Palestinian population by means available to every individual, such as stones, Molotov cocktails, barricades, and burning tires. The difficulty was to devise a means to defuse the violence. For both sides the intifada became a test of political wills portending continuing confrontations over time.

By the time of the Madrid Peace Conference* and the Israel-PLO Declaration of Principles* the intifada had petered out, though periodic clashes between Palestinian demonstrators and IDF soldiers and settlers continued to occur. Moreover, Muslim extremist groups such as Hamas and Palestine Islamic Jihad (PIJ), both of which grew to prominence during the intifada, continued to wage a terrorist war of attrition against Israel.

For further information see: Robert Owen Freedman, editor, *The Intifada: Its Impact on Israel, the Arab World, and the Superpowers* (Miami: Florida International University Press, 1991); Shlomo Gazit, "Israel and the Palestinians: Fifty Years of Wars and Turning Points," *The Annals of* the American Academy of Political and Social Science 555 (January 1998): 82-96; Giora Goldberg, Gad Barzilai, and Efraim Inbar, The Impact of Intercommunal Conflict: The Intifada and Israeli Public Opinion (Jerusalem: Leonard Davis Institute for International Relations, Hebrew University of Jerusalem Press, February 1991); F. Robert Hunter, The Palestinian Uprising: A War by Other Means, Revised Edition (Berkeley: University of California Press, 1993); Efraim Inbar, "Israel's Small War: The Military Response to the Intifada," Armed Forces and Society 18:1 (Fall 1991): 29-50; Zachary Lockman and Joel Beinin, editors, Intifada: The Palestinian Uprising against Israeli Occupation (Boston: South End Press, 1989); Yossi Melman and Dan Raviv, Behind the Uprising: Israelis, Jordanians, and Palestinians (Westport, CT: Greenwood, 1989); Don Peretz, Intifada: The Palestinian Uprising (Boulder, CO: Westview, 1990); Ze'ev Schiff and Ehud Ya'ari, Intifada: The Palestinian Uprising— Israel's Third Front (New York: Simon and Schuster, 1990); Aryeh Shalev, The Intifada: Causes and Effects (Boulder, CO: Westview, 1991).

IRAN. Iran is a non-Arab state located in the predominantly Arab Middle East. Iran opposed the creation of the Jewish state in the United Nations General Assembly vote in November 1947 on the Palestine Partition Plan* but, subsequently, established diplomatic relations with Israel. During the reign of Mohammed Reza Shah Pahlavi, mutually beneficial relations developed between Israel and Iran that involved, among other activities, the sale of oil to Israel and Israeli assistance with various developmental projects in Iran. Positive, if low profile, political linkages were established. Following the Iranian Revolution, diplomatic relations between the two states were broken as the Islamic Republic of Iran established close formal links with the Palestine Liberation Organization*. Under the Ayatollah Khomeini, Iran called for the termination of the Jewish state and the liberation of Jerusalem* from Israeli control. Despite this hostile rhetoric Israel was involved in U.S. efforts to transfer weapons to Teheran during the Iran-Iraq War of the 1980s ("Irangate") in exchange for the release of American hostages held in Lebanon* by Iranian-backed forces. Hostility and vituperative rhetoric have been the hallmarks of Iran's approach to Israel since the accession of the Islamic Republic regime in Teheran. This hostility is manifested in Iran's active support for Muslim extremist groups such as Hezbollah*, Hamas, and Palestine Islamic Jihad that commit acts of terror against Israel and against Israeli and Jewish targets internationally. Teheran also remains opposed to the Arab-Israel peace process and is doing all that it can to destabilize the entire Middle East, including acquiring and/or developing weapons of mass destruction and the long-range missile capability to deliver those weapons. These circumstances, combined with continued hostile rhetoric from Teheran, diminish the credibility of occasional rumors of positive change in Israel-Iran relations.

For further information see: Michael Eisenstadt, *Iranian Military Power: Capabilities and Intentions* (Washington, DC: The Washington Institute for Near East Policy, 1996); David Menashri, *Revolution at a Crossroads: Iran's Domestic Politics and Regional Ambitions* (Washington, DC: The Washington Institute for Near East Policy, 1997).

IRAQ. An Arab state in the Middle East situated in the northeastern portion of the Arabian Peninsula on the Persian Gulf. Although Iraq does not border Israel, it has been an active participant in the Arab-Israeli conflict for much of the period since 1947, and has fought against Israel in Israel's War of Independence*, the Six Day War*, and the Yom Kippur War*. It remains in a state of war with Israel and has been associated with the Arab confrontation states. Iraq was among those Arab states that took the lead against Egyptian President Anwar Sadat's* overtures to Israel in 1977 and 1978, it opposed the Egypt-Israel Peace Treaty of 1979*, and it harbored and supported anti-Israel Palestinian terrorist groups. In 1981 Israel destroyed Iraq's Osirak* nuclear reactor arguing it was developing nuclear weapons. At the same time, during the course of the Iran-Iraq War (from 1980 to the cease-fire of 1988), Baghdad was preoccupied with developments in the Gulf area and the cause against Israel became of much lesser consequence. With the end of Gulf hostilities, Israel became increasingly concerned about Iraqi intentions, particularly with the large size, capability, and battle experience of Iraq's military, its ability and willingness to use missiles and chemical-biological warfare in its war with Iran, and its support of the Palestinian cause against Israel. The Iraqi attack against and occupation of Kuwait in August 1990 and the crisis which followed confirmed many Israeli fears. During the Persian Gulf War between Iraq and the international coalition that began in January 1991, Iraq launched 39 Scud missiles* against Israel that killed and wounded Israelis and caused substantial property damage. This unprovoked attack occasioned substantial concern and debate in Israel about an appropriate response. The Shamir*-led Government decided that it would accede to requests by the United States* that it not respond militarily to the aggressive acts by Iraq. Though weakened by international sanctions, Saddam Hussein's Iraq continued to be considered a military threat by Israel.

For further information see: Moshe Arens "Unfinished Business," *Jerusalem Post,* November 21, 1997; Gad Barzilai, "Society and Politics in War: The Israeli Case," in *The Gulf Crisis and Its Global Aftermath,* edited by Gad Barzilai, Aharon Klieman, and Gil Shidlo (London: Routledge, 1993): 129-145; Gad Barzilai and Efraim Inbar, "Do Wars Have an Impact?: Israeli Public Opinion after the Gulf War," *Jerusalem Journal of International Relations* 14:1 (March 1992): 48-64; Seth Carus, *The Genie Unleashed: Iraq's Chemical and Biological Weapons Production* (Washington, DC: The Washington Institute for Near East Policy, 1989); Shai Feldman, *The Raid on Osiraq: A Preliminary Assessment* (Tel Aviv: Jaffee Center for Strategic Studies, Tel Aviv University, 1981); Lawrence Freedman and Efraim Karsh, *The Gulf Conflict 1990-1991: Diplomacy and War in the New World Order* (London: Faber and Faber, 1993); Dore Gold, *Israel and the Gulf: New Security Frameworks for the Middle East* (Washington, DC: The Washington Institute for Near East Policy, November 1996); David H. Goldberg, "The Iraqi Invasion of Kuwait: The Implications for Israel," *Middle East Focus* 12:3 (Fall 1990): 2-5, 27; Mark A. Heller, "Of Israel-bashing and the Iraqi Crisis," *Jerusalem Post,* December 7, 1997; Efraim Inbar, "Strategic Consequences for Israel," in *The Gulf Crisis and Its Global Aftermath,* edited by Gad Barzilai, Aharon Klieman, and Gil Shidlo (London: Routledge, 1993): 146-159; Amos Perlmutter, Michael Handel, and Uri Bar-Joseph, *Two Minutes Over Baghdad* (London: Valentine, Mitchell, 1982); Yitzhak Rabin, "Israel's Security Policy after Desert Storm," in *Thoughts on the National Security Concept of Israel* (Ramat Gan: Begin and Sadat Center for Strategic Studies, Bar Ilan University, August 1991, Hebrew); Bernard Reich, "Israel and the Iraq-Iraq War," in *The Persian Gulf War: Lessons for Strategy, Law, and Diplomacy,* edited by Christopher C. Joyner (New York: Greenwood, 1990): 75-90.

IRGUN (IRGUN TZVAI LEUMI—ETZEL). Also called Hagana Bet*. A Jewish military organization in Palestine* formed in 1931 and headed by Abraham Tehomi (formerly Silber), organized on a military basis and stressed military training and discipline. In its early years, civilian backing was provided by a broadly based board consisting of representatives of all non-socialist parties in the Yishuv*. The rank and file of the organization consisted overwhelmingly of members of Betar* and young Revisionists*, but the Revisionist movement had at that stage no decisive influence over the body. In 1937 Tehomi reached an agreement with the Hagana* for the merger of the two defense bodies. This led to a split in Etzel in April 1937. Etzel asserted that only active retaliation would deter the Arabs. Its ideology, based on the teachings of Vladimir Zeev Jabotinsky*, was built on the principle that armed Jewish force was the prerequisite for the Jewish State and that every Jew had a natural right to enter Palestine. Irgun's first commander was Robert Bitker, who was succeeded by Moshe Rosenberg and then by David Raziel. Its symbol was a hand holding a rifle over the map of the original Palestine mandate, including Transjordan, with the motto "rak kach" ("only thus"). The Jewish Agency* strongly denounced Irgun's "dissident activities," which the British administration countered by suppression and mass arrests. Until May 1939, Irgun's activities were limited to retaliation against Arab attacks. After the publication of the British White Paper of 1939*, the British Mandatory* authorities became Irgun's main target. Another major field of activity was the organization of Aliya Bet* (illegal immigration) and helping "illegal" immigrants land safely.

With the outbreak of World War II, Irgun announced the cessation of anti-British action and offered its cooperation in the common struggle against Nazi Germany. Its commander in chief, David Raziel, was killed in Iraq* in May 1941 while leading Irgun volunteers on a special mission for the British. Raziel's successor was Yaakov Meridor*, who in turn was replaced by Menachem Begin* in December 1943, who remained in command until 1948.

In January 1944, Irgun declared that the truce was over and that a renewed state of war existed with the British. Irgun demanded the liberation of Palestine from British occupation. Its attacks were directed against government institutions such as immigration, land registry, and income tax offices and police and radio stations. Limited cooperation was established in the late fall of 1945 between Irgun, LEHI*, and Hagana with the formation of the Hebrew Resistance Movement. Cooperation between the three forces lasted, with occasional setbacks, until August 1946. On July 22 of that year, Etzel blew up the British Army headquarters and the Secretariat of the Palestine Government in the King David Hotel* in Jerusalem*.

When, after the United Nations adopted the Palestine Partition Plan* on November 29, 1947, organized Arab bands launched murderous anti-Jewish attacks, Irgun vigorously counterattacked. Among these was the capture, on April 10, 1948, of the village of Deir Yassin by Irgun-LEHI forces, which resulted in a reported 240 Arab civilian casualties, although recent Palestinian research suggests that the actual number of casualties may have been exaggerated.

When the State of Israel was proclaimed on May 14, Irgun announced that it would disband and transfer its men to the Israel Defense Forces*. For several weeks, however, until full integration was completed, Irgun formations continued to function as separate units.

On June 20, 1948, a cargo ship, the *Altalena**, purchased and equipped in Europe by Irgun and its sympathizers and carrying 800 volunteers and large quantities of arms and ammunition, reached Israel's shores. Irgun demanded that 20% of the arms be allocated to its still independent units in Jerusalem, but the Israeli Government ordered the surrender of all arms and of the ship. When the order was not complied with, Government troops opened fire on the ship, which consequently went up in flames off Tel Aviv*. On September 1, 1948, the remaining units disbanded and joined the Israel Defense Forces.

For further information see: Yaacov Banai, *Unknown Soldiers* (Tel Aviv: Hag Yedidim, 1958, Hebrew); Menachem Begin, *The Revolt: Story of the Irgun* (New York: Nash, 1981); J. Bowyer Bell, *Terror Out of Zion: Irgun Tzva'i Le'umi, Lehi, Palestine Underground, 1929-1949* (New York: St. Maitin's, 1977); Yitzhak Ben-Ami, *Years of Wrath, Days of Glory: Memoirs from the Irgun* (New York: Speller, 1982); Thurston Clarke, *By Blood and Fire: The Attack on the King David Hotel* (New York: Putnam, 1982); Joseph Heller, "The Zionist Right and National Liberation: From Jabotinsky to Avraham Stern," *Israel Affairs* 1:3 (Spring 1995): 85-109; Samuel Katz, *Days of Fire: The Secret History of the Irgun Zva'i Leumi* (Garden City, NY: Doubleday, 1968); Shlomo Nakdimon, *Altalena* (Jerusalem: Edanim, 1978, Hebrew); David Niv, *Battle of Freedom: The Irgun Tzva'i Le'umi*, 3 volumes (Tel Aviv: Klausner Institute, 1963-1967); Joseph Schechtman and Yehuda Benari, *A History of the Revisionist Movement* (Tel Aviv: Hadar, 1970, Hebrew); Yaacov Shavit, *Revisionism in Zionism* (Tel Aviv: Yariv, 1978, Hebrew); Yaacov Shavit, *Jabotinsky and the Revisionist Movement, 1925-1948*

(London: Frank Cass, 1988); Yaacov Shavit, "Fire and Water: Ze'ev Jabotinsky and the Revisionist Movement," in *Essential Papers on Zionism*, edited by Jehuda Reinharz and Anita Shapira (New York: New York University Press, 1996): 544-566.

IRGUN TZVAI LEUMI (NATIONAL MILITARY ORGANIZATION, ETZEL) *see* IRGUN

ISRAEL AHAT *see* ONE ISRAEL

ISRAEL AIRCRAFT INDUSTRIES (IAI). Israel Aircraft Industries is the centerpiece of Israel's armaments industry. It has grown rapidly, from a company of less than one hundred employees when founded to more than twenty thousand by the 1980s. IAI produces a wide range of items, some under license, including aircraft (such as the Fouga-Magister), ammunition, armor, radar/sonar, and gyroscopes.

The idea to form an aircraft industry combining the special security needs of Israel with the development of industry originated in the Ministry of Defense during the 1950s. The reasons were that Israel's strategic situation depended on a capability to manufacture arms, the high costs of foreign-made arms, and the fear of an arms embargo. Maintenance was a problem for both the air force and El Al*, which was dependent upon maintenance facilities abroad. The need to establish an aeronautical and technological center in Israel was acute.

Al Shwimmer, an American aeronautical engineer who served in the Israeli air force, established a small factory in California called Intercontinental Airways, which dealt mainly with repairing old airplanes. In 1951, he met with Shimon Peres*, then the head of an Israeli arms acquisition delegation, and proposed that his company look for scrap metal for Mustang planes (which were then very popular in the Israeli air force), renovate the planes, and send them to Israel. The idea was broached to David Ben-Gurion* who accepted it. Ben-Gurion proposed that Shwimmer relocate the factory to Israel. This was the beginning of Israel Aircraft Industries. Shwimmer submitted his proposal for the establishment of an aircraft industry to the Prime Minister. The proposal included two projects calling for the establishment of a base in Israel that would be able to repair and overhaul all types of aircraft, both military and civilian, including engines; and the independent production of planes in Israel. The second project was not accepted by the Government since it seemed unrealistic. The first, however, was to be fulfilled by creating Bedek, a company established in 1951 according to a special agreement between Shwimmer and the Government. The factory grew quickly. In the early 1960s Bedek's management decided to proceed with the original proposal to attempt to produce new aircraft in Israel. Among the problems they encountered was the lack of a crystallized and experienced engineering body. This problem was reflected in the manufacturing of the Fuga and the "Stratocruiser." However, this problem was solved by the mid-1960s.

On March 31, 1968, Bedek was transformed from a subdivision of the Ministry of Defense to an independent company. It then was divided into three units: the Bedek-Metosim unit, which primarily dealt with the repair and rebuilding of airplanes; the aircraft manufacturing unit, which focused on the manufacture of new aircraft; and the engineering unit, which dealt with research and development. That same year for the first time the company assumed responsibility for the design and manufacture of a whole plane, the Arava, which was a light plane carrying up to 20 people that could land and take off on short runways. The Arava was produced in both a civilian and military version. In the early 1970s Bedek revised its goals and decided to produce a fighter plane. The first such plane was the Kfir*.

Other than production and repair of aircraft, Israel Aircraft Industries also deals with the production of other sophisticated weapons systems, such as the Mazlat (the Hebrew acronym for pilotless aircraft). These weapons systems have included the Gabriel*, a sea-to-sea missile. The Gabriel later became one of IAI's primary export items. In addition, IAI produces several ships, such as the Dabour class corvettes, armored vehicles, electrical and communication systems, helicopters, etc. Many of these products are produced by one of the company's numerous subsidiaries, including Alta, Tama, Mabat, Shahal, Pamal, and others.

In the mid-1990s IAI came under the scrutiny of a government commission mandated to examine the future of Israel's defense industry. The Peled Commission concluded that in order to compete in the future, the Israeli defense industry will have to undergo significant structural change. At the core of this change will be IAI, which, according to the commission's recommendations, will have concentrated into it all aviation and space technology research and development, including aircraft upgrades, avionics and photographic systems, developing and manufacturing pilotless aircraft, missiles and missile launchers, and satellites.

For further information see: Benjamin Beit-Hallahmi, *The Israeli Connection: Who Israel Arms and Why* (New York: Pantheon, 1987); Eitan Berglas, *Defense and the Economy: The Israeli Experience* (Jerusalem: The Maurice Falk Institute for Economic Research, January 1983); Aharon S. Klieman, *Israel's Global Reach: Arms Sales as Diplomacy* (McLean, Virginia: Pergamon-Brassey, 1985); Shimon Peres, *David's Sling: The Arming of Israel* (London: Weidenfeld and Nicolson, 1970); Stewart Reiser, *The Israeli Arms Industry: Foreign Policy, Arms Transfers, and Military Doctrine of a Small State* (New York: Holmes and Meier, 1989).

ISRAEL B'ALIYA (ISRAEL FOR IMMIGRATION/ISRAEL MOVING UPWARD). A political party headed by Natan (Anatoly) Sharansky* and comprised mostly of immigrants from the former Soviet Union that ran candidates for the first time in the 1996 election and won seven Knesset* seats. It participated in the governing coalition formed by Benjamin Netanyahu*, with Sharansky serving as Minister of Industry and Trade and Yuli Edelstein as Immigrant Absorption Minister. Israel B'Aliya advocated increased funding for the absorption of immigrants. It also adopted a liberal perspective on domestic economic and social issues, including the recognition by religious authorities of conversions to Judaism performed by non-Orthodox rabbis and the patrilineal line of Jewish descent. On foreign and security policy it sought to present itself as a centrist party – contending that future Israeli Governments must be prepared to abide by international obligations entered into by previous Governments (e.g., the Oslo Accords*) but at the same time demanding full compliance from the Arab side in all peace agreements. Israel B'Aliya won six seats in the elections for the 15th Knesset that occurred on May 17, 1999; it ran on a campaign that emphasized the need for the Russian immigrant community to have greater control over agencies of government that most effect their daily lives, including and especially the Interior Ministry. In the governing coalition presented by Ehud Barak* on July 6, 1999, Israel B'Aliya's Natan Sharansky* was named Interior Minister and MK Marina Solodkin was appointed deputy minister of immigrant absorption. However, only days after the new Government was formed, Israel B'Aliya was rocked by the departure of two members of Knesset (Roman Bronfman and Alexander Tsinker) who moved to set up an independent faction in the Knesset.

For further information see: Etta Bick, "Sectarian Party Politics in Israel: The Case of Yisrael Ba'Aliya, The Russian Immigrant Party," *Israel Affairs* (Special Issue: "Israel at the Polls 1996") 4:1 (Autumn 1997): 121-145; Bernard Reich, Meyrav Wurmser, and Noah Dropkin, "Playing Politics in Moscow and Jerusalem: Soviet Jewish Immigrants and the 1992 Knesset Election," in *Israel at the Polls 1992*, edited by Daniel J. Elazar and Shmuel Sandler (Lanham, MD: Rowman and Littlefield, 1995): 127-154.

ISRAEL BEITEINU (ISRAEL OUR HOME). A Russian immigrant party headed by former Likud* Party insider and Netanyahu* adviser Avigdor Lieberman, that won four Knesset* seats in the elections of May 1999. Lieberman stresses that the party's intention is to bring about public unity and peace agreements with a consensus. The platform centers on immigrant needs, including housing, strengthening of development towns, fighting unemployment, education, employment equality, and immigration absorption. On February 1, 2000 it joined with the National Union* faction in the 15th Knesset to form the National Home Party.

ISRAEL BONDS *see* STATE OF ISRAEL BONDS

ISRAEL COMMUNISTS *see* COMMUNIST PARTY

ISRAEL DEFENSE FORCES (ZAHAL) (IDF). Israel's military is under a unified command of land, air, and sea forces. It is subject to the authority of the Government* and carries out its policy. The Minister of Defense is in charge of the IDF. The Minister is a civilian, although he or she may have had a previous career in the professional military (e.g., Moshe Dayan*, Ezer Weizman*, Yitzhak Rabin*, Yitzhak Mordechai*, Amnon Lipkin-Shahak*, and Ehud Barak*). A special ministerial committee generally headed by the Prime Minister deals with security matters on behalf of the Government. Military service in the armed forces is compulsory and eligible men and women are drafted at 18. Men serve for three years, women for two. Men remain liable for reserve duty until the age of 45 while women remain liable until they reach 24. Israel's Arab* citizens are not required to serve but they can, and some do, volunteer.

Druze* men have been drafted into the IDF since 1957 at the request of their communities. The IDF is composed of a small standing force consisting of career officers, noncommissioned officers and draftees, as well as reserve officers. The reserve forces are regularly called to active status for training and service and they constitute the bulk of the military personnel. The IDF is responsible for the security of the country and its primary task is to defend the state from the enemy. Nevertheless, it performs other tasks which serve the public good. It helps in the absorption of new immigrants, the enhancement of education for recruits, and the provision of teachers to some developing areas.

In the 1990s the IDF was subjected to significant scrutiny and review, mostly for the purpose of confronting the strategic challenges posed in the twenty-first century, but also to address apparent changes in popular attitudes about the role of the military in Israeli society. In 1999 the IDF was comprised of 175,000 active soldiers and some 430,000 reservists, with national defense expenditures of $6.6 billion, constituting about 12% of GNP.

For further information see: Yigal Allon, *Shield of David: The Story of Israel's Armed Forces* (London: Weidenfeld and Nicolson, 1970); Yigal Allon, *The Making of Israel's Army* (London: Valentine, Mitchell, 1970); Gad Barzilai and Efraim Inbar, "The Use of Force: Israeli Public Opinion of Military Options," *Armed Forces and Society* 23:1 (Fall 1996): 49-80; Yehuda Ben-Meir, *National Security Decision-Making: The Israeli Case* (Boulder, CO: Westview, 1986); Yehuda Ben-Meir, *Civil-Military Relations in Israel* (New York: Columbia University Press, 1995); Eitan Berglas, *Defense and the Economy: The Israeli Experience* (Jerusalem: The Maurice Falk Institute for Economic Research, January 1983); Tom Bowden, *Army in the Service of the State* (Tel Aviv: University Publishing Projects, 1976); Stuart A. Cohen, "The Hesder Yeshivot in Israel: A Church-State Military Arrangement," *Journal of Church and State* (Winter 1993): 113-130; Stuart A. Cohen, *"Mista'arvim*—IDF 'Masqueraders': The Military Unit and the Public Debate," *Low Intensity Conflict and Law Enforcement* 2:2 (Autumn 1993): 282-300; Stuart A. Cohen, "How Did the Intifada Affect the IDF?" *Conflict Quarterly* 14:3 (Summer 1994): 7-22; Stuart A. Cohen, "The IDF: From a 'People's Army' to a 'Professional Army'—Causes and Implications," *Armed Forces and Society* 21:2 (Winter 1995): 237-254; Stuart A. Cohen, "The Peace Process and Its Impact on the Development of a 'Slimmer' and

'Smarter' IDF," *Israel Affairs* 1:4 (Summer 1995): 1-21; Stuart A. Cohen, "Towards a New Portrait of the (New) Israeli Soldier," *Israel Affairs* 3:3&4 (Spring/Summer 1997): 77-114; Stuart A. Cohen, *The Scroll or the Sword? Dilemmas of Religion and Military Service in Israel* (London: Harwood Academic Publishers, 1997); Ze'ev Drori, "Utopia in Uniform," in *Israel: The First Decade of Independence*, edited by S. Ilan Troen and Noah Lucas (Albany: State University of New York Press, 1995): 593-613; D. Eshel, *Israel's Air Force Today* (Hod Hasharon, Israel: Eshel Dramit Ltd., 1981); Edward B. Glick, *Between Israel and Death* (Harrisburg, PA: Stackpole, 1974); Michael J. Handel, *Israel's Political-Military Doctrine* (Cambridge, MA: Harvard Center for International Affairs, 1973); Chaim Herzog, *The Arab-Israeli Wars: War and Peace in the Middle East* (London: Arms and Armour Press, 1982); Efraim Inbar, "Israel's Small War: The Military Response to the Intifada," *Armed Forces and Society* 18:1 (Fall 1991): 29-50; Efraim Inbar, "Yitzhak Rabin and Israeli National Security: An Analysis of the late Prime Minister's Strategic Legacy," (Ramat Gan: Begin and Sadat Center for Strategic Studies, January 1996); Efraim Inbar, "Contours of Israel's New Strategic Thinking," *Political Science Quarterly* 111:1 (Spring 1996): 41-64; Robert Jackson, *The Israeli Air Force: The Struggle for Middle East Aircraft Supremacy Since 1948*, Second Edition (London: Stacey, 1972); Ariel Levite, *Offense and Defense in Israeli Military Doctrine* (Boulder, CO: Westview, 1989); Moshe Lissak, "The Civilian Component of Israel's Security Doctrine: The Evolution of Civil-Military Relations in the First Decade," in *Israel: The First Decade of Independence*, edited by S. Ilan Troen and Noah Lucas (Albany: State University of New York Press, 1995): 575-591; Edward Luttwak and Dan Horowitz, *The Israeli Army* (New York: Harper and Row, 1975); Moshe Pearlman, *The Army of Israel* (New York: Philosophical Library, 1950); Shimon Peres, *David's Sling: The Arming of Israel* (London: Weidenfeld and Nicolson, 1970); Yoram Peri, *Between Battles and Ballots: Israel's Military in Politics* (Cambridge: Cambridge University Press, 1983); Amos Perlmutter, *Military and Politics in Israel, 1948-1967: Nation-Building and Role Expansion* (London: Frank Cass, 1969); Amos Perlmutter, *Politics and the Military in Israel, 1967-1977* (London: Frank Cass, 1978); Gunther E. Rothenberg, *Anatomy of the Israeli Army* (London: Batsford, 1979); Murray Rubinstein and Richard Goldman, *The Israeli Air Force Story* (London: Arms and Armour Press, 1979); Ze'ev Schiff, *A History of the Israeli Army (1874 to the Present)* (New York: Macmillan, 1985); Jehuda L. Wallach, *Israeli Military History: A Guide to the Sources* (New York: Garland, 1984); Avner Yaniv, *Deterrence without the Bomb: The Politics of Israeli Strategy* (Lexington, MA: Lexington Books, 1986).

ISRAEL ECHAD *see* **ONE ISRAEL**

ISRAEL-EGYPT DISENGAGEMENT OF FORCES AGREEMENT (1974). In late October 1973 the United Nations Security Council adopted Resolution 338*, which called for an immediate cease-fire in the Yom Kippur War*, the implementation of United Nations Security Council Resolution 242*, and explicitly required negotiations "between the parties." Subsequently, United States* Secretary of State Henry Kissinger negotiated the Israel-Egypt Disengagement of Forces Agreement of 1974. It brought about the reaffirmation of the cease-fire achieved at the end of the Yom Kippur War, the disengagement and separation of Israeli and Egyptian military forces, and the creation of disengagement zones between the opposing forces.

ISRAEL GREEN PARTY (HAYERUKIM). Environmentalist party led by former Meretz* MK and one of the founders of Peace Now*, Dedi Zucker. The party, according to Zucker, places "equal importance on fighting for human rights, community-based economic enterprises, feminist and gay rights, multiculturalism and the decentralization of government power into more grass-roots movements." It failed to win a Knesset seat in the May 17, 1999 elections.

ISRAEL-JORDAN PEACE TREATY. On October 17, 1994, Israeli and Jordanian negotiators initialed a peace agreement in Amman, Jordan*. The treaty was formally signed by Prime Minister Abdul-Salam Majali of Jordan and Prime Minister Yitzhak Rabin* of Israel, in a gala ceremony on October 26, 1994, in the Jordan Valley. The treaty consists of 30 articles and five annexes, which address such diverse issues as boundary demarcations, water issues, policy cooperation, environmental issues, refugees, and mutual border crossings. The international border (left undefined since the 1948 war and the 1949 Armistice Agreements*) was to be based on maps dating from the British Mandate for Palestine*. In a novel move, Jordan agreed to lease back (for 25 years, with an option to renew) to Israel farm land in the Arava* that was returned to Jordan in the treaty. Yet another interesting element was Israel's commitment to respect Jordan's special interests in Muslim holy places in Jerusalem* in any peace agreement affecting the city. The treaty also formalized cooperation between Israel and Jordan in the areas of tourism and other economic endeavors, the exploiting and distribution of water and other natural resources, and combating terrorism.

For further information see: Robert Satloff, "The Jordan-Israel Peace Treaty: A Remarkable Document," *Middle East Quarterly* 2:1 (March 1995): 47-51; Samuel Segev, *Crossing the Jordan: Israel's Hard Road to Peace* (New York: St. Martin's, 1998); Moshe Zak, "The Jordan-Israel Peace Treaty: Thirty Years of Clandestine Meetings," *Middle East Quarterly* 2:1 (March 1995): 53-57; Laura Zittrain Eisenberg and Neil Caplan, *Negotiating Arab-Israeli Peace: Patterns, Problems, Possibilities* (Bloomington: Indiana University Press, 1995): chapter 5.

ISRAEL LABOR PARTY (MIFLEGET HAAVODA HAISRAELIT). The successor to MAPAI* that dominated the politics of the pre-state Yishuv and the first three decades of independence. On January 21, 1968, Mapai merged with two other labor parties, Ahdut Haavoda* and Rafi*, to form the Israel Labor Party. The merger of the labor parties did not eliminate the differences between the coalition's components, but instead shifted the quarrels to the intraparty sphere. It was within the confines of the Labor Party that the problems of political leadership and succession for the Government of Israel were resolved. Beginning with the 1969 Knesset* election, the Labor Party was joined in an election alliance (the Alignment*) with Mapam*, although both parties retained their own organizational structures and ideological positions. The new party retained Labor's dominant position until 1977, when lackluster leadership, corruption scandals, and the founding of the Democratic Movement for Change*, made way for the Likud* victory. Mapam left the Alignment in 1984 to protest the party's agreement to form a National Unity Government* with Likud.

Labor's policies are Zionist* and socialist. They include: support for the immigration of Jews to Israel; establishment of a social welfare state; and a state-planned and publicly regulated economy with room for the participation of private capital, full employment, minimum wages, and the right to strike. Labor stands for the separation of religion and the state, although it has historically made major concessions to the religious parties in this area. It supports equality for minorities, including the Arabs of Israel*.

Historically the "Jordan Option"* was the cornerstone of Labor's approach for resolving the dispute over territories occupied in 1967. Viewing the PLO* as a terrorist organization, Labor preferred to negotiate with Jordan's* King Hussein*. This approach changed in 1993 when, in the context of the Declaration of Principles* negotiated with the PLO at Oslo, Prime Minister Yitzhak Rabin* agreed to recognize the PLO and to undertake a complex negotiating formula that required Israel to cede territory in the West Bank* and Gaza Strip* to an elected Palestinian self-governing authority, in return for normalized relations and an end to terrorism and all other forms of violence. In 1999, Labor—under the expanded One Israel* banner—campaigned on the themes of "an Israel of change and hope" and "a revolution in the State of Israel." Its domestic policy platform emphasized national unity and the breaking down of economic barriers. These goals were to be achieved by "changing the national priorities ... by slashing ... subsidies to privileged sectors, such as settlements." In addition, party leader Ehud Barak* declared that savings would be accrued through reducing what he called "corruption" in terms of state funding for the ultra-Orthodox community and its institutions; Haredim will be entitled to exactly the same rights as all other citizens, Barak said, "but there will be no more corruption." A centerpiece of One Israel's domestic policy platform was Barak's pledge to severely redefine the status quo agreement* that had conditioned Israel's religious affairs since independence, beginning with a move to end most deferments from military service for men studying in orthodox rabbinical institutions. In terms of foreign and security policy, in 1999 Labor/One Israel laid forth the following "red lines" for final status negotiations* with the Palestinians: Jerusalem* will remained united under Israeli sovereignty; there will be no return to the pre-Six Day War* lines; there will be no Arab or Palestinian army west of the Jordan River; and most Jewish residents of the West Bank will live in large settlement blocs under Israeli sovereignty. Barak also pledged that his Government will hold a national referendum on a final-status agreement with the Palestinians. Barak pledged to withdraw the IDF* from Lebanon* within one year of taking office, and to resume meaningful negotiations with Syria* toward an agreement effecting both the south Lebanon security zone* and the Golan Heights*.

For many years Labor Party politics were characterized by an intense power struggle between Yitzhak Rabin and Shimon Peres*. Peres, once an ally of Moshe Dayan* and David Ben-Gurion* in the breakaway Rafi* faction, served as Defense Minister in Rabin's first Government (1974-1977). In 1977 Peres replaced Rabin as Labor chairman when on the eve of national elections Rabin was forced to step down after admitting that he and his wife had maintained an illegal bank account in the United States* while he was serving as Israel's ambassador there. Under Peres, Labor was defeated in the 1977 election, but Peres retained the leadership of the party, withstanding a challenge by Rabin at Labor's December 1980 national convention. Rabin served as Defense Minister in the Government of National Unity* formed by Peres in 1984 and continued in that position in the unity government formed in 1988, with Peres as Finance Minister. The second Likud*-Labor National Unity Government lasted until the spring of 1990 when, in the context of intense disputes between the two parties over peacemaking, Prime Minister Yitzhak Shamir* dismissed Peres from the Government and the other Labor members resigned. A subsequent Knesset* vote of no-confidence terminated the Shamir-led Government and Peres, as Labor Party leader, was given the opportunity to form a new Government. When Peres failed in this task, Shamir succeeded in crafting together a narrow coalition.

After several tries Rabin finally succeeded in ousting Peres as Labor Party leader in early 1992 and led his party to victory in the June 23, 1992, election of the 13th Knesset. In the new Government Rabin served as both Prime Minister and Defense Minister and appointed Peres as Foreign Minister. To the surprise of many observers, the two old rivals achieved a modus vivendi and together set Israel on a new course that resulted in a series of interim agreements with the PLO, the Peace Treaty with Jordan, and the opening of substantive negotiations with a number of Arab countries (including Syria).

Following the November 1995 assassination of Rabin the leadership of the Labor Party reverted to Shimon Peres, who was defeated by Benjamin Netanyahu* in the first direct election of the Prime Minister on May 29, 1996. Peres resigned as party leader in June 1997 and was replaced by former IDF* Chief of Staff Ehud Barak*. Prior to the 1999 elections, Barak signed separate agreements to draw Gesher* and Meimad* into the One Israel* party. The expanded party won 26 seats in the elections held on May 17, 1999, becoming the single largest party in the 15th Knesset, while in the direct election for Prime Minister, Ehud Barak defeated Likud leader Benjamin Netanyahu* by a count of 56.08% to 43.92%.

Barak presented his seven-party coalition and its program before the Knesset on July 6, 1999.

For further information see: Myron J. Aronoff, *Power and Ritual in the Israel Labor Party: A Study in Political Anthropology* (Assen/Amsterdam: Van Gorcum, 1977); Yossi Beilin, "A Dominant Party in Opposition: The Israeli Labor Party, 1977-1988," *Middle East Review* 17:4 (Summer 1985): 34-44; David H. Goldberg, *Democracy in Action 1999: A Guide to the Participants and Issues in Israeli Politics* (Toronto: The Canada-Israel Committee, May 1999); Giora Goldberg, "The Electoral Fall of the Israeli Left," *Israel Affairs* (Special Issue: "Israel at the Polls 1996") 4:1 (Autumn 1997): 52-72; Efraim Inbar, *War and Peace in Israeli Politics: Labor Party Positions on National Security* (Boulder, CO: Lynne Rienner, 1991); Efraim Inbar, "Labor's Return to Power," in *Israel at the Polls 1992*, edited by Daniel J. Elazar and Shmuel Sandler (Lanham, MD: Rowman and Littlefield, 1995): 27-44; Gershon R. Kieval, *Party Politics in Israel and the Occupied Territories* (Westport, CT: Greenwood, 1983); Gershon R. Kieval, "The Foreign Policy of the Labor Party," in *Israeli National Security Policy: Political Actors and Perspectives*, edited by Bernard Reich and Gershon R. Kieval (New York: Greenwood, 1988): 19-54; Peter Y. Medding, *Mapai in Israel: Political Organization and Government in a New Society* (Cambridge, MA: Harvard, 1972); Jonathan Mendilow, "Israel's Labor Alignment in the 1984 Elections: Catch-All Tactics in a Divided Society," *Comparative Politics* 20 (July 1988); Yonathan Shapiro, "The End of a Dominant Party System," in *The Elections in Israel—1977*, edited by Asher Arian (Jerusalem: Jerusalem Academic Press, 1980); Yonathan Shapiro, *The Formative Years of the Israeli Labour Party* (London: Sage, 1976); Efraim Torgovnik, "Party Organization and Electoral Politics: The Labor Alignment," in *Israel at the Polls 1981*, edited by Howard R. Penniman and Daniel J. Elazar (Washington, DC: American Enterprise Institute, 1986); Yael Yishai, "The Israeli Labor Party and the Lebanon War," *Armed Forces and Society* 11 (Spring 1985); David Wurmser, "Israel's Collapsing Labor Party," *Middle East Quarterly* 2:3 (September 1995): 37-46.

ISRAEL LANDS AUTHORITY. Agency responsible for administering state-owned land, which comprised some 90% of pre-1967 Israel. In the pre-state period responsibility for purchasing and reclaiming areas of Palestine* for Jewish settlement was held by the Jewish National Fund*.

After independence, many of these functions passed naturally to state institutions, including the Israel Lands Authority, with the efforts of the JNF directed to the reclamation of uncultivable land. Though initially part of the Ministry of Agriculture, the Lands Authority was placed under the jurisdiction of the new Ministry of National Infrastructure established in 1996 by the Netanyahu* Government.

ISRAEL-LEBANON AGREEMENT OF MAY 17, 1983. In the wake of the War in Lebanon* in 1982, Israel engaged in negotiations with Lebanon* under the auspices of the United States*, concerning the withdrawal of foreign forces from Lebanon and related arrangements. After months of discussion, an agreement was reached. The May 17, 1983 agreement provided for the withdrawal of Israeli forces from Lebanon and noted that "they consider the existing international boundary between Israel and Lebanon inviolable." Israel committed itself to withdraw from southern Lebanon in return for specific security arrangements in the south and some elements of normalization approaching, but not quite becoming, a peace treaty. It was an important milestone in Israel's relations with the Arab states. Although signed and ratified by both states, Lebanon abrogated the agreement in March 1984 under heavy pressure from Syria.

For further information see: Yair Evron, *War and Intervention in Lebanon: The Israeli-Syrian Deterrence Dialogue* (Baltimore: Johns Hopkins, 1987); Moshe Ma'oz, *Syria and Israel: From War to Peace-Making* (London: Oxford University Press, 1996); Itamar Rabinovich, *The War for Lebanon, 1970-1985*, Revised Edition (Ithaca: Cornell University Press, 1985); Laura Zittrain Eisenberg, "Israel's Lebanon Policy," *MERIA Journal* 3:3 (Ramat Gan: BESA Center for Strategic Studies, Bar Ilan University, September 1997); Laura Zittrain Eisenberg and Neil Caplan, *Negotiating Arab-Israeli Peace: Patterns, Problems, Possibilities* (Bloomington: Indiana University Press, 1997).

ISRAEL OUR HOME *see* ISRAEL BEITEINU

ISRAEL-PLO DECLARATION OF PRINCIPLES *see* DECLARATION OF PRINCIPLES

ISRAEL PRIZE. An award given by the Israel Ministry of Education and Culture on Independence Day annually for outstanding achievement in various fields, including Jewish studies, Torah, humanities, sciences, and the arts.

ISRAEL-SYRIA DISENGAGEMENT OF FORCES AGREEMENT (1974). An agreement between Syria and Israel achieved in May 1974 through the shuttle diplomacy of United States* Secretary of State Henry Kissinger. It brought about the reaffirmation of the cease-fire achieved at the end of the Yom Kippur War*, the disengagement and separation of Israeli and Syrian military forces on the Golan Heights*, and the creation of disengagement zones between the opposing armies.

ISRAELI ARABS *see* ARABS IN ISRAEL; DRUZE

ITZIK, DALIA. Born in 1952 in Jerusalem* and teacher by training, Dalia Itzik served from 1982 to 1988 as chairperson of the Jerusalem Teachers' Association. Member of the Jerusalem City Council and Deputy Mayor of the city from 1989-1993 she was first elected to the Knesset* in 1992 on the Israel Labor* party list. Reelected in 1996 and 1999, she was appointed Environment Minister on July 6, 1999, the only female member of the original cabinet formed by Ehud Barak*.

IVAN THE TERRIBLE *see* DEMJANJUK, IVAN (JOHN)

J

JABAL ABU GHNEIM *see* HAR HOMA

JABOTINSKY, VLADIMIR ZE'EV. Born in Odessa, Russia, in 1880, Vladimir Jabotinsky was the founder of the World Union of Zionist Revisionists* in 1925, which later branched off into the New Zionist Organization*. The union advocated the establishment of a Jewish state, increased Jewish immigration, and militant opposition to the British Mandatory* authorities in Palestine*. His philosophy provided the ideological basis for the Herut Party*. He studied law in Bern and Rome, but became interested in the Zionist cause with the growth of pogroms in Russia. After the beginning of World War I, Jabotinsky promoted the idea of a Jewish Legion* as a component of the British army and he later joined it. In March 1921 he joined the Zionist Executive but resigned in January 1923 to protest the perceived lack of resistance on the part of the Zionist leadership to British Middle East policy, specifically the unilateral secession of Transjordan from the Palestine Mandate in 1922. In 1923 Jabotinsky founded Brit Trumpeldor (Betar)* and in 1925 the World Union of Zionists-Revisionists was formed in Paris and he became President. Jabotinsky later seceded from the World Zionist Organization* and founded (in Vienna in 1935) the New Zionist Organization, of which he became President. He campaigned against the British plans for the partition of Palestine and advocated and promoted illegal Jewish immigration to Palestine. He died in New York in 1940. Jabotinsky's remains were transferred to Israel and reburied on Mount Herzl* in Jerusalem* in July 1964. His influence on Israel's history and politics is substantial as indicated by his role as the ideological forebear of the Herut* and Likud* political parties and especially the influence of his ideas on the thinking and policies of Menachem Begin*, Yitzhak Shamir* and Benjamin Netanyahu*.

For further information see: Joseph Heller, "The Zionist Right and National Liberation: From Jabotinsky to Avraham Stern," *Israel Affairs* 1:3 (Spring 1995): 85-109; Vladimir Jabotinsky, *The Jewish War Front* (London: Allen and Unwin, 1940); Vladimir Jabotinsky, *The Story of the Jewish Legion* (New York: Ackerman, 1945); Samuel Katz, *Lone Wolf: A Biography of Vladimir (Ze'ev) Jabotinsky*, 2 volumes (New York: Barricade Books, 1996); Joseph B. Schechtman, *The Vladimir Jabotinsky Story*, 2 volumes (New York: Yoseloff, 1956-1961); Joseph B. Schechtman and Yehuda Benari, *A History of the Revisionist Movement* (Tel Aviv: Hadar, 1970, Hebrew); Yaacov Shavit, *Revisionism in Zionism* (Tel Aviv: Yariv, 1978, Hebrew); Yaacov Shavit, *Jabotinsky and the Revisionist Movement, 1925-1948* (London: Frank Cass, 1988); Yaacov Shavit, "Ze'ev Jabotinsky and the Revisionist Movement," in *Essential Papers on Zionism*, edited by Jehuda Reinharz and Anita Shapira (New York: New York University Press, 1996): 544-566.

JARRING, GUNNAR. Then Swedish Ambassador to the USSR* who was appointed by United Nations Secretary General U Thant in November 1967 as a Special Representative to assist in Arab-Israeli peace efforts based on the principles in United Nations Security Council Resolution 242* of November 22, 1967.

JEBEL ABU-GHNEIM *see* HAR HOMA

JERICHO. Located northwest of the northern end of the Dead Sea*, ancient Jericho is considered by some to be the oldest city in the world—dating back to 7,000 BCE. It is mentioned in the Bible and was conquered by the Israelites led by Joshua when they entered the Land of Canaan*. The city has been built and rebuilt throughout the centuries. Control over Jericho was transferred to the PLO* under the terms of the May 1994 Cairo Agreement*.

JERICHO MISSILE. An Israeli-produced surface-to-surface ballistic missile. The short-range version, the Jericho I, was said to have a range of up to 500 km and to be armed with a conventional warhead. Its intermediate-range counterpart, the Jericho II, was a two-stage missile with a range of about 1,500 km, and was capable of carrying a conventional warhead or a nonconventional (chemical or nuclear) warhead. Israeli development of the Jericho began in 1963, in cooperation with France*. Development of the Jericho II began in the mid-1970s with Israel Aircraft Industries* as the prime contractor. The Jericho has never been tested in combat, although there were reports of plans to deploy it in both the Yom Kippur War of 1973* and the Persian Gulf War of 1991*. Israel viewed the Jericho as a vital component of its deterrence and defense capability.

For further information see: Jon J. Peterson and Stephen H. Gotowicki, "Jericho Missile," in *An Historical Encyclopedia of the Arab-Israeli Conflict*, edited by Bernard Reich (Westport, CT: Greenwood, 1996): 265-266; *The Middle East Military Balance 1997/98* (London: International Institute for Strategic Studies, 1998).

JERUSALEM. Jerusalem is Israel's largest city and its declared capital. It is a Holy City for Jews, Christians, and Muslims. In 1947, when the United Nations voted to partition Palestine* into a Jewish state and an Arab state, Jerusalem was to be internationalized. However, the city was divided between Jordan* (East Jerusalem, including the walled old city) and Israel (West Jerusalem, the new city) during Israel's War of Independence*. Israel made its portion of Jerusalem its capital. Nevertheless, most countries did not accept that decision and many retained their embassies in Tel Aviv*. In the Six Day War* Israel gained control of East Jerusalem and merged it with the western portion of the city.

On July 30, 1980, the Knesset* passed the Basic Law*: Jerusalem, Capital of Israel, 5740-1980. It declared: "Jerusalem united in its entirety is the capital of Israel. Jerusalem is the seat of the President of the State, the Knesset, the Government and the Supreme Court. The Holy Places shall be protected from desecration and any other violation and from anything likely to violate the freedom of access of the members of the different religions to the places sacred to them or their feelings with regard to those places." It also provided that the Government would work for the development and prosperity of the city and the welfare of its inhabitants and would give special priority to this activity.

West Jerusalem is the modern part of the city. East Jerusalem includes the walled old city, the site of many ancient holy places. Jews consider Jerusalem a holy city because it was their political and religious center in biblical times. About 1000 BCE King David made Jerusalem the capital of the united Israelite tribes. David's son, King Solomon, built the first Temple of the Jews in the city. Christians consider Jerusalem holy because Jesus was crucified there and many events in his life took place in the city. Muslims believe that Muhammed, the founder of Islam, ascended to heaven from Jerusalem, and the city is the third holiest in Islam after Mecca and Medina in Saudi Arabia. The city is the site of numerous holy places. Among the more prominent are the Wailing Wall* and the Church of the Holy Sepulcher (which is believed to stand on the hill of Calvary, or Golgotha, where Jesus was crucified and buried). The church is shared by several Christian sects, and the Dome of the Rock (which stands near the Wailing Wall) was built over the rock from which, according to Muslim belief, Muhammed rose to heaven. In Jewish tradition it was on this rock that Abraham prepared to sacrifice his son Isaac as God commanded.

In the Oslo Accords* Israel and the PLO agreed to defer discussions about Jerusalem until the "final status" stage of negotiations. In the Israel-Jordan Peace Treaty (1994)* it was agreed that Jordanian interests in Jerusalem's Muslim holy places would be taken into account in a final settlement affecting the city.

For further information see: M. A. Aamiry, *Jerusalem: Arab Origins and Heritage* (London: Longman, 1978); Ziad Abu-Amr, "The Significance of Jerusalem: A Muslim Perspective," *Palestine-Israel Journal of Politics, Economics and Culture* 2:2 (1995); Adnan Abu-Odeh, "Two Capitals in an Undivided Jerusalem," *Foreign Affairs* 71:2 (Spring 1992): 183-188; Dan Bahat, *The Historical Atlas of Jerusalem: A Brief Illustrated Survey* (New York: Scribner, 1975); Meron Benvenisti, *City of Stone: The Hidden History of Jerusalem* (Berkeley: University of California Press, 1997); Meron Benvenisti, *Jerusalem: The Torn City* (Jerusalem: University of Minneapolis Press, 1977); Yehuda Blum, *The Juridical Status of Jerusalem* (Jerusalem: Leonard Davis Institute of International Relations, Hebrew University of Jerusalem, 1974); H. Eugene Bovis, *The Jerusalem Question, 1917-1968* (Stanford, CA: Hoover Institution, 1971); Marshall J. Breger, "The New Battle for Jerusalem," *Middle East Quarterly* 1:4 (December 1994); Henry Cattan, *Jerusalem* (London: Croom Helm, 1981); Naomi Chazan, *Negotiating the Non-Negotiable: Jerusalem in the Framework of an Israeli-Palestinian Settlement* (Cambridge, MA: American Academy of Arts and Sciences, 1991); Amir Cheshin, Bill Hutman, and Avi Melamed, *Separate and Unequal* (Cambridge, MA: Harvard, 1999); Saul B. Cohen, *Jerusalem: Bridging the Four Walls: A Geopolitical Perspective* (New York: Herzl, 1977); Amos Elon, *Jerusalem: City of Mirrors* (Boston: Little, Brown, 1989); Yossi Feintuch, *U.S. Policy on Jerusalem* (Westport, CT: Greenwood, 1987); Martin Gilbert, *Jerusalem: Illustrated History Atlas* (Jerusalem: Steimatsky, 1994); Martin Gilbert, *Jerusalem in the Twentieth Century* (London: Chatto and Windus, 1997); Dore Gold, *Jerusalem* (Tel Aviv: Jaffee Center for Strategic Studies, Final Status Issues: Israel-Palestinians Study No. 7, Tel Aviv University, 1995); David H. Goldberg, *Jerusalem* (Toronto: Foundation for Middle East Studies, Middle East Peace Process Issue Brief No. 2, February 1997); Mark A. Heller and Sari Nusseibeh, *No Trumpets, No Drums: A Two-State Settlement of the Israeli-Palestinian Conflict* (New York: Hill and Wang, 1991); Moshe Hirsch, Deborah Housen-Couriel and Ruth Lapidoth, *Whither Jerusalem?: Proposals and Positions concerning the Future of Jerusalem* (The Hague: Kluwer, 1995); Bernard Joseph, *The Faithful City: The Siege of Jerusalem, 1948* (New York: Simon and Schuster, 1960); Nazmi Ju'beh, "The Palestinian Attachment to Jerusalem," *Palestine-Israel Journal of Politics, Economics and Culture* 2:2 (1995); Ghada Karmi, editor, *Jerusalem Today: What Future for the Peace Process?* (Reading: Ithaca Press, 1996); Kathleen M. Kenyon, *Digging Up Jerusalem*

(London: Benn, 1974); Teddy Kollek, *Jerusalem, Sacred City of Mankind: A History of Forty Centuries* (New York: Random House; Jerusalem: Steimatzky, 1968); Teddy Kollek, "Sharing United Jerusalem," *Foreign Affairs* 67:2 (Winter 1988/1989): 156-168; Teddy Kollek, *Jerusalem* (Washington, DC: The Washington Institute for Near East Policy, Policy Papers No. 22, 1990); Teddy Kollek, "Jerusalem Voices: Tolerant, Inclusive, Fair-Minded—But Ours," *Moment*, December 1995; Norman Kotker, *The Earthly Jerusalem* (New York: Scribner, 1969); Joel Kramer, editor, *Jerusalem: Problems and Prospects* (New York: Praeger, 1980); Jonathan Kuttab, "The Legal Status of Jerusalem," *Palestine-Israel Journal of Politics, Economics and Culture* 2:2 (1995); Ruth Lapidoth, *Jerusalem and the Peace Process* (Jerusalem: The Jerusalem Institute for Israel Studies, 1994); Elihu Lauterpacht, *Jerusalem and the Holy Places* (London: Geerings of Ashford, 1968); Ian Lustick, "Reinventing Jerusalem," *Foreign Policy* 93 (Winter 1993-1994): 41-59; Donald Neff, "Jerusalem in U.S. Policy," *Journal of Palestine Studies* 23:1 (Autumn 1993); Sari Nusseibeh, "On Jerusalem," *Palestine-Israel Journal of Politics, Economics and Culture* 2:2 (1995); John M. Oesterreicher and Anne Sinai, editors, *Jerusalem* (New York: John Day, 1974); Richard H. Pfaff, *Jerusalem: Keystone of an Arab-Israeli Settlement* (Washington, DC: American Enterprise Institute for Public Policy Research, 1969); Terence Prittie, *Whose Jerusalem?* (London: Muller, 1981); Abraham Rabinovich, *Jerusalem on Earth: People, Passions, and Politics in the Holy City* (New York: Free Press, 1988); Edward Said, "Projecting Jerusalem," *Journal of Palestine Studies*, 25 (Autumn 1995): 5-14; Ira Sharkansky, *Governing Jerusalem: Again on the World's Agenda* (Detroit: Wayne State University Press, 1996); Andrew Sinclair, *Jerusalem: The Endless Crusade: The Struggle for the Holy City from Its Foundation to the Modern Era* (New York: Crown, 1995); Emanuel Sivan, "The Sanctity of Jerusalem in Islam in the Period of the Crusades," in *Sefer Yerushalaim 1099-1250*, edited by Yehoshua Praver and Hagai Ben-Shamai (Jerusalem: Yad Yitzhak Ben-Zvi, 1991, Hebrew); Shlomo Slonim, *Jerusalem in America's Foreign Policy, 1947-1997* (The Hague: Kluwer Law International, 1999); A.L. Tibawi, *Jerusalem: Its Place in Islam and Arab History* (Beirut: The Institute for Palestine Studies, 1969); U.S. Congress, *Jerusalem: The Future of the Holy City for Three Monotheisms* (Washington, DC: U.S. Congress, Committee on Foreign Affairs, Subcommittee on the Near East, 1971); Zvi Weblowsky, *The Meaning of Jerusalem to Jews, Christians, and Muslims* (Jerusalem: Intratypset, 1977).

JERUSALEM POST. English-language daily newspaper founded in 1932 in Jerusalem* as the *Palestine Post*. Its founding editor was Gershon Agron. It has no formal political party affiliation. It was renamed the *Jerusalem Post* on April 23, 1950.

JERUSALEM PROGRAM. In 1968 the Zionist movement adopted the Jerusalem Program which essentially replaced the Basle Program* of 1897. The Jerusalem Program provided: "The aims of Zionism are: The Unity of the Jewish people in its historic homeland Eretz Israel through Aliyah from all countries; The strengthening of the State of Israel which is based on the prophetic vision of justice and peace; The preservation of the identity of the Jewish people through the fostering of Jewish and Hebrew* education and of Jewish spiritual and cultural values; The protection of Jewish rights everywhere."

JEWISH AGENCY (JEWISH AGENCY FOR PALESTINE, JEWISH AGENCY FOR ISRAEL). Agency established in the 1920s under the terms of the British Mandate for Palestine* to advise and cooperate with the British authorities in the task of establishing the Jewish National Home in Palestine*. Article 4 of the Mandate for Palestine provided for the recognition of an appropriate "Jewish Agency" as a "public body for the purpose of advising and cooperating with the Administration of Palestine in such economic, social and other matters as may affect the establishment of the Jewish National Home and the interests of the Jewish population in Palestine, and subject always to the control of the Administration, to assist and take part in the development of the country." Article 6 of the Mandate stipulated that the British administration of Palestine should, "in cooperation with the Jewish Agency," encourage settlement by Jews on the land. Article 11 provided that the administration might arrange with the Jewish Agency "to construct or operate, upon fair and equitable terms, any public works, services and utilities, and to develop any of the natural resources of the country, insofar as these matters are not directly undertaken by the Administration." The Mandate itself recognized the World Zionist Organization (WZO)* as such Jewish Agency (article 4) and directed the WZO to "take steps in consultation with His Britannic Majesty's Government to secure the cooperation of all Jews who are willing to assist in the establishment of the Jewish National Home." The WZO, on its part, undertook to take steps to secure such cooperation.

The Zionist Organization performed its functions until a Jewish Agency for Palestine (which included non-Zionist and Zionist Jews) was formally constituted in 1929. It provided the apparatus for worldwide Jewish participation in the building of the Jewish home in Palestine. The Jewish Agency worked with the government of the Yishuv* and, particularly, with the Vaad Leumi*. Generally, the Agency promoted immigration, settlement, economic development, and mobilized support for Jewish efforts in Palestine. Its political department acted as the "foreign ministry" of the quasigovernment in Palestine. It negotiated with the Palestine Government and Great Britain*, and it represented the cause of the Jewish national home before appropriate organs of the League of Nations and the United Nations. The Jewish Agency's officials, along with those of the Vaad Leumi and other organs of the Yishuv, provided Israel's ministries with a trained core of civil servants and political leaders. David Ben-Gurion*, who served as Israel's first Prime Minister and Minister of Defense, was Chairman of the Executive of the Jewish Agency and Moshe Shertok (later Sharett)* was a director of the Agency's political department. One of the main tasks of the Jewish Agency during the period of the British administration of Palestine was to represent the Zionist movement and world Jewry before the Mandatory Government, the League of Nations, and the British Government in London. It also served as part of the governing structure of the Yishuv. It promoted Zionism, encouraged and facilitated immigration, raised funds, engaged in social-welfare activities, promoted Jewish culture, developed economic enterprises, and formulated domestic and external policies for the Jewish community.

It was realized long before May 15, 1948, that the future independent and sovereign Jewish state would be fully responsible for the conduct of its domestic and foreign affairs and that some functions hitherto exercised by the Jewish Agency would have to be transferred to the state. On the other hand, it was obvious that the state would not and could not deal with all matters that had been in the purview of the Jewish Agency (in particular, immigration, absorption of immigrants, and settlement), not only for financial reasons but also because they were a global Jewish responsibility and not an internal affair of Israel. It was felt that the Jewish Agency would be needed to express the partnership of the Jewish people all over the world with Israel in the historic enterprise of building the state and to channel and utilize properly the aid that was expected and forthcoming from Diaspora* Jewry.

The Jewish Agency/World Zionist Organization, even though nongovernmental, performs functions instrumental to Zionism and important to the government's activities; its personnel often move to and from positions of responsibility within the government. Upon independence the Government of Israel began to assume many of the functions previously performed by this institution and formalized its relationship with it through legislation and administrative decisions. The Jewish Agency today is responsible for the organization of Jewish immigration to Israel; the reception, assistance, and settlement of immigrants; care of children; and aid to cultural projects and institutions of higher learning. It fosters Hebrew* education and culture in the Diaspora, guides and assists Zionist youth movements, and organizes the work of the Jewish people in support of Israel.

The mutual relations of the state and the Jewish Agency were put on a firm legal basis by the Law on the Status of the World Zionist Organization—Jewish Agency of 5713 (1952), Article 4 of which declares: "The State of Israel recognized the WZO as the authorized agency that will continue to operate in the State of Israel for the development and settlement of the country, the absorption of immigrants from the Diaspora and the coordination of the activities in Israel of Jewish institutions and organizations active in those fields." After the Six Day War* of 1967 it was suggested that while the WZO-Jewish Agency should remain in charge of immigration, the absorption and integration of immigrants should become largely a responsibility of the Government. A new Ministry for the Absorption of Immigrants was established.

In recent years the Jewish Agency and the World Zionist Organization have been restructured to reflect changes in Israel-Diaspora relations.

When Sallai Meridor took over as head of the Jewish Agency in June 1999 he said that while the Agency would continue to help Jews settle in Israel, it would expand its mission into strengthening Jewish identity and sense of peoplehood, especially among young Jews.

For further information see: Avraham Burg, *Brit Am—A Covenant of the People: Proposed Policy Guidelines for the National Institutions of the Jewish People* (Jerusalem: The Jewish Agency, 1995); Daniel J. Elazar, *The Jewish Agency within the World Polity* (Jerusalem: The Jerusalem Center for Public Affairs, 1994); Daniel J. Elazar, "Tremors in Israel-

Diaspora Relations," *Jerusalem Letter* (Jerusalem Center for Public Affairs, October 16, 1994); Yosef Gorny, "The Zionist Movement and the State of Israel, 1948-1952: A Formation of Normal Interrelations," in *Israel: The First Decade of Independence*, edited by S. Ilan Troen and Noah Lucas (Albany: State University of New York Press, 1995): 683-698; Arthur Hertzberg, "Israel and the Diaspora: A Relationship Reexamined," *Israel Affairs* 2:3/4 (Spring/Summer 1996): 169-183; Charles S. Liebman, "Restructuring Israeli-Diaspora Relations," *Israel Studies* 1:1 (Spring 1996): 315-322; Sam Norwich, *What Will Bind Us Now? A Report on the Institutional Ties between Israel and American Jewry* (New York: Center for Middle East Peace and Economic Cooperation, 1994); Ernest Stock, "Philanthropy and Politics: Modes of Interaction between Israel and the Diaspora," in *Israel: The First Decade of Independence*, edited by S. Ilan Troen and Noah Lucas (Albany: State University of New York Press, 1995): 699-711; David Vital, "Israel and the Jewish Diaspora: Five Comments on the Political Relationship," *Israel Affairs* 1:2 (Winter 1994): 171-187.

JEWISH BRIGADE. Established formally by a decision of the British Government in September 1944 to join in the Allied fight against the Axis in World War II, the Brigade's origins go back to 1939 when some 130,000 Palestinian Jews registered as volunteers for military service against the Axis. During the war the members of the unit served in various capacities in the fight against Nazi Germany and its allies.

For further information see: Efraim Dekel, *SHAI: The Exploits of the Hagana Intelligence* (New York: Yoseloff, 1959); Zerubavel Gilad, editor, *Hidden Shield: The Secret Military Efforts of the Yishuv during the War, 1939-1945* (Jerusalem: Jewish Agency, 1951).

JEWISH LEGION. Military units formed by Jewish volunteers in World War I to fight alongside British troops for the liberation of Palestine* from the Turks.

For further information see: Vladimir Jabotinsky, *The Story of the Jewish Legion* (New York: Ackerman, 1945); Samuel Katz, *A Biography of Vladimir (Ze'ev) Jabotinsky*, 2 volumes (New York: Barricade Books, 1996).

JEWISH NATIONAL FUND (JNF) (KEREN KAYEMET LE ISRAEL). Various organizations and units were created to carry on the work of the World Zionist Organization*. The Jewish National Fund (JNF) was founded in 1901 at the Fifth Zionist Congress. It was charged with land purchases and development in Palestine*. It now focuses on afforestation and reclamation of land in Israel. In 1960, the Knesset passed the Israel Lands Administration* Act, which transferred ownership of the land owned by the Keren Kayemet to the State of Israel.

For further information see: Henriette Hannah Bodenheimer, "The Status of the Keren Kayemeth," in *Herzl Year Book* (New York: Herzl Press, 1964-1965): 153-181; and Ira Hirschman, *The Awakening: The Story of the Jewish National Fund* (New York: Shengold, 1981).

JEWISH QUESTION. For centuries European society had sought to find an appropriate means for addressing the so-called Jewish Question, the relationship between the Christian majority and the Jewish minority. When various remedies—including emancipation, assimilation, separation, and overt persecution and discrimination (in the form of state-sponsored pogroms and other forms of anti-Semitism*)—failed to "solve" the problem, a growing number of Jews turned to political Zionism* and independent statehood.

THE JEWISH STATE see DER JUDENSTAAT

JNF *see* JEWISH NATIONAL FUND

JOINT EMERGENCY COMMITTEE. A Joint Emergency Committee, composed of members of the Executive of the Jewish Agency* and the Vaad Leumi (National Council)* of the Jewish community in Palestine*, was formed in the autumn of 1947, at which time the United Nations was considering the future of the British Mandate* and it had become obvious that the British were intent on withdrawal. The Committee was formed to make appropriate arrangements for the transfer of power from the Mandatory administration to the government of the proposed Jewish State and it sought to fill the void created by the disintegration of the British role. It drafted a legal code and a proposed constitution; it developed a roster of experienced civil servants willing to serve the future government; and it instituted vigorous recruitment for the Hagana* to preserve the security of the Jewish community of Palestine. It disbanded in March 1948 and was succeeded by the Peoples Council, which became the de facto Government of Israel upon independence.

JORDAN (FORMERLY TRANSJORDAN). The Hashemite Kingdom of Jordan is Israel's neighbor to the east with which it has fought in several wars and with which it has been in a formal state of peace since 1994. Following the War of Independence*, Jordan and Israel signed an Armistice Agreement* which established the frontiers between the two states during the period from 1949 to 1967. During the war Jordan occupied a portion of the territory of the Palestine Mandate* that had been allocated to the Arab state of Palestine and retained control of that area which became known as the West Bank*, as well as the eastern part of Jerusalem* (including the "Old City"). It later annexed that territory. The frontier condition between the two states varied from peaceful to one across which raids and reprisals took place. Jordan joined in the Arab fighting against Israel in the Six Day War* during which time Israel took control of the West Bank and East Jerusalem from Jordan, but abstained during both the Sinai War* and the War of Attrition*. During the Yom Kippur War* King Hussein* committed only token forces to the battle against Israel and these fought alongside Syrian troops in the Golan Heights*.

Negotiations between senior Israeli officials and King Abdullah took place prior to the creation of Israel and substantial high level contacts between the two states continued over the years since. The open bridges policy* of Moshe Dayan* increased the flow of people and goods across the Jordan River between Jordan and Israel after the Six Day War. Numerous other contacts of various kinds at various levels and on numerous themes also took place. The concept of a Jordan option*, which assumed that Jordan could represent the Palestinians as a means of resolving the Arab-Israeli conflict*, was for many years a core component of the Labor Party's* approach to peacemaking.

On September 14, 1993 (one day after the signing of the Israel-PLO Declaration of Principles*), Israel and Jordan initialed a substantive common agenda for peacemaking. The following July 25, Prime Minister Yitzhak Rabin* and King Hussein* signed the Washington Declaration* symbolizing the completion of this agenda. On October 17, 1994, Israel and Jordan initialed a peace treaty in Amman; the official signing ceremony, witnessed by U.S. President Bill Clinton, took place on

October 26, 1994. Although based on common interests and long-standing understandings (especially concerning issues of security), the Israeli-Jordanian relationship is not without its occasional stresses and strains. For example, in early March 1997 King Hussein* sent a pointed letter to Prime Minister Benjamin Netanyahu* expressing "distress" over the course of Israeli-PLO* peace negotiations. A few days later (March 13, 1997) seven Israeli schoolgirls were killed when a deranged Jordanian soldier shot at their bus at the Naharayim border stop (a place known by both sides as the "peace island"); King Hussein* subsequently made unprecedented condolence calls on the families of the victims of the attack. A temporary crisis in bilateral relations arose in the fall of 1997 when Mossad* agents, carrying forged Canadian passports, tried to assassinate Khaled Mashaal*, head of the Hamas political office in Amman. Despite occasional disruptions the peace with Jordan remains the most secure of Israel's treaty relationships with its Arab neighbors. The death of King Hussein* in February 1999 and his choice of Abdullah as the new king raised questions about the continuation of the positive relationship between the two states. Abdullah II pledged to continue his father's efforts to sustain peace with Israel and initial indications suggested a continuation of the process.

For further information see: Uri Bar-Yoseph, *The Best of Enemies: Israel and Transjordan in the War of 1948* (London: Frank Cass, 1987); El Hassan Bin Talal, "Jordan's Quest for Peace," *Foreign Affairs* 60:4 (Spring 1982): 804-809; Adam Garfinkle, *Israel and Jordan in the Shadow of War: Functional Ties and Futile Diplomacy in a Small Place* (New York: St. Martin's, 1992); Adam Garfinkle, "The Transformation of Jordan, 1991-1995," in *The Middle East and the Peace Process: The Impact of the Oslo Accords*, edited by Robert O. Freedman (Gainsville: University Press of Florida, 1998): 101-133; Yoav Gelber, *Jewish-Transjordanian Relations, 1921-1948* (London: Frank Cass, 1997); Aharon S. Klieman, "The Israel-Jordan Tacit Security Regime," in *Regional Security Regimes: Israel and Its Neighbors*, edited by Efraim Inbar (Albany: State University of New York Press, 1995): 127-149; Samir A. Mutawi, *Jordan in the 1967 War* (Cambridge: Cambridge University Press, 1987); Daniel Pipes and Adam Garfinkle, "Is Jordan Palestine?" *Commentary* 86 (October 1988): 35-42; Emile Sahliyeh, "Jordan and the Question of Confidence Building: The Politics of Ambivalence," in *Confidence-Building Measures in the Middle East*, edited by Gabriel Ben-Dor and David B. Dewitt (Boulder, CO: Westview,

1994): 179-198; Robert Satloff, "The Jordan-Israel Peace Treaty: A Remarkable Document," *Middle East Quarterly* 2:1 (March 1995): 47-51; Dan Schueftan, "Jordan's 'Israeli Option,'" in *Jordan in the Middle East: The Making of a Pivotal State*, edited by Joseph Nevo and Ilan Pappe (London: Frank Cass, 1994): 254-282; Dan Schueftan, "Jordan's Motivation for a Settlement with Israel," *Jerusalem Quarterly* 44 (Fall 1987): 79-120; Avraham Sela, "Transjordan, Israel and the 1948 War: Myth, Historiography and Reality," *Middle Eastern Studies* 28:4 (October 1992): 623-688; Zev Sharef, "Negotiations with King Abdullah and the Formation of a Governmental Structure," in *Israel in the Middle East: Documents and Readings on Society, Politics and Foreign Relations, 1948-Present*, edited by Itamar Rabinovich and Jehuda Reinharz (New York: Oxford University Press, 1984): 32-36; Avi Shlaim, *Collusion across the Jordan: King Abdullah, The Zionist Movement, and the Partition of Palestine* (Oxford: Clarendon, 1988); Martin Sicker, *Between Hashemites and Zionists: The Struggle for Palestine, 1908-1988* (New York: Holmes and Meier, 1989); Asher Susser, *In through the Out Door: Jordan's Disengagement and the Middle East Peace Process* (Washington, DC: The Washington Institute for Near East Policy, 1990); Moshe Zak, "A Survey of Israel's Contacts with Jordan," in *Israel in the Middle East: Documents and Readings on Society, Politics and Foreign Relations, 1948-Present*, edited by Itamar Rabinovich and Jehuda Reinharz (New York: Oxford University Press, 1984): 337-342; Moshe Zak, "The Ambivalent Diplomacy of King Hussein," *Global Affairs* 4:2 (Spring 1989): 111-128; Moshe Zak, "The Jordan-Israel Peace Treaty: Thirty Years of Clandestine Meetings," *Middle East Quarterly* 2:1 (March 1995): 53-57; Moshe Zak, "The Shift in Ben-Gurion's Attitude toward the Kingdom of Jordan," *Israel Studies* 1:2 (Fall 1996): 140-169.

JORDAN IS PALESTINE. A philosophy, espoused mainly by the political right in Israel, which viewed the Hashemite Kingdom of Jordan* as a Palestinian state. From this perspective, the Balfour Declaration* and the British Mandate for Palestine* applied to areas on both sides of the Jordan River, and Great Britain's decisions to unilaterally separate the area east of the river from the Mandate and to establish Transjordan in the early 1920s were illegitimate. Revisionist Zionism* viewed the Zionist leadership's acceptance of this state of affairs as a capitulation. Nationalist Zionists continued to contend that the Arab demand for a Palestinian state was unnecessary, inasmuch as one already existed in Jordan. Hence, there was no need for another Palestinian state west of the

Jordan River, where Israel was located. This view was never accepted by either the Palestinian leadership or the King of Jordan. In renouncing Jordan's claim to the West Bank in July 1988, King Hussein* specifically noted that "Jordan is not Palestine." With the Israel-PLO Declaration of Principles* and the Peace Treaty with Jordan*, the "Jordan is Palestine" argument lost much of its appeal among average Israelis.

For further information see: Raphael Israeli, *Palestinians between Israel and Jordan: Squaring the Triangle* (New York: Praeger, 1991); Daniel Pipes and Adam Garfinkle, "Is Jordan Palestine?" *Commentary* 86 (October 1988): 35-42.

JORDAN OPTION. An approach to a peaceful resolution of the Arab-Israeli conflict which suggested that Israel and Jordan would negotiate to determine the future of the West Bank* (Judea and Samaria*) and Gaza* since Jordan between 1949 and 1967 had been the power controlling the West Bank and appeared amenable to possible participation in a peace process. It had been a major element of Labor Party* policy until the Oslo Accords* and the Jordan-Israel Peace Treaty*.

JORDAN RIVER. The Jordan, some 205 miles long, flows north to south through the Sea of Galilee* and ends in the Dead Sea* and forms the boundary between Palestine* and Transjordan. The Jordan originates in the snows and rains of Mount Hermon* and its sources are the Hasbani River in Lebanon, the Banias River in Syria, and the Dan in Israel.

JORDANIAN OPTION *see* JORDAN OPTION

JUDAH *see* JUDEA

JUDEA. The Kingdom of Judah (Judea) maintained its capital at Jerusalem* until 586 BCE, when the Babylonians destroyed the Temple, ended the kingdom, and took the leadership and much of the Jewish population in exile to Babylon. Under Cyrus of Persia the Jews were allowed to return to Jerusalem, and the rebuilding of the Temple began. Its area is approximately 1,750 square miles (4,550 square kilometers), 56 miles (90 kilometers) long and 34 miles (55 kilometers) wide. It constitutes the southern portion of the area known as the West Bank* that was taken by Israel from Jordan*, in the Six Day War*. It is heavily populated and is a source of contention between Israelis and Palestinians, much of it centered on the status of the city of Hebron*. Parts of Judea have been transferred, in whole or in part, to Palestinian control, pursuant to the Oslo Accords*.

JUDEA AND SAMARIA. Terms used in Israel to refer to the West Bank*.

JUNE WAR (1967) *see* SIX DAY WAR

K

KACH (THUS). A political movement on the extreme right of Israel's political spectrum founded and led by Rabbi Meir Kahane* until his death. It is essentially a secular nationalist movement that focuses on the Arab challenges to Israel and its Jewish character. In the 1984 election, after failure in previous attempts, Kach succeeded in gaining nearly 26,000 votes and a seat in the Knesset*. Kahane had campaigned on a theme of "making Israel Jewish again" by seeking the expulsion of the Arabs from Israel, as well as from the West Bank* and Gaza Strip*. Initially, the party was banned from participation in the election by the Central Elections Committee, but the ruling was reversed by the Supreme Court*—a move that gained the party additional publicity and probably facilitated its efforts to secure a Knesset seat. Despite Kahane's success in the 1984 elections he was considered an extremist, even by many on the right, and his political ideology and programs remain marginal in Israel and are considered by the majority of Israelis in that vein. He was ruled out as a political ally and coalition partner by all the major factions in the Knesset, including Tehiya*. Kach was banned from participation in the 1988 Knesset election by the Central Elections Committee on the grounds that it was racist; similar grounds were cited for banning it from participating in the 1992 and 1996 elections. After the murder of Rabbi Kahane, Rabbi Avraham Toledano was chosen as his successor in March 1991.

Disputes over tactics and personal rivalries within Kach led to the formation of a breakaway faction calling itself Kahane Chai* (Kahane Lives) and headed by Benjamin Kahane, son of Rabbi Meir Kahane. Both Kach and Kahane Chai were outlawed and disarmed after the February

1994 massacre of Arab worshippers in Hebron* by Baruch Goldstein*, a Kach activist. Followers of Rabbi Meir Kahane are among the most militant opponents of the Oslo Accords* and of territorial compromise in the West Bank.

For further information see: S. Daniel Breslauer, *Meir Kahane: Ideologue, Hero, Thinker* (Lewiston, NY: Edwin Mellen Press, 1986); Rael Jean Isaac, *Israel Divided: Ideological Politics in the Jewish State* (Baltimore: Johns Hopkins, 1976); Gershon R. Kieval, *Party Politics in Israel and the Occupied Territories* (Westport, CT: Greenwood, 1983); Yair Kolter, *Heil Kahane* (New York: M. Rachlin Printing, 1986); Jay Shapiro, *Meir Kahane: The Litmus Test of Democracy in Israel* (Montreal: Dawn Publications, 1988); Ehud Sprinzak, *The Ascendance of Israel's Radical Right* (New York: Oxford University Press, 1991); Ehud Sprinzak, "Extremism and Violence in Israel: The Crisis of Messianic Politics," *The Annals of the American Academy of Political and Social Science* 555 (January 1998): 114-126; Ehud Sprinzak, *Kach and Meir Kahane: The Emergence of Jewish Quasi-Fascism* (New York: American Jewish Committee, 1985).

KAHALANI, AVIGDOR. Born in 1944 in Palestine* he holds a BA degree in general history from Tel Aviv University and an MA in political science from Haifa University. He served in the IDF* and rose to rank of Brigadier General. In the Yom Kippur War*, he served as commander of an armored battalion on the Golan Heights*. He became a Labor* MK in the 13th Knesset* but quit to protest Labor's apparent flexibility vis-à-vis the Golan Heights*. He helped found and headed a new party, The Third Way*, that won four seats in the 14th Knesset. He served as Minister of Internal Security in the Netanyahu* Government established in 1996. Kahalani headed The Third Way in the May 1999 elections, but the party failed to pass the threshold for winning seats in the Knesset.

KAHAN COMMISSION OF INQUIRY. Toward the end of the War in Lebanon* Christian Phalangist forces massacred Palestinians at the Sabra and Shatila* refugee camps in the Beirut area. Some alleged that the Israeli army should have known and could have prevented the massacres since the camps were within the army's supposed range of control. The resultant anguish within Israel led to the decision, taken by the Cabinet on September 28, 1982, to create a Commission of Inquiry. Its terms of reference were described this way: "The matter which will be subjected to inquiry is: all the facts and factors connected with the atrocity carried out by a unit of the Lebanese Forces against the civilian population in the Shatila and Sabra camps." The Commission of Inquiry consisted of Yitzhak Kahan, President of the Supreme Court*, who served as Commission Chairman; Aharon Barak, Justice of the Supreme Court; and Yona Efrat, a reserve Major General in the Israel Defense Forces*. Its final report was issued in February 1983. Among other recommendations it was suggested that Major General Yehoshua Saguy not continue as Director of Military Intelligence* and that Division Commander Brigadier General Amos Yaron not serve in the capacity of a field commander in the Israel Defense Forces*. Among other results of the report and recommendations was the resignation of Ariel Sharon* as Minister of Defense.

For further information see: Martin Edelman, "The Kahan Commission of Inquiry," *Midstream* (June-July 1983): 11-14; R. T. Naylor, "From Bloodbath to Whitewash," *Arab Studies Quarterly* 5 (Fall 1983): 337-361; David Pollock, "Israel since the Lebanon War," in *The Middle East after the Israeli Invasion of Lebanon*, edited by Robert O. Freedman (Syracuse, NY: Syracuse, 1986): 255-298; Avner Yaniv, *Dilemmas of Security: Politics, Strategy and the Israeli Experience in Lebanon* (Oxford: Oxford University Press, 1987); Avner Yaniv and Robert J. Leiber, "Personal Whim or Strategic Imperative? The Israeli Invasion of Lebanon," *International Security* 8:(Fall 1983): 117-142; *The Beirut Massacre: The Complete Kahan Commission Report* (Princeton, NJ: Karz-Cohl, 1983).

KAHANE, RABBI MEIR. He was born in Brooklyn, New York, in 1932, the son of an Orthodox Rabbi, and became an ordained rabbi in the 1950s. In 1946 he joined Betar*. He studied at the Mirrer Yeshiva in Brooklyn and later attended Brooklyn College and then studied law at New York University. He founded the Jewish Defense League in 1968 as a response to vicious outbreaks of anti-Semitism* in New York and a perceived need to change the Jewish image. The Jewish Defense League became known for its violent methods, especially those designed to call attention to the plight of Soviet Jewry. He moved to Israel in 1971. In Israel he was arrested numerous times and served some months in prison in 1981 under preventive detention for threatening violence against Palestinian protesters in the West Bank*. He headed the Kach Party* which he founded. He was elected to the Knesset* in 1984. A prolific author,

Kahane advocated the necessity of retaining Israel's Jewish character as its first priority. Thus, he proposed that the Arabs should leave Israel and go to other locations in the Arab world because of the violence they have perpetrated against the Jews, and because their growing numbers would threaten the Jewish nature of the Israeli state. Kahane was assassinated while on a speaking engagement in New York City in the fall of 1990.

For further information see: S. Daniel Breslauer, *Meir Kahane: Ideologue, Hero, Thinker* (Lewiston, NY: Edwin Mellen Press, 1986); Meir Kahane, *Our Challenge: The Chosen Land* (Radnor, PA: Chilton, 1974); Yair Kolter, *Heil Kahane* (New York: M. Rachlin Printing, 1986); Jay Shapiro, *Meir Kahane: The Litmus Test of Democracy in Israel* (Montreal: Dawn Publishers, 1988); Meir Kahane, *The Story of the Jewish Defense League* (Radnor, PA: Chilton Books, 1975); Meir Kahane, *They Must Go* (New York: Grosset and Dunlap, 1981); Meir Kahane, *Forty Years* (Miami: Institute of the Jewish Idea, 1983); Meir Kahane, *Uncomfortable Questions for Comfortable Jews* (Secaucus, NJ: Lyle Stuart, 1987); Ehud Sprinzak, *Kach and Meir Kahane: The Emergence of Jewish Quasi-Fascism* (New York: American Jewish Committee, 1985); Ehud Sprinzak, "Violence and Catastrophe in the Theology of Rabbi Kahane: The Ideologization of the Mimetic Desire," *Terrorism and Political Violence* 3:3 (Autumn 1991); Ehud Sprinzak, *The Ascendance of Israel's Radical Right* (New York: Oxford University Press, 1991); Ehud Sprinzak, "Extremism and Violence in Israel: The Crisis of Messianic Politics," *The Annals of the American Academy of Political and Social Science* 555 (January 1998): 114-126.

KAHANE CHAI (KAHANE LIVES). A splinter group from the militant Kach* movement founded by the late Rabbi Meir Kahane* in the 1980s. It was headed by Rabbi Kahane's son, Benjamin. Both it and Kach were outlawed and disarmed in the immediate aftermath of the February 1994 Hebron Massacre*. Nevertheless, Benjamin Kahane and his followers continued to operate underground.

For further information see: Yasha Manuel Harari, "Kahane Chai," in *An Historical Encyclopedia of the Arab-Israeli Conflict*, edited by Bernard Reich (Westport, CT: Greenwood, 1996).

KAPLAN, ELIEZER. Born in Minsk, Russia, in 1891, he was educated in Russia and became active in Zionist affairs. He visited Palestine* briefly in 1920 and settled there in 1923. In 1933 he became a member of the Executive of the Jewish Agency*, becoming the head of its Finance and Administrative Department. He was a central figure in the planning and organizing of economic and development projects in Palestine. After the independence of Israel he became the first Minister of Finance and later Deputy Prime Minister. He died in Genoa, Italy, while on a trip in 1952.

KATYUSHA ROCKET. A small-caliber, unguided, Soviet-made ground-to-ground rocket. Variants were used against Israeli targets by the Egyptian army in the Six Day War* and the Yom Kippur War* and by the PLO* during its years of presence in southern Lebanon*. Beginning in the mid-1980s, Katyushas were fired at Israeli positions in southern Lebanon and at Israeli towns and villages in the northern Galilee by Lebanon-based Hezbollah, AMAL Shi'ite guerillas, and the Popular Front for the Liberation of Palestine-General Command (PFLP-GC).

For further information see: Jon J. Peterson, "Katyusha Rocket," in *An Historical Encyclopedia of the Arab-Israeli Conflict*, edited by Bernard Reich (Westport, CT: Greenwood, 1996): 293-295.

KATZAV, MOSHE. Born in 1945 in Iran*, he graduated from the Hebrew University of Jerusalem* and served as mayor of Kiryat Malachi. He was first elected to the Knesset* in 1977. He was Minister of Labor and Social Affairs in the National Unity Government* established in 1984 and became Minister of Transport in the Government established in December 1988. He retained the latter position in the Shamir-led* Government established in June 1990. He served as Minister of Tourism and Deputy Prime Minister (and the Cabinet Minister responsible for liaising with Israel's Arab community) in the Government formed after the 1996 election. On May 17, 1999, he was reelected to the 15th Knesset, ranking third on the Likud* list.

KATZIR, EPHRAIM (FORMERLY KATCHALSKI). Born in Kiev, Russia, on May 16, 1916. He was brought to Palestine* by his parents in 1922 and was educated at the Hebrew University of Jerusalem*, where he received his master's degree in 1937 and his doctorate in 1941. From 1941 to 1948 he held posts at Hebrew University and as a research fellow at Brooklyn Polytechnic Institute and at Columbia University. During Israel's War of Independence* he headed the science corps of the Hagana*. In 1949 he joined the Department of Biophysics at the Weizmann Institute of

Science* in Rehovot and became department head. He did research on proteins and polyamino acids and is a member of numerous scientific organizations. He became President* of Israel in April 1973 and remained in that position until 1978. In keeping with government policy that government officials adopt Hebrew names, he changed his name from Katchalski to Katzir. In 1978 he became the head of the Center for Biotechnology at Tel Aviv University and a professor at the Weizmann Institute.

KATZ-OZ, AVRAHAM. Born in Tel Aviv* in 1934 and a member of Kibbutz Nahal Oz. He was educated at the Hebrew University* where he received an MSc in agriculture. He was a Labor Alignment* member of the Knesset* since 1981. He became Minister of Agriculture in the Government established in December 1988. He did not contest the 1996 elections to the 14th Knesset.

KEREN HAYESOD (PALESTINE FOUNDATION FUND). The major fund-raising and financial institution of the World Zionist Organization* that financed its activities in Palestine*. The 1920 Zionist conference created the fund to finance immigration to Palestine and rural settlement there and in March 1921 it was registered as a British company. In the subsequent years it was the agency that funded the building of the Jewish State in Palestine and Israel. Its funds came from contributions and financed activities in the areas of immigration, absorption, settlement, water resource development, and economic investment. Keren Hayesod was incorporated as an Israeli company by a special act of the Knesset*, the Keren Hayesod Law of January 18, 1956.

KEREN KAYEMET LE ISRAEL *see* JEWISH NATIONAL FUND

KESSAR, ISRAEL. Born in 1931 in Sana, Yemen, he immigrated to Palestine* in 1933 and was educated in Jerusalem*. He received a BA in economics and sociology and an MA in labor studies from Tel Aviv University*. Beginning in 1984 he served as a Member of the Knesset* on the Maarach* list and as Secretary General of the Histadrut*. Ousted in 1992 in the shake-up in the Histadrut power restructuring that occurred in the early 1990s, Kessar retired from party politics but retains influence in Labor* Party circles.

KFIR. An Israeli-designed and Israeli-produced fighter aircraft, initially developed in the early 1970s. First used in combat missions in 1977, it had a maximum speed of Mach 2.3 and an operational altitude of 58,000 feet. It was designed to be employed in either an air-defense or ground-attack role. Depending on its role the Kfir had an unrefueled range of between 548 and 737 miles. It was air-refuelable.

For further information see: Stephen H. Gotowicki, "Kfir Fighter Aircraft," in *An Historical Encyclopedia of the Arab-Israeli Conflict*, edited by Bernard Reich (Westport, CT: Greenwood, 1996): 297-298.

KHARTOUM ARAB SUMMIT. At the Khartoum Arab Summit held at Sudan's capital at the end of the summer of 1967, the Arab states agreed to unite their efforts "to eliminate the effects of the [Israeli] aggression" in the Six Day War* and to secure Israeli withdrawal from the occupied territories* within the framework of "the main principles" to which they adhere: "no peace with Israel, no recognition of Israel, no negotiation with it, and adherence to the rights of the Palestinian people in their country."

For further information see: Avner Cohen, *Israel and the Arab World* (New York: Funk and Wagnalls, 1970); Yehoshafat Harkabi, *Arab Attitudes to Israel* (London: Valentine, Mitchell, 1972); Yehoshafat Harkabi, *Arab Strategies and Israel's Response* (New York: The Free Press, 1977); Mohamed Heikal, *The Road to Ramadan* (New York: Ballantine, 1975); Bernard Reich, editor, *Arab-Israeli Conflict and Conciliation: A Documentary History* (Westport, CT: Praeger, 1995): 101.

KIBBUTZ (PL. KIBBUTZIM). The kibbutz (a word meaning collective settlement that comes from the Hebrew* for group) is a socialist experiment—a voluntary grouping of individuals who hold property in common and have their needs satisfied by the commune. Every kibbutz member participates in the work. All the needs of the members, including education, recreation, medical care, and vacations, are provided by the kibbutz. The earliest kibbutzim were founded by pioneer immigrants from Eastern Europe who sought to join socialism and Zionism* and thus build a new kind of society. They have been maintained by a second and third generation as well as by new members. Initially, the kibbutzim focused on the ideal of working the land and became known for their crops, poultry, orchards, and dairy farming. As modern techniques, especially automation, were introduced and as land and water became less available, many of the kibbutzim shifted their activities or branched out into new areas, such as industry and tourism, to supplement the agricultural pursuits. Kibbutz factories now manufacture electronic products, furniture, plastics, household appliances, farm machinery, and irrigation-system components. *See also* HAKIBBUTZ HAARTZI; HAKIBBUTZ HAMEUHAD; IHUD HAKVUTZOT VEHAKIBBUT-ZIM; UNITED KIBBUTZ MOVEMENT.

For further information see: Haim Barkai, *Growth Patterns of the Kibbutz Economy* (Amsterdam: North-Holland, 1977); Eliezer Ben-Rafael, "The Kibbutz in the 1950s: A Transformation of Identity," in *Israel: The First Decade of Independence*, edited by S. Ilan Troen and Noah Lucas (Albany: State University of New York Press, 1995): 265-278; Avraham C. Ben-Yosef, *The Purest Democracy in the World* (New York: Herzl and Yoseloff, 1963); Bruno Bettelheim, *The Children of the Dream* (London: Macmillan, 1969); Joseph Blasi, *The Communal Experience of the Kibbutz* (New Brunswick, NJ: Transaction, 1986); Alison M. Bowes, "The Experiment That Did Not Fail: Image and Reality in the Israeli Kibbutz," *International Journal of Middle East Studies* 22 (February 1990): 85-104; H. Darin Drabkin, *The Other Society* (London: Gollancz, 1962); Aryeh Fishman, editor, *The Religious Kibbutz Movement* (Jerusalem: 1957); Eliyahu Kanovsky, *The Economy of the Israeli Kibbutz* (Cambridge, MA.: Harvard University Press, 1966); Ernest Krausz, editor, *Sociology of the Kibbutz* (New Brunswick, NJ: Transaction Books, 1983); Dan Leon, *The Kibbutz: A New Way of Life* (Oxford, UK: Pergamon Press, 1969); Dan Leon, *The Kibbutz: A Portrait from Within* (Tel Aviv: Israel Horizons, 1964); David Mittelberg, *Strangers in Paradise: The Israeli Kibbutz Experience* (New Brunswick, NJ: Transaction Books, 1988); Henry Near, "Black Holes and Galaxies in Kibbutz History," *Israel Affairs* 1:2 (Winter 1994): 309-321; Henry Near, *The Kibbutz Movement: A History*, 2 volumes (London: The Littman Library of Jewish Civilization, 1992, 1997); Henry Near, "The Crisis in the Kibbutz Movement, 1949-1961," in *Israel: The First Decade of Independence*, edited by S. Ilan Troen and Noah Lucas (Albany: State University of New York Press, 1995): 243-263; Albert I. Rabin, *Growing Up in the Kibbutz* (New York: Springer, 1965); Shimon Shur, et al., *The Kibbutz: A Bibliography of Scientific and Professional Publications in English* (Darby, PA: Norwood, 1981); Melford E. Spiro, *Children of the Kibbutz* (Cambridge, MA: Harvard University Press, 1958); Melford E.

Spiro, *Gender and Culture: Kibbutz Women Revisited* (Durham, NC: Duke University Press, 1979); Melford E. Spiro, *Kibbutz: Venture in Utopia* (Cambridge, MA: Harvard University Press, 1979); Boris Stern, *The Kibbutz That Was* (Washington, DC: Public Affairs Press, 1965); Lionel Tiger and Joseph Shepher, *Woman in the Kibbutz* (New York: Harcourt, Brace, Jovanovich, 1975); Murray Weingarten, *Life in a Kibbutz* (New York: The Reconstructionist Press, 1955).

KIBYA (QIBYA). The Jordanian village that was the site of the first major retaliatory raid by Israel to terrorist incursions from neighboring Arab countries. On October 15, 1953, Palestinian infiltrators from Jordan* murdered a young woman and two of her children in the Israeli settlement of Yehud. Israeli intelligence identified the Jordanian village of Kibya as one of the bases used by the infiltrators for this and other attacks. Despite the opposition of Prime Minister Moshe Sharett* (who reportedly preferred to work with the Jordanian government in stopping the terrorist incursions), a special anti-terrorist squad of Israeli soldiers, Unit 101, commanded by Ariel Sharon*, raided Kibya on October 14-15, 1953. In the course of the attack about 12 Jordanian soldiers were killed along with some 60 Jordanian civilians. Though the Kibya raid produced the short-term benefit of temporarily deterring cross-border terrorist incursions, the diplomatic costs to Israel were substantial, including condemnations by the United States*, Great Britain*, and the United Nations Security Council.

For further information see: Joseph E. Goldberg, "Kibya," in *An Historical Encyclopedia of the Arab-Israeli Conflict*, edited by Bernard Reich (Westport, CT: Greenwood, 1996): 300-302; Benny Morris, *Israel's Border Wars: 1949-1956* (Oxford: Oxford University Press, 1993).

KILOMETER 101. The point along the Cairo-Suez road where, after the Yom Kippur War*, Israeli and Egyptian military officials met for negotiations toward implementing the conditions of United Nations Security Council Resolution 338*, beginning on October 28, 1973. The talks, mediated by U.S. Secretary of State Henry Kissinger, resulted in a six-point agreement, signed by Egyptian general Abdul Ghani Gamassy and Israeli general Aharon Yariv, on November 11, 1973. The Kilometer 101 talks set the stage for the Israeli-Egyptian Disengagement of Forces Agreement* of 1974.

For further information see: Matti Golan, *The Secret Conversations of Henry Kissinger: Step-by-Step Diplomacy in the Middle East* (New York: Quadrangle, 1976).

KING-CRANE COMMISSION. At the time of World War I, perhaps the most significant American concern and its first political involvement in the Middle East was the formation of an investigating commission that was sent to the region and offered suggestions concerning its future. At a meeting of the Big Four in March 1919, U.S. President Woodrow Wilson proposed that a commission visit Syria* to elucidate the state of opinion in the region and report on its findings to the Versailles peace conference. The United States* sent two Americans, Henry C. King, President of Oberlin College, and Charles R. Crane, a manufacturer, to the area but neither the British nor the French joined the commission. The King-Crane Commission was the first significant American involvement in the political affairs of the area although, in the final analysis, the inquiry had no real impact. Neither the Allies nor the United States gave it serious consideration. King and Crane arrived in Palestine* in June 1919, conducted interviews and studied reports and documents. In August the Commission submitted its report to the American delegation for use at the peace conference. Generally, it argued against the Zionist objectives and sought to include Palestine within a larger Syrian mandate that would include Lebanon* and Palestine.

For further information see: Neil Caplan, *Futile Diplomacy, Vol. 1—Early Arab-Zionist Negotiation Attempts, 1913-1931* (London: Frank Cass, 1983); Harry N. Howard, *The King-Crane Commission: An American Inquiry in the Middle East* (Beirut: Khayats, 1963); Walid Khalidi, editor, *From Haven to Conquest: Readings in Zionism and the Palestine Question until 1948* (Washington, DC: The Institute for Palestine Studies, 1987): 213-218; Bernard Wasserstein, "Patterns of Communal Conflict in Palestine," in *Essential Papers on Zionism*, edited by Jehuda Reinharz and Anita Shapira (New York: New York University Press, 1996): 671-688.

KING DAVID HOTEL. Built in 1930, after World War II it housed the headquarters of the British military and civilian command in Palestine*. On July 22, 1946, the south-west corner of the building was destroyed by a bombing committed by the Irgun Tzvai Leumi*. A total of 91 people were killed in the attack: 41 Arabs, 28 British, 17 Jews, and five others.

According to the Irgun's leader, Menachem Begin*, the bombing was a political act, a demonstration that the Irgun could strike at the very heart of the British Mandate* in Palestine. The attack was condemned by the Jewish Agency* leadership. Nevertheless, it prompted a crackdown by British security authorities of Zionist activities in Palestine. The King David Hotel was rebuilt in 1948. *See also* IRGUN TZVAI LEUMI.

For further information see: Menachem Begin, *The Revolt: Story of the Irgun* (New York: Nash, 1981); Thurston Clarke, *By Blood and Fire: The Attack on the King David Hotel* (New York: Putnam's, 1981).

KIRYAT ARBA. A Jewish settlement established at Hebron* after the Six Day War*. The name Kiryat Arba or Kiryat Haarbah, is mentioned in the Bible: "Kiryat Arba, that is Hebron" (Joshua, 15:54), "Hebron, formally called Kiryat Arba" (Judges, 1:10), "Kiryat Arba, that is Hebron" (Genesis, 35:27), and "some of the men of Judah lived in Kiryat Arba and its villages" (Nehemiah, 11:25). In the Cave of Machpela in Hebron are the tombs of Abraham, Isaac, and Jacob and their wives (Sarah, Rebecca and Leah, respectively). An old Jewish tradition has it that this cave is also the burial place of Adam and Eve who lived in Hebron after their banishment from the Garden of Eden. The name Kiryat Arba (Town of the Four) was chosen to allude to the four pairs who are buried there.

KITCHEN CABINET. Although the cabinet* has been the primary policy-making body of Israel and it decides Israel's policies in all areas of activity subject to the approval of the Knesset*, at times much of the cabinet's work has been conducted by a small and select group of ministers meeting informally. When Golda Meir* was Prime Minister these informal meetings generally were referred to as the kitchen cabinet.

KNESSET (PARLIAMENT). The Knesset is the supreme authority in the state, and its laws are theoretically the source of all power and authority, although in reality decisions are made by the Prime Minister and the Government (or Cabinet)* and ratified by the Knesset. The Knesset's name is derived from the Knesset Hagedola* (Great Assembly), the supreme legislative body of the Jewish people after the biblical period and prior to the Maccabean Revolt. The modern body is based, to a large extent, on the British model, adapted to Israel's needs and special requirements. It is a unicameral body of 120 members elected for four-year terms by general, national, direct, equal, secret, and proportional suffrage in accordance with the Knesset Elections Law. Citizens may be elected to the Knesset if they are at least 21 years of age. The entire country elects all members; there are no separate constituencies. This system derives from that used by the World Zionist Organization (WZO)* and the Histadrut* and other elements in the Yishuv* prior to Israel's independence. All Israeli citizens age 18 and over may vote in Knesset elections without regard to sex, religion, or other factors, unless deprived of that right by a court of law. Voters cast their ballots for individual parties, each with rival lists of candidates, rather than for individual candidates. According to the revised Basic Law: The Government (1992)* voters also simultaneously cast a second ballot for the direct election of the Prime Minister. Each party may present the voter with a list of up to 120 names—its choices for Knesset seats. An important part of the Knesset's work is done within the framework of its major committees: House Committee, Finance Committee, Economics Committee, Foreign Affairs and Defense Committee, Internal Affairs and Environment Committee, Constitution, Law and Justice Committee, Immigration and Absorption Committee, Education and Culture Committee, Labor and Welfare Committee, and State Control Committee.

For further information see: Asher Arian, *The Second Republic: Politics in Israel* (Chatham, NJ: Chatham House, 1998); Eliahu S. Likhovski, *Israel's Parliament: The Law of the Knesset* (Oxford: Clarendon Press, 1971); Gregory S. Mahler, *The Knesset: Parliament in the Israeli Political System* (Rutherford, NJ: Fairleigh Dickinson University Press, 1981); Samuel Sager, *The Parliamentary System of Israel* (Syracuse, NY: Syracuse University Press, 1985); State of Israel, *The Knesset, Rules of Procedure* (Jerusalem, 1995); Asher Zidon, *Knesset: The Parliament of Israel*, Translated from the Hebrew by Aryeh Rubinstein and Gertrude Hirschler (New York: Herzl Press, 1967).

KNESSET ELECTIONS. The Knesset* is elected every four years, but may dissolve itself and call for new elections before the end of its term. Elections to the Knesset are general, nationwide, direct, equal, secret, and proportional. The entire country is a single constituency. According to the Basic Law: The Knesset (1958)*, every citizen is eligible to vote from age 18, provided the courts have not deprived the individual of this right by law, and to be elected from age 21. Prior to elections, each party presents its list of candidates and its platform. There is no rule regarding the way candidates are to be chosen and the order in which they are to be presented in each list, since this is the sole prerogative of the parties or the groups submitting the list. Some parties make use of an organizing committee, while others select candidates in the party centers or in the branches. In some instances the person at the head of the list decides who should follow him on the list and in what order, while in others secret elections are held beforehand, with the participation of all the members of the group or party in question. In recent years lists comprising several parties generally reserve certain places on the lists for each of the parties they contain, each such party filling those places in its own way or according to its own regulations. Also, in recent years a number of parties have chosen their electoral lists through primary elections.

Parties represented in the outgoing Knesset are automatically eligible to stand for reelection. Additional parties may stand for election, provided they obtain the requisite number of signatures of eligible voters and deposit a bond, which is refunded if they succeed in receiving at least 1.5% of the national vote. A Treasury allocation for each Knesset member is granted to each party represented in the outgoing Knesset, in order to wage their election campaign. New parties receive a similar allocation retroactively for each Knesset member they actually elect. The State Comptroller* reviews the disbursement of all campaign expenditures. The President*, the State Comptroller, judges and other senior public officials, as well as the Chief of Staff of the Israel Defense Forces* and other high-ranking army officers, are disqualified from presenting their candidacy for the Knesset, unless they have resigned their positions by a specified date (one hundred days) prior to the elections.

The Central Elections Committee, headed by a justice of the Supreme Court* and including representatives of the parties holding seats in the Knesset, is responsible for conducting the elections. The 11th Knesset barred the submission of lists whose platform negated the existence of the Jewish State or its democratic character. On election day, each voter casts a ballot for one party—its list of candidates and its platform as a whole, having been presented prior to the election. Beginning in 1996 a second ballot is cast for the direct election of the Prime Minister. Knesset seats are assigned in proportion to each party's percentage of the total national vote. Knesset seats are allocated according to the sequence in which the candidates appear on their respective party lists. Ever since the establishment of Israel, a large number of small parties have received representation in the Knesset, thus ensuring the representation of a wide spectrum of political views.

For further information see: Asher Arian, "The Israeli Election for Prime Minister and the Knesset 1996," *Electoral Studies* 17 (1996): 574; Asher Arian, *The Second Republic: Politics in Israel* (Chatham, NJ: Chatham House, 1998); Basic Law: The Government (1992); Avraham Brichta, "Proposed Electoral Reforms in Israel," *Jewish Journal of Sociology* 33:2 (1991); Avraham Brichta, "The New Premier-Parliamentary System in Israel," *The Annals of the American Academy of Political and Social Science* 555 (January 1998): 180-192; Abraham Diskin, *Elections and Voters in Israel* (Westport, CT: Praeger, 1991); Reuven Y. Hazan, "Presidential Parliamentarianism: Direct Popular Election of the Prime Minister, Israel's New Electoral and Political System," *Electoral Studies* 15 (1996): 21-37; Bernard Susser, "The Direct Election of the Prime Minister: A Balance Sheet," *Israel Affairs* (Special Issue: "Israel at the Polls 1996") 4:1 (Autumn 1997): 237-257.

KNESSET HAGEDOLA. (Literally "The Great Assembly"). The supreme legislative body of the Jewish people at the beginning of the Second Temple period in ancient Israel, following the return from the Babylonian exile (from c. 538 BCE). The name of the modern parliament of Israel—the Knesset—is derived from it.

KNESSET YISRAEL. The term used to refer to the organizational structure of the Yishuv* during the British Mandate*.

KOL ISRAEL (THE VOICE OF ISRAEL). The cornerstone of electronic media in Israel, governed by the Israel Broadcasting Authority (IBA) Act of 1965. Broadcasting in Israel had its roots both in the official service operating under the British Mandate* and the clandestine Jewish broadcasts set up by paramilitary underground organizations (for example, Kol Israel ha-Lohemet—The Voice of Fighting Zion, established by the Irgun Tzvai Leumi* in March 1939). In 1940, Kol Israel—The Voice of Israel, was used for the first time: it was the radio broadcasting station of the Hagana*. In 1950, this became the Israel army broadcasting station, Galei Tzahal*. Kol Israel came into existence in 1948 with a live broadcast of the Proclamation of Independence and the ceremony of signing the Declaration at the Tel Aviv Museum. The first broadcast of Kol Israel television occurred on Independence Day, 1968. Early on, efforts were made to have Kol Israel serve as a national institution with an emphasis on Zionist education and educational programing. Broadcasts were aired in Hebrew*, Arabic, and English. Additional programing in Russian and other languages was introduced to accommodate immigrant waves. Until the late 1980s broadcasting in Israel was a monopoly controlled tightly by the state. However, in the early 1990s legislation was changed to permit the opening-up of the system, including a second television channel and local radio stations, privately run, and cable television.

For further information see: Dan Caspi and Yehiel Limor, *The Mass Media in Israel 1948-1990* (Tel Aviv: Am Oved, 1995, Hebrew); Rachel Lael, editor, *Channel 2—The First Year* (Jerusalem: Israel Democracy Institute, 1994, Hebrew).

KOLLEK, THEODORE (TEDDY). Born in Vienna in 1911 he early became involved in Zionism*. He settled in Palestine* in 1934 and was one of the founders of Kibbutz Ein Gev. From 1940 to 1947 he served on the staff of the Political Department of the Jewish Agency*. After Israel's independence he became the number two official in Israel's embassy in Washington. He served as Director General of the Prime Minister's Office from 1952 to 1964. Affiliated with Mapai* he followed David Ben-Gurion* when he left the party and founded Rafi*. At the head of the Rafi ticket, he was elected Mayor of Jerusalem* in 1965. Kollek remained Mayor of Jerusalem until November 1993 when he was defeated by Likud* candidate Ehud Olmert*. When Jerusalem was reunited as a consequence of the 1967 Six Day War* it posed a particular challenge to the Mayor who had to extend the services of the city to East Jerusalem and was now Mayor of the entire city. He led the One Jerusalem party, a loose coalition of Labor* party members and personal supporters of Kollek, that established control of Jerusalem's city council in 1978.

For further information see: Teddy Kollek and Amos Kollek, *For Jerusalem: A Life* (New York: Random House, 1978); Teddy Kollek, "Sharing United Jerusalem," *Foreign Affairs* 67:2 (Winter 1988/1989): 156-168; Teddy Kollek, *Jerusalem* (Washington, DC: The Washington Institute for Near East Policy, 1990).

KOOK, RABBI AVRAHAM YITZHAK HACOHEN. Chief Ashkenazi Rabbi of Palestine* (1921-1935). He was born in Griva, Latvia, in 1865 and died in Jerusalem* in 1935. He studied in various Eastern European yeshivot and served as Rabbi for a number of communities. In 1904 he settled in Palestine where he served as Rabbi of the Jewish community of Jaffa*. Stranded in Europe during World War I, he returned to Palestine in 1919 and became the Rabbi of the Ashkenazi* community of Jerusalem. When the Chief Rabbinate* of Palestine was established in 1921 he was chosen Ashkenazi Chief Rabbi and held that position until his death. He developed a nationalist-religious philosophy and pursued the Zionist ideal. He established his own yeshiva in Jerusalem (Merkaz Harav) where he focused on the ideal of a religious-national renaissance for the Jewish people. He was outspoken in his criticism of the administration of the British Mandate for Palestine*.

For further information see: Shlomo Avineri, *The Making of Modern Zionism: The Intellectual Origins of the Jewish State* (New York: Basic, 1981): 187-197; Arthur Hertzberg, editor, *The Zionist Idea: A Historical Analysis and Reader* (New York: Atheneum, 1979): 416-431.

KOOK, RABBI ZVI YEHUDA. Born in Lithuania in 1891 he was educated at Jewish religious schools as well as at universities in Germany. He immigrated with his parents to Palestine* in 1904 where his father, Rabbi Avraham Yitzhak Hacohen Kook*, later became Chief Ashkenazi Rabbi. He became head of the Merkaz Harav Yeshiva and published numerous religious and other commentaries. He was an ardent Zionist. He participated in Gush Emunim* activities and became the movement's spiritual mentor. He died in 1982.

For further information see: Shmuel Almog, "People and Land in Modern Jewish Nationalism," in *Essential Papers on Zionism*, edited by Jehuda Reinharz and Anita Shapira (New York: New York University Press, 1996): 46-62; Zvi Yehuda Kook, "Honest We Shall Be in the Land and in the Torah," in *A Land of Settlement*, edited by Yaacov Shavit (Jerusalem: Har Zion, 1977, Hebrew): 106-110.

KOOR INDUSTRIES. An umbrella organization for industrial and craft concerns. It was established in 1944 as part of Solel Boneh*, a construction concern whose aim was to develop heavy industry factories. The establishment of Koor was part of the Histadrut's* general plan to ensure basic industry for the Yishuv* which would maximize the use of existing raw materials, would enable a planned distribution of the factories such that they would provide employment in development towns and areas, and would help the balance of payments both by creating local products to replace imports, and in supporting the export industry. Such an industry was also to be the basis for an independent security industry, a source of training for Jewish workers, and it was hoped that it would ensure the labor movement's special place in defining the direction and development of the economy in the future. In 1958, Solel Boneh was reorganized and divided into three companies: (1) construction and public works throughout the country; (2) construction and pavement abroad; and (3) different types of industrial production. This made Koor an independent company, which rapidly became the largest concern in Israel. Despite its status as Israel's largest conglomerate, Koor experienced severe economic difficulties in the late 1980s. It sold off various subsidiaries, closed unprofitable units, and defaulted on some bank loans. In the fall of 1991 United States* and Israeli banks, the Government of Israel, and Hevrat Ovdim* signed a financial restructuring agreement designed to rescue Koor. In the 1990s large segments of the company were sold off to private investors in the context of the general trend toward privatizing the Israeli economy and the breaking up of monopolies.

KUPAT HOLIM (SICK FUND). A comprehensive health insurance scheme of the Histadrut* founded in 1911. When the Histadrut was formed in 1920 two health insurance schemes merged into a joint sick fund which maintained its own medical staff. It provided medical services for its members and new immigrants who were given Kupat Holim coverage on arrival. It has clinics throughout Israel as well as numerous other facilities, including hospitals. In recent years the role of the Kupat Holim has changed significantly as Israel's entire health care system has undergone radical restructuring. *See also* HEALTH.

KWARA JEWS. In June 1999 Foreign Minister Ariel Sharon* was appointed to coordinate the overall Israeli activity for bringing about the speedy arrival of the approximately 3,500 Kwara Jews from Ethiopia* to Israel. Immigrant Absorption Minister Yuli Edelstein* was to head an inter-ministerial team for coordinating absorption of the immigrants in to Israeli Society. Also it was decided to dispatch medical aid and food to the Jews in Kwara.

L

LA'AM PARTY (TOWARD THE PEOPLE). One of the components that formed Likud* in 1973. It was composed of parts of the Free Center Party*, the State List*, and the Land of Israel Movement*.

LABOR ALIGNMENT *see* ALIGNMENT

LABOR PARTY *see* ISRAEL LABOR PARTY

LAHAD, ANTOINE. Christian Lebanese commander of the South Lebanese Army* since January 1984, following the death of the army's founder, Major Saad Georges Haddad. One of Lahad's first moves as commander was to change his force's name, from the Christian Free Lebanon Militia to the South Lebanese Army, to reflect the fact that it was not just for Christians but for all Lebanese who opposed the Palestine Liberation Organization* and Syrian* presence in the country. With the reduced influence of the PLO in Lebanon following Operation Peace for Galilee* (1982), the primary activity for Lahad and the SLA became cooperating with the Israel Defense Forces* in combating Hezbollah and other Shi'ite Muslim militias operating in and around the security zone*. In the late 1990s, Lahad expressed reservations about a proposed unilateral Israeli withdrawal from the security zone, fearful of reprisal attacks against SLA fighters and their families by rival Lebanese forces. *See also* LEBANON.

LAKE KINNERET *see* SEA OF GALILEE

LAKE TIBERIAS *see* SEA OF GALILEE

LAND DAY. An annual commemoration by Israel's Arab* population of the killing on March 30, 1976, of six demonstrators who had been protesting the confiscation of Arab land in the Galilee*. Though historically restricted to peaceful marches, Land Day in recent years has been characterized by violent demonstrations by segments of the Arab community.

LAND FOR PEACE. The general concept that Israel would return land (the amount subject to negotiations) occupied during the Six Day War*, in exchange for peace, recognition, and normalization of relations with the

Arab states. The principle was enshrined in United Nations Security Council resolutions 242* (1967) and 338* (1973). It was accepted as the framework for Arab-Israeli negotiations by all parties to the Madrid Middle East Peace Conference* of 1991.

LAND OF ISRAEL *see* ERETZ ISRAEL

LAND OF ISRAEL MOVEMENT. A political movement, established in the aftermath of the Six Day War*, that argued in favor of Israel's retaining most of the territories occupied in the war. Many of the movement's guiding principles found political expression in the Gush Emunim* settler movement and the Tehiya Party*.

For further information see: Rael Jean Isaac, *Israel Divided: Ideological Politics in the Jewish State* (Baltimore: Johns Hopkins, 1976); Ehud Sprinzak, *The Ascendance of Israel's Radical Right* (New York: Oxford University Press, 1991).

LANDAU, HAIM. Born in Cracow, Poland, in 1916, Landau immigrated to Palestine* and in 1935 enrolled at the Technion* in Haifa*, where he received a degree in construction engineering in 1944. Shortly after his arrival in Palestine, he joined the Irgun Tzvai Leumi*. In 1944 he served as Deputy Commander of the Irgun and was subsequently appointed chief of its general command, a post which he held until 1948. One of the founding members of the Herut Party*, he was elected to the First Knesset* in January 1949, and reelected to all subsequent Knessets until the Ninth. In December 1969 he joined the Government of National Unity* as Minister of Development, a position he held until the resignation of Gahal* from that Government in August 1970. He was appointed Minister without Portfolio in January 1978. In January 1979 he was appointed Minister of Transport. He died in 1981.

LANDAU, MOSHE. Born in Danzig, Germany, in 1912 and educated in law at the University of London, he settled in Palestine* in 1933. In 1948 he was appointed a judge of the Haifa* District Court, an office he held until 1953 when he was appointed a justice of the Supreme Court of Israel*. He was the presiding judge at the trial of the Nazi war criminal Adolf Eichmann*, and served as President of the Supreme Court from 1980 to 1982. In 1987 he was appointed to head a commission of inquiry to examine the methods used by the Shin Bet-General Security Service

(Shabak)* in interrogating suspected terrorists. The Landau Commission determined that in dealing with dangerous terrorists who represent a grave threat to the safety and security of the State of Israel and its citizens, "the use of a moderate degree of pressure, including physical pressure" in order to obtain crucial information, was unavoidable under certain circumstances. Although it established specific measures and parameters for guarding against the inappropriate use of interrogation methods, the Landau Commission was accused by the United Nations and international human rights monitoring agencies of having legitimized activities often defined as torture.

For further information see: Mordechai Kremnitzer, "National Security and the Rule of Law: A Critique of the Landau Commission's Report," in *National Security and Democracy in Israel*, edited by Avner Yaniv (Boulder, CO: Lynne Rienner, 1993): 153-172; Moshe Landau, "The Limits of Pressure," *Israeli Democracy* (Fall 1990): 32-34.

LAPID, YOSEF TOMMY. Born in 1931 he grew up as Tomislav Lampel in Novi Sad, Yugoslavia. His father was killed in the Mauthausen concentration camp. He and his mother survived World War II in the Jewish ghetto in Budapest, Hungary. He emigrated to Israel in 1948. He changed his name to Lapid, served in the IDF*, and studied law. He became a journalist and author and served as an editor and editorial writer at *Maariv**. He also appeared on the prime-time, political talk show "Popolitika," which was important in his political life. In March 1999 he was approached to head the Shinui Party* and he agreed. He campaigned for the Knesset* as the head of the Shinui Party. His theme centered on the inanities of the religious Jews of Israel—he ran a political campaign bashing ultra-Orthodox Jews, railing against their "medieval," anti-democratic ways, special privileges and raids on the public trough. Under Lapid's leadership, Shinui won six seats in the 15th Knesset.

LASKOV, CHAIM. Laskov was born in Russia and immigrated to Palestine* with his parents in 1925. His father was murdered by Arabs in 1930 in Haifa*, where he studied in the "Reali" high school. He joined the Hagana* at a young age and entered Orde Wingate's "Special Night Squadrons". Following the outbreak of World War II, he joined the British army and served in North Africa and Europe. He was released from the army with the rank of Major. After World War II, he organized the purchasing of weapons in Europe to be smuggled into Israel. When he returned to Israel, he became the chief training and education officer of the Hagana. He commanded the first armored battalion of the Israel Defense Forces* in the War of Independence*, and later the Seventh Brigade during the battles to free the Galilee*. After the war, he attained the rank of Major General, and became the head of the training and education branch of the IDF. He was appointed head of the air force in 1953, the armored corps in 1956, the commander of a division in the Sinai War*, and later the commander of the southern command. He served as Chief of Staff of the IDF between 1958-1961, and in November 1972 he became the Commissioner of Soldiers' Complaints in the Defense Ministry. He was a member of the Agranat Commission of Inquiry* that was established after the Yom Kippur War*. He died in 1982.

LATRUN. A locality with a monastery at the foot of the Judean* hills on the road from Tel Aviv* to Jerusalem*. The monastery was founded in the nineteenth century by French Trappist monks. It is located at a strategic crossroads linking the Mediterranean coast to Jerusalem where the coastal plain meets the Judean hills. The Ayalon Valley where Joshua completed the conquest of Canaan* is here. During the British Mandate* a police fortress was built at the strategic location as was a detention camp where many Jewish political prisoners were held. A major effort was made by the Jews during Israel's War of Independence* to take this area in order to open the road from Tel Aviv to Jerusalem, but it failed and an alternative "Burma Road" had to be built to transport vital supplies to the city's embattled Jewish sector. The area was captured by Israel during the Six Day War*.

LAU, RABBI ISRAEL MEIR. Born in 1937 in Pyotrekov, Poland, Rabbi Meir is a survivor of the Buchenwald Concentration Camp. In 1946 he immigrated to Israel. Before being elected Ashkenazi Chief Rabbi in 1993, Rabbi Lau was Chief Rabbi and President of the Rabbinical Court of Tel Aviv-Yafo from 1988-1993.

LAVI. On February 8, 1980, Defense Minister Ezer Weizman* approved plans for the development and production by Israel Aircraft Industries* of a single-engine fighter aircraft, to be known as the Lavi. Although intended to be Israeli-developed and Israeli-built, much of the funding for the project was to come from the United States*. The first full scale mock-up of the Lavi was revealed at the beginning of 1985. The first Lavi (B-01) flew on December 31, 1986, piloted by IAI chief test pilot

Menachem Schmoll. The project was cancelled on August 30, 1987, against the background of massive cost overruns ($1.5 billion had already been expended on research and development) in a period of severe fiscal austerity introduced in 1985 by the Government of National Unity*. Prominent Israelis, including former Defense Minister Moshe Arens*, charged that the United States pressured Israel to cancel production of the Lavi because it represented significant competition for the American arms and aircraft industry and because production of an Israeli jet fighter would reduce the country's dependence on the United States for maintaining its qualitative military advantage.

For further information see: Moshe Arens, *Broken Covenant: American Foreign Policy and the Crisis Between the US and Israel* (New York: Simon and Schuster, 1995); Duncan L. Clarke and Alan S. Cohen, "The Lavi Fighter," *The Middle East Journal* 40:1 (Winter 1986): 16-32; Hirsch Goodman and W. Seth Carus, *The Future Battlefield and the Arab-Israeli Conflict* (New Brunswick, NJ: Transaction, 1990): 58-62; Bernard Reich, *Securing the Covenant: United States-Israel Relations after the Cold War* (Westport, CT: Praeger, 1995); Dov S. Zakheim, *Flight of the Lavi: A US-Israeli Crisis* (London: Brassey's, 1996).

LAVON, PINHAS (FORMERLY LUBIANIKER). He was the key figure in the "affair" that clouded Israel's political life for almost a decade from the mid-1950s to the mid-1960s, and resulted in the downfall of a Government and the splitting-up of the country's ruling Mapai* party. He was born in Poland and attended Lvov University. He immigrated to Palestine* at 25. He became active in the Mapai Party and served as its Secretary from 1935 to 1937. After Israel's independence he was elected to the First Knesset*. He served as Minister of Agriculture and then of Supply and Rationing before becoming Minister of Defense in 1953. He died on January 24, 1976. *See also* LAVON AFFAIR.

LAVON AFFAIR. Pinhas Lavon* was Israel's Defense Minister in 1954 when Israeli agents were arrested in Egypt*, apparently for trying to bomb United States* facilities in Cairo and Alexandria and other targets in an effort to turn Great Britain* and the United States against Egypt. The Government of Prime Minister Moshe Sharett* had not been consulted and Lavon claimed that he had not been aware of the plan. However, Colonel Binyamin Gibli, head of military intelligence, insisted that Lavon had personally instructed him to proceed. An inquiry was ordered but no conclusion was reached. Lavon resigned from the Government and was elected Secretary General of the Histadrut*. As a consequence of later revelations the Cabinet was convinced that the evidence against Lavon had been fabricated and the Government issued a statement that the 1954 operation had been ordered without Lavon's knowledge. Prime Minister David Ben-Gurion*, who had been outvoted in the Cabinet, called the resolution a miscarriage of justice. In protest against the intrusion of the executive into the sphere of the judiciary, Ben-Gurion resigned and brought down the Government. He told his party that he would not accept a mandate to form a new Government as long as Lavon represented the party as Secretary General of the Histadrut. The party's central committee ousted Lavon in 1961.

For further information see: S. Z. Abramov, "The Lavon Affair," *Commentary* 31 (February 1961): 100-105; Moshe Bar-Natan, "The Lavon Affair," *Jewish Frontier* 28 (January 1961): 4-6; Erwin Frenkel, "The Lavon Affair: Its Political Implications," *Midstream* 7 (April 1961): 60-69; Amos Perlmutter, *Military and Politics in Israel, 1948 to 1967: Nation-Building and Role Expansion* (London: Frank Cass, 1969); Dan Raviv and Yossi Melman, *Every Spy a Prince: The Complete History of Israel's Intelligence Community* (Boston: Houghton Mifflin, 1990); Gabriel Sheffer, *Moshe Sharett: Biography of a Political Moderate* (Oxford: Clarendon, 1996); J. L. Talmon, "Lavon Affair—Israeli Democracy at the Crossroads," *New Outlook* 4 (March-April 1961): 23-32; Shabtai Teveth, *Ben-Gurion's Spy: The Story of the Political Scandal That Shaped Modern Israel* (New York: Columbia University Press, 1996).

LAW OF RETURN (1950). The law was adopted by the Knesset* on July 5, 1950. It assures virtually unlimited and unfettered Jewish immigration to Israel by providing that every Jew has the right to immigrate to Israel and to settle there unless the applicant is engaged in an activity "directed against the Jewish people" or one that may "endanger public health or the security of the state." An amendment in 1954 also restricted those likely to endanger public welfare. The 1950 law has provided the formal basis for the substantial immigration (aliya*) that has taken place since independence. The concept of unlimited immigration, which has been reinforced by the programs and actions of successive Governments and has had overwhelming support in parliament and from Israel's Jewish population, has brought hundreds of thousands of Jewish immigrants to Israel from more than 70 countries. In recent years there has been much debate about possible changes to the Law of Return in reaction to the arrival in Israel of thousands of immigrants who are not considered Jewish according to Halacha* but nevertheless are receiving generous benefits under the Law of Return.

LEBANON. Israel's neighbor to the north. During the War of Independence* Lebanon joined in the fighting against Israel despite that country's Christian majority and the control of the body politic by that segment of the Lebanese population. Lebanon essentially abstained from participation in the Sinai* and Six Day Wars* and the War of Attrition*. After the Palestine Liberation Organization* was ousted from Jordan in September 1970 it moved into Lebanon via Syria* and established a base of operations and a virtual "state-within-a-state" in the south. Attacks against targets in Israel by the PLO from Lebanon led to Israeli retaliatory strikes as well as two major military operations: Operation Litani* and Operation Peace for Galilee*. While the PLO was building its base of operations and striking against Israel, these developments were contributing to the disintegration of Lebanon, a process that had already begun because of disagreements among the various Lebanese indigenous factions over the distribution of socioeconomic and political power. A civil war broke out in Lebanon in 1975 and did not end until an Arab League* sponsored agreement of 1989. In the intervening years some 40,000 Syrian troops entered Lebanon, ostensibly as peacekeepers and at the invitation of the Lebanese government and the Arab League. Under the terms of the Taif agreement, Syrian forces were to be withdrawn incrementally from Lebanon, but this provision was not implemented. Meanwhile, with the absence of effective control from Beirut, the PLO was able to use Lebanese territory for attacks into Israel. After a number of these strikes Israel launched Operation Litani* in March 1978. Despite the subsequent establishment of the United Nations Interim Force in Lebanon (UNIFIL*) in the border region, periodic attacks into Israel continued. In June 1982 Israel launched Operation Peace for Galilee, the War in Lebanon*, to rectify the situation. A cease-fire brokered by the United States* permitted the PLO to evacuate its forces from Lebanon. Subsequently the United States brokered an agreement between Israel and Lebanon—the May 17, 1983, agreement* —which called for the withdrawal of Israeli forces from Lebanon. The agreement was subsequently abrogated by the Lebanese government under pressure from

Syria. Israel completed its withdrawal from Lebanon in 1985 while a security zone* was established in Lebanon along Israel's northern border.

However, since then Israel has fought a war of attrition against Iranian-sponsored militant Shi'ite forces such as Hezbollah and Amal. Attacks by these groups on Israeli forces and forces of the pro-Israeli South Lebanon Army (SLA)*, and Katyusha missile* strikes into northern Israel, prompted two major IDF operations in southern Lebanon: Operation Accountability* (1992) and Operation Grapes of Wrath* (1996). Continuing IDF losses led to increased public debate about Israel's status in southern Lebanon. Early in its tenure the Government of Benjamin Netanyahu* floated a "Lebanon First" idea, whereby negotiations with the Lebanese government over an IDF withdrawal from the south would pave the way for broader negotiations with Syria over security arrangements in Lebanon and over the Golan Heights* and related issues. This proposal was rejected by the Syrians, who feared that a separate Lebanese-Israeli deal would alleviate the pressure on Jerusalem* to negotiate with Damascus over the Golan Heights on terms preferable to Syria. In the absence of any immediate prospect for a negotiated settlement with either Beirut or Damascus, Israel in the spring of 1998 announced its readiness to withdraw unilaterally from southern Lebanon, on the basis of United Nations Security Council Resolution 425*, but conditioned this withdrawal on the readiness and the ability of the Lebanese government to apply its sovereign authority in the border region. During the 1999 election campaign, Labor*/One Israel* candidate Ehud Barak* pledged to withdraw Israeli forces from Lebanon within one year of being elected Prime Minister.

For further information see: Latif Abul-Husn, *The Lebanese Conflict: Looking Inward* (Boulder, CO: Lynne Rienner, 1998); Rex Brynen, *Sanctuary and Survival: The PLO in Lebanon* (Boulder, CO: Westview, 1990); Neil Caplan and Ian Black, "Israel and Lebanon: Origins of a Relationship," *Jerusalem Quarterly* 27 (Spring 1983): 48-58; Laura Zittrain Eisenberg, "Desperate Diplomacy: The Zionist-Maronite Treaty of 1946," *Studies in Zionism* 13:2 (Autumn 1992); Laura Zittrain Eisenberg, *My Enemy's Enemy: Lebanon in the Early Zionist Imagination, 1900-1948* (Detroit: Wayne State University Press, 1994); Laura Zittrain Eisenberg, "Israel's South Lebanon Imbroglio," *Middle East Quarterly* 4:2 (June 1997): 60-69; Laura Zittrain Eisenberg, "Israel's Lebanon Policy," *MERIA Journal* 3:3 (Ramat Gan: Begin-Sadat Center for Strategic Studies, Bar Ilan University, September 1997); Yair Evron, *Lebanon: The Israeli-Syrian Deterrence Dialogue* (London: Croom Helm, 1987); Shlomo Gazit, "The Security Zone Has Served Us Faithfully—But Its Time Has Passed," *Ha'aretz*, September 8, 1997; Beate Hamizrachi, *The Emergence of the South Lebanon Security Belt: Major Saad Haddad and the Ties with Israel, 1975-1978* (New York: Praeger, 1988); Mark Heller, "Weighing Israel's Options Now," in *Lebanon on Hold: Implications for Middle East Peace*, edited by Rosemary Hollis and Nadim Shehadi (London: The Royal Institute of International Affairs, 1996): 52-55; Raphael Israeli, editor, *PLO in Lebanon: Selected Documents* (London: Weidenfeld and Nicolson, 1983); Benny Morris, "Israel and the Lebanese Phalange: The Birth of a Relationship, 1948-1951," *Studies in Zionism* 5:1 (Spring 1984): 125-144; Fida Nasrallah, "The Way Ahead: Restoring the Lebanese State," in *Lebanon on Hold: Implications for Middle East Peace*, edited by Rosemary Hollis and Nadim Shehadi (London: The Royal Institute of International Affairs, 1996): 82-85; Augustus Richard Norton (with Jillian Schwedler), "(In)security Zones in South Lebanon," *Journal of Palestine Studies* 23:89 (Autumn 1993): 61-79; Walid Phares, "Liberating Lebanon," *Middle East Quarterly* 3:4 (December 1996): 21-30; Itamar Rabinovich, *The War for Lebanon, 1970-1985*, Revised Edition (Ithaca, NY: Cornell University Press, 1985); Barry Rubin and Laura Blum, *The May 1983 Agreement Over Lebanon* (Baltimore: Johns Hopkins, 1988); Ze'ev Schiff, "Lebanon: Motivation and Interests in Israel's Policy," *Middle East Journal* 38 (Spring 1984): 220-227; Ze'ev Schiff, "A Ball in Lebanon's Court," *Ha'aretz*, January 14, 1998; Ze'ev Schiff and Ehud Ya'ari, *Israel's Lebanon War* (New York: Simon and Schuster, 1984); Avner Yaniv, *Dilemmas of Security: Politics, Strategy and the Israeli Experience in Lebanon* (Oxford: Oxford University Press, 1987); Avner Yaniv and Robert J. Lieber, "Personal Whim or Strategic Imperative? The Israeli Invasion of Lebanon," *International Security* 8:2 (Fall 1983): 117-142.

LEBANON WAR (1982) *see* WAR IN LEBANON

LEHI (LOHAMEI HERUT YISRAEL—FIGHTERS FOR THE FREEDOM OF ISRAEL, STERN GROUP) *see* STERN (GANG) GROUP

LEVINGER, RABBI MOSHE. Born in Jerusalem* in 1935, Rabbi Levinger planned and initiated the Jewish return to Hebron* at Passover in 1968

and continues to live there. He was involved in the creation of Gush Emunim* and has been among its leaders and activists. In May 1990 he entered Eyal prison to begin serving a five-month jail sentence for causing the death of an Arab shopkeeper in Hebron in September 1988. He and his followers are among the most militant opponents of the Oslo* process, and especially the agreement to withdraw the IDF from much of Hebron.

LEVY, DAVID. David Levy was born in Rabat, Morocco, on December 12, 1937, and has lived in the development town* of Beit She'an* since immigrating to Israel in 1957. A former construction worker, he began his political career in the Histadrut* and served as chairman of its Likud* faction and also as deputy head and head of Beit She'an Local Council (1964-1977). He was the Likud candidate for the position of Secretary General of the Histadrut in the 1977 and 1981 elections. He was first elected on behalf of the Herut Party* faction of Gahal* to the Seventh Knesset* in October 1969, and has been reelected to all subsequent Knessets. Levy was appointed Minister of Immigrant Absorption in June 1977, and Minister of Construction and Housing in January 1978. In August 1981 he became Deputy Prime Minister and Minister of Construction and Housing and retained those posts in the National Unity Government* established in 1984. In the Government established in December 1988 he became Deputy Prime Minister and Minister of Construction and Housing. He served as Deputy Prime Minister and Minister of Foreign Affairs in the Shamir*-led Government established in June 1990.

In 1993 Levy lost a bitter race to succeed Yitzhak Shamir as Likud leader, to Benjamin Netanyahu*. He and his followers subsequently withdrew from Likud to form the Gesher* (Bridge) Party and proposed to run an independent slate in the 1996 Knesset election. In addition, Levy declared his candidacy for Prime Minister. Gesher subsequently agreed to participate in a joint electoral list along with Likud and Tsomet*. In return for receiving "safe" slots on the list for himself and his cohorts, Levy agreed to pull out from the prime ministerial race. After the 1996 election he was appointed Foreign Minister and Deputy Prime Minister, positions he held until his resignation in January 1998 ostensibly due to disputes with Netanyahu over control of the peace negotiations with the Palestinians as well as over perceived discriminatory treatment of disadvantaged sectors of the Israeli society—including Moroccans and other Sephardim*—in the proposed 1998 state budget. In the spring of

1999, Gesher joined with Labor* and Meimad* to form the One Israel* Party that successfully contested the May 17, 1999, elections for the 15th Knesset, with David Levy installed in the third slot on the joint list. He was appointed Foreign Minister in the Government headed by Ehud Barak*, and was subsequently named deputy Prime Minister.

For further information see: Aryeh Avneri, *David Levy* (Tel Aviv: Revivim Publishing, 1983, Hebrew).

LEVY, MOSHE. Born in 1936 in Tel Aviv* he studied economics and the history of Islamic countries at the Hebrew University*. He joined the Israel Defense Forces* in 1954 and served in the Golani Brigade and in the paratroopers and held a series of commands. He was in command of the Central Command from 1977 to 1982 and from 1982 to 1983 served as Deputy Chief of Staff of the Israel Defense Forces. He served as Chief of Staff of the IDF from 1983 to 1987.

LEVY, YITZHAK. Levy was born in 1947 in Morocco and immigrated to Israel in 1957. He was educated at the orthodox Yeshivot Hakotel, where he received his rabbinical ordination and served in the Israel Defense Forces (IDF)*, achieving the rank of Major. An educator by profession, and member of the executive of the Bnai Akiva youth movement and its World Secretariat, Levy is one of the founders of the West Bank* settlement of Elon Moreh. First elected to the Knesset* in 1988 on the National Religious Party* list, he served as the party's secretary-general from 1986-1995. He was appointed Minister of Transportation by Benjamin Netanyahu* in June 1996. In February 1998, he was elected NRP leader, succeeding the late Zevulun Hammer*; he completed Hammer's term as Minister of Education and Culture. He also served as Minister of Religious Affairs until August 1998 when the position rotated to Eli Suissa*. Reelected to the 15th Knesset in 1999 on the NRP list, he was appointed Minister of Housing and Construction on July 6, 1999, by Ehud Barak*.

LIBERAL CENTER PARTY. This party was formed in 1985 by Liberal Party* members who left the Likud*. Its leaders included former Tel Aviv* Mayor Shlomo Lahat and then Jewish Agency* Chairman Arye Leon Dulzin*, as well as former minister and Knesset Speaker Yitzhak Berman*. Its political platform opposed the annexation of the occupied territories* as well as the "binational state" which would result from such annexation. It argued that Israel must be a Jewish and Zionist state and should be prepared to give up territories for peace. Jerusalem* was not a matter for negotiation, and the party rejected the creation of an independent Palestinian state between Israel and Jordan*. The party's platform also stressed the equality of all Israeli citizens regardless of religion, race, or sex. It became part of the Center Shinui* political bloc.

LIBERAL PARTY (HAMIFLAGA HALIBERALIT). The Liberal Party was established during the Fifth Knesset* by a merger of the General Zionist Party (Hatzionim Haklaliyim)* and the Progressive Party (Hamiflaga Haprogressivit)*. The party's beginnings can be traced to middle-of-the-road Zionists* who wanted to unify all Zionists without regard to socialist, Revisionist*, or religious feelings. They stressed industrial development and private enterprise. This group split into two wings in 1935: General Zionists A, the larger of the two groups which was led by Chaim Weizmann*, on the left; and General Zionists B, on the right. Both were comprised of industrialists, merchants, landlords, white-collar professionals, and intellectuals. The two factions merged in 1946 to form the General Zionist Party; split again in 1948, when the one group formed the Progressive Party; and then merged once again in 1961 as the Liberal Party. The party won 17 seats in the 1961 Knesset election, the same as Herut*. In 1965, Herut and the Liberals set up an electoral alliance called Gahal*. Seven Liberals in the Knesset refused to join Gahal and formed the Independent Liberal Party*. From 1965 to 1977, the Independent Liberals averaged about 3.5% of the vote and retained four or five Knesset seats. In 1971, they won only one seat, and in 1981, with only 0.6% of the vote, they disappeared from the Knesset. In the meantime, in 1973, retired General Ariel Sharon*, then a member of the Liberal Party within Gahal, advocated a wider union of parties which could present itself as a genuine alternative to the Labor Alignment*. Sharon and Ezer Weizman* successfully brought the Free Center Party*, the State List*, and the Land of Israel Movement* (a nonparty group advocating immediate Israeli settlement and development of the occupied territories*) into the Herut-Liberal alliance to form Likud*.

LIEBERMAN, AVIGDOR. Born in the Soviet Union in 1958 Lieberman immigrated to Israel from Moldova, then part of the USSR*, in 1978 and became a right-wing student activist in Israel. Chief of staff (actually director general of the Prime Minister's office) of Prime Minister Netanyahu* who resigned on November 23, 1997, under pressure from elements of the Likud Party*. He was accused of improperly influencing a party conference to strengthen Netanyahu's control of the party. Lieberman was a gatekeeper and political aide to Netanyahu. He was a founder of the Israel Beiteinu* political party and became a member of the 15th Knesset* in the 1999 elections.

LIKUD (UNION) PARTY. Likud was established in 1973 and the alliance crystalized at the time of the 1977 elections. It consisted of: the Gahal* alliance (Herut* and the Liberals*); the La'am* alliance (the State List* and the Free Center*); Ahdut (a one-man faction in the Knesset*); and Shlomzion*, Ariel Sharon's* former party.

Likud came to power in Israel in 1977, ousting the Labor* Party-led Government for the first time since Israel became independent. Although it retained its Government position after the 1981 elections, its majority in the Knesset* seldom exceeded two or three votes. In 1984, it lost its plurality and joined with the Labor Alignment* to form a Government of National Unity* in which it shared power and ministerial positions. In the 1988 Knesset election it again emerged as the dominant party but without a majority. A Likud-dominated Government with Yitzhak Shamir* as Prime Minister and with Labor as the junior partner was formed in December 1988. In 1992 Likud, under the leadership of Yitzhak Shamir, was narrowly defeated by a revitalized Labor Party headed by Yitzhak Rabin*.

Likud is right-of-center, strongly nationalist, and assertive in foreign policy. In 1996, it formed a "national camp" joint electoral slate with Gesher* and Tsomet*. An attempt to revive this coalition with Tsomet failed in the spring of 1999, and Likud ran for the 15th Knesset on its own. Its domestic policy platform emphasized continued efforts to sustain the growth of the Israeli economy, containing the country's rate of inflation, progress in the areas of privatization of state-owned businesses and foreign investment, and continued support and encouragement of the country's high-tech industrial sector. With regard to foreign and security policy, Likud's 1999 platform emphasized two essential themes: the success of Prime Minister Benjamin Netanyahu's* effort to have the concept of "reciprocity" incorporated into the lexicon of Middle East diplomacy—by demanding, and receiving, assurances of enhanced efforts by the Palestinian Authority* to abide by its commitments to fight terrorism, end the use of inflammatory language, and educate its own population about the benefits of peace; and Netanyahu's pledge to protect Israel's vital strategic and historical interests in the context of projected final status negotiations* with the Palestinians. Final status negotiations with the Palestinian Authority would be conducted on the following principles: self-rule, rather than an independent state, for Palestinian residents of the West Bank* and Gaza Strip*; a united Jerusalem* under exclusive Israeli sovereignty; the Jordan River* as Israel's permanent border to the east; Israeli security zones in the West Bank and Gaza Strip, to protect vital Israeli interests, including exclusive protection of Jewish settlements; the Palestinian Authority will be expected to fulfill all of its obligations under the Oslo* and Wye River* accords. With regard to relations with Syria*, Likud called for strengthening Jewish settlements on the Golan Heights* but also called for negotiations with Damascus over the status of the Heights, without preconditions.

From the first Knesset Likud and its predecessors had been led by Menachem Begin*. With Begin's retirement in 1983 leadership was passed to Yitzhak Shamir, who in turn was succeeded by Benjamin Netanyahu in 1993. In a nationwide primary of Likud members on January 26, 1999, Benjamin Netanyahu was confirmed as party leader and its candidate for Prime Minister. However, Netanyahu resigned as party leader, and quit the Knesset, after his defeat by Labor* leader Ehud Barak* on May 17, 1999, in an election in which Likud won only 19 seats in the 15th Knesset.

For further information see: Asher Arian, *The Second Republic: Politics in Israel* (Chatham, NJ: Chatham House, 1998); Dan Caspi, Abraham Diskin and Emanuel Gutmann, editors, *The Roots of Begin's Success: The 1981 Israeli Elections* (New York: St. Martin's, 1984); Daniel Gavron, *Israel after Begin* (Boston: Houghton Mifflin, 1984); David H. Goldberg, *Democracy in Action 1999: A Guide to the Participants and Issues in Israeli Politics* (Toronto: Canada-Israel Committee, May 1999); Rael Jean Isaac, *Israel Divided: Ideological Politics in the Jewish State* (Baltimore: Johns Hopkins, 1976); Gershon R. Kieval, *Party Politics in Israel and the Occupied Territories* (Westport, CT: Greenwood, 1983); Elfi Pallis, "The Likud Party: A Primer," *Journal of Palestine Studies* 21 (Winter 1992): 41-60; Ilan Peleg, "The Foreign Policy of Herut and the Likud," in *Israeli National Security Policy: Political Actors and Perspectives*, edited by Bernard Reich and Gershon R. Kieval (New York: Greenwood, 1988):

55-78; Bernard Reich and Gershon R. Kieval, *Israel: Land of Tradition and Conflict*, Second Edition (Boulder, CO: Westview, 1993).

LIPKIN-SHAHAK, AMNON. Born in Tel Aviv* in 1944 to an affluent seventh-generation Israeli family, at the age of 14 he entered a military boarding school in Haifa*. A graduate of the Israel Defense Force's* Command and Staff College and the National Defense College, he joined the paratroop brigade in 1962 and served as a paratroop commander in the Six Day War*. He was decorated for his role in extricating tanks and soldiers during the ill-fated operation against Palestine Liberation Organization* fighters at Karameh* in Jordan* in 1968. He was again decorated for leading a squad that blew up the headquarters of a Palestinian terrorist faction in Beirut under heavy enemy fire in the spring of 1973. In the 1973 Yom Kippur War*, Lipkin-Shahak served as deputy commander of a paratroop brigade; he also participated in one of the bloodiest clashes in Israeli military history: the battle for the "Chinese farm" during the crossing of the Suez Canal. He moved rapidly up the ranks of the IDF, becoming head of the OC Central Command in 1983, Director of Military Intelligence* in 1986, Deputy Chief of Staff under Ehud Barak* in 1991, and Chief of Staff in 1995. His long-standing friendship with fellow career soldier Yitzhak Mordechai* became strained in 1994, when Lipkin-Shahak, about to take over as IDF Chief of Staff, vetoed the appointment of Mordechai as his deputy. In a twist of fate, Lipkin-Shahak subsequently found himself serving under Mordechai when, in the summer of 1996, the latter was named Minister of Defense.

Lipkin-Shahak formally retired from active military service on December 24, 1998; only days later, on January 6, 1999, he announced his candidacy for the post of Prime Minister, as the head of the new Center Party*. His campaign was premised on the themes of the need for national unity and for a return to honesty and integrity in Israeli political life; he also was highly critical of the political policies and personal behavior of the incumbent Prime Minister, Benjamin Netanyahu*. Though he initially scored very well in public opinion surveys, his campaign for Prime Minister rapidly lost steam and he eventually relinquished to Yitzhak Mordechai his leadership of the Center Party and its nomination for Prime Minister. On May 17, 1999, Lipkin-Shahak was elected to the Knesset* for the first time, from the Center Party list. He became Deputy Minister of Tourism in the Government formed by Ehud Barak* in 1999, but he was subsequently made Minister of Tourism when the Basic Law: The

Government* was amended to permit the expansion of the cabinet* from 18 to 24 ministers.

LITANI OPERATION see OPERATION LITANI

LOHAMEI HERUT YISRAEL *see* STERN (GANG) GROUP

LUBAVITCH HASIDIC SECT. A movement founded in Eastern Europe in the eighteenth century (around 1734) by Israel Ba'al Shem Tov. Emerging as a conservative backlash to the liberal enlightenment (*Haskala*) beginning to prevail among the European Jewish intelligentsia, it emphasized a spiritual and emotional renewal of the connection between Jews and God. Beginning in 1764 small groups of Hasidim* made their way to Palestine*, establishing Ashkenazi* communities in Safed, Hebron*, B'nai Brak, Tiberias, and Jerusalem*. The first Hasidic Rabbinical Court in Jerusalem was established in 1855. Most Hasidic leaders, with the exception of extremist groups, welcomed the Balfour Declaration*. Among the most active proponents of Hasidic immigration to Palestine was the influential Rabbi Avraham Mordechai Alter of Gur (the Gur Rebbe). Nevertheless, the leaders of some Hasidic sects were anti-Zionist in orientation (based on the belief that Jewish national renewal only was possible when the Messiah arrived) and actively opposed aliya*. The Holocaust* caused a practical acceptance of Zionism* by most Hasidic leaders and the postwar years witnessed a significant growth in the Hasidic movement in Israel. Among the most important aspects of this growth was the establishment in 1949 of Kfar Habad, under the auspices of the Lubavitch Rabbi Yosef Yitzhak Schneerson. Under the leadership of his successor, Rabbi Menachem Mendel Schneerson*, the influence in Israeli politics of the Lubavitch Hasidim grew tremendously, impacting on the outcome of several elections in the 1980s and the 1990s. The political interests of the movement are represented for the most part by Agudat Israel*.

For further information see: Charles S. Liebman, *Religion, Democracy and Israeli Society* (Amsterdam: Harwood Academic Publishers, 1997); Gary S. Schiff, *Tradition and Politics: The Religious Parties of Israel* (Detroit: Wayne State University Press, 1977).

LUBRANI, URI. Israel's Ambassador to Iran* prior to the 1979 revolution, he subsequently served as chief advisor to successive Israeli Governments on military and political relations with Iran, Syria*, and Lebanon*.

M

MAABAROT (TRANSIT CAMPS). Temporary accommodations provided by Israel for mass immigration between 1950 and 1954 to facilitate absorption of new immigrants into the Israeli system. The conditions in the camps were problematic and demonstrations and other difficulties resulted. More permanent housing was soon constructed and a new system for immigrant absorption was devised and put into effect in 1954. *See also* ALIYA.

For further information see: Elazar Leshem and Judith T. Shuval, editors, *Immigration to Israel: Sociological Perspectives* (New Brunswick, NJ: Transaction, 1998); "Refugee Settlement and Resettlement in Israel," *Refuge: Canada's Periodical on Refugees* (Special Issue) 14:6 (November 1994); Eli Tzur, "Mapam and the European and Oriental Immigrations in Israel," in *Israel: The First Decade of Independence*, edited by S. Ilan Troen and Noah Lucas (Albany: State University of New York Press, 1995): 543-556; Alex Weingrod, "Struggles of Ethnic Adaptation: Interpreting Iraqi and Moroccan Settlement in Israel," in *Israel: The First Decade of Independence*, edited by S. Ilan Troen and Noah Lucas (Albany: State University of New York Press, 1995): 523-542; Oren Yiftachel and Avinoam Meir, *Ethnic Frontiers and Peripheries: Landscapes of Development and Inequality in Israel* (Boulder, CO: Westview, 1998).

MA'ALOT MASSACRE. On May 13, 1974, a series of terrorist incidents near the town of Ma'alot-Tarshisah, in the western Upper Galilee, left a total of 35 dead and 70 others wounded. Israeli soldiers, searching for the terrorist assailants of two civilians near Moshav Elkosh, caught up with the three-man PLO* squad near Ma'alot. Killing three residents of a private home and then a street sweeper, the terrorists took hostage 85 students and teachers at the Nativ Meir School. Demanding the release of 20 of their comrades from Israeli prisons and safe passage for themselves and their hostages to Damascus, Syria*, the terrorists concentrated all their hostages in one classroom and wired it with explosives. The Israeli Government allowed the release of the 20 prisoners but refused to accede to the terrorists' demand to take the hostages to Damascus. Having reached an impasse in the negotiations, the Israeli Government ordered the military to storm the school. In the raid, 21 children, three terrorists, and a soldier died. In total, the series of terrorist incidents claimed 35 lives and 70 more were wounded. *See also* TERRORISM.

For further information see: David Wurmser, "Ma'alot," in *An Historical Encyclopedia of the Arab-Israeli Conflict*, edited by Bernard Reich (Westport, CT: Greenwood, 1996): 332-333.

MAAPILIM. The illegal immigrants who entered Palestine* despite the strict immigration quotas imposed by the British Mandatory* authorities. The beginning of such immigration, called *haapalah**, dates to 1934. It peaked in the immediate post-World War II period, with the aim of providing refuge for Holocaust* survivors. *See also* ALIYA BET.

MAARACH *see* ALIGNMENT

MA'ARIV **(EVENING).** An afternoon daily Hebrew language*. It is a politically independent and secular newspaper which first appeared on February 15, 1948, published in Tel Aviv.

MACDONALD PAPER *see* WHITE PAPER OF 1939

MACMICHAEL, SIR HAROLD ALFRED. He was born in Britain in October 1882 and died in September 1969, he served as High Commissioner and Commander in Chief for Palestine* (and also as high commissioner for Transjordan*) from 1938 to 1944. His tenure in Palestine was characterized by increasing tension between Arab and Jewish communities as well as between the Zionists and the British Mandate*. As High Commissioner for Palestine MacMichael oversaw implementation of the White Paper of 1939*, which called for severe restrictions on Jewish immigration and land purchases in Palestine. By the time of his departure from Palestine at the end of August 1944, there was virtually no contact between the Mandate and the Jewish leadership, many of whom held MacMichael personally responsible for the fate of Jewish refugees fleeing Nazi oppression yet denied admittance to Palestine.

For further information see: Gavriel Cohen, "Harold MacMichael and Palestine's Future," *Zionism* 3 (April 1981): 133-155; Dan Horowitz and Moshe Lissak, *Origins of the Israeli Polity: Palestine under the Mandate* (Chicago: University of Chicago Press, 1978); William Roger Louis and Robert W. Stookey, editors, *The End of the Palestine Mandate* (Austin: University of Texas Press, 1986); Ze'ev Sharef, *Three Days: An Account of the Last Days of the British Mandate and the Birth of Israel* (New York: Doubleday, 1962); A. J. Sherman, *Mandate Days: British Lives in Palestine 1918-1948* (London: Douglas and McIntyre, 1998); Christopher Sykes, *Crossroads to Israel 1917-1948* (Bloomington: Indiana University Press, 1973); Bernard Wasserstein, "Patterns of Communal Conflict in Palestine," in *Essential Papers on Zionism*, edited by Jehuda Reinharz and Anita Shapira (New York: New York University Press, 1996): 671-688.

MADRID PEACE CONFERENCE. An Arab-Israeli peace conference convened in Madrid, Spain, beginning October 30, 1991, at the invitation of the United States* and the USSR*. In an opening plenary session, Israeli, Syrian, Egyptian, Lebanese, and Jordanian-Palestinian delegations met and delivered speeches and responses. These were followed by bilateral negotiations between Israel and each of the Arab delegations. The conference was an important step on the road to peace in that it involved direct, bilateral, public, and official peace negotiations between Israel and its Arab neighbors.

MAFDAL *See* NATIONAL RELIGIOUS PARTY

MAGEN DAVID (SHIELD OF DAVID). A Jewish symbol. It appears on the flag of the state of Israel as it did on the flag of the Zionist movement. It consists of two superimposed triangles which form a six-pointed star. Although an ancient symbol it became widely used in Europe for the Jewish communities in the sixteenth and seventeenth centuries. In 1897 the First Zionist Congress chose it as the symbol of the movement and of the World Zionist Organization*. It was employed by the Nazis during the Holocaust* as a means of identifying Jews. The Flag and Emblem Law of Israel of May 24, 1949, incorporated the Magen David into the official flag of Israel.

MAGEN DAVID ADOM (RED SHIELD OF DAVID). Israel's equivalent of the Red Cross which provides emergency medical services. The first group was founded in Tel Aviv* in 1930 and in 1935 a national organization was formed. After Israel's independence it sought to affiliate with the International Red Cross, but this was rejected as the Red Cross refused to recognize the Magen David Adom symbol, a red six-pointed star. This remains the case although there are some cooperative relations between the two organizations.

MAGIC CARPET *see* OPERATION MAGIC CARPET

MAGNES, JUDAH LEON. Born in San Francisco in 1877, he died in New York in 1948. He was ordained as a rabbi at Hebrew Union College in 1900. An ardent Zionist, he was active in many of the Zionist organizations prior to his settling in Palestine* in 1922. He helped found the American Jewish Committee, which sought to speak for the Jewish community in the United States* and to act in its defense against anti-Semitism*, and served on its Executive Committee from 1906 to 1918. He helped found Hebrew University* and became its Chancellor in 1925. After reorganization he became the President of the University in 1935, a post in which he remained until he died. He became an advocate of a binational state in Palestine as a means of preventing bloodshed which he believed would be associated with efforts to establish a Jewish State and in 1929 helped found Brit Shalom*. In 1942 he founded the Ihud* (Unity) organization for better understanding between Arabs and Jews. He continued to advocate a binational state until after the establishment of Israel.

For further information see: Norman Bentwich, *For Zion's Sake: A Biography of Judah L. Magnes* (Philadelphia: The Jewish Publication Society of America, 1954); Ben Halpern, "The Americanization of Zionism, 1880-1930," in *Essential Papers on Zionism*, edited by Jehuda Reinharz and Anita Shapira (New York: New York University Press, 1996): 318-336; Susan Lee Hattis, *The Bi-National Idea in Palestine during Mandatory Times* (Haifa: Shikmona, 1970); Judah L. Magnes, *Like All Nations?* (Jerusalem: Weiss Press, 1930).

MAHAL. Acronym for Mitnadvei Hutz Laeretz (foreign volunteers). A group of some 3,000 Jewish and non-Jewish soldiers who came to Palestine* to fight in Israel's War of Independence*.

For further information see: David Bercuson, *The Secret Army* (Toronto: Lester and Orpen Dennys, 1983); A. Joseph Heckelman, *American Volunteers and Israel's War of Independence* (New York: Ktav, 1974); Joseph Hockstein and Murray S. Greenfield, *The Jews' Secret Fleet: The Untold Story of North American Volunteers Who Smashed the British Blockade* (Jerusalem: Gefen, 1988).

MAKI *see* COMMUNIST PARTY

MAKLEFF, MORDECHAI. Born in Palestine* in 1920, he volunteered in the 1930s to serve in the Hagana*. During World War II, he served in the British army in Orde Wingate's "Special Night Squadrons." Following the war, he left the British army with the rank of Major. In the War of Independence*, he took part in combat as a brigade commander along the northern front. He became commander of military intelligence and served as the Deputy Chief of Staff in 1951-1952. He served as Chief of Staff of the Israel Defense Forces* in 1952-1953. Following his retirement from the military, he became General Manager of Israel's electric company, the Israel Chemicals Company, and held other public posts. He died in 1978.

MANDATE *see* BRITISH MANDATE

MANDELBAUM GATE. The sole access point between Israeli- and Jordanian-held parts of Jerusalem* between 1948 and 1967. Although according to the 1949 Armistice Agreement* with Jordan*, Israelis and other Jews were to have access to religious holy places in the Old City via the Mandelbaum Gate, in reality access was made available only to non-Jews. The gate was one of the fronts used by Israeli forces that retook the Old City in the Six Day War*.

For further information see: Martin Gilbert, *Jerusalem: Illustrated History Atlas* (Jerusalem: Steimatsky, 1994).

MAPAI (MIFLEGET POALEI ERETZ YISRAEL—ISRAEL WORKERS PARTY). Mapai originated with the union of two smaller political parties, Ahdut Haavoda* and Hapoel Hatzair*, in 1930, but the roots of the movement can be traced to the turn of the century in Europe, especially Russia. Its program focused on the development of the Jewish people in Israel as a free working people rooted in an agricultural and industrial economy and developing its own Hebrew* culture. It supported membership in the world movement of the working class and cooperation in the struggle to eliminate class subjugation and social injustice in any form. It endorsed the building of a Jewish commonwealth focusing on labor, equality, and freedom. Its program was a combination of Zionist and socialist ideologies. Mapai soon became the dominant party in the Yishuv*. The two parties which formed it had established the Histadrut* in 1920, and under their leadership it became the embodiment of the Jewish community in Palestine*. Mapai controlled the Histadrut as well as the National Council* and the Jewish Agency*. Many of the noted figures in the creation of Israel came from Mapai, including David Ben-Gurion*, Moshe Sharett* (formerly Shertok), Golda Meir* (formerly Meyerson), Moshe Dayan*, and others. In the elections for the Knesset* from Israel's independence until 1965, when it ran in the framework of the Alignment*, Mapai won the largest number of seats and its leader was given the mandate to form the Government. All of Israel's Prime Ministers and Histadrut Secretaries General as well as many other senior members of the Israeli administrations and political elite were Mapai members in the period from its founding until its merger into the Israel Labor Party*. It was the leading member of all Government coalitions and generally held the key portfolios of Defense, Foreign Affairs, and Finance as well as the post of Prime Minister. The party permeated the Government, the bureaucracy, the economy, and most of the other institutions of Israel. Political advancement in Israel and party membership were generally coincident. In 1965 Mapai joined with Ahdut Haavoda to form the Alignment to contest the Knesset election. In 1968 the Alignment joined with Rafi* to form the Israel Labor* Party.

For further information see: Myron J. Aronoff, *Power and Ritual in the Israel Labor Party: A Study in Political Anthropology* (Assen/Amsterdam: Van Gorcum, 1977); Gershon R. Kieval, *Party Politics in Israel and the Occupied Territories* (Westport, CT: Greenwood, 1983); Gershon R. Kieval, "The Labor Party," in *Israeli National Security Policy: Political Actors and Perspectives*, edited by Bernard Reich and Gershon R. Kieval (New York: Greenwood, 1988); Peter Y. Medding, *Mapai in Israel: Political Organization and Government in a New Society* (Cambridge, MA: Harvard, 1972).

MAPAM (MIFLEGET POALIM HAMEUHEDET—UNITED WORKERS PARTY). Mapam was organized in 1948 when Hashomer Hatzair* merged with radical elements from Ahdut Haavoda*. It is a left-wing socialist-Zionist Jewish-Arab party. From its beginnings, the party was more Marxist than Mapai*. The former Ahdut Haavoda members left in 1954 because of Mapam's pro-Soviet orientation and acceptance of Arabs* as party members. Although the party's domestic policy was essentially indistinguishable from Mapai's, Mapam's share of the vote in national elections declined steadily before it joined the Alignment* for the 1969 elections. Mapam ended its alliance with Labor* in September 1984 over the issue of the formation of a Government of National Unity* with Likud*. The veteran leader, Victor Shemtov*, retired as party head. It has supported the principle of compromise concerning the trade of territories for peace in the Arab-Israeli conflict*. It supports the return of most of the territories, except for minor border changes required for security, in exchange for peace. It has expressed its readiness to negotiate with any authorized Palestinian* element that will declare its willingness to recognize Israel and to cease terrorism. Drawing support primarily from the socialist Kibbutz* movement as well as segments of the Israeli Arab community, Mapam historically advocated a policy of compromise in relations with the Palestinians. Domestically, it championed freedom of religious expression among Israeli Jews and the extension of equal rights for all Israelis. In 1992 it joined with the Citizens' Rights Movement* and Shinui* to form the Meretz/Democratic Israel* faction that won 12 seats in the 13th Knesset* and participated in the coalition Governments headed by Yitzhak Rabin (1992-1995) and Shimon Peres (1995-1996). Mapam and Meretz won nine seats in the 14th Knesset (1996) and 10 in the 15th (1999).

For further information see: Gershon R. Kieval, *Party Politics in Israel and the Occupied Territories* (Westport, CT: Greenwood, 1983); Peretz Merhav, *The Israeli Left: History, Problems, Documents* (San Diego: A. S. Barnes, 1980); Eli Tzur, "Mapam and the European and Oriental Immigrations," in *Israel: The First Decade of Independence*, edited by S. Ilan Troen and Noah Lucas (Albany: State University of New York Press, 1995): 543-556.

MASHAAL AFFAIR. A bungled Mossad* attempt at assassinating Khaled Mashaal, a Hamas political leader. Israel described Mashaal, a political leader of the Islamic group Hamas, as "responsible for the murder of innocent civilians." The incident occurred on September 25, 1997, in Amman, and seriously soured relations with Jordan*. The two Mossad agents, carrying forged Canadian passports, were taken prisoner, and in return for their release Israel had to free Hamas founder Sheikh Ahmed Yassin* and dozens of other Palestinian and Jordanian prisoners. The affair ultimately forced the resignation of Mossad chief Danny Yatom* and his director of operations. The Ciechanover Commission* reported in February 1998 to the Prime Minister that the Mossad* and its head (Danny Yatom*) bore full responsibility for the failed assassination attempt.

MASSADA. A natural rock fortress in the Judean desert on the shore of the Dead Sea*, located south of Ein Gedi, where a group of Jewish Zealots held out against a Roman siege for seven months in AD 73. When the Romans finally entered the fortress they found that the defenders had committed suicide rather than be taken alive. This heroic stand has led to the pledge of Israeli youngsters that "Massada shall not fall again." Excavations of the site by archaeologist Yigael Yadin* documented much of the historical writings of Josephus concerning Massada.

For further information see: Josephus, *The Jewish War* (New York: Penguin Books, 1970); Yigael Yadin, *Massada: Herod's Fortress and the Zealots' Last Stand* (New York: Random House, 1966).

MAY 17, 1983 AGREEMENT *see* ISRAEL-LEBANON AGREEMENT OF MAY 17, 1983

MEA SHEARIM (HUNDRED GATES). A neighborhood of Jerusalem* located near the pre-June 1967 "Green Line*'" with Jordan* and the Mandelbaum Gate*. It was one of the first neighborhoods built outside the walls of the old city of Jerusalem, around 1874. The first residents were Orthodox Jews who sought to escape the crowded conditions in the old Jerusalem community. The name is derived from the book of Genesis in the Bible. It has become the symbol of religious extremism because the neighborhood is under the influence of the Neturei Karta*, though not all who live there are members of that group. The inhabitants of the area tend to be traditional and religious in their outlook.

MECHDAL. A Hebrew* word meaning omission. A term widely used in Israel in the aftermath of the Yom Kippur War* to refer to the failures of the Government and of the military to have been fully prepared for the outbreak of the War and to have responded to the initial attacks. *See also* AGRANAT COMMISSION OF INQUIRY.

MEIMAD (DIMENSION/MOVEMENT FOR THE RELIGIOUS CENTER).
Acronym for Tenua Mercazit Datit (Movement for the Religious Center).
Founded in 1988 as a reaction to the sharp move to the political right of
the National Religious Party* (NRP), it is a dovish religious party
drawing much of its membership from those formerly affiliated with the
NRP. Meimad seeks to promote dialogue and lessen polarization within
Israeli society. On matters of peace and security it follows the principle
that "the good of the people and State of Israel takes precedence over
political control over the entire Land of Israel." Its founder and spiritual
leader is Rabbi Yehuda Amital*, the prominent head of the Har Etzion
yeshiva in the West Bank* settlement of Alon Shvut. It did not win any
seats in the 1988 or 1992 Knesset elections. But Rabbi Amital agreed to
serve as Minister without Portfolio in the Government formed by Shimon
Peres* following the November 1995 assassination of Prime Minister
Yitzhak Rabin*. Meimad did not submit a list of candidates for the 14th
Knesset elections (1996) but it did publicly endorse the prime ministerial
candidacy of Shimon Peres, in part to demonstrate that "the whole
religious community is not on one side" of the political debate. It
continues to work with other groups in Israel and the Diaspora* toward
the goal of achieving reconciliation both on the peace process and the
contentious "Who is a Jew*?" debate. Rabbi Amital and other Meimad
activists have also participated in meetings with the religious leaders of
the Muslim and Christian communities in Israel. In the spring of 1999,
Meimad agreed to join with Labor* and Gesher* to form the One Israel*
Party that contested the May 17, 1999, elections, winning 26 seats in the
15th Knesset and forming the new Government, under the leadership of
Ehud Barak*, with Meimad represented by its political leader, Rabbi
Michael Melchior, who was appointed a minister in the Prime Minister's
office with responsibility for Israel-Diaspora relations and social affairs.

For further information see: Charles S. Liebman, *Religion, Democracy
and Israeli Society* (Amsterdam: Harwood Academic, 1997); Stewart
Reiser, "The Religious Parties and Israel's Foreign Policy," in *Israeli
National Security Policy: Political Actors and Perspectives*, edited by
Bernard Reich and Gershon R. Kieval (New York: Greenwood, 1988):
105-121; "Rabbi Amital: Religious Zionism Is Looking More Like Kach
than NRP," *Ha'aretz*, August 5, 1997; "Meimad leader Amital Calls
Conversion Bill 'Hitler's work,'" *Ha'aretz*, January 20, 1998.

MEIR, GOLDA (FORMERLY MEYERSON). Born Golda Mabovitch on May 3, 1898, in Kiev, Russia. In 1903 her family moved to Pinsk and, three years later, settled in Milwaukee. She graduated from high school in Milwaukee and attended the Milwaukee Normal School for Teachers. At age 17 she joined the Poalei Zion (Workers of Zion) Party*. She married Morris Meyerson in December 1917 and in 1921 they moved to Palestine*. They settled in Kibbutz Merhaviah, but later moved to Tel Aviv* and then to Jerusalem*. In 1928 she became Secretary of the Women's Labor Council of the Histadrut* in Tel Aviv. When Mapai* was formed in 1930 by the merger of Ahdut Haavoda* and Hapoel Hatzair* (The Young Worker), she quickly became a major figure in the new party.

In 1934 she was invited to join the Executive Committee of the Histadrut and became head of its Political Department. In 1946, when the British Mandatory* authorities arrested virtually all the members of the Jewish Agency* Executive and the Vaad Leumi* that they could find in Palestine, she became acting head of the Political Department of the Jewish Agency replacing Moshe Shertok (later Sharett)*, who was imprisoned in Latrun*. In the months immediately preceding Israel's Declaration of Independence* she met secretly with King Abdullah of Transjordan to dissuade him from joining the Arab League* in attacking Jewish Palestine, but her efforts failed. In early June 1948, she was appointed Israel's first Minister to Moscow, but returned to Israel in April 1949. She was elected to the First Knesset* in 1949 on the Mapai* ticket and became Minister of Labor in the Government, a post she held until 1956, when she became Foreign Minister for a decade under Prime Ministers David Ben-Gurion* and Levi Eshkol*. As Minister of Labor her principal function was the absorption of hundreds of thousands of immigrants who arrived in Israel in the first years after independence. She initiated large-scale housing and road-building programs and strongly supported unlimited immigration, and she helped to provide employment and medical care for the immigrants.

When she succeeded Moshe Sharett as Foreign Minister in 1956, she Hebraicized her name and became known as Golda Meir. As Foreign Minister she concentrated on Israel's aid to African and other developing nations as a means of strengthening Israel's international position. She resigned as Foreign Minister in January 1966 and was succeeded by Abba Eban*. Because of her enormous popularity in Mapai, she was prevailed on to accept appointment as General Secretary of the party, and, in that position, was Prime Minister Levi Eshkol's closest adviser. In January 1968 she was instrumental in facilitating the union of Mapai, Rafi*, and Ahdut Haavoda as the Israel Labor Party*. After serving for two years as Secretary General, she retired from public life.

Following Eshkol's death in February 1969, party leaders prevailed upon her to succeed Eshkol and she became Israel's fourth Prime Minister in March 1969. She retained the National Unity Government that Eshkol had constructed at the time of the Six Day War*. In the Knesset election at the end of October, the Labor Party won 56 seats, and Meir once again became Prime Minister. She led Israel through the trauma of the Yom Kippur War* and its aftermath. Following the 1973 election, which was postponed until December 31, she had great difficulty in forming a Government with Moshe Dayan* continuing in his role as Minister of Defense. In April 1974 she resigned. She died on December 8, 1978.

For further information see: Michael Bar-Zohar, *Lionhearts: Heroes of Israel* (New York: Warner, 1998); Marver H. Bernstein, "Golda Meir," in *Political Leaders of the Contemporary Middle East and North Africa*, edited by Bernard Reich (Westport, CT: Greenwood, 1990): 325-332; Henry M. Christman, editor, *This Is Our Strength: Selected Papers of Golda Meir* (New York: Macmillan, 1962); Golda Meir, *My Life: The Autobiography of Golda Meir* (London: Weidenfeld and Nicolson, 1975); Golda Meir, "Israel in Search of Lasting Peace," *Foreign Affairs* 51 (April 1973): 447-461; Menahem Meir, *My Mother, Golda Meir: A Son's Evocation of Life with Golda Meir* (New York: Arbor House, 1983); Marie Syrkin, *Golda Meir: Woman with a Cause* (New York: Putnam, 1973); Marie Syrkin, editor, *A Land of Our Own: An Oral Autobiography by Golda Meir* (Philadelphia: The Jewish Publication Society of America; New York: Putnam, 1973).

MELCHIOR, MICHAEL. Born in Denmark in 1954, Melchior immigrated to Israel in 1985. He has been the Chief Rabbi of Norway, is the International Director of the Elie Weisel Foundation, and Chairman of the Secretariat of Meimad since 1995. He was elected to the 15th Knesset on the One Israel* list. He became minister in the Prime Minister's office with responsibility for Diaspora relations and social affairs.

MEMORANDUM OF UNDERSTANDING (MOU). In November 1981, Israel and the United States* negotiated and signed a Memorandum of Understanding on Strategic Cooperation in which it was agreed that United States-Israel strategic cooperation "is designed against the threat to peace and security of the region caused by the Soviet Union or Soviet-controlled forces from outside the region introduced into the region." The MOU was suspended in December 1981 in the wake of Israel's extension of its law and jurisdiction to the Golan Heights*, but additional memoranda were signed in subsequent years. A new MOU, emphasizing cooperation against the threat of long-range ballistic missiles, was signed on October 30, 1998.

MERETZ/DEMOCRATIC ISRAEL. An electoral list formed prior to the 1992 Knesset* election through the amalgamation of three left-wing Zionist parties: Mapam*, the Citizens' Rights Movement*, and Shinui*. The movement's platform was liberal in character. On the domestic front, it advocated the complete separation of religion from political affairs and the enacting of a formal, written constitution to "protect the democratic character of the country, the freedom of the individual, the rule of law and the rights of the minority." Its 1992 platform viewed continued settlement activity in the West Bank* and Gaza Strip* as an "obstacle to peace", and it proposed a peace agreement with the Palestinians based on "mutual recognition of the right to self-determination of both peoples." It held that Jerusalem* must remain unified under Israeli administration but recommended that the city's "special national and religious links" be reflected in any final status agreement. In 1999, Meretz's domestic policy platform emphasized the need to end the "special privileges" accorded to the ultra-orthodox political parties by the Netanyahu* Government, including deferments from military service for most men studying in orthodox yeshivas. It also demanded that the formal separation of religion from politics be codified in a written constitution: "While Jewish law and tradition are the cornerstone of our national culture... [Israel is] a country of law and not of Halacha." The key change in Meretz's 1999 foreign policy platform related to Jerusalem; while adhering to the national consensus that the city must remain unified under Israeli sovereignty, Meretz "recognizes the need for a compromise that will give expression to religious and national concerns... as a first indication of that, we call for recognition of the Orient House as the legitimate representative of the PA in Jerusalem.... Meretz believes that Palestinian representation in Jerusalem does not harm the city's status as the Israeli capital, and would actively serve the interests of Palestinian residents of Jerusalem, many of whom are not Israeli citizens." Under the leadership of the veteran CRM leader, Shulamit Aloni*, Meretz won 12 seats in the 1992 Knesset election and joined the governing coalition headed by Yitzhak Rabin* and the Israel Labor* Party. The party slipped to nine seats in the 14th Knesset under the leadership of Yossi Sarid*, who had succeeded Aloni in 1996. In the spring of 1999, Shinui left Meretz in order to run independently in the election to the 15th Knesset, winning six seats. Despite the loss of Shinui, Meretz went on to win 10 seats in the May 17, 1999, vote. On July 6, 1999, it joined the coalition Government headed by Ehud Barak*, with Yossi Sarid* serving as Education Minister, and Ran Cohen as Minister of Industry and Trade.

For further information see: Asher Arian, *The Second Republic: Politics in Israel* (Chatham, NJ: Chatham House, 1998); David H. Goldberg, *Democracy in Action 1999: A Guide to the Participants and Issues in Israeli Politics* (Toronto: Canada-Israel Committee, May 1999); Gershon R. Kieval, *Party Politics in Israel and the Occupied Territories* (Westport, CT: Greenwood, 1983).

MERIDOR, DAN. Born in Jerusalem* on April 23, 1947, he is the son of former Irgun* commander and Herut* MK, Yaakov Meridor*, making the younger Meridor a "Likud* prince*." A graduate of the Faculty of Law at the Hebrew University of Jerusalem*, he served as Government Secretary from 1982 to 1984. He was first elected to the Knesset* on the Likud list in 1984. He became Minister of Justice in the Government established in December 1988 and retained that position in the Government of June 1990. In July 1996 he agreed to join the governing coalition headed by Benjamin Netanyahu*, as Finance Minister. He resigned in June 1997 to protest the perceived lack of support from the Prime Minister for the package of economic reforms that he sought to institute. On December 22, 1998, he quit the Likud in order to form his own centrist party that would contest elections to the 15th Knesset; he also announced his candidacy for the position of Prime Minister. He subsequently joined with Ronnie Milo*, Yitzhak Mordechai* and Amnon Lipkin-Shahak* to form the new Center* Party that won six seats in the May 17, 1999, Knesset elections.

MERIDOR, YAAKOV. Born in Poland in 1913 he emigrated to Palestine* in 1932, where in the following year, he joined the Irgun*, which he commanded from 1941 to 1943. He served in the First through the Sixth Knessets*. He was the founder and chairman of the Board of Directors of Maritime Fruit Carriers Ltd., and served on the Board of Directors of the Atlantic Fisheries and Shipping Co., Ltd. On August 5, 1981, following his election to the 10th Knesset, he was sworn in as Minister of Economic Affairs. He is the author of *Long Is the Road to Freedom*. He died on June 30, 1995.

MESHAL, KHALED *see* MASHAAL AFFAIR

MIFLEGET HOK HATEVA *see* NATURAL LAW PARTY

MILITARY *see* HAGANA, ISRAEL DEFENSE FORCES

MILO, RONNIE. Born in Tel Aviv* on November 26, 1949, Milo was educated at the Faculty of Law of Tel Aviv University. First elected to the Knesset* on the Likud* list in 1977, he became Minister of Ecology and Environmental Protection in the Government established in December 1988 and assumed the position of Minister of Police in the Government established in June 1990. Mayor of Tel Aviv* since November 1993, in May 1998 Milo announced his candidacy for Prime Minister as the leader of a new centrist political movement—called "Atid*"—committed to "bridging gaps" among Israelis on political, religious, and social grounds. Milo subsequently joined with Dan Meridor*, Yitzhak Mordechai* and former IDF* chief of staff Amnon Lipkin-Shahak* in forming the new Center* Party that won six seats in the 15th Knesset, with Milo returning to the Knesset on the Center list.

MIZRAHI. Mizrahi came into being in 1902, although its central concept can be identified as early as the 1880s. The founders of the movement did not see an inherent contradiction between traditional Judaism and Zionism*. Mizrahi and its labor offshoot, Hapoel Hamizrahi (founded in 1922), functioned as part of the World Zionist Organization* and the Yishuv* institutions in Palestine*. The fundamental principle on which the Mizrahi and Hapoel Hamizrahi were based is adherence to Jewish religion and tradition. Both parties sought to secure the adoption of the religious precepts of Judaism in the everyday life of the Yishuv*, and to found the State of Israel constitutionally upon Jewish religious law.

The difference between the two parties was in the social composition of their membership, which gave each a distinctive social outlook. The attitude of Mizrahi on internal social issues was largely determined by the fact that its members were drawn almost entirely from the middle-class element. As distinct from the Mizrahi, Hapoel Hamizrahi was composed exclusively of Orthodox working-class elements. In addition to being a political party, Hapoel Hamizrahi served as a professional organization, fulfilling all the functions which the Histadrut* performs for its members. In the 1951 Knesset* election Mizrahi won two seats and Hapoel Hamizrahi won eight seats. In 1955 Mizrahi and Hapoel Hamizrahi formed the National Religious Party* to contest the Knesset election as a religious party seeking to combine religious concerns and a moderate socialist orientation in economic matters within a Zionist framework. A centerpiece of Mizrahi's religious-Zionist philosophy is the hesder yeshiva system which combines military service with religious studies.

For further information see: Menachem Friedman, "The Structural Foundation for Religious-Political Accommodation in Israel: Fallacy and Reality," in *Israel: the First Decade of Independence*, edited by S. Ilan Troen and Noah Lucas (Albany: State University of New York Press, 1995): 51-81; Gershon R. Kieval, *Party Politics in Israel and the Occupied Territories* (Westport, CT: Greenwood, 1983); Stewart Reiser, "The Religious Parties in Israel: Social Significance and Policy Implications," *Middle East Focus* 12:2 (Summer/Fall 1990): 9-16; Yosef Salmon, "Tradition and Nationalism," in *Essential Papers on Zionism*, edited by Jehuda Reinharz and Anita Shapira (New York: New York University Press, 1996): 94-116; Gary S. Schiff, *Tradition and Politics: The Religious Parties of Israel* (Detroit: Wayne State University Press, 1977).

MODA'I, YITZHAK. Born in Tel Aviv* in 1926, he received a BSc in chemical industrial engineering from the Technion* in 1947, a graduate degree in economics from the University of London in 1957, and a law degree from the Tel Aviv* branch of Hebrew University* in 1959. He served as Israel's Assistant Military Attaché in London in 1951-1952, on the Israel-Syria* and Israel-Lebanon* Mixed Armistice Commissions, and as an observer, on behalf of Israel, at several sessions of the Council of Europe. After the Six Day War* he served as Military Governor of Gaza* and was involved in private industry. First elected on behalf of the Liberal Party* faction of Likud* to the 8th Knesset* in December 1973, and reelected to the 9th, he served on the Economics and State Control Committees of the Knesset. He served as President of the Israel-America Chamber of Commerce and General Manager of Revlon (Israel) Ltd. Moda'i served as Minister of Energy and Infrastructure from 1977 to 1981, and as Minister of Communications from 1979 to 1981. On August 5, 1981 he was sworn in as Minister without Portfolio. He became Minister of Finance in the National Unity Government* established in 1984 and later served as Minister without Portfolio in that Government. He became Minister of Economics and Planning in the Government established in December 1988. In June 1990 he assumed the position of Minister of Finance in the new Shamir*-led Government. He died in May 1998.

MOETZET GEDOLEI HATORAH *see* COUNCIL OF TORAH SAGES

MOETZET HACHMEI HATORAH *See* SEPHARDI TORAH GUARDIANS

MOFAZ, SHAUL. Born in Iran* in 1948 to a teacher in an Organization for Rehabilitation Through Training (ORT) vocational school, he immigrated with his family to Israel in 1957 and entered the Israel Defense Forces (IDF) in 1966. He grew up in Eilat* and went to Nahalal agricultural high school. Fought as a paratrooper in the Six Day War*; as a unit commander along the Suez Canal during the War of Attrition*; and as a commander of the paratrooper reconnaissance unit in the Yom Kippur War*. He commanded the cover unit in the 1976 IDF operation to free hostages being held at the Entebbe airport in Uganda (Entebbe Operation*), and he was an infantry brigade commander in the 1982 Lebanon War (Operation Peace for Galilee*). Key postings included deputy commander of the elite General Staff Reconnaissance Unit (Sayeret Matkal); commander of the IDF officers' school; commander of the Paratrooper Brigade; commander of IDF forces in the West Bank* and Gaza Strip*; OC Southern Command; head of the IDF Planning Branch; Israeli representative to security negotiations with the Palestinians; and Deputy Chief of the General Staff. He became the IDF's Chief of Staff on July 9, 1998, succeeding the retiring Amnon Lipkin-Shahak*.

MOKED. A political party formed by the combination of the Israel Communist Party* and Tchelet Adom (Blue-Red) Movement that won a seat in the Knesset* in the 1973 election. It later merged into Shelli*.

MOLEDET (HOMELAND) PARTY. A political party created for the 1988 Knesset* election by Israel Defense Forces* Reserve General Rehavam ("Gandhi") Zeevi*. It advocates the transfer of the Arab population of the occupied territories* to Arab countries. In 1991 it joined the narrow coalition formed by Yitzhak Shamir*, but it subsequently quit to protest Israel's participation in the Madrid Peace Conference*. In 1992 there was a petition to the Central Elections Committee to disqualify Moledet on the grounds that its program to transfer Arabs from the West Bank* was anti-democratic and racist; Moledet spokesmen countered that transfer would be instituted exclusively on a voluntary basis. The Central Elections Committee held in favor of Moledet and it went on to win three seats in the 13th Knesset. It won two seats in the 14th Knesset (1996). It is strongly opposed to the Oslo* peace process. Moledet joined with the New Herut* party and Tekuma* to form the new National Union* Party that won four seats in the 15th Knesset (May 1999).

MONTEFIORE, SIR MOSES HAIM. Born in Italy in 1784 and died in England* in 1885, he was a major benefactor of early Zionist* settlement of Palestine*. A member of a wealthy Sephardic* family, he was brought to England in infancy and rose to become one of London's most successful financiers. He served as president of the influential Board of Deputies of British Jews from 1835 to 1874. During a visit to Palestine in 1839 he sponsored the first census taken of the Jewish population there since biblical times. In 1849 he established a small textile plant in Jerusalem* and in 1854 he initiated a fund-raising drive for the relief of the victims of a famine in Palestine. In 1855 he purchased land near Jaffa* that ultimately became the first Jewish orange orchard in Palestine. In addition, he established Mishkenot Sha'ananim, the first Jewish residential community outside the walls of Jerusalem's Old City. A fund established by Montefiore to mark his ninetieth birthday (in 1874) was instrumental in facilitating the establishment of early Hoveve Zion* agricultural settlements in Palestine.

For further information see: Shmuel Ettinger and Israel Bartal, "The First Aliya: Ideological Roots and Practical Accomplishments," in *Essential Papers on Zionism*, edited by Jehuda Reinharz and Anita Shapira (New York: New York University Press, 1996): 63-93.

MORASHA (HERITAGE) PARTY. A political party created by a religious-nationalist splinter group from the National Religious Party*

(NRP) that joined with Poalei Agudat Israel* to contest the 1984 Knesset* election. The party advocated more Jewish settlement of the West Bank* and claimed the support of Gush Emunim*. Hanan Porat and Rabbi Haim Druckman*, formerly of the NRP, were leaders of the party, which combined religious orthodoxy and a demand for more territory. It merged with the NRP faction in the Knesset in July 1986.

For further information see: Gershon R. Kieval, *Party Politics in Israel and the Occupied Territories* (Westport, CT: Greenwood, 1983); Stewart Reiser, "The Religious Parties and Israel's Foreign Policy," in *Israeli National Security Policy: Political Actors and Perspectives*, edited by Bernard Reich and Gershon R. Kieval (New York: Greenwood, 1988): 105-121; Ehud Sprinzak, "Extremist Inputs into Israel's Foreign Policy: The Case of Gush Emunim," in *Israeli National Security Policy: Political Actors and Perspectives*, edited by Bernard Reich and Gershon R. Kieval (New York: Greenwood, 1988): 123-146; Ehud Sprinzak, *The Ascendance of Israel's Radical Right* (New York: Oxford University Press, 1991).

MORDECHAI, YITZHAK. Born in Kurdish Iraq in 1944, he immigrated to Israel in 1950 and entered the army at 18. During a 33-year (1962-1995) career in the Israel Defense Forces* he held a number of important positions, including chief infantry and paratroops officer, head of Headquarters Training Development, OC Southern Command, OC Central Command, and OC Northern Command. He retired from the military, with the rank of Major-General, in 1995. Entering party politics, he ranked fourth on the joint Likud*-Tsomet*-Gesher* list for election to the 14th Knesset* in 1996. In June of that year he was named Minister of Defense, and served as a key member of Benjamin Netanyahu's* "kitchen cabinet"* on peace and security matters. Publicly fired by Netanyahu on January 23, 1999, Mordechai joined Ronnie Milo*, Dan Meridor*, and Amnon Lipkin-Shahak* in forming the new Center* party, becoming the party's leader and its candidate for Prime Minister. He was thus the first serious Sephardic* candidate for Prime Minister. On the eve of the May 17, 1999, general election, he withdrew from the prime ministerial race and threw his support behind One Israel* candidate Ehud Barak*. Under Mordechai's leadership, the Center Party won six seats in the 15th Knesset, and on July 6, 1999, it joined the governing coalition headed by Barak, with Mordechai serving as Transportation Minister. On July 11, 1999, he was named Deputy Prime Minister (one of three Deputy Prime

Ministers in Barak's Government). He holds a BA degree in history from Tel Aviv University and an MA in political science from Haifa University.

MORESHET AVOT *see* TRADITION OF THE FATHERS

MOSHAV (MOSHAV OVDIM). A cooperative agricultural settlement. A moshav is a village composed of a number of families—the average is about 60—each of which maintains its own household, farms its own land, and earns its income from what it produces. The moshav leases its land from the Israel Lands Authority* or the Jewish National Fund* (Keren Kayemet Le Israel) and, in turn, distributes land to each of its members. Each family belongs to the cooperative that owns the heavy machinery and deals collectively with marketing and supplies and provides services such as education and medical care. Families are duty-bound to mutual assistance in cases of need as a result of some misfortune or national service. Hired labor is forbidden except under special circumstances and then only after the village committee has given its approval. Full response is expected to the needs of the nation and the labor movement. However, over the years there have appeared some deviations from the principles of moshav living. Some now engage in industry under similar conditions. The first moshav, Nahalal*, was founded in 1921 in the Jezreel Valley*. Private homes, rather than communal living, are the rule, as are private plots of land and individual budgets. Moshavim (plural of moshav) have become more numerous than kibbutzim*. Many of the post-independence immigrants to Israel were attracted to the concept of cooperative activity based on the family unit rather than the kibbutz's socialist communal-living approach. The moshavim are organized in the countrywide Tnaut Moshavei Haovdim—the Moshav Movement. They belong to the Agricultural Workers Union and to the Histadrut*.

For further information see: Jay S. Abarbanel, *The Cooperative Farmer and the Welfare State: Economic Change in an Israeli Moshav* (Manchester, UK: Manchester University Press, 1974); Elaine Baldwin, *Differentiation and Cooperation in an Israeli Veteran Moshav* (Manchester: Manchester University Press, 1972); Joseph Blasi, *The Communal Experience of the Kibbutz* (New Brunswick, NJ: Transaction, 1995); Maxwell I. Klayman, *The Moshav in Israel: A Case Study of Institution-Building for Agricultural Development* (New York: Praeger,

1970); Leonard Mars, *The Village and the State: Administration, Ethnicity and Politics in an Israeli Cooperative Village* (Westmead, UK: Gower, 1980); Henry Near, *The Kibbutz Movement: A History*, 2 volumes (London: The Littman Library of Jewish Civilization, 1992, 1997); Harry Viteles, *A History of the Co-Operative Movement in Israel: A Source Book*, 7 volumes (London: Vallentine, Mitchell, 1966-1968).

MOSHAV SHITUFI. It is the middle way in settlement between the kibbutz* and the moshav ovdim*. It resembles the kibbutz in its communal production and is like the moshav in its individual family-consumer framework. The first moshav shitufi was set up in 1936 at Kfar Hittim.

MOSHAVA (LITERALLY "COLONY"). A private farming village. The first was founded in Palestine* in 1878 and known as Petah Tikva*. Others included Rishon Le Zion*, Rosh Pina, and Nes Ziona.

MOSSAD—HAMOSSAD LEMODIIN VETAFKIDIM MEYUHADIM. The Institute for Intelligence and Special Missions. Created on September 1, 1951, it is Israel's equivalent of the United States* Central Intelligence Agency. Among its missions are the collection of political, social, economic, and military information in and on foreign countries, especially all aspects of Arab politics, society, and foreign policy. For many years the Mossad was headed by Reuven Shiloah*. In the 1990s its chiefs included Shabtai Shavit, Danny Yatom, and Ephraim Halevy. Though shaken by a series of highly publicized operational failures and personnel shakeups, it remains an important component of Israel's intelligence and security community.

For further information see: Michael Bar-Zohar, *Spies in the Promised Land: Isar Harel and the Israeli Secret Service* (Boston: Houghton Mifflin, 1972); Ian Black and Benny Morris, *Israel's Secret Wars: A History of Israel's Intelligence Services* (London: Grove Weidenfeld, 1991); Stanley Blumberg and Gwinn Owens, *The Survival Factor: Israeli Intelligence from World War I to the Present* (New York: Putnam, 1981); Richard Deacon, *The Israeli Secret Service* (New York: Taplinger, 1978); Dennis Eisenberg, Uri Dan, and Eli Landau, *The Mossad Inside Stories: Israel's Secret Intelligence Service* (London: Paddington, 1978); Haggai Eshed, *Reuven Shiloah—The Man Behind the Mossad: Secret Diplomacy in the Creation of Israel* (London: Frank Cass, 1997); Dan Raviv and

Yossi Melman, *Every Spy a Prince: The Complete History of Israel's Intelligence* Community (Boston: Houghton Mifflin, 1990); Stewart Stevens, *The Spymasters of Israel* (New York: Macmillan, 1980); Gordon Thomas, *Gideon's Spies: The Secret History of the Mossad* (New York: St. Martin's, 1999).

MOU *see* MEMORANDUM OF UNDERSTANDING

MOUNT HERZL (HAR HERZL). A hill on the western outskirts of Jerusalem* on which is located the grave of Theodor Herzl* whose remains were transferred there from Vienna in 1949. Other prominent Zionist and Israeli figures, including the assassinated Prime Minister Yitzhak Rabin*, are also buried there.

MOUNT SCOPUS (HAR HATZOFIM). A hill in Jerusalem*. Site of the first campus of the Hebrew University* of Jerusalem which was cut off from Jewish Jerusalem* during the War of Independence*, but remained under Israel's control. The enclave was held by a small contingent of Israelis who were periodically relieved by convoys under United Nations escort. In the Six Day War*, Israel recaptured the surrounding territory and the Hebrew University began to rebuild and expand its facilities on Mt. Scopus.

MOUNT ZION. A hill in Jerusalem* located outside of Zion Gate of the old walled city. An old tradition places the tomb of King David on Mount Zion.

MOVEMENT FOR DISCHARGED SOLDIERS. A party led by Ben-Zion Koren created to contest the 1988 Knesset election*. It failed to secure sufficient votes to win a seat in parliament.

MOVEMENT FOR MOSHAVIM, DEVELOPMENT TOWNS AND NEIGHBORHOODS. A political party, led by Raanan Zaim, which contested the 1988 Knesset* election but failed to secure a seat.

MULTILATERAL TALKS. At the Moscow Middle East Peace Conference of January 1992 a multilateral diplomatic track was established to complement the bilateral negotiating process between Israelis and Arabs initiated at the Madrid Conference* of October 1991. The 36 parties attending the Moscow meetings agreed on the establishment of five working groups (comprised of Middle East parties and others) to deal with: arms control and regional security; economic development; the environment; water resources; and refugees. Each working group had a designated gavel-holder and facilitators, and each working group was represented on a steering group—co-chaired by the United States* and Russia*—that guided the multilateral negotiating process. Although designed to operate parallel to the bilateral negotiations, the activities of the multilateral talks were directly affected by the shifting fortunes of Israel's direct separate negotiations with its various Arab neighbors.

For further information see: Joel Peters, *Building Bridges: The Arab-Israeli Multilateral Talks* (London: Royal Institute of International Affairs, 1994).

MUNICH MASSACRE. On September 5, 1972, eight members of the Black September* PLO* faction broke into the competitors' residence at the Munich, Germany*, Summer Olympic Games and took 13 Israeli athletes hostage. Two of the athletes escaped while two others were killed in countering the initial attack. The remaining nine Israelis were held hostage by the terrorists who sought to exchange them for Israeli and West German cooperation in releasing 234 of their comrades incarcerated in Israeli and West German prisons, and in providing the terrorists with three airplanes and safe passage out of Germany. Faced with the refusal of both Israel and West Germany to release the 234 prisoners, the terrorists reduced their demands to one plane, which was to fly them to Cairo, Egypt*, where they threatened to execute the Israeli hostages if Israel did not release the Palestinian prisoners. While boarding the aircraft at the Munich airport the terrorists were attacked by a West German anti-terrorism unit. In the ensuing firefight the terrorists killed their nine Israeli hostages and the German soldiers killed five of the eight terrorists; the other three terrorists were captured. (But they were subsequently released in exchange for a hijacked Lufthansa airplane.) The Government of Prime Minister Golda Meir* responded to the Munich attack by forming a special secret anti-terrorist unit mandated to hunt down and assassinate those responsible for organizing the Olympic massacre.

For further information see: Mark Daryl Erickson and Simeon Manickavasagam, "Munich Olympics Massacre (1972)," in *An Historical Encyclopedia of the Arab-Israeli Conflict*, edited by Bernard Reich (Westport, CT: Greenwood, 1996): 364-365; Serge Groussard, *The Blood of Israel: The Massacre of the Israeli Athletes, The Olympics, 1972* (New York: Morrow, 1975); George Jonas, *Vengeance: The True Story of an Israeli Counter-Terrorist Team* (New York: Simon and Schuster, 1984).

N

NAHAL. (Derived from the Hebrew* words—Noar Halutzi Lohaim—meaning Fighting Pioneering Youth.) A formation within the Israel Defense Forces* which combines military training and operations with pioneering settlement and agricultural training. After completing basic training Nahal groups are allocated to settlements for a period of combined agriculture and military training. The Nahal program derived from the security needs of the pioneering agricultural settlements that developed from the immigration to Palestine* starting in the latter part of the nineteenth century. The hostile environment and security situation in Palestine helped to dictate the requirement for self-defense against armed attack. The Nahal program was formalized in the summer of 1948 by Prime Minister David Ben-Gurion* for the specific purpose of encouraging the flow of people into the agricultural settlements and maintaining the pioneering spirit. The Nahal was the natural continuation of the pioneering traditions of the waves of immigration to Israel. Since its establishment Nahal has created new settlements and assisted in the establishment of others. It has opened up undeveloped areas and created a presence at sensitive border points. Originally a unit within Gadna* it was separated from it in September 1949. On August 1, 1998, Nahal officially disappeared as a separate branch of the IDF and became a part of the Education and Gadna branch.

For further information see: Yigal Allon, *The Making of Israel's Army* (New York: Bantam, 1971); Stuart A. Cohen, "The IDF: From a 'People's Army' to a 'Professional Military'—Causes and Implications," *Armed Forces and Society* 21:2 (Winter 1995): 237-254; Ze'ev Drori, "Utopia in Uniform," in *Israel: The First Decade of Independence*, edited by S. Ilan Troen and Noah Lucas (Albany: State University of New York Press, 1995): 593-613; Moshe Lissak, "The Civilian Component of Israel's Civil-Military Relations in the First Decade," in *Israel: The First Decade of Independence*, edited by S. Ilan Troen and Noah Lucas (Albany: State

University of New York Press, 1995): 575-592; Gunter E. Rosenberg, *Anatomy of the Israeli Army* (London: Batsford, 1979); Ze'ev Schiff, *A History of the Israeli Army, 1870-1974* (New York: Simon and Schuster, 1974).

NAHALAL. An agricultural settlement in the western Jezreel Valley*. Founded in 1921, it was the first moshav ovdim* and became the prototype of this type of settlement. It was laid out in a circle with the houses grouped around a central section of public buildings.

NARKISS, UZI. Born in Jerusalem* in 1925, he began his military career as a teenager in the Haganah*, participating in the 1946 demolition of the bridges across the Jordan River* that were used by Arab irregulars. Later he was in brief command of the Etzion bloc*. Later in 1948 he became an operations officer and then a battalion commander under Yigal Allon* in the south. He also was assigned to Yitzhak Sadeh*. Uzi Narkiss was a deputy battalion commander in the Palmah* brigade commanded by Yitzhak Rabin* and was ordered in May 1948 to break through to the besieged Jewish quarter of Jerusalem. His men succeeded in blowing a hole in Zion Gate and linking up with the beleaguered defenders. But the force that was to relieve Narkiss and his men did not materialize and he ordered his men out. Lacking reinforcements and ammunition he ordered his troops to break out of Jerusalem's Old City in 1948. The Jewish quarter soon fell. When the war ended, he was a battalion commander in the Negev* division. He served in various command positions and established Israel's National Security College. In the 1967 Six Day War* he headed the Central Command and directed the battle for the liberation of Jerusalem*. As OC Central Command in 1967 he commanded the brigades that retook the Old City, reentering the walled city together with Moshe Dayan* and Rabin in June 1967. After retiring from the Israel Defense Forces* in 1968 he worked for 25 years with the Jewish Agency*, serving as director general of the information department and the immigration and absorption department. He also served as chairman of the Government Coins and Medals Corporation and devoted himself to maintaining the soldiers' memorial on Ammunition Hill in Jerusalem. He died in December 1997.

For further information see: Uzi Narkiss, *Soldier of Jerusalem*. Foreword by Herman Wouk. Translated by Martin Kett (London: Vallentine Mitchell, 1998).

NASI *see* PRESIDENT

NATIONAL COUNCIL *see* VAAD LEUMI

NATIONAL COUNCIL OF STATE *see* CONSTITUENT ASSEMBLY

NATIONAL DEMOCRATIC ALLIANCE-BALAD. An Arab political party headed by Azmi Bishara*. In 1996 it ran as part of an electoral coalition with the Democratic Front for Peace and Equality-Hadash*. It ran independently in 1999, winning two seats in the 15th Knesset*. Its policy platform emphasized the granting of full civil and political rights to Israeli Arabs, and the need for Israel to "become a state of [all] its citizens, not a Jewish state." *See also* ARAB POLITICAL PARTIES.

NATIONAL HOME PARTY. Nationalist political party formed on February 1, 2000 by the amalgamation of much of Israel Beiteinu* and National Union* factions in the 15th Knesset*.

NATIONAL MILITARY ORGANIZATION *see* IRGUN

NATIONAL RELIGIOUS PARTY (NRP) (MIFLAGA DATIT LEUMIT—MAFDAL). The National Religious Party was founded in 1956 by Mizrahi* as a religious party seeking to combine religious concerns and a moderate socialist orientation in economic matters within a Zionist framework. It was a merger of Mizrahi, formally established as a party in Palestine* in 1918, and Hapoel Hamizrahi (Mizrahi Worker), founded in 1922. Hapoel retained a degree of independence as the trade-union section of the party responsible for immigration and absorption, labor and vocational affairs, housing, settlement, culture, pension funds, and economic affairs, etc. The central NRP organization was responsible for policy, party organization, religion and rabbinical relations, and publications.

From its beginning, this party of Orthodox religious Zionists began to have an impact, electing 19% of the delegates to the Twelfth Zionist Congress in 1921. After Israel's independence, the NRP served in every Government except for a brief period from 1958 to 1959, when it left the coalition over the question of who should be considered a Jew for purposes of immigration. The party is overseen by the World Center, a council elected by the world conference of the party. The conference also elects the chairman of the World Center, the party leader. Delegates to the conference are elected from local party branches by the party members. The party also has a very active youth wing, Bnai Akiva, as well as a sports organization and a vast network of nurseries/day care centers, kindergartens, and educational institutions. Bar Ilan University* and the Mosad HaRav book publishing house were established by Mizrahi and are part of the NRP operation.

The NRP was founded to emphasize the need for legislation based on Jewish religious law (Halacha*) and protective of a "Torah true" tradition. It actively supports Jewish immigration, the development of the private sector, and government support of all Halachically necessary religious activities, including a religious school system and rabbinical councils in every city. These aims have been constant since the founding of the NRP's predecessors, and they have been realized to a large degree. With only some minor intraparty disagreement, the NRP view was that it was organized for religious purposes and had no particular role to play in political, economic, or foreign affairs. It was able to cooperate effectively with Mapai* and the Israel Labor Party* primarily because of its willingness to defer to the left on foreign and defense questions in return for support in religious matters. At the same time, the party's commitment to religious Zionism was reflected in the establishment of the Hesder yeshiva system, combining religious studies with military service.

With Israel's capture of the West Bank* and the Sinai Peninsula* in 1967, however, NRP political attitudes began to change. The capture of ancient Israeli cities—Hebron*, Shechem (Nablus), and Old Jerusalem*—was seen as a miraculous achievement in fulfillment of the covenant between God and the Jewish people. The NRP believed that the return of any of the territory of historic Israel would be a repudiation of that covenant. On that basis, NRP hawks sought to focus the party's efforts on the rapid settlement of the new territory with the aim of securing it for Israel in perpetuity. Most of the party's efforts in this regard were spearheaded by its Bnai Akiva youth wing, which after 1967 sought to appeal to nontraditional voters with the slogan "no return of any part of Eretz Israel." Largely because both groups are composed of the same people, the Youth Faction has strong but informal ties with Gush Emunim*, the most militant of West Bank settlers. In some respects, the Youth Faction considers itself the political representation of the Gush Emunim.

Youth Faction leaders have come to increasing prominence in both the NRP and the Government. Nevertheless, the NRP also encompasses other factions which represent more flexible (i.e. moderate) points of view on the future of the West Bank. The factionalism of the NRP reflects both personal conflicts and differing policy perspectives. Yosef Burg* served as the party leader from its founding to the mid-1980s and also served in many Israeli cabinets. A man of great political skill, he worked successfully to maintain and expand the religious foundation of the state. His seniority and role as head of the largest faction (Lamifneh) secured his dominant position in the party, but he did not dictate its positions or policies. His influence was, in part, the result of his shrewd use of patronage in allocating jobs in the party and the party-controlled institutions. As a Government minister, he was also able to distribute many public jobs in the religious and educational establishments and a variety of posts controlled by the Ministry of the Interior.

The long-time leader of the party's Bnai Akiva youth wing, Zevulun Hammer*, became NRP General Secretary in 1984. Between the 1984 and 1988 elections the NRP went through a significant reorganization and there was a clear move to the right on political and educational issues. In 1988 Professor Avner Shaki* was elected to head the ticket and Zevulun Hammer was placed in the second position. The party's election platform reflected a hawkish tendency, with great emphasis on the party's relationship with Jewish settlers in Judea* and Samaria* and permanent Israeli retention of these areas. As a member of the Government at the time, the NRP had supported the Camp David Accords* in the late 1970s, including the plan to accord limited self-governing authority to West Bank and Gaza* Palestinians. However, the party's discernible shift to the right in the mid-1980s caused some internal divisions, as reflected in the formation of the breakaway dovish Meimad* faction prior to the 1988 Knesset election. Led by Shaki in the 1988 Knesset election, the NRP supported a program that stipulated there would be only one state between the Jordan River and the Mediterranean Sea—the State of Israel. No independent national Arab entity will exist within the limits of the Land of Israel. No part of Israel will be given over to a foreign government or authority and no Jewish settlement will be uprooted. The NRP, however, was prepared for direct negotiations with neighboring Arab states based on any realistic peace proposal. In 1992, the party platform reflected a continued shift to the right, with the membership all but ruling out the possibility of joining a governing coalition headed by Labor. In elections to the 13th Knesset the NRP won six seats but did not join the Rabin*-led Government. The credibility of the party was to some extent shaken by the assassination of Yitzhak Rabin by Yigal Amir*, a member of the religious Zionist community and a graduate of the Hesder yeshiva system. However, under the careful and pragmatic leadership of Zevulun Hammer the party reasserted its commitment to Zionist values and, having taken nine seats in the 14th Knesset (1996), the NRP was accorded two ministries in the coalition headed by Benjamin Netanyahu*. Many analysts expressed uncertainty about the direction the party would take following the death of Zevulun Hammer in January 1998. The NRP voiced strong opposition within the Netanyahu Government to the Hebron* and Wye River* diplomatic protocols, frequently threatening to bring the Government down if the territorial concessions addressed in those agreements were implemented fully. This threat was finally fulfilled in late December 1998, when, faced with the NRP's likely support for a non-confidence motion, Netanyahu approved the dissolution of his Government and the call for new elections for both Prime Minister and the 15th Knesset on May 17, 1999. The party's 1999 policy platform emphasized "The NRP—giving the state a soul." It also emphasized the need to protect Israeli vital interests in the West Bank and Gaza Strip, including all Jewish settlements, in the context of projected final status negotiations with the Palestinians. Despite its reputation for hawkishness, the NRP in the spring of 1999 suffered the defections of two of its stalwarts, who shifted allegiance to the new Tekuma* faction that ultimately was incorporated into the right-wing National Union* Party headed by Ze'ev Binyamin Begin*. The NRP won five seats in the 15th Knesset and, after much internal debate, it joined the governing coalition headed by Ehud Barak*, with party leader Yitzhak Levy serving as Minister of Construction and Housing, Shaul Yahalom as Deputy Education Minister, and Yigal Bibi as Deputy Religious Affairs Minister.

For further information see: Ervin Birnbaum, *The Politics of Compromise: State and Religion in Israel* (Rutherford, NJ: Fairleigh Dickinson University Press, 1970); Eliezer Don-Yehiya, "Origins and Development of the *Aguda* and *Mafdal* Parties," *Jerusalem Quarterly*, No. 20 (Summer 1981): 49-64; Eliezer Don-Yehiya, "Religion and Coalition: The National Religious Party and Coalition Formation in Israel," in *The Elections in Israel*, edited by Asher Arian (Jerusalem: Academic Press, 1975): 255-284; Eliezer Don-Yehiya, "Religion, Social Cleavages and Political Behavior: The Religious Parties in the Israeli

Elections," in *Who's the Boss? The Elections in Israel, 1988 and 1989,* edited by Daniel J. Elazar and Shmuel Sandler (Detroit: Wayne State University Press, 1993): 83-129; Eliezer Don-Yehiya, "The Religious Parties and the 1996 Elections," *Israel Affairs* (Special Issue: "Israel at the Polls 1996") 4:1 (Autumn 1997): 73-102; Menachem Friedman, "The Structural Foundation for Religio-Political Accommodation in Israel: Fallacy and Reality," in *Israel: The First Decade of Independence,* edited by S. Ilan Troen and Noah Lucas (Albany: State University of New York Press, 1995): 51-81; Gershon R. Kieval, *Party Politics in Israel and the Occupied Territories* (Westport, CT: Greenwood, 1983); Charles S. Liebman, *Religion, Democracy and Israeli Society* (Amsterdam: Harwood Academics, 1997); Stewart Reiser, "The Religious Parties and Israel's Foreign Policy," in *Israeli National Security Policy: Political Actors and Perspectives,* edited by Bernard Reich and Gershon R. Kievel (New York: Greenwood, 1988): 105-121; Stewart Reiser, *The Politics of Leverage: The National Religious Party of Israel and Its Influence on Foreign Policy,* Harvard Middle East Papers, Modern Series, No. 2 (Cambridge, MA: Center for Middle Eastern Studies, Harvard University Press, 1984); Stewart Reiser, "The Religious Parties in Israel: Social Significance and Policy Implications," *Middle East Focus* 12:2 (Summer/Fall 1990): 9-16; Shmuel Sandler, "The National Religious Party: Towards a New Role in Israel's Political System," in *Public Life in Israel and the Diaspora,* edited by Sam N. Lehman-Wilzig and Bernard Susser (Jerusalem: Bar Ilan University, 1981); Gary S. Schiff, *Tradition and Politics: The Religious Parties of Israel* (Detroit: Wayne State University Press, 1977).

NATIONAL UNION (HAICHUD HALEUMI). A coalition of right-wing political parties that ran for the first time in the May 1999 elections for the 15th Knesset*, winning four seats. It was comprised of Moledet*, the New Herut Party*, and Tekuma*, and headed by former Likud* MK and cabinet minister Ze'ev Binyamin Begin*. Opposition to further territorial concessions in the West Bank* and the Gaza Strip* was the major plank of its policy platform.

Its platform provided, in part: "The Land of Israel is the homeland of the Jewish People, from the authority of its Torah and heritage, home of the returnees to Zion. The faction will act to encourage immigration and absorption and strengthen Jewish settlement in all areas of the Land of Israel. The faction will aim for the establishment of Jewish sovereignty over every part of the Land of Israel under our control. Jerusalem, eternal capital, will be completely kept under Israeli sovereignty. The faction will act diligently for the strengthening and development of Jewish settlement in all of its parts. The right of the Jewish People to the Land of Israel is inseparably connected to the right to peace and security. The Wye, Hebron and Oslo agreements, that violate this basic right, are not bringing peace rather bloodshed. No area in the Land of Israel will be transferred to foreign rule, including the Golan Heights. The faction rejects the claim of the 'right of return' of the Arab population to the Land of Israel. The State of Israel shall strive to reach peace agreements with all of its neighbors but not at the expense of the security of the state and its residents. ... Israel is a Jewish and democratic state. As such it will protect equal rights for all its citizens and residents. The standing of the legislative authority will be strengthened and the independence of the judiciary will be honored. The faction will advance the eternal values of the Torah of Israel in the life of the nation. The faction will maintain the status quo on matters of religion and state that are meant to insure the Jewish character of the State. The addition of legislation in these matters will not be done except with broad national agreement."

For further information see: David H. Goldberg, *Democracy in Action 1999: A Guide to the Participants and Issues in Israeli Politics* (Toronto: Canada-Israel Committee, May 1999).

NATIONAL UNITY GOVERNMENT (NUG) *see* GOVERNMENT OF NATIONAL UNITY

NATIONAL WATER CARRIER. The national water carrier, put into operation in 1964, brings water from Lake Tiberias* through a series of pipes, aqueducts, open canals, reservoirs, tunnels, dams, and pumping stations to various parts of the country, including the northern Negev*.

NATURAL LAW PARTY—MIFLEGET HOK HATEVA. A small political party established by Reuven Zelinkovsky. It believes that meditation is the answer to Israel's problems, both in the peace process and domestically as well as for environmental issues. It failed to receive enough votes in the May 17th, 1999, elections to secure a seat in the Knesset.

NAVEH, DANNY. Born in 1960, he graduated from the faculty of law at the Hebrew University of Jerusalem*. He served as an advisor to Likud's* Moshe Arens* during his tenures as Foreign Minister and

Defense Minister in the 1980s. From June 1996 to July 1999, he served as Cabinet Secretary for the Government headed by Benjamin Netanyahu*. In this capacity, he served for a time as head of the Israeli team in negotiations with the Palestinians toward implementing the Oslo Accords*. He was elected to the 15th Knesset*, on the Likud list, on May 17, 1999.

NAVON, YITZHAK. Born in Jerusalem* on April 19, 1921, of prominent Sephardi* lineage. The Navon family is one of the oldest and most distinguished Jerusalem families. On his father's side he came from a wealthy Sephardi family which arrived in Palestine* from Constantinople in the seventeenth century. On his maternal side he is of Moroccan background. Navon received an education at religious schools and at Hebrew University*, where he studied Hebrew literature, Arabic, Islamic culture, and pedagogy. In 1951, he became political secretary to Foreign Minister Moshe Sharett*. He served as head of Prime Minister David Ben-Gurion's* office from 1952 to 1963. In 1965, after resigning from the civil service, he was elected to the Knesset* on the Rafi* ticket. In 1972 he was elected Chairman of the World Zionist Council*. He served from 1978 to 1983 as the fifth President* of Israel. He became Deputy Prime Minister and Minister of Education and Culture in the 1984 National Unity Government* and retained those posts in the Government established in December 1988. He tended to combine liberal values and Labor socialist ideology with dovish views on foreign policy issues. He often expressed his views publicly during his tenure as President and was a very popular figure in that position.

NAZARETH. A town in northern Israel that was the home of Jesus Christ during his early youth. It is the principal Arab city in Israel and most of its inhabitants are Christian, although there is a small Muslim minority.

NE'EMAN COMMITTEE. Committee established by the Netanyahu* Government, comprised of representatives of the Orthodox, Conservative, and Reform streams of Judaism in Israel and under the chairmanship of Finance Minister Yaacov Ne'eman*. It was mandated to achieve consensus on interdenominational disputes over such issues as the right of non-Orthodox rabbis to perform conversions and marriages and to sit on influential local religious councils, in order to preempt petitions on these issues before the Supreme Court of Israel*. Despite limited successes, including the agreement to establish an institute for religious conversions that will be operated by representatives of all streams of Judaism, the overall effectiveness of the work of the Ne'eman Committee was marred by continuing mistrust among its participants. *See also* LAW OF RETURN; WHO IS A JEW.

NE'EMAN, YAACOV. Born in Tel Aviv* in 1940 to immigrants from Hungary, he was educated in law at the Hebrew University of Jerusalem* and at New York University (where he also taught). An expert in the field of tax law, in 1972 he joined the prestigious Tel Aviv law firm headed by Chaim Herzog* and Michael Fox. In the early 1980s he served as Director-General of the Finance Ministry under finance minister Yigael Hurvitz*. Despite having not been nominated to any electoral list, he was appointed Justice Minister by Benjamin Netanyahu* in June 1996. However, weeks later he resigned amidst allegations of perjury and obstruction of justice in the trial of Shas* MK Arye Deri*. After being acquitted of all charges in the spring of 1997 he was appointed Finance Minister, filling the cabinet position left vacant by the resignation of Likud* MK Dan Meridor*. As Finance Minister, Ne'eman moved aggressively to slash government spending and to reform Israel's tax system. He also served as the Netanyahu Government's point-man in efforts to find a workable compromise on the contentious issue of religious conversions. Ne'eman resigned as Finance Minister on December 18, 1998, citing disarray in Netanyahu's coalition that prevented passage of the 1999 state budget.

NEEMAN, YUVAL. Born in Tel Aviv* in 1925, he was educated at the Technion* and holds a PhD from London University. He is a Professor of physics and served as President of Tel Aviv University. He was the founder and chairman of the Tehiya* movement from its inception in 1979. He served as Minister of Science and Development in the Government from 1982 to 1984. He previously served as chief scientist of the Ministry of Defense and is the recipient of numerous awards and prizes in science. He became Minister of Science and Development in the Government established in June 1990. Tehiya subsequently quit the Government to protest Israel's participation in the Madrid Peace Conference*. It failed to win any seats in the 13th Knesset (1992) and Neeman retired from party politics. However, Tehiya's political philosophy continues to color important aspects of the foreign and security policy debate in Israel.

For further information see: Aaron David Rosenbaum, "Tehiya as a Permanent Nationalist Phenomenon," in *Israeli National Security Policy: Political Actors and Perspectives*, edited by Bernard Reich and Gershon R. Kieval (New York: Greenwood, 1988): 147-167.

NEGEV. The triangular southern half of Israel. It extends from Beersheva* south to the port of Eilat* on the Gulf of Aqaba*. The Negev is a semidesert tableland from 1,000 to 2,000 feet (300 to 610 meters) above sea level. It has limestone mountains and flatlands and is covered by a layer of fertile loam, which must have water to grow crops. The Israelis have farmed part of the Negev by irrigation with water brought through the National Water Carrier* from Lake Kinneret (the Sea of Galilee*) through canals and pipelines. They have also mined phosphates and copper.

NEGEV PARTY. Led by Pini Badash, a former Tzomet* MK, this party was created to promote the needs of Negev* residents. Its concerns included opposition to the decision to bring Tel Aviv garbage to Dudaim, as well as a proposed toxic waste dump. They are also trying to relieve the encroachment of Bedouin in the Negev and reduce crime. The Negev Party did not win a mandate in the 15th Knesset.

NETANYAHU, BENJAMIN ("BIBI"). Born in Tel Aviv* on October 21, 1949. Raised partly in the United States* where his father, Professor Benzion Netanyahu, a strong supporter of Ze'ev Jabotinsky* and Revisionist Zionism*, taught medieval Jewish history. From 1967 to 1972 he served in the elite Sayeret Metkal anti-terrorism unit of the Israel Defense Forces*. Having graduated from the Massachusetts Institute of Technology (MIT) with degrees in architecture and business administration, he was pursuing a business career in the United States when his older brother, Jonathan ("Yoni"), was killed in the Israeli raid on a hijacked airplane in Entebbe*, Uganda, in July 1976 where hostages from a hijacked aircraft were being held. He returned to Israel and established the Jonathan Institute, a foundation devoted to studying ways to fight international terrorism. As director of the institute he edited several major publications, including: *International Terrorism: Challenge and Response* (Jerusalem: The Jonathan Institute, 1980) and *Terrorism: How the West Can Win* (Jerusalem: The Jonathan Institute; New York: Farrar, Straus, and Giroux, 1986). In 1982 he was recruited by Ambassador Moshe Arens* to serve as deputy chief of mission at the

Israeli Embassy to the United States. From 1984 to 1988 he served as Israel's Permanent Representative to the United Nations. First elected to the Knesset*, on the Likud* list, he served as Deputy Foreign Minister from 1988 to 1991 and as Deputy Minister in the Prime Minister's office from 1991 to 1992. He gained international prominence during the 1991 Persian Gulf War, when he was interviewed live on American television as Iraqi Scud missiles* fell on Israel, and then as Israel's chief spokesman at the October 1991 Madrid Middle East Peace Conference*. On March 25, 1993, he was elected to succeed Yitzhak Shamir* as Likud* Party leader, defeating David Levy*. In June 1996 he defeated Labor* Party leader Shimon Peres* in the first direct election of the Prime Minister. On June 18, 1996, he presented his Government to the Knesset*. The first Prime Minister to be born in Israel since independence, he was generally viewed as representative of the new generation of Israeli politicians. Despite having been caught up in a series of political controversies, the Netanyahu Government had important accomplishments. Domestically, it stimulated high levels of foreign investment in the Israeli economy, especially in the "high-tech" sector, and it made serious efforts (through the Ne'eman Committee*) to facilitate a rapprochement between the Orthodox and non-Orthodox elements of Israeli Jewish society with regard to the sensitive "Who is a Jew"* issue. In the foreign policy domain, the Netanyahu Government withdrew from 80% of the city of Hebron* and agreed, in the Wye River Memorandum*, to undertake further redeployments in the West Bank*. But, it made the fulfilment of additional concessions conditional on the Palestinians abiding by their obligation to combat terrorism in a consistent and comprehensive manner, thereby introducing the concept of "reciprocity" into the lexicon of Arab-Israeli peacemaking. However, the concessions undertaken by Netanyahu's Government in negotiations with the Palestinians were viewed with enthusiasm by right-wing and religious elements of the cabinet, and this contributed to the Government's downfall. The Government fell, through a consensus agreement among Knesset members, on December 21, 1998. On May 17, 1999, he was defeated in the direct election for Prime Minister, receiving 43.92% of the popular vote compared to the 56.08% taken by One Israel* leader Ehud Barak*. Netanyahu immediately resigned as Likud leader and subsequently relinquished his seat in the Knesset. *Ha'aretz** editorialized (on May 16) "Benjamin Netanyahu brought to the role of Prime Minister a style of rule, if not traits of character, extraordinary in their destructiveness. He was not your typical Prime Minister, striking a reasonable balance between his failures and successes." Nevertheless, he hinted that he might return telling his followers: "The course we charted together will triumph in the end, and we will all witness this victory. ... With God's help, we shall yet return." The essence of his political philosophy was outlined in his book, *A Place among the Nations: Israel and the World* (New York: Bantam, 1993).

For further information see: Avishai Margalit, "The Terror Master," *The New York Review of Books* (October 5, 1995): 17-22; David Remnick, "The Outsider," *New Yorker* (May 25, 1998); Pamela Rivers, "Benjamin Netanyahu," in *An Historical Encyclopedia of the Arab-Israeli Conflict*, edited by Bernard Reich (Westport, CT: Greenwood, 1996): 372-373.

NETUREI KARTA (ARAMAIC: GUARDIANS OF THE CITY). A group of religious extremists who live primarily in the Mea Shearim* section of Jerusalem* and in Bnei Brak. It derives its name from a passage in the Talmud which refers to those who devote themselves to the study of the Torah as the guardians of the city. The group adheres to strict Orthodox views and follows the lifestyles that were brought to Israel from Eastern Europe. Their dress codes are the traditional long coat and black hats of Eastern European origin. They oppose Zionism* and have refused to accept Israel as a Jewish state. They oppose the use of the Hebrew* language for everyday communication because it is the holy language and because to do so would imply acceptance of Israel as the Jewish state. They believe that a Jewish state can be established only by God. Neturei Karta strongly opposes Israel and has indicated a willingness to work with groups such as the Palestine Liberation Organization* and the Arab states to oppose the Zionist enterprise.

The group has close ties with the Satmar Rebbe and those of similar views who are headquartered in Brooklyn, New York. According to their doctrine, any attempt to regain the Holy Land by force or against the will of God is considered a sin. The Zionists, in their view, have usurped the holy name "Israel" and have exploited the Jewish religion and the Holy Land to reinforce their positions. Neturei Karta spokespersons have made clear their opposition to Israel and political Zionism in numerous ways. They do not recognize Israel, do not use its currency, do not speak its language (speaking Yiddish* instead), do not go to its schools or hospitals, do not pay taxes, and do not accept any assistance or social security from the state. They see themselves as the original Jewish settlers, the Palestinian Jews who made their way to the Holy Land with the clear intent of worshiping God in his "back yard". They claim to have no political ambitions. They do not recognize the Israeli flag and have no "right" to a flag of their own. They have raised the Palestinian flag because they have said it is a flag of a state they consider to be theirs. They have indicated that they wish to be part of a proposed Palestinian state and to be represented in a joint Palestinian-Jordanian delegation to struggle against the common Zionist enemy.

For further information see: Charles S. Liebman, *Religion, Democracy and Israeli Society* (Amsterdam: Harwood Academics, 1997); David J. Schnall, *Radical Dissent in Contemporary Israeli Politics: Cracks in the Wall* (New York: Praeger, 1979); Gary S. Schiff, *Tradition and Politics: The Religious Parties of Israel* (Detroit: Wayne State University Press, 1977).

NEW COMMUNIST LIST (RAKAH). Descended from the Socialist Workers' Party of Palestine* (founded in 1919), the party was renamed the Communist Party of Palestine in 1921 and the Communist Party of Israel (Maki) in 1948. A pro-Soviet, anti-Zionist group formed Rakah in 1965. It had both Jewish and Arab members and campaigned for a socialist system in Israel, a lasting peace between Israel and the Arab countries, and the Palestinian Arab people. It favored full implementation of United Nations Security Council Resolutions 242* and 338*; Israel's withdrawal from all Arab territories occupied since 1967; formation of a Palestinian Arab state in the West Bank* and Gaza Strip*; recognition of the national rights of the State of Israel and of the Palestinian people; democratic rights and defense of working-class interests; and an end of alleged discrimination against the Arab minority in Israel and against Sephardic* Jewish communities. It contested the 1984 Knesset* election as Hadash (Democratic Front for Peace and Equality)*, an alliance with the Black Panther* movement of Sephardic Jews, winning four seats in the Knesset*. It won one seat in the 1988 Knesset election, three in 1992, and five in 1996. The party's long-time Secretary-General, Meir Wilner*, retired in the early 1990s. As a component of the Democratic Front for Peace and Equality (Hadash)*, it won three seats in the 15th Knesset (1999). *See also* COMMUNIST PARTY; DEMOCRATIC FRONT FOR PEACE AND EQUALITY.

For further information see: Gershon R. Kieval, *Party Politics in Israel and the Occupied Territories* (Westport, CT: Greenwood, 1983); Peretz Merhav, *The Israeli Left: History, Problems, Documents* (San Diego: A. S. Barnes, 1980); Dunia H. Nahas, *The Israeli Communist Party* (London: Croom Helm, 1976); Sandra Miller Rubenstein, *The Communist Movement in Palestine and Israel, 1919-1984* (Boulder, CO: Westview, 1985); David J. Schnall, *Radical Dissent in Contemporary Israeli Politics: Cracks in the Wall* (New York: Praeger, 1979).

NEW HERUT (HERUT HAHADASHA). A right-wing political party headed by former Likud* MK and cabinet minister Ze'ev Binyamin Begin* that competed for the first time in the May 1999 elections for the Knesset* as part of the National Union* coalition. Emerging in late 1998, it was comprised primarily of former Likud politicians such as Begin who had become disenchanted with either the leadership of Benjamin Netanyahu* or the decision of the Netanyahu-led governing coalition to agree to significant territorial concessions in the Hebron* agreement of January 1997 and the Wye River Memorandum* of October 23, 1998. On March 12, 1999, an agreement was established to have New Herut contest the elections to the 15th Knesset as part of a joint National Union list with Moledet* and Tekuma*, winning four seats.

For further information see: David H. Goldberg, *Democracy in Action 1999: A Guide to the Participants and Issues in Israeli Politics* (Toronto: Canada-Israel Committee, May 1999).

NEW LIBERAL PARTY. A political party founded in 1987 as a merger of three groups: Shinui*, the Liberal Center Party*, and the Independent Liberal Party*. Its leaders included Amnon Rubinstein*, Yitzhak Berman*, and Moshe Kol.

NEW ZIONIST ORGANIZATION (NZO). A worldwide Zionist organization created after members of the Union of Zionists-Revisionists voted to secede from the World Zionist Organization*. Its aims, articulated at its Constituent Congress in September 1935, included the creation of a Jewish majority on both sides of the Jordan River and the establishment of a Jewish state in Palestine*.

For further information see: Joseph Heller, "The Zionist Right and National Liberation: From Jabotinsky to Avraham Stern," *Israel Affairs*

1:3 (Spring 1995): 85-109; Samuel Katz, *A Biography of Vladimir (Ze'ev) Jabotinsky*, 2 volumes (New York: Barricade Books, 1996); Yaacov Shavit, *Ze'ev Jabotinsky and the Zionist Movement, 1925-1948* (London: Frank Cass, 1988); Yaacov Shavit, "Ze'ev Jabotinsky and the Revisionist Movement," in *Essential Papers on Zionism*, edited by Jehuda Reinharz and Anita Shapira (New York: New York University Press, 1996): 544-566.

NISSIM, MOSHE. Born in Jerusalem* in 1935, he received a law degree from Hebrew University* in 1957. He was first elected on behalf of the General Zionists* to the Fourth Knesset* in November 1959. He was elected to all Knessets since 1969 on behalf of the Liberal Party* faction of Gahal* and the Likud* bloc, respectively, until he retired from party politics following the 1992 Knesset election.

NOBEL PEACE PRIZE. On two occasions Israeli political leaders have been awarded the Nobel Prize for Peace. In 1978 Prime Minister Menachem Begin* and Egypt's President Anwar Sadat* shared the prize for their breakthrough agreements at the September 1978 Camp David summit meeting* with U.S. President Jimmy Carter*. In December 1994 Prime Minister Yitzhak Rabin*, and Foreign Minister Shimon Peres*, along with Palestine Liberation Organization (PLO)* Chairman Yasser Arafat*, were awarded the Nobel Peace Prize for concluding the Oslo Accords* of 1993.

NRP *see* **NATIONAL RELIGIOUS PARTY**

NUCLEAR RESEARCH AND DEVELOPMENT *see* ATOMIC RESEARCH AND DEVELOPMENT

O

OCCUPIED TERRITORIES. In the Six Day War* Israel occupied various Arab and Arab-held territories, including the Sinai Peninsula*, the Gaza Strip*, the West Bank*, East Jerusalem* and the Golan Heights*. Although commonly referred to as the occupied territories they are often referred to in Israel as "the administered areas."

For further information see: William W. Harris, *Taking Root: Israeli Settlement in the West Bank, the Golan and Gaza-Sinai, 1967-1980* (New York: Wiley, 1980); Bernard Reich, *Israel and Occupied Territories* (Washington, DC: U.S. Department of State, 1973).

OCTOBER WAR (1973) *see* **YOM KIPPUR WAR**

OFEQ (HORIZON) SATELLITES. A long term project intended to provide Israel with an independent space satellite capability. OFEQ1, produced by Israel Aircraft Industries*, was tested in September 1988. OFEQ2 was tested in April 1990. Both projects reentered the earth's atmosphere within six months of being launched. OFEQ3, also known as EROS (Earth Resources Observation System), was launched in April 1995; it was designed to last two years in orbit but was kept in service longer pending the successful development of the next generation (OFEQ4). As with many other projects of Israel's military-industrial complex, OFEQ is shrouded in secrecy. It is generally assumed that the goal of the project is to accord the Israeli military an independent reconnaissance satellite capability. Israel began pursuing its own spy satellite capability over two decades ago when the United States* turned down Jerusalem's request for satellite-generated satellite intelligence data. The pace of research and development associated with OFEQ was accelerated in the early 1990s in the context of the reported refusal of the United States to provide Israel with satellite data about Iraqi ballistic missile emplacements during the Persian Gulf War. On April 5, 1995, Israel launched its first spy satellite on a three-stage Shavit launch rocket. OFEQ2 was launched in April 1990. The satellite was to travel east to west on a latitude of 37 degrees, and would fly over Iran*, Iraq*, and Syria*. Formally the Government said that it was "an experimental satellite intended for scientific and technological purposes." On January 22, 1998, OFEQ4 failed to reach its intended low Earth orbit and dropped into the Mediterranean Sea. Despite this setback, senior officials reaffirmed Israel's commitment to the satellite project.

For further information see: Moshe Arens, *Broken Covenant: American Foreign Policy and the Crisis between the United States and Israel* (New York: Simon and Schuster, 1995); Efraim Inbar and Shmuel Sandler, "Israel's Deterrence Strategy Revisited," *Security Studies* 3:2 (Winter 1993/1994): 330-358; Avner Yaniv, "Non-Conventional Weapons and the Future of Arab-Israeli Deterrence," *Israel Affairs* 2:1 (Autumn 1995):

137-152; "OFEQ Satellite Program Facing Serious Delay," *Jerusalem Post,* April 13, 1998; "Outer Space—Clean Up Your Act," *Ha'aretz,* July 28, 1998.

OLEH (JEWISH IMMIGRANT TO ISRAEL) *see* ALIYA

OLMERT, EHUD. Born in the Revisionist Zionism* settlement of Nahalat Jabotinsky (today part of Binyamina) on September 30, 1945, he is one of the "princes*" of the Likud* party, the son of former Irgun* fighter and Herut* MK Mordechai Olmert. After army service he received a BA in psychology and a law degree from Hebrew University of Jerusalem*; he was elected to the Knesset* in 1973 on the Likud list. He became Minister without Portfolio in the Government established in December 1988, and became Minister of Health in the June 1990 Government. Returned to the Knesset on the Likud list in 1992 and 1996, he was elected Mayor of Jerusalem* in November 1993, ousting the long-time incumbent, Teddy Kollek*. Reelected as Mayor in November 1998, he was compelled (by a new law) to relinquish his seat in the 14th Knesset. Following the May 17, 1999, general elections, he declared his candidacy to replace Benjamin Netanyahu* as leader of the Likud Party, but he was defeated by Ariel Sharon* on September 2, 1999.

OMETZ (COURAGE TO CURE THE ECONOMY). A political party founded in 1982 by Yigael Hurvitz*, an industrialist who had served, under Likud*, as Minister of Industry, Commerce, and Tourism and, later, as Minister of Finance. The party's primary position was that drastic measures were needed to deal with Israel's substantial economic problems. The party won one Knesset* seat in the 1984 election and Hurvitz joined the Government of National Unity* as Minister without Portfolio in 1984.

ONE ISRAEL (ISRAEL AHAT). An electoral coalition comprised of the Israel Labor Party*, Gesher*, and Meimad*, that took 20.2 % of the popular vote in the May 17, 1999, elections, translating to 26 seats in the 15th Knesset*. Its leader, Ehud Barak*, defeated Likud* leader Benjamin Netanyahu* in the direct election for Prime Minister. One Israel's policies were essentially those of Labor, though Labor's traditional base of electoral support was expanded through the incorporation under the One Israel banner of the Sephardi*-dominated Gesher and the moderate

Orthodox Meimad. Its representatives dominated the governing coalition presented by Barak to the Knesset* on July 6, 1999.

For further information see: David H. Goldberg, *Democracy in Action 1999: A Guide to the Participants and Issues in Israeli Politics* (Toronto: Foundation for Middle East Studies, May 1999).

ONE PEOPLE (AM ECHAD). Workers' party headed by Histadrut* chairman and former Labor* MK Amir Peretz*, that broke from Labor and ran independently in the May 17, 1999, elections to the Knesset*, winning two seats. The party platform stressed increased privatization without increased unemployment and an increased minimum wage.

OPEN BRIDGES POLICY. The term refers to the bridges across the Jordan River* between Jordan* and the West Bank* and Israel as well as to the links between Israel and Jordan developed after the Six Day War* of 1967. Moshe Dayan*, who was Minister of Defense, allowed the shipment of goods (mostly agricultural produce) and later the crossing of people between the two sides of the river.

OPERATION ACCOUNTABILITY. In July 1993, Israel sent forces into southern Lebanon* in response to the launching of mortar shells and Katyusha rockets* on Israeli civilian population centers in the northern Galilee region. The purpose of the operation was to punish the Iranian-backed Hezbollah and the militant Popular Front for the Liberation of Palestine-General Command (PFLP-GC). By disrupting the lives of the civilian population in southern Lebanon Israel sought to achieve two goals: to dissuade local villagers from cooperating with the terrorist groups (for example, by allowing them to store weapons and fire missiles at Israeli targets from the relative safety of villages and/or providing safe haven to the terrorists); and to pressure the Lebanese central Government to impose order over the terrorist factions operating with impunity in the border region. The operation ended when the United States* helped broker a general agreement between Israel and Hezbollah to avoid targeting civilians in their continuing conflict in southern Lebanon.

For further information see: Laura Zittrain Eisenberg, "Israel's South Lebanon Imbroglio," *Middle East Quarterly* 4:2 (June 1997): 60-69; Augustus Richard Norton (with Jullian Schwedler), "(In)Security Zones in South Lebanon," *Journal of Palestine Studies* 23:1 (Autumn 1993): 61-79.

OPERATION ALI BABA (OPERATION EZRA AND NEHEMIA). The airborne transfer to Israel of virtually all of Iraq's ancient Jewish community (about 123,000), which migrated to Israel in 1950. *See also* ALIYA.

OPERATION ENTEBBE *see* ENTEBBE OPERATION

OPERATION EXODUS. The name given to the effort begun in 1990 to achieve the emigration of Soviet Jews from the USSR* and to resettle them in Israel. In 1990-1991 more than 350,000 Soviet Jews arrived in Israel for resettlement and absorption. Between 1990 and 1996 some 750,000 new immigrants arrived from the former Soviet Union. *See also* ALIYA.

For further information see: David H. Goldberg, "Soviet Jewish Immigration: The Challenges for Israel," *Middle East Focus*, 12:1 (Summer 1990): 2-5; Baruch Gur-Gurevitz, *After Gorbachev —History in the Making: Its Effects on the Jews in the Former Soviet Union 1989-1994* (Jerusalem: The Jewish Agency for Israel, 1995); Bernard Reich, Meyrav Wurmser, and Noah Dropkin, "Playing Politics in Moscow and Jerusalem: Soviet Jewish Immigrants and the 1992 Knesset Elections," in *Israel at the Polls 1992*, edited by Daniel J. Elazar and Shmuel Sandler (Lanham, MD: Rowman and Littlefield, 1995): 127-155; Stewart Reiser, *Soviet Jewish Immigration to Israel: Political and Economic Implications* (Los Angeles: The Susan and David Wilstein Institute of Jewish Policy Studies, Spring 1992); Naomi Sheppard, "Ex-Soviet Jews in Israel: Asset, Burden, or Challenge?" *Israel Affairs* 1:2 (Winter 1994): 245-266.

OPERATION EZRA AND NEHEMIA *see* OPERATION ALI BABA

OPERATION GRAPES OF WRATH. Israeli actions in Lebanon in the spring of 1996 in response to Hezbollah attacks on northern Israel. The Israeli government had been under pressure to take action toward improving security. Rocket attacks and suicide bombings in Israel by Palestinians claimed more than 50 victims in February and March 1996. Israeli actions included artillery shelling and the use of helicopter gunships attacking Hezbollah targets. Israel used its air force and artillery corps, but decided not to utilize ground forces. In early April 1996, Israel fired missiles and launched air strikes on southern Lebanon* bases of the Iranian-backed Hezbollah and the Popular Front for the Liberation of Palestine-General Command (PFLP-GC), in response to an increase in terrorist attacks on Israeli forces in and around the south Lebanon security zone* and Katyusha missile* firings on Israeli population centers in the northern Galilee. The declared intent of the operation was to protect Israeli towns, villages, and kibbutzim by pushing the terrorists out of firing range. By hitting major infrastructure projects in southern Lebanon (such as hydroelectric facilities and highways) and forcing the temporary relocation of the local population northward toward Beirut, Israel sought to achieve two additional goals: to separate the guerrilla factions from the local villages where they were hiding weapons and launching missiles at Israel, and to compel the Lebanese central Government to take steps to apply sovereign authority over the border region (including disarming and disbanding Hezbollah and other guerrilla factions).

Although Operation Grapes of Wrath was initially supported by much of the Israeli public as necessary to ensure the safety of the northern population, the popular mood toward the operation shifted significantly after an errant Israeli missile killed more than 100 Lebanese refugees at a United Nations station at Kfar Qana on April 18, 1996. This incident elicited strong condemnation of Israel by the United Nations General Assembly and by the Secretary General. Operation Grapes of Wrath ended with a United States*-brokered cease-fire on April 26, 1996. According to this agreement, Israel and Hezbollah (represented in the understanding by the Government of Lebanon) reiterated their commitment (initially established in the context of Operation Accountability* of July 1993) to avoid firing on each other's civilian populations. In addition, the April 26, 1996, agreement provided for the establishment of a multiparty monitoring group that would hear and adjudicate complaints of violations of the cease-fire, and a consultative group to assist reconstruction in Lebanon.

For further information see: Laura Zittrain Eisenberg, "Israel's South Lebanon Imbroglio," *Middle East Quarterly* 4:2 (June 1997): 60-69.

OPERATION JONATHAN *see* ENTEBBE OPERATION

OPERATION LITANI. In 1978 Israel launched an invasion of southern Lebanon to drive the PLO* from their positions close to the Israeli border from which they had been launching attacks against Israel since before the Yom Kippur War*.

OPERATION MAGIC CARPET. The airborne transfer to Israel in 1949-1950 of virtually the entire Jewish community of Yemen. *See also* ALIYA.

For further information see: Shlomo Barer, *The Magic Carpet* (London: Secker and Warburg, 1952).

OPERATION MOSES. A massive airlift in late 1984 and early 1985 that brought thousands of Falashas* (Jews of Ethiopia*) to Israel from refugee camps in Sudan. *See also* ALIYA.

For further information see: Ruth Gruber, *Rescue: The Exodus of the Ethiopian Jews* (New York: Atheneum, 1988); Shmuel Yilma, *From Falasha to Freedom: An Ethiopian Jew's Journey to Jerusalem* (Jerusalem: Gefen, 1996).

OPERATION PEACE FOR GALILEE *see* WAR IN LEBANON

OPERATION SHEBA. On January 5, 1985, the Sudanese Government suspended Operation Moses* following an Israeli press conference revealing details of the airlift of Ethiopian Jews* from refugee camps in Sudan. The airlift was to have been kept a secret, but foreign news agencies had already leaked reports of the project. The untimely disruption of Operation Moses left several hundred Jews stranded in Sudan. The further Beta Israel were removed from Sudan in a CIA-sponsored airlift labeled Operation Sheba or Operation Joshua. *See also* ETHIOPIA, ETHIOPIAN JEWS; FALASHAS; OPERATION MOSES; OPERATION SOLOMON.

For further information see: Ruth Gruber, *Rescue: The Exodus of Ethiopian Jews* (New York: Atheneum, 1988).

OPERATION SOLOMON (ALSO KNOWN AS OPERATION SHLOMO). An airlift of some 14,500 Ethiopian* Jews from Addis Ababa, Ethiopia, to Israel carried out by the Government of Israel on the weekend of May 24-25, 1991.

For further information see: Ruth Gruber, *Rescue: The Exodus of the Ethiopian Jews* (New York: Atheneum, 1988); Shmuel Yilma, *From Falasha to Freedom: An Ethiopian Jew's Journey to Jerusalem* (Jerusalem: Gefen, 1996). *See also* OPERATION SHEBA.

ORIENT HOUSE. A building in East Jerusalem* owned by the family of veteran PLO* member and Palestinian Authority* official Faisal Husseini; it served as the effective headquarters for the Palestinian delegation to the 1991 Madrid Peace Conference*. Since the start of the Oslo* peace process the Palestinians continued to use Orient House as a seat of their political activities in East Jerusalem, insisting on holding meetings there with foreign diplomats and journalists. That this activity took place despite the fact that the Declaration of Principles* and subsequent implementing agreements specifically restricted Palestinian political affairs to areas outside of Jerusalem and prevented the Palestinian Authority from conducting foreign and defense policy was viewed by Israel as a direct challenge to its sovereignty over the unified city. In response, successive Israeli Governments since 1993 introduced legislation granting police the authority to close Orient House. However, Israel was under pressure not to implement this legislation for fear of provoking a diplomatic crisis.

ORIENTAL JEWS. Israel's non-Ashkenazi Jews are referred to as Edot Hamizrach (eastern, or Oriental, communities), Sephardim, or Oriental Jews. The term Sephardim (derived from the Hebrew name for Spain) is often used to refer to all Jews whose origin is in the Arab world and Muslim lands, although it properly refers to the Jews of Spain and the Iberian Peninsula and the communities they established in areas to which they migrated after their expulsion from the Iberian peninsula during the Spanish Inquisition. The Iberian Jews generally spoke Ladino*, a Judeo-Spanish language originally written in medieval Hebrew letters and later in Latin letters (much as the Ashkenazi Jews spoke Yiddish*), whereas those of the Middle Eastern communities did not. They hold strong traditional beliefs of the Sephardim* and often their educational and living standards are lower than the Ashkenazi* Jews. They constitute a majority of the country's population. Most of the Oriental immigration came after Israel's independence from the eastern Arab states (such as Iraq*) and from Iran*, where the Jews had resided for more than two thousand years and often had substantial centers of learning. The community is diverse and pluralistic, although a collective "Oriental" identity appears to be emerging. Historically, the political interests of the Oriental Jews coalesced with those of the Likud Party*, which shared their sense of disillusionment toward the Mapai Party* establishment. However, since the mid-1980s a growing proportion of the Oriental community has found political expression through Sephardic political parties, especially the Sephardic Torah Guardians-Shas Party*.

"ORIENTAL REVOLT". The lack of substantial political organization in the Oriental Jewish* population in the first decades after Israel's independence meant that its method of expression was by casting votes for, or withholding them from, the major established political parties. This seemed to reach a plateau in the 1981 Knesset* elections, when the Oriental vote for Likud* led the Israeli media to speak of an "Oriental revolt," and the Jewish ethnic issue became more public during the campaign. It seemed to suggest full-scale Oriental efforts to be heard in the electoral process and to follow the pattern foreshadowed in the 1977 election and replicated in the 1984 election, although the ethnic issue was all but eliminated from the latter campaign.

For further information see: Dan Caspi, Abraham Diskin, and Emanuel Gutmann, *The Roots of Begin's Success: The 1981 Israeli Elections* (London: Croom Helm, 1984); Daniel J. Elazar, *The Other Jews: The Sephardim Today* (New York: Basic, 1989); Calvin Goldscheider, *Israel's Changing Society: Population, Ethnicity, and Development* (Boulder, CO: Westview, 1996); Oren Yiftachel and Avinoam Meir, *Ethnic Frontiers and Peripheries: Landscapes of Development and Inequality in Israel* (Boulder, CO: Westview, 1998).; Yael Yishai, *Land of Paradoxes: Interest Politics in Israel* (Albany: State University of New York Press, 1991).

OSIRAK (OSIRAQ) NUCLEAR REACTOR. On June 7, 1981, the Israel air force bombed Iraq's* nuclear reactor at Osirak, claiming that it was developing nuclear weapons.

For further information see: Shai Feldman, "The Bombing of Osiriq—Revisited," *International Security* 7 (Fall 1982); 114-142; Amos Perlmutter, Michael Handel, Uri Bar-Joseph, *Two Minutes Over Baghdad* (London: Vallentine, Mitchell, 1982).

OSLO ACCORDS. In the spring and summer of 1993 Israeli and Palestine Liberation Organization* officials met secretly in various European locales in an effort to establish the framework for negotiations leading to a permanent peace agreement. These talks occurred under the auspices of the Norwegian Government and its foreign minister, Johan Jorgen Holst. The final series of talks took place near the Norwegian capital, Oslo, and concluded with the exchange of letters of recognition between Israel's Prime Minister Yitzhak Rabin* and PLO Chairman Yasser Arafat* on September 9, 1993, and the formal signing of the Israel-PLO Declaration of Principles* by Israeli Foreign Minister Shimon Peres* and PLO official Mahmoud Abbas (Abu Mazen)* at the White House on September 13, 1993. The Declaration of Principles established the goal of an Israeli-PLO peace agreement and set the framework and timetable for achieving it. It was followed by a series of partial interim agreements, including the Cairo Agreement* of May 4, 1994 (also referred to as the "Gaza-Jericho First" Agreement, or the Oslo I Implementing Agreement); an Early Empowerment Agreement signed on August 24, 1994; the Israeli-Palestinian Interim Agreement on the West Bank and the Gaza Strip* of September 28, 1995 (also known as the Oslo II Agreement*); the Protocol Concerning the Redeployment in Hebron*, signed by Israel and the Palestinian Authority* on January 17, 1997, and the Wye River Memorandum* signed by Israel and the Palestinian Authority on October 23, 1998.

For further information see: Mahmoud Abbas, *Through Secret Channels* (London: Garnet Publishing, 1985); Jane Corbin, *Gaza First: The Secret Norway Channel to Peace between Israel and the PLO* (London: Bloomsbury, 1994); Amos Elon, "The Peacemakers," *New Yorker*, December 30, 1993: 77-85; David Makovsky, *Making Peace with the PLO: The Rabin Government's Road to the Oslo Accords* (Boulder, CO: Westview, 1996); Uriel Savir, *The Process: 1,100 Days That Changed the Middle East* (New York: Random House, 1998).

OSLO II ACCORDS. Short form for the Israeli-Palestinian Agreement on the West Bank and Gaza Strip, signed by Israel's Prime Minister Yitzhak Rabin* and PLO* Chairman Yasser Arafat* in Washington, DC, on September 28, 1995. A detailed, lengthy document, it is comprised of five main chapters, dealing with the arrangements for electing the Palestinian Legislative Council* and the powers and responsibilities of the council; redeployment and security arrangements in the West Bank*; legal affairs;

cooperation between Israel and the Palestinian Legislative Council ; and miscellaneous provisions. In addition, there are a total of seven annexes to the agreement, comprised of ten appendices, as well as nine detailed maps of the West Bank* and the Gaza Strip*. Major elements of the Accords include: the arrangements for transferring control over six West Bank towns and cities (Bethlehem*, Jenin, Nablus, Ramallah, Qalkilieh, Tulkarm) and surrounding Arab villages to the administration of the Palestinian self-government authority* and arrangements for the future redeployment of Israeli forces in part of Hebron* and security arrangements in the city; the division of the West Bank and the Gaza Strip into three categories [Area A (areas transferred completely to Palestinian authority for the duration of the interim autonomy period), Area B (areas of shared Israeli and Palestinian jurisdiction), and Area C (areas remaining under full Israeli control and to be gradually transferred to Palestinian jurisdiction with the exception of areas deemed by Israel to be crucial to security)]; and the arrangements for electing the Palestinian Legislative Council. The Accord also stipulated that further redeployment of Israeli military forces to specified military locations would be gradually implemented in accordance with the terms of reference agreed to in the Declaration of Principles* in three phases, each to take place after an interim of six months, after the inauguration of the Palestinian Legislative Council, and to be completed within 18 months from the date of the inauguration of the Council.

OZ, AMOS. Born in Jerusalem* in 1939, he was educated at the Hebrew University* and at Oxford University Press University. A member of Kibbutz Hulda, Amos Oz is a widely published author of novels, short stories, essays, and articles in Israel and abroad, including: *In the Land of Israel* (1983); *The Slopes of Lebanon* (1989); *To Know a Woman* (1991); *FIMA* (1993); *Israel, Palestine and Peace Essays* (1994); *Under This Blazing Light* (1995); and *Don't Call It Night* (1995).

P

PALESTINE. The geographical area of which part is occupied by the State of Israel. Palestine is one of the names for the territory that has also been known as the Holy Land or the Land of Israel (Eretz Israel*). The name is derived from the fact that it was called *Palestina* by the Greeks and the Romans because of the Philistines who lived in part of the region. During the period of Ottoman control it was generally known by the Arabic *Filastin*, although it was part of the province of Syria*. The League of Nations' Palestine Mandate awarded to Great Britain* included territory on both sides of the Jordan River but Transjordan was soon separated and only the area west of the river was referred to as the British Mandate for Palestine*between 1922 and 1948. With the establishment of Israel and the first Arab-Israeli War* Palestine ceased to exist as a geographical or political unit.

PALESTINE LIBERATION ORGANIZATION (PLO). An organization originally created and established by the Arab League*in 1964 which claims to represent the Palestinian people wherever they may live. Its original leader was Ahmed Shukeiri, but after the Six Day War* and the substantial Israeli victory with its occupation of the West Bank* and Gaza Strip*, Yasser Arafat* took over the leadership of Fatah*, the largest faction, and subsequently of the PLO. He has remained its Chairman since and has been the international representative and symbol of the PLO. He gives voice to its demands and guides its overall direction and policy. Israel's relationship with the PLO was slow to develop inasmuch as it was viewed by most Israelis as a terrorist organization bent on Israel's destruction. For many years it was illegal for Israelis to have any contact with anyone suspected of membership in the PLO or the PLO's governing body, the Palestine National Council (PNC). The majority of Israelis were unmoved by the November 1988 resolution passed by the PNC declaring an independent Palestinian state in the West Bank and Gaza. Israel conditioned its participation in the Madrid Peace Conference* on the Palestinian delegation being comprised of individuals ostensibly unaffiliated with the PLO and subsumed within a joint delegation with the Jordanians. The first substantive change in policy occurred in January 1993 when the Knesset* passed legislation lifting the ban on innocent contacts with PLO members. The next breakthrough came on September 9, 1993, when Prime Minister Yitzhak Rabin*and PLO Chairman Arafat exchanged letters of recognition. In the Declaration of Principles* (September 13, 1993) Israel and the PLO outlined the terms of reference for achieving a negotiated permanent settlement of their dispute and began to gradually implement those terms of reference. In January 1996 Arab residents of the West Bank, Gaza Strip, and East Jerusalem*elected a Palestinian Legislative Council* and Executive Committee, headed by

President Yasser Arafat. With this election, responsibility for areas of the West Bank and Gaza ceded to Palestinian control was transferred from the PLO to the Palestinian Authority*. But the PLO was still considered the effective sovereign authority in these areas as well as the representative of Palestinians residing outside of the West Bank and Gaza. Leadership over the PLO remains firmly in the hands of Yasser Arafat, and there is much speculation about which groups will constitute the next generation of PLO leadership. *See also* PALESTINE NATIONAL COVENANT.

For further information see: Yonah Alexander and Joshua Sinai, *Terrorism: The PLO Connection* (New York: Crane Russak, 1989); Jillian Becker, *The PLO: The Rise and Fall of the Palestine Liberation Organization* (London: Weidenfeld and Nicolson, 1984); Laurie Brand, *Palestinians in the Arab World: Institution Building and the Search for State* (New York: Croom Helm, 1988); Rex Brynen, *Sanctuary and Survival: The PLO in Lebanon* (Boulder, CO: Westview, 1990); Helena Cobban, *The Palestinian Liberation Organization: People, Power and Politics* (New York: Cambridge University Press, 1984); Helena Cobban, "Israel and the Palestinians: From Madrid to Oslo and Beyond," in *Israel under Rabin*, edited by Robert O. Freedman (Boulder, CO: Westview, 1995); Jane Corbin, *Gaza First: The Secret Norway Channel to Peace Between Israel and the PLO* (London: Bloomsbury, 1994); Hillel Frisch, *Countdown to Statehood: Palestinian State Formation in the West Bank and Gaza* (Albany: State University of New York Press, 1998); Shlomo Gazit, "Israel and the Palestinians: Fifty Years of Wars and Turning Points," *Annals of the American Academy of Political and Social Science* 555 (January 1998): 82-96; Rashid Khalidi, *Palestinian Identity: The Construction of Modern National Consciousness* (New York: Columbia University Press, 1997); Baruch Kimmerling and Joel S. Migdal, *Palestinians: The Making of a People* (New York: Free Press, 1993); Kemal Kirisci, *The PLO and World Politics: A Study of the Mobilization and Support for the Palestinian Cause* (London: Frances Pinter, 1986); Neil C. Livingstone and David Halevy, *Inside the PLO* (New York: Morrow, 1990); David Makovsky, *Making Peace with the PLO: The Rabin Government's Road to the Oslo Accord* (Washington, DC: Washington Institute for Near East Policy; Boulder, CO: Westview, 1996); Aaron David Miller, *The PLO and the Politics of Survival* (Washington, DC: Center for Strategic and International Studies, Georgetown University Press; New York: Praeger, 1983); Muhammad

Muslih, *Toward Coexistence: An Analysis of the Resolutions of the Palestine National Council* (Washington, DC: The Institute for Palestine Studies, 1990); Jamal R. Nassar, *The Palestine Liberation Organization: From Armed Struggle to the Declaration of Independence* (New York: Praeger, 1991); Cheryl Rubenberg, *The Palestine Liberation Organization: Its Institutional Infrastructure* (Belmont, MD: Institute of Arab Studies, 1983); Barry Rubin, *The Arab States and the Palestine Conflict* (Syracuse, NY: Syracuse University Press, 1981); Barry Rubin, *Revolution Until Victory? The Politics and History of the PLO* (Cambridge, MA: Harvard University Press, 1994); Barry Rubin, *Israel, The Palestinian Authority and the Arab States* (Ramat Gan: Begin-Sadat Center for Strategic Studies Security and Policy Studies No. 36, Bar Ilan University, January 1998); Barry Rubin, "Who Will Succeed Yasser Arafat?" *Middle East Quarterly* 5:1 (March 1998): 3-9; Barry Rubin, "Palestinian Politics and the Peace Process," *Peacewatch: Special Policy Forum Report* (Washington, DC: Washington Institute for Near East Policy, April 23, 1998); Uriel Savir, *The Process: 1,100 Days That Changed the Middle East* (New York: Random House, 1998); Avraham Sela and Moshe Ma'oz, editors, *The PLO and Israel: From Armed Conflict to Political Solution, 1964-1994* (New York: St. Martin's, 1997); Mark Tessler, *A History of the Israeli-Palestinian Conflict* (Bloomington: Indiana University Press, 1994); John Wallach and Janet Wallach, *The New Palestinians: The Emerging Generation of Leaders* (Rocklin, CA: Prima Publishing, 1992).

PALESTINE MANDATE *see* BRITISH MANDATE FOR PALESTINE

PALESTINE NATIONAL COVENANT. The Covenant was adopted by the Palestine Liberation Organization (PLO)* in 1964. Its central theme is the elimination of Israel and its replacement by a Palestinian state established in all of Palestine*. It was rewritten by the Palestine National Council in Cairo in July 1968. At the core of the Covenant is Article 20 which declares that the "Balfour Declaration, the Mandate for Palestine and everything that has been based upon them, are deemed null and void." Although various Palestinian leaders have suggested that the Covenant has been superseded in part by subsequent statements and declarations, the Covenant remained formally unchanged as the guide to Palestinian objectives until December 14, 1998.

In his letter of recognition to Prime Minister Yitzhak Rabin* of September 9, 1993, PLO Chairman Yasser Arafat* pledged to take the necessary steps to formally repeal those provisions of the PNC Covenant calling for Israel's destruction. This commitment was reiterated on several occasions by the PLO leadership. On April 24, 1996, the PNC meeting in Gaza* passed a resolution declaring null and void "the articles [of the PNC Covenant] that are contrary to the [September 9, 1993] letters of mutual recognition." However, this declaration was rejected by many Israelis as vague and imprecise. On January 22, 1998, Arafat wrote to U.S. President Bill Clinton specifying which provisions of the Covenant the PNC was prepared to modify or rescind. On December 10, 1998, the Palestine Central Committee meeting in Gaza, by a vote of 81 to 7 (with 7 abstentions) voted to revoke the specific clauses of the Covenant referred to in Arafat's letter to Clinton. This decision was ratified on December 14, 1998, by members of the Palestine National Council meeting in Gaza; the decision, adopted by a show of hands rather than a formal vote, was witnessed by President Clinton. The Government of Israel expressed its satisfaction with the PNC decision, calling it "an important and crucial step in the carrying out of basic Palestinian commitments undertaken in agreements with Israel."

For further information see: Yehoshafat Harkabi, *The Palestine Covenant and Its Meaning* (London: Vallentine, Mitchell, 1979).

PALESTINE PARTITION PLAN. A plan adopted by the United Nations General Assembly—Resolution 181*—on November 29, 1947. Based on the majority recommendation of the United Nations Special Committee on Palestine (UNSCOP)*, it called for dividing the British Mandate* into an Arab state, a Jewish state and an internationalized sector (*corpus separatum*) including Jerusalem*, with an economic union linking the two states. Its terms of reference were accepted by the Yishuv* which, though unhappy with the exclusion of Jerusalem, nevertheless viewed partition as an important step toward independent statehood and a practical necessity for providing refuge for survivors of the Holocaust*. The partition plan was rejected unconditionally by the Arab leadership in Palestine and by the League of Arab States*. These clashing perspectives provided a basis for the ongoing Arab-Israeli conflict.

For further information see: Yossi Katz, *Partner to Partition: The Jewish Agency's Partition Plan in the Mandate Era* (London: Frank Cass, 1998);

Walid Khalidi, "Revisiting the UNGA Partition Resolution," *Journal of Palestine Studies* 27:1 (Autumn 1997): 5-21; David Kimche and Jon Kimche, *A Clash of Destinies: The Arab-Jewish War and the Founding of the State of Israel* (New York: Praeger, 1960); William Roger Louis and Robert W. Stookey, *The End of the Palestine Mandate* (Austin: University of Texas Press, 1986); Zeev Sharef, *Three Days: An Account of the Last Days of the British Mandate and the Birth of Israel* (New York: Doubleday, 1962).

PALESTINIAN AUTHORITY. The name initially given to the Palestinian self-Government authority established in 1994 with the implementation of the "Gaza-Jericho First Agreement" (Cairo Agreement)*. The name was subsequently applied to the body administering affairs of the West Bank* and the Gaza Strip* that were transferred to Palestinian jurisdiction pursuant to the Early Empowerment Agreement (August 24, 1994)*, the Israeli-Palestinian Agreement on the West Bank and the Gaza Strip (Oslo II) Accords* of September 28, 1995, the Protocol concerning the Redeployment in Hebron* of January 17, 1997, and the Wye River Memorandum* of October 1998. Under the terms of Article 4 of the Cairo Agreement, "the Palestinian Authority will consist of one body of 24 members which shall carry out and be responsible for all the legislative and executive powers and responsibilities transferred to it under the Agreement ... and shall be responsible for the exercise of judicial functions...." These terms of reference were subsequently superseded by Chapter One of the Oslo II Agreement*, which permitted the election of a Palestinian Legislative Council* comprised of 82 representatives from which would be constituted of an Executive Authority composed of a *Ra'ees* (Chairman or President) who was to be directly elected in a separate simultaneous vote, and an indeterminate number of members. *See also* PALESTINIAN LEGISLATIVE COUNCIL.

PALESTINIAN LEGISLATIVE COUNCIL. Chapter One of the Israeli-Palestinian Interim Agreement on the West Bank* and the Gaza Strip*(Oslo II Accords*) of September 28, 1995, stipulated the conditions for electing a Palestinian Legislative Council and the powers and responsibilities of this body. In accordance with the agreed provisions of the Oslo II Agreement, Palestinian residents of the West Bank, Jerusalem* and the Gaza Strip elected their first Legislative Council on January 20, 1996. In a simultaneous vote, PLO* Chairman Yasser Arafat* was elected *Ra'ees* of the Palestinian Legislative Council's Executive

Authority. Arafat subsequently appointed a committee from the Legislative Council to serve as the Executive Authority. The Palestinian Legislative Council was formally installed on March 7, 1996, with its first working session beginning on March 21, 1996.

PALMAH (ACRONYM FOR PLUGOT MAHAT—ASSAULT COMPANIES). Commando units of the Hagana* in Palestine* and later the shock batallions of the Israel Defense Forces*. In May 1941 the Hagana created a full-time military force of volunteers, something of a professional and elite unit. The Palmah played a key role in Israel's War of Independence* but afterward its units were integrated into the Israel Defense Forces with former Palmah members occupying many senior command positions.

PARLIAMENT *see* KNESSET

PARTITION PLAN *see* PALESTINE PARTITION PLAN

PATRIOT MISSILE. An anti-ballistic missile system, batteries of which were sent by the United States* during the Persian Gulf War to help Israel defend against Scud missiles* being fired by Iraq*.

PATT, GIDEON (FORMERLY GIDEON MARCUS). (After his mother died and his Aunt Haya Patt adopted him his name was changed.) Born in Jerusalem* in 1933, Gideon Patt studied in religious schools and at the Merkaz Harav yeshiva. After serving in the army he entered politics. He went to the United States* to work for Nahum Goldmann, then Chairman of the World Zionist Organization*. He received a BSc in economics, international trade and labor relations from New York University in 1963. He entered the Knesset* on behalf of the Liberal Party* faction of Gahal* in January 1970. In January 1979 he was appointed Minister of Industry, Commerce, and Tourism and on August 5, 1981, he was sworn in as Minister of Commerce and Industry. Patt served as Minister of Science and Development in the National Unity Government* established in 1984. In December 1988 he became Minister of Tourism and retained that portfolio in the Government established by Yitzhak Shamir* in June 1990. A member of the 13th Knesset, he retired from party politics prior to the 1996 election and was appointed CEO of the International Office of Israel Bonds*.

PEACE FOR GALILEE *see* WAR IN LEBANON

PEACE MOVEMENT. Within Israel, between the Six Day* and Yom Kippur Wars*, two alternatives to the official position developed that focused on the occupied territories* and their disposition. Some argued that Israel should retain the territories occupied in 1967 and establish settlements there. The Peace Movement, which was composed of a number of small groups on the left, took time to become established, in part because the official position preempted the Movement's main arguments by making overtures to the Arab states that indicated Israel was prepared to return territory for peace and to be magnanimous in victory. When it became clear that Israel's insistence on direct negotiations for peace was unsuccessful and when the Government began to show an interest in establishing settlements and retaining territories, the Peace Movement was energized and became more prominent. It argued that the failure of the peace process could be attributed in large measure to the Government of Israel for not taking greater initiatives. *See also* PEACE NOW.

For further information see: Myron J. Aronoff and Pierre M. Atlas, "The Peace Process and Competing Challenges to the Dominant Zionist Discourse," in *The Middle East Peace Process: Interdisciplinary Perspectives*, edited by Ilan Peleg (Albany: State University of New York Press, 1998): 41-60; Myron J. Aronoff and Yael S. Aronoff, "Domestic Determinants of Israeli Foreign Policy: The Peace Process from the Declaration of Principles to the Oslo II Interim Agreements," in *The Middle East and the Peace Process: The Impact of the Oslo Accords*, edited by Robert O. Freedman (Gainesville: University Press of Florida, 1998): 11-34; Mordechai Bar-On, *In Pursuit of Peace: A History of the Israeli Peace Movement* (Washington, DC: The United States Institute of Peace, 1996); Rael Jean Isaac, *Israel Divided: Ideological Politics in the Jewish State* (Baltimore: Johns Hopkins, 1976); Yael Yishai, *Land of Paradoxes: Interest Politics in Israel* (Albany: State University of New York Press, 1991).

PEACE NOW (SHALOM ACHSHAV). An interest group established in the spring of 1978 when reserve army officers wrote to Prime Minister Menachem Begin* urging him to pursue peace vigorously. It has worked to keep the subject on the public agenda with rallies and demonstrations. Among its positions is the view that there should be territorial compromise and Israel should relinquish some of the occupied territories*. It was prominent in protests against the War in Lebanon* and the Sabra and Shatila* camp massacres.

For further information see: Mordechai Bar-On, *In Pursuit of Peace: A History of the Israeli Peace Movement* (Washington, DC: The United States Institute of Peace, 1996).

PEEL COMMISSION. A British Royal Commission, chaired by Lord Robert Peel, appointed in 1936 to investigate the cause of Arab unrest in Palestine*. After much consultation it recommended partition of the Palestine Mandate* into an Arab state united with Transjordan, and a Jewish state, while retaining a British enclave that included Jerusalem*. The partition idea generated heated debate among the leadership of he Yishuv*. Many Zionists viewed it as a reversal of British commitments to Zionism undertaken in the Balfour Declaration* and a step away from the goal of achieving a Jewish National Home in all of Palestine. At the end of the day, the Zionists accepted partition as a practical step toward independent statehood in at least part of Palestine, even though they were unhappy with the exclusion of Jerusalem* and the small amount of territory allotted to the Jewish state. For their part, the Arabs adamantly rejected partition and reacted to the idea by launching a new, more violent phase of the Arab Revolt. Confronted with Arab opposition, along with the disapproval of the Permanent Mandate Commission of the League of Nations*, Great Britain ultimately dropped the partition idea. Two years later, in 1939, it issued a new White Paper* which sought to appease Arab rioters by dramatically restricting Jewish immigration to Palestine. *See also* BRITISH MANDATE FOR PALESTINE.

For further information see: Nancy Hasanian and Mark Daryl Erickson, "Peel Commission," in *An Historical Encyclopedia of the Arab-Israeli Conflict*, edited by Bernard Reich (Westport, CT: Greenwood Press, 1996): 406-408.

PELED, MATITYAHU. Born in Jerusalem* in January 1923, he joined the Palmah* in 1941. Following independence he helped found the IDF* Staff and Command College. He was among the first high-ranking officers, immediately after the 1967 Six Day War*, to call upon Israel to help the Palestinians create their own state in much of the West Bank* and Gaza Strip*. Retiring from the IDF in 1975 at the rank of Brigadier General, he became one of the first prominent Israelis to advocate direct negotiations with the PLO*. He held secret meetings with PLO representatives and helped found the Israel Council for Israeli-Palestinian Peace. In 1984 he (along with the Israeli journalist and political activist Uri Avneri and the Israeli Arab lawyer Muhammad Miari) helped found the Progressive List for Peace* and was elected to the Knesset* on the PLP slate. He was one of the founders of the Israeli peace movement Gush Shalom. He also advocated on behalf of Israeli soldiers who refused to serve in the West Bank and Gaza during the intifada*. He died in March 1995.

PERES, SHIMON (FORMERLY PERSKY). Born on August 16, 1923, in the town of Vishneva, Poland, to Isaac and Sarah Persky. Because of British restrictions and the financial burdens associated with immigration, Isaac Persky emigrated to Palestine* in 1931, leaving his wife and two sons behind. The family was reunited in Palestine in 1934. Shimon Peres became involved in the largest of the Zionist movements, Hashomer Hatzair* (Young Guard), and later joined Hanoar Haoved (Working Youth). By 1941 Peres was a leader in the kibbutz* movement in Palestine and he continued his efforts within Hanoar Haoved. In 1942 he joined Kibbutz Alumot and he remained a member until 1957. Peres's military career began in the Hagana*. He rose to the rank of commander by his late teens, and in 1947 he accepted Levi Eshkol's* offer to serve as Director of Manpower and in that capacity was active in the procurement and manufacture of arms for the Israel Defense Forces (IDF)*. His successful efforts to develop and acquire arms both at home and abroad gained him recognition as one of the pioneers of Israel's defense industry. After Israel's War of Independence* in 1949, Peres asked Prime Minister David Ben-Gurion* for a leave of absence to study abroad. Ben-Gurion granted the leave provided Peres continue his arms acquisition efforts in the United States* where he chose to study at Harvard University and New York University. He returned to Israel and in February 1952 was appointed to serve as Deputy Director-General of the Defense Ministry. In October 1952 he became Acting Director-General of the Defense Ministry. As Director-General of the Defense Ministry Peres continued his efforts to acquire high-quality weapons for the IDF. Peres spent much of his time fostering Franco-Israeli relations and France* remained Israel's primary supplier of major weapons systems until after the Six Day War* of 1967. Peres's efforts included gaining French consent to provide Israel with an atomic reactor located at Dimona*. Peres was instrumental in the creation of

Bedek, which later came to be known as the Israel Aircraft Industries (IAI)*.

Peres's Knesset* career began in 1959 when he was elected to parliament as a member of the Mapai* Party although he continued to serve as Deputy Minister of Defense. Peres was included in Ben-Gurion's cabinet which gave him a larger role in policy debates. In 1963 Ben-Gurion resigned and was replaced by Levi Eshkol* as Prime Minister and Minister of Defense. Ben-Gurion's retirement from politics lasted only two years before he returned to the political arena in June 1965 as the leader of a new political party called Rafi*. Peres resigned his position in the Government to join Ben-Gurion and become Secretary General of the new party. He managed the party's campaign efforts in the 1965 election in which it won 10 seats. But the new Government did not include Rafi or any of its members. In 1968, Rafi joined with Mapai and Ahdut Haavoda* to form the Israel Labor Party*. Between 1969 and 1973 Peres held a variety of cabinet posts, including Minister of Absorption, Minister of Transport, Minister of Information, Minister of Communications, and Minister without Portfolio with responsibility for economic development in the occupied territories.

In April 1974 Golda Meir* submitted her resignation as Prime Minister. The two candidates to succeed her were Peres, who was serving as Minister of Information, and Yitzhak Rabin*, Minister of Labor. Rabin, who was the preferred choice of the party establishment, won a close vote over Peres in the Labor Party's central committee. However, Peres's performance established him as the number two man in the party. The new Government was established in June 1974 with Rabin as Prime Minister and Peres as Minister of Defense. Relations between Peres and Rabin were strained during the term of the Government. Disputes arose over domestic and foreign policy, the selection of personnel, and the scope of their authority.

Peres formally announced his intention to challenge Rabin for the party leadership in January 1977. The showdown took place at the Labor Party convention the following month where Rabin prevailed by a slim majority. However, a series of scandal, including the disclosure that Rabin's wife maintained bank accounts in the United States in violation of Israeli currency laws, led Rabin to resign from the chairmanship of the Labor Party in April 1977, just one month prior to the Knesset elections.

Peres became the party's new leader and candidate for the premiership. Despite Peres's efforts, Likud* won a plurality of Knesset seats and succeeded in forming the Government headed by Menachem Begin*. In June 1977 Peres was elected Labor Party Chairman. The 1981 election was Peres's second loss to Begin. In the 1984 election Labor secured 44 seats to Likud's 41, and although he received the mandate to form the Government Peres was unable to form a majority coalition. This led to the formation of a National Unity Government (NUG)*, which was a new experiment in Israeli politics. A rotation* agreement was adopted which called for Peres to serve as Prime Minister for the first half of the 50-month term while the Likud's Yitzhak Shamir* served as Foreign Minister. After 25 months the two rotated positions for the balance of the term. During his tenure as Prime Minister, Peres presided over Israel's withdrawal from Lebanon* and confronted the economic problems with austerity measures. Peres also actively sought to establish diplomatic contacts with Arab leaders such as King Hassan II of Morocco and King Hussein* of Jordan*, and tried to improve relations with the United States* that had been strained under Begin and Shamir. The 1988 Knesset election, as in 1984, did not produce a clear victory for either Labor or Likud. Shamir was given the mandate to form a coalition by President Chaim Herzog*. Shamir chose to form a second National Unity Government coalition with Labor. The central difference between the 1988 coalition agreement and the 1984 agreement was that Shamir would serve as Prime Minister for the duration of the Government. Peres accepted the position of Finance Minister. Peres and the other Labor Party ministers left the Government in the spring of 1990 and forced a vote of confidence in the Knesset which the Shamir-led Government lost. Peres subsequently sought to form a narrow coalition during the spring of 1990, but was unsuccessful. In June 1990 Shamir was able to form a Government which gained the confidence of the Knesset. Peres reverted to the role of leader of the opposition in the Knesset.

After several tries Yitzhak Rabin finally succeeded in ousting Peres as Labor Party Chairman in early 1992 and he led his party to victory in the elections to the 13th Knesset. Peres served as Foreign Minister in the new governing coalition. To the surprise of many, Peres and Rabin achieved a modus vivendi and together they set Israel on a new course that resulted in a series of interim agreements with the PLO*, the 1994 Peace Treaty with Jordan, and the opening of commercial relations and substantive diplomatic discussions with a number of other Arab countries, including

Syria*. For his efforts Peres received the 1994 Nobel Peace Prize* (an award that he shared with Rabin and the PLO's Yasser Arafat*). Peres actively promoted the vision of "a new Middle East", one premised on the completion of formal peace agreements and the full political, social, and economic integration of Israel into the Middle East. He became Interim Prime Minister and Defense Minister following the November 1995 assassination of Yitzhak Rabin. Seeking a mandate of his own he opted for early elections in the spring of 1996. However, by less than 1% of the popular vote he lost the direct election of the Prime Minister to the Likud's Benjamin Netanyahu*. Peres subsequently relinquished the chairmanship of the Labor Party and he was succeeded by Ehud Barak*. He remained active both in Labor Party politics and in advocating for peace. He established an institute bearing his name that is dedicated to promoting economic cooperation between Israelis and Palestinians. Peres was accorded the second slot on the One Israel* electoral slate for the May 17, 1999, elections to the 15th Knesset. As the longest-serving member of the Knesset, he was appointed interim Speaker of the 15th Knesset following the elections, a position he held until the election of the new speaker, One Israel* MK Avraham Burg*, on July 6, 1999. Peres was named to a new cabinet portfolio, that of Regional Cooperation Minister, in the coalition formed by Ehud Barak.

For further information see: Matti Golan, *Shimon Peres: A Biography*, translated by Ina Friedman (New York: St. Martin's, 1982); Giora Goldberg, "The Electoral Fall of the Israeli Left," *Israel Affairs* (Special Issue: "Israel at the Polls 1996") 4:1 (Autumn 1997): 53-72; Jacob Heilbrunn, "Shimon Peres's Neighborhood," *New Republic* (July 10, 1995): 14-18; Joseph Helman, "Shimon Peres," in *Political Leaders of the Contemporary Middle East and North Africa*, edited by Bernard Reich (Westport, CT: Greenwood, 1990): 403-412; Avishai Margalit, "The Chances of Shimon Peres," *New York Review of Books*, April 11, 1996; Shimon Peres, *David's Sling: The Arming of Israel* (New York: Random House, 1970); Shimon Peres, *From Those Men: Seven Founders of the State of Israel*, translated by Philip Simpson (New York: Wyndham, 1979); Shimon Peres (with Arye Naor), *The New Middle East* (New York: Henry Holt, 1993); Shimon Peres, *Battling for Peace: A Memoir from Israel's Birth to Today's Struggle for Peace in the Middle East*, edited by David Landau (New York: Random House, 1995); Shimon Peres, "The Middle East in a New Era," *Mediterranean Quarterly* 2 (Fall 1991): 1-14; "Shimon Peres: The Unloved Visionary," *The Jerusalem Report*

(December 15, 1994): 11-17; Michal Yaniv, "Peres the Leader, Peres the Politician," in *The Elections in Israel 1996*, edited by Asher Arian and Michal Shamir (Albany: SUNY Press, 1999): 211-239; "Farewell to the Last of the Young Men," *Ha'aretz*, June 3, 1997; "New Peres Center to Focus upon Economic Projects," *Jerusalem Post*, September 23, 1997; "Peres Steals Labor Convention Limelight by Backing Palestinian Statehood," *Jerusalem Post*, December 8, 1997; "Peres's New Plans," *Ha'aretz*, January 8, 1998.

PERETZ, AMIR. Born in Morocco in 1952, he immigrated to Israel in 1956. Peretz was elected to the Knesset* in 1988 on the Labor* party list, and reelected in 1996. He was elected Chairman of the Histadrut* in 1995 and reelected in June 1998. Peretz established the break-away One Nation (Am Echad)* workers' party that won two seats in the 15th Knesset in elections held on May 17, 1999.

PERETZ, YITZHAK HAIM. Born in 1939 in Morocco, Peretz served as Chief Rabbi of Raanana. Elected to the Knesset* on the Shas* list, he served in the Government of National Unity* established in 1984 as a Minister without Portfolio (until December 1984); as Minister of the Interior (from December 1984 to January 1987); and as Minister without Portfolio (from May 1987 to December 1988). He became Minister of Immigration and Absorption in the Government formed in December 1988 and retained that position in the Government established in June 1990.

PERMANENT STATUS TALKS *see* FINAL STATUS TALKS

PETAH TIKVA. A city on the coastal plain of Israel northeast of Tel Aviv*. It was founded in 1878 as an agricultural settlement and developed into the first modern Jewish moshava* (private village) in the country and became known as the "mother of moshavot". It has become a growing and thriving city.

PLO *see* PALESTINE LIBERATION ORGANIZATION

PNINA ROSENBLUM *see* ROSENBLUM, PNINA

POALEI AGUDAT ISRAEL (WORKERS OF THE ASSOCIATION OF ISRAEL). A religious labor movement dedicated to building the Land of Israel in the spirit of the Torah. Founded in 1922 in Poland to counteract the growth of secularism, socialism, and antireligious tendencies among Jewish workers, this organization was the labor wing of Agudat Israel*. Within Agudat Israel, it fought for the development of the land and the building of a Jewish state in the spirit of the Torah and tradition. In the late 1920s the first Poalei Agudat Israel pioneers arrived in Palestine*. In 1933 they founded Kibbutz Hafetz Hayim. In 1946, the World Union of Poalei Agudat Israel was founded . Its members joined the Hagana* to fight the Arab invasion in 1948 and it joined the trade union department of the Histadrut* under a special arrangement. In 1960 it officially split from Agudat Israel and became independent. It joined with a splinter group from the National Religious Party* to form Morasha* to contest the 1984 Knesset* election.

POALEI ZION. Literally "workers of Zion." A Zionist socialist workers' party which began in Russia*, Austria, and the United States* in the late nineteenth and early twentieth centuries. Influenced by the writings of the socialist Zionist theoretician, Dov Ber Borochov, Poalei Zion's platform was based on Marxist principles developed along nationalist lines. The party's worldwide movement was continually involved in arguments on such fundamental issues as cooperative settlement activity in Eretz Israel* initiated by the labor class; membership in the Zionist* movement (which included members of the bourgeoisie); and the party's relationship to the Communist International.

POGROMS. Organized, state-sanctioned acts of violent anti-Semitism* in nineteenth-century Eastern Europe that contributed to the evolution of modern political Zionism* and Jewish immigration to Palestine.

"POLITICIDE." A term developed to describe the destruction of a state, that is, the Arab goal of destroying Israel. Between 1949 and 1967 Israel was prepared for peace with the Arab states on the basis of the 1949 armistice* lines with minor modifications. After the events of May and June 1967, including the Six Day War*, the stark reality of "politicide" began to enter into these considerations, and many argued for a need to change the security situation. Opposition among many Israelis to territorial concessions in the West Bank*, Gaza Strip* and Golan Heights* is fueled by continuing concerns that the Arab countries will use these territories as military bases for achieving their ultimate goal of destroying Israel.

For further information see: Yehoshafat Harkabi, *Arab Strategies and Israel's Response* (New York: The Free Press, 1971); Yehoshafat Harkabi, *Fedayeen Action and Arab Strategy*, Adelphi Papers, No. 53 (London: Institute for Strategic Studies, 1968); Yehoshafat Harkabi, *Palestinians and Israel* (Jerusalem: Keter, 1974); Yehoshafat Harkabi, *Arab Attitudes to Israel* (London: Valentine, Mitchell; New York: Hart, 1967).

POLLARD, JONATHAN JAY. A United States* Navy civilian intelligence analyst who was arrested in November 1985 outside the gates of the Israeli Embassy in Washington, DC, and charged with passing confidential information to Israel. His wife, Anne Henderson Pollard, also was arrested. He was reportedly trying to seek refuge there but was denied admittance by Embassy officials who apparently did not know who he was. Israeli officials denied that he was working for them, suggesting that he might have been operating on his own. He pleaded guilty in June 1986, claiming that the information he passed to Israel was vital to its security and was being deliberately withheld by the United States. He was sentenced to life in prison. His wife received a five-year sentence and was released in early 1989. Senior Israeli officials and representatives of American Jewish organizations charged that he was being subjected to excessive and unfair treatment compared to the sentences given to Americans convicted of spying for the Soviet Union at the height of the Cold War.

Under heavy pressure from Israel and supporters of Mr. Pollard in the United States, President Bill Clinton reviewed the case in 1993 and again in 1996. Each time, he decided against clemency after receiving recommendations from cabinet officials and agencies involved in the case.

On November 21, 1995, Interior Minister Ehud Barak* decided to grant Israeli citizenship to Jonathan Pollard. On May 12, 1998, the Government of Israel formally acknowledged that Pollard had served as an Israeli agent handled by senior members of the Scientific Liaison Bureau (Lakam). Despite speculation that this admission was the first step on the road to Pollard's ultimate release, he remained in an American prison.

Israeli Prime Minister Benjamin Netanyahu* asked President Clinton to grant clemency to Pollard during the Wye River* peace talks in October

1998, and the President said he would review the Pollard case. Those supporting clemency argue that Pollard has served long enough, that he spied for a friendly nation, not an enemy, that his release will help the peace process, and that the United States reneged on the plea bargain agreement. Those who oppose clemency argue that Pollard's spying exposed U.S. intelligence methods and personnel, that the Pollard case is not related to the peace process, that who he spied for is irrelevant, and that the judges' sentence was justified by the magnitude of the crime.

For further information see: Wolf Blitzer, *Territory of Lies: The Exclusive Story of Jonathan Jay Pollard: The American Who Spied on His Country for Israel and How He Was Betrayed* (New York: Harper and Row, 1989).

PORUSH, MENACHEM. An ordained rabbi. Born in Jerusalem* on April 2, 1916, he was educated at religious schools. He served as a correspondent for foreign newspapers from 1932 to 1938 and as an editor for *Kol Israel** from 1936 to 1949. He was first elected to the Knesset* as a member for Agudat Israel* in 1959. He served as Vice Mayor of Jerusalem from 1969 to 1974. He served as Deputy Minister of Labor and Social Affairs in the National Unity Government* established in 1984. He was reelected to the Knesset in 1988 and 1992.

POWER FOR PENSIONERS. An issue-specific party led by Gideon Ben-Yisrael, head of the Pensioners Association, to run in the May 17, 1999, Knesset* elections. The party is in favor of a national pension law and social welfare policy. Members advocate increased state funding for nursing homes. The party did not win a seat in the election.

PRESIDENT (NASI). Nasi in Hebrew means "prince" or, now, President. The title Nasi is derived from the head of the Sanhedrin, the assembly of Jewish scholars which served as both a legislature and supreme court until the fifth century. The President is elected by a simple majority of the Knesset* for a five-year term and may be elected for no more than two consecutive terms. He is Head of State and has powers that are essentially representative in character. In the sphere of foreign affairs these functions include signing instruments that relate to treaties ratified by the Knesset; appointing diplomatic and consular representatives; receiving foreign diplomatic representatives; and issuing consular exequaturs (official written accreditations). In the domestic sphere, the President has the power to grant pardons and reprieves and to commute sentences. Subsequent to nomination by the appropriate body, the Head of State appoints civil judges; *dayanim* (judges of the Jewish religious courts); *kadis* (judges of Muslim religious courts); the state comptroller*, the president of the Magen David Adom Association*; and the Governor of the Bank of Israel*, as well as other officials as determined by law. The President signs all laws passed by the Knesset, with the exception of those relating to presidential powers, and all documents to which the state seal is affixed. Official documents signed by the President require the countersignature of the Prime Minister or other duly authorized minister, with the exception of those where another procedure is laid down, as in the case of judges.

The President's powers and functions relating to the formation of the Government fall into a different category. Historically, after elections or the resignation or death of the Prime Minister, the President consulted with representatives of the parties in the Knesset and selected a member of the Knesset to form a Government. This responsibility was particularly germane in the aftermath of the close elections of 1984 and 1988. The President's functions in the formation of Governments were restricted with the direct election of the Prime Minister and other aspects of the revised Basic Law: The Government (1992)*. However, the President may still formally receive the resignation of the Government. Another aspect of the presidential role that could have potential political significance in the future is the office's public position and prestige potential—the President makes visits throughout the country, delivers speeches, and formally opens the first session of each Knesset. Though the president's legal authority is largely ceremonial in nature, the President's power to speak out on social and political issues can have significant impact on public opinion.

Since statehood Israel has had seven Presidents: Chaim Weizmann* (1948-1952), Yitzhak Ben-Zvi* (1952-1963), Shneor Zalman Shazar* (1963-1973), Ephraim Katzir* (1973-1978), Yitzhak Navon* (1978-1983), Chaim Herzog* (1983-1993), and Ezer Weizman* (since 1993). In the spring of 1998 Ezer Weizman was elected by the Knesset to serve a second five year term as President of Israel. According to preliminary legislation adopted by the Knesset in late December 1998, future presidents of Israel will serve for one seven-year term.

PRIME MINISTER The Prime Minister is Israel's head of Government. From 1948 to 1996 the President* was empowered to designate a member of Knesset*, almost always the leader of the party holding the most seats, to serve as Prime Minister and to form a Government. Pursuant to the revised Basic Law: The Government (1992), the Prime Minister is now chosen through direct popular election. The Prime Minister must be a citizen of Israel of at least 30 years of age and a member of the Knesset. The Prime Minister-elect has 45 days within which to form a Government and present that Government and its guiding principles to the Knesset for a vote of confidence. If within that period a Government cannot be formed, a brief extension may be granted, after which time new elections for both the Prime Minister and Knesset must be held. As the only directly elected politician in Israel, the Prime Minister's power and influence is significant. He or she is empowered to form a Cabinet and dominates the process in which the Government's program of action is formulated and implemented. However, while significant, the powers of the Prime Minister are not all-encompassing. According to the new Basic Law: The Government, the Prime Minister may be ousted from office if he loses the confidence of 80 members of the Knesset. Moreover, the Prime Minister is constrained by the need to accommodate the competing interests of the various parties that usually are involved in forming governing coalitions in Israel. Unlike any other political institution in Israel, the office of the Prime Minister has been shaped by the men or women who have occupied it. Since independence, Israel has had 10 Prime Ministers: David Ben-Gurion* (1948-1954 and 1955), Moshe Sharett* (1954-1955), Levi Eshkol* (1963-1969), Golda Meir* (1969-1974), Yitzhak Rabin* (1974-1977 and 1992-1995), Menachem Begin* (1977-1983), Yitzhak Shamir* (1983-1984 and 1986-1992), Shimon Peres* (1984-1986 and 1995-1996), Benjamin Netanyahu* (1996-1999), and Ehud Barak* (1999-). Having held the office for most of the country's turbulent early years, as well as his dominance of the political institutions of the pre-state Yishuv*, David Ben-Gurion established the standard of strong and decisive leadership against which all subsequent Israeli Prime Ministers have tended to be measured.

"PRINCES OF THE PARTY." The name applied to generally well-educated, politically sophisticated and financially secure Likud* activists whose fathers (or mothers) had been prominent in Revisionism*, Herut*, or Irgun*. Among those fitting this description were Ze'ev Binyamin

Begin*, Tzachi Hanegbi*, Uri Landau, Limor Livnat, Dan Meridor*, Ronnie Milo*, Benjamin Netanyahu*, and Ehud Olmert*.

PRISONERS OF ZION. The name applied to Jews who were persecuted and often imprisoned or subjected to internal exile by the USSR* for studying Hebrew*, practicing Judaism, or requesting to emigrate to Israel.

PROGRESSIVE CENTER PARTY. Romanian immigrants party created to run in the May 17, 1999, elections. Led by Adrian Ionovici, he feels that Romanian immigrants had always supported Labor without being given positions on its lists, or ministerial positions. He would like to see the Romanian immigrants begin to receive a place in the Government as the Russian immigrants already have. The party did not receive enough votes to secure a Knesset seat.

PROGRESSIVE LIST FOR PEACE (PLP). A mixed Arab-Jewish political party established in 1984 by Israeli Arab lawyer Muhammad Miari from Haifa* and two prominent Jewish leftists, Matityahu Peled* and Uri Avneri, but supported primarily by Israeli Arabs*. The party held its first convention in August 1985. In 1992 the party ran on a platform that advocated full equality for Jewish and Arab citizens (within the state's pre-1967 boundaries); recognized the right of both Jewish Israelis and Palestinians to national self-determination; formally recognized the PLO*; and advocated total Israeli withdrawal from the West Bank* and Gaza Strip* as well as from East Jerusalem* and the establishment in those areas of an independent Palestinian state. In 1988 there was an appeal to the Central Elections Committee to have the PLP disqualified on the grounds that its policy platform was contrary to the security interests of the state. This appeal was rejected and the PLP won one seat in the 12th Knesset*. It failed to cross the threshold of 1.5% of the popular vote in the 1992 elections, and its supporters drifted to other Arab or non-Zionist Arab-Jewish parties.

PROGRESSIVE PARTY (HAMIFLAGA HAPROGRESSIVIT). A political party established in October 1948 by combining Haoved Hazioni, Aliya Hadasha, and the left wing of the General Zionists*. Its focus was on domestic social and related issues. Pinhas Rosen represented the party in Government coalitions and served as Minister of Justice. In April 1961 the Progressive Party united with the General Zionist Party to form the Liberal Party*. In 1965 the former General Zionists decided to establish a parliamentary bloc with the Herut Party*. The former Progressives opposed this move and many split from the Liberal Party to establish the Independent Liberal Party*.

Q

QIBYA *see* KIBYA

QWARA JEWS *see* KWARA JEWS

R

RABBINATE (CHIEF) OF ISRAEL. The origins of the institution of the Chief Rabbinate of Israel date back to when Palestine* was part of the Ottoman Empire. According to Ottoman regulations, the Sultan would appoint one eminent Turkish rabbi as Chief Rabbi of the Jews of the Ottoman Empire, which included Palestine. Residing in Constantinople and bearing the title *Hakham (Haham) Bashi* (literally, "Chief Sage"), he was the official spokesman of the Jewish community to the authorities, and by *firman* (the Sultan's command) he exercised broad authority over all the religious activities and spiritual concerns of members of the Jewish community throughout the Ottoman Empire. The *Hakham Bashi* of Jerusalem* had the title *Rishon Le-Zion* (First in Zion). The *Rishon Le-Zion* gradually came to assume authority over all the religious affairs of the Jews of Palestine. The post of *Hakham Bashi* was always held by a rabbi of the Sephardi* community in Jerusalem, which originally constituted the majority of the Yishuv*.

Sir Herbert Samuel*, the first High Commissioner for Palestine under the British Mandate*, appointed a commission headed by Norman Bentwich, then Legal Secretary of the Mandatory Government, which recommended the establishment of an electoral college of 100 members to choose two Chief Rabbis and a Council of the Chief Rabbinate*. In 1921 the electoral college met in Jerusalem and it elected Avraham Yitzhak Hacohen Kook* and Yaakov Meir as Chief Rabbis and presidents of the Council of the Chief Rabbinate of Palestine. The Mandatory Government accepted the newly organized Chief Rabbinate of Palestine as exercising sole jurisdiction in matters of personal status. The office of Hakham Bashi was abolished, and the judgments of the Rabbinate were enforced by the civil courts. On January 12, 1936, new elections were held and Rabbi Yitzhak Halevi Herzog* was chosen Ashkenazi Chief Rabbi and Rabbi Meir was reelected Sephardi Chief Rabbi. As Rabbi Meir was ill, Rabbi Ben-Zion Meir Hay Uziel was elected his acting representative. In 1945 Chief Rabbis Herzog and Uziel were reelected.

After the independence of Israel, the first elections for the Council of the Chief Rabbinate were held in March 1955. Chief Rabbi Herzog was reelected and Rabbi Yitzhak Rahamim Nissim was chosen to replace Rabbi Uziel, who had died in 1953. Ashkenazi Chief Rabbis have included Avraham Yitzhak Kook, Yitzhak Halevi Herzog, Issar Yehuda Unterman, Shlomo Goren, Avraham Elkana Kahana-Shapiro, and Yisrael Lau (1993-). Sephardi Chief Rabbis have included Ya'akov Meir, Ben-Zion Meir Hai Uziel, Yitzhak Rahamim Nissim, Ovadia Yosef, Mordechai Eliyahu, and Eliyahu Bakshi-Doron (1993-).

RABIN, LEAH. The wife of Yitzhak Rabin* who began to emerge in her own right after Rabin's assassination in November 1995. She directly linked Likud* and Netanyahu* with the assassination and accused the right wing of fostering a bitter political climate from which the assassination sprang. Prior to the murder she basically played a social role and was involved in charitable activities, but not engaged directly in politics. Her autobiography is entitled *Rabin: Our Life, His Legacy* (New York: Putnam's, 1997).

RABIN, YITZHAK. Born in Jerusalem* on March 1, 1922, to Russian immigrants to Palestine*. He entered the prestigious Kadourie Agricultural School in the Galilee* in 1937 and, after graduation in 1940, he moved to Kibbutz Ramat Yohanan. He joined the Hagana* in May 1941 and subsequently served in the Palmah*. Later, he was arrested in a massive sweep by British Mandatory* authorities and he spent a brief period in a British prison. In October 1947, he was appointed Deputy Commander of the Palmah. A month before Israel declared its independence on May 14, 1948, he was put in charge of the Palmah's

Harel Brigade and was assigned the task of eliminating Arab strongholds along the Tel Aviv*-Jerusalem road.

Rabin's military career included a variety of positions in the Israel Defense Forces* during Israel's formative years, including head of the army's tactical operations division from 1950 to 1952, head of the training branch from 1954 to 1956, and Commanding Officer of the northern command from 1956 to 1959. He was then appointed Army Chief of Operations and came into conflict with then Deputy Defense Minister Shimon Peres* over the question of who should determine the priorities in the acquisition and manufacture of arms. Rabin believed that the decision should be made by professional soldiers rather than by civilians in the Defense Ministry. The political rivalry with Peres developed into a bitter personal feud. Rabin was appointed Chief of Staff of the IDF in January 1964 and during his tenure focused on the restructuring of the army and on acquiring more advanced weaponry. In the Six Day War* Rabin's army won a decisive victory over its Arab adversaries in six days, radically transforming the situation in the Middle East. In February 1968 he became Israel's Ambassador to the United States* and, in March 1973, he returned to Israel.

After the Knesset* election of December 1973 Rabin was invited by Golda Meir* to join the new cabinet as Defense Minister because of Moshe Dayan's* refusal to serve in the new Government. When Dayan suddenly announced his willingness to join, Rabin became Minister of Labor. But, Meir resigned following publication of the Agranat Commission's* interim report. On April 22, 1974, Rabin was chosen by the Labor Party* central committee to succeed Meir as Prime Minister, whereas Shimon Peres's strong showing in the vote earned him the post of Defense Minister, from which he tried to undermine Rabin's authority at almost every turn in the hope of replacing him. Rabin served as Prime Minister from June 1974 to May 1977 during which time he concentrated on rebuilding the IDF to which the successful raid at Entebbe* airport contributed by restoring the army's and nation's self-confidence. He also successfully negotiated a second disengagement of forces agreement with Egypt* brokered by the United States. Rabin's term as Prime Minister ended prematurely in 1977 after a cabinet dispute led to the scheduling of early elections. A month before the election, Rabin was forced to step down after admitting that his wife had maintained an illegal bank account in the United States. Peres was designated to head the Labor Party list in the election, but Labor was defeated at the polls. For the next four years, Rabin found himself in Peres's political shadow and the relationship between the two was highly contentious. Rabin challenged Peres for the party's leadership at its national convention in December 1980 but lost. In 1984, Rabin became Minister of Defense in the National Unity Government* that was formed following the July 1984 election and remained in that position under both Peres and Yitzhak Shamir*. He once again became Minister of Defense in the Government established in December 1988. As Defense Minister in the early phases of the intifada*, he was responsible for quelling the demonstrations and restoring order. He left the Government with the other Labor ministers in the spring of 1990. Rabin failed in his challenge to Shimon Peres in the summer of 1990 for the leadership of the party.

In early 1992 Rabin finally succeeded in ousting Peres as Labor Party Chairman. Exploiting his reputation as "Mr. Security," Rabin led his party to victory in the election to the 13th Knesset. In the new Government he served as both Prime Minister and Defense Minister and appointed Peres as Foreign Minister. Though skeptical about dealing with the PLO*, Rabin approved transforming the secret private discussions in Oslo between Israelis and Palestinians into formal negotiations culminating with the Israeli-PLO Declaration of Principles*. Unlike his contacts with the PLO's Yasser Arafat*, which remained cool and formal, Rabin's relationship with Jordan's* King Hussein* was warm and personal. During his tenure important progress was also reported in achieving commercial and/or diplomatic contacts with Arab countries, including Syria*. In 1994 Rabin received the Nobel Peace Prize*, along with Peres and Arafat. On November 4, 1995, at the conclusion of a mass peace rally in Tel Aviv*, Rabin was assassinated by Yigal Amir*. The social and political implications of his murder continue to be felt in Israel and throughout the Middle East.

For further information see: Hemda Ben-Yehuda, "Attitude Change and Policy Transformation: Yitzhak Rabin and the Palestinian Question, 1967-95," *Israel Affairs* 3:3/4 (Spring/Summer 1997): 201-224; David Horovitz, editor, *Yitzhak Rabin: Soldier of Peace* (London: Peter Halban, 1996); Efraim Inbar, *War and Peace in Israeli Politics: Labor Party Positions on National Security* (Boulder, CO: Lynne Rienner, 1991); Efraim Inbar, "Labor's Return to Power," in *Israel at the Polls 1992*, edited by Daniel J. Elazar and Shmuel Sandler (Lanham, MD: Rowman and Littlefield, 1995): 27-43; Efraim Inbar, "Yitzhak Rabin and Israeli National Security," Begin-Sadat Center for Strategic Studies Study and Policy Studies, No. 25 (Ramat Gan: Bar Ilan University, January 1996); Gershon R. Kieval, "The Foreign Policy of the Labor Party," in *Israeli National Security Policy: Political Actors and Perspectives*, edited by Bernard Reich and Gershon R. Kieval (New York: Greenwood, 1988): 19-54; Gershon R. Kieval, "Yitzhak Rabin," in *Political Leaders of the Contemporary Middle East and North Africa*, edited by Bernard Reich (Westport, CT: Greenwood, 1990): 441-448; Dan Kurzman, *Soldier of Peace: The Life of Yitzhak Rabin, 1922-1995* (New York: HarperCollins, 1998); David Makovsky, *Making Peace with the PLO: The Rabin Government's Road to the Oslo Accord* (Washington, DC: Washington Institute for Near East Policy; Boulder, CO: Westview, 1996); Leah Rabin, *Rabin: Our Life, His Legacy* (New York: Putnam's, 1997); Yitzhak Rabin, *The Rabin Memoirs* (Boston: Little, Brown, 1979); Yitzhak Rabin, "In the Aftermath of the War in Lebanon: Israel's Objectives," in *Israel's Lebanon Policy: Where To?* edited by Joseph Alpher (Tel Aviv: Jaffee Center for Strategic Studies, August 1984); Robert Slater, *Rabin of Israel: A Biography*, Revised Edition (London: Robson Books, 1993).

RABIN-PELOSOFF, DALIA. Born March 19, 1950, in Israel, Dalia Rabin Pelosoff is the daughter of the late Prime Minister Yitzhak Rabin*. A lawyer and former legal advisor for the Histadrut, she joined the Center Party* for the May 1999 elections and secured a Knesset* seat. She is also the Chairperson of the Administrative Committee for the Yitzhak Rabin Center for Israel Studies.

RABINOVICH, ITAMAR. Born in Jerusalem* in 1942, he was educated at the Hebrew University of Jerusalem*, Tel Aviv University, and University of California, Los Angeles. Professor of Middle East history at Tel Aviv University and founding member of the Shiloah Institute and the Moshe Dayan Center for Middle Eastern and African Studies, Rabinovich was named Israel's Ambassador to the United States* (1992-1996) and chief negotiator in this period in talks with Syria* sponsored by the United States. In his book, *The Brink of Peace: The Israeli-Syrian Negotiations and the Israeli-Arab Peace Process* (Princeton, NJ: Princeton University Press, 1998) he described the progress achieved by Israeli and Syrian negotiators toward an agreement affecting the Golan Heights* in the months preceding the assassination of Prime Minister

Yitzhak Rabin*, as well as the failure of Syrian President Hafez Assad to continue the negotiations when offered the same terms by Rabin's successor, Shimon Peres*. Rabinovich became president of Tel Aviv University in May 1999.

RABINOWITZ, YEHOSHUA. Born in Poland on November 13, 1911, he immigrated to Palestine* in 1934 and joined Mapai* in the mid-1950s. He was elected to the Tel Aviv* city council in 1956, became Deputy Mayor in 1959, and Mayor of Tel Aviv-Jaffa in 1969. He was defeated for reelection in 1973. He became Finance Minister in the Government established by Yitzhak Rabin* in 1974 and remained in office until 1977.

RACHEL, TOMB OF. The Bible relates that Rachel, one of the matriarchs of the Jewish people, was buried on the way to Bethlehem and a site near that city has been regarded as that spot since ancient times. It has been a place of Jewish pilgrimage.

RAFAEL, GIDEON. Born in Berlin in 1913, he left Germany after Hitler's rise to power and immigrated to Palestine* in 1934. In 1940 he was sent to Europe by the Hagana* to negotiate with the Nazis for the rescue of some 40,000 German Jews but his negotiations failed. He served with the British army in World War II. He later joined the political department of the Jewish Agency*, where he worked in intelligence and directed efforts to recover Jewish property lost in Europe. In 1947 he was a member of the Jewish Agency delegation to the United Nations when the General Assembly voted for the partition of Palestine. He helped to found the Foreign Ministry when Israel became independent. He became an adviser to the Israeli delegation to the United Nations and from 1953 to 1957 he was in charge of Middle Eastern and United Nations affairs at the Foreign Ministry. He later served in a series of Foreign Ministry positions at home and abroad. After working as Director General for the Foreign Ministry from 1968 to 1972 he became Ambassador to Great Britain from 1973 to 1978. He then retired. He died in Jerusalem* in February 1999.

For further information see: Gideon Rafael, *Destination Peace—Three Decades of Israeli Foreign Policy* (London: Weidenfeld and Nicolson, 1981).

RAFI (RESHIMAT POALEI ISRAEL—ISRAEL LABOR LIST). A political party founded in July 1965 by David Ben-Gurion* and seven other

Knesset* members. The founders seceded from Mapai* over the issue of the Lavon Affair*. Teddy Kollek*, its candidate, was elected Mayor of Jerusalem* in 1965. It secured 10 seats in the Knesset in 1965. It remained in opposition to the Government until the eve of the Six Day War* when it joined the Government of National Unity* and Moshe Dayan* (a member) became Minister of Defense. In January 1968 it joined Mapai and Ahdut Haavoda* to form the Israel Labor Party*. Ben-Gurion and some of his followers opposed Rafi joining in the Israel Labor Party and established a new party—Reshima Mamlakhtit (State List)*. In the Knesset elections of 1969 it won four seats.

For further information see: Myron J. Aronoff, *Power and Ritual in the Israel Labor Party: A Study in Political Anthropology* (Assen/Amsterdam: Van Gorcum, 1977); Gershon R. Kieval, "The Foreign Policy of the Labor Party," in *Israeli National Security Policy: Political Actors and Perspectives*, edited by Bernard Reich and Gershon R. Kieval (New York: Greenwood, 1988): 19-54; Efraim Inbar, *War and Peace in Israeli Politics: Labor Party Positions on National Security* (Boulder, CO: Lynne Rienner, 1991); Gabriel Sheffer, *Moshe Sharett: Biography of a Political Moderate* (Oxford University Press: Clarendon, 1996); Shabtai Teveth, *Ben-Gurion's Spy: The Story of the Political Scandal That Shaped Modern Israel* (New York: Columbia University Press, 1996); Ronald W. Zweig, editor, *David Ben-Gurion: Politics and Leadership in Israel* (London: Frank Cass; Jerusalem: Yad Itzhak Ben-Zvi, 1991).

RAKAH (RESHIMA KOMUNISTIT HADASHA—NEW COMMUNIST LIST)
see NEW COMMUNIST LIST AND COMMUNIST PARTY

RAMADAN WAR *see* YOM KIPPUR WAR

RAMAT GAN. A city on the outskirts of Tel Aviv* founded in 1914 and into which the first settlers moved in 1922. Since Israel's independence it has become one of the most important industrial centers of the country. Among its important activities is the Diamond Center—the focal point of Israel's diamond* industry. Bar Ilan University* is located here.

RAMON, HAIM. Born in 1950 in Tel Aviv* to Sephardic* immigrants from Morocco, Haim Ramon was educated at Tel Aviv University as a lawyer. He was first elected to the Knesset*, on the Labor Party* list, in

1983, and served as Minister of Health from 1992 to February 1994, but resigned from the Government and quit the Labor Party to protest the proposed reform of Israel's health care system. Heading an independent political party, he won the chairmanship of the powerful Histadrut* labor federation in May 1994, defeating the incumbent Labor Party candidate (Haim Haberfeld*) and disrupting Labor's 75-year monopoly over the federation. He served as Histadrut chairman from May 1994 to November 1995, clearing up many financial and administrative problems and streamlining the organization, and in the process building up his base of political support. In November 1995 he agreed to rejoin Labor and served as Minister of the Interior until 1996. He surprised many observers by not entering the race to succeed Shimon Peres* as Labor Party leader in 1997. On May 17, 1999, Ramon was reelected to the Knesset, on the One Israel* list. On July 6, 1999, he was appointed Minister without Portfolio in the Prime Minister's Office, with responsibility for Jerusalem* affairs, Government reform, and liaison between the Government and the Knesset.

RAS AL-AMUD. A site a few hundred yards east of the Temple Mount* and south of the Mount of Olives. In July 1997 Jerusalem* Mayor Ehud Olmert* granted permission for a developer to break ground and begin construction on a Jewish housing project in an Arab neighborhood. Palestinian leaders described the plan as evidence of Israeli bad faith in the peace process and protested the decision to build. The project was subsequently postponed. In January 1998 the Interior Ministry announced that it had approved plans for Ras al-Amud. Netanyahu's* office said he would block the project because of its political sensitivity. In August 1998 Jerusalem city authorities approved plans to build 132 apartments for Jewish families in Ras al-Amud. Netanyahu's office again minimized the possibility that the project would go ahead arguing that "public order and safety" powers of the Government could be used to prevent it.

RATZ see CITIZENS' RIGHTS AND PEACE MOVEMENT

RELIGIOUS AFFAIRS, MINISTRY OF. The Ministry of Religious Affairs has primary responsibility for meeting Jewish religious requirements, such as the supply of ritually killed and prepared (kosher) meat, for overseeing rabbinical courts and religious schools, as well as for looking after the autonomous religious needs of the non-Jewish communities.

RENEWAL PARTY *see* TEKUMA

RESOLUTION 242 *see* UNITED NATIONS SECURITY COUNCIL RESOLUTION 242

RESOLUTION 338 *see* UNITED NATIONS SECURITY COUNCIL RESOLUTION 338

REVISIONISTS. A Zionist political party, founded in 1925 by Vladimir Zeev Jabotinsky*. It reflected the demand for a revision of the Zionist Executive's conciliatory policy toward the British Mandatory* Government and toward the system and pace of Zionist activity in Palestine*. In the Revisionist conception, the Zionist aim was to provide an integral solution to the worldwide Jewish problem in all its aspects — political, economic, and spiritual. To attain this objective, the Revisionists demanded that the entire mandated territory of Palestine, on both sides of the Jordan River, be turned into a Jewish state with a Jewish majority. The contention of the Revisionists was that worldwide political pressure must be exerted to induce Britain* to abide by the letter and spirit of the Palestine Mandate. They stressed the imperative necessity of bringing to Palestine the largest number of Jews within the shortest possible time. The financial instrument of the movement was the Keren Tel Hai (Tel Hai Fund). Within the World Zionist Organization (WZO)*, Revisionism met with increasingly strong resistance, particularly from the labor groups. The World Union of Zionists-Revisionists was founded in 1925 as an integral part of the WZO with Jabotinsky as President. The Revisionists strongly opposed expansion of the Jewish Agency* through inclusion of prominent non-Zionists, which, they felt, would impair the national character, independence, and freedom of political action of the Zionist movement. From 1929, when the expanded Jewish Agency took over the political prerogatives of the WZO, Jabotinsky consistently urged increasing independence for the Revisionists. In 1935 a referendum held among Revisionists resulted in their secession from the World Zionist Organization and the establishment of an independent New Zionist Organization (NZO)*. Eleven years later, when ideological and tactical differences between the NZO and the WZO had diminished, the NZO decided to give up its separate existence. The United Zionists-Revisionists (the merger of the Revisionist Union and the Jewish State party) participated in the elections to the twenty-second Zionist Congress in Basle in 1946.

For more information see: Shlomo Avineri, *The Making of Modern Zionism: The Intellectual Origins of the Jewish State* (New York: Basic, 1981); Menachem Begin, *The Revolt: Story of the Irgun* (New York: Nash, 1981); Joseph Heller, "The Zionist Right and National Liberation: From Jabotinsky to Avraham Stern," *Israel Affairs* 1:3 (Spring 1995): 85-109; Arthur Hertzberg, editor, *The Zionist Idea: A Historical Analysis and Reader* (New York: Atheneum, 1979);Vladimir Jabotinsky, *The Story of the Jewish Legion* (New York: Ackerman, 1945); Samuel Katz, *A Biography of Vladimir (Ze'ev) Jabotinsky*, 2 volumes (New York: Barricade, 1996); Joseph B. Schechtman, *The Vladimir Jabotinsky Story*, 2 volumes (New York: Yoseloff, 1956-1961); Joseph B. Schechtman and Yehuda Benari, *A History of the Revisionist Movement* (Tel Aviv: Hadar, 1970); Yaacov Shavit, *Revisionism in Zionism* (Tel Aviv: Yariv, 1978); Yaacov Shavit, *Jabotinsky and the Revisionist Movement, 1925-1948* (London: Frank Cass, 1988); Yaacov Shavit, "Ze'ev Jabotinsky and the Revisionist Movement," in *Essential Papers on Zionism*, edited by Jehuda Reinharz and Anita Shapira (New York: New York University Press, 1996): 544-566.

RIGHT OF RETURN. The term applied to the long-standing Palestinian demand for the absolute return to Israel of Arab refugees from the 1948 Arab-Israeli War*. Israel has consistently rejected this as impractical and as a direct threat to its national security.

For further information see: Rashid Khalidi, "Observations on the Right of Return," *Journal of Palestine Studies* 21:2 (Winter 1992): 29-40.

RISHON LE ZION (FIRST IN ZION). Title of the Sephardi* Chief Rabbi of Israel*. Prior to the creation of the Chief Rabbinate the title was used for the head of the Sephardi rabbis of Jerusalem*. *See also* CHIEF RABBINATE OF ISRAEL.

RISHON LE ZION (FIRST IN ZION). A city founded in 1882 by immigrants from Russia. The name is derived from the Bible.

ROSENBLUM, PNINA. Pnina Rosenblum, a former model and owner of her own line of cosmetics, led this party bearing her name into the May 17, 1999, elections. The party did not win a Knesset* seat, failing to meet the threshold by a few thousand votes. She took no stance on the issues of the peace process her party platform was, rather, based on women's rights and a better economy.

ROSENNE, MEIR. Born in Iasi, Romania, on February 19, 1931, and immigrated to Palestine* at the age of 13, Meir Rosenne studied at the Sorbonne where he received his MA in political science and his PhD with honors in international law. He is a graduate of the Institute for Advanced International Studies in Paris. Rosenne joined the Israel Government service in 1953 and served in a variety of positions. Between 1971 and 1979 he was legal adviser to the Israel Foreign Ministry. In this capacity he served as the legal adviser to the Israel delegation to the negotiations at Kilometer 101*, the Geneva Peace Talks (1973), and the related negotiations with the Egyptian and Syrian delegations following the Yom Kippur War*. He participated in the negotiations leading to the Egypt-Israel Peace Treaty* in 1979 and, until September 1979, he was head of the Israeli team to the autonomy negotiations with Egypt. He became Ambassador to France* in 1979 and served in that capacity until May 1983, when he was nominated to be Israel's Ambassador to the United States*. Subsequent to his service as Ambassador to the United States he became head of the Israel Bonds Organization*.

ROSH HANIKRA. Border point on the Israel-Lebanon frontier at the Mediterranean Sea.

ROTATION. The coalition agreement between Labor* and Likud* which established the Government of National Unity* in 1984 provided for the "rotation" of the positions of Prime Minister and Foreign Minister between Yitzhak Shamir* of Likud and Shimon Peres* of the Labor Alignment. During the first 25 months of the Government, Peres was to serve as Prime Minister and Shamir as Foreign Minister. They would then "rotate" and Shamir would become Prime Minister and Peres Foreign Minister for the second 25 months. Despite dire predictions concerning the fate of the agreement and the Government established under its terms, the rotation took place in October 1986 as scheduled and the Government served its full term.

RUBINSTEIN, AMNON. Born in 1931 in Tel Aviv*, he graduated in law from Hebrew University of Jerusalem* and received a PhD from the London School of Economics. He served as professor of law and dean of the faculty of law at Tel Aviv University and participated in the founding of Democratic Movement for Change (DASH)* in the period following the 1973 Yom Kippur War*. He was the chairman of the Shinui* faction in the 10th Knesset* (1981). He served as Minister of Communications in the 1984 Government of National Unity* and as Minister of Education in the Labor*-led governing coalition between 1992 and 1996. Rubenstein was reelected to the 14th Knesset in 1996 on the joint Meretz/Democratic Israel* list and was reelected to the 15th Knesset in 1999, again on the Meretz list.

For further information see: Amnon Rubinstein, *A Certain Political Experience* (Jerusalem: Idanim, 1982) (In Hebrew).

RUBINSTEIN, ELYAKIM (ELI). Born in Tel Aviv* in 1947, he graduated as a lawyer from the Hebrew University of Jerusalem*. He served in the legal department and as deputy legal adviser in the Ministry of Defense from 1973 to 1977. From 1977 to 1981, he served as senior adviser to Foreign Minister Moshe Dayan*. He was involved in the Camp David* negotiations with Egypt* and from 1981 to 1985 he served as the Foreign Ministry's legal adviser. In 1986 he served briefly as political counselor at the Israeli Embassy in Washington, DC. In November 1986 he became secretary of the cabinet, a position he held for seven-and-one-half years, serving under Likud* Prime Minister Yitzhak Shamir* and Labor* Prime Ministers Shimon Peres* and Yitzhak Rabin*. In 1991 he was appointed by Shamir to head the early Washington rounds of negotiations with the joint Jordanian-Palestinian delegation ensuing from the Madrid Peace Conference*; he also was involved in talks with the Jordanians after the Oslo Accords* were signed. He resigned as cabinet secretary in April 1994, reportedly because he was upset at having been left in the dark over the Oslo negotiations. However, in November 1994 he was appointed by Yitzhak Rabin to head a committee to oversee implementation of the Peace Treaty with Jordan*, a position he held until June 1995 when he was appointed a Jerusalem District Court judge. On January 27, 1997, he was appointed Attorney-General.

RUSSIA *see* UNION OF SOVIET SOCIALIST REPUBLICS

S

SABRA. A term commonly used to refer to native born Israelis. It is derived from the name of the cactus plant (in Hebrew*, *tzabar*) which grows in Israel. The plant has a sweet and juicy fruit encased in a tough skin that has numerous thorns. This is supposed to characterize the Israelis who are seen as tough on the outside but gentle inside.

SABRA AND SHATILA REFUGEE CAMPS. Among the tragic aspects of the War in Lebanon* of 1982 was the massacre by Christian Phalangist forces of Palestinians at the Sabra and Shatila refugee camps in the Beirut area. The resultant anguish within Israel over possible Israeli involvement led to the decision to create a Commission of Inquiry, headed by Supreme Court* Chief Justice Yitzhak Kahan. *See also* KAHAN COMMISSION OF INQUIRY.

For further information see: Martin Edelman, "The Kahan Commission of Inquiry," *Midstream* (June-July 1983): 11-14; R. T. Naylor, "From Bloodbath to Whitewash," *Arab Studies Quarterly* 5 (Fall 1983): 337-361; Ze'ev Schiff and Ehud Ya'ari, *Israel's Lebanon War* (New York: Simon and Schuster, 1984); Avner Yaniv, *Dilemmas of Security: Politics, Strategy and the Israeli Experience in Lebanon* (Oxford University Press: Clarendon, 1987).

SADAT, ANWAR. The President of Egypt* after the death of Gamal Abdul Nasser who led Egypt in the Yom Kippur War*. He proposed direct negotiations with Israel to resolve the Arab-Israeli conflict and visited Israel in November 1977. He signed the Camp David Accords* of 1978 and the Egypt-Israel Peace Treaty* of 1979 and established the process of peace and normalization of relations between Egypt and Israel. Sadat was assassinated by Muslim militants while reviewing a military parade in Cairo in October 1981. He shared the Nobel Peace Prize for 1978 with Menachem Begin.*

For further information see: Butros Butros-Ghali, *Egypt's Road to Jerusalem: A Diplomat's Story of the Struggle for Peace in the Middle East* (New York: Random House, 1997); Marius Deeb, "Anwar al-Sadat," in Bernard Reich, Editor, *Political Leaders of the Contemporary Middle East and North Africa* (Westport, CT: Greenwood, 1990): 453-460;

Anwar Sadat, *In Search of Identity: An Autobiography* (New York: Harper and Row, 1978).

SADEH, YITZHAK. Born in Lublin in Russian Poland in 1890, he served in the Russian Army in World War I, but settled in Palestine* in 1920. He soon became active in the Hagana* and in 1941 founded the Palmah* and served as its commander until 1945. At the beginning of the War of Independence* he served in the command of the Hagana and when the Israel Defense Forces* was established he became commander of the 8th Armored Brigade. After the war he resigned from the Israel Defense Forces and assumed a leading role in the Mapam Party*. He died in Petah Tikva* in 1952.

SAFED (TZEFAT). A city in upper Galilee* in which Jews have lived for centuries. Beginning in the sixteenth century it became an important center of Jewish learning. It has become a center for artists and tourists.

SAMARIA. Northern section of the highlands of Palestine*, north of Judea*. Its area is approximately 1,000 square miles, 31 miles long and 23 miles wide. It was part of the West Bank* occupied by Jordan* in Israel's War of Independence* and was taken by Israel in the Six Day War*. Already densely populated by Arabs, since the Six Day War it has been heavily populated by Jewish settlers* especially in areas abutting the former Green Line*. The large concentration of Jewish settlers, the area's proximity to Jerusalem* and to the country's industrial heartland, its historical significance, and its strategic value are among the factors cited by those who demand Israel's permanent retention of much of Samaria in negotiations with the PLO*.

SAMUEL, HERBERT LOUIS. First Viscount. Born in Liverpool, England, in 1870, he entered politics and with the outbreak of World War I developed an interest in the subject of Zionism* and the creation of a Jewish national home. He was appointed the first High Commissioner of Palestine* under the British Mandate* and served from 1920 to 1925, during which time he established the foundations of the civil administration of Palestine.

For further information see: Elie Kedourie, "Sir Herbert Samuel and the Government of Palestine," in *The Chatham House Version and Other Middle Eastern Studies*, edited by Elie Kedourie (London: Weidenfeld and Nicolson, 1970): 52-81; M. Mossek, *Palestine Immigration Policy under Sir Herbert Samuel: British, Zionist and Arab Attitudes* (London: Frank Cass, 1978); Edwin Samuel, *A Lifetime in Jerusalem: The Memoirs of the Second Viscount Samuel* (Jerusalem: Israel Universities Press, 1970); Herbert L. S. Samuel, *Memoirs* (London: Cresset, 1945); A. J. Sherman, *Mandate Days: British Lives in Palestine 1918-1948* (London: Douglas and McIntyre, 1998); Bernard Wasserstein, "Herbert Samuel and the Palestine Problem," *English Historical Review* 91 (October 1976): 753-775.

SAN REMO. A conference held in the Italian town of San Remo on April 16-26, 1920, to consider the future of Middle East territories that had been under Turkish rule prior to World War I. The conference—attended by Great Britain*, France*, Italy, and Japan—ratified decisions taken in secret war-time negotiations involving Britain and France (such as the Sykes-Picot Agreement* of May 1916) to divide former Turkish holdings in the Middle East into spheres of influence. According to these agreements, France was given Mandatory rights in Lebanon and Syria, and Britain Mandatory rights to Palestine* and Iraq*/Mesopotamia. A second San Remo conference, eight months later, further defined the boundaries of these areas. The Mandate proposals were formally approved by the League of Nations on July 24, 1922, and became official on September 29, 1923.

For further information see: David Fromkin, *A Peace to End All Peace: Creating the Modern Middle East 1914-1922* (New York: Henry Holt, 1989).

SAPIR, PINHAS (FORMERLY KOSLOWSKY). Born in Suwalki, Russian Poland, on October 15, 1907, he immigrated to Palestine* in 1929, took the name Sapir, and settled in Kfar Saba where he worked in the orange groves. He held a number of local positions and worked with the Mekorot Water Company from 1937 to 1947. In February 1948 he was put in charge of the quartermaster branch of the Hagana*. During the War of Independence* he traveled abroad to purchase arms. Later in 1948 he was appointed Director-General of the Ministry of Defense and from 1953 to 1955 he served as Director-General of the Ministry of Finance. In 1955 he was appointed Minister of Commerce and Industry and in 1963 became Minister of Finance. In 1968 he became Secretary General of the Israel Labor Party*. In 1969 he again became Minister of Finance until

June 1974. He died in 1975 while serving as Chairman of the Jewish Agency* and the World Zionist Organization*.

SARID, YOSSI. Born in 1940 in Rehovot worked as a journalist. A member of the Knesset* since 1974, originally on the Labor Alignment* list, he shifted to the Citizens' Rights Movement* after the 1984 election to protest Labor's participation with Likud* in the National Unity Government*. A founder of the Meretz/Democratic Israel* coalition, he participated in the Labor-led governing coalition between 1992 and 1996, serving as Environment Minister from January 1993 to June 1996. As a Government minister he played an increasingly active part in negotiations with the PLO*. He became leader of the CRM and Meretz upon the retirement of Shulamit Aloni* prior to the 1996 election. Under Sarid's leadership, Meretz won nine seats in the 14th Knesset (1996) and 10 seats in the 15th Knesset (1999). On July 6, 1999, Sarid was appointed Minister of Education in the Government headed by Prime Minister Ehud Barak*.

SAVIDOR, MENACHEM. Born in Russia in 1918, he became active in the Betar* youth movement after moving with his family to Poland in 1923. After high school he completed studies in philology in Vilna. In 1941 he immigrated to Palestine* and joined the British army, serving in the Jewish Brigade*. He later served in the Israel Defense Forces* where he rose to the rank of Lieutenant Colonel. He became Director-General of the Transport Ministry and Director-General of Israel Railways. After running unsuccessfully for Mayor of Tel Aviv* in 1973 he was elected in 1977 to the Knesset* and in 1981 became Speaker. He left politics in 1984 and died in November 1988.

SAVIR, URIEL (URI). Born in 1952 in Jerusalem*, he joined the Israeli Foreign Ministry in 1975. From 1984 to 1988, he was media adviser and bureau chief for Shimon Peres* in the latter's capacities as Prime Minister and Foreign Minister. In November 1988 he was named Consul-General in New York, a position he held until May 1993 when he was appointed Director-General of the Foreign Ministry, again under Shimon Peres. He was involved in the final, crucial stages of the negotiations in Oslo that culminated with the September 1993 Israel-PLO* Declaration of Principles* and he participated in subsequent negotiations with the PLO concerning the Cairo Agreement* of May 1994. Leaving government service in 1996 he became the founding Executive Director of the Peres Institute for Peace, a Tel Aviv*-based institute established by Shimon

Peres to encourage economic cooperation between Israelis and Palestinians. Savir's experiences in negotiating the Declaration of Principles were described in his book, *The Process: 1,100 Days That Changed The Middle East* (New York: Random House, 1998). On May 17, 1999, Savir was elected to the 15th Knesset* on the Center* Party list.

For further information see: Michael Keren, "Israeli Professionals and the Peace Process," *Israel Affairs* 1:1 (Autumn 1994): 149-163; Michael Keren, *Professionals against Populism: The Peres Government and Democracy* (Albany: State University of New York Press, 1995); David Makovsky, *Making Peace with the PLO: The Rabin Government's Road to the Oslo Accords* (Boulder, CO: Westview, 1996); Uriel Savir, "Why Oslo Still Matters," *New York Times Magazine* (May 3, 1998): 50-54.

SCHACH, ELIEZER. Born in Lithuania in 1897, he was educated in Orthodox yeshivas in Lithuania and Russia. In 1940, he and his family escaped to Palestine*. He became head of the Ponevezh Yeshiva in Bnai Brak, a stronghold of the *misnagdim*, the branch of ultra-Orthodox Ashkenazic Jewry that opposed the Hasidim*. He was for many years co-chairman of the Council of Torah Sages*, the ruling body of the Agudat Israel* movement. His co-chairman was Rabbi Simcha Bunim Alter*, the head of the Ger (or Gur) Hasidic dynasty. The tension inherent in this relationship was given political expression in intense internal divisions within Agudat Israel. His concern about the growing influence of the Hasidic wing over Agudat Israel's Sephardic* followers prompted Schach to help form the Sephardi Torah Guardians (Shas)* breakaway faction which won four seats in the 1984 Knesset* elections, compared to only two for Agudat Israel. In 1988, alarmed by the growing influence of his arch rival, Rabbi Menachem Mendel Schneerson*, the head of the world Lubavitch* Hasidic sect, Schach and his followers left Agudat Israel and formed the Degel Hatorah* Party that won two seats in the 12th Knesset. In 1992, on the eve of the elections for the 13th Knesset, he agreed to have Degel Hatorah participate with Agudat Israel in a joint list called United Torah Judaism*. However, he made a serious tactical error by permitting Agudat Israel to hold the lion's share of power in the alliance. Moreover, in public statements prior to the election he implied that Sephardim were not yet ready to take on leadership responsibilities, thereby prompting many Sephardic voters to shift their support to Shas. Despite this estrangement from the Sephardic community, as well as his advancing age, Schach remained a dominant force in the ultra-Orthodox community's political campaign to have Halacha* imposed on ever-greater aspects of daily life in Israel.

SCHNEERSON, RABBI MENACHEM MENDEL. He was the seventh in a line of Grand Rabbis, or Rebbes, of the Lubavitch Hasidic* movement who died on June 12, 1994. He was born on April 14, 1902, in Ukraine. He studied mathematics and science in Berlin and at the Sorbonne, fled the Nazis in 1941, and immigrated to the United States* where he settled in New York. He rebuilt the movement, which had nearly perished in the Holocaust*, into a worldwide movement with substantial influence. In the 1980s, Rabbi Schneerson directed his followers to become actively engaged in Israeli electoral politics—primarily through support for Agudat Israel*—in order to block the formation of Governments that might be inclined to relinquish territory in the West Bank*, and in order to promote the introduction of legislation designed to strengthen the authority of Jewish law (Halacha*). He was a major political force in Israel, both in the Knesset and among the electorate, although he never went there. In fact, except to pray at the Queens cemetery where his father-in-law and wife were buried, he had not ventured beyond his Crown Heights stronghold in 37 years. Rabbi Schneerson taught that Jews could hasten the arrival of the Messiah if they practiced the traditions laid out in the Hebrew Bible and interpreted by the rabbis in the Talmud and other classical texts. Some of the Rebbe's followers believed that he was the Messiah, the savior promised by the prophets, but Rabbi Schneerson discouraged such talk. His critics charged that his disclaimers were too mild and that he should have put an end to such speculation long ago. His interventions helped influence the results of the 1984 and 1988 elections in Israel.

SCOPUS, MOUNT *see* MOUNT SCOPUS

SCUD MISSILES. Land-based, surface-to-surface, short-range ballistic missiles, first designed by the Soviet Union* in the late 1950s. Over the years three variants of the missile were introduced: the Scud A, with a range of approximately 81 miles and capable of carrying a high-explosive conventional warhead; the Scud B, with a range of 174 miles and capable of carrying a conventional warhead or a nonconventional (nuclear or chemical) warhead; and the Scud C, with a range of nearly 280 miles. The Scud missile was first introduced to the Middle East battlefield prior to the 1973 Yom Kippur War* by the Egyptians to deter Israeli combat aircraft strikes deep into Egyptian territory by threatening ballistic missile use against Israeli civilian population centers. However, the Scud played only a small part in the Yom Kippur War. In the late 1980s Iraq* developed two extended-range variants of the missile: the *Al-Husseini*, with a range of about 375 miles; and the *Al-Abbas*, with an anticipated range of up to 560 miles. Both models were capable of carrying conventional and nonconventional warheads. During the Persian Gulf War of 1991, Iraq fired a total of 39 of these missiles into Israel, inflicting only limited physical damage but causing a great deal of psychological trauma among the Israeli population. A number of Iraqi Scud missiles were also fired at Saudi Arabia. Many of Iraq's Scud missiles and their mobile launchers withstood strategic bombings by the U.S.-led multinational forces during the Persian Gulf conflict; most were reportedly destroyed by UN arms inspectors in the months and years after the war.

For further information see: Jon J. Peterson and Stephen H. Gotowicki, "Scud Missiles," in *An Historical Encyclopedia of the Arab-Israeli Conflict*, edited by Bernard Reich (Westport, CT: Greenwood, 1996): 456-457.

SDE BOKER. A kibbutz in the Negev* founded in 1952 and chosen by David Ben-Gurion* as his residence when not in Tel Aviv* or Jerusalem*. His house remains and he is buried at the kibbutz.

SEA OF GALILEE. The Sea of Galilee is a small (14 miles long and 8 miles across at its broadest point) freshwater lake in northern Israel and is often mentioned in the Bible. It is called the Sea of Kinnereth (Lake Kinneret) in the Old Testament. The name Galilee is used in the New Testament. It is also called Lake Tiberias for a city on its shore. The Sea of Galilee lies on the Jordan plain in Israel 30 miles from the Mediterranean Sea. It touches the Golan Heights* on the northeast. The Jordan River* flows southward through it. *See also* GALILEE.

SECOND ALIYA. The Second Aliya (1904-1914) was the most significant in terms of Israel's future political system. Some 40,000 immigrants of Russian and Eastern European origin laid the foundations of the labor movement and established the first Jewish labor parties and kibbutzim*. They were secularists who sought to modernize and secularize Jewish life in the Diaspora*, and they brought their political ideas, especially socialist ideology, to Palestine* and thereby provided the foundations of the future political system. *See also* ALIYA.

For further information see: Yosef Gorny, "Changes in the Social and Political Structure of the Second Aliya between 1904 and 1940," in *Essential Papers on Zionism*, edited by Jehuda Reinharz and Anita Shapira (New York: New York University Press, 1996): 371-421.

SECOND ISRAEL. A reference to Israel's Sephardim* and their perceived second-class status in Israel. Shas* was seen as representing Sephardim, whether Orthodox or not, and their success in the 1999 Knesset election was viewed as a victory for the Second Israel.

For further information see: Daniel J. Elazar, *The Other Jews: The Sephardim Today* (New York: Basic, 1989).

SECURITY ZONE. A narrow strip (three to nine miles wide) of land north of the Israel-Lebanon* border retained by Israel following the unilateral withdrawal of most IDF* troops from Lebanon in the spring of 1985. The area was patrolled by small contingents of IDF soldiers and by units of the Israel-backed South Lebanese Army*. The purpose of the security zone was to be a buffer to protect the towns and villages of northern Israel by keeping militant forces—such as the PLO* and Hezbollah—out of Katyusha* missile range of the border region, and by creating a physical barrier to terrorist incursions. However, the growing number of Israeli casualties in the security zone caused a heated public debate in the late 1990s about withdrawing IDF forces completely from the area. In the 1999 election campaign, Ehud Barak* pledged to withdraw the IDF from the security zone within one year of taking office. *See also* FATAHLAND.

For further information see: Laura Zittrain Eisenberg, "Israel's South Lebanon Imbroglio," *Middle East Quarterly* 4:2 (June 1997): 61-69; Beate Hamizrachi, *The Emergence of the South Lebanon Security Belt: Major Saad Haddad and the Ties with Israel, 1975-1978* (New York: Praeger, 1988).

SEPARATION. The ambiguous and vague concept of Israelis and West Bank*-Gaza* Palestinians living their lives apart. Severing ties between Arabs and Jews has been part of Israel's political discourse since the

Persian Gulf War. Opinion in Israel is divided between those who envision a final peace settlement premised on a complete separation from the Palestinians, and those who perceive the need for continued economic contacts across the political borders.

SEPHARDI, SEPHARDIM *see* ORIENTAL JEWS

SEPHARDI TORAH GUARDIANS (SHAS). A political party established by individuals of Sephardic* background who split from Agudat Israel* and first contested the 1984 Knesset* election. While ideologically close to Agudat Israel positions, the founders of this party perceived discrimination against Sephardim and consequently wished to get the funds, political jobs, and other forms of support of which they had felt deprived. Among the founders of the party was Rabbi Nissim Zeev of Jerusalem*, while Rabbi* Yitzhak Haim Peretz* was the leader of the Knesset* list. Shas formed a council of sages known as Moetzet Hachmei Hatorah and its leadership was closely linked to the former Sephardic Chief Rabbi* of Israel, Ovadia Yosef*. It argued that the Torah was its platform and regarded itself as a movement of spiritual awakening. Despite a split in the party and the creation of Yahad Shivtei Yisrael (Yishai*), it won six seats in the 1988 Knesset election to emerge as the third-largest party in the parliament and the largest of the religious parties. Rabbi Ovadia Yosef resigned his position on the Supreme Rabbinical Court in order to campaign actively for Shas. In the spring of 1990 five of the six Shas members of the Knesset abstained in the vote of confidence that led to the ouster of the Shamir*-led Government. In June 1990 Shas joined the newly established Likud*-led Government of Yitzhak Shamir. It won six seats in the 13th Knesset (1992) and agreed to join the coalition headed by Yitzhak Rabin*. It subsequently left the Government over disputes with cabinet members from Meretz* and the left wing of the Labor* Party over religious legislation; also contributing to Shas's departure from the Government was the criminal case against party leader Arye Deri* on charges of fraud and corruption. Though no longer part of the coalition, Shas continued to serve as a "safety net" for Rabin and Shimon Peres* by abstaining from Knesset votes relating to the Middle East peace process. Shas won 10 seats in the 14th Knesset (1996) and occupied two seats in the governing coalition headed by Benjamin Netanyahu*.

On matters of foreign and security policy Shas has traditionally taken a somewhat more accommodative line than the other ultra-Orthodox religious parties. Its long-time spiritual leader, Rabbi Ovadia Yosef, has emphasized that *pikuah nefesh*—"the saving of human life"—takes precedence over all the other commandments in the Torah, including the retention of all of Eretz Israel*. In terms of its domestic policy platform Shas advocates increased respect and representation for Sephardic Jews and the maximum incorporation of Orthodox Jewish practices in Israeli daily life.

Elections in the 1990s witnessed a significant increase in support for Shas even among non-Orthodox Sephardic Jews. Analysts attributed this to Shas's deliberate strategy of defining itself as an "ethnic" political movement, as well as to the vast network of quality subsidized educational institutions and day-care centers established by Shas, especially in poorer parts of the country. Shas has used its growing political influence to aggressively push successive Governments for legislation affecting religious affairs generally and the "Who is a Jew"* question in particular.

Shas won 17 seats in the May 17, 1999, elections to the Knesset; this despite the March 17, 1999, conviction of party leader Arye Deri and the evidence of widespread corruption amongst the party's leadership and despite popular criticism of the party's alleged anti-democratic ideology. On June 16, 1999, Deri formally resigned as the political leader of Shas, thereby opening the way for the party to join the coalition Government named by Ehud Barak* on July 6, 1999, with Eli Suissa* serving as Minister of National Infrastructure, Eli Yishai* (who replaced Deri as Shas's political leader) as Labor and Social Affairs Minister, Shlomo Benizri as Health Minister, Yitzhak Cohen as Minister of Religious Affairs, and Nissim Dahan as Deputy Interior Minister.

For further information see: Eliezer Don-Yehiya, "Religion, Social Cleavages and Political Behavior: The Religious Parties in the Israeli Elections," in *Who's the Boss? The Elections in Israel, 1988 and 1989*, edited by Daniel J. Elazar and Shmuel Sandler (Detroit: Wayne State University Press, 1993): 83-129; Eliezer Don-Yehiya, "The Religious Parties in the 1996 Elections," *Israel Affairs* (Special Issue: "Israel at the Polls 1996") 4:1 (Autumn 1997): 73-102; Daniel J. Elazar, *The Other Jews: The Sephardim Today* (New York: Basic, 1989); Charles S.

Liebman, *Religion, Democracy and Israeli Society* (Amsterdam: Harwood Academics, 1997); Stewart Reiser, "The Religious Parties and Israel's Foreign Policy," in *Israeli National Security Policy: Political Actors and Perspectives*, edited by Bernard Reich and Gershon R. Kieval (New York: Greenwood, 1988): 105-122; Stewart Reiser, "The Religious Parties in Israel: Social Significance and Policy Implications," *Middle East Focus* 12:2 (Summer/Fall 1990): 9-16; Ira Sharkansky, *Rituals of Conflict: Religion, Politics and Public Policy in Israel* (Boulder, CO: Lynne Rienner, 1996); Aaron P. Willis, "SHAS—The Sephardic Torah Guardians: Religious Movement and Political Power," in *The Elections in Israel 1992*, edited by Asher Arian and Michael Shamir (Albany: State University of New York Press, 1995); Oren Yiftachel and Avinoam Meir, *Ethnic Frontiers and Peripheries: Landscapes of Development and Inequality in Israel* (Boulder, CO: Westview, 1998); Yael Yishai, *Land of Paradoxes: Interest Politics in Israel* (Albany: State University of New York Press: 1991).

SEPHARDIM PARTY. An ethnic-based political party that represented an effort to organize Sephardic* and Oriental Jews* and succeeded in electing four members to the First Knesset* and two to the Second Knesset. Toward the end of the tenure of the First Knesset the party split along economic lines and it eventually disappeared when one of its most prominent leaders, Bechor Shitreet, was coopted by Mapai* to serve as Minister of Police in a series of Governments led by David Ben-Gurion*.

SETTLEMENTS. Beginning in the second half of the nineteenth century Jewish immigrants began to establish settlements throughout Palestine*. The purpose of these settlements was to provide security to civilian settlements, kibbutzim*, and moshavim* in far-flung areas of Palestine and to establish permanent Zionist "facts" on the ground. The paramilitary Nahal* program combined military service with agricultural activities in support of these settlements. Several of the early settlements were destroyed or evacuated in the 1948 Arab-Israeli War*. Many of them, especially the Etzion Bloc* and Hebron*, were reestablished in the immediate aftermath of the 1967 Six Day War*, while new settlements were established in the Sinai*, Gaza Strip* and Golan Heights*.

A great deal of settlement activity occurred between 1967 and 1977 under Labor*-led Governments, but the emphasis in that period tended to be on using settlements to reinforce Israel's strategic interests in the occupied territories* and around Jerusalem*. Under Labor, most settlement activity was state-sponsored and -funded; however, in some cases (such as the small settlement established by Rabbi Moshe Levinger* in Hebron* on the eve of Passover, 1968), settlements were established as a result of private initiatives and against government wishes. The pace and scope of settlement activity changed substantially with the ascendance of Likud* to power in 1977, with an emphasis on encouraging maximum Jewish presence in all parts of the occupied territories so as to make it difficult to evacuate from them in the context of future peace agreements. Nevertheless, it was under Likud that all settlements in the Sinai Desert (such as Yamit*) were evacuated in the early 1980s in fulfilment of the Peace Treaty with Egypt*.

Since 1967 no Israeli Government has formally introduced as policy the prospect of disbanding and evacuating settlements in the West Bank*. The Galili Document* of 1973 preempted an apparent move by Labor Party doves to place the status of settlements on the negotiating table. During the campaign preceding the 1992 Knesset election, Labor Party chairman Yitzhak Rabin* made vague references to the possibility of Israel's eventually evacuating *political settlements* (that is, settlements established provocatively alongside or amidst Arab population centers in the West Bank or in far-flung parts of the territories and offering no strategic value to Israel) while maintaining permanent control over *security settlements* (that is, those settlements vital to the security of Israeli populations in the West Bank, and of Jerusalem). However, Rabin never specified which settlements he placed in each category.

At Israel's insistence, discussion of the permanent status of settlements was deferred until the final status* phase of the Oslo* process. Nevertheless, the settlements issue was a source of controversy between Israeli and Palestinian negotiators from the outset. There were some 170,000 Jewish settlers in the West Bank and Gaza Strip at the end of 1999, constituting about 2.7% of Israel's total population.

In October 1999 Prime Minister Ehud Barak* reached an understanding with the Council of Jewish Communities in Judea*, Samaria* and Gaza whereby YESHA* agreed to voluntarily disband a small number of unauthorized mini-settlements in the West Bank. On December 7, 1999 Barak offered to refrain from issuing additional housing tenders in the territories in the period leading up to the Israeli-Palestinian final-status "framework agreement" though existing contracts would be honored and the prohibition on new housing would not affect settlements abutting Jerusalem. However, Israeli officials emphasized that this confidence building gesture was not inconsistent with Barak's "red line" that envisioned the vast majority of Jewish residents of the occupied territories living in large settlement blocs under Israeli sovereignty in a permanent peace agreement with the Palestinians.

For further information see: Joseph Alpher, *Settlements and Borders—Final Status Issues—Israelis-Palestinians*, Study No. 3 (Tel Aviv: The Jaffee Center for Strategic Studies, Tel Aviv University, 1994); Elisha Efrat, "Jewish Settlements in the West Bank: Past, Present, Future," *Israel Affairs* 1:1 (Autumn 1994): 135-148; Herb Keinon, *Israeli Settlements: A Guide* (New York: Anti-Defamation League of B'nai Brith, 1995); David Newman, "Boundaries in Flux: The 'Green Line' Boundary between Israel and the West Bank—Past, Present and Future," *Boundary and Territory Briefing* 1:7 (Durham, UK: International Boundaries Unit, University of Durham Press, 1995).

SHABAK *see* SHIN BET

SHACH, ELIEZER *see* ELIEZER SCHACH

SHAHAK, AMNON *see* AMNON LIPKIN-SHAHAK

SHAHAL, MOSHE. Born in Iraq* on May 20, 1935, he studied at Haifa* University and graduated from the Law Faculty of Tel Aviv University*. Shahal is a lawyer by profession and was a member of the Knesset* since 1969 on the Labor Alignment* list. He became Minister of Energy and Infrastructure in 1984 and retained that post in the Government established in December 1988. He served as Internal Security Minister in the Labor-led coalition of 1992-1996, and was reelected to the Knesset on the Labor list in 1996. He did not seek election to the Knesset in 1999.

SHAI. Acronym for Sherut Yediot (information service). The intelligence service of the Hagana* established in 1940. *See also* ISRAEL DEFENSE FORCES.

For further information see: Yigal Allon, *Shield of David: The Story of Israel's Armed Forces* (London: Weidenfeld and Nicolson, 1970); Efraim

Dekel, *SHAI: The Exploits of Haganah Intelligence* (New York: Yoseloff, 1959); Zerubavel Gilad, editor, *Hidden Shield: The Secret Military Efforts of the Yishuv during the War, 1939-1945* (Jerusalem: The Jewish Agency for Israel, 1951); Ze'ev Schiff, *A History of the Israeli Army, 1870-1974* (New York: Simon and Schuster, 1974).

SHAKI, AVNER. Born in Safed* in 1928, he graduated from the Faculty of Law of Hebrew University*. Shaki served as a member of the Knesset* from 1969 to 1973 and again beginning in 1984. He became a Minister without Portfolio in the Government established in December 1988. He served as leader of the National Religious Party* in the late 1980s and early 1990s, and was appointed Minister of Religious Affairs in the Shamir*-led Government. Under his leadership the National Religious Party adopted an increasingly hawkish perspective on foreign and national security policy. Shaki was reelected to the 13th (1992) and the 14th (1996) Knessets on the NRP list. He was a strong critic of the Oslo Accords* and was a leader of the faction that threatened to have the party leave the Netanyahu*-led Government in response to IDF* redeployments in Hebron* and elsewhere in the West Bank*. Shaki was not accorded a "secure" slot on the National Religious Party list that contested election to the 15th Knesset on May 17, 1999.

SHALIT CASE. In 1968, Benjamin (Binyamin) Shalit, an Israeli-born Jewish naval officer married to a non-Jew abroad, applied to have his two children registered by the Israeli Government as Jews. The request was denied by the Interior Ministry, which wanted to leave blank both the "religion" and "nationality" categories of the children's registration cards due to the fact that, having been born to a non-Jewish mother, they were not Jewish according to Halacha*. Shalit, himself an atheist, was prepared to leave the religious category blank but he wanted his children registered as being of the Jewish nation. The Supreme Court*, by a 5-4 decision, supported Shalit's request. The Knesset*, under pressure from the National Religious Party*, subsequently amended the Law of Return* to read that a Jew is one born of a Jewish mother or a woman converted to Judaism according to Halacha. This amended legislation caused the Court to deny a second request by Shalit, in 1972, to register his third child as a member of the Jewish nation. *See also* WHO IS A JEW.

SHALOM ACHSHAV *see* PEACE NOW

SHAMGAR, MEIR. Born in Danzig in 1925, he studied history and philosophy at the Hebrew University of Jerusalem* and law at the government Law School of London University. In the years leading to statehood, he was a member of the Irgun* and was placed in administrative detention in British colonies in Africa. Returning to Palestine*, he served in the Israel Defense Forces*, attaining the rank of Brigadier-General. He served as Military Advocate General from 1961 to 1968. In 1967-1968, he created the legal framework of the Israeli military government in the West Bank* and Gaza Strip*. From 1968 to 1975 he served as Attorney-General*. Appointed a Justice of the Supreme Court of Israel*in 1975, he became President of the Court in 1983. In 1994, he chaired the Commission of Inquiry into the killing of Palestinian worshippers in Hebron* (the Hebron Massacre*). He retired from the Supreme Court in August 1995. On November 8, 1995, he was appointed to head the State Commission of Inquiry into the November 5 assassination of Prime Minister Yitzhak Rabin*. He was the recipient of the 1996 Israel Prize* for Special Contribution to the State and Society. *See also* SHAMGAR COMMISSION OF INQUIRY.

SHAMGAR COMMISSION OF INQUIRY. On November 8, 1995, a State Commission of Inquiry was established to investigate the circumstances surrounding the assassination of Prime Minister Yitzhak Rabin* by Yigal Amir*. It was chaired by the recently retired President of the Supreme Court* Justice Meir Shamgar*. Its other members were Zvi Zamir (Mossad* director, 1968-1974), and Ariel Rosen-Zvi (Professor of Law at Tel Aviv University). It submitted its 332-page report on March 28, 1996, two days after Yigal Amir's conviction. Its main conclusions fell into two categories. Concerning the assassination itself, it concluded that the General Security Service/Shin Bet* had no prior knowledge of Yigal Amir, though it was criticized for not taking seriously a general description of Amir and his intentions that it received some five months before the assassination. Otherwise, the intelligence units were generally exonerated. The Shamgar Commission totally rejected any suggestion of a broad-based conspiracy surrounding the Rabin assassination. The second section of the report was highly critical of the special unit of the Shin Bet assigned to protect Very Important People (VIPs), including and especially the Prime Minister. According to the Shamgar Report, "thinking and performance [of the VIP unit] were extremely flawed, and the management culture of Government authorities ... was weak." It declared that if Shin Bet director Carmi Gillon and the chief of the agency's Protection Unit had not already resigned, it would have recommended their dismissal. The Commission did recommend the dismissal of the three next-highest-ranking Shin Bet officials in the protection unit, barring two others from command positions for specified periods of time, and lesser sanctions for officials of the next two echelons down. A 118-page classified appendix to the report recommended stronger intelligence liaison and cooperation between the police and the Shin Bet, more intensive surveillance of subversive Jewish organizations, and better control of undercover agents by the Shin Bet. On March 31, 1996, the Government of Israel adopted the recommendations of the Shamgar report.

SHAMIR, YITZHAK (FORMERLY YZERNITZKY). Born in Rozhinay (or Rozhnoi) in eastern Poland in 1915, Yitzhak Shamir was educated at a Hebrew* secondary school in Bialystok, where he became a disciple of Vladimir Ze'ev Jabotinsky* and joined the Revisionist youth movement, Betar*. He studied law at Warsaw University until 1935 when he emigrated to Palestine* and changed his name to Shamir. He completed his studies at Hebrew University* of Jerusalem*.

Shamir joined the Irgun* in 1937 and rose through the ranks of the organization into leadership positions. In 1940 the Irgun suspended attacks against the British Mandatory* authorities in Palestine and offered its cooperation in the war effort against Germany. This action caused a split in the organization and led to the creation of a smaller and more militant group which Shamir joined. This faction, LEHI* (Lohamei Herut Yisrael—Israel Freedom Fighters), was known as the "Stern Gang"*, named after Abraham Stern (Yair), the group's first leader, and viewed the British as the main obstacle to the establishment of a Jewish state in Palestine. After Stern was killed by British police in 1942, Shamir helped to reorganize LEHI, establishing a high command known as LEHI Central which included Shamir, Nathan Yellin-Mor, and Dr. Israel Scheib (Eldad). Shamir directed LEHI's operations, which became increasingly violent. A terror campaign was conducted against the British which included the assassination of Lord Moyne, Britain's senior Middle East official who was stationed in Cairo, in 1944. Two LEHI members were captured, tried, convicted, and executed for the crime. The Stern Gang was also suspected in the assassination of Swedish Count Folke Bernadotte, who sought to mediate an end to Israel's War of Independence* on behalf of the United Nations*. But, these charges were never substantiated and Shamir has refused to comment on the matter. He was arrested twice by British authorities, in 1941 and 1946, but managed to escape both times. He was sent to a detention camp in Eritrea, but he escaped and traveled through Ethiopia to Djibouti, ultimately arriving in France* where he was given political asylum. He remained in France until he returned to the newly established State of Israel in May 1948.

Shamir found it difficult to enter Israel's new political system, which was dominated by former Hagana* members and others who had been associated with the Labor Zionist* movement. Shamir sought election to the Knesset* in 1949 with a list of candidates comprised of former LEHI members, but this effort failed. Shamir did not pursue elective office again until he joined the Herut Party* of Menachem Begin* in 1970. During the period from 1948 to 1955 he remained in private life where he was active in a number of commercial ventures, including directing an association of cinema owners. These were not particularly successful. Isser Harel*, then head of the Mossad*, recruited Shamir into the organization in 1955 where his operational experience from the Mandate period could be put to use. He spent a decade with the Mossad and rose to a senior position. For a part of that time he was stationed in Paris. Shamir left the Mossad in 1965 and returned to private life where he pursued commercial interests but with only moderate success. He remained active in public life primarily through his efforts at increasing Soviet Jewish immigration to Israel. In 1970 Menachem Begin offered him a position in Herut*, which Shamir had recently joined, and he was elected to the Executive Committee and became the Director of the Immigration Department.

Shamir successfully ran for election to the Knesset for the first time on the Herut list in 1973 and became a member of the State Comptroller Committee and the Defense and Foreign Affairs Committee. He directed the party's Organization Department, and in 1975 he was elected Chairman of Herut's Executive Committee, a post to which he was reelected unanimously two years later. The 1977 Knesset election was a watershed in Israeli politics. Likud*, into which Herut had merged, secured the largest number of votes and Menachem Begin became Israel's first non-Labor Prime Minister. Shamir was elected Speaker of the Knesset in June 1977 and continued to be a loyal supporter of Begin. Loyalty characterized Shamir's service to Begin both within the party and in the Begin-led Governments in which he served. The most significant issue which separated the two was Begin's decision to negotiate and sign the Camp David Accords* and the Egypt-Israel Peace Treaty*. Shamir opposed the treaty (as did other Likud leaders including Moshe Arens* and Ariel Sharon*) because he believed Israel was sacrificing too much in return for what he viewed as uncertain guarantees of peace. The withdrawal from the Sinai Peninsula* and the relinquishing of the security buffer it provided and the sophisticated air bases located there, as well as the dismantling of Jewish settlements, was seen as too high a price for Israel to pay. Shamir abstained on the final Knesset vote when the treaty was approved.

Begin appointed Shamir as his Foreign Minister in March 1980. Shamir's view of the Camp David process changed during his tenure as Foreign Minister when he was responsible for implementing the agreements reached, and he became an advocate of that approach for future negotiations between Israel and the Arab states. Shamir was also active in efforts to reestablish diplomatic relations with several African states, which had been severed at the time of the Yom Kippur War*. He also supported legislation declaring united Jerusalem* the eternal capital of Israel, as well as the bombing of the Iraqi nuclear reactor in June 1981, and the annexation of the Golan Heights* in December 1981. He saw these actions as contributing to Israel's security. After the 1981 Knesset election Shamir continued to serve as Foreign Minister. During this term in office Shamir was criticized by the Kahan Commission* because he failed to pass on to appropriate individuals information he received from Communications Minister Mordechai Zipori* suggesting that massacres were taking place in the Sabra and Shatila* camps near Beirut in September 1982.

Menachem Begin resigned from office in September 1983. Shamir was the compromise choice to follow Begin and he formed the new Government. On October 10, 1983, the Knesset endorsed the Government and its programs and Yitzhak Shamir became the Prime Minister of Israel, but many viewed him as an interim leader who would last only until the next Knesset election in 1984. The 1984 Knesset election results were inconclusive, and after a period of intense, lengthy, and complex negotiations, Labor and Likud formed, in September 1984, a Government of National Unity*, the basis of which was a series of compromises and concessions. According to the terms of the agreement, Shamir and Labor's Shimon Peres* each were to serve for 25 months as Prime

Minister while the other held the position of Vice Prime Minister and Foreign Minister. Peres was Prime Minister during the first period, and rotated* positions with Shamir as agreed in October 1986. The 1988 Knesset election, as in 1984, did not demonstrate a clear preference for either Likud or Labor among the electorate. After weeks of intensive negotiations Shamir entered into a new coalition agreement with Labor which placed Labor in an equal position with Likud in the Government. The distribution of cabinet portfolios among the two blocs was to be equal, but Shamir would remain the Prime Minister for the full tenure of the Government. In the spring of 1989, under persistent pressure from the United States*, Shamir (along with Defense Minister Yitzhak Rabin*), developed a complex peace initiative focusing on negotiations with the Palestinians. Building on the idea of Palestinian elections in the West Bank* and Gaza* and a five-year transitional period of local self-government, the Shamir Proposal was approved by the Likud-Labor National Unity Government on May 14, 1989. However, disagreements with the Bush Administration over specific aspects of the proposal and the absence of a positive response from the Arab side combined to scuttle the plan. Disagreement within the cabinet over the peace process reached a climax in the spring of 1990 that led to a vote of no confidence in the Government. Shamir headed a caretaker Government and, after an abortive effort by Shimon Peres to form a new Government, formed a Likud-led Government composed of right of center and religious political parties that won Knesset approval in June 1990.

Shamir governed Israel during the Persian Gulf War and took the difficult decision to abide by the American request to not respond militarily to Iraqi Scud missile* attacks. Following the end of the Gulf War, his Government agreed to participate in the Madrid Peace Conference*. Shamir became embroiled in a prolonged dispute with the Bush Administration and elements of the American Jewish community over U.S. loan guarantees for absorbing Soviet Jewish immigrants and over Likud policy toward Jewish settlements in the West Bank. Shamir announced his resignation as Likud leader following the party's defeat in the 1992 election of the 13th Knesset. He was succeeded by Benjamin Netanyahu* in the spring of 1993. He retired from party politics in 1996 but remained an active commentator on Israeli foreign and domestic affairs. He remained a strong critic of the Oslo Accords* and of Netanyahu's performance as Prime Minister. His autobiography, *Summing Up* (Boston: Little, Brown, 1994), provoked considerable controversy. In March 1999 he quit the Likud Party to join the newly established Herut Party of Benny Begin*.

For further information see: J. Bowyer Bell, *Terror Out of Zion: Irgun Tzva'i Le'umi: LEHI, Palestine Underground, 1929-1949* (New York: St. Martin's, 1977); Yitzhak Ben-Ami, *Years of Wrath, Days of Glory: Memoirs from the Irgun* (New York: Speller, 1982); Joel Brinkley, "The Stubborn Strength of Yitzhak Shamir," *New York Times Magazine* (August 21, 1988): 26-29, 68, 70, 72, 74, 76, 77; Joseph Heller, "The Zionist Right and National Liberation: From Jabotinsky to Avraham Stern," *Israel Affairs* 1:3 (Spring 1995): 85-109); Samuel Katz, *Days of Fire: The Secret History of the Irgun Tzva'i Le'umi* (New York: Doubleday, 1968); David Niv, *Battle of Freedom: The Irgun Tzva'i Le'umi*, 3 volumes (Tel Aviv: Klausner Institute, 1963-1967); Ilan Peleg, "The Foreign Policy of Herut and the Likud," in *Israeli National Security Policy: Political Actors and Perspectives*, edited by Bernard Reich and Gershon R. Kieval (New York: Greenwood, 1988): 55-78; Bernard Reich and Joseph Helman, "Yitzhak Shamir," in *Political Leaders of the Contemporary Middle East and North Africa*, edited by Bernard Reich (Westport, CT: Greenwood, 1990): 486-494; Yitzhak Shamir, "Israel's Role in a Changing Middle East," *Foreign Affairs* 60:4 (Spring 1982): 789-801; Yitzhak Shamir, "Israel at 40: Looking Back, Looking Ahead," *Foreign Affairs* 66:3 (1987/88): 574-590.

SHAPIRA, YOSEF. Born in Jerusalem* in 1926, Shapira graduated from yeshiva. He served as the World Secretary of the Bnei Akiva youth movement and of the World Executive of the Mizrahi* movement. Additionally, he served in the Government of National Unity* established in 1984 as Minister without Portfolio representing the Morasha* Party.

SHAPIRO, AVRAHAM. Born in Romania, Shapiro made aliya* in 1949. An ordained rabbi, he entered politics as a member of Agudat Israel* at the summons of the Gerer Rebbe (the Rabbi of Gur). In 1983 he was elected Ashkenazi* Chief Rabbi* of Israel, a position he held until 1993.

SHARANSKY, ANATOLY (NATAN). Born in Donetsk, Ukraine, in 1948, he was one of the most famous of the Prisoners of Zion* who were denied the right to emigrate from the Soviet Union and persecuted and imprisoned by the Soviets because of their avowed commitment to Zionism*. He graduated from the Physical Technical Institute in Moscow with a degree in computer science. In 1973 Sharansky's refusenik experience began. He applied for an exit visa to Israel but was denied for "security" reasons. Soon after this incident, in July 1974, he married Avital Shteiglitz. The Soviet authorities forced her, a few hours after their wedding, to leave the country for Israel. In March 1977, *Izvestia* published an article in which Sharansky was accused of collaborating with the CIA. Within 10 days, he was arrested on charges of treason and espionage and imprisoned in Moscow's Lefortovo Prison. Sharansky remained in complete isolation for one-and-a-half years before he was even brought to trial. During this period, hundreds of Soviet Jews were interrogated in connection with his case. The false accusations foreshadowed the threats and intimidation Jews faced in applying to emigrate to Israel. Sharansky was denied counsel of choice and so served as his own defense. Although the U.S.* Government categorically denied any connection between Sharansky and the CIA—including a statement by President Jimmy Carter—Sharansky was found guilty of the charges and sentenced to 13 years imprisonment: three years in isolation and 10 years of hard labor. In his last words to the Court, Sharansky spoke of the two thousand years of exile of the Jewish people. "Next Year in Jerusalem", were his final words to the Court in the face of persecution. An international campaign calling for Natan's release was waged by Avital in conjunction with organizations around the world. Sharansky's name featured prominently in petitions, demonstrations, and meetings at the highest levels. Finally released from the Soviet Union on February 11, 1986 (in exchange for a Soviet spy being held by the United States), he went directly to Israel where he was reunited with his wife, Avital. In 1986 he was elected president of the Soviet Jewry Zionist Forum, an umbrella organization of groups lobbying on behalf of Soviet Jewish immigrants in Israel. Reluctant to enter party politics, he resisted pressure to lead the Russian immigrant Da* list that unsuccessfully contested the 1992 Knesset* election. However, in 1996 he agreed to head the Israel B'Aliya* party that won seven seats in the 14th Knesset and joined the governing coalition formed by Benjamin Netanyahu*. In June 1996 he was appointed Minister of Industry and Trade and in addition served as a member of Netanyahu's kitchen cabinet* on security policy and the peace process, and was Israel's point man on political, economic, military, and cultural relations with Russia and other areas of the former Soviet Union. On May 17, 1999, Israel B'Aliya , under Sharansky's leadership, won six seats in the 15th Knesset. On July 6, 1999, it joined the coalition

Government headed by Ehud Barak*, with Sharansky serving as Interior Minister.

For further information see: Martin Gilbert, *Sharansky: Hero of Our Time* (New York: Viking, 1986); David Remnick, "The Afterlife," *The New Yorker* (August 11, 1997): 50-63.

SHAREF, ZE'EV. Born in Izvor-Szeletin, Romania, in 1906, Sharef became active in the Poalei Zion* youth movement in Romania. He migrated to Palestine* in 1925 and subsequently held a series of official and semiofficial posts in support of the Zionist movement and the Jewish community in Palestine. From 1943 to 1947 he served as secretary of the Political Department of the Jewish Agency*. He then was charged by the Provisional Council of State with the task of preparing the administrative machinery essential for the functioning of the new state upon termination of the British Mandate for Palestine*. From 1948 to 1957 he was Secretary of the Cabinet and from 1957 to 1959 he served as Director-General of the Prime Minister's Office. He held a number of other civil service positions and in 1965 was elected to the Knesset* on the Labor Alignment* list. He held a number of cabinet portfolios in the late 1960s and early 1970s. He died in Jerusalem* in 1984. His book, *Three Days* (New York: Doubleday, 1962) described the crucial events surrounding the termination of the British Mandate and the proclamation of the State of Israel in May 1948.

SHARETT, MOSHE (FORMERLY SHERTOK). Born in Kherson, Russia, in 1894 and raised in a Zionist household, Moshe Sharett immigrated with his family to Palestine* in 1906, settling in an Arab village in the Samarian Hills. In 1908 the family moved to Jaffa* where his father was a founder of the Ahuzat Bayit quarter, which later became Tel Aviv*. After high school, Sharett studied law in Constantinople and then volunteered as an officer in the Turkish army during World War I. In 1920, while studying at the London School of Economics, he joined the British Poalei Zion* movement. In 1931 he became Secretary of the Jewish Agency's* Political Department, and in 1933, at the 18th Zionist Conference, was elected head of the Political Department after the assassination of Chaim Arlosoroff. On June 29, 1946, Sharett and other leaders of the Jewish Agency were arrested by the British in Palestine and were imprisoned in the Latrun* camp for four months. During 1947 he sought approval at the United Nations for the United Nations Special

Committee on Palestine* Partition Plan*. Sharett became Israel's first Foreign Minister in 1948. Generally perceived as a relative moderate on peace and security issues (especially in comparison to David Ben-Gurion's* more hawkish approach), Sharett promoted a diplomatic solution to the dispute with Israel's neighbors. In addition, as Foreign Minister, he initially sought a nonaligned status for Israel, but after the Korean War he promoted closer ties with Western democratic countries. He sought contacts with developing nations in Asia and Africa and also signed the Luxembourg Agreement with West Germany's* Konrad Adenauer. In January 1954, after Prime Minister David Ben-Gurion* temporarily retired from office, Sharett became Prime Minister but retained the Foreign Affairs portfolio. With Ben-Gurion's return as Prime Minister in November 1955 against the background of the Lavon Affair* and the likelihood of renewed hostilities with Egypt*, disagreements surfaced between the two men and Sharett resigned. In 1960, Sharett was elected Chairman of the Executive of the World Zionist Organization* and Jewish Agency* and remained active in Mapai* party activities. He died in 1965.

For further information see: Ilan Pappe, "Moshe Sharett, David Ben-Gurion and the 'Palestinian Option', 1948-1956," *Studies in Zionism* 7:1 (1987); Menachem L. Rosensaft, *Moshe Sharett: Statesman of Israel* (New York: Shengold, 1966); Moshe Sharett, *A Personal Diary*, 8 volumes (Tel Aviv: Sifriat Ma'ariv, 1978, Hebrew); Gabriel Sheffer, *Resolution versus Management of the Middle East Conflict. A Reexamination of the Confrontation between Moshe Sharett and David Ben-Gurion* (Jerusalem: Magnes, 1980); Gabriel Sheffer, "Moshe Sharett (Shertok)," in *New Encyclopedia of Zionism and Israel*, edited by Geoffrey Wigoder (New York: Herzl Press, 1994): 1185-1186; Gabriel Sheffer, "Sharett's 'Line', Struggles, and Legacy," in *Israel: The First Decade of Independence*, edited by S. Ilan Troen and Noah Lucas (Albany: State University of New York Press, 1995): 143-169; Gabriel Sheffer, *Moshe Sharett: Biography of a Political Moderate* (Oxford University Press: Clarendon, 1996); Avi Shlaim, "Conflicting Approaches to Israel's Relations with the Arabs: Ben-Gurion and Sharett, 1953-1956," *Middle East Journal* 37:2 (1983): 180-201.

SHARIR, AVRAHAM. Born in 1932 in Tel Aviv*, he studied law at the Hebrew University* of Jerusalem, and became an attorney. He was active in youth and student circles of the General Zionist* Organization and served as Parliamentary Secretary of the Liberal Party* until 1964 and as its Secretary General from 1974. From 1964 to 1967 he headed the Jewish Agency* Economic Department in the United States* and served there as an economic consul for Israel from 1970 to 1974. From 1967 to 1970 he was Director General of the Employers' Organization, a member of the High Court for Labor Relations, and a member of the government Committee on Pensions. Sharir was first elected to the Ninth Knesset* in May 1977, after serving as Liberal Party* National Elections Manager. On August 5, 1981, following his reelection to the Tenth Knesset, he was sworn in as Minister of Tourism. He served as Minister of Tourism in the Government of National Unity* established in 1984, as well as Justice Minister from July 30, 1986, until the formation of the second unity Government in December 1988. Reelected to the 12th Knesset in 1988 on the Likud* list, he did not contest the 1992 elections.

SHARM EL-SHEIKH. A point on the southern tip of the Sinai Peninsula* which allows control of the passage of shipping through the Strait of Tiran* between the Red Sea and the Gulf of Aqaba*. Egypt* used its control of this geographic position to prevent shipping to Israel. The United Nations Emergency Force* (UNEF) was introduced to that location following Israel's withdrawal from Sinai in 1957 and remained there, guaranteeing freedom of navigation, until May 1967. Israel captured the position during the Six Day War* and remained there until after the Egypt-Israel Peace Treaty* which guaranteed freedom of passage.

For further information see: Mordechai Abir, *Sharm el-Sheikh—Bab al-Mandeb: The Strategic Balance and Israel's Southern Approaches* (Jerusalem: The Leonard Davis Institute for International Relations, Hebrew University of Jerusalem, March 1974); Ruth Lapidoth, *Freedom of Navigation with Special Reference to International Waterways in the Middle East* (Jerusalem: The Leonard Davis Institute for International Relations, Hebrew University of Jerusalem, 1975).

SHARON, ARIEL (NICKNAMED ARIK) (FORMERLY SHEINERMAN). He was born in 1928 in Kfar Malal, a farm village not far from present-day Tel Aviv*. At the age of 14 he joined the Hagana*, was wounded during the War of Independence* in 1948, and subsequently rose swiftly in the ranks of the Israel Defense Forces*. In 1952 he established the "101 Unit" for special operations (a special commando force known for its daring counter-terrorist operations behind enemy lines), and in 1956 he commanded a paratroop brigade, units of which parachuted into the Mitla Pass to mark the beginning of the Sinai War*. He then studied at the British Staff College in Camberley and, upon his return, was appointed head of the Israel Defense Forces School of Infantry. In 1962 he became Director of Military Training of the IDF and, that same year, he graduated from the law school of the Hebrew University*. In the Six Day War* of 1967 he commanded an armored division which fought in the Sinai Peninsula* and, in 1969, became commanding officer of the Southern Command.

In June 1973 Sharon resigned from the IDF, joined the Liberal Party*, and was instrumental in bringing about the alignment of Herut*, the Free Center*, the State List*, and the Liberal Party* within the framework of the Likud bloc*. The Yom Kippur War* brought him back to active military service as a reserve officer in command of an armored division, units of which were the first to cross the Suez Canal and establish an Israeli bridgehead on the Egyptian side. In December 1973 he stood for election to the Knesset*, and was elected on behalf of the Liberal Party faction of the Likud bloc. In December 1974 Sharon resigned from the Knesset, in order that his reserve commission with the IDF might be reinstated. In June 1975 he was appointed adviser to Prime Minister Yitzhak Rabin* on security affairs and held that position until April 1976, when he resigned to form the Shlomzion Party*, which gained two seats in the elections to the Ninth Knesset in May 1977. Immediately following the elections, the Shlomzion Party merged with the Herut Party faction of the Likud bloc, and it was on this ticket that he was reelected to the Tenth Knesset on May 30, 1981. He was appointed Minister of Agriculture in June 1977. On August 5, 1981, he was sworn in as Minister of Defense, but was forced from this position in February 1983 after the Kahan Commission of Inquiry* report concerning the massacre at the Sabra and Shatila* refugee camps in Lebanon* was published. But he remained in the Cabinet. He later became Minister of Industry and Trade and in December 1988 was reappointed to that position. In June 1990 he became Minister of Construction and Housing. In that capacity he instituted a plan to increase substantially the number of Jewish settlers in Judea* and Samaria*. Although he initially announced his intention to vie for the prime ministership in 1996, he subsequently withdrew and instead concentrated on unifying the center-right vote behind the Likud's Prime Ministerial candidate, Benjamin Netanyahu*. Sharon played an important role in facilitating the formation of the joint "national camp" list for the 1996 Knesset election involving the Likud, Gesher*, and Tsomet*. He was initially not included in the cabinet formed by Netanyahu but after intense negotiations he agreed to accept a new portfolio, that of Minister of National Infrastructure. He also was named a member of Netanyahu's kitchen cabinet* on foreign and security policy and in that capacity formulated a model of "strategic interests" in the West Bank* that helped to set the parameters for the internal debate in Israel over the future nature of relations with the Palestinians. Appointed Foreign Minister in October 1998, he joined Netanyahu in negotiations with the Palestinians that culminated with the Wye River Memorandum* of October 23, 1998. On May 17, 1999, Sharon was reelected to the 15th Knesset on the Likud list, and he was chosen temporary leader of the party after Benjamin Netanyahu's resignation following his defeat to One Israel's* Ehud Barak* in the direct election for Prime Minister and Likud's defeat in the Knesset election. On September 2, 1999, he was elected party leader, defeating Ehud Olmert* and Meir Shitreet*.

For further information see: Uzi Benziman, *Sharon: An Israeli Caesar* (New York: Adama, 1986).

SHAS *see* SEPHARDI TORAH GUARDIANS

SHAVIT, SHABTAI. Born in Nesher, near Haifa*, he served in the IDF's* General Staff Reconnaissance Unit and joined the Mossad* in 1964. He was appointed its head in 1989. He ended his 32-year career in the Mossad on June 2, 1996. He earned a BA in Arabic language and literature and Middle East history and received his MA in public administration from Harvard University.

SHAZAR, SHNEOR ZALMAN (FORMERLY RUBASHOV). Born in Mir in the Minsk Province of Russia, on October 6, 1889, he later moved with his family to Stolbtsy, where he received a traditional *heder* education. Encouraged by his parents' Zionism*, he entered the Poalei Zion* movement in Russia in 1905. During the unsuccessful Russian revolution of 1905 he participated in Jewish self-defense groups. In 1907, he moved to Vilna, where he wrote for Yiddish* newspapers in Russia and in the United States*. He left for Palestine* in 1911 but returned to Russia and then, beginning in 1912, he studied at several German universities. In 1916, he became one of the founders of the Labor Zionist movement in

Germany*, and the next year helped found the Hehalutz movement in Germany. At the Poalei Zion conference in Vienna in 1920 he gained notice as a prominent spokesman for the right wing. He was responsible for the first conference of the World Hehalutz Organization in 1921. He settled in Palestine* in 1924, and became a member of the secretariat of the Histadrut* and joined the editorial board of *Davar*. In 1949, he was elected to Israel's First Knesset* and served as Minister of Education and Culture, in which capacity he was responsible for the 1949 Compulsory Education Law. In 1952, the Soviet Government refused to accept him as Israel's Ambassador to Moscow. He became a member of the Executive of the Jewish Agency* in 1952 and headed the Department of Information, and after 1954 the Department of Education and Culture in the Diaspora*. Between 1956 and 1960, he was acting chairman of the Jewish Agency's Jerusalem* Executive. Shazar was elected the third President of Israel on May 21, 1963, and reelected in March 1968 and served until 1973. As President, he sponsored the Bible Study Circle and the Circle for the Study of the Diaspora. He wrote voluminously on political, social, and historical themes. In January 1964 he was awarded the Bialik Prize for his book on Jewish personalities. He died in Jerusalem* on October 5, 1974.

SHEINBEIN, SAMUEL. Samuel Sheinbein was accused of killing, dismembering, and burning Alfredo Enrique Tello, Jr., in Maryland. He fled to Israel, claimed citizenship, and sought to avoid facing trial in the United States. Although Israeli prosecutors sought extradition, the Israeli Supreme Court* decided that he would not be returned to the United States to stand trial under existing law. It ruled that he could not be extradited because of an Israeli law that prohibited the extradition of Israeli citizens. He was to be tried in Israel. The issue generated tension in United States-Israel relations. Prior to his trial he agreed to a plea bargain deal in which he admitted to the murder and received a 24-year jail sentence.

The Knesset* later amended Israel's extradition statute that blocked his return to the United States. Israelis who live in Israel and are accused of crimes abroad can be extradited under a valid extradition treaty under certain circumstances. However, the law offers no protection to someone who did not reside in Israel whether or not that person was an Israeli citizen.

SHELLI (SHALOM LEYISRAEL; PEACE FOR ISRAEL). After the split with the New Communist* List in 1965, Maki* became more moderate in its opposition to Government policies and became primarily Jewish in membership. In 1975, it merged with Moked* (Focus), a socialist party, and in 1977, Moked united with other noncommunist groups to form Shelli. The new party was founded by Arie Eliav*, a former Labor Party* Secretary General. The party's platform called for the establishment of a Palestinian Arab state, the withdrawal of Israel to its pre-1967 borders, and political negotiations with the Palestine Liberation Organization* on the basis of mutual recognition. Shelli's campaign for the 1977 election secured it two seats—Arie Eliav and Meir Pail, the former Moked leader—but the party was unsuccessful in the 1981 election.

SHEMTOV, VICTOR. Born in 1918 in Sofia, Bulgaria, he became involved in socialist Zionism* at an early age. He immigrated to Palestine* in 1939 and soon became active in the Hagana*. He entered politics in 1944, joining the Socialist League which later helped to form Mapam*. He became Secretary General of the party in 1979 and served as a member of the Knesset* since 1961. Following the Yom Kippur War*, Shemtov and fellow cabinet minister Aharon Yariv advocated Israel's recognition of the PLO* in exchange for PLO recognition of Israel and disengagement from terror. The so-called Yariv-Shemtov formula was rejected by the Rabin*-led coalition Government in 1974 and by the Labor Party* platform committee. Nevertheless, the core components of the Yariv-Shemtov formula—mutual recognition between Israel and the PLO and an end to PLO terrorism—was instituted in the context of the Oslo peace accords* of September 1993.

For further information see: Mordechai Bar-On, *In Pursuit of Peace: A History of the Israeli Peace Movement* (Washington, DC: U.S. Institute of Peace, 1996); Efraim Inbar, *War and Peace in Israeli Politics: Labor Party Positions on National Security* (Boulder, CO: Lynne Rienner, 1991); Peretz Merhav, *The Israeli Left: History, Problems, Documents* (San Diego: A. S. Barnes, 1980).

SHERTOK, MOSHE *see* MOSHE SHARETT

SHILOAH, REUVEN. An intelligence official in the Yishuv*, Reuven Shiloah was involved in the Rhodes and Lausanne talks following Israel's War of Independence* and in the secret negotiations between Israel and

King Abdullah of Jordan* in 1949-1950. He was the founder and first director of the Mossad* (March 1951 to September 1952). He served as Minister in Israel's Embassy in Washington (1953-1957) and as an adviser to then Foreign Minister Golda Meir* (1958-1959). He died in 1959 at age 49. An institute of Middle Eastern and African Studies at Tel Aviv University was named in his memory; it subsequently was incorporated into the Moshe Dayan Center for Middle Eastern and African Studies. See also MOSSAD.

For further information see: Haggai Eshed, Reuven Shiloah—The Man behind the Mossad: Secret Diplomacy in the Creation of Israel (London: Frank Cass, 1997).

SHIN BET (SHABAK). Acronym for Sherut Bitahon Klali (General Security Services). The organization responsible for prevention of hostile secret activity in Israel including espionage and sabotage. It was founded in 1948 and headed by Isser Harel* until 1954. Carmi Gillon was named head of the Shin Bet in early 1995, replacing Yaacov Peri; however, Gillon was forced to resign less than one year later following the November 1995 assassination of Prime Minister Yitzhak Rabin* and was replaced by the former chief of the Israeli navy, Ami Ayalon. Though badly shaken by controversies surrounding the Rabin assassination and by a number of other operational failures in recent years, as well as by greater public scrutiny of its methods of operation (including its methods for interrogating terrorists), the Shin Bet remains an important component of Israel's intelligence and national security community.

SHINUI (CHANGE). In the wake of the Yom Kippur War* a small protest group called "Shinui—The Political and Social Revival Movement" was founded by Professor Amnon Rubinstein* of Tel Aviv University. It sought to effect changes in the Israeli political system and political life and developed a party organization, but did not have a candidate of imposing stature. In 1976, it joined with others to form the Democratic Movement for Change* (DASH) which secured 15 seats in the 1977 Knesset* election under the leadership of Professor Yigael Yadin*, who agreed to serve as Deputy Prime Minister in the coalition formed by Menachem Begin*. The party included Shinui, Yadin's own Democratic Movement*, and individuals and groups form both within and outside the existing political parties. Although composed mostly of elements of the center-left, Shinui could not be classified in terms of traditional Israeli political ideology.

It sought to present itself as a "centrist" alternative to both Labor* and Likud*. It focused on the need for electoral reform and general improvement in the political life of the country, and encouraged a free enterprise economy, the protection of individual rights (to be enshrined in a formal, written constitution), and opposition to religious coercion. In the foreign policy realm Shinui favored a negotiated peace agreement with the Arabs, arguing that this would free Israel from the cycle of war and bloodshed and prevent it from becoming a binational state which would rule over another people. Israel's security would be guaranteed by secure border adjustment, security arrangements, and the demilitarization of evacuated areas. After DMC's dissolution, Shinui again emerged as an independent party and won two seats in the 1981 elections. It won three seats in the 1984 election and was a junior partner in the 1984-1988 National Unity Government*. It joined with the Independent Liberal* and the Liberal Center* parties to form the Center-Shinui movement and won two seats in the 12th Knesset (1988). In 1992 it joined with two other Zionist-left parties (the Citizens' Rights Movement* and Mapam*) to form the Meretz/Democratic Israel* coalition that won 12 seats in the 13th Knesset and participated in the coalition headed by Yitzhak Rabin*, with party leader Amnon Rubinstein* serving as Minister of Education. Shinui and Meretz won nine seats in the 14th Knesset (1996). Prior to the May 17, 1999, elections to the 15th Knesset, Shinui went its own way. In the beginning of 1997, the Citizens' Rights Movement and Mapam decided to formally unite Meretz into one political party. A group of Shinui members led by Amnon Rubinstein left Shinui and joined Meretz. Running independently under the leadership of the prominent journalist and television personality, Yosef (Tommy) Lapid*, and on a platform dominated by opposition to what Lapid called the "religious coercion" employed by the ultra-Orthodox parties and the unfair special privileges accorded the Haredi parties in order to secure their support in governing coalitions. Shinui campaigned for an end to wide-scale deferments from military service accorded to students in ultra-Orthodox yeshivas and an end to overly generous financial concessions to the ultra-Orthodox parties and their institutions. It advocated a formal separation of religion that would in turn be incorporated into a written constitution that would "retain the Jewish and Zionist nature of the State, while ensuring the rights of minorities and individual rights, in the spirit of Israel's

Declaration of Independence." In foreign and security policy, Shinui's 1999 platform endorsed the Oslo Peace Accords and pledged support for "future agreements with the Palestinians which will ensure peace and secure borders for Israel in which a united Jerusalem is the capital of Israel alone." Shinui won six seats in the 15th Knesset. However, unable to reconcile its opposition to working with the ultra-Orthodox political parties, Shinui remained outside of the governing coalition formed by Labor's Ehud Barak*.

For further information see: David H. Goldberg, *Democracy in Action 1999: A Guide to the Participants and Issues in Israeli Politics* (Toronto: Canada-Israel Committee, May 1999).

SHITREET (OR SHEETRIT), MEIR. Born in 1948 in Morocco, he immigrated to Israel in 1957. Educated at Bar Ilan University*, he served as Mayor of Yavneh from 1974 to 1987 and as Treasurer of the Jewish Agency for Israel* from 1988 to 1992. First elected to the Knesset* in 1981, on the Likud* list, he sat on many Knesset committees, including: Finance; Constitution; Law and Justice; and Education and Culture. During the 14th Knesset (1996-1999), he served as Deputy Speaker of the Knesset and as Knesset Coalition Leader. He served as Minister of Finance from February to July 1999. He was reelected to the 15th Knesset on May 17, 1999, on the Likud list. He vied to succeed Benjamin Netanyahu* as Likud leader, but was defeated by Ariel Sharon*.

SHLEMUT HAMOLEDET. The concept of the right of the Jewish people to all of Eretz Israel*. The Revisionist Party*, established by Vladimir Jabotinsky* in 1925, and his New Zionist Organization* supported the principle of Shlemut Hamoledet, and rejected Arab claims for national and political sovereignty in Palestine*.

SHLOMZION PARTY. A political party formed by Ariel Sharon* which contested the 1977 Knesset* election and won two seats in parliament. It then joined the Likud*.

SHOAH *see* HOLOCAUST

SHOCHAT, AVRAHAM ("BEIGE"). Born in Tel Aviv in 193, he was educated as a construction engineer at the Technion*. One of the founders of the southern city of Arad and former head of its local council, Shochat was first elected to the Knesset* in 1988 on the Israel Labor* Party list and from 1992 to 1996 he served as Finance Minister. He was appointed Finance Minister again on July 6, 1999, by Ehud Barak*.

SHOMRON, DAN. Born in 1937 in Ashdot Yaacov, he joined the Israel Defense Forces* in 1956. He holds a BA degree in geography from Tel Aviv University. As chief infantry and paratrooper officer of the IDF, he was placed in overall command of the Entebbe Operation*, the July 1976 operation to rescue hostages being held by Palestinian and German terrorists at the airport at Entebbe, Uganda. Shomron became chief of staff of the IDF in 1987 and retained that post until retiring from active service in April 1991. He was involved in the early organizing of The Third Way (Derech HaSlisheet)* Party that made a successful entry into the electoral process in the Knesset* elections of 1996. In late 1996, Shomron served briefly as Israel's chief negotiator in security talks with the Palestinian Authority*.

SHOSTAK, ELIEZER. He was born in Poland on December 16, 1911, and emigrated to Palestine* in 1935. From 1957 to 1959 he studied philosophy and Kabala at Hebrew University*. He was one of the founders of the Herut Party*, from which he resigned in 1966, and subsequently was a member of the La'am* faction of the Likud* bloc. First elected on behalf of Herut to the Second Knesset* in July 1951, and reelected to subsequent Knessets, he served on the Labor, Economics, Public Services, and Finance Committees of the Knesset. He also was Secretary General of the National Federation of Labor and Chairman of the National Health Insurance Fund. He became Minister of Health in June 1977, serving in that post until 1984.

SHOVAL, ZALMAN (ORIGINALLY FINKELSTEIN). He was born in Danzig on April 28, 1930, but left with his family before World War II for Tel Aviv*. He served in the army and studied economics and international affairs at the University of California at Berkeley and at the Graduate Institute of International Studies in Geneva. He started his career in the Israeli foreign ministry in the 1950s but left to enter a family business. He later entered politics, beginning his affiliation with Rafi* and the State List* under Ben-Gurion*. He became a member of the Knesset* in 1970. The State List* later moved to Likud* and Shoval shifted as well. He later joined the Knesset on the Likud list. From 1990 to 1992 he served as Ambassador of Israel to the United States*, a posting he resumed in July

1998. He declared his intention to resign as ambassador following the May 17, 1999, elections in Israel and completed his term in Washington in January 2000.

SINAI CAMPAIGN *see* SINAI WAR

SINAI PENINSULA. The land bridge between Asia and Africa, some 23,000 square miles in size. It has the shape of a triangle bounded by the Gulf of Suez in the West, the Gulf of Aqaba* in the East, and the Mediterranean Sea in the North. Its highest point is Jebel Musa (the Biblical Mount Sinai). The peninsula was occupied by Israel in the Sinai War* and, after its return to Egypt* in 1957 it was captured again in the Six Day War*. It was evacuated by Israel and returned to Egypt in accordance with the Egypt-Israel Peace Treaty of 1979*.

SINAI II ACCORDS (1975). A complex of agreements between Israel and Egypt* achieved through the shuttle diplomacy of United States* Secretary of State Henry Kissinger. They were signed in Geneva on September 4, 1975, by representatives of Egypt and Israel, and constituted a significant accomplishment. The agreements consisted of a formal agreement between the two parties, an annex, and a proposal for an American presence in Sinai in connection with an early-warning system. In addition there were memoranda of agreement between the United States and Israel and separate United States assurances to Israel and Egypt. This was more than a simple disengagement of military forces since the parties agreed that "the conflict between them and in the Middle East shall not be resolved by military force but by peaceful means." These were the first steps toward increased accommodation between the parties and it moved in the direction of a peace settlement. It was in the Memorandum of Agreement between the United States and Israel regarding the Geneva Peace Conference that the United States pledged that it "will continue to adhere to its present policy with respect to the Palestine Liberation Organization*, whereby it will not recognize or negotiate with the Palestine Liberation Organization so long as the Palestine Liberation Organization does not recognize Israel's right to exist and does not accept Security Council Resolutions 242* and 338*."

For further information see: Boutros Boutros-Ghali, *Egypt's Road to Jerusalem: A Diplomat's Story of the Struggle for Peace in the Middle East* (New York: Random House, 1997); Matti Golan, *The Secret*

Conversations of Henry Kissinger: Step-by-Step Diplomacy in the Middle East (New York: Quadrangle, 1976); Henry A. Kissinger, *Years of Upheaval* (Boston: Little, Brown, 1982); William B. Quandt, *Decade of Decisions: American Policy toward the Arab-Israeli Conflict, 1967-1976* (Berkeley: University of California Press, 1977); Yitzhak Rabin, *The Rabin Memoirs* (Boston: Little, Brown, 1979); Bernard Reich, editor, *Arab-Israeli Conflict and Conciliation: A Documentary History* (Westport, CT: Praeger, 1995); Edward R. F. Sheehan, *The Arabs, Israelis, and Kissinger: A Secret History of American Diplomacy in the Middle East* (New York: Reader's Digest Press, 1976); Robert Slater, *Rabin of Israel: A Biography*, Revised Edition (London: Robson, 1993); Steven L. Spiegel, *The Other Arab-Israeli Conflict: Making America's Middle East Policy, from Truman to Reagan* (Chicago: University of Chicago Press, 1985).

SINAI WAR (1956). The war had its origins in the regional tensions which were common after the Egyptian Revolution of 1952. The arms race was continuing, and tension grew further when the Czechoslovakian-Egyptian arms deal*, announced in September 1955, introduced the Soviet Union as a major arms supplier to the Arab-Israeli sector of the Middle East. Palestinian fedayeen* (commando) attacks into Israel were on the increase. At the same time Britain* and France* opposed Egypt's* nationalization of the Suez Canal and its support of anti-French rebels in North Africa. Britain and France agreed with Israel that action against the dangers posed by President Gamal Abdul Nasser of Egypt and his policies was essential, and the three powers secretly organized a coordinated operation. Israel moved into the Sinai Peninsula* on October 29, 1956, and by the afternoon of the next day Britain and France issued an ultimatum (as previously agreed) calling on both sides to stop fighting and to withdraw to positions 10 miles (16 kilometers) on either side of the Suez Canal. Israel accepted, but Egypt rejected the proposal. By November 5 Israel had occupied Sharm el-Sheikh*, and the fighting ended. Israel eventually withdrew from all of the territory its forces had occupied during the conflict under the weight of United Nations resolutions but especially under pressure from the Eisenhower Administration. The United States* provided assurances to Israel concerning freedom of navigation through the Strait of Tiran* and in the Gulf of Aqaba*. The United Nations Emergency Force* (UNEF) was created to patrol the Egyptian side of the Egypt-Israel armistice line, which it did until the days immediately preceding the Six Day War*.

For further information see: Mordechai Bar-On, *The Gates of Gaza: Israel's Road to Suez and Back, 1955-1957* (London: Macmillan, 1994); Shlomo Barer, *The Weekend War* (New York: Yoseloff, 1960); A. J. Barker, *Suez: The Seven Day War* (London: Faber and Faber, 1964); Robert R. Bowie, *Suez, 1956: International Crisis and the Role of Law* (New York: Oxford University Press, 1975); Michael Brecher, *Decisions in Israel's Foreign Policy* (London: Oxford University Press, 1974); Merry Bromberger and Serge Bromberger, *Secrets of Suez* (London: Pan Books and Sidgwick and Jackson, 1957); E. L. M. Burns, *Between Arab and Israeli* (Beirut: The Institute for Palestine Studies, 1969); Peter Calvocoressi, *Suez Ten Years Later* (New York: Random House, 1967); Erskine B. Childers, *The Road to Suez* (London: MacGibbon and Kee, 1962); Moshe Dayan, *Diary of the Sinai Campaign, 1956* (London: Sphere Books, 1967); Anthony Eden, *Full Circle* (Boston: Houghton Mifflin, 1960); Anthony Eden, *The Suez Crisis of 1956* (Boston: Beacon, 1968); Herman Finer, *Dulles Over Suez* (Chicago: Quadrangle Books, 1964); Motti Golani, *Israel in Search of a War: The Sinai Campaign, 1955-1956* (Brighton, UK: Sussex Academic Press, 1998); Robert Henriques, *A Hundred Hours to Suez: An Account of Israel's Campaign in the Sinai Peninsula* (New York: Pyramid Books, 1967); Chaim Herzog, *The Arab-Israeli Wars* (New York: Random House, 1982); Paul Johnson, *The Suez War* (New York: Greenberg, 1957); Selwyn Lloyd, *Suez: The Twice-Fought War* (New York: McGraw-Hill, 1969); Selwyn Lloyd, *Suez 1956: A Personal Account* (New York: Mayflower, 1978); William Roger Louis and E. Roger Owen, editors, *Suez 1956: The Crisis and Its Consequences* (London: Oxford University Press, 1989); S. L. A. Marshall, *Sinai Victory: Command Decisions in History's Shortest War, Israel's Hundred-Hour Conquest of Sinai* (New York: William Morrow, 1958); Benny Morris, *Israel's Border Wars, 1949-1956: Arab Infiltration, Israeli Retaliation and the Countdown to the Suez War* (Oxford University Press: Clarendon, 1994); Donald Neff, *Warriors at Suez: Eisenhower Takes America into the Middle East* (New York: Linden, 1981); Anthony Nutting, *I Saw for Myself* (New York: Doubleday, 1958); Edgar O'Ballance, *The Sinai Campaign* (London: Faber and Faber, 1959); Nadav Safran, *From War to War: The Arab-Israeli Confrontation, 1948-1967* (New York: Praeger, 1969); Ernest Stock, *Israel on the Road to Sinai, 1949-1956* (Ithaca, NY: Cornell University Press, 1967); S. Ilan Troen, "The Protocol of Sevres: British/French/Israeli Collusion against Egypt, 1956," *Israel Studies* 1:2 (Fall 1996): 122-139.

SINGER, JOEL *see* YOEL ZINGER

SIX DAY WAR (1967). In mid-May 1967, Egypt* (goaded by Arab criticism for its passivity vis-à-vis Israel and false Soviet* information about Israeli military mobilizations) proclaimed a state of emergency, mobilized its army, and moved troops across the Sinai Peninsula* toward the border with Israel. President Gamal Abdul Nasser requested the removal of the United Nations Emergency Force (UNEF)* from the Egypt-Israel frontier, and United Nations Secretary General U Thant complied. The UNEF positions were then manned by contingents of the Egyptian armed forces and of the Palestine Liberation Organization*. Egypt and Israel faced each other with no buffer, and Nasser announced that the Strait of Tiran* would be closed to Israeli shipping and to strategic cargoes bound for Israel's port of Eilat*. Israel regarded these actions as *casus belli*, illegal, and aggressive.

On May 30, 1967, Jordan* entered into a defense pact with Syria* and Egypt, and Iraqi* troops were stationed along the Israel-Jordan front. In response to the failure of the international community to take any tangible action to support Israel in the developing crisis, Israel decided to act on its own. It created a "wall-to-wall*" political coalition (excluding the Communists) in a Government of National Unity*, and Moshe Dayan* became the Defense Minister. On June 5, 1967, Israel launched a preemptive strike against Egyptian air forces and bases. The war was broadened after Jordan and Syria joined in the conflict, initiating their participation by shelling Israeli positions in Jerusalem* and from the Golan Heights* respectively. Israel decisively defeated Egypt, Jordan, Syria, and their allies, and in six days radically transformed the situation in the Middle East: It was in control of territories stretching from the Golan Heights* in the north to Sharm el-Sheikh* in the Sinai Peninsula, and from the Suez Canal to the Jordan River*. The territories included the Sinai Peninsula*; the Gaza Strip*; the West Bank*, referred to by Israel as Judea* and Samaria*; the Golan Heights; and East Jerusalem*.

For further information see: Alex Benson, editor, *The 48 Hour War* (New York: IN Publishing Corporation, 1967); Ruth Bondy, Ohad Zemora, and Raphael Bashan, editors, *Mission Survival* (New York: Sabra, 1968); Michael Brecher, *Decisions in Crisis: Israel, 1967 and 1973* (Berkeley: University of California Press, 1980); Randolph A. Churchill and Winston S. Churchill, *The Six Day War* (London: Heinemann, 1967);

David Dayan, *Strike First: A Battle History of the Six-Day War* (New York: Pitman, 1967); Robert J. Donovan and the Staff of the *Los Angeles Times*, *Israel's Fight for Survival: Six Days in June: June 5-10, 1967* (New York: New American Library, 1967); Theodore Draper, *Israel and World Politics: Roots of the Third Arab-Israeli War* (New York: Viking, 1968); Janice Gross Stein and Raymond Tanter, *Rational Decision-Making: Israel's Security Choices 1967* (Columbus: Ohio State University Press, 1980); Chaim Herzog, *The Arab-Israeli Wars* (New York: Random House, 1982); Michael Howard and Robert Hunter, *Israel and the Arab World: The Crisis of 1967* (London: Adelphi Papers, International Institute of Strategic Studies, 1967); Keesing's Research Report, *The Arab-Israeli Conflict: The 1967 Campaign* (New York: Scribner, 1968); David Kimche and Dan Bavly, *The Six Day War: Prologue and Aftermath* (New York: Stein and Day, 1971); Hal Kosut, editor, *Israel and the Arabs: The June 1967 War* (New York: Facts On File, 1968); Walter Laqueur, *The Road to War: The Origins and Aftermath of the Arab-Israeli Conflict 1967-68* (Baltimore: Penguin, 1969); Robert Moskin, *Among Lions: The Battle for Jerusalem, June 5-7, 1967* (New York: Arbor House, 1982); Edgar O'Ballance, *The Third Arab-Israeli War* (London: Faber and Faber, 1972); Richard B. Parker, *The Six Day War: A Retrospective* (Gainesville: University Press of Florida, 1996); Glubb Pasha, *The Middle East Crisis: A Personal Interpretation* (London: Hodder and Stoughton, 1967); Indar J. Rihkye, *The Sinai Blunder: Withdrawal of the Force Leading to the Six Day War* (London: Cass, 1980); Donald B. Robinson, *Under Fire: Israel's 20 Year Struggle for Survival* (New York: W.W. Norton, 1968); Menahem Z. Rosensaft, *Not Backward to Belligerency: A Study of Events Surrounding the Six-Day War of June 1967* (New York: Yoseloff, 1969); Nadav Safran, *From War to War: The Arab-Israeli Confrontation, 1947-1967* (New York: Pegasus, 1969); Avraham Shapira, editor, *The Seventh Day: Soldiers' Talk about the Six-Day War* (New York: Scribner's, 1970); William Stevenson, *Strike Zion!* (New York: Bantam Books, 1967); Fred Wehling, *Irresolute Princes: Kremlin Decision Making in Middle East Crises, 1967 and 1973* (New York: St. Martin's, 1997).

SMALL CONSTITUTION. Israel's system of government is based on an unwritten constitution. The first legislative act of the Constituent Assembly* in February 1949 was to enact a Transition Law, often referred to as the Small Constitution, that became the basis of constitutional life in the state. Administrative and executive procedures were based on a combination of past experience in self-government, elements adapted from the former Mandatory structure, and new legislation. According to the Small Constitution, Israel was established as a republic with a weak president* and a strong cabinet* and parliament (Knesset*). It was anticipated that this document would be replaced in due course by a more extensive and permanent one. A "constitutional revolution" occurred in the late 1980s and early 1990s, against the background of growing popular pressure for the promulgation of a formal written constitution and bill of rights. *See also* BASIC LAWS.

SNEH, EFRAIM. Born in 1944 in Tel Aviv*, Efraim Sneh was trained as a physician at Tel Aviv Medical School. For many years he served as a career soldier in the Israel Defense Forces*. Medical officer of the paratroops corps during the 1973 Yom Kippur War* and Chief Medical Officer of the paratroops and infantry corps (1974-1978), he commanded the medical team in the Entebbe Operation* in July 1976. He was a commander of an elite IDF unit (1978-1980) and the Chief Medical Officer of IDF Northern Command (1980-1981) as well as the Commander of the South Lebanon security zone* (1981-1982). He then was named head of Civil Administration in the West Bank* (1985-1987). He retired from active military service in 1987 with the rank of Brigadier-General. He became director of the Golda Meir* Association for the education and promotion of democratic values and was first elected to the Knesset*, on the Labor* list, in 1992, and served as a member of the Knesset Foreign Affairs and Defense Committee. He was appointed Minister of Health by Yitzhak Rabin* on June 1, 1993, remaining in that position in the Government formed by Shimon Peres* on November 22, 1995, following Rabin's assassination. In the 14th Knesset (1996-1999), he sat on the influential Knesset State Audit Committee. He vied for the leadership of the Labor Party in June 1997, but was defeated by Ehud Barak*. On May 17, 1999, Sneh was reelected to the 15th Knesset on the One Israel* list, and on July 6, 1999, he was appointed Deputy Defense Minister under Ehud Barak, who served as both Defense Minister and Prime Minister.

SOLEL BONEH. Literally "paves and builds." A roadbuilding and construction company belonging to the Histadrut*. During the Arab riots in Palestine* from 1936 to 1939, Solel Boneh helped build farm settlements, pave security roads, construct airfields, and erect fortifications. During World War II it helped the British army pave roads and construct airfields, bridges, and army camps. Solel Boneh subsidiaries supply much of the Israeli national demand for stone, gravel, marble, and cement, as well as most of its plumbing and bathroom fittings. The company employs many factory workers in its various enterprises. Its activities have become international and since the 1960s considerable contract work has been carried out in Africa. Its overseas activities are often coordinated with Mashav, the international development assistance arm of the Israel Foreign Ministry.

For further information see: Michael Curtis and Susan Aurelia Gitelson, editor, *Israel in the Third World* (New Brunswick, NJ: Transaction, 1976); Samuel Decalo, *Israel and Africa: Forty Years, 1956-1996* (Gainesville: Florida Academic Press, 1998); Samuel Kurland, *Cooperative Politics: The Story of the Histadrut* (New York: Sharon Books of the National Committee For Labor of Palestine, 1947); Noah Malkoah, *Histadrut in Israel: Its Aims and Achievements* (Tel Aviv: Histadrut, 1961); Ze'ev Tzahor, "The Histadrut: From Marginal Organization to 'State-in-the-Making,'" in *Essential Papers on Zionism*, edited by Jehuda Reinharz and Anita Shapira (New York: New York University Press, 1996): 473-508.

SOUTH LEBANESE ARMY (SLA) (ALSO KNOWN AS THE FREE LEBANON MILITIA AND THE ARMY OF FREE LEBANON). A mostly Christian militia, armed and funded by Israel and operating in Israel's security zone* in southern Lebanon*. The close working relationship between it and Israel dates from the mid-1970s when Israel and the Lebanese Christians found common cause in curbing PLO* terrorist activity in southern Lebanon—terrorism that provoked Israeli responses that would invariably harm the interests of the local, mainly Christian, population in the border region. The SLA also opposed the growing autonomous influence of the PLO presence in southern Lebanon—"Fatahland"*—that threatened to disrupt the delicate political balance in the country between Christians and Muslims. In addition, Israel and the SLA shared an opposition to Syria's* overwhelming military presence in and political influence over Lebanon. The first formal funding by Israel of the SLA forces headed by Major Saad Georges Haddad occurred in June 1978 (although informal ties with Haddad's militia existed as early as 1975 and the outbreak of the civil war in Lebanon). Following Haddad's death from cancer in January 1984 leadership over the movement passed to Major General Antoine Lahad*. He immediately changed the official name of the movement from the Free

Lebanon Military to the South Lebanese Army, to reflect the fact that the SLA was no longer just for Christians but for all Lebanese who opposed the PLO and Syrian presence in their country. With the reduced influence of the PLO in Lebanon following the 1982 Operation Peace for Galilee*, the primary focus of SLA activities became cooperating with Israeli forces in combating Shi'ite Muslim militant groups such as Hezbollah and Amal. A major Hezbollah strategy was to target SLA fighters, in the hopes of demoralizing them and weakening their ties to Israel. One of the arguments used by those Israelis opposed to an IDF withdrawal from the security zone is concern about what will happen to Israel's allies in the South Lebanese Army.

For further information see: Yasha Manuel Harari, "South Lebanese Army," in *An Historical Encyclopedia of the Arab-Israeli Conflict*, edited by Bernard Reich (Westport, CT: Greenwood, 1996): 490-491; Beate Hamizrachi, *The Emergence of the South Lebanon Security Belt: Major Saad Haddad and the Ties with Israel, 1975-1978* (New York: Praeger, 1988).

SOVIET UNION see USSR

SPECIAL RELATIONSHIP see GERMANY; UNITED STATES OF AMERICA

STATE COMPTROLLER. In May 1949 the Knesset* passed the State Comptroller Law of 5709 (1949) which established, under its aegis, the Office of the State Comptroller to supervise the activities of the Government, the ministries, local authorities, government corporations, and other bodies, if the Government or the Knesset so desires. The Comptroller is appointed by the President* upon recommendation of the Knesset but is independent of the Government and responsible only to the Knesset, a regulation that is strictly interpreted. Its annual report is published and presented to the Knesset. The State Comptroller also serves as an ombudsman, dealing with the public's complaints against any institution of the state. Under an amendment to the State Comptroller Law, comptrollers now serve one term of seven years; previously the State Comptroller was elected by the Knesset for a five-year term and was eligible for reelection to a second five-year term. In July 1998 Miriam Ben-Porat completed her second term as State Comptroller and was succeeded by former Supreme Court* Justice Eliezer Goldberg.

The function of the State Comptroller is to examine the efficiency, legality; and ethical probity with which the government operates. The Comptroller is appointed by the Knesset and submits an annual report to it as well as any specially requested reports that might be prepared at its request from time to time. The report contains details on all agencies audited. It provides specific findings and is published.

The State Comptroller engages in critical review of the administration of the assets, physical plant, finances, and obligations of the state. The Comptroller audits the operations of government ministries, state-owned enterprises and institutions, corporations in whose operations the government is involved, local authorities, and other agencies subject to inspection under law. The powers vested in the Comptroller and the variety of agencies audited are extensive. State Comptroller audits are not restricted to accounting matters. The Comptroller examines the legality, integrity, management, efficiency, and economy of the operations of agencies audited. The Comptroller inspects parties' books of account and monitors parties' compliance with the ban on receiving contributions from corporations, expenditure ceilings stipulated by law, and bookkeeping in accordance with guidelines laid down by the Comptroller. The Comptroller discharges a similar duty concerning local authorities and enforces rules meant to prevent conflicts of interest on the part of ministers and deputy ministers.

When the Comptroller's Office completes its audits of other agencies, a report is compiled and submitted to the Knesset Control Committee. When a local authority is audited, the Comptroller reports to the head of the authority reviewed. These reports are also published, ordinarily upon presentation.

The Knesset Control Committee holds annual discussions on State Comptroller reports. The Comptroller always takes part in the discussions and invites relevant senior civil servants to attend the committee's deliberations. The committee submits its conclusions and proposals regarding the report to the Knesset plenum for approval. The Knesset, the Control Committee, and the Government are entitled to ask the Comptroller for an opinion on any matter pertaining to Comptroller duties.

Since 1971, the State Comptroller has also served as the Public Complaints Commissioner, in effect functioning as an ombudsman, in which role he or she investigates complaints by the public. In this the Comptroller is assisted by a special Public Complaints Commission attached to the office. Anyone may petition the Public Complaints Commissioner. Complaints may be filed against agencies legally subject to auditing by the State Comptroller or against persons who work for such agencies. Complaints may cover any action contrary to law, without legal basis, contrary to the principles of sound administration, or involving excessive severity or flagrant injustice. "Actions" may include action taken late or failure to act. The State Comptroller and Public Complaints Commissioner is accountable only to the Knesset, and is not dependent on the Government. The Comptroller maintains liaison with the Knesset's State Control Committee. The Commissioner submits an annual report to the Knesset, which is then published and brought to public attention.

For further information see: Asher Arian, *The Second Republic: Politics in Israel* (Chatham, NJ: Chatham House, 1998), chapter 9; Joseph Badi, editor, *Fundamental Laws of the State of Israel* (New York: Twayne, 1961); Gad Yaacobi, *The Government of Israel* (New York: Praeger, 1982).

STATE LIST. Originally founded in 1968 by David Ben-Gurion*, when he and some of his followers in Rafi* refused to join in the new Israel Labor Party*. The State List won four seats in 1969 when it could still be considered a party of the left. In 1973, sizable remnants of the party joined the Likud* alliance, eventually merging with other groups to form La'am*.

STATE OF ISRAEL BONDS. In 1950 Prime Minister David Ben-Gurion* proposed that an Israel bond be floated in the United States* as a means of securing urgently needed funds for the new state. He visited the United States in May 1951 to launch the bond drive. The bonds were later sold in other countries as well. An Israel Bonds Organization was created and billions of dollars of bonds were sold.

For further information see: Ernest Stock, "Philanthropy and Politics: Modes of Interaction between Israel and the Diaspora," in *Israel: The First Decade of Independence*, edited by S. Ilan Troen and Noah Lucas (Albany: State University of New York Press, 1995): 699-711.

STATUS QUO AGREEMENT. Israel's religious structure stems partly from a compromise to obviate clashes that took the form of a so-called status quo agreement worked out by David Ben-Gurion* on the eve of Israel's independence. It retained the situation as it had existed upon independence: individuals would be free to pursue their religious practices in private as they saw fit while in the public domain there would be no changes in the prevailing situation. This arrangement thus continued the Ottoman Empire's millet system which allowed each religious community to control its own affairs. This allowed preservation of a large system of religious (especially rabbinical) courts and other government-supported religious institutions. The status quo agreement allowed the Orthodox community to maintain and expand its efforts to assert control over various activities, periodically engendering public conflict and discussion. A particularly controversial dimension of the status quo agreement was the granting of deferments from military service for men studying in ultra-Orthodox rabbinical institutions. In December 1998, the Supreme Court of Israel* ruled that the status quo agreement initially negotiated between Ben-Gurion and the ultra-Orthodox political parties, to grant exemptions from military service to yeshiva students, was unconstitutional; the Court gave the Knesset* one year in which to formulate new legislation affecting the question of deferrals from military service for yeshiva students. During the 14th Knesset (1996-1999) Labor* party leader Ehud Barak* sought to introduce legislation in the Knesset that would effectively end most exemptions from military duty on religious grounds. This determination to change the status quo agreement was reiterated by Barak both prior to and since his election as Prime Minister on May 17, 1999. The question of how to achieve this change was a key component of Barak's coalition negotiations with both Shas* and the United Torah Judaism* parties in June-July of 1999.

For further information see: Stuart A. Cohen, *The Scroll or the Sword? Dilemmas of Religion and Military Service in Israel* (Amsterdam: Harwood Academic Publishers, 1997); Charles S. Liebman and Eliezer Don-Yehiya, *Religion and Politics in Israel* (Bloomington: Indiana University Press, 1984); Ira Sharkansky, *Rituals of Conflict: Religion, Politics, and Public Policy in Israel* (Boulder, CO: Lynne Rienner, 1996).

STERN (GANG) GROUP. Also known as LEHI (Lohamei Herut Yisrael—Fighters for the Freedom of Israel*). The Stern gang was a Jewish underground fighting force in Palestine* that was formed by

Abraham Stern (Yair) in 1940 after a split in the Irgun Tzvai Leumi*. At the outbreak of World War II, Vladimir Jabotinsky*, supreme commander of the Irgun, ordered the cessation of hostile activities against the British Mandatory Government* in Palestine*. Stern, insisting that Great Britain's involvement in the war presented the Jewish national movement with the opportunity to force the British to honor their obligations toward the Jewish people, advocated the intensification of anti-British activities. LEHI's activities were strongly opposed and condemned by the majority of the Yishuv*, including the Hagana*, and its policies were in contradiction even to those of the Irgun. In February 1942, British police officers found Stern and shot him and, subsequently, many leaders and members of the group were arrested. A command composed of Nathan Friedmann-Yellin, Yitzhak Yzernitsky (Shamir)*, and Dr. Israel Scheib (Eldad) took over responsibility for the military and political activities of the organization, which became known as the "Stern Gang." LEHI adopted a policy of individual acts of terrorism. In the summer of 1944 the LEHI command decided to extend anti-British hostilities beyond Palestine. In November 1944 Lord Moyne was assassinated in Cairo. LEHI attacked the oil refineries in Haifa* and various British military installations, businesses, government offices, British military and police personnel, and army trains and other vehicles, increasingly harassing the administration. Following the United Nations Palestine partition* decision of November 1947, LEHI fought the Arab irregulars who attacked the Yishuv. After the proclamation of Israel's independence, LEHI was disbanded as an independent fighting force and its units were incorporated into the Israel Defense Forces*. Friedmann-Yellin was elected on a LEHI slate to the First Knesset*, but attempts to develop a cohesive political program and to form a political party proved ineffectual.

For further information see: Yaacov Banai, *Unknown Soldiers* (Tel Aviv: Hag Yedidim, 1958, Hebrew); Menachem Begin, *The Revolt: Story of the Irgun* (New York: Nash, 1981); J. Bowyer Bell, *Terror Out of Zion: Irgun Tzva'i Leumi: LEHI and the Palestine Underground, 1919-1949* (New York: St. Martin's, 1977); Yitzhak Ben-Ami, *Years of Wrath, Days of Glory: Memoirs of the Irgun* (New York: Speller, 1982); Yigal Elam, "Haganah, Irgun and 'Stern': Who Did What?" *Jerusalem Quarterly* 23 (Spring 1982): 70-78; Gerold Frank, *The Deed* (New York: Simon and Schuster, 1963); Miriam Getter, "The Arab Problem in the Ideology of LEHI," *Zionism* 1 (Spring 1980): 129-139; Giora Goldberg, "Rejoinder: Haganah, Irgun and 'Stern': Who Did What?" *Jerusalem Quarterly* 25

(Fall 1982): 116-120; Joseph Heller, "Avraham Stern ('Yair')," in *New Encyclopedia of Zionism and Israel*, 2 volumes, edited by Geoffrey Wigoder (Teaneck, NJ: Herzl Press, 1994): 1233; Joseph Heller, "Lohamei Herut Yisrael," in *New Encyclopedia of Zionism and Israel*, 2 volumes, edited by Geoffrey Wigoder (Teaneck, NJ: Herzl Press, 1994): 886-888; Joseph Heller, "The Zionist Right and National Liberation: From Jabotinsky to Avraham Stern," *Israel Affairs* 1:3 (Spring 1995): 85-109; Joseph Heller, *The Stern Gang: Ideology, Politics and Terror, 1940-1949* (London: Frank Cass, 1996); Samuel Katz, *Days of Fire: The Secret History of the Irgun Tzva'i Le'umi* (New York: Doubleday, 1968); David Niv, *Battle of Freedom: The Irgun Tzva'i Le'umi*, 3 volumes (Tel Aviv: Klausner Institute, 1963-1967); Yitzhak Shamir, *Summing Up: An Autobiography* (Boston: Little, Brown, 1994).

STRAIT OF TIRAN. Body of water connecting the Red Sea and the Gulf of Aqaba* (Gulf of Eilat). The Strait is narrow and constricted by islands (Tiran and Sanafir) and reefs. From the Egyptian Sinai Peninsula* to Tiran Island the distance is approximately five miles. Coral formations constrict the seaway into two navigable channels: Enterprise Passage, which borders the Sinai coast, is 1,300 yards wide, while Grafton Passage, about one mile from the island of Tiran, is about 900 yards wide. Israel has argued that the Gulf of Aqaba should be treated as an international waterway and that no state has the right to deny passage through the Strait of Tiran. The Arab argument is that the Gulf of Aqaba consists of Arab territorial waters and that passage through it and the Strait of Tiran therefore cannot be undertaken without the consent of the Arab states. Until 1956 Egypt* prevented shipping to Israel by placing military positions along the Sinai shore. These were destroyed by Israel during the Sinai War* of 1956. The announcement by President Nasser of Egypt in May 1967 that the Strait were blockaded was a proximate cause of the Six Day War*. *See also* SHARM EL-SHEIKH.

SUEZ CRISIS (1956) *see* SINAI WAR (1956)

SUISSA, ELI. Born in Morocco in 1956, he immigrated to Israel that same year. He had an Orthodox religious education, and completed his service in the Israel Defense Forces* in the elite Golani Brigade and as an officer in the army's chaplaincy. A founding member of the Sephardic Torah Guardian/Shas* party, he was appointed to the Shas-controlled Interior Ministry, first in charge of the Jerusalem* district and later as Deputy

Director-General of the ministry. Though not a member of Knesset*, he served as Interior Minister under Benjamin Netanyahu* (July 1996-June 1999). He also served as Minister of Religious Affairs from August 1998-June 1999. On May 17, 1999, he was elected to the 15th Knesset on the Shas list, and he was appointed Minister of National Infrastructure in the Government named by Ehud Barak* on July 6, 1999.

SUPREME COURT. At the top of the judicial hierarchy in Israel is the Supreme Court. There is a President or Chief Justice and a number (determined by the Knesset*) of associate justices. The Court has original and appellate jurisdiction. It hears appeals from lower courts in civil and criminal matters. It has original jurisdiction in matters seeking relief against administrative decisions that are not within the jurisdiction of any court. In this instance it may restrain or direct government agencies or other public bodies. It also plays a role in certain instances with regard to actions of religious courts. The Supreme Court serves as a guardian of fundamental rights protecting individuals from arbitrary actions by public officials or state bodies or agencies. While it does not formally have the power of judicial review and cannot invalidate the legislation of the Knesset, the Supreme Court has in recent years adopted a more active role for itself in defining general social mores. This increased activism has prompted a forceful response by more conservative elements of Israeli society, especially the ultra-Orthodox Jewish community.

For further information see: Asher Arian, *The Second Republic: Politics in Israel* (Albany, NY: State University of New York, 1998): chapter 9; Gad Barzilai, "Courts as Hegemonic Institutions: The Israeli Supreme Court in a Comparative Perspective," *Israel Affairs* 5:2&3 (Winter-Spring 1999): 15-33; Gad Barzilai, Ephraim Yuchtman-Yaar, and Ze'ev Segal, *The Israeli Supreme Court and the Israeli Public* (Tel Aviv: Papyrus, 1994 [in Hebrew]); Martin Edelman, *Courts, Politics, and Culture in Israel* (Charlottesville: University Press of Virginia, 1994); Hillel Neuer, "Israel's Imperial Judiciary," *Commentary* 108:3 (October 1999), 28-31.

SYKES-PICOT AGREEMENT. A World War I agreement between Great Britain* and France* to divide into spheres of control and influence areas of the Middle East held by the Ottoman Empire. The agreement, negotiated for Great Britain by Sir Mark Sykes and François-Georges Picot for France, was completed in January 1916 and ratified in May 1916 in an exchange of letters between British Foreign Secretary Sir Edward

Grey and France's Ambassador to London, Paul Cambon. The agreement defined areas of British and French control as well as spheres of influence. Britain's authority was to extend over southern Mesopotamia (Iraq*) and from the Egyptian border to Iraq (this area was to be identified as a "red zone"). In addition, the Mediterranean ports of Acre* and Haifa* were to be under British control. The French sphere of influence (the "blue zone") was to include a coastal strip of Syria* and Lebanon* as well as a portion of Palestine* west of the Jordan River*. Most of Palestine, including Jerusalem*, was to be part of an area that was to be administered internationally (the "brown zone"). The agreement superseded commitments made by Great Britain to Arab nationalism earlier in World War I (in the form of an exchange of letters between Britain's High Commissioner in Cairo, Sir Henry McMahon, and Hussein*, the Sherif of Mecca in October 1915). With only minor adjustments the Sykes-Picot Agreement was the basis of the Mandates in the former Turkish areas accorded to Great Britain and to France by the League of Nations at the San Remo Conference* of April 1920. *See also* BRITISH MANDATE FOR PALESTINE.

For further information see: David Fromkin, *A Peace to End All Peace. Creating the Modern Middle East, 1914-1922* (New York: Henry Holt, 1989); Joseph Goldberg, "Sykes-Picot Agreement," in *An Historical Encyclopedia of the Arab-Israeli Conflict*, edited by Bernard Reich (Westport, CT: Greenwood, 1996): 504 505; Elie Kedourie, "Sir Mark Sykes and Palestine 1915-1916," *Middle Eastern Studies* 6 (October 1970): 340-345.

SYRIA. Syria is Israel's neighbor to the northeast and has been a major antagonist of Israel since the Jewish state achieved its independence. The two countries have fought in the War of Independence*; the Six Day War*, during which Israel captured the Golan Heights*; the Yom Kippur War*, in which there were some additional Israeli territorial gains; and the War in Lebanon*. United States* Secretary of State Henry Kissinger brokered a disengagement of forces agreement* between the two states in the spring of 1974. No further progress toward peace between the two states was made and Syria continued to strive for "strategic parity" between the two states. The two states remained in confrontation until the fall of 1991 when Syria was among the Arab states that met with Israel at the Madrid Peace Conference*. However Syria (and Lebanon*) chose to boycott meetings of the multilateral track of negotiations initiated at the

Moscow Conference (January 1992). Under U.S. prodding, Israelis and Syrians met sporadically between 1993 and 1996 in Washington, DC, and at the nearby Wye Plantation* in Maryland. Yitzhak Rabin's* terms of reference—i.e., that the depth of Israeli withdrawal on or from the Golan Heights* would be determined by the depth of peace and normalized relations offered by Syria in return—was apparently accepted by Syrian President Hafez al-Asad as the basis for more substantive negotiations. There is evidence suggesting that Rabin had agreed in principle to the phased complete withdrawal of Israeli forces from the Golan and had conveyed this decision to his Syrian counterpart via the Americans. After Rabin's assassination Interim Prime Minister Shimon Peres* sought to resume negotiations with Syria on these same terms. However, in the final analysis Asad drew back from the proposed deal. In 1996 the new Government headed by Benjamin Netanyahu* declared that, while it sought to resume negotiations with Damascus, it would not necessarily be bound by the terms of reference agreed to in principle by the previous Government. It is widely assumed that an Israeli-Syrian agreement vis-à-vis the Golan Heights will also affect Israel's status with regard to Lebanon. Labor* leader Ehud Barak*, who as IDF* chief of staff in the mid-1990s had participated in security talks with his Syrian counterpart, following his election as Prime Minister on May 17, 1999, declared his interest in resuming substantive talks with Damascus. Those negotiations, involving Barak and Syria's Foreign Minister Farouk al-Shaara, were finally resumed in Washington, DC, on December 15-16, 1999. Reiterating a commitment first undertaken by Yitzhak Rabin, Barak pledged to hold a national referendum on a final peace agreement with Syria.

For further information see: Yaacov Bar-Siman-Tov, *Linkage Politics in the Middle East—Syria between Domestic and External Conflict, 1961-1970* (Boulder, CO: Westview, 1983); Nissim Bar-Yaakov, *The Israeli-Syrian Armistice: Problems of Implementation, 1949-1966* (Jerusalem: Magnes; London: Oxford University Press, 1967); John F. Devlin, "Syrian Policy in the Aftermath of the Israeli Invasion of Lebanon," in *The Middle East after the Israeli Invasion of Lebanon*, edited by Robert O. Freedman (Syracuse, NY: Syracuse University Press, 1986): 299-322; M. Zuhair Diab, "Syrian Security Requirements in a Peace Settlement with Israel," *Israel Affairs* 1:4 (Summer 1995): 71-88; Alasdair Drysdale and Raymond A. Hinnesbusch, *Syria and the Middle East Peace Process* (New York: Council on Foreign Relations, 1991); Michael Eisenstadt,

Arming for Peace? Syria's Elusive Quest for 'Strategic Parity' (Washington, DC: Washington Institute for Near East Policy, 1992); Raymond A. Hinnesbusch, "Does Syria Want Peace? Syrian Policy in the Syrian-Israeli Peace Negotiations," *Journal of Palestine Studies* 26:1 (Autumn 1996): 42-57; Raymond A. Hinnesbusch, "Syria and the Transition to Peace," in *The Middle East and the Peace Process: The Impact of the Oslo Accords*, edited by Robert O. Freedman (Gainesville: University Press of Florida, 1998): 134-153; Efraim Inbar, "Israeli Negotiations with Syria," *Israel Affairs* 1:4 (Summer 1995): 89-100; Moshe Ma'oz, *Syria under Hafiz al-Assad: New Domestic and Foreign Policies* (Jerusalem: The Leonard Davis Institute for International Relations, Jerusalem Papers on Peace Problems 15, Hebrew University of Jerusalem Press, 1975); Moshe Ma'oz, *Asad: The Sphinx of Damascus* (London: Weidenfeld and Nicolson, 1987); Moshe Ma'oz, *Syria and Israel: From War to Peacemaking* (London: Oxford University Press, 1996); Moshe Ma'oz and Avner Yaniv, editors, *Syria under Asad: Domestic Constraints and Regional Risks* (New York: St. Martin's, 1986); Yoel Marcus, "A Cold Peace Is the Best We Can Hope For," *Ha'aretz*, December 21, 1999; Mohammed Muslih, "Dateline Damascus: Asad Is Ready," *Foreign Policy* 96 (Fall 1994): 145-183; Daniel Pipes, *Syria beyond the Peace Process* (Washington, DC: Washington Institute for Near East Policy, Policy Papers No. 40, 1996); Itamar Rabinovich, "Controlled Conflict in the Middle East: The Syrian-Israeli Rivalry in Lebanon," in *Conflict Management in the Middle East*, edited by Gabriel Ben-Dor and David B. Dewitt (Lexington, MA: Lexington Books, 1987): 97-111; Itamar Rabinovich, *The Road Not Taken: Early Arab-Israeli Negotiations* (New York: Oxford University Press, 1991); Itamar Rabinovich, *The Brink of Peace: The Israeli-Syrian Negotiations and the Israeli-Arab Peace Process* (Princeton, NJ: Princeton University Press, 1998); Ze'ev Schiff, *Peace with Security: Israel's Minimal Security Requirements in Negotiations with Syria* (Washington, DC: Washington Institute for Near East Policy, Policy Papers No. 34, 1993); Ze'ev Schiff, "What a Good Agreement Means," *Ha'aretz*, December 21, 1999; Patrick Seale, *The Struggle for Syria: A Study of Post-War Arab Politics, 1945-1958* (New Haven, CT: Yale, 1986); Patrick Seale, *Asad: The Struggle for the Middle East* (Berkeley: University of California Press, 1988); Patrick Seale, "Asad's Regional Strategy and the Challenge from Netanyahu," *Journal of Palestine Studies* XXVI:1 (Autumn 1996): 27-41; Aryeh Shalev, *The Israel-Syria Armistice Regime 1949-1955* (Tel Aviv: Jaffee Center for Strategic Studies, Study No. 21, Tel Aviv University;

Boulder, CO: Westview, 1993); Aryeh Shalev, *Israel and Syria: Peace and Security on the Golan* (Tel Aviv: Jaffee Center for Strategic Studies, Tel Aviv University; Boulder, CO: Westview, 1994); Avner Yaniv and Moshe Ma'oz, editors, *Syria and Israel's National Security* (Tel Aviv, Maarachot, 1991, Hebrew); Eyal Zisser, "Asad Inches toward Peace," *Middle East Quarterly* 1:3 (September 1994): 37-44; Eyal Zisser, "Syria and Israel: Toward a Change?" in *Regional Security Regimes: Israel and Its Neighbors*, edited by Efraim Inbar (Albany: State University of New York Press, 1995): 151-174.

SYRIA-ISRAEL DISENGAGEMENT OF FORCES AGREEMENT *See* ISRAEL-SYRIA DISENGAGEMENT OF FORCES AGREEMENT

T

TAAS (TAASIYA TZVAIT). Literally "military industry." An enterprise devoted to development and manufacture of weapons and munitions for the Israel Defense Forces* and the defense establishment. It was initiated in the aftermath of the anti-Jewish riots of 1921, when the need arose for guns and ammunition to arm the Hagana*. *See also* ISRAEL AIRCRAFT INDUSTRIES.

TABA. A small (1.2 square kilometer) enclave on the border between Egypt* and Israel which remained in dispute when the international boundary was established between the two countries following the Egypt-Israel Peace Treaty* of 1979. Israel retained the area after withdrawing from Sinai in 1982, arguing that the maps showed incorrect lines. After years of fruitless negotiations the issue was submitted to international arbitration. The arbitrators reported in September 1988 that the area belonged to Egypt. Israel and Egypt signed agreements on February 26, 1989, that turned Taba back to Egypt. Egypt thus regained control of all of the Sinai Peninsula* captured by Israel in the Six Day War*. Taba itself was an insignificant piece of land, but it became symbolic of a number of difficulties in the Egypt-Israel relationship following the signing of the peace treaty.

TAMI (TENUAH LEMASSORET ISRAEL; MOVEMENT FOR JEWISH TRADITION). A political party founded in May 1981 by then Religious Affairs Minister Aharon Abuhatzeira*. The party drew support mainly from Sephardim*, and claimed to seek the elimination of anti-Moroccan sentiment in Israel, but it was created primarily because of Abuhatzeira's personal political ambition and his antipathy toward the National Religious Party* leaders, especially Yosef Burg*. Abuhatzeira left the NRP after receiving what he regarded as insufficient support during his trial on various criminal charges. He accused the NRP leadership of ethnic discrimination. Tami sought to appeal to followers of the NRP and Agudat Israel* by stressing the Moroccan connection, intending thereby to draw voters from Israel's large Moroccan community to fellow Moroccan Abuhatzeira. Abuhatzeira had strong support from Nissim Gaon, a Swiss-Jewish millionaire of Sudanese origin, who had been active in Sephardic causes. He had hoped for a sizable victory which would give him significant bargaining power after the election, but his efforts suffered a number of crucial setbacks, including repudiation by his venerable uncle, Rabbi Yisrael Abuhatzeira, a leader of Moroccan Jews in Israel. In addition, it became clear that he had created a party with a narrow sectarian base and thus lost any chance for a broader appeal to others, especially Sephardim of non-African origin. The number-two candidate on Tami's original list, Aharon Uzan, was a former Agriculture Minister in Labor* Governments, who noted that the party's purpose "is to right the glaring wrongs perpetrated against us North Africans and against the Sephardim in general." By the 1988 Knesset election Tami had dissolved and its supporters drifted to other political parties, primarily Shas*.

For further information see: Yoram Bilu and Eyal Ben-Ari, "The Making of Modern Saints: Manufactured Charisma and the Abu-Hatseiras of Israel," *American Ethnologist* 19:4 (1992): 672-687; Daniel J. Elazar, *The Others Jews: The Sephardim Today* (New York: Basic, 1989); Gershon R. Kieval, *Party Politics in Israel and the Occupied Territories* (Westport, CT: Greenwood, 1983); Oren Yiftachel and Avinoam Meir, *Ethnic Frontiers and Peripheries: Landscapes of Development and Inequality in Israel* (Boulder, CO: Westview, 1998).

TAMIR, SHMUEL (FORMERLY KATZENELSON). Born in Jerusalem* on March 10, 1923, Shmuel Tamir studied at the Government School of Law in Jerusalem and passed his last examinations while a prisoner in an internment camp in Kenya. In his youth he joined the Irgun* and was its second in command in the Jerusalem District. He was detained a number of times by the British authorities and the last time was exiled and imprisoned in Kenya. In 1948 he was among the founders of the Herut Party*, but in the 1950s he retired from it. In 1964 he returned to activities in the Herut Party and was among the founders of Gahal*. In 1965 he was elected to the Sixth Knesset*. Tamir, Eliezer Shostak*, and others formed the Free Center*. The Free Center joined the Likud* when it was established in 1973. In 1976 Tamir and his colleagues of the Free Center terminated the partnership with the Likud after differences of opinion with Menachem Begin*. When the Democratic Movement for Change* was established a few months later, Tamir united with it in the elections for the Ninth Knesset. He served as Minister of Justice from 1977 to 1980.

TARSHISH. A small political party, headed by Moshe Dweck, which contested the 1988 Knesset election* on a platform demanding greater economic rights for Israelis of Sephardic* descent, but failed to gain a seat in parliament.

TECHNION. The Israel Institute of Technology is located in Haifa*, and is Israel's leading university in engineering. It is also the oldest institution of higher learning in the country. Construction was begun in 1912, but various factors delayed its formal opening. The first classes were held in 1924. The school grew slowly until the independence of Israel when the significance of science and technology for the development and the security of the new state became apparent. The Technion was envisaged as the institution to provide Israel with the engineers, architects, and research scientists essential for the country's technical advance. It has since become an internationally recognized institution in its areas of specialty. *See also* EDUCATION.

TEHIYA (RENAISSANCE). Founded in 1979, Tehiya was a political party of "true believers" focused on the Land of Israel* with an ideological fervor reminiscent of Israel's political parties in the early years of independence and before. It was composed of both religious and secular elements and appealed strongly to Israel's youth. It had a component from Gush Emunim* (Bloc of the Faithful), but various secularists and secular-oriented groupings were also involved.

Tehiya included old associates of Menachem Begin* from the anti-British underground and former Herut* Knesset* members such as Geula Cohen* and Land of Israel Movement* personalities also joined. Included among its prominent members were Moshe Shamir, General Avraham Yoffe, Dr. Zeev Vilnay, and Dr. Israel Eldad. Tehiya's origins were based in opposition to the Camp David Accords* and the Egypt-Israel Peace Treaty*, which called for total withdrawal from the Sinai Peninsula* and commitment to autonomy for the Arabs residents in the West Bank* and Gaza Strip*. Tehiya members charged that Begin had sold out to international pressure and demanded that all of the occupied territories* must remain in Israel's hands. The party's head was Professor Yuval Neeman*, a physicist from Tel Aviv University, a leading nuclear scientist with a long-standing role in the defense establishment. In July 1982, Tehiya joined the ruling coalition of Menachem Begin's Likud* with Neeman serving as Minister of Science and Technology. This move seemed to help ensure Tehiya's future and to help strengthen the opposition in the Government to concessions concerning Palestinian autonomy in the West Bank. Rafael Eitan*, former Chief of Staff of the Israel Defense Forces*, assumed the leadership of the Tehiya-Tsomet* alliance and the combined party won five Knesset seats in the 1984 election. The coalition was disbanded in 1987 when Eitan established his own party, Tsomet. Tehiya campaigned in the 1988 election on a platform that called for "peace for peace," without Israel yielding any portion of the Land of Israel, and for increasing settlement in the territories as a guarantee of peace. It supported having Israeli sovereignty applied to Judea*, Samaria*, and Gaza.

In 1990 Tehiya joined the narrow coalition formed by Yitzhak Shamir* but it subsequently left the Government to protest Israel's participation in the Madrid Peace Conference*. It failed to pass the threshold of 1.5% of the popular vote in the 1992 election and it did not contest the 1996 or 1999 elections. The core of its support shifted either to one of the other secular-nationalist parties (Likud*, Tsomet, or Moledet*) or to the National Religious Party (NRP*). However, its political philosophy continues to color important aspects of the foreign and security policy debate in Israel.

For further information see: Etta Bick, "Fragmentation and Realignment: Israel's Nationalist Parties in the 1992 Elections," in *Israel at the Polls 1992*, edited by Daniel J. Elazar and Shmuel Sandler (Lanham, MD:

Rowman and Littlefield, 1995), 67-101; Gershon R. Kieval, *Party Politics in Israel and the Occupied Territories* (Westport, CT: Greenwood, 1983); Aaron D. Rosenbaum, "Tehiya as a Permanent Nationalist Phenomenon," in *Israeli National Security Policy: Political Actors and Perspectives*, edited by Bernard Reich and Gershon R. Kieval (New York: Greenwood, 1988): 147-167.

TEKUMA (RENEWAL). A small right-wing political faction that broke away from the National Religious Party* prior to the May 17, 1999, elections. It was founded by two former NRP Knesset* members, Hanan Porat and Zvi Handel, both of whom criticized the NRP for not quitting the Government of Benjamin Netanyahu* to protest the agreements to cede territory in Hebron* and elsewhere in the West Bank*. Tekuma's policy platform expressed strong support for Jewish settlers and firm opposition to further territorial concessions to Israel's Arab negotiating partners. It joined with New Herut* and Moledet* to form the National Union* party that won four seats in the 15th Knesset.

For further information see: David H. Goldberg, *Democracy in Action 1999: A Guide to the Participants and Issues in Israeli Politics* (Toronto: Canada-Israel Committee, May 1999).

TEL AVIV-YAFO. Tel Aviv-Yafo is the second-largest city of Israel and the nation's chief financial, commercial, and industrial center. It is one of the most modern cities in the Middle East and lies on the eastern shore of the Mediterranean Sea. The southwestern section of the city was formerly a separate town called Jaffa*. Cultural attractions in Tel Aviv-Yafo include the Museum Haaretz and the Tel Aviv Museum. Tel Aviv University is one of the city's several institutions of higher learning. Tel Aviv-Yafo is the center of Israel's primary manufacturing district. About half the nation's business companies are in the area. Their products include building materials, chemicals, clothing, electronic equipment, machine tools, and processed foods. The city is also the nation's leading center for such activities as banking, publishing, and trade. Israel's political parties have their headquarters in Tel Aviv-Yafo. In 1909, Jewish immigrants from Europe founded Tel Aviv northeast of Jaffa. Tel Aviv was administered as part of Jaffa at first, but it became a separate town in 1921. Tel Aviv grew rapidly as Jewish immigrants arrived mainly from Europe. It became Israel's first capital when the nation was established in 1948. The capital was moved to Jerusalem* in 1949, but the Israeli

Ministry of Defense and many foreign embassies remained in Tel Aviv. Most government departments maintain offices in Tel Aviv. In 1950, Tel Aviv and Jaffa merged to form Tel Aviv-Yafo.

TELEM. A political party which was formed by Moshe Dayan* in the spring of 1981 and contested the Knesset* election that summer, winning two seats. After Dayan's death in October 1981 its two Knesset members joined Likud* and the party dissolved.

TEMPLE MOUNT FAITHFUL *see* AL-AKSA MOSQUE

TEMPORARY INTERNATIONAL PRESENCE IN HEBRON (TIPH). A small force of unarmed international (primarily European) observers deployed in Hebron* in the aftermath of the February 1994 massacre of 29 Moslem worshipers by the Jewish settler, Baruch Goldstein*.

TERRITORIES *see* OCCUPIED TERRITORIES

TERRORISM. One of the more important factors shaping political life in Israel has been the ever-present threat of terrorism. The pre-state Yishuv* was confronted with extended periods of violence perpetrated by elements of the local Arab community in Palestine*. Initially, the Zionist response was a policy of "restraint" (*havlagah*), premised on passive defense of Jewish settlements and cooperation with the British Mandatory authorities. However, the response became progressively more forceful, especially during the Arab Revolt of 1936-1939 and following the Arabs's rejection of the November 1947 United Nations Palestine Partition Plan*. Following statehood, the primary terrorism threat was posed by fedayeen raids out of the Egyptian-controlled Gaza Strip* and from the Jordanian-held West Bank*. In reaction, the IDF* undertook a policy of vigorous retaliation, the goal of which was twofold: first, to punish the perpetrators of terrorist attacks, and second, to deter neighboring Arab countries from offering the terrorists support and safe haven. In the early 1970s much of the terrorist threat originated in southern Lebanon*, where the base of operations of the Palestine Liberation Organization* shifted following its eviction from Jordan following Black September*. Escalating levels of terrorism across its northern border, combined with sensational attacks on Israeli targets internationally, prompted major IDF offensives on PLO bases in Lebanon in 1978 (Operation Litani*) and 1982 (Operation Peace for Galilee*). The

PLO evacuation from Lebanon in September 1982 shifted the focus on terrorism to the West Bank and Gaza Strip where, beginning with the outbreak of the intifada* in December 1987, the IDF was confronted with widespread Palestinian violent demonstrations. Since the signing of the Oslo Accords* in 1993 there was a significant upswing in the number of and severity of terrorist attacks on Israelis, committed in the main by Islamic extremist groups and PLO rejectionist factions opposed to reconciliation with Israel. In addition, beginning in the mid-1980s the IDF fought a war of attrition against the Iranian-backed Hezbollah and other extremist groups in southern Lebanon. Over the decades, large numbers of Palestinian groups, sometimes assisted by regional states, have joined in anti-Israel terrorist activities designed to pursue the goal of restoring Palestine to the Palestinians. From Israel's perspective, there is a clear correlation between the prospects for achieving permanent peace and a substantial reduction in the threat to the physical security of Israelis posed by terrorism.

THE THIRD WAY (DERECH HASHLISHIT). A political party comprised mainly of former members of the Israel Labor Party* who left out of concern about the territorial concessions the Governments of Yitzhak Rabin* and Shimon Peres* were reportedly considering making to Syria* in negotiations over the Golan Heights*. It promoted a third way—not that of Labor or Likud*. Under the leadership of former Labor MK Avigdor Kahalani* (a hero of the Golan campaign during the Yom Kippur War* and a leader of the Knesset's* "Golan caucus") the party won four seats in the 1996 election and joined the governing coalition formed by Benjamin Netanyahu*, with Kahalani serving as Public Security Minister. Its centrist policy platform was encapsulated in the slogan "Peace with Secure Borders"—it supported peace negotiations with Israel's Arab neighbors on the basis of the land-for-peace* concept but it demanded that any concessions be reciprocal and conditioned on Israel's national security requirements.

In addition to its concern about the status of the Golan Heights, it expressed reservations about the way in which the Rabin-Peres Governments had implemented the Oslo Accords* with the PLO*. While acknowledging that Israel must find a way to end its administration over the Palestinian residents of the West Bank* and Gaza Strip*, leaders of the new political movement feared that the level and scope of IDF* redeployments in the occupied territories* were weakening Israel's ability to protect its vital security assets.

In its approach to the Palestinian track, The Third Way drew inspiration from the Allon Plan*. In July 1995 it published a Peace Map that would see the overwhelming majority of Jewish settlers in the West Bank incorporated into three major blocs that would then be annexed by Israel. Control of the balance of the West Bank (about 51%) and its Arab population would be transferred to the Palestinian autonomous areas. Jewish settlers remaining outside of areas annexed by Israel would be given the option of relocating to one of the settlement blocs or remaining in areas administered by the Palestinian Authority* but protected by the extra-territorial application of Israeli law. As part of the Government, The Third Way also adopted a centrist position on the contentious "Who is a Jew" debate*. It failed to win a seat in the 1999 Knesset election.

TIBI, AHMED. Born on December 19, 1958 in Israel, Ahmed Tibi is an Israeli Arab (who defines himself as a Palestinian with Israeli citizenship). Dr. Ahmed Tibi, a gynecologist by profession, served as advisor to Palestinian Authority Chairman Yasser Arafat. He joined the Balad Party* list prior to the May 1999 elections and received a seat in the 15th Knesset. On December 21, 1999, the Knesset House Committee approved Tibi's request to have his Arab Movement for Renewal* recognized as an independent Knesset faction.

TICHON, DAN. Born in Kiryat Haim on January 15, 1937, he is a graduate of Hebrew University* in economics and international relations. Chairman of the Board (1971-1981) and Director-General (1977) of a private construction firm, Housing and Development for Israel, Ltd, Tichon has been a member of the Knesset* on the Likud* list since 1981. He served as Deputy Speaker of the Knesset and Chairman of the Knesset State Audit Committee. Elected Speaker of the 14th Knesset in June 1996, he retired from party politics prior to the 1999 Knesset election.

TIRAN, STRAIT OF *see* STRAIT OF TIRAN

TORAH FLAG (DEGEL HATORAH) *see* DEGEL HATORAH

TORAH RELIGIOUS FRONT. A joint election list formed by Agudat Israel* and Poalei Agudat Israel* to contest the Knesset* elections in 1951, 1955,

1959, and 1973. As a result of these elections, it won five, six, six, and five seats, respectively.

TOUBI, TAWFIK. Born on May 11, 1922, in Haifa* Tawfik Toubi is a Christian Arab journalist and active member of the Communist Party* since 1940. A Knesset* member since the first Knesset was elected in 1949, he retired in July 1990.

TRADITION OF THE FATHERS (MORESHET AVOT). Party led by former Moledet MK Rabbi Yosef Ba-Gad (considered the clown of the Knesset) who was disqualified for the Prime Minister race for allegedly faking one-third of the 61,000 signatures he presented to the Central Elections Committee. A right wing group that did not win any mandates in the May 17th elections.

TREATY OF PEACE BETWEEN THE ARAB REPUBLIC OF EGYPT AND THE STATE OF ISRAEL *see* EGYPT-ISRAEL PEACE TREATY

TRUMPELDOR, JOSEPH. A Zionist* pioneer born in Russia in 1880 who settled in Palestine* in 1912. He worked in Kibbutz Degania* and participated in the defense of Jewish settlements. Trumpeldor helped to organize the Jewish Legion* which served with the British army during World War I. He returned briefly to Russia in 1917, but then returned to Palestine in 1919. Trumpeldor died in 1920 while defending the northern settlement of Tel Hai against Arab attackers and this action made him a legendary hero. The Revisionist* youth movement and its sports organization are named after him—Betar* (acronym for Brit Yosef Trumpeldor).

TSABAN, YAIR. Born in Jerusalem* in 1930, Tsaban was a member of the Hagana* from 1945 to 1947 and of the Palmah* from 1948 to 1949. He helped to found Kibbutz Zorah. He served in the Knesset* as a member of Maki* and helped to found Moked* and Shelli*. Tsaban joined Mapam* in 1980 and represented it in the Knesset (and subsequently the Meretz/Democratic Israel* faction) since 1981. He served as Minister of Immigration between 1992 and 1996, and retired from party politics prior to the election to the 14th Knesset in 1996.

TSOMET (TZOMET) (MOVEMENT FOR ZIONIST REVIVAL). Founded in November 1987 as a breakaway from Tehiya*, it won two seats in the

1988 Knesset* election. Led by former Israel Defense Forces* Chief of Staff Rafael (Raful) Eitan*, the party advocated the retention of much of the West Bank*. Domestically, it called for the strict separation of religion from politics, an end to the practice of granting deferments from military service for students in Orthodox rabbinical institutions, and a return to integrity in governmental affairs. Tsomet joined the narrow Shamir*-led coalition in 1990, and it won a surprising eight seats in the 13th Knesset (1992). It ran in the 1996 election as part of a joint national camp list along with Likud* and Gesher*. Eitan was appointed Minister of Agriculture and Environment and Deputy Prime Minister in the coalition headed by Benjamin Netanyahu*. In the general elections that occurred on May 17, 1999, Tsomet failed to cross the threshold for winning seats in the 15th Knesset.

For further information see: Etta Bick, "Fragmentation and Realignment: Israel's Nationalist Parties in the 1992 Elections," in *Israel at the Polls 1992*, edited by Daniel J. Elazar and Shmuel Sandler (Lanham, MD: Rowman and Littlefield, 1995): 67-101.

TSUR, YAACOV. Born in 1937 in Haifa*, Yaacov Tsur graduated from Hebrew University of Jerusalem*. He is a member of Kibbutz Netiv Halamed Heh. He served as Secretary General of Hakibbutz Hameuhad* movement. He was a Labor Alignment* member of the Knesset* since 1981. He served as Minister of Immigrant Absorption until 1988 and became Minister of Health in the Government established in December 1988 and remained in that position until the spring of 1990 when Labor left the Government.

TSUR, ZVI. Born in Saslav, Russia, on April 17, 1923, Zvi Tsur joined the Israel Defense Forces*, rising through the ranks to become Chief of Staff from 1961 to 1964. He later served as assistant Minister of Defense and then served with the senior management of Clal Industries.

TURKEY. From independence, Israeli officials saw the need to establish positive relations with Moslem, non-Arab countries of the Middle East, to offset Israel's isolation from, and encirclement by, hostile Arab neighbors. As part of this strategy ties were developed with pre-revolutionary Iran*, Ethiopia*, and Turkey.

Because of pressure from its Arab and Muslim neighbors Turkey voted against the partition of Palestine* in 1947. However, it did extend de jure recognition to Israel in 1949 and established diplomatic relations. A bilateral trade agreement was signed in 1950, followed by a transportation agreement in 1951. Early on, the Turks viewed Israel as a potential military ally in their ongoing territorial disputes with Syria* (especially over the sanjak of Alexandretta and over the distribution of the waters of the Tigris and Euphrates river system) and in combating Kurdish and Armenian terrorism.

Beginning in the mid-1950s, Turkey began to move closer to the Arab countries and to diminish relations with Israel. In the wake of the 1956 Sinai War* it reduced to chargé d'affaires the level of its diplomatic representation in Israel. However, Arab pressure for a complete severing of relations was resisted. Turkey joined much of the Arab and Moslem world in criticizing Israel's occupation of Muslim territory in the 1967 Six Day War* and there was a perceptible softening of Ankara's attitude toward Palestinian terrorist groups operating on Turkish soil. In 1971 the Israeli consul in Istanbul, Ephraim Elrom, was kidnaped and murdered, and in September 1986 22 Jews were massacred in an Istanbul synagogue by members of the Palestinian terrorist Abu Nidal Organization.

The Knesset's passage of the Basic Law: Jerusalem*, Capital of Israel* in 1980, led to a further diminishing of Turkey's diplomatic representation in Israel, to the level of second secretary. However, by the mid-1980s, the decline in the importance of the Arab market and Arab and Islamic oil opened the way for an improvement in bilateral relations with Israel. The first expression of this new attitude was in trade. Bilateral commercial exchange totaled $54 million in 1987. By 1998 this figure had increased to approximately $750 million, with expectations of trade reaching $2 billion by the year 2000. In November 1993 Turkey's foreign minister, Hikmet Cetin, became the highest ranking Turkish official to ever visit Israel. During Cetin's visit the two countries set up working groups to establish a bilateral free-trade zone. (This agreement was formally ratified in April 1997.) In addition, Cetin and Foreign Minister Shimon Peres* signed a memorandum of understanding laying the foundation for future cooperation between the two countries particularly in economic matters. There were also high level discussions about cooperation in security and the combating of terrorism. In late January 1994 President Ezer Weizman* became the first Israeli Head of State to visit Turkey, at the head of a large Israeli trade delegation. Subsequently, reciprocal visits by top Israeli and Turkish officials and by commercial delegations became routine.

In addition to commercial exchange, significant growth occurred in security cooperation, joint military training, and counter-terrorism. The first joint training exercise involving the air forces of Israel and Turkey took place in June 1994. Also in 1994 the two sides reached a draft agreement on joint efforts to combat international terrorism. In 1996 it was revealed that Turkish and Israeli officials had quietly forged a series of secret military and intelligence agreements. These improving strategic relations were sustained in the mid-1990s (often at the insistence of the Turkish military) during the brief tenure of the Islamist government headed by Necmettin Erbakan. Beginning on January 6, 1998, Israel, Turkey, and the United States* participated in large-scale naval search-and-rescue exercises in the eastern Mediterranean. The exercises, codenamed *Reliant Mermaid*, were observed by the commander of the Jordanian* navy. Israeli and Turkish officials were at pains to emphasize that the exercises were designed to strengthen cooperation between the two countries in the performance of humanitarian services and were not meant to threaten third parties. Nevertheless, the Turkish-Israeli strategic alliance was strongly criticized by many Arab countries, such as Egypt*, Iraq* and Syria, as well as by Iran.

Turkish President Suleyman Demirel made an official visit to Israel in July 1999 for talks with Prime Minister Ehud Barak* and others aimed at reaffirming the U.S.-backed strategic partnership between the two regional powers and to show that the recent change in government both in Turkey and Israel will not affect their core relations. In December 1999, Turkish, Israeli, and U.S. naval forces again participated in joint search-and-rescue exercises in the eastern Mediterranean.

For further information see: Bulent Aras, *The Palestinian-Israeli Peace Process and Turkey* (New York: NOVA, 1998); Mahmut Bali Aykan, "The Turkey-U.S.-Israel Triangle: Continuity, Change and Implications for Turkey's Post-Cold War Middle East Policy," *Journal of South Asian and Middle Eastern Studies* 22:4 (Summer 1999): 1-31; Michael Eisenstadt, "Turkish-Israeli Military Cooperation," *Policywatch*, No. 262 (Washington, DC: Washington Institute for Near East Policy, July 24, 1997); George Emanuel Gruen, *Turkey, Israel and the Palestine Question,*

1948-1960: A Study in the Diplomacy of Ambivalence, PhD Dissertation (New York: Columbia University Press, 1970); George Emanuel Gruen, "Turkey's Relations with Israel and its Arab Neighbors: The Impact of Basic Interests and Changing Circumstances," *Middle East Review* 17 (Spring 1985): 33-43; Alan Makovsky, "Israeli-Turkish Relations: A Turkish 'Periphery Strategy'?" in *Reluctant Neighbor: Turkey's Role in the Middle East,* edited by Henri Barkey (Washington, DC: The United States Institute of Peace, 1996); Alan Makovsky, "Israeli-Turkish Cooperation: Full Steam Ahead," *Policywatch,* No. 292 (Washington, DC: Washington Institute for Near East Policy, January 6, 1997); Amikam Nachmani, "Bridge across the Middle East: Turkey and Israel in the 1990's," *Middle East Quarterly* 5:2 (June 1998): 19-29; Daniel Pipes, "A New Axis: The Emerging Turkish-Israel Entente," *The National Interest* (Winter 1997/1998): 31-38; Brent Sasley, *Structural Reinterpretation of Power in the Middle East: Explanations and Implications of the Evolving Military Relationship between Turkey and Israel,* MA Thesis (Winnipeg, Manitoba: University of Manitoba Press, October 1998).

TZVAH HAGANA LE YISRAEL *see* ISRAEL DEFENSE FORCES

U

UNEF *see* UNITED NATIONS EMERGENCY FORCE

UNITED ARAB LIST. An Arab political party that contested the 1977 Knesset* election and won a single seat in parliament.

UNITED ARAB LIST/ARAB DEMOCRATIC PARTY. A joint Arab list that won four seats in the 14th Knesset* (1996); this number increased to five in the 15th Knesset that was elected on May 17, 1999.

UNITED ISRAEL APPEAL (UIA). Successor organization to the United Palestine Appeal*.

UNITED JEWISH APPEAL (UJA). A fund-raising campaign organized for the development of the Jewish national home in Palestine* and, later,

Israel, as well as for Jewish communities and concerns worldwide. It began to function as a permanent organization in 1938.

For further information see: Menahem Kaufman, "Envisioning Israel: The Case of the United Jewish Appeal," in *Envisioning Israel: The Changing Ideals and Images of North American Jews*, edited by Allon Gal (Jerusalem: Magnes; Detroit: Wayne State University Press, 1996): 219-253; Herbert Parzen and Ernest Stock, "United Jewish Appeal," in *New Encyclopedia of Zionism and Israel*, 2 volumes, edited by Geoffrey Wigoder (Teaneck, NJ: Herzl Press, 1994): 1296-1297; Ernest Stock, "Philanthropy and Politics: Modes of Interaction between Israel and the Diaspora," in *Israel: The First Decade of Independence*, edited by S. Ilan Troen and Noah Lucas (Albany: State University of New York Press, 1995): 699-711.

UNITED KIBBUTZ MOVEMENT (HATNUA HAKIBBUTZIT HAMEUHEDET). In 1979 the national conventions of Ihud Hakvutzot Vehakibbutzim and Hakibbutz Hameuhad* decided to merge into the United Kibbutz Movement. *See also* KIBBUTZ.

UNITED KINGDOM *see* GREAT BRITAIN

UNITED NATIONS DISENGAGEMENT OBSERVER FORCE (UNDOF). United Nations peacekeeping force established to monitor the Israel-Syria Disengagement Agreement* of May 31, 1974. The force was authorized by Security Council Resolution 350. Its area of operations extended 80 miles from Mount Hermon* in the north to the Jordan River* in the south. Its original mandate was for six months. This has been extended every six months since 1974. It is considered one of the most successful long-term UN peacekeeping efforts.

For further information see: Stephen H. Gotowicki and Matthew Dorf, "United Nations Disengagement Observer Force (UNDOF)," in *An Historical Encyclopedia of the Arab-Israeli Conflict*, edited by Bernard Reich (Westport, CT: Greenwood, 1996): 523-525.

UNITED NATIONS EMERGENCY FORCE (UNEF). The United Nations peacekeeping force that was inserted between Israeli and Egyptian armies at the end of the Sinai War* of 1956. General Assembly Resolution 1000 (ES-1) of November 5, 1956, empowered the Secretary General to establish an international emergency force with the capabilities of keeping the Egyptian-Israeli front at peace until a political settlement could be reached. UNEF was created as an armed police force, though it was authorized to use force only in self-defense. Its mandate was premised on four major objectives: secure the cessation of hostilities and supervise the cease-fire; ensure the orderly withdrawal of Israeli, British, and French forces from Egyptian territory; patrol the border between Israel and Egypt*; and ensure the observance of the Egypt-Israel armistice.

The first UNEF unit was deployed to the Suez Canal on November 15, 1956. On March 7, 1957, the force became operational in the Gaza Strip* with the permission of Egypt following the Israeli withdrawal. Israel never permitted UNEF to operate on its soil. At its strength, UNEF forces were deployed along the 145 miles of international frontiers connecting Israel and Egypt.

The force functioned successfully for 10 years, until May 18, 1967, when Secretary General U Thant acquiesced to an Egyptian request to terminate UNEF's presence in Egypt. When, on the same day, Israel declined a request to allow UNEF to redeploy to the Israeli side of the international boundary, U Thant felt there was no choice but to terminate the force's operation. He was widely criticized for moving prematurely in this matter, thereby complicating diplomatic efforts to forestall hostilities in the spring of 1967. *See also* SIX DAY WAR.

For further information see: Michael Comay, *U.N. Peacekeeping in the Israeli-Arab Conflict, 1948-1975: An Israeli Critique* (Jerusalem: Hebrew University of Jerusalem, 1974); Elihu Lauterpacht, *The United Nations Emergency Force: Basic Documents* (New York: Praeger, 1960); Indar Jit Rikhye, *The Sinai Blunder: Withdrawal of the United Nations Emergency Force Leading to the Six-Day War of June 1967* (London: Frank Cass, 1980); Susan L. Rosenstein, Stephen H. Gotowicki, and Matthew Dorf, "United Nations Emergency Force (UNEF)," in *An Historical Encyclopedia of the Arab-Israeli Conflict*, edited by Bernard Reich (Westport, CT: Greenwood, 1996): 525-527.

UNITED NATIONS EMERGENCY FORCE II (UNEF II). The second United Nations peacekeeping force inserted between Israel and Egypt*. It was established by Security Council Resolution 340 on October 25, 1973, at the end of the Yom Kippur War*. Unlike its predecessor, UNEF*, which maintained relative peace and stability until it was unceremoniously withdrawn by Secretary General U Thant on May 18, 1967, at the request of Egypt, UNEF-II could not be withdrawn unilaterally and without action by the Security Council. Its mandate was expanded to supervise the Israel-Egypt Disengagement Agreement* signed at Kilometer 101* on January 18, 1974.

The first UNEF-II troops were deployed on October 27, 1973, on the west bank of the Suez Canal and under the command of a Finnish officer, Major General Ensio Siilasvuo. At its maximum strength, it consisted of nearly 7,000 soldiers drawn from 12 contributing countries. Its mandate was for a period of six months but was extended eight times. On July 24, 1979, the Security Council declined to extend UNEF II's mandate, its functions having been superseded by the security provisions of the Egypt-Israel Peace Treaty* of March 26, 1979.

For further information see: Ensio Siilasvuo, *In the Service of the Middle East, 1967-1979* (New York: Hurst, 1992).

UNITED NATIONS GENERAL ASSEMBLY RESOLUTION 3379. On November 10, 1975, the United Nations General Assembly, by a vote of 72 in favor, 35 against, with 32 abstentions, adopted Resolution 3379, in which it declared, inter alia: "*Determines* that Zionism is a form of racism and discrimination." The passage of the so-called "Zionism is racism" resolution marked a nadir in Israel's relationship with the United Nations. On December 16, 1991, a brief statement in the General Assembly revoking the resolution was supported by 111 countries. But the statement revoking the resolution was opposed by most Arab states, which either voted against or were absent from the General Assembly chamber when the vote was called.

UNITED NATIONS INTERIM FORCE IN LEBANON (UNIFIL). The peacekeeping force created on March 19, 1978, by United Nations Security Council Resolution 425* in response to Israel's incursion into southern Lebanon* in pursuit of the PLO* (Operation Litani*). It was mandated to be an interim force, with its field of operations originally envisioned as bounded by the Israel-Lebanon border in the south, the Litani River in the north, the Mediterranean Sea in the west, and the Lebanon-Syria border on the east. However, it was never allowed by Israel to operate in its southernmost zone—the mainly Christian border region which in 1985 became Israel's security zone* that was patrolled by Israeli troops and forces of the Israel-supported South Lebanese Army*. It was mandated to pursue the achievement of three goals: confirming the withdrawal of Israeli forces from Lebanon; restoring international peace and security in the border region; and assisting the Government of Lebanon in ensuring the return of its effective authority in the area. The achievement of these goals was constrained by a number of factors, including: Israel's mistrust of the United Nations; the absence of a strong Lebanese sovereign authority with which UNIFIL could interact; and the difficulty experienced by UNIFIL in applying its mandate with respect to the numerous extra-governmental armed militias operating in southern Lebanon, including the PLO, Hezbollah, Shi'ite Amal, and the South Lebanese Army*. Nevertheless, UNIFIL experienced some success in reducing the chances of war in the border region. Its original mandate was for six months. It has been renewed every six months since 1978.

For further information see: Laura Zittrain Eisenberg, "Israel's South Lebanon Imbroglio," *Middle East Quarterly* 4:2 (June 1997): 61-69; Stephen H. Gotowicki and Matthew Dorf, "United Nations Interim Force in Lebanon (UNIFIL)," in *An Historical Encyclopedia of the Arab-Israeli Conflict*, edited by Bernard Reich (Westport, CT: Greenwood, 1996): 534-535.

UNITED NATIONS PALESTINE COMMISSION. Shortly after the Palestine Partition Plan* vote of November 1947, the United Nations established a Palestine Commission to effect the transfer from the British Mandatory power to the proposed Arab and Jewish states. *See also* PALESTINE PARTITION PLAN.

UNITED NATIONS PARTITION PLAN *see* PALESTINE PARTITION PLAN

UNITED NATIONS SECURITY COUNCIL RESOLUTION 242. The United Nations Security Council, on November 22, 1967, adopted a British-sponsored resolution designed to achieve a solution to the Arab-Israeli conflict. The resolution was deliberately vague, but emphasized an exchange of territory for peace. The full text of the resolution reads as follows:

"The Security Council, Expressing its continuing concern with the grave situation in the Middle East. Emphasizing the inadmissibility of the acquisition of territory by war and the need to work for a just and lasting peace in which every State in the area can live in security. Emphasizing further that all Member States in their acceptance of the Charter of the United Nations have undertaken a commitment to act in accordance with Article 2 of the Charter. 1. Affirms that the fulfillment of Charter principles requires the establishment of a just and lasting peace in the Middle East which should include the application of both the following principles: (i) Withdrawal of Israeli armed forces from territories occupied in the recent conflict; (ii) Termination of all claims or states of belligerency and respect for and acknowledgment of the sovereignty, territorial integrity and political independence of every State in the area and their right to live in peace within secure and recognized boundaries free from threats or acts of force; 2. Affirms further the necessity (a) For guaranteeing freedom of navigation through international waterways in the area; (b) For achieving a just settlement of the refugee problem; (c) For guaranteeing the territorial inviolability and political independence of every State in the area, through measures including the establishment of demilitarized zones; 3. Requests the Secretary-General to designate a Special Representative to proceed to the Middle East to establish and maintain contacts with the States concerned in order to promote agreement and assist efforts to achieve a peaceful and accepted settlement in accordance with the provisions and principles in this resolution; 4. Requests the Secretary-General to report to the Security Council on the progress of the efforts of the Special Representative as soon as possible."

Gunnar Jarring*, then Sweden's Ambassador to Moscow, was appointed by the United Nations Secretary General in November 1967 to implement the resolution, but ultimately he failed to secure meaningful movement toward peace. UNSC Resolution 242 has been the basis of all subsequent peace efforts. Its guiding principle of land-for-peace was institutionalized at the Madrid Peace Conference* and in the Oslo Accords*.

For further information see: David H. Goldberg, editor, *United Nations Security Council Resolution 242: A Twenty-Five Year Retrospective* (Toronto: Foundation for Middle East Studies, June 1993); Robert Satloff, editor, *United Nations Security Council Resolution 242: The Building Block of Peacemaking* (Washington, DC: Washington Institute for Near East Policy, 1993).

UNITED NATIONS SECURITY COUNCIL RESOLUTION 338. On October 22, 1973, the United Nations Security Council adopted Resolution 338, which called for an immediate cease-fire in the Yom Kippur War* and the implementation of United Nations Security Council Resolution 242*, and explicitly required negotiations "between the parties." The full text reads as follows:

"The Security Council 1. Calls upon all parties to the present fighting to cease all firing and terminate all military activity immediately, no later than 12 hours after the moment of the adoption of this decision, in the positions they now occupy; 2. Calls upon the parties concerned to start immediately after the cease-fire the implementation of Security Council resolution 242 (1967) in all of its parts; 3. Decides that, immediately and concurrently with the cease-fire, negotiations start between the parties concerned under appropriate auspices aimed at establishing a just and durable peace in the Middle East."

The resolution provided the basis for the initial postwar military disengagement negotiations involving Israel, Egypt*, and Syria*.

UNITED NATIONS SECURITY COUNCIL RESOLUTION 425. The resolution adopted on March 19, 1978, in response to Israel's March 14, 1978, incursion into southern Lebanon* in pursuit of PLO* terrorists (Operation Litani*). The resolution called "for strict respect for the territorial integrity, sovereignty and political independence of Lebanon within its internationally recognized boundaries." It also called "upon Israel immediately to cease its military action against Lebanese territorial integrity and withdraw forthwith its forces from all Lebanese territory." Resolution 425 also approved the establishment of the United Nations Interim Force in Lebanon* for the purpose of confirming the withdrawal of Israeli forces, restoring international peace and security, and assisting the Government of Lebanon in ensuring the return of its effective authority in the area. From the outset, Israel objected to these terms of reference. The Government of Menachem Begin* stated that withdrawal of Israeli forces from Lebanon would be contingent upon the removal of PLO forces from the area and the withdrawal of all other foreign forces from Lebanon (especially Syrian). This conditionality was restated by all successive Israeli Governments until, in early 1998, when Defense Minister Yitzhak Mordechai* declared Israel's readiness to negotiate the withdrawal of its forces from Lebanon on the basis of Security Council Resolution 425.

UNITED NATIONS SPECIAL COMMITTEE ON PALESTINE (UNSCOP). Unable to satisfy the conflicting views of the Arab and Jewish communities of Palestine* and to ensure public safety because of the conflicts between them, and faced with the heavy burden entailed in retaining the Palestine Mandate (British Mandate*), which compounded the extensive costs of World War II, the British conceded that the Mandate was unworkable and turned the Palestine problem over to the United Nations in the spring of 1947. The United Nations Special Committee on Palestine (UNSCOP) examined the issues and recommended that the Mandate be terminated and that the independence of Palestine be achieved without delay. However, it was divided on the future of the territory. The majority proposed partition into a Jewish state and an Arab state linked in an economic union, with Jerusalem* and its environs established as an international enclave. The minority suggested that Palestine become a single federal state, with Jerusalem as its capital and with Jews and Arabs enjoying autonomy in their respective areas. The majority proposal was adopted by the United Nations General Assembly on November 29, 1947. *See also* PALESTINE PARTITION PLAN.

UNITED NATIONS TRUCE SUPERVISION ORGANIZATION (UNTSO). The first United Nations peacekeeping operation established in the Middle East, it was originally constituted by Security Council Resolution 50 (May 29, 1948), to provide advisory and observation support to the Jerusalem-based Palestine Truce Commission. In August 1949, the Truce Commission observers were reassigned formally as UNTSO by United Nations Security Council Resolution 73 and assigned the mission of supervising the Armistice Agreements* signed at the end of the 1948-1949 War of Independence between Israel and Egypt*, Lebanon*, Syria*, and Jordan*. After each of the Arab-Israeli wars, the mission of UNTSO was slightly modified. Following the 1956 Sinai War*, its personnel patrolled the Sinai Peninsula* even though the 1949 Israeli-Egyptian armistice was declared dead because of Egypt's support for fedayeen* terror raids into Israel, and UNTSO peacekeepers supported the United Nations Emergency Force* interposed between Israeli and Egyptian forces. After the 1967 Six Day War*, UNTSO remained in place to supervise the cease-fires between Israel and its Arab interlocutors. After the 1973 Yom Kippur War*, UNTSO staffers were used as an

experienced manpower pool for disengagement forces established in the
Sinai (UNEF II*) and on the Golan Heights* (UNDOF*).

For further information see: Rosalyn Higgins, *United Nations
Peacekeeping 1946-1967: Documents and Commentary* (London: Oxford
University Press, 1969); Ensio Siilasvuo, *In the Service of Peace in the
Middle East, 1967-1979* (New York: St. Martin's Press, 1992).

UNITED PALESTINE APPEAL (UPA). An American organization
established in 1925 to coordinate the various Zionist fund-raising efforts
primarily to support the establishment of Jewish settlements in Palestine*.
In 1950 it was renamed the United Israel Appeal*.

UNITED RELIGIOUS FRONT. In the elections to the First Knesset* in 1949
the various religious groups—Mizrahi*, Hapoel Hamizrahi*, Agudat
Israel*, and Poalei Agudat Israel*— all ran on a single electoral list
known as the United Religious Front. The Front won 16 seats in the
Knesset but was not sustained and the religious parties ran individually or
in smaller combinations in subsequent elections.

For further information see: Charles S. Liebman and Eliezer Don-Yehiya,
Religion and Politics in Israel (Bloomington: Indiana University Press,
1984); Gary S. Schiff, *Tradition and Politics: The Religious Parties of
Israel* (Detroit: Wayne State University Press, 1977).

UNITED STATES OF AMERICA. The relationship between the United
States and Israel antedates the independence of Israel. President
Woodrow Wilson endorsed the Balfour Declaration* soon after its
issuance in 1917 and the United States Congress did so in the 1920s.
Despite these and other statements of support for a Jewish state or
homeland in Palestine*, no substantial gestures of U.S. support for Zionist
aspirations took place until after World War II when the status of
Palestine became a matter of considerable international attention. The
administration of President Harry Truman sought a significant increase in
Jewish immigration to Palestine immediately after World War II as a
means of providing a refuge for displaced persons and other survivors of
the Nazi Holocaust*. When the British turned the Palestine Mandate over
to the United Nations in 1947, the United States supported the concept of
partition and lobbied extensively to achieve that objective. After Israel

declared its independence in May 1948, the United States was the first state to grant recognition, although it was de facto and not de jure.

In the decades since Israel's independence the two states developed a diplomatic-political relationship that focused on the need to resolve the Arab-Israeli conflict*, as well as to maintain the survival and security of Israel. Nevertheless, while they agreed on the general concept, they often differed on the precise means of achieving the desired result. The bilateral relationship became especially close after the Six Day War*, when a congruence of policy prevailed on many of their salient concerns. In the wake of the Yom Kippur War* and the shuttle diplomacy undertaken by Secretary of State Henry Kissinger that followed, United States economic and military assistance to Israel reached very significant levels.

In the 1980s the relationship took on an added dimension as President Ronald Reagan saw Israel as a strategic asset against Soviet incursion in the Middle East. An element of tension existed between the Bush Administration and the coalition Government headed by Yitzhak Shamir* over such issues as Jewish settlements, the status of Jerusalem*, and Palestinian representation in proposed peace negotiations. But there was a high degree of common interest between the two Governments during the Persian Gulf War and in the post-war diplomacy that culminated with the Madrid Peace Conference*. There was a very high degree of cooperation between the Clinton Administration and the Labor*-led coalitions headed by Yitzhak Rabin* and (then) Shimon Peres*. Strains in the bilateral relationship reemerged with the change in Government in Israel from Labor to the Likud* under Benjamin Netanyahu* in 1996, especially over peace talks with the Palestinians. Even then, however, the disputes between Jerusalem and Washington were said to be more of tactics rather than overall strategy (that is, over the specific steps toward achieving the shared goal of secure peace for Israel and its neighbors), and efforts were made to resolve the disputes in an atmosphere characterized by deep mutual respect and understanding. Despite tension between the Clinton and Netanyahu administrations over the pace of Middle East diplomacy, the United States and Israel on October 30, 1998, signed an important memorandum of understanding on strategic cooperation against long-range missiles and weapons of mass destruction.

The relationship between the Clinton Administration and the Government of Prime Minister Ehud Barak*, elected on May 17, 1999, was markedly more positive than had been the relationship with the Netanyahu-led Government. With the concurrence of the Barak regime, the U.S. brokered additional talks with the Palestinians, resulting in the September 1999 agreement signed by Barak and Yasser Arafat* at Sharm el-Sheikh, Egypt, toward implementing outstanding elements of the Wye River Memorandum* and fast-tracking negotiations toward an Israeli-Palestinian final status agreement. Again in collaboration with the new Israeli Government, the United States convened substantive talks involving Barak and Syria's Foreign Minister Farouk Sharaa, first in Washington, DC, and then in Shepherdstown, West Virginia, in late December 1999 and early January 2000.

The United States and Israel are linked in a complex and multifaceted "special relationship*" that has focused on the continuing United States support for the survival, security, and well-being of Israel. The relationship revolves around a broadly conceived ideological factor and is based on substantial positive perception and sentiment evidenced in public opinion and other statements. It is also manifest in United States political-diplomatic support as well as substantial military and economic assistance to Israel. United States commitments to Israel's security and defense are not formally enshrined, but there is a general perception that the United States would prevent Israel's destruction. The United States is an indispensable, if not fully dependable, ally. It provides economic, technical, military, political, diplomatic, and moral support and there are broad areas of agreement with Israel on many issues. Divergence on some issues derives from a difference of perspective and from the overall policy environments in which the two states operate.

For further information see: Yaacov Bar-Siman-Tov, *Israel, The Superpowers, and the War in the Middle East* (New York: Praeger, 1987); Avraham Ben-Zvi, *The United States and Israel: The Limits of the Special Relationship* (New York: Columbia University Press, 1993); Avraham Ben-Zvi, "Paradigm Lost? The Limits of the American-Israeli Special Relationship," *Israel Affairs* 4:2 (Winter 1997): 1-25; Avraham Ben-Zvi, *Decade of Transition: Eisenhower, Kennedy, and the Origins of the American-Israeli Alliance* (New York: Columbia University Press, 1998); Wolf Blitzer, *Between Washington and Jerusalem: A Reporter's Notebook* (New York: Oxford University Press, 1985); Shai Feldman, *The Future of US-Israel Strategic Cooperation* (Washington, DC: Washington Institute for Near East Policy, 1996); Allon Gal, editor, *Envisioning*

Israel: The Changing Ideals and Images of North American Jews (Jerusalem: Magens; Detroit: Wayne State University Press, 1996); Zvi Ganin, *American Jewry and Israel, 1945-1948* (New York: Holmes and Meier, 1979); Edward B. Glick, *The Triangular Connection: America, Israel and American Jews* (London: Allen and Unwin, 1982); Dore Gold, *Israel as an American Non-NATO Ally: Parameters of Defense-Industrial Cooperation* (Tel Aviv: Jaffee Center for Strategic Studies, 1992); Dore Gold, *US Forces on the Golan Heights and Israeli-Syrian Security Arrangements* (Tel Aviv: Jaffee Center for Strategic Studies, Memorandum No. 44, Tel Aviv University, August 1994); David H. Goldberg, *Foreign Policy and Ethnic Interest Groups: American and Canadian Jews Lobby for Israel* (Westport, CT: Greenwood, 1990); Peter Grose, *Israel in the Mind of America* (New York: Knopf, 1983); I.L. Kenen, *Israel's Defense Line: Her Friends and Foes in Washington* (Buffalo: Prometheus, 1981); James G. MacDonald, *My Mission in Israel, 1948-1951* (New York: Simon and Schuster, 1951); David W. Lesch, editor, *The Middle East and the United States: A Historical and Political Reassessment*, Second Edition (Boulder, CO: Westview Press, 1999); Karen L. Puschel, *US-Israel Strategic Cooperation in the Post-Cold War Era: An American Perspective* (Tel Aviv: Jaffee Center for Strategic Studies, Tel Aviv University, 1992); William B. Quandt, *Decade of Decisions: American Policy toward the Arab-Israeli Conflict, 1967-1976* (Berkeley: University of California Press, 1977); William B. Quandt, *Peace Process: American Diplomacy and the Arab-Israeli Conflict since 1967* (Washington, DC: Brookings Institution; Berkeley: University of California Press, 1993); David Rodman, "Patron-Client Dynamics: Mapping the American-Israeli Relationship," *Israel Affairs* 4:2 (Winter 1997): 26-46; Bernard Reich, *Quest for Peace: United States-Israel Relations and the Arab-Israeli Conflict* (New Brunswick, NJ: Transaction, 1977); Bernard Reich, *The United States and Israel: Influence in the Special Relationship* (New York: Praeger, 1984); Bernard Reich, "The United States and the Arab-Israeli Peace Process," in *Confidence Building Measures in the Middle East*, edited by Gabriel Ben-Dor and David B. Dewitt (Boulder, CO: Westview, 1994): 221-247; Bernard Reich, "Reassessing the US-Israeli Special Relationship," *Israel Affairs* 1:1 (Autumn 1994): 64-83; Bernard Reich, *Securing the Covenant: United States-Israel Relations after the Cold War* (Westport, CT: Praeger, 1995); Nadav Safran, *The United States and Israel* (Cambridge, MA: Harvard, 1963); Nadav Safran, *Israel: The Embattled Ally* (Cambridge, MA: The Belknap Press of Harvard University Press,

1981); Joseph B. Schechtman, *The United States and the Jewish State Movement: The Crucial Decade, 1939-1949* (New York: Herzl and Yoseloff, 1966); David Schoenbaum, *The United States and the State of Israel* (New York: Oxford University Press, 1993); Haim Shaked and Itamar Rabinovich, editors, *The Middle East and the United States: Perceptions and Policies* (New Brunswick, NJ: Transaction, 1980); Gabriel Sheffer, editor, "US-Israel Relations at the Crossroads," *Israel Affairs* (Special Issue) 2:3 & 4 (Spring/Summer 1996); John Snetsinger, *Truman, the Jewish Vote and the Creation of Israel* (Stanford, CA: Hoover Institution, 1974); Steven L. Spiegel, *The Other Arab-Israeli Conflict: Making America's Middle East Policy, From Truman to Reagan* (Chicago: University of Chicago Press, 1985); Steven L. Spiegel, Mark A. Heller, and Jacob Goldberg, editors, *The Soviet-American Competition in the Middle East* (Lexington, MA: Lexington Books, 1988); Melvin I. Urofsky, *We Are One: American Jewry and Israel* (Garden City, NY: Anchor, 1978); Evan M. Wilson, *Decision in Palestine: How the United States Came to Recognize Israel* (Stanford, CA: Hoover Institution, 1979).

UNITED TORAH JUDAISM (UTJ). A joint electoral list comprised of two mainly Ashkenazi* ultra-Orthodox political parties, Agudat Israel* and Degel Hatorah*. In its first election, in 1992, the joint list won four seats in the 13th Knesset*. It replicated this success in 1996, and it participated in the Likud*-led coalition formed by Benjamin Netanyahu*. UTJ won five seats in the 15th Knesset (1999) and it joined the Government headed by Ehud Barak*.

UNITED WORKERS PARTY *see* MAPAM

UNSCOP *see* UNITED NATIONS SPECIAL COMMITTEE ON PALESTINE

USSR (THE SOVIET UNION). The relationship between the Union of Soviet Socialist Republics and Israel underwent substantial change over the years. The Soviet Union and the Communist Party were opposed ideologically to Zionism*, but in 1947 the Soviet Union's representative at the United Nations, Andrei Gromyko, supported the Palestine Partition Plan* which led to the creation of Israel. In 1948 the Soviet Union became one of the first states to recognize the new state of Israel and was instrumental in assuring arms from the Soviet bloc to Israel via Czechoslovakia during its War of Independence*.

However, positive relations in the first years soon gave way to a deterioration of the relationship in the early 1950s that culminated in Soviet arms supply to Egypt announced in 1955. A factor in the relationship then, as later, was the relationship between Israel and the Soviet Jewish population. Israel's desire to ensure the well-being internally of the Soviet Jewish population and to ensure the right of emigration for those who wished to leave the USSR led to conflicts with Soviet authorities and Moscow's official position. Despite the growing relationship between the Soviet Union and the Arab states in the decade following the Sinai War* of 1956, correct if cool relations were retained with Israel. The Soviet Union contributed to the Six Day War* of 1967 through circulation of a fallacious rumor concerning Israeli military mobilization. At this time the Soviet Union and its East European allies (except Romania) broke diplomatic relations with Israel. Since the 1967 conflict the Soviet Union had attempted to become a more significant factor in the peace process. At the same time, since the advent of the Gorbachev approach to foreign policy there had been an improvement in the relationship of the two states. Consular contacts and exchanges took place, Soviet Jewish emigration increased substantially, and several East European states restored diplomatic relations with Israel. Nevertheless, the Soviet Union maintained the position that it could not reestablish relations with Israel until such time as there was substantial movement toward peace and the withdrawal of Israel from the occupied territories*. On October 18, 1991, the USSR and Israel reestablished diplomatic relations. This was part of the process of preparation for the Madrid Peace Conference* that convened at the end of October 1991 to negotiate a solution to the Arab-Israeli conflict.

Upon the collapse of the USSR in December 1991, Russia took over most of the Soviet Union's functions in Middle East diplomacy, including co-sponsoring (with the United States) the Madrid process. In January 1992, Moscow hosted the first session of the multilateral talks of the Madrid Peace Process. From the early 1990s some 750,000 citizens of the former Soviet Union emigrated to Israel and there was significant growth in bilateral relations with Russia and several of the former Soviet republics in the cultural and commercial domains. Nevertheless Israel remained skeptical about Russia's ambitions in the region, as reflected in its relations with militant Arab regimes (including Syria*, Libya, and Iraq*) and its transfer of military technology to Iran*.

For further information see: Uri Bialer, *Between East and West: Israel's Foreign Policy Orientation, 1948-1956* (Cambridge: Cambridge University Press, 1990); Avigdor Dagan, *Moscow and Jerusalem: Twenty Years of Relations between Israel and the Soviet Union* (London: Abelard-Schuman, 1970); Robert O. Freedman, "Russia and the Middle East: The Primakov Era," *MERIA Journal* 2:2 (Ramat Gan, Israel: Begin and Sadat Center for Strategic Studies, Bar Ilan University, May 1998); Robert O. Freedman, "Russia and the Middle East under Yeltsin," in *The Middle East and the Peace Process: The Impact of the Oslo Accords*, edited by Robert O. Freedman (Gainesville: University Press of Florida, 1998): 365-412; Galia Golan, *The Soviet Union and the Palestine Liberation Organization: An Uneasy Alliance* (New York: Praeger, 1980); Galia Golan, *Soviet Policies in the Middle East from World War Two to Gorbachev* (Cambridge, UK: Cambridge University Press, 1990); Galia Golan, *Moscow and the Middle East* (London: Royal Institute of International Affairs, 1992); David H. Goldberg and Paul Marantz, editors, *The Decline of the Soviet Union and the Transformation of the Middle East* (Boulder, CO: Westview, 1994); Baruch A. Hazan, *Soviet Propaganda: A Case Study of the Middle East Conflict* (New York: Wiley, 1976); K. Ivanov and Z. Sheinis, *The State of Israel: Its Position and Policies* (Moscow: State Publication of Political Literature, 1958); Arthur Jay Klinghoffer (with Judith Apter), *Israel and the Soviet Union: Alienation or Reconciliation* (Boulder, CO: Westview, 1985); Arnold P. Krammer, *The Forgotten Friendship: Israel and the Soviet Bloc, 1947-53* (Urbana: University of Illinois Press, 1974); Victor A. Kremenyuk, "Russia's Role in Peacemaking and Confidence Building in the Middle East: Present and Future," in *Confidence Building Measures in the Middle East*, edited by Gabriel Ben-Dor and David B. Dewitt (Boulder, CO: Westview, 1994): 249-266; Yaacov Ro'i, *Soviet Decision Making in Practice: The USSR and Israel, 1947-1954* (New Brunswick, NJ: Transaction, 1980); Yaacov Ro'i, editor, *The Limits of Power: Soviet Policy in the Middle East* (London: Croom Helm, 1979); Amnon Sela, *Soviet Policy and Military Conduct in the Middle East* (London: Macmillan, 1981); Judd L. Teller, *The Kremlin, the Jews, and the Middle East* (New York: Yoseloff, 1957); Fred Wehling, *Irresolute Princes: Kremlin Decision Making in Middle East Crises, 1967 and 1973* (New York: St. Martin's, 1997).

V

VAAD LEUMI (NATIONAL COUNCIL). Under the terms of the British Mandate for Palestine*, Jewish and Arab quasigovernments were established in Palestine* in the 1920s. As early as 1920 the Jewish community of Palestine (Yishuv*) elected by secret ballot an Assembly of the Elected* or parliament. Between sessions its powers were exercised by the National Council appointed by the Elected Assembly from among its members. The National Council, in turn, selected an Executive from among its membership to exercise administrative executive power over the Jewish community. Its role was tantamount to that of a cabinet and its authority was generally accepted in the Yishuv and was recognized by the Mandate authorities. At first its jurisdiction was confined essentially to social and religious matters, but by the 1930s it also functioned in the fields of education, culture, health, and welfare. Through administration of the Jewish community's affairs, the members of the National Council and the Elected Assembly gained valuable experience in self-rule. The Council's departments, staffed by members of the Jewish community, provided a trained core of civil servants for the post-Mandate period of independence. Political experience was also gained as political parties developed to contest the elections for office. When Israel became independent, many of the ministries of the Provisional Government were transformations of departments and bureaus that had functioned under the auspices of the National Council. The National Council formed the basis of Israel's Provisional State Council (which exercised legislative authority as the predecessor of Israel's Knesset* or parliament) and the Executive of the National Council formed the basis of the Provisional Government or Cabinet*.

For further information see: Dan Horowitz and Moshe Lissak, *Origins of the Israeli Polity: Palestine under the Mandate* (Chicago: University of Chicago Press, 1978).

VANUNU, MORDECHAI. Israeli who disclosed that Israel had nuclear bombs to the *Sunday Times* of London. The *Sunday Times* of October 5, 1986, ran a lengthy story under a front page banner headline "Revealed: The Secrets of Israel's Nuclear Arsenal". On March 24, 1988, he was convicted by a Jerusalem* court of treason. The lengthy trial was held in secrecy and the only sentence made public from the court's verdict was "we decided the defendant is guilty on all three counts." Vanunu was a nuclear technician who left Israel with highly classified data and later was lured back to Israel and put on trial. He had worked at Israel's Dimona* nuclear reactor but was laid off in 1985 and, shortly thereafter, left Israel. *See also* ATOMIC RESEARCH AND DEVELOPMENT.

VATICAN. After intense and lengthy negotiations, Israel and the Vatican formally recognized each other and signed an agreement, on December 30, 1993, to establish diplomatic relations. The agreement was signed first in the Vatican and then in Jerusalem*.The Israel-Vatican agreement provided, in part: "The Holy See and the State of Israel, Mindful of the singular character and universal significance of the Holy Land; Aware of the unique nature of the relationship between the Catholic Church and the Jewish people, and of the historic process of reconciliation and growth in mutual understanding and friendship between Catholics and Jews; Having decided on 29 July 1992 to establish a "Bilateral Permanent Working Commission," in order to study and define together issues of common interest, and in view of normalizing their relations; Recognizing that the work of the aforementioned Commission has produced sufficient material for a first and Fundamental Agreement; Realizing that such Agreement will provide a sound and lasting basis for the continued development of their present and future relations and for the furtherance of the Commission's task, Agree upon the following Articles: ... The State of Israel, recalling its Declaration of Independence, affirms its continuing commitment to uphold and observe the human right to freedom of religion and conscience, as set forth in the Universal Declaration of Human Rights and in other international instruments to which it is a party. ... The Holy See, recalling the Declaration of Religious Freedom of the Second Vatican Ecumenical Council, "Dignitatis humanea," affirms the Catholic Church's commitment to uphold the human right to freedom of religion and conscience, as set forth in the Universal Declaration of Human Rights and in other international instruments to which it is a party. The Holy See wishes to affirm as well the Catholic Church's respect for other religions and their followers as solemnly stated by the Second Vatican Ecumenical Council in its Declaration on the Relation of the Church to Non-Christian Religions, "Nostra aetate." ... The Holy See and the State of Israel are committed to appropriate cooperation in combatting all forms of antisemitism and all kinds of racism and of religious intolerance, and in promoting mutual understanding among nations, tolerance among communities and respect for human life and dignity. ... The Holy See takes this occasion to reiterate its condemnation of hatred, persecution and all other manifestations of antisemitism directed against the Jewish people and individual Jews anywhere, at any time and by anyone. In particular, the Holy See deplores attacks on Jews and desecration of Jewish synagogues and cemeteries, acts which offend the memory of the victims of the Holocaust, especially when they occur in the same places which witnessed it. ... The State of Israel affirms its continuing commitment to maintain and respect the "Status quo" in the Christian Holy Places to which it applies and the respective rights of the Christian communities thereunder. The Holy See affirms the Catholic Church's continuing commitment to respect the aforementioned "Status quo" and the said rights. ..."

On June 15, 1994, Israel and the Vatican announced agreement on opening full diplomatic relations. They agreed to exchange ambassadors and open embassies. Until then the Vatican had withheld formal recognition of Israel citing such issues as the state's disputed borders, the unsettled status of Jerusalem, and concerns about the protection of Catholic institutions under Israeli law. The Vatican had also called on Israel to recognize the legitimate rights of the Palestinians. The agreement also opened the way for an increased Vatican role in the Arab-Israeli peace process. For Israel there was some expectation that the agreement would help eliminate anti-Semitism* and encourage more church action against that phenomenon. In January 1996 the Vatican published documents showing that during the last years of World War II it opposed the creation of a Jewish state in Palestine.

VILNAI, MATAN. Born in Israel on May 20, 1944, Matan Vilnai was a General in the IDF after 30 years of service before joining the One Israel Party list for the May 1999 elections. He received a seat in the 15th Knesset and became Minister of Science in Ehud Barak's* Government.

VILNER, MEIR see MEIR WILNER

VOICE OF PEACE. The name of a ship, owned by veteran Israeli peace activist Abie Nathan that, beginning shortly after the 1967 Six Day War*, transmitted messages of peace and calls for Arab-Israeli reconciliation from positions just beyond Israel's territorial waters in the Mediterranean Sea. It concluded its broadcasting in September 1993, shortly after the signing of the Israel-PLO Declaration of Principles*.

W

WADI SALIB. An Oriental Jewish (primarily North African) slum neighborhood in Haifa* in which there were riots in July 1959 in the wake of a rumor that a police officer had killed a local resident. Subsequently other riots in Wadi Salib and elsewhere also drew attention to the poor economic and social conditions in which many Oriental immigrants were living. Wadi Salib became a symbol of Oriental discontent. *See also* ORIENTAL JEWS.

WAILING WALL (WESTERN WALL). The Wall, located on Mount Moriah in Jerusalem's* Old City, is all that remains of the Temple of biblical times. The Temple was destroyed and rebuilt several times, with the last destruction at the hands of the Romans in AD 70. The Wall, which is some 160 feet long, was the western wall of the Temple courtyard. It has been a symbol of Jewish faith. Its alternate name ("Wailing Wall") is derived from the sorrowful prayers said there in mourning for the destruction of the Temple. According to legend, the Wall itself weeps over the destruction of the Temple.

WALL-TO-WALL COALITION. During the crisis preceding the Six Day War* of June 1967, Israel created a "wall-to-wall" political coalition incorporating virtually all of Israel's political parties in a Government of National Unity*. The Communists* were pointedly excluded but, for the first time, Gahal* and Menachem Begin* joined Israel's coalition Government. Begin and his political allies remained in the Government until the summer of 1970 when they withdrew because of opposition to Government policy concerning the terms associated with the cease-fire in the War of Attrition* that had been arranged by the United States*.

WAR IN LEBANON (1982). Also known as Operation Peace for Galilee. On June 6, 1982, Israel began a major military action against the Palestine Liberation Organization (PLO)* in Lebanon*. The announced immediate goal was to put the Galilee* out of the range of PLO shelling. It sought to remove the PLO military and terrorist threat to Israel and to reduce the PLO's political capability. It was described as a major response to years of PLO terrorist attacks against Israel and its people. The Israeli incursion into Lebanon came suddenly and Israeli forces moved swiftly north of the Israel-Lebanon border, capturing and destroying numerous PLO strongholds and positions. Within a week Israel was in control of much of the southern portion of the country and thousands of PLO fighters were killed or captured. By the middle of June Israel had virtually laid siege to Beirut. The war enjoyed widespread initial support but later occasioned major debate and demonstration (much relating to Sabra and Shatila*), and led to Israel's increased international political and diplomatic isolation. It also brought about major political and diplomatic clashes with the United States. An agreement of May 17, 1983, between Israel and Lebanon providing for the withdrawal of Israeli forces from Lebanon noted that "they consider the existing international boundary between Israel and Lebanon inviolable." Although it was signed and ratified by both states, Lebanon, under substantial pressure from Syria*, abrogated the agreement in March 1984. All Israeli forces were withdrawn from Lebanon, except for a security zone* in southern Lebanon along the border with Israel, by 1985. *See also* LEBANON AND ISRAEL-LEBANON AGREEMENT OF MAY 17, 1983.

For further information see: Dan Bavly and Eliahu Salpeter, *Fire in Beirut: Israel's War in Lebanon with the PLO* (New York: Stein and Day, 1984); Yair Evron, *War and Intervention in Lebanon: The Israeli-Syrian Deterrence Dialogue* (Baltimore: Johns Hopkins University Press, 1987); Shai Feldman and Heda Rechnitz-Kijner, *Deception, Consensus and War: Israel in Lebanon* (Tel Aviv: Jaffee Center for Strategic Studies, Paper No. 27, October 1984); Richard A. Gabriel, *Operation Peace for Galilee: The Israeli-PLO War in Lebanon* (New York: Hill and Wang, 1984); Raphael Israeli, editor, *PLO in Lebanon: Selected Documents* (London: Weidenfeld and Nicolson, 1983); John Bulloch, *Final Conflict: The War in Lebanon* (London: Century, 1983); Yitzhak Kahan, Aharon Barak, and Yona Efrat, *Commission of Inquiry into the Events at the Refugee Camps in Beirut. Final Report.* Authorized Translation (Jerusalem: Government Printer, 1983); John Laffin, *The War of Desperation: Lebanon, 1982-1985* (London: Osprey, 1985); Itamar Rabinovich, *The War for Lebanon, 1970-1985*, Revised Edition (Ithaca, NY: Cornell University Press, 1985); Ze'ev Schiff, "Green Light, Lebanon," *Foreign Policy* 50 (Spring 1983): 73-85; Ze'ev Schiff and Ehud Ya'ari, *Israel's Lebanon War* (New York: Simon and Schuster, 1989); Jacobo Timmerman, *The Longest War: Israel in Lebanon* (New York: Alfred Knopf, 1982); Avner Yaniv, *Dilemmas of Security: Politics, Strategy and the Israeli Experience in Lebanon*

(Oxford University Press: Clarendon, 1987); Avner Yaniv and Robert J. Lieber, "Personal Whim or Strategic Imperative? The Israeli Invasion of Lebanon," *International Security* 8:2 (Fall 1983): 117-142.

WAR OF ATTRITION (1969-1970). In the first years after the Six Day War*, Israel retained control of the occupied territories*, and despite various efforts, no significant progress was made toward the achievement of peace. The Palestinians became more active — initially gaining publicity and attention through terrorist acts against Israel, some of which were spectacular in nature. However, the most serious threat to Israel came from Egypt*, which embarked on the War of Attrition in the spring of 1969 in an effort, as President Gamal Abdul Nasser put it, "to wear down the enemy." But the war soon took on a broader scope as the Egyptians faced mounting losses and minimal successes, and Nasser sought and received assistance from the USSR*. The Soviets soon were involved as advisers and combatants, and Israeli aircraft flying over the Suez Canal Zone were challenged by Russian-flown Egyptian planes. The War of Attrition was ended by a United States*-sponsored cease-fire in August 1970, and talks under Ambassador Gunnar Jarring's* auspices were restarted, but no significant progress toward peace followed.

For further information see: Yaacov Bar-Siman-Tov, *The Israeli-Egyptian War of Attrition, 1967-1970: A Case Study of Limited Local Wars* (New York: Columbia University Press, 1980); Chaim Herzog, *The Arab-Israeli Wars* (New York: Random House, 1982); David A. Korn, *Stalemate: The War of Attrition and Great Power Diplomacy in the Middle East, 1967-1970* (Boulder, CO: Westview, 1992); Edgar O'Ballance, *The Electronic War in the Middle East, 1968-1970* (London: Faber and Faber, 1974); Fred Wehling, *Irresolute Princes: Kremlin Decision Making in Middle East Crises, 1967-1973* (New York: St. Martin's, 1997).

WAR OF INDEPENDENCE (1948-1949). As Israel declared its independence in May 1948, armies of the Arab states entered Palestine* and engaged in open warfare with the defense forces of the new state, with the stated goals of preventing the establishment of a Jewish state and of assuring that all of Palestine would be in Arab hands. This first Arab-Israeli war (known in Israel as the War of Independence) involved troops from Egypt*, Syria*, Jordan*, Iraq*, and Lebanon*, with assistance from other Arab quarters, against Israel. The war was long and costly: Israel lost some 4,000 soldiers and 2,000 civilians, about 1% of the Jewish population, and each side had successes and failures. The war ended in 1949 when Armistice Agreements* were signed with the neighboring Arab states. Peace did not follow and additional wars between Israel and the Arabs were fought over the ensuing decades.

For further information see: Lynne Reid Banks, *Torn Country: An Oral History of the Israeli War of Independence* (New York: Franklin Watts, 1982); David Roy Elston, *No Alternative: Israel Observed* (London: Hutchinson, 1960); Chaim Herzog, *The Arab-Israeli Wars* (New York: Random House, 1982); Benjamin Kagan, *The Secret Battle for Israel* (Cleveland: World, 1966); Walid Khalidi, *All That Remains: The Palestinian Villages Occupied and Depopulated by Israel in 1948* (Washington, DC: Institute for Palestine Studies, 1971); David Kimche and Jon Kimche, *A Clash of Destinies: The Arab-Jewish War and the Founding of the State of Israel* (New York: Praeger, 1960); Dan Kurzman, *Genesis 1948: The First Arab-Israel War* (London: Vallentine, Mitchell, 1970); Netanel Lorch, *The Edge of the Sword: Israel's War of Independence, 1947-1949* (New York: Putnam's, 1961); Benny Morris, *The Birth of the Palestinian Refugee Problem, 1947-1949* (Cambridge: Cambridge University Press, 1987); Edgar O'Ballance, *The Arab-Israeli War, 1948* (London: Faber and Faber, 1956); Ze'ev Sharef, *Three Days: An Account of the Last Days of the British Mandate and the Birth of Israel* (New York: Doubleday, 1962); Avi Shlaim, *Collusion across the Jordan* (New York: Columbia University Press, 1988); Constantine N. Zurayk, *Palestine: The Meaning of the Disaster* (Beirut: Khayat's, 1956).

"WARS OF THE JEWS" *see* YOM KIPPUR WAR

WASHINGTON DECLARATION. On September 14, 1993, one day after the signing of the Israel-PLO Declaration of Principles*, representatives of Israel and Jordan initialed a common agenda for future peace negotiations. The declaration generated from these negotiations was formally signed by Jordan's King Hussein* and Israel's Prime Minister Yitzhak Rabin* in Washington, DC, on July 25, 1994. The Washington Declaration became the basis of the Israel-Jordan Peace Treaty*, initialed on October 17, 1994, in Amman, Jordan, and formally signed on October 26, 1994, in the Jordan Valley.

WAXMAN, NAHSHON (WACHSMAN). An Israel Defense Forces* corporal kidnaped by Hamas terrorists on October 9, 1994. The kidnappers threatened to murder him unless Israel agreed to free Hamas's founder and spiritual leader, Sheikh Ahmed Yassin*, and other imprisoned Palestinians. Waxman was killed during a rescue attempt by IDF commandos in the West Bank* village of Bir Nabala on October 14, 1994.

WEIZMAN, EZER. A nephew of Chaim Weizmann*, who spells his name with one "n" to avoid benefiting from the family connection. Born in 1924 in Tel Aviv*, he was educated at the Reali School in Haifa*, and joined the Hagana* in 1939. In 1942 he enlisted in the British Royal Air Force and in 1948 served as a Squadron Commander in the Israel Defense Forces* and rose through the ranks. He studied with the British Royal Air Force from 1951 to 1953 and in 1958 he became Commander in Chief of the Israel Air Force. From 1966 to 1969 he served as Chief of the General Staff Branch of the IDF and in that capacity was involved in planning Israel's victory in the Six Day War*. He resigned from the IDF in December 1969, apparently convinced that he would not be made Chief of Staff, and immediately entered political life. In 1969-1970 he served as Minister of Transport in the National Unity Government led by Golda Meir* in one of the six seats allocated to Gahal*. In the Government formed by Menachem Begin* in 1977 he served as Minister of Defense (as a Likud* member) but resigned in 1980. In 1984 he founded his own centrist political party, Yahad*, that won three Knesset seats and joined the Government of National Unity* with Weizman serving as Minister in the Prime Minister's Office. He became Minister of Science and Development in the Government established in December 1988.

After retiring from party politics in February 1992 he was elected President* of Israel in 1993 and was reelected for a second five-year term in March 1998. Renowned as a populist politician, he was credited with opening up the office of the presidency, making it an institution more accessible to the average Israeli. He also sought to transform the presidency into a "bully pulpit" for expressing popular sentiment about controversial aspects of domestic politics and foreign and security policy (an exercise that found Weizman clashing on occasion with Labor* and Likud Prime Ministers alike).

For further information see: Ezer Weizman, *On Eagles' Wings* (New York: Macmillan, 1979); Ezer Weizman, *The Battle for Peace* (New York: Bantam, 1981).

WEIZMANN, CHAIM. Chaim Weizmann was born in Motol, near Pinsk, Russia, on November 27, 1874. The Weizmann family were ardent Zionists and belonged to the Hoveve Zion*. He was educated in Germany* where he received a Doctor of Science degree from the University of Freiburg in 1900. In 1904 Weizmann moved to England, where he began his career as a faculty member in biochemistry at the University of Manchester. As director of the Admiralty Laboratories during 1919 he discovered a process for producing acetone (a vital ingredient of gunpowder). Weizmann became the leader of the English Zionist movement and was instrumental in securing the Balfour Declaration*. In 1918 he became chairman of the Zionist Commission to Palestine*. Following World War I, Weizmann emerged as the leader of the World Zionist Organization* and built a home in Palestine* near Rehovot. He served as President of the World Zionist Organization from 1920 to 1946, except for the years 1931-1935. He helped found the Jewish Agency*, the Hebrew University* of Jerusalem, and the Sieff Research Institute at Rehovot (now the Weizmann Institute of Science*). In 1919 Weizmann headed the Zionist delegation to the Paris Peace Conference and in the fall of 1947 he addressed the United Nations General Assembly to plead for the establishment of a Jewish state. Weizmann also appealed (successfully) to United States* President Harry Truman for assistance in the effort to secure a Jewish state and to override support in the United States Department of State for a plan that would have omitted the Negev from the proposed state. With the declaration of Israel's independence and the establishment of a Provisional Government in May 1948, Weizmann became President of Israel's Provisional Government, and in February 1949, the first elected Knesset* selected Weizmann as the first President* of Israel. He was reelected in November 1951, but died on November 9, 1952.

For further information see: Sir Isaiah Berlin, *Chaim Weizmann* (London: Weidenfeld and Nicolson, 1958); Ben Halpern, *A Clash of Heroes* (New York: Oxford University Press, 1987); Arthur Hertzberg, editor, *The Zionist Idea: A Historical Analysis and Reader* (New York: Atheneum, 1979): 572-588; Barnet Litvinoff, *Weizmann: Last of the Patriarchs* (New York: Holt, Rinehart and Winston, 1972); Jehuda Reinharz, *Chaim*

Weizmann: The Making of a Zionist Leader (New York: Oxford University Press, 1985); Jehuda Reinharz, "The Balfour Declaration in Historical Perspective," in *Essential Papers on Zionism*, edited by Jehuda Reinharz and Anita Shapira (New York: New York University Press, 1996): 587-616; Norman Rose, *Chaim Weizmann: A Biography* (New York: Viking, 1986); Samuel Shihor, *Hollow Glory: The Last Days of Chaim Weizmann* (New York: Yoseloff, 1960); Melvin I. Urosky, "Chaim Weizmann," in *Contemporary Political Leaders of the Middle East and North Africa*, edited by Bernard Reich (New York: Greenwood, 1990): 495-502; Meyer W. Weisgal and Joel Carmichael, editors, *Chaim Weizmann—A Biography by Several Hands* (New York: Atheneum, 1963); Chaim Weizmann, *Trial and Error* (New York: Harper and Brothers, 1949); Chaim Weizmann, *The Letters and Papers of Chaim Weizmann*, 2 Volumes (Jerusalem: Israel Universities Press; Oxford University Press, 1968-1984); Vera Weizmann, *The Impossible Takes Longer* (New York: Harper and Row, 1967).

WEIZMANN INSTITUTE OF SCIENCE. A major scientific institution located in Rehovot, focusing on fundamental research and higher education in the sciences. It developed out of the Daniel Sieff Research Institute, which was founded in 1934. It was conceived in the 1940s and the first building of the Weizmann Institute was dedicated in 1949. It is named after Chaim Weizmann*.

WEST BANK. The area of historical Palestine* lying west of the Jordan River* and the Dead Sea*. Designated by the United Nations Palestine Partition Plan* to become part of an Arab state, it—along with the eastern half of Jerusalem*—was occupied by Jordan* during the 1948-1949 Arab-Israeli War*. On April 24, 1950, the parliament of Jordan passed legislation designed to unite the West Bank and East Jerusalem with Jordanian territory east of the Jordan; however, this annexation was largely ignored by the international community. The area came under Israeli control during the June 1967 Six Day War*, although Jordan continued to maintain an administrative presence in the West Bank. In the summer of 1988, King Hussein* announced that Jordan was disengaging politically and administratively from the area. Pursuant to the Oslo Accords*, areas of the West Bank were transferred by Israel to the control of the Palestinian Authority*.

WESTERN WALL *see* WAILING WALL

WHITE PAPER OF 1939. A statement of policy, also known as the MacDonald White Paper (after Colonial Secretary Malcolm MacDonald), that was issued by the British Government on May 17, 1939. It called for one independent state in all of Palestine*, to be established incrementally over the next 10 years and, under the prevailing demographic conditions, it would be Arab-controlled. It imposed severe restrictions on Jewish immigration to Palestine. For five years, a maximum of 15,000 Jews per year, for a total of 75,000, would be permitted to immigrate to Palestine. After that, no further Jewish immigration would be permitted without the consent of the Arab community. Moreover, the number of Jews entering Palestine illegally would be deducted from the 75,000 quota. Restrictions were imposed on the purchase of land in Palestine by Jewish immigrants. The Zionist leadership rejected the White Paper; leaders accused Britain of reneging on its commitments to Zionism (articulated in the Balfour Declaration* and the League of Nations Mandate for Palestine*) and of betraying the Jewish people in their "darkest hour", when they were in desperate need of a safe haven from Nazi oppression. From the Zionist perspective, the White Paper constituted the death knell of the British Mandate*.

WHO IS A JEW. In 1950 the Knesset* passed the Law of Return*, granting any Jew immigrating to Israel the right to immediate citizenship. The law did not define a Jew and left it to the Minister of the Interior to interpret the clause as he saw fit. In 1958, the then-Interior Minister Yisrael Bar Yehuda issued a directive to ministry officials instructing them to register as Jewish any person who sincerely declared himself to be a Jew. The National Religious Party* subsequently resigned from the Government in protest. In 1970, the Supreme Court* ordered the Interior Ministry's registrar in Haifa* to record as Jewish nationals the children of Binyamin Shalit*, whose wife was not Jewish. The case aroused controversy and led to the amendment of the Law of Return defining a Jew as "a person born of a Jewish mother or who has been converted to Judaism and who does not profess another religion." Agudat Israel* demanded that the amendment stipulate that the conversion be "according to Halacha"*—the formulation the religious parties have been fighting for ever since. Such a stipulation would exclude conversions by other than recognized Orthodox rabbis. Since then, the issue has come up after every parliamentary election in coalition negotiations with the religious parties. In 1974, a compromise formula drafted by Rabbi Shlomo Goren*, which called for conversion "according to the manner practiced and accepted among the Jewish people from generation to generation", failed to win support among religious and secular parties. Over the years, the religious parties have made numerous attempts to have their proposed amendment approved by the Knesset. All have failed, but the margin of defeat has narrowed. In June 1988, the effort was rejected by 60 votes to 53. When Shas* took over the Interior Ministry after the 1984 elections, there were several attempts to circumvent the Law of Return. Under Rabbi Yitzhak Peretz*, Interior Ministry officials refused to register Shoshana Miller, an American-born Reform convert to Judaism, as Jewish. Miller appealed the case to the Supreme Court and won, prompting Peretz to resign. During coalition negotiations over the establishment of the December 1988 Government, it appeared that the religious parties might finally succeed, provoking an outcry of crisis proportions from world Jewry. In the summer of 1989 the Supreme Court ordered the Interior Ministry to accept non-Orthodox converts to Judaism as immigrants according to the Law of Return and register them as Jews. The ruling on the registration of non-Orthodox converts came at a time when the Interior Ministry had begun to reverse its former practice of allowing such converts to come as immigrants, even though it did not register them as Jews. The ministry had excluded them by demanding that all conversion certificates must be validated by the local rabbinical courts, which accepted only Orthodox conversions. Other prominent cases have included the Brother Daniel case* (1962); the status of the Falashas* of Ethiopia*; and the status of the Bnai Israel* of India*.

The issue took on a new political imperative against the background of the arrival in Israel in the late 1980s and 1990s of some 800,000 new immigrants from the former Soviet Union and Ethiopia.

For further information see: Charles S. Liebman, *Religion, Democracy and Israeli Society* (Amsterdam: Harwood Academic Publishers, 1997); Charles S. Liebman and Eliezer Don-Yehiya, *Religion and Politics in Israel* (Bloomington: Indiana University Press, 1984); Gary S. Schiff, *Tradition and Politics: The Religious Parties of Israel* (Detroit: Wayne State University Press, 1977).

WILNER, MEIR. Born in Vilnius on October 23, 1918, Wilner was educated at a Hebrew* high school in Vilnius and at the Hebrew University of Jerusalem*. A signer of the Declaration of Independence* and a journalist by profession, he was a Knesset* member beginning with the First Knesset until his resignation in January 1990. At the time he was Secretary General of the Israel Communist Party* and a member of the Rakah* faction in the parliament. He participated in the symbolic fiftieth anniversary re-signing of the Declaration of Independence in 1998.

WOMEN'S INTERNATIONAL ZIONIST ORGANIZATION (WIZO). The Women's International Zionist Organization was founded in July 1920 in London and in 1949 the seat of its Executive moved to Israel. The organization seeks to unite Jewish women in participating actively in the upbuilding and consolidation of Israel through various activities, including education and training of youth and women in agriculture, home economics, and, more generally, in other areas relating to social welfare. It also seeks to strengthen the cultural and spiritual links between the Diaspora* and Israel.

For further information see: Dafna N. Izraeli, "The Zionist Women's Movement in Palestine, 1911-1927: A Sociological Analysis," *SIGNS* 7 (1981): 87-114.

WORLD ZIONIST ORGANIZATION (WZO). The official organization of the Zionist movement founded at the initiative of Theodor Herzl* at the first Zionist Congress in Basle, Switzerland, in August 1897. The World Zionist Organization conducted the political, economic, and settlement activities leading to the establishment of Israel. The right of membership in the Zionist Organization was accorded to every Jew who subscribed to the Organization's program—the Basle Program*—and who paid the one shekel dues. Each shekel holder who was at least 18 years of age was entitled to elect delegates to the Zionist Congress, or to be elected to Congress once having attained the age of 24. Over the years, the center of the Zionist movement was shifted from place to place until it was transferred permanently to Jerusalem*. Since 1952, the Zionist Organization has functioned in the framework of the Status Law. In 1960, various changes were introduced in its Constitution (which had been in force since 1899). In 1951, the Jerusalem Program* was adopted in addition to the Basle Program. This Jerusalem Program was subsequently superseded by the new Jerusalem Program of 1968.

The Zionist Congress is the supreme body of the Zionist Organization. It is the Congress that is empowered to elect the President, the Chairman, the General Council, and the members of the Zionist Executive, the

Congress Attorney, and the Comptroller. The Congress deals with, and determines, all basic matters relating to the activities of the World Zionist Organization. It is composed of delegates elected in all countries, except Israel where the Zionist parties in the country receive their representation in the Congress on the basis of elections to the Knesset*. In its current configuration (since 1997), the World Zionist Congress is composed of 750 delegates of whom 503 have voting rights. Also represented are organizations such as Hadassah* and WIZO*. Israel provides 38% of the delegates, the United States* 29%, and the remaining countries of the Diaspora* 33%. The Congress receives and discusses reports from the Zionist General Council and the Executive. The Congress met annually until 1901, when it was resolved to meet every two years. Subsequently, until 1939, it met every other year (except during World War I). According to the Constitution adopted in 1960, the Zionist Congress convenes every four years.

The Zionist Congresses were held as follows: 1st Congress: Basle, August 29-31, 1897; 2d Congress: Basle, August 28-31, 1898; 3d Congress: Basle, August 15-18, 1899; 4th Congress: London, August 13-16, 1900; 5th Congress: Basle, December 26-30, 1901; 6th Congress: Basle, August 23-28, 1903; 7th Congress: Basle, July 27-August 2, 1905; 8th Congress: The Hague, August 14-21, 1907; 9th Congress: Hamburg, December 26-30, 1909; 10th Congress: Basle, August 9-15, 1911; 11th Congress: Vienna, September 2-9, 1913; 12th Congress: Karlovy Vary (Carlsbad), September 1-14, 1921; 13th Congress: Karlovy Vary, August 6-18, 1923; 14th Congress: Vienna, August 18-31, 1925; 15th Congress: Basle, August 30-September 11, 1927; 16th Congress: Zurich, July 29-August 10, 1929; 17th Congress: Basle, June 30-July 15, 1931; 18th Congress: Prague, August 21-September 4, 1933; 19th Congress: Lucerne, August 20-September 4, 1935; 20th Congress: Zurich, August 3-16, 1937; 21st Congress; Geneva, August 16-25, 1939; 22d Congress: Basle, December 9-24, 1946; 23d Congress: Jerusalem, August 14-30, 1951; 24th Congress: Jerusalem, April 24-May 7, 1956; 25th Congress: Jerusalem, December 27, 1960-January 11, 1961; 26th Congress: Jerusalem, December 30, 1964-January 11, 1965; 27th Congress: Jerusalem, June 9-19, 1968; 28th Congress: Jerusalem, January 1-28, 1972; 29th Congress: Jerusalem, February 20-March 1, 1978; 30th Congress: Jerusalem, December 7-16, 1982; 31st Congress Jerusalem, 1987; 32nd Congress Jerusalem, July 26-30, 1992; and 33rd Congress Jerusalem, December 23-25, 1997.

The Zionist General Council, which is elected by the Zionist Congress, functions in the period between Congresses and is empowered to deliberate and decide on all matters affecting the Zionist Organization and its institutions, including the budget, with the exception of matters relegated solely to the authority of the Congress. Its composition reflects the relative strength of forces in the Congress. The Zionist General Council supervises the activities of the Zionist Executive by means of its various committees.

The Zionist Executive is the executive arm of the World Zionist Organization, and is elected by the Congress for a period of four years. Some of its members are placed in charge of the various departments of the Executive, others serve as members without portfolio. The Executive reflects the relative strength of forces in the Congress.

The World Zionist Organization is now a full partner in the Jewish Agency for Israel*, which is an umbrella institution for a number of agencies and functional departments responsible for activities such as the facilitation of aliya*, immigration absorption and resettlement, and other social services in Israel; the promotion of Zionist education; and advocating on behalf of Diaspora* Jewish communities in distress. In recent years steps have been taken to restructure the World Zionist Organization to reflect the current balance of financial and political interests between Israel and Diaspora Jewish communities. In 1997, the Jewish Agency for Israel and World Zionist Organization had an approved budget totaling about $500 million (US). In 1995 Labor* Member of Knesset Avraham Burg* was elected to the position of Chairman of the Executive of the World Zionist Organization and the Jewish Agency for Israel, permanently replacing Simha Dinitz*. In December 1997 Burg was reelected to a second two-year term. In December 1997 the chairmanship of the WZO shifted to Salai Meridor.

For further information see: Avraham Burg, *Brit Am—A Covenant of the People: Proposed Policy Guidelines for the National Institutions of the Jewish People* (Jerusalem: The Jewish Agency for Israel, 1995); Daniel J. Elazar, *The Jewish Agency within the World Polity* (Jerusalem: Jerusalem Center for Public Affairs, 1994); Yosef Gorny, "The Zionist Movement and the State of Israel, 1948-1952: A Formation of Normal Interrelations," in *Israel: The First Decade of Independence*, edited by S. Ilan Troen and Noah Lucas (Albany: State University of New York Press,

1995): 683-698; Charles S. Liebman, "Restructuring Israeli-Diaspora Relations," *Israel Studies* 1:1 (Spring 1996): 315-322; Ernest Stock, "Philanthropy and Politics: Modes of Interaction between Israel and the Diaspora," in *Israel: The First Decade of Independence*, edited by S. Ilan Troen and Noah Lucas (Albany: State University of New York Press, 1995): 699-711.

WYE RIVER MEMORANDUM. The agreement signed by Israel's Prime Minister Benjamin Netanyahu*, Palestinian Authority* Chairman Yasser Arafat* and U.S. President Bill Clinton, on October 23, 1998. It concluded nine days of intensive negotiations between Israeli, Palestinian, and American delegations. The memorandum effectively provided for the implementation of the terms of the Oslo II Accords* of September 1995 and the Hebron Protocol* of January 1997. Major aspects of the memorandum included the phased redeployment of Israel Defense Forces* personnel from an additional 13% of the West Bank* and the transfer to full Palestinian control ("Area A") of another 14% of the West Bank that had heretofore been under joint Israeli-Palestinian jurisdiction ("Area B"); pledges of enhanced efforts on the part of the Palestinian Authority in the fighting of terrorism and the establishment of tripartite (Israeli, Palestinian, and American) committees for verifying Palestinian compliance with these commitments; commitments by the Palestinian Authority to finally and unconditionally amend the Palestine National Covenant*; and the immediate start of negotiations between Israel and the Palestinian Authority on permanent status issues such as Jerusalem*, settlements, water, refugees, and the nature and precise configuration of political boundaries between Israel and areas of the West Bank and the Gaza Strip* under the jurisdiction of the Palestinian Authority.

WYE RIVER PLANTATION. A former colonial plantation and conference center in rural Maryland. It was the site of a series of meetings between Israeli and Syrian political and military officials that occurred under U.S. auspices between December 1995 and March 1996. It was also the location of nine days of intensive talks between Israel and the Palestinian Authority* that culminated with the Wye River Memorandum* signed by Israel's Prime Minister Benjamin Netanyahu*, Palestinian Authority Chairman Yasser Arafat*, and U.S. President Bill Clinton on October 23, 1998.

WZO *see* WORLD ZIONIST ORGANIZATION

Y

YAACOBI, GAD. Born on January 18, 1935 in Kfar Vitkin, Yaacobi graduated from the Faculties of Law and Commerce of Tel Aviv University. He was a Labor Alignment* member of the Knesset* since 1969. He served as Minister of Transport. Then, in the Government of National Unity* established in 1984, Yaacobi served as Minister of Economics and Planning and later became Minister of Communications in the Government established in December 1988. He served as Israel's Ambassador to the United Nations from 1992 to 1996.

For further information see: Gad Yaacobi, *The Government of Israel* (New York: Praeger, 1982); Gad Yaacobi, *Wanted: A New Course* (B'nei Brak: Steimatzky, 1991, Hebrew); Gad Yaacobi, *Breakthrough: Israel in a Changing World* (New York: Cornwall Books, 1996).

YAD VASHEM (THE HEROES' AND MARTYRS' AUTHORITY). The official Israeli authority to commemorate the heroes and martyrs who died in the Holocaust*. The name, meaning monument and memorial, is derived from the Bible. The Authority was created by an act of the Knesset* in 1953. It has archives and a library on the Nazi era and publishes on the Holocaust. Among its buildings is a memorial hall, dedicated in 1961, in which there is a memorial flame and inscriptions on the floor listing the names of the most notorious of the extermination camps. A section of the memorial is dedicated to "Righteous Gentiles", non-Jews who helped save the lives of Jews during the Nazi reign of terror.

YADIN, YIGAEL (FORMERLY SUKENIK). He was the son of the noted archaeologist Eliezer Lipa Sukenik. Born in Jerusalem* on March 21, 1917, he joined the Hagana* at age 15. He left the Hagana in 1945 to pursue his education at Hebrew University*, but returned to active duty at the time of preparations for Israel's independence. He became Chief of General Staff Branch of Hagana headquarters in 1947 and Chief of Operations of the Israel Defense Forces (IDF)* General Staff in 1948, a post he held during the War of Independence*. In 1949 he became Chief of Staff of the IDF at age 32 and began to develop the foundations for the reorganization of the IDF into a regular army. He served as head of one of Israel's negotiating teams in the armistice negotiations at Rhodes.

Yadin resigned his military post in December 1952 in protest over cuts in the military budget and to resume his research as an archaeologist. He received his PhD in archaeology from the Hebrew University and later became professor of archaeology at that institution. From 1955 to 1958 he directed the excavations at Hazor and from 1960 to 1961 he led explorations of the Judean Desert caves where the Bar Kochba* documents were discovered. From 1963 to 1965 he directed the Masada* expedition. He was awarded the Israel Prize* in Jewish Studies in 1956 and the Rothschild Science Prize in 1964. He was the author of numerous publications in the field of archaeology.

After the Yom Kippur War*, Yadin served as one of the members of the Agranat Commission* appointed to look into Israel's state of readiness at the time of the outbreak of the war. In 1976 he decided to reenter public life and seek the position of Prime Minister, arguing that Israel urgently needed political and economic reforms. He seemed to appeal to the Israeli public as a trusted and untainted but fresh political face. In 1976 he helped to form a new political party—Democratic Movement for Change*. The party won 15 seats in the 1977 Knesset* election and joined the coalition Government led by Menachem Begin*, with Yadin serving as Deputy Prime Minister until 1981. He died on June 28, 1984.

For further information see: Gershon R. Kieval, *Party Politics in Israel and the Occupied Territories* (Westport, CT: Greenwood, 1983); Nachman Orieli and Amnon Barzilai, *The Rise and Fall of the DMC* (Tel Aviv: Reshafim, 1982, Hebrew); Neil Asher Silberman, *A Prophet from amongst You: The Life of Yigael Yadin: Soldier, Scholar, and Mythmaker of Modern Israel* (Reading, MA: Addison-Wesley, 1993); Yigael Yadin, *The Art of Warfare in Biblical Lands in the Light of Archaeological Study*, 2 volumes (New York: McGraw-Hill, 1963); Yigael Yadin, *Masada: Herod's Fortress and the Zealots' Last Stand* (New York: Random House, 1966); Yigael Yadin, *Bar-Kokhba: The Rediscovery of the Legendary Hero of the Second Jewish Revolt against Rome* (London: Weidenfeld and Nicolson, 1971).

YAHAD. A party at the center of the political spectrum founded in 1984 and led by Ezer Weizman*. The party won three seats in the 1984 Knesset* election on a platform that advocated a peace settlement with the Arabs and the Palestinians. It joined the Government of National Unity* in which Weizman served as Minister in the Prime Minister's office.

YAHAD SHIVTEI YISRAEL *see* YISHAI

YAHALOM, SHAUL. Born in 1947 in Tel Aviv*, he served in the Israel Defense Forces* and studied education and economics at Bar Ilan University*. He became chairman of the board of directors of the Hebrew*-language daily newspaper, *Hatzofeh**, the voice of the Mizrachi* movement and the National Religious Party*. Political Secretary of the NRP from 1987-1995, he was first elected to the Knesset* in 1992 on the NRP list. In the 13th Knesset (1992-1996), he served as a member of the Knesset committees on State Control and Education and Culture, and as chairman of the Knesset Subcommittee on Special Education. Reelected to the 14th Knesset in 1996, he served as chairman of the Knesset Committee on the Constitution, Law, and Justice; chairman of the Knesset Subcommittee on Education and Culture in the IDF; and as a member of the Knesset Committee on Foreign Affairs and Security. In February 1998, he was appointed Minister of Transportation, replacing fellow NRP MK Yitzhak Levy*, who became Minister of Education and Culture following the death of Zevulun Hammer*. Reelected to the 15th Knesset, on July 6, 1999, Ehud Barak* appointed him Deputy Minister of Education, Culture, and Sports.

YAMIT. The largest of a series of settlements on the northern coast of the Sinai Peninsula* that were established by Israel after the 1967 Six Day War*. The readiness of the Government of Menachem Begin* to evacuate the city and all other Sinai settlements as part of the Peace Treaty with Egypt* evoked significant political opposition in Israel, especially among Gush Emunim* and its offshoot, the Movement to Halt the Retreat at Sinai. These groups feared that the full evacuation of settlements would weaken Israel's ability to defend against future attack from Egypt; there was also a concern that it would set a dangerous precedent for future negotiations over the West Bank* and the Gaza Strip*. The plan was to prevent the evacuation of Yamit by concentrating 100,000 settlers there on April 22, 1982, the day the Israel Defense Forces* were scheduled to complete the evacuation of the city. In the end, however, only a few thousand protesters took up positions at Yamit, and the evacuation was completed by unarmed soldiers and without serious opposition or injury. Once the evacuation was completed, all buildings at Yamit were leveled by IDF bulldozers.

For further information see: Monica M. Boudjouk, "Yamit," in *An Historical Encyclopedia of the Arab-Israeli Conflict*, edited by Bernard Reich (Westport, CT: Greenwood, 1996): 591-592; Gadi Wolfsfeld, "Collective Political Action and Media Strategy: The Case of Yamit," *Journal of Conflict Resolution* 28 (September 1984): 363-381.

YASSIN, SHEIKH AHMED ISMAIL. Born in Ashkelon in 1933 or 1934, he became a quadriplegic due to serious illness at a young age. An Islamic scholar, he was a founder of the Gaza wing of the Egyptian-based Muslim Brotherhood. In 1984, he was sentenced to 13 years in Israeli prison for possession of arms, but was released a year later as part of an exchange in which six Israeli soldiers captured in Lebanon* were traded for 1,000 Palestinian security prisoners. Yassin is the principal founder of the Islamic Resistance Movement-Hamas, begun on December 14, 1987, only days after the start of the intifada*. In 1989 he was sentenced to a life term in prison for issuing orders to kidnap and kill four Israeli soldiers. He was released into Jordanian hands on October 1, 1997, in the aftermath of the Mashaal affair*, the Mossad's* botched attempted assassination of Hamas official Khaled Mashaal, in Amman, Jordan*, on September 25, 1997. Initially transported to Jordan, he was subsequently permitted to return to his home in Gaza, from where he continued to inspire Hamas's political and military resistance against Israel; he also was openly critical of the Oslo* peace accords and Yasser Arafat's* administration of areas of the West Bank* and Gaza Strip* transferred to Palestinian control.

For further information see: Ziad Abu-Amr, "Hamas: A Historical and Political Background," *Journal of Palestine Studies* 22:4 (Summer 1993): 5-19; Nancy Hasanian, "Sheik Ahmed Ismail Yassin," in *An Historical Encyclopedia of the Arab-Israeli Conflict*, edited by Bernard Reich (Westport, CT: Greenwood Press, 1996): 593-594; Shaul Mishal, "Intifada Discourse: The Hamas and UNL Leaflets," in *The PLO and Israel: From Armed Conflict to Political Solution, 1964-1994*, edited by Avraham Sela and Moshe Ma'oz (New York: St. Martin's Press, 1997): 197-212; Don Peretz, *Intifada: The Palestinian Uprising* (Boulder, CO: Westview Press, 1990); Barry Rubin, *Revolution until Victory? The Politics and History of the PLO* (Cambridge, MA: Harvard University Press, 1994); Ze'ev Schiff and Ehud Ya'ari, *Intifada: The Palestinian Uprising—Israel's Third Front*, translated by Ina Friedman (New York: Simon and Schuster, 1989); John Wallach and Janet Wallach, *The New*

Palestinians: The Emerging Generation of Leaders (Rocklin, CA: Prima Publishing, 1992); "Charter of the Islamic Resistance Movement (Hamas) of Palestine," *Journal of Palestine Studies* 22:4 (Summer 1993): 122-134; "Release of a Hamas leader: A Tangle of Mideast Intrigue," *New York Times*, October 2, 1997.

YATOM, DANNY. Yatom was born in Netanya. He studied mathematics, physics, and computer science at Hebrew University*. He joined the army in 1963. He was a commando in the General Staff Reconnaissance Unit (Sayeret Matkal) where he served together with Benjamin Netanyahu* and Ehud Barak*. He held a number of key combat and planning positions in the army, including the position of armored corps commander and head of the Army Planning Branch. In 1991 he was appointed as chief of the Central Command, a position requiring extensive efforts to deal with the intifada*. Prime Minister Yitzhak Rabin* appointed him as his chief military aide in 1992, but he returned as head of the Central Command in 1993. Yatom returned to work for Rabin in April 1994 and continued working with Shimon Peres* when he replaced Rabin as Prime Minister. Peres appointed Yatom to head the Mossad* in 1996 replacing Shabtai Shavit*. He resigned in February 1998 following publication of the report of the Ciechanover Commission's* investigation of the Mashaal Affair*, the botched September 1997 Mossad attempted assassination of Hamas official Khaled Mashaal* in Amman, Jordan*. The commission had noted that Yatom "had erred in his handling of the operation." In his letter of resignation to Netanyahu, Yatom wrote: "I do not accept the findings of the Ciechanover Commission report regarding faults in my performance...." On May 30, 1999, Yatom was appointed by Prime Minister-elect Ehud Barak* to a new position, head of the political security branch of the Prime Minister's Office; his responsibilities included advising the Prime Minister on security matters and acting as liaison between the PMO and the various branches of the country's intelligence and security community. (Ironically, the creation of such a position was one of the principal recommendations of the Ciechanover Commission.)

YEDIOT AHRONOT **(LATEST INFORMATION—NEWS).** Hebrew* daily afternoon newspaper published in Tel Aviv*. It was founded in Palestine* in 1939. It has an independent, center-right editorial line.

YEHOSHUA, AVRAHAM B. (A. B. YEHOSHUA). Part of the "young guard" of Israeli writers whose works were published beginning in the late 1950s. A strong critic of Israel's administration of the occupied territories*, and of the seemingly disproportionate influence of Orthodox and ultra-Orthodox political parties in Israeli political affairs. He has also advocated fundamental structural reform of Israel's relationship with Diaspora* Jewish communities. He was born in Jerusalem* in 1936 to parents native to the city for six generations, was educated there, and eventually graduated from the Hebrew University of Jerusalem* where he majored in philosophy and Hebrew* literature. He lived in Paris for several years as the General Secretary of the World Organization of Jewish Students, but returned to Israel in 1967 to live in Haifa*. He served as Dean of Students at Haifa University, and since 1972, he has been on the faculty there as a professor of literature. His first stories were published in 1957, and since then he has published numerous stories in *Keshet Quarterly,* and various literary-supplement sections of newspapers. In 1962, he published his first full-length book, *The Death of an Old Man.* His other books include *In Front of the Forests* (1968), *Nine Stories* (1971), *In Early Summer 1970* (1972), *Until Winter* (1974), *A Late Divorce* (1985), *The Lover* (1986), *Five Seasons* (1991), *Mr. Mani* (1992), and others. Among his plays are *A Night in May* and *Last Treatment.*

YEMENITE ASSOCIATION OF ISRAEL. A party led by Salah Mansoura that contested the 1988 Knesset* election, but failed to secure a mandate.

YEMENITE PARTY. An ethnic political party that won one seat in each of the first two Knesset* elections, but was unsuccessful in sustaining or expanding its political base.

YERIDA ("GOING DOWN"). Refers to emigration from Israel. Yerida became a salient issue of public concern in the late 1970s and continued into the 1980s despite uncertainty as to its exact dimensions and the fact that during each of the major waves of aliya* there was also emigration. Nevertheless yerida was seen as something of a measure of well-being in Israel.

YESHA. The name adopted by the Council of Jewish Communities in Judea*, Samaria* and Gaza*, the umbrella group representing the majority of settlers in the occupied territories*. It is an acronym of

Yehuda, Shomron, and Aza (the Hebrew names for the areas) and also translates as "salvation."

YISHAI. Acronym for Yahad Shivtei Yisrael ("The Tribes of Israel Together"). A Sephardic* ethnic political party oriented toward the Yemenite community formed by a breakaway group from Shas* to contest the 1988 Knesset* elections and led by Rabbi Shimon Ben Shlomo. Ben Shlomo had served in the previous Knesset and he formed the new party after he was removed from the Shas electoral list. It failed to secure a seat in parliament.

YISHAI, ELIYAHU (ELI). Yishai was born in 1963 in Jerusalem*. Following service in the Israel Defense Forces*, he served as head of the office of the Interior Minister, member of the Jerusalem* City Council in 1987-1988, acting Secretary General of the Sephardic Torah Guardian*/Shas Party (1990-1996), Director-General of Shas's El Hama'ayan network of educational and social services (1994-1996). First elected to the 14th Knesset* on the Shas list in 1996, he served as Minister of Labor and Social Affairs in the coalition headed by Benjamin Netanyahu* (July 1996-June 1999). Reelected to the 15th Knesset on May 17, 1999, he became Shas's political leader after the resignation of Arye Dori*. He was reappointed Minister of Labor and Social Affairs in the Government named by Ehud Barak* on July 6, 1999.

YISHUV (SETTLEMENT). The Jewish community in Palestine* in the period of the British Mandate*. The yishuv was an autonomous political body which gained valuable experience in political procedures and self-rule. A political elite emerged, civil servants gained experience, and political parties were established and developed procedures for working together. An educational system was built. The Histadrut* was founded and became a major political, economic, and social force. A self-defense capability was created and became the basis of the Israel Defense Forces*. It provided the foundation for the Governmental institutions and political processes of Israel after independence.

For further information see: Dan Horowitz and Moshe Lissak, *Origins of the Israeli Polity: Palestine under the Mandate* (Chicago: University of Chicago Press, 1978).

YISRAEL BA'ALIYA *see* ISRAEL B'ALIYA

YOM KIPPUR WAR (1973). On October 6, 1973 (Yom Kippur), Egypt* and Syria* launched a coordinated attack on Israeli positions on the Suez Canal and Golan Heights* fronts. Taking Israel by surprise, the Arab armies crossed the Suez Canal, secured a beachhead in the Sinai Peninsula*, and advanced into the Golan Heights while—during the first three days of combat—a skeletal Israeli force sought to withstand the invasion until additional troops could be mobilized. Ultimately Israel stopped the Arab forces and reversed their initial military successes; it retook the Golan Heights and some additional territory, while Egypt and Israel traded some territory along the Suez Canal following Israel's crossing of the Canal and its advance toward Cairo. The United Nations Security Council adopted Resolution 338*, which called for an immediate cease-fire and the implementation of United Nations Security Council Resolution 242* and explicitly required negotiations "between the parties." Subsequently, United States* Secretary of State Henry Kissinger negotiated the Israel-Egypt Disengagement of Forces Agreement* of 1974 and the Sinai II Accords* of 1975 between Egypt and Israel, as well as the Israel-Syria Disengagement of Forces Agreement* of 1974. These involved Israeli withdrawals from territory in the Suez Canal Zone in the two agreements with Egypt and in the Golan Heights in the arrangement with Syria.

The Yom Kippur War resulted in an Israeli military victory, but that victory was accompanied by significant political and diplomatic disappointments and by domestic economic, psychological, and political stress. In purely tangible terms the 1973 war had perhaps the most far-reaching effects on Israel of any conflict to that time. Personnel losses and overall casualty rates were substantial. The mobilization of the largest part of the civilian reserve army of several hundred thousand caused dislocations in agriculture and industry. Tourism and diamond sales fell, and the sea passage to Eilat* was blockaded at the Bab el-Mandeb. Numerous other aspects of the war added to the economic costs of the conflict, and austerity was the logical result. At the same time Israel's international position deteriorated. Although it was not the initiator of the war, Israel was condemned, and numerous states (particularly in Africa) broke diplomatic relations. The ruptures with Africa were a disappointment, but a shift in the attitudes and policies of the European states and Japan was perhaps more significant. The war also increased Israel's dependence on the United States. No other country could provide Israel, or was prepared to do so, with the vast quantities of modern and sophisticated arms required for war or the political and moral support necessary to negotiate peace.

The cease-fire of October 22, 1973, was followed by what Israelis often refer to as the "Wars of the Jews"—internal political conflicts and disagreements. The initial domestic political effect of the war was to bring about the postponement to December 31 of the elections originally scheduled for October 30 and the suspension of political campaigning and electioneering for the duration of the conflict. The war not only interrupted the campaign for the Knesset* elections, it also provided new issues for the opposition to raise, including the conduct of the war and the "mistakes" that preceded it. In November 1973 the Government appointed a Commission of Inquiry, headed by Chief Justice Shimon Agranat* of the Supreme Court*, to investigate the events leading up to the hostilities (including information concerning the enemy's moves and intentions), the assessments and decisions of military and civilian bodies in regard to this information, and the Israel Defense Forces' deployments, preparedness for battle, and actions in the first phase of the fighting. *See also* AGRANAT COMMISSION OF INQUIRY.

For further information see: Avraham Adan, *On the Banks of the Suez* (San Rafael, CA: Presidio, 1980); Michael Brecher, *Decision in Crisis: Israel, 1967 and 1973* (Berkeley: University of California Press, 1980); Michael I. Handel, *Perception, Deception and Surprise: The Case of the Yom Kippur War* (Jerusalem: The Leonard Davis Institute for International Relations, Jerusalem Papers on Peace Problems 19, Hebrew University of Jerusalem, 1976); Mohammed Heikal, *The Road to Ramadan* (New York: Ballantine, 1975); Chaim Herzog, *The War of Atonement: October 1973* (Boston: Little, Brown, 1975); Edgar O'Ballance, *No Victor, No Vanquished: The Yom Kippur War* (San Rafael, CA: Presidio, 1978); Ze'ev Schiff, *October Earthquake: Yom Kippur 1973* (Tel Aviv: University Publications Project, 1974); Arnold Sherman, *When God Judged and Men Died: A Battle Report of the Yom Kippur War* (New York: Bantam Books, 1973); Lester A. Sobel, editor, *Israel and the Arabs: The October 1973 War* (Oxford University Press, UK: Clio, 1974); Sunday Times, *Insight on the Middle East War* (London: Deutsch, 1974); Fred Wehling, *Irresolute Princes: Kremlin Decision Making in Middle East Crises, 1967-1973* (New York: St. Martin's, 1997); "The October War and Its Aftermath," *Journal of Palestine Studies* (Special Issue) 3:2 (Winter 1974).

YOSEF, RABBI OVADIA. Born in Baghdad in 1920, he was taken by his parents to Jerusalem* when he was four years old. He was ordained as a Rabbi at the age of 20. In 1945 he was appointed a judge in the Sephardi* religious court in Jerusalem*. In 1947 he was elected head of the Cairo religious court and deputy Chief Rabbi of Egypt*. In 1950 he returned to Israel and was appointed a member of the rabbinical court of Petah Tikva* and of Jerusalem. In 1965 he was appointed a member of the Supreme Rabbinical Court of Appeals in Jerusalem and in 1968 became Sephardi Chief Rabbi* of Tel Aviv-Yafo*. From 1972 to 1983 he served as the Sephardi Chief Rabbi of Israel. In 1970 he was awarded the Israel Prize* for Torah Literature. He was instrumental in the founding of Shas* and remains the party's chief spiritual and political adviser.

Yosef prefers compromise; his religious rulings, for example, invoke the language of conciliation. He lives in a self-contained world of religious affairs and Shas politics. Yosef is one of the current generation's leading Torah scholars. So why did the scholar end up in politics? In a word: for honor—both his own and that of the Sephardi community.

Shas was formed in late 1983 by disaffected Sephardi members of Agudat Israel. Though initially hesitant about its success, Yosef soon gave his blessing to the new party, which he saw as a means of redressing discrimination against religious Sephardim.

At a conference on Halacha on August 13, 1989, Yosef declared it permissible to return parts of the Land of Israel if that would prevent war and save lives.

Z

ZAHAL *see* ISRAEL DEFENSE FORCES

ZE'EVI, REHAVAM (NICKNAME GANDHI). Born in 1926 in Jerusalem* and educated at Givat Hashlosha Local School, he entered the IDF* and rose to the rank of Major General. He later entered politics and became leader of the Moledet Party*, a party that advocates the transfer of the Arab population of the occupied territories* to Arab countries. In

February 1991 Ze'evi entered the cabinet as the representative of the party after it agreed to join the Shamir-led coalition. Ze'evi and Moledet subsequently quit the Government to protest Israel's participation in the Madrid Peace Conference*. Ze'evi was reelected to the Knesset* in 1992 and 1996. On May 17, 1999, Ze'evi was reelected to the 15th Knesset on the list of the National Union* coalition headed by Ze'ev Binyamin Begin*.

ZINGER, YOEL (ALSO KNOWN AS JOEL SINGER). As a senior legal adviser in the Ministry of Foreign Affairs, he was a principal author for Israel of the Israel-PLO Declaration of Principles* of September 13, 1993. He was also involved in subsequent negotiations toward implementing the Cairo ("Gaza-Jericho First") Agreement* of May 4, 1994.

ZION. The term was used by the Hebrew* prophets to refer to Jerusalem* as a spiritual symbol. As a symbol of the Holy Land it became central in the religious life of Jews outside of Israel and eventually became the basis of Zionism*.

ZIONISM. A term coined by Nathan Birnbaum in 1890 for the movement seeking the return of the Jewish people to Palestine*. After 1896 Zionism referred to the political movement founded by Theodor Herzl* seeking a Jewish National Home in Palestine*. The term is derived from Mount Zion*, one of the hills of Jerusalem*. Zion came to symbolize for the Jews their desire to return to their homeland, which dated at least as far back as the Babylonian exile in the sixth century BC. Psalm 137 says: "By the waters of Babylon, there we sat down and wept, when we remembered Zion." In the latter part of the nineteenth century the eastern European movement that promoted settlement in the Land of Israel called itself Hibbat Zion* (Love of Zion). The term Zionism was used for the first time in 1890 in a Hebrew* periodical. Theodor Herzl adopted it to refer to his political movement, which sought the return of the Jews to the Holy Land.

For further information see: Shlomo Avineri, *The Making of Modern Zionism: The Intellectual Origins of the Jewish State* (New York: Basic Books, 1981); Martin Buber, *Israel and Palestine: The History of an Idea* (London: East and West Library, 1952); Israel Cohen, *A Short History of Zionism* (London: Muller, 1951); Allon Gal, *Socialist Zionist Theory and*

Issues in Contemporary Jewish Nationalism (Cambridge: Schenkman Publishing Company, 1973); Martin Gilbert, *Exile and Return* (Philadelphia: Lippincott, 1978); Jay Y. Gonen, *A Psychohistory of Zionism* (New York: Mason/Charter, 1975); Haim Gordon, *Make Room for Dreams: Spiritual Challenges to Zionism* (Westport, CT: Greenwood Press, 1989); Ahad Ha'am, *Selected Essays* (Cleveland and New York and Philadelphia: World Publishing Company and The Jewish Publication Society of America, 1962); Abraham S. Halkin, editor, *Zion in Jewish Literature* (New York: Herzl, 1961); Ben Halpern, *The Idea of the Jewish State*, Second Edition (Cambridge, MA: Harvard University Press, 1970); Ben Halpern and Jehuda Reinharz, *Zionism and the Creation of a New Society* (Oxford, UK: Oxford University Press, 1998); Joseph Heller, *The Zionist Idea* (New York: Schocken, 1949); Arthur Hertzberg, editor, *The Zionist Idea: An Historical Analysis and Reader* (New York: Doubleday, 1959); Theodor Herzl, *The Jewish State: An Attempt at a Modern Solution of the Jewish Question* (London: R. Searl, 1934); Theodor Herzl, *Old New Land* (New York: Herzl, 1960); Moses Hess, *Rome and Jerusalem* (New York: Bloch, 1945); Walter Laqueur, *A History of Zionism* (London: Weidenfeld and Nicolson, 1972); Rufus Learsi, *Fulfillment: The Epic Story of Zionism* (New York: World, 1951); Barnet Litvinoff, *The Road to Jerusalem: Zionism's Imprint on History* (London: Weidenfeld and Nicolson, 1965); Jacob J. Petuchowski, *Zion Reconsidered* (New York: Twayne, 1966); Oskar K. Rabinowicz, *Fifty Years of Zionism: A Historical Analysis of Dr. Weizmann's "Trial and Error"* (London: Robert Anscombe, 1950); Joseph Schechtman and Yehuda Benari, *History of the Revisionist Movement* (Tel Aviv: Hadar Publishing House, 1970); Dan V. Segre, *A Crisis of Identity: Israel and Zionism* (Oxford, UK: Oxford University Press, 1980); Yaacov Shavit, *Revisionism in Zionism* (Tel Aviv: Yariv, 1978); Gary V. Smith, *Zionism the Dream and the Reality: A Jewish Critique* (Newton Abbot, UK: David and Charles, 1974); Nahum Sokolow, *Hibbath Zion (The Love of Zion)* (Jerusalem: Rubin Mass, 1941); Nahum Sokolow, *History of Zionism, 1600-1918* (New York: Ktav, 1969); Alan R. Taylor, *Prelude to Israel: An Analysis of Zionist Diplomacy 1897-1947*, Revised Edition (Beirut: The Institute for Palestine Studies, 1970); David Vital, *The Origins of Zionism* (Oxford, UK: Oxford University Press, 1975); David Vital, *Zionism: The Formative Years* (New York: Oxford University Press, 1982).

ZIONISM IS RACISM RESOLUTION *See* UNITED NATIONS GENERAL ASSEMBLY RESOLUTION 3379.

ZIPORI, MORDECHAI. Zipori was born in Tel Aviv* in 1924 and was educated in religious schools. In 1939 he joined the Irgun* and, in 1945, was deported to Eritrea, where he remained until 1948. From 1948 to 1977 Zipori served in the Israel Defense Forces*, reaching the rank of Brigadier General and the position of Assistant Chief of Operations in the General Staff. In 1977 Zipori joined the Herut Party* and was elected on behalf of that faction of the Likud* to the Ninth Knesset* in May 1977. He served as Deputy Minister of Defense throughout the duration of the Ninth Knesset, from 1977 to 1981. On August 5, 1981, after having been reelected to the 10th Knesset, he was sworn in as Minister of Communications and served in that position until 1984.

ZUABI, ABDEL RAHMAN. In May 1998 Justice Minister Tzachi Hanegbi* announced the first appointment of an Arab to the Supreme Court of Israel*. Abdel Rahman Zuabi was born in Nazareth* and studied law at Tel Aviv University. He worked in private practice until he was appointed to the Nazareth District Court in the 1970s. He also served as a member of the Shamgar Commission of Inquiry* that probed the 1994 massacre of Palestinians at the Machpela Cave in Hebron*.

BIBLIOGRAPHY

DIRECTORIES, YEARBOOKS, AND ENCYCLOPEDIAS

Bank of Israel. *Annual Report.* Jerusalem: 1955- .
Bridger, David and Samuel Wolk, eds. *The New Jewish Encyclopedia.* New York: Behrman, 1976.
Encyclopedia Judaica. 16 vols. Jerusalem: Keter, 1972.
Hill, Helen, ed. *Zionist Year Book. London: Zionist Federation of Great Britain & Ireland,* 1951- .
Israel. Central Bureau of Statistics. *Statistical Abstract of Israel.* Jerusalem: Central Bureau of Statistics, 1949- .
Israel Government Yearbook. Jerusalem: Government Printer, 1950- .
The Israel Yearbook. Tel-Aviv: Israel Yearbook Publishers, 1950- .
Patai, Raphael, ed. *Encyclopedia of Zionism and Israel,* 2 vols. New York: Herzl, McGraw-Hill, 1971.

GENERAL

Aharoni, Yohanan and Michael Avi-Yonah, eds. *The Macmillan Bible Atlas.* New York: Macmillan, 1968.
Atlas of Israel. New York: Macmillan, 1985.
Ben-Gurion, David. *Israel: A Personal History.* New York: Funk and

Wagnalls; New York and Tel Aviv: Sabra Books, 1971.

Ben-Meir, Alon. *Israel: The Challenge of the Fourth Decade.* New York and London: Cyrco Press, Inc., 1978.

Bentwich, Norman. *Israel Resurgent.* New York: Praeger, 1960.

Bermant, Chaim. *Israel.* New York: Walker, 1967.

Cameron, James. *The Making of Israel.* London: Secker and Warburg, 1976.

Chafets, Ze'ev. *Heroes and Hustlers, Hard Hats and Holy Men: Inside the New Israel.* New York: Morrow, 1986.

Cooke, Hedley V. *Israel: A Blessing and a Curse.* London: Stevens and Sons Limited, 1960.

Cragg, Kenneth. *This Year in Jerusalem.* London: Darton Longman and Todd, Ltd., 1982.

Crossman, Richard H. S. *A Nation Reborn: The Israel of Weizmann, Bevin, and Ben-Gurion.* London: Hamish Hamilton, 1960.

Davis, Moshe, ed. *Israel: Its Role in Civilization.* New York: Harper and Row, 1956.

DeGaury, Gerald. *The New State of Israel.* New York: Praeger, 1952.

Dunner, Joseph. *Democratic Bulwark in the Middle East: A Review and Analysis of Israel's Social, Economic, and Political Problems during the Period From 1948 to 1953.* Grinnell, IA: Grinnell College Press, 1953.

Eisenstadt, Samuel N. *Israeli Society.* New York: Praeger, 1967.

_____. *The Transformation of Israeli Society.* London: Weidenfeld and Nicolson, 1985.

Elon, Amos. *The Israelis: Founders and Sons.* New York: Bantam Books, 1972.

Elston, D. R. *No Alternative: Israel Observed.* London: Hutchinson, 1960.

_____. *Israel: The Making of a Nation.* Oxford: Oxford University Press, 1963.

Farrell, James T. *It Has Come to Pass.* New York: Herzl, 1958.

Feis, Herbert. *The Birth of Israel: The Tousled Diplomatic Bed.* New York: W. W. Norton, 1969.

Flink, Salomon J. *Israel, Chaos and Challenge: Politics vs. Economics.* Ramat Gan, Israel: Turtledove, 1980.

Friedlander, Dov and Calvin Goldscheider. *The Population of Israel.* New York: Columbia University Press, 1979.

Frank, Waldo. *Bridgehead: The Drama of Israel.* New York: George Braziller, Inc., 1957.

Frankel, William. *Israel Observed: An Anatomy of the State*. London: Thames and Hudson, 1980.

Frischwasser-Ra'anan, H. F. *The Frontiers of a Nation*. London: Batchworth, 1955.

Garcia-Granados, Jorge. *The Birth of Israel: The Drama and I Saw It*. New York: Alfred Knopf, 1948.

Gavron, Daniel. *Israel after Begin*. Boston: Houghton Mifflin, 1984.

Gilbert, Martin. *The Atlas of Jewish History*, Fifth Edition. London: J. M. Dent, 1993.

_____. *Atlas of the Arab-Israeli Conflict*, Sixth Edition. New York: Oxford University Press, 1993.

Grose, Peter. *A Changing Israel*. New York: Vintage Books, 1985.

Heschel, Abraham H. *Israel: An Echo of Eternity*. New York: Farrar, Straus, and Giroux, 1969.

Heubner, Theodore and Carl Hermann Voss. *This Is Israel*. New York: Philosophical Library, 1956.

Heydemann, Steven, ed. *Issues in Contemporary Israel: The Begin Era*. Boulder, CO: Westview Press, 1984.

Historical Atlas of Israel. Jerusalem: Carta, 1983.

Janowsky, Oscar I. *Foundations of Israel: Emergence of a Welfare State*. Princeton, NJ: D. Van Nostrand, 1959.

Kraines, Oscar. *Israel: The Emergence of a New Nation*. Washington, DC: Public Affairs Press, 1954.

Lehman-Wilzig, Sam N. and Bernard Susser, eds. *Public Life in Israel and the Diaspora*. Jerusalem: Bar-Ilan University Press, 1981.

Lehrman, Hal. *Israel, The Beginning and Tomorrow*. New York: William Sloane Assoc., 1951.

Marx, Emanuel, ed. *A Composite Portrait of Israel*. London and New York: Academic Press, 1980.

Meinertzhagen, Richard. *Middle East Diary: 1917-1956*. New York: Yoseloff, 1960.

Metz, Helen Chapin, Editor. Israel: A Country Study. Washington, DC: Federal Research Division, Library of Congress, 1990.

Meyer, Herrmann M. Z., comp. *Israel: Pocket Atlas and Handbook*. Jerusalem: Universitas Booksellers, 1961.

Meyer, Lawrence. *Israel Now: Portrait of a Troubled Land*. New York: Delacorte, 1982.

Naamani, Israel T. *Israel: A Profile*. New York: Praeger, 1972.

_____, David Rudavsky and Abraham Katsh, eds. *Israel: Its Politics and Philosophy: An Annotated Reader*. New York: Behrman, 1974.

Orni, Ephraim and Elisha Efrat. *Geography of Israel*, Third Revised Edition. Jerusalem: Keter, 1971.

Oz, Amos. *In the Land of Israel*. New York: Harcourt, Brace and Jovanovich, 1983.

Postal, Bernard and Henry W. Levy. *And the Hills Shouted for Joy: The Day Israel Was Born*. New York: David McKay, 1973.

Prittie, Terence. *Israel: Miracle in the Desert*. New York: Praeger, 1967.

Rabinovich, Itamar and Jehuda Reinharz, eds. *Israel in the Middle East: Documents and Readings on Society, Politics, and Foreign Relations, 1948-Present*. New York: Oxford University Press, 1984.

Reich, Bernard. *Historical Dictionary of Israel*. Lanham, MD: Scarecrow Press, 1992.

Reich, Bernard and Gershon R. Kieval. *Israel: Land of Tradition and Conflict, Second Edition*. Boulder, CO: Westview Press, 1993.

_____ and Gershon R. Kieval, eds. *Israel Faces the Future*. New York: Praeger, 1986.

Safran, Nadav. *Israel: The Embattled Ally*. Cambridge, MA: Belknap Press of Harvard University Press, 1981.

Schoenbrun, David, with Robert Szekely, Lucy Szekely. *The New Israelis*. New York: Atheneum, 1973.

Segev, Tom. *1949: The First Israelis*. New York: The Free Press and London: Collier Macmillan, 1986.

St. John, Robert. *Tongue of the Prophets: The Life Story of Eliezer Ben-Yehuda*. New York: Doubleday, 1952.

Vilnay, Zev. *The New Israel Atlas: Bible to Present Day*. New York: McGraw-Hill, 1969.

Waxman, Charles I. and Rafael Medoff. *Historical Dictionary of Zionism*. Lanham, MD: Scarecrow Press, 2000.

Williams, L. F. Rushbrook. *The State of Israel*. New York: Macmillan, 1957.

DEFENSE AND SECURITY

Ben-Meir, Yehuda. *National Security Decision-Making: The Israeli Case*. Boulder, CO: Westview Press, 1986.

Cohen, Avner. *Israel and the Bomb*. Cambridge, MA: Harvard University Press, 1998.

Feldman, Shai. *Israeli Nuclear Deterrence: A Strategy for the 1980s.*

New York: Columbia University Press, 1982.

Ilan, Amitzur. *The Origins of the Arab-Israeli Arms Race: Arms, Embargo, Military Power and Peace in the 1948 Palestine War*. New York: New York University Press, 1996.

Klieman, Aaron and Ariel Levite, eds. *Deterrence in the Middle East: Where Theory and Practice Converge*. JCSS Study no. 22. Tel Aviv: Jaffee Center for Strategic Studies, Tel Aviv University; Boulder, CO: Westview Press, 1993.

Levite, Ariel. *Offense and Defense in Israeli Military Doctrine*. Boulder, CO: Westview Press, 1989.

Middle East Military Balance. Tel Aviv: Jaffee Center for Strategic Studies, Tel Aviv University, 1979-.

Reich, Bernard and Gershon R. Kieval, eds. *Israeli National Security Policy: Political Actors and Perspectives*. New York, Westport, CT: and London: Greenwood, 1988.

Reiser, Stewart. *The Israeli Arms Industry: Foreign Policy, Arms Transfers, and Military Doctrine of a Small State*. New York: Holmes and Meier, 1989.

Schiff, Ze'ev. *A History of the Israeli Army: 1874 to the Present*. New York: Macmillan Publishing, 1985.

Tamir, Avraham. *A Soldier in Search of Peace: An Inside Look at Israel's Strategy*. New York: Harper and Row, 1988.

Van Creveld, Martin. *The Sword and the Olive: A Critical History of the Israeli Defense Force*. New York: Public Affairs, Perseus Books Group, 1998.

GOVERNMENT AND POLITICS

Akzin, Benjamin and Yehezkel Dror. *Israel: High-Pressure Planning*. Syracuse: Syracuse University Press, 1966.

Arian, Asher (Alan). *The Choosing People: Voting Behavior in Israel*. Cleveland and London: Case Western Reserve University Press, 1973.

_____. *The Second Republic: Politics in Israel*. Chatham, NJ: Chatham House Publishers, 1998.

_____, ed. *The Elections in Israel: 1969*. Israel: Jerusalem Academic Press, 1972.

_____, ed. *The Elections in Israel: 1973*. New Brunswick, NJ:

Transaction Books, 1975.

_____, ed. *The Elections in Israel: 1977.* New Brunswick, NJ: Transaction Books, 1980.

_____, ed. *The Elections in Israel: 1981.* New Brunswick, NJ: Transaction Books, 1984.

_____. *Ideological Change in Israel.* Cleveland: Case Western Reserve University Press, 1968.

_____, ed. *Politics in Israel: The Second Generation.* Chatham, NJ: Chatham House, 1985.

Arian, Alan and Michal Shamir, eds. *The Elections in Israel: 1984.* New Brunswick, NJ: Transaction Books, 1986.

_____, eds. *The Elections in Israel, 1988.* Boulder, CO: Westview Press, 1990.

_____, eds. *The Elections in Israel, 1992.* Albany, NY: State University of New York Press, 1995.

_____, eds. *The Elections in Israel, 1996.* Albany, NY: State University of New York Press, 1999.

Aronoff, Myron J. *Frontiertown: The Politics of Community Building in Israel.* Manchester, UK: Manchester University Press, 1974.

Badi, Joseph. *The Government of the State of Israel: A Critical Account of Its Parliament, Executive and Judiciary.* New York: Twayne, 1963.

_____, ed. *Fundamental Laws of the State of Israel.* New York: Twayne, 1961.

Baker, Henry E. *The Legal System of Israel.* Jerusalem: Israel Universities Press, 1968.

Bayne, E.A. *Four Ways of Politics: State and Nation in Italy, Somalia, Israel, Iran.* New York: American Universities Field Staff, 1965.

Ben-Meir, Yehuda. *Civil-Military Relations in Israel.* New York: Columbia University Press, 1995.

Bernstein, Marver H. *The Politics of Israel: The First Decade of Statehood.* Princeton: Princeton University Press, 1957.

Bilinsksi, R., et al. *Can Planning Replace Politics? The Israeli Experience.* The Hague: Martinus Nijhoff, 1980.

Bradley, C. Paul. *Electoral Politics in Israel.* Grantham, NH: Tompson and Rutter, 1981.

Caiden, Gerald E. *Israel's Administrative Culture.* Berkeley, CA: Institute of Governmental Studies, University of California Press, 1970.

Caspi, Dan, Abraham Diskin and Emanuel Gutmann, eds. *The Roots of*

Begin's Success: The 1981 Israeli Elections. London and Canberra: Croom Helm and New York: St. Martin's Press, 1984.

Deshen, Shlomo. *Immigrant Voters in Israel.* Manchester, UK: Manchester University Press, 1970.

Dror, Yehezkel and Emanuel Gutmann, eds. *The Government of Israel.* Jerusalem: The Eliezer Kaplan School of Economics and Social Sciences, The Hebrew University, 1961.

Eisenstadt, S.N. *Israeli Society.* London: Weidenfeld and Nicolson, 1967.

Elazar, Daniel J. and Howard R. Penniman, eds. *Israel at the Polls 1981.* Bloomington: Indiana University Press, 1986.

Elazar, Daniel J., and Shmuel Sandler, eds. *Israel's Odd Couple: The Nineteen Eighty-Four Knesset Elections and the National Unity Government.* Detroit, MI: Wayne State University Press, 1990.

_____. *Who's the Boss in Israel: Israel at the Polls, 1988-89.* Detroit MI: Wayne State University Press, 1992.

_____. *Israel at the Polls, 1992.* Lanham, MD: Rowman and Littlefield, 1995.

Elizur, Yuval and Eliahu Salpeter. *Who Rules Israel?* New York: Harper and Row, 1973.

Etzioni-Halevy, Eva, with Rina Shapira. *Political Culture in Israel: Cleavage and Integration Among Israel's Jews.* New York: Praeger, 1977.

Fein, Leonard J. *Israel: Politics and People.* Boston: Little, Brown, 1968.

Freudenheim, Yehoshua. *Government in Israel.* Dobbs Ferry, NY: Oceana, 1967.

Gerson, Allan. *Israel, the West Bank and International Law.* Totowa, NJ: Cass, 1978.

Harkabi, Yehoshafat. *The Bar-Kokhba Syndrome: Risks and Realism in International Politics.* Chappaqua, NY: Rossel, 1983.

Horowitz, Dan and Moshe Lissak. *The Origins of the Israeli Polity.* Chicago: University of Chicago Press, 1978.

_____. *Trouble in Utopia: The Overburdened Polity of Israel.* Albany: State University of New York Press, 1989.

Horowitz, David. *State in the Making.* New York: Alfred Knopf, 1953.

Isaac, Rael Jean. *Israel Divided: Ideological Politics in the Jewish State.* Baltimore, MD: Johns Hopkins University Press, 1976.

_____. *Party and Politics in Israel: Three Visions of a Jewish State.* New York: Longman, 1981.

Israel. Ministry of Justice. *Laws of the State of Israel: Authorized Translation.* Jerusalem: Government Printer, 1948-.

Kieval, Gershon R. *Party Politics in Israel and the Occupied Territories.* Westport, CT: Greenwood, 1983.

Kimmerling, Baruch. *Zionism and Territory: The Socio-Territorial Dimension of Zionist Politics.* Berkeley, CA: Institute of International Studies, 1983.

Kraines, Oscar. *Government and Politics in Israel.* Boston: Houghton Mifflin, 1961.

Liebman, Charles S. and Eliezer Don-Yehiya. *Religion and Politics in Israel.* Bloomington: Indiana University Press, 1984.

Mahler, Gregory S. *Israel: Government and Politics in a Maturing State.* San Diego, CA: Harcourt Brace Jovanovich, 1990.

Merhav, Peretz. *The Israeli Left: History, Problems, Documents.* Cranbury, NJ: A. S. Barnes, 1980.

Penniman, Howard R. and Daniel Elazar, eds. *Israel at the Polls, 1981.* Washington, DC: American Enterprise Institute for Public Policy Research, 1986.

Peri, Yoram. *Between Battles and Ballots: Israeli Military in Politics.* Cambridge, UK: Cambridge University Press, 1983.

Perlmutter, Amos. *Military and Politics in Israel.* London: Frank Cass, 1969.

_____. *Anatomy of Political Institutionalization: The Case of Israel and Some Comparative Analyses.* Cambridge, MA: Center for International Affairs, Harvard University, 1970.

_____. *Israel: The Partitioned State.* New York: Scribner, 1985.

Rackman, Emmanuel. *Israel's Emerging Constitution, 1948-51.* New York: Columbia University Press, 1955.

Rubinstein, Amnon. *The Zionist Dream Revisited: From Herzl to Gush Emunim and Back.* New York: Schocken, 1984.

Samuel, Edwin. *Problems of Government in the State of Israel.* Jerusalem: Rubin Mass, 1956.

Schnall, David J. *Radical Dissent in Contemporary Israeli Politics: Cracks in the Wall.* New York: Praeger, 1979.

Seligman, Lester G. *Leadership in a New Nation: Political Development in Israel.* New York: Atherton, 1964.

Sharkansky, Ira. *The Political Economy of Israel.* New Brunswick, NJ: Transaction Books, 1987.

_____. *What Makes Israel Tick? How Domestic Policy-Makers Cope with Constraints.* Chicago: Nelson-Hall, 1985.

_____. *Wither the State? Politics and Public Enterprise in Three Countries.* Chatham, NJ: Chatham House Publishers, 1979.

Shimshoni, Daniel. *Israel Democracy: The Middle of the Journey.* New York: Free Press, 1982.

Vlavianos, Basil J. and Feliks Gross, eds. *Struggle for Tomorrow: Modern Political Ideologies of the Jewish People.* New York: Arts, 1954.

Wolfsfeld, Gadi. *The Politics of Provocation : Participation and Protest in Israel.* Albany: State University of New York Press, 1988.

Yaacobi, Gad. *The Government of Israel.* New York: Praeger, 1982.

Yanai, Nathan. *Party Leadership in Israel.* Philadelphia: Turtledove, 1981.

Yishai, Yael. *Between the Flag and the Banner: Women in Israeli Politics.* Albany: State University of New York Press, 1997.

_____. *Land of Paradoxes: Interest Politics in Israel.* Albany: State University of New York Press, 1991.

Zohar, David M. *Political Parties in Israel: The Evolution of Israeli Democracy.* New York: Praeger, 1974.

HISTORY

Barbour, Neville. *Palestine, Star or Crescent?* New York: Odyssey, 1947.

Bauer, Yehuda. *From Diplomacy to Resistance: A History of Jewish Palestine, 1939-1945.* Philadelphia: Jewish Publication Society, 1970.

Ben-Gurion, David. *Israel: Years of Challenge.* New York: Holt, Rinehart, and Winston, 1963.

_____. *The Jews in Their Land.* Garden City, NY: Doubleday, 1966.

Bentwich, Norman and Helen Bentwich. *Mandate Memories, 1918-1948.* London: Hogarth, 1965.

Buber, Martin. *Israel and Palestine.* New York: Farrar, Straus, and Young, 1952.

Cohen, Amnon. *Palestine in the 18th Century: Patterns of Government and Administration.* Jerusalem: Magnes, 1973.

Crossman, Richard H.S. *A Nation Reborn.* New York: Atheneum, 1960.

Dunner, Joseph. *Republic of Israel: Its History and Its Promise.* New York: McGraw-Hill, 1950.

Garcia-Granados, Jorge. *The Birth of Israel, The Drama as I Saw It.* New York: Alfred Knopf, 1948.

Gilbert, Martin. *Israel: A History.* London: Doubleday, 1998.

Horowitz, Dan and Moshe Lissak. *Origins of the Israeli Polity: Palestine under the Mandate.* Chicago: Chicago University Press, 1978.

Hurewitz, Jacob C. *The Struggle for Palestine.* New York: W.W. Norton, 1950.

Jones, Philip, comp. *Britain and Palestine 1914-1948: Archival Sources for the History of the British Mandate.* London: Oxford University Press, 1979.

Katznelson, Rachel Shazar. *The Plough Woman: Memoirs of the Pioneer Women of Palestine*, Second Edition. New York: Herzl, 1975.

Koestler, Arthur. *Promise and Fulfillment: Palestine 1917-1949.* New York: Macmillan, 1949.

Lowdermilk, W. C. *Palestine: Land of Promise.* New York: Harper and Row, 1944.

Lucas, Noah. *The Modern History of Israel.* New York and Washington, DC: Praeger, 1975.

Maoz, Moshe, ed. *Studies on Palestine during the Ottoman Period.* Jerusalem: Magnes, 1975.

Marlowe, John. *The Seat of Pilate: An Account of the Palestine Mandate.* London: Cresset Press, 1959.

Nathan, Robert, Oscar Gass, and Daniel Kraemer. *Palestine: Problem and Promise.* Washington, DC: Public Affairs Press, 1946.

Parkes, James. *A History of Palestine from 135 A.D. to Modern Times.* Oxford: Clarendon, 1949.

Sachar, Howard M. *A History of Israel: From the Rise of Zionism to Our Time.* New York: Alfred Knopf, 1976.

_____. *A History of Israel. Volume II: From the Aftermath of the Yom Kippur War.* New York: Oxford University Press, 1987.

Sacher, Harry. *Israel: The Establishment of a State.* London: Weidenfeld and Nicolson, 1952.

Samuel, Maurice. *Harvest in the Desert.* Philadelphia: Jewish Publication Society, 1944.

_____. *Level Sunlight.* New York: Alfred Knopf, 1953.

Sanders, Ronald. *The High Walls of Jerusalem: A History of the Balfour Declaration. The Birth of the British Mandate for Palestine.* New York: Holt, Rinehart, and Winston, 1984.

Sanger, Richard H. *Where the Jordan Flows.* Washington, DC: Middle

East Institute, 1963

Sharef, Zeev. *Three Days: An Account of the Last Days of the British Mandate and the Birth of Israel*. New York: Doubleday, 1962.

Sykes, Christopher. *Crossroads to Israel*. Cleveland and New York: World Publishing, 1965.

Tuchman, Barbara W. *Bible and Sword: England and Palestine from the Bronze Age to Balfour*. New York: Minerva Press, 1968.

INTERNATIONAL RELATIONS

Amir, Shimeon. *Israel's Development Cooperation with Africa, Asia and Latin America*. New York: Praeger, 1974.

Argov, Shlomo. *An Ambassador Speaks Out*. London: Weidenfeld and Nicolson, with the Van Leer Institute, 1983.

Bialer, Uri. *Between East and West: Israel's Foreign Policy Orientation, 1948-1956*. Cambridge: Cambridge University Press, 1990.

Bialer, Uri. *Mapai and Israel's Foreign Policy, 1947-1952*. Jerusalem: Hebrew University, 1981.

Brecher, Michael. *The Foreign Policy System of Israel: Setting, Images, Process*. New Haven: Yale University Press, 1972.

_____. *Israel, The Korean War, and China*. New Brunswick, NJ: Transaction Books, 1974.

_____. *Decisions in Israel's Foreign Policy*. New Haven: Yale University Press, 1975.

Brecher, Michael with Benjamin Geist. *Decisions in Crisis: Israel, 1967 and 1973*. Berkeley, CA: University of California Press, 1980.

Curtis, Michael R. and Susan Aurelia Gitelson, eds. *Israel in the Third World*. New Brunswick, NJ: Transaction Books, 1976.

Decalo, Samuel. *Israel and Africa: Forty Years, 1956-1996*. Gainesville, FL: Florida Academic Press, 1998.

Draper, Theodore. *Israel and World Politics: Roots of the Third Arab-Israeli War*. New York: Viking Press, 1968.

Eban, Abba. *Voice of Israel*. New York: Horizon, 1957.

Elath, Eliahu. *Israel and Her Neighbors*. London: James Barrie, 1956.

Eytan, Walter. *The First Ten Years: A Diplomatic History of Israel*. New York: Simon and Schuster, 1958.

Glick, Edward B. *Latin America and the Palestine Problem*. New York: Theodor Herzl Foundation, 1958.

Golan, Galia. *Yom Kippur and After.* Cambridge, UK: Cambridge University Press, 1977.

Heller, Mark A. *A Palestinian State: The Implications for Israel.* Cambridge, MA: Harvard University Press, 1983.

Herzog, Chaim. *Who Stands Accused? Israel Answers Its Critics.* New York: Random House, 1978.

Hillel, Shlomo. *Operation Babylon.* New York: Doubleday, 1987.

Joseph, Benjamin M. *Besieged Bedfellows: Israel and the Land of Apartheid.* Westport, CT: Greenwood, 1988.

Kaufman, Edy, Yoram Shapira, and Joel Barromi. *Israel-Latin American Relations.* New Brunswick, NJ: Transaction Books, 1979.

Kay, Zachariah. *Canada and Palestine: The Politics of Non-Commitment.* Jerusalem: Israel Universities Press, 1974.

_____. *The Diplomacy of Prudence: Canada and Israel, 1948-1958.* Montreal & Kingston: Queen's University Press, 1996.

Klieman, Aaron. *Israel's Global Reach: Arms Sales as Diplomacy.* Elmsford, NY: Pergamon-Brassey's International Defense Publishers, 1985.

Krammer, Arnold P. *The Forgotten Friendship: Israel and the Soviet Bloc, 1947-1953.* Urbana: University of Illinois Press, 1974.

Kreinin, Mordechai. *Israel and Africa: A Study in Technical Cooperation.* New York: Praeger, 1964.

Laufer, Leopold. *Israel and the Developing Countries: New Approaches to Cooperation.* New York: Twentieth Century Fund, 1967.

Liebman, Charles. *Pressure without Sanctions: The Influence of World Jewry on Israeli Policy.* Rutherford, NJ: Fairleigh Dickinson University Press, 1977.

Peleg, Ilan. *Begin's Foreign Policy, 1977-1983: Israel's Move to the Right.* Westport, CT: Greenwood, 1987.

Raphael, Gideon. *Destination Peace: Three Decades of Israeli Foreign Policy.* New York: Stein and Day, 1981.

Roberts, Samuel J. *Survival or Hegemony? The Foundations of Israeli Foreign Policy.* Baltimore and London: Johns Hopkins University Press, 1973.

Romberg, Otto R. and George Schwinghammer, eds. *Twenty Years of Diplomatic Relations between the Federal Republic of Germany and Israel.* Frankfurt-am-Main: Tribune Books, 1985.

Slater, Robert. *Israel's Aid to Developing Nations.* New York: Friendly House Publishers, 1973.

Tekoah, Yosef. *In the Face of Nations: Israel's Struggle for Peace.* New

York: Simon and Schuster, 1976.

Wilson, Harold. *The Chariot of Israel: Britain, America and the State of Israel.* London: Weidenfeld and Nicolson, 1981.

RELIGION

Abramov, S. Zalman. *Perpetual Dilemma: Jewish Religion in the Jewish State.* Rutherford, NJ: Fairleigh Dickinson University Press, 1979.

Aviad, Janet. *Return to Judaism: Religious Renewal in Israel.* Chicago: University of Chicago Press, 1983.

Badi, Joseph. *Religion in Israel Today: The Relationship between State and Religion.* New York: Bookman Associates, 1959.

Birnbaum, Ervin. *The Politics of Compromise: State and Religion in Israel.* Rutherford, NJ: Fairleigh Dickinson University Press, 1970.

Don-Yehiya, Eliezer. "The Politics of Religious Parties." In *Public Life in Israel and the Diaspora*, edited by Sam N. Lehman-Wilzig and Bernard Susser. Jerusalem: Bar-Ilan University Press, 1981.

Kraines, Oscar. *The Impossible Dilemma: Who Is a Jew in the State of Israel.* New York: Bloch, 1976.

Leslie, Samuel C. *The Rift in Israel: Religious Authority and Secular Democracy.* New York: Schocken, 1971.

Liebman, Charles S. and Eliezer Don-Yehiya. *Civil Religion in Israel: Traditional Judaism and Political Culture in the Jewish State.* Berkeley, Los Angeles, London: University of California Press, 1983.

———. *Religion and Politics in Israel.* Bloomington: Indiana University Press, 1984.

Liebman, Charles S. and Elihu Katz, eds. *The Jewishness of Israel.* Albany: State University of New York Press, 1997.

Marmorstein, Emile. *Heaven at Bay: The Jewish Kulturkampf in the Holy Land.* London: Oxford University Press, 1969.

Rabinowicz, Harry M. *Hasidism and the State of Israel.* Rutherford, NJ: Fairleigh Dickinson University Press, 1982.

Schiff, Gary S. *Tradition and Politics: The Religious Parties of Israel.* Detroit: Wayne State University Press, 1977.

Sharansky, Ira. *Rituals of Conflict: Religion, Politics, and Public Policy in Israel.* Boulder, CO: Lynne Rienner Publishers, 1996.

Weiner, Herbert. *The Wild Goats of Ein Gedi: A Journal of Religious*

Encounters in the Holy Land. Cleveland, New York, and
Philadelphia: World Publishing Company and Jewish Publication
Society of America, 1963.

Zucker, Norman L. *The Coming Crisis in Israel: Private Faith and
Public Policy.* Cambridge: MIT Press, 1973.

ABOUT THE AUTHORS

BERNARD REICH is Professor of Political Science and International Affairs and former Chairman of the Department of Political Science at George Washington University in Washington, D.C. He serves as a consultant to various United States government agencies and is Chairman of Advanced Area Studies (Middle East–Fertile Crescent) at the Department of State's Foreign Service Institute, and a member of the adjunct faculty of the United States Air Force Special Operations School and the Naval School of Health Sciences. He is a member of the Board of Advisory Editors of the *Middle East Journal* and of the International Editorial Board of *Israel Affairs*. Among other works, Professor Reich is the author of *Quest for Peace: United States-Israel Relations and the Arab-Israeli Conflict*, *The United States and Israel: Influence in the Special Relationship*, *Israel: Land of Tradition and Conflict* (2 editions), *Historical Dictionary of Israel*, *Securing the Covenant: United States-Israel Relations After the Cold War*, and *Arab-Israeli Conflict and Conciliation: A Documentary History*; coauthor of *The United States and the Israel-Arab Conflict*, *United States Foreign Policy and the Middle East/North Africa: A Bibliography of Twentieth-Century Research*, *U.S. Foreign Relations with the Middle East and North Africa: A Bibliography*, and *Asian States' Relations with the Middle East and North Africa: A Bibliography, 1950-1993*; editor and coauthor of *Government and Politics of the Middle East and North Africa* (3 editions); *Israel Faces the Future, The Powers in the Middle East: The Ultimate Strategic*

Arena, Israeli National Security Policy: Political Actors and Perspectives, Political Leaders of the Contemporary Middle East and North Africa: A Biographical Dictionary, Israeli Politics in the 1990s: Key Domestic and Foreign Policy Factors, An Historical Encyclopedia of the Arab-Israeli Conflict, and *Handbook of Political Science Research on the Middle East and North Africa*; as well as the author of numerous articles, book chapters and monographs on Israel, Middle East politics, international politics, and United States foreign policy.

DAVID HOWARD GOLDBERG (Ph.D., McGill University) currently serves as Director of Research for the Canada-Israel Committee in Toronto. He has taught political science and international relations at York University and has held professional appointments with the Foundation for Middle East Studies and Canadian Professors of Peace in the Middle East, and was publisher of *Middle East Focus.* He is the author of *Foreign Policy and Ethnic Interest Groups: American and Canadian Jews Lobby for Israel* (1990) and *Democracy in Action 1999: A Guide to the Participants and Issues in Israeli Politics* (May 1999), and contributing coeditor of *The Domestic Battleground: Canada and the Arab-Israeli Conflict* (1989) and *The Decline of the Soviet Union and The Transformation of the Middle East* (1994).